Introduction to
3D GAME PROGRAMMING
WITH DIRECTX® 11

Frank D. Luna

MERCURY LEARNING AND INFORMATION
Dulles, Virginia
Boston, Massachusetts

-14

#754724429

Publisher: David Pallai
MERCURY LEARNING AND INFORMATION
22841 Quicksilver Drive
Dulles, VA 20166
info@merclearning.com
www.merclearning.com
1-800-758-3756

This book is printed on acid-free paper.

Frank D. Luna. *Introduction to 3D GAME PROGRAMMING WITH DIRECTX 11*

ISBN: 978-1-9364202-2-3

Library of Congress Control Number: 2012931119

1314 3

To my nieces and nephews,
Marrick, Hans, Max, Anna, Augustus, and Presley

CONTENTS

PART II   DIRECT 3D FOUNDATIONS

PART III   TOPICS

ACKNOWLEDGMENTS

I would like to thank Rod Lopez, Jim Leiterman, Hanley Leung, Rick Falck, Tybon Wu, Tuomas Sandroos, and Eric Sandegren for reviewing earlier editions of the book, and I would like to thank Jay Tennant and William Goschnick for reviewing select chapters of the current edition. I want to thank Tyler Drinkard for building some of the 3D models and textures used in the demo programs of this book. I also want to thank Dale E. La Force, Adam Hoult, Gary Simmons, James Lambers, and William Chin for their assistance. Lastly, I want to thank the staff at Mercury Learning and Information, in particular, David Pallai.

INTRODUCTION

Direct3D 11 is a rendering library for writing high performance 3D graphics applications using modern graphics hardware on the Windows platform. (A modified version of DirectX 9 is used on the XBOX 360.) Direct3D is a low-level library in the sense that its application programming interface (API) closely models the underlying graphics hardware it controls. The predominant consumer of Direct3D is the games industry, where higher level rendering engines are built on top of Direct3D. However, other industries need high performance interactive 3D graphics as well, such as medical and scientific visualization and architectural walkthrough. In addition, with every new PC being equipped with a modern graphics card, non-3D applications are beginning to take advantage of the GPU (graphics processing unit) to offload work to the graphics card for intensive calculations; this is known as *general purpose GPU computing*, and Direct3D 11 provides the compute shader API for writing general purpose GPU programs. Although Direct3D is usually programmed from native C++, stable .NET wrappers exist for Direct3D (e.g., http://slimdx.org/) so that you can access this powerful 3D graphics API from managed applications. Finally, at their 2011 BUILD conference (http://www.buildwindows.com/), Microsoft recently showed that Direct3D 11 will play the key role in writing high performance 3D "Metro" applications in Windows 8. All-in-all, the future looks bright for Direct3D developers.

This book presents an introduction to programming interactive computer graphics, with an emphasis on game development, using Direct3D 11. It teaches the fundamentals of Direct3D and shader programming, after which the reader will be prepared to go on and learn more advanced techniques. The book is divided into three main parts. Part I explains the mathematical tools that will be used throughout this book. Part II shows how to implement fundamental tasks in Direct3D, such as initialization, defining 3D geometry, setting up cameras, creating vertex, pixel, geometry, and compute shaders, lighting, texturing, blending, stenciling, and tessellation. Part III is largely about applying Direct3D to implement a variety of interesting techniques and special effects, such as working with meshes, terrain rendering, picking, particle systems, environment mapping, normal mapping, displacement mapping, real-time shadows, and ambient occlusion.

For the beginner, this book is best read front to back. The chapters have been organized so that the difficulty increases progressively with each chapter. In this way, there are no sudden jumps in complexity leaving the reader lost. In general, for a particular chapter, we will use the techniques and concepts previously developed. Therefore, it is important that you have mastered the material of a chapter before continuing. Experienced readers can pick the chapters of interest.

Finally, you may be wondering what kinds of games you can develop after reading this book. The answer to that question is best obtained by skimming through this book and seeing the types of applications that are developed. From that you should be able to visualize the types of games that can be developed based on the techniques taught in this book and some of your own ingenuity.

INTENDED AUDIENCE

This book was designed with the following three audiences in mind:

1. Intermediate level C++ programmers who would like an introduction to 3D programming using the latest iteration of Direct3D.

2. 3D programmers experienced with an API other than DirectX (e.g., OpenGL) who would like an introduction to Direct3D 11.

3. Experienced Direct3D 9 and Direct3D 11 programmers wishing to learn the latest iteration of Direct3D.

PREREQUISITES

It should be emphasized that this is an introduction to Direct3D 11, shader programming, and 3D game programming; it is *not* an introduction to general computer programming. The reader should satisfy the following prerequisites:

1. High School mathematics: algebra, trigonometry, and (mathematical) functions, for example.

2. Competent with Visual Studio: should know how to create projects, add files, and specify external libraries to link, for example.

3. Intermediate C++ and data structure skills: comfortable with pointers, arrays, operator overloading, linked lists, inheritance, and polymorphism, for example.

4. Familiarity with Windows programming with the Win32 API is helpful, but not required; we provide a Win32 primer in Appendix A.

REQUIRED DEVELOPMENT TOOLS AND HARDWARE

To program Direct3D 11 applications, you will need the DirectX 11 SDK; the latest version can be downloaded from http://msdn.microsoft.com/en-us/directx/default.aspx. Once downloaded, follow the instructions given by the installation wizard. At the time of this writing, the latest SDK version is the June 2010 DirectX SDK. All of our sample programs were written using Visual Studio 2010.

Direct3D 11 requires Direct3D 11 capable hardware. The demos in this book were tested on a Geforce GTX 460.

USE OF THE D3DX LIBRARY

Since version 7.0, DirectX has shipped with the D3DX (Direct3D Extension) library. This library provides a set of functions, classes, and interfaces that simplify common 3D graphics related operations, such as math operations, texture and image operations, mesh operations, and shader operations (e.g., compiling and assembling). That is to say, D3DX contains many features that would be a chore to implement on your own.

We use the D3DX library throughout this book because it allows us to focus on more interesting material. For instance, we would rather not spend pages explaining how to load various image formats (e.g., .bmp, .jpeg) into a Direct3D texture interface when we can do it in a single call to the D3DX function `D3DX11CreateTextureFromFile`. In other words, D3DX makes us more productive and lets us focus more on actual content rather than spending time reinventing the wheel.

Other reasons to use D3DX:

1. D3DX is general and can be used with a wide range of different types of 3D applications.

2. D3DX is fast, at least as fast as general functionality can be.

3. Other developers use D3DX. Therefore, you will most likely encounter code that uses D3DX. Consequently, whether you choose to use D3DX or not, you should become familiar with it so that you can read code that uses it.

4. D3DX already exists and has been thoroughly tested. Furthermore, it becomes more improved and feature rich with each iteration of DirectX.

USING THE DIRECTX SDK DOCUMENTATION AND SDK SAMPLES

Direct3D is a huge API and we cannot hope to cover all of its details in this one book. Therefore, to obtain extended information it is imperative that you learn how to use the DirectX SDK documentation. You can launch the C++ DirectX online documentation by executing the *windows_graphics.chm* file in the *DirectX SDK\Documentation\DirectX9* directory, where *DirectX SDK* is the directory you installed DirectX to. In particular, you will want to navigate to the Direct3D 11 section (see Figure 1).

The DirectX documentation covers just about every part of the DirectX API; therefore it is very useful as a reference, but because the documentation doesn't go into much depth, or assumes some previous knowledge, it isn't the best learning tool. However, it does get better and better with every new DirectX version released.

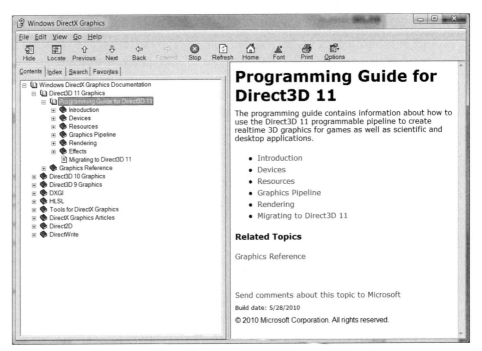

Figure 1. Direct3D Programming Guide in the DirectX documentation.

As said, the documentation is primarily useful as a reference. Suppose you come across a DirectX related type or function, say the function **ID3D11Device::CreateBuffer**, for which you would like more information. You simply do a search in the documentation index and you get a description of the object type, or in this case function; see Figure 2.

Note: ▶ *In this book we may direct you to the documentation for further details from time to time.*

We would also like to point out the available Direct3D sample programs that ship with DirectX SDK. The C++ Direct3D samples are located in the *DirectX SDK\ Samples\C++\Direct3D10* and *DirectX SDK\Samples\C++\Direct3D11* directories. Each sample illustrates how to implement a particular effect in Direct3D. These

Figure 2. Index of the DirectX documentation.

samples are fairly advanced for a beginning graphics programmer, but by the end of this book you should be ready to study them. Examination of the samples is a good "next step" after finishing this book. Note that we mentioned both the Direct3D 10 and Direct3D 11 samples. Direct3D 11 extends Direct3D 10 with new features, so Direct3D 10 techniques still apply when making a Direct3D 11 application; hence, it is still worthwhile to study the Direct3D 10 samples to see how a particular effect can be implemented.

CLARITY

We want to emphasize that the program samples for this book were written with clarity in mind and not performance. Thus, many of the samples may be implemented inefficiently. Keep this in mind if you are using any of the sample code in your own projects, as you may wish to rework it for better efficiency. Moreover, in order to focus on the Direct3D API, we have built minimal infrastructure on top of Direct3D. In a large 3D application, you will likely implement a rendering engine on top of Direct3D; however, the topic of this book is the Direct3D API, not rendering engine design.

SAMPLE PROGRAMS AND ONLINE SUPPLEMENTS

The companion DVD and Web sites for this book (www.d3dcoder.net and www.merclearning.com) play an integral part in getting the most out of this book. On the DVD and Web site you will find the complete source code and project files for every sample in this book. In many cases, DirectX programs are too large to fully embed in a textbook; therefore, we only embed relevant code fragments based on the ideas being shown. It is highly recommended that the reader study the corresponding demo code to see the program in its entirety. (We have aimed to make the demos small and focused for easy study.) As a general rule, the reader should be able to implement a chapter's demo(s) on his or her own after reading the chapter and spending some time studying the demo code. In fact, a good exercise is trying to implement the samples on your own using the book and sample code as a reference.

In addition to sample programs, the website also contains a message board. We encourage readers to communicate with each other and post questions on topics they do not understand or on topics for which they need clarification. In many cases, getting alternative perspectives and explanations to a concept speeds up the time it takes to comprehend it. And lastly, additional program samples and tutorials are planned to be added to the web site on topics that we could not fit into this book.

DEMO PROJECT SETUP IN VISUAL STUDIO 2010

The demos for this book can be opened simply by double-clicking the corresponding project file (.vcxproj) or solution file (.sln). This section describes how to create and build a project from scratch using the book's demo application framework using Visual Studio 2010 (VS10). As a working example, we will show how to recreate and build the "Box" demo of Chapter 6.

It is assumed that the reader has already successfully downloaded and installed the latest version of the DirectX SDK (available at http://msdn.microsoft.com/directx/), which is needed to program DirectX applications. The installation of the SDK is straightforward, and the installation wizard will walk you through it.

Create a Win32 Project

First, launch VS10, then go to the main menu and select **File >New >Project,** as shown in Figure 3.

The New Project dialog box will appear (Figure 4). Select **Visual C++ > Win32** from the Visual C++ Project Types tree control on the left. On the right, select **Win32 Project.** Next, give the project a name and specify the location you wish to store the project folder. Also uncheck **Create directory for solution,** if it is initially checked by default. Now hit **OK.**

A new dialog box will appear. On the left, there are two options: Overview and Application Settings. Select **Application Settings,** which produces the dialog box shown in Figure 5. From here, be sure that **Windows application** is chosen, and the **Empty project** box is checked. Now press the **Finish** button. At this point, you have successfully created an empty Win32 project, but there are still some things to do before you can build a DirectX project demo.

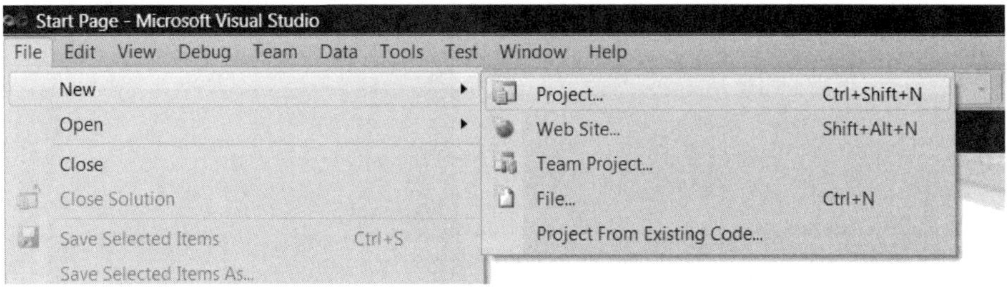

Figure 3. **Creating a new project.**

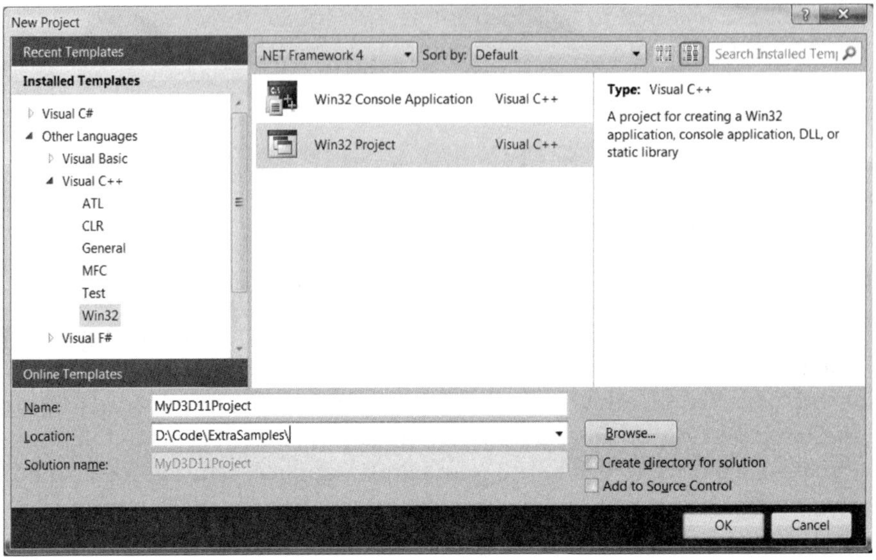

Figure 4. **New Project settings.**

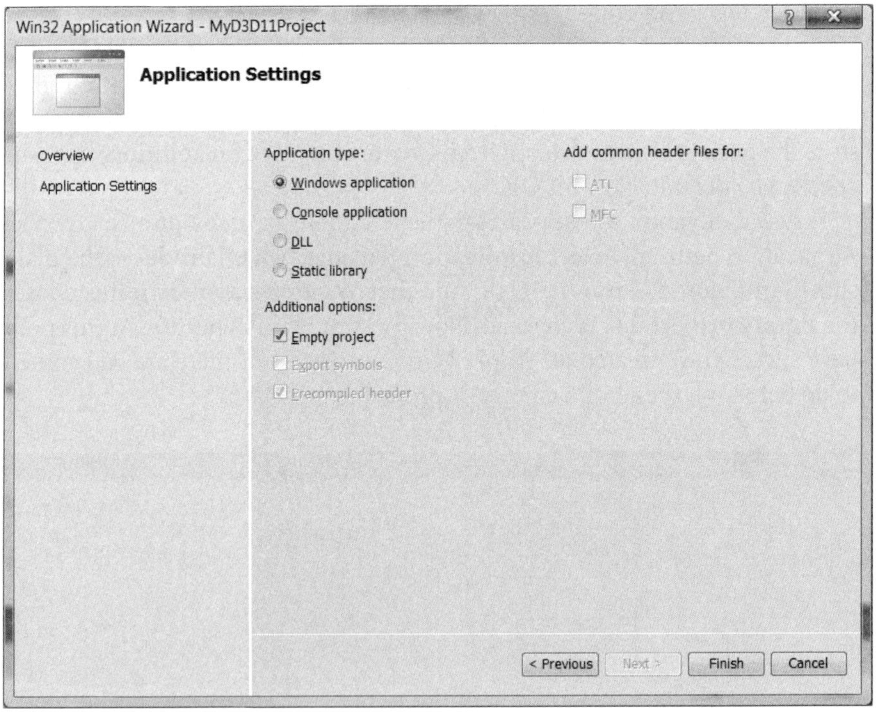

Figure 5. **Application settings.**

Linking the DirectX Libraries

We now need to link the DirectX libraries to our project. For a debug build, add the additional libraries:

```
d3d11.lib;
d3dx11d.lib;
D3DCompiler.lib;
Effects11d.lib;
dxerr.lib;
dxgi.lib;
dxguid.lib;
```

For a release build, add the same libraries above, but remove the 'd' character at the end of `d3dx11d.lib` and `Effects11d.lib`, so that they are just `d3dx11.lib` and `Effects11.lib`.

To link the library files, right-click on the project name under the Solution Explorer and select **Properties** from the dropdown menu (Figure 6). This launches the dialog

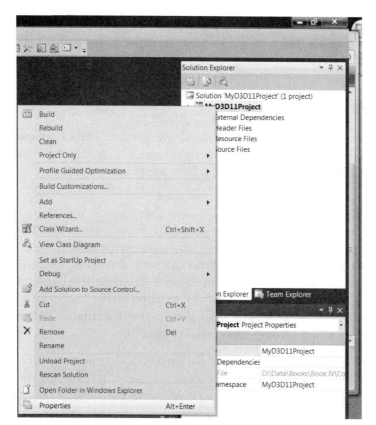

Figure 6. **Right-click on the project and select Properties from the context menu.**

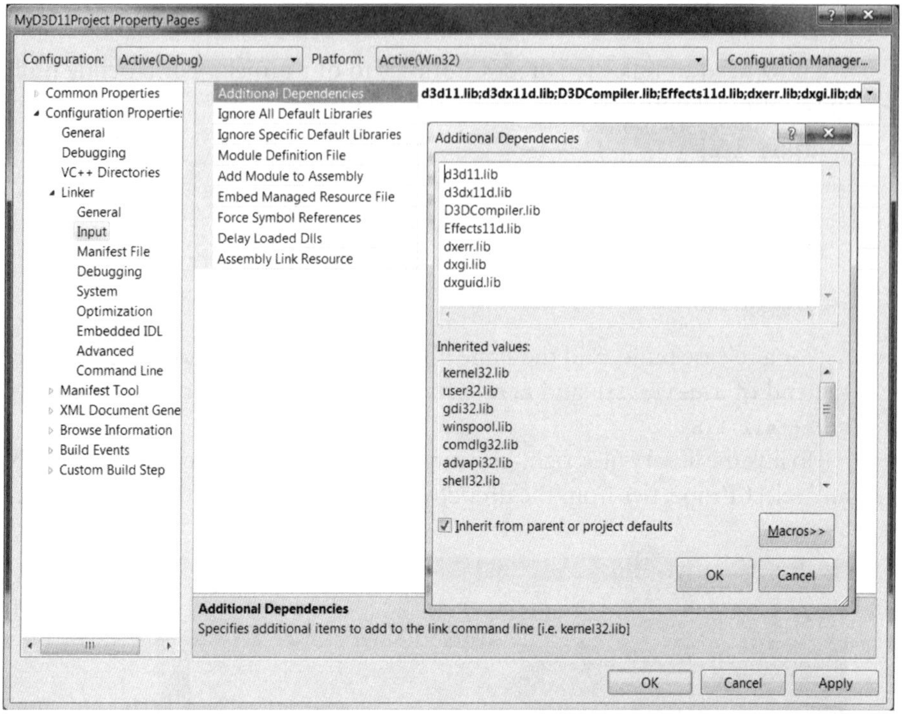

Figure 7. Link the DirectX libraries.

box shown in Figure 7. From the left-hand-side tree control, select **Configuration Properties > Linker >Input.** Then on the right-hand-side, specify the library file names on the **Additional Dependencies** line. Press **Apply** and then **OK.**

Setting up the Search Paths

We now need to make sure Visual Studio knows the directories in which to search for DirectX header and library files. Again, right-click on the project name under the Solution Explorer and select **Properties** from the dropdown menu (Figure 6). This launches the dialog box shown in Figure 7. From the left-hand-side tree control, select **Configuration Properties > VC++ Directories.** Then on the right-hand-side, you will need to add additional items for **Executable Directories**, **Include Directories,** and **Library Directories** (Figure 8).

Note: *Keep in mind that the exact path for the DirectX SDK depends on where you installed the DirectX SDK, and the exact path for the Common directory depends on where you extract the sample programs. Furthermore, you are free to move the Common directory, but you must remember to update the search paths in Visual Studio accordingly.*

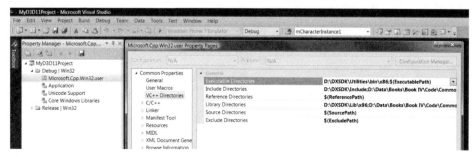

Figure 8. Setting the search paths per project.

Category	Additional Items
Executable Directories	1. D:\DXSDK\Utilities\bin\x86 – DirectX utility programs. In particular, we run the *fxc* utility program from the IDE.
Include Directories	1. D:\DXSDK\Include – DirectX header files. 2. D:\Data\Books\Book IV\Code\Common – Path to shared sample code for all of our demos (see "Note" following).
Library Directories	1. D:\DXSDK\Lib\x86 – DirectX library files. 2. D:\Data\Books\Book IV\Code\Common – Path to shared sample code for all of our demos (see "Note" following).

Note: *When you download the book's source code, there will be a folder for each chapter, and a Common directory. The Common directory contains reusable framework code that all the demos can share; this prevents duplication of source code across projects. In order for VC++ to find header files and libraries in the Common folder, we need to add it to the search paths.*

In Visual Studio 2010, the directory paths are per project settings (this differs from Visual Studio 2008 behavior). This means you need to set the search paths for every project when you make a new project. If you make many demo projects, this can be annoying. However, there is a way to make these settings permanent for a user. Under the Visual Studio menu, select **View > Other Windows > Property Manager.** Expand the property manager as in Figure 9, and double-click the

Figure 9. Setting the search paths per user.

Microsoft.Cpp.Win32.user item. You get a dialog box similar to the one in Figure 8, except that the paths you set here will persist across projects, so that you do not need to add them every time. More specifically, every new project you make will inherit the values set here.

Adding the Source Code and Building the Project

Finally, our project setup is complete. We can now add our source code files to the project and build it. First, copy the "Box" source code files to your project's directory, as well as the FX folder. We also assume that you have placed the *Common* directory somewhere on your hard drive and have added the appropriate search paths, as described in the previous section.

After you copy the files, your project directory should look like the one in Figure 10. Now, follow these steps to add the code to your project.

1. Right-click on the project name under the Solution Explorer and select **Add > Existing Item…** from the dropdown menu, and add *BoxDemo.cpp* to the project.

2. Right-click on the project name under the Solution Explorer and select **Add > New Filter,** and name the filter *FX*. Right-click on the FX filter and select **Add > Existing Item…** from the dropdown menu, and add *FX\color.fx* to the project.

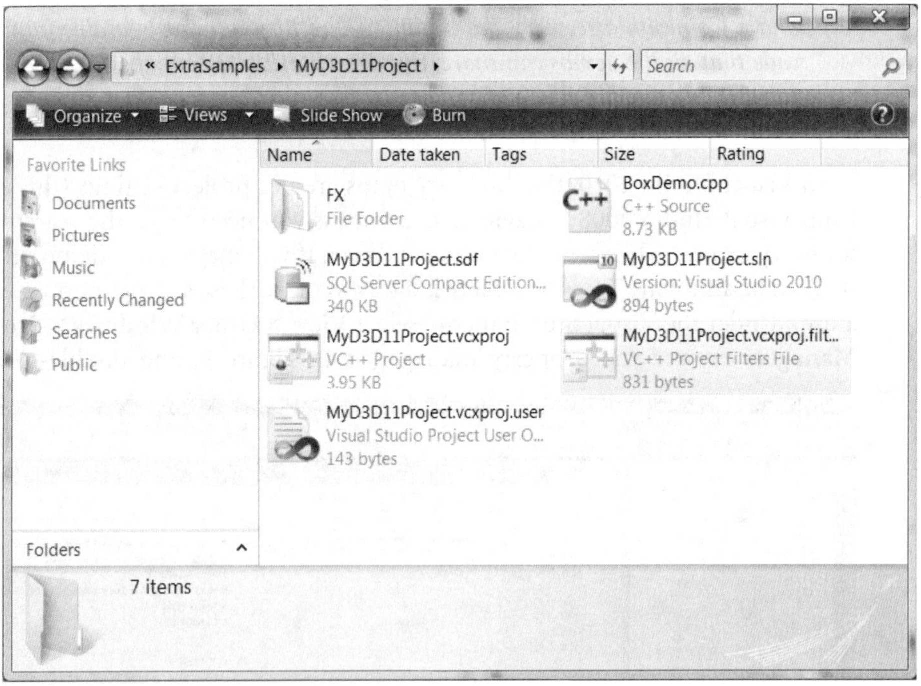

Figure 10. **The project directory after copying the files.**

3. Right-click on the project name under the Solution Explorer and select **Add >
    New Filter,** and name the filter *Common*. Right-click on the *Common* filter and
    select **Add > Existing Item...** from the dropdown menu, navigate to where you
    placed the book's *Common* directory code, and add all the *.h/.cpp* files from that
    directory to the project.

4. The source code files are now part of the project, and your Solution Explorer
    should look like Figure 11. You can now go to the main menu, and select **Debug >
    Start Debugging** to compile, link, and execute the demo. The application in Figure
    12 should appear.

Figure 11. Solution Explorer after adding all the files.

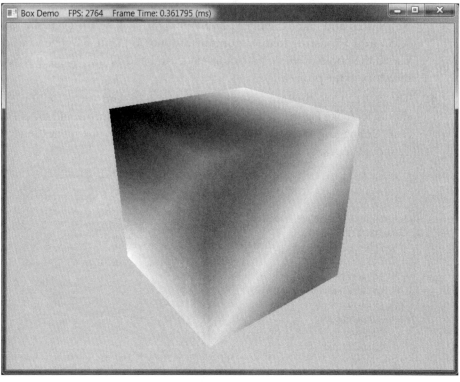

Figure 12. Screenshot of the "Box" demo.

Note: *A lot of the code in the Common directory is built up over the course of the book. So we recommend that you do not start looking through the code. Instead, wait until you are reading the chapter in the book where that code is covered.*

Note: *Most of the other samples invoke a shader compiler tool at build time. You do not need to do this to run the existing demos because we have already configured this step. However, we explain how to do this in your own projects in §6.9.5.*

Part 1   *MATHEMATICAL PREREQUISITES*

*"For the things of this world cannot be made
known without a knowledge of mathematics."*

Roger Bacon, Opus Majus part 4 Distinctia Prima cap 1, 1267.

Video games attempt to simulate a virtual world. However, computers, by their very nature, crunch numbers. Thus the problem of how to convey a world to a computer arises. The answer is to describe our worlds, and the interactions therein, completely mathematically. Consequently, mathematics plays a fundamental role in video game development.

In this prerequisites part, we introduce the mathematical tools that will be used throughout this book. The emphasis is on vectors, coordinate systems, matrices, and transformations, as these tools are used in just about every sample program of this book. In addition to the mathematical explanations, a survey and demonstration of the relevant classes and functions from the XNA math library are provided.

Note that the topics covered here are only those essential to understanding the rest of this book; it is by no means a comprehensive treatment of video game mathematics, as entire books are devoted to this topic. For readers desiring a more complete reference to video game mathematics, we recommend [Verth04] and [Lengyel02].

Chapter 1, Vector Algebra: Vectors are, perhaps, the most fundamental mathematical objects used in computer games. We use vectors to represent positions, displacements, directions, velocities, and forces, for example. In this chapter, we study vectors and the operations used to manipulate them.

Chapter 2, Matrix Algebra: Matrices provide an efficient and compact way of representing transformations. In this chapter, we become familiar with matrices and the operations defined on them.

Chapter 3, Transformations: This chapter examines three fundamental geometric transformations: scaling, rotation, and translation. We use these transformations to manipulate 3D objects in space. In addition, we explain change of coordinate transformations, which are used to transform coordinates representing geometry from one coordinate system into another.

1

VECTOR
ALGEBRA

Vectors play a crucial role in computer graphics, collision detection, and physical simulation, all of which are common components in modern video games. Our approach here is informal and practical; for a book dedicated to 3D game/graphics math, we recommend [Verth04]. We emphasize the importance of vectors by noting that they are used in just about every demo program in this book.

Objectives:

1.   To learn how vectors are represented geometrically and numerically.
2.   To discover the operations defined on vectors and their geometric applications.
3.   To become familiar with the XNA Math library's vector functions and classes.

1.1 VECTORS

A *vector* refers to a quantity that possesses both magnitude and direction. Quantities that possess both magnitude and direction are called *vector-valued quantities*. Examples of vector-valued quantities are forces (a force is applied in a particular direction with a certain strength—magnitude), displacements (the net direction and distance a particle moved), and velocities (speed and direction). Thus, vectors are used to represent forces, displacements, and velocities. In addition, we also use vectors to specify pure directions, such as the direction the player is looking in a 3D game, the direction a polygon is facing, the direction in which a ray of light travels, or the direction in which a ray of light reflects off a surface.

A first step in characterizing a vector mathematically is geometrically: We graphically specify a vector by a directed line segment (see Figure 1.1), where the length denotes the magnitude of the vector and the aim denotes the direction of the vector. We note that the location in which we draw a vector is immaterial because changing the location does not change the magnitude or direction (the two properties a vector possesses). Therefore, we say two vectors are equal if and only if they have the same length and they point in the same direction. Thus, the vectors **u** and **v** drawn in Figure 1.1*a* are actually equal because they have the same length and point in the same direction. In fact, because location is unimportant for vectors, we can always translate a vector without changing its meaning (because a translation changes neither length nor direction). Observe that we could translate **u** such that it completely overlaps with **v** (and conversely), thereby making them indistinguishable—hence their equality. As a physical example, the vectors **u** and **v** in Figure 1.1*b* both tell the ants at two different points A and B to move north ten meters from where they are. Again we have **u** = **v**. The vectors themselves are

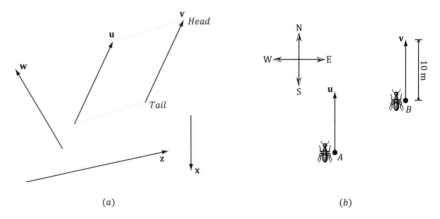

(a)   (b)

Figure 1.1. (a) Vectors drawn on a 2D plane. (b) Vectors instructing ants to move 10 meters north.

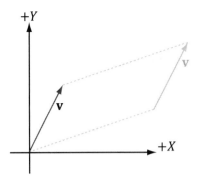

Figure 1.2. We translate v so that its tail coincides with the origin of the coordinate system. When a vector's tail coincides with the origin, we say that it is in standard position.

independent of position; they simply instruct the ants how to move from where they are. In this example, they tell the ants to move north (direction) ten meters (length).

1.1.1 Vectors and Coordinate Systems

We could now define useful geometric operations on vectors, which can then be used to solve problems involving vector-valued quantities. However, because the computer cannot work with vectors geometrically, we need to find a way of specifying vectors numerically instead. So what we do is introduce a 3D coordinate system in space, and translate all the vectors so that their tails coincide with the origin (Figure 1.2). Then we can identify a vector by specifying the coordinates of its head, and write $\mathbf{v} = (x, y, z,)$ as shown in Figure 1.3. Now we can represent a vector with three **floats** in a computer program.

Note: *If working in 2D, then we just use a 2D coordinate system and the vector only has two coordinates: $\mathbf{v} = (x, y)$ and we can represent a vector with two **floats** in a computer program.*

Consider Figure 1.4, which shows a vector **v** and two frames in space. (Note that we use the terms *frame, frame of reference, space,* and *coordinate system* to all mean the

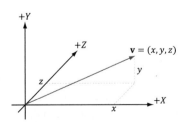

Figure 1.3. A vector specified by coordinates relative to a coordinate system.

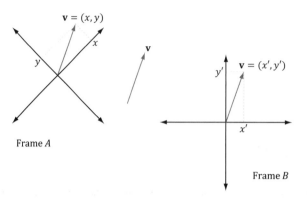

Figure 1.4. The same vector v has different coordinates when described relative to different frames.

same thing in this book.) We can translate **v** so that it is in standard position in either of the two frames. Observe, however, that the coordinates of the vector **v** relative to frame *A* are different than the coordinates of the vector **v** relative to frame *B*. In other words, the *same* vector **v** has a different coordinate representation for distinct frames.

The idea is analogous to, say, temperature. Water boils at 100° Celsius or 212° Fahrenheit. The physical temperature of boiling water is the *same* no matter the scale (i.e., we can't lower the boiling point by picking a different scale), but we assign a different scalar number to the temperature based on the scale we use. Similarly, for a vector, its direction and magnitude, which are embedded in the directed line segment, does not change; only the coordinates of it change based on the frame of reference we use to describe it. This is important because it means whenever we identify a vector by coordinates, those coordinates are relative to some frame of reference. Often in 3D computer graphics, we will utilize more than one frame of reference and, therefore, we will need to keep track of which frame a vector's coordinate are relative to; additionally, we will need to know how to convert vector coordinates from one frame to another.

Note: ▶ *We see that both vectors and points can be described by coordinates (x, y, z) relative to a frame. However, they are not the same; a point represents a location in 3-space, whereas a vector represents a magnitude and direction. We will have more to say about points in §1.5.*

1.1.2 Left-Handed Versus Right-Handed Coordinate Systems

Direct3D uses a so-called left-handed coordinate system. If you take your left hand and aim your fingers down the positive *x*-axis, and then curl your fingers towards the positive *y*-axis, your thumb points roughly in the direction of the positive *z*-axis. Figure 1.5 illustrates the differences between a left-handed and right-handed coordinate system.

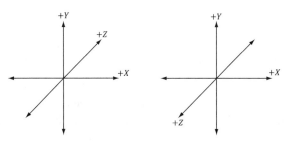

Figure 1.5. On the left we have a left-handed coordinate system. Observe that the positive z-axis goes into the page. On the right we have a right-handed coordinate system. Observe that the positive z-axis comes out of the page.

Observe that for the right-handed coordinate system, if you take your right hand and aim your fingers down the positive x-axis, and then curl your fingers towards the positive y-axis, your thumb points roughly in the direction of the positive z-axis.

1.1.3 Basic Vector Operations

We now define equality, addition, scalar multiplication, and subtraction on vectors using the coordinate representation. For these four definitions, let $\mathbf{u} = (u_x, u_y, u_z)$ and $\mathbf{v} = (v_x, v_y, v_z)$.

1. Two vectors are equal if and only if their corresponding components are equal. That is, $\mathbf{u} = \mathbf{v}$ if and only if $u_x = v_x$, $u_y = v_y$, and $u_z = v_z$.

2. We add vectors component wise: $\mathbf{u} + \mathbf{v} = (u_x + v_x, u_y + v_y, u_z + v_z)$. Observe that it only makes sense to add vectors of the same dimension.

3. We can multiply a scalar (i.e., a real number) and a vector and the result is a vector. Let k be a scalar, then $k\mathbf{u} = (ku_x, ku_y, ku_z)$. This is called *scalar multiplication*.

4. We define subtraction in terms of vector addition and scalar multiplication. That is, $\mathbf{u} - \mathbf{v} = \mathbf{u} + (-1 \cdot \mathbf{v}) = \mathbf{u} + (-\mathbf{v}) = (u_x - v_x, u_y - v_y, u_z - v_z)$.

☞ Example 1.1

Let $\mathbf{u} = (1,2,3), \mathbf{v} = (1,2,3), \mathbf{w} = (3,0,-2)$, and $k = 2$. Then,

1. $\mathbf{u} + \mathbf{w} = (1, 2, 3) + (3, 0, -2) = (4, 2, 1)$;

2. $\mathbf{u} = \mathbf{v}$;

3. $\mathbf{u} - \mathbf{v} = \mathbf{u} + (-\mathbf{v}) = (1, 2, 3) + (-1, -2, -3) = (0, 0, 0) = 0$;

4. $k\mathbf{w} = 2(3, 0, -2) = (6, 0, -4)$.

The difference in the third item illustrates a special vector, called the *zero-vector*, which has zeros for all of its components and is denoted by $\mathbf{0}$.

☞ Example 1.2

We will illustrate this example with 2D vectors to make the drawings simpler. The ideas are the same as in 3D; we just work with one less component in 2D.

1. Let $\mathbf{v} = (2,1)$. How do $\mathbf{v}$ and $-\frac{1}{2}\mathbf{v}$ compare geometrically? We note that $-\frac{1}{2}\mathbf{v} = \left(-1, -\frac{1}{2}\right)$. Graphing both $\mathbf{v}$ and $-\frac{1}{2}\mathbf{v}$ (Figure 1.6a), we notice that $-\frac{1}{2}\mathbf{v}$ is in the direction directly opposite of $\mathbf{v}$ and its length is 1/2 that of $\mathbf{v}$. Thus, geometrically, negating a vector can be thought of as "flipping" its direction, and scalar multiplication can be thought of as scaling the length of a vector.

2. Let $\mathbf{u} = \left(2, \frac{1}{2}\right)$ and $\mathbf{v} = (1, 2)$. Then $\mathbf{u} + \mathbf{v} = \left(3, \frac{5}{2}\right)$. Figure 1.6b shows what vector addition means geometrically: We parallel translate $\mathbf{u}$ so that its *tail* coincided with the *head* of $\mathbf{v}$. Then, the sum is the vector originating at the tail of $\mathbf{v}$ and ending at the head of the translated $\mathbf{u}$. (We get the same result if we keep $\mathbf{u}$ fixed and translate $\mathbf{v}$ so that its tail coincides with the head of $\mathbf{u}$. In this case, $\mathbf{u} + \mathbf{v}$ would be the vector originating at the tail of $\mathbf{u}$ and ending at the head of the translated $\mathbf{v}$.) Observe also that our rules of vector addition agree with what we would intuitively expect to happen physically when we add forces together to produce a net force: If we add two forces (vectors) in the same direction, we get another stronger net force (longer vector) in that direction. If we add two forces (vectors) in opposition to each other, then we get a weaker net force (shorter vector). Figure 1.7 illustrates these ideas.

3. Let $\mathbf{u} = \left(2, \frac{1}{2}\right)$ and $\mathbf{v} = (1, 2)$. Then $\mathbf{v} - \mathbf{u} = \left(-1, \frac{3}{2}\right)$. Figure 1.6c shows what vector subtraction means geometrically. Essentially, the difference $\mathbf{v} - \mathbf{u}$ gives us a vector aimed from the head of $\mathbf{u}$ to the head of $\mathbf{v}$. If we instead interpret $\mathbf{u}$ and $\mathbf{v}$ as points, then $\mathbf{v} - \mathbf{u}$ gives us a vector aimed from the point $\mathbf{u}$ to the point $\mathbf{v}$; this interpretation is important as we will often want the vector aimed from one point to another. Observe also that the length of $\mathbf{v} - \mathbf{u}$ is the distance from $\mathbf{u}$ to $\mathbf{v}$, when thinking of $\mathbf{u}$ and $\mathbf{v}$ as points.

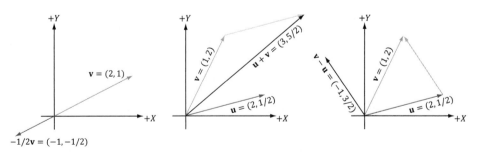

Figure 1.6. (a) The geometric interpretation of scalar multiplication. (b) The geometric interpretation of vector addition. (c) The geometric interpretation of vector subtraction.

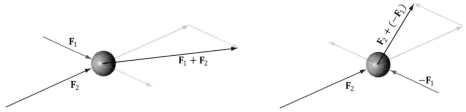

Figure 1.7. Forces applied to a ball. The forces are combined using vector addition to get a net force.

1.2 LENGTH AND UNIT VECTORS

Geometrically, the magnitude of a vector is the length of the directed line segment. We denote the magnitude of a vector by double vertical bars (e.g., $\|\mathbf{u}\|$ denotes the magnitude of $\mathbf{u}$). Now, given a vector $\mathbf{u} = (x, y, z)$, we wish to compute its magnitude algebraically. The magnitude of a 3D vector can be computed by applying the Pythagorean theorem twice; see Figure 1.8.

First, we look at the triangle in the xz-plane with sides x, z, and hypotenuse a. From the Pythagorean theorem, we have $a = \sqrt{x^2 + z^2}$. Now look at the triangle with sides a, y, and hypotenuse $\|\mathbf{u}\|$. From the Pythagorean theorem again, we arrive at the following magnitude formula:

$$\|\mathbf{u}\| = \sqrt{y^2 + a^2} = \sqrt{y^2 + \left(\sqrt{x^2 + z^2}\right)^2} = \sqrt{x^2 + y^2 + z^2} \qquad \textbf{(eq. 1.1)}$$

For some applications, we do not care about the length of a vector because we want to use the vector to represent a pure direction. For such direction-only vectors, we want the length of the vector to be exactly one. When we make a vector

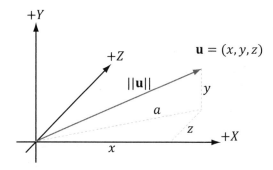

Figure 1.8. The 3D length of a vector can be computed by applying the Pythagorean theorem twice.

unit length, we say that we are *normalizing* the vector. We can normalize a vector by dividing each of its components by its magnitude:

$$\hat{\mathbf{u}} = \frac{\mathbf{u}}{\|\mathbf{u}\|} = \left(\frac{x}{\|\mathbf{u}\|}, \frac{y}{\|\mathbf{u}\|}, \frac{z}{\|\mathbf{u}\|} \right) \qquad \textbf{(eq. 1.2)}$$

To verify that this formula is correct, we can compute the length of $\hat{\mathbf{u}}$:

$$\|\hat{\mathbf{u}}\| = \sqrt{\left(\frac{x}{\|\mathbf{u}\|}\right)^2 + \left(\frac{y}{\|\mathbf{u}\|}\right)^2 + \left(\frac{z}{\|\mathbf{u}\|}\right)^2} = \frac{\sqrt{x^2 + y^2 + z^2}}{\sqrt{\|\mathbf{u}\|^2}} = \frac{\|\mathbf{u}\|}{\|\mathbf{u}\|} = 1$$

So $\hat{\mathbf{u}}$ is indeed a unit vector.

☞ Example 1.3

Normalize the vector $\mathbf{v} = (-1, 3, 4)$. We have $\|\mathbf{v}\| = \sqrt{(-1)^2 + 3^2 + 4^2} = \sqrt{26}$. Thus, $\hat{\mathbf{v}} = \frac{\mathbf{v}}{\|\mathbf{v}\|} = \left(-\frac{1}{\sqrt{26}}, \frac{3}{\sqrt{26}}, \frac{4}{\sqrt{26}} \right)$.

To verify that $\|\hat{\mathbf{v}}\|$ is indeed a unit vector, we compute its length:

$$\|\hat{\mathbf{v}}\| = \sqrt{\left(-\frac{1}{\sqrt{26}}\right)^2 + \left(\frac{3}{\sqrt{26}}\right)^2 + \left(\frac{4}{\sqrt{26}}\right)^2} = \sqrt{\frac{1}{26} + \frac{9}{26} + \frac{16}{26}} = \sqrt{1} = 1.$$

1.3 THE DOT PRODUCT

The dot product is a form of vector multiplication that results in a scalar value; for this reason, it is sometimes referred to as the scalar product. Let $\mathbf{u} = (u_x, u_y, u_z)$ and $\mathbf{v} = (v_x, v_y, v_z)$, then the dot product is defined as follows:

$$\mathbf{u} \cdot \mathbf{v} = u_x v_x + u_y v_y + u_z v_z \qquad \textbf{(eq. 1.3)}$$

In words, the dot product is the sum of the products of the corresponding components.

The dot product definition does not present an obvious geometric meaning. Using the law of cosines (see Exercise 10), we can find the relationship,

$$\mathbf{u} \cdot \mathbf{v} = \|\mathbf{u}\| \|\mathbf{v}\| \cos \theta \qquad \textbf{(eq. 1.4)}$$

where θ is the angle between the vectors $\mathbf{u}$ and $\mathbf{v}$ such that $0 \le \theta \le \pi$; see Figure 1.9. So, Equation 1.4 says that the dot product between two vectors is the cosine of the angle between them scaled by the vectors' magnitudes. In particular, if both

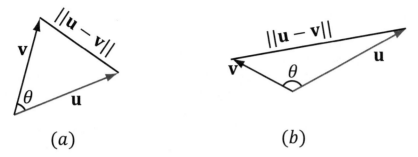

Figure 1.9. In the left figure, the angle θ between u and v is an acute angle. In the right figure, the angle θ between u and v is an obtuse angle. When we refer to the angle between two vectors, we always mean the smallest angle, that is, the angle θ such that $0 \le \theta \le \pi$.

u and **v** are unit vectors, then **u** · **v** is the cosine of the angle between them (i.e., **u** · **v** = cos θ).

Equation 1.4 provides us with some useful geometric properties of the dot product:

1. If **u** · **v** = 0, then **u** ⊥ **v** (i.e., the vectors are orthogonal).

2. If **u** · **v** > 0, then the angle θ between the two vectors is less than 90 degrees (i.e., the vectors make an acute angle).

3. If **u** · **v** < 0, the angle θ between the two vectors is greater than 90 degrees (i.e., the vectors make an obtuse angle).

Note: *The word "orthogonal" can be used as a synonym for "perpendicular."*

☞ Example 1.4

Let **u** = (1, 2, 3) and **v** = (−4, 0, −1). Find the angle between **u** and **v**. First we compute:

$$\mathbf{u} \cdot \mathbf{v} = (1,2,3) \cdot (-4,0,-1) = -4 - 3 = -7$$

$$\| \mathbf{u} \| = \sqrt{1^2 + 2^2 + 3^2} = \sqrt{14}$$

$$\| \mathbf{v} \| = \sqrt{(-4)^2 + 0^2 + (-1)^2} = \sqrt{17}$$

Now, applying Equation 1.4 and solving for theta, we get:

$$\cos\theta = \frac{\mathbf{u}\cdot\mathbf{v}}{\| \mathbf{u} \|\| \mathbf{v} \|} = \frac{-7}{\sqrt{14}\sqrt{17}}$$

$$\theta = \cos^{-1}\frac{-7}{\sqrt{14}\sqrt{17}} \approx 117°$$

☞ Example 1.5

Consider Figure 1.10. Given **v** and the *unit* vector **n**, find a formula for **p** in terms of **v** and **n** using the dot product.

First, observe from the figure that there exists a scalar k such that $\mathbf{p} = k\mathbf{n}$; moreover, because we assumed $\|\mathbf{n}\| = 1$, we have $\|\mathbf{p}\| = \|k\mathbf{n}\| = |k|\|\mathbf{n}\| = |k|$. (Note that k may be negative if and only if **p** and **n** aim in opposite directions.) Using trigonometry, we have that $k = \|\mathbf{v}\| \cos\theta$; therefore, $\mathbf{p} = k\mathbf{n} = (\|\mathbf{v}\| \cos\theta)\mathbf{n}$. However, because **n** is a unit vector, we can say this in another way:

$$\mathbf{p} = (\|\mathbf{v}\| \cos\theta)\mathbf{n} = (\|\mathbf{v}\| \cdot 1 \cos\theta)\mathbf{n} = (\|\mathbf{v}\| \|\mathbf{n}\| \cos\theta)\mathbf{n} = (\mathbf{v} \cdot \mathbf{n})\mathbf{n}$$

In particular, this shows $k = \mathbf{v} \cdot \mathbf{n}$, and this illustrates the geometric interpretation of $\mathbf{v} \cdot \mathbf{n}$ when **n** is a unit vector. We call **p** the *orthogonal projection* of **v** on **n**, and it is commonly denoted by

$$\mathbf{p} = \text{proj}_{\mathbf{n}}(\mathbf{v})$$

If we interpret **v** as a force, **p** can be thought of as the portion of the force **v** that acts in the direction **n**. Likewise, the vector $\mathbf{w} = \text{perp}_{\mathbf{n}}(\mathbf{v}) = \mathbf{v} - \mathbf{p}$ is the portion of the force **v** that acts orthogonal to the direction **n** (which is why we also denote it by $\text{perp}_{\mathbf{n}}(\mathbf{v})$ for perpendicular). Observe that $\mathbf{v} = \mathbf{p} + \mathbf{w} = \text{proj}_{\mathbf{n}}(\mathbf{v}) + \text{perp}_{\mathbf{n}}(\mathbf{v})$, which is to say we have decomposed the vector **v** into the sum of two orthogonal vectors **p** and **w**.

If **n** is not of unit length, we can always normalize it first to make it unit length. Replacing **n** by the unit vector $\dfrac{\mathbf{n}}{\|\mathbf{n}\|}$ gives us the more general projection formula:

$$\mathbf{p} = \text{proj}_{\mathbf{n}}(\mathbf{v}) = \left(\mathbf{v} \cdot \frac{\mathbf{n}}{\|\mathbf{n}\|}\right)\frac{\mathbf{n}}{\|\mathbf{n}\|} = \frac{(\mathbf{v} \cdot \mathbf{n})}{\|\mathbf{n}\|^2}\mathbf{n}$$

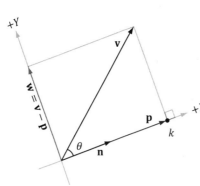 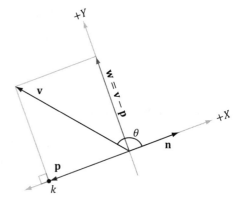

Figure 1.10. The *orthogonal projection* of v on n.

1.3.1 Orthogonalization

A set of vectors $\{\mathbf{v}_0,\ldots,\mathbf{v}_{n-1}\}$ is called *orthonormal* if the vectors are mutually orthogonal (every vector in the set is orthogonal to every other vector in the set) and unit length. Sometimes we have a set of vectors that are almost orthonormal, but not quite. A common task is to orthogonalize the set and make it orthonormal. In 3D computer graphics we might start off with an orthonormal set, but due to numerical precision issues, the set gradually becomes un-orthonormal. We are mainly concerned with the 2D and 3D cases of this problem (that is, sets that contain two and three vectors, respectively).

We examine the simpler 2D case first. Suppose we have the set of vectors $\{\mathbf{v}_0,\mathbf{v}_1\}$ that we want to orthogonalize into an orthonormal set $\{\mathbf{w}_0,\mathbf{w}_1\}$ as shown in Figure 1.11. We start with $\mathbf{w}_0 = \mathbf{v}_0$ and modify $\mathbf{v}_1$ to make it orthogonal to $\mathbf{w}_0$; this is done by subtracting out the portion of $\mathbf{v}_1$ that acts in the $\mathbf{w}_0$ direction:

$$\mathbf{w}_1 = \mathbf{v}_1 - \text{proj}_{\mathbf{w}_0}(\mathbf{v}_1)$$

We now have a mutually orthogonal set of vectors $\{\mathbf{w}_0,\mathbf{w}_1\}$; the last step to constructing the orthonormal set is to normalize $\mathbf{w}_0$ and $\mathbf{w}_1$ to make them unit length.

The 3D case follows in the same spirit as the 2D case, but with more steps. Suppose we have the set of vectors $\{\mathbf{v}_0,\mathbf{v}_1,\mathbf{v}_2\}$ that we want to orthogonalize into an orthonormal set $\{\mathbf{w}_0,\mathbf{w}_1,\mathbf{w}_2\}$ as shown in Figure 1.12. We start with $\mathbf{w}_0 = \mathbf{v}_0$ and

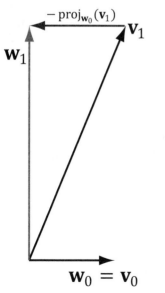

Figure 1.11. 2D orthogonalization.

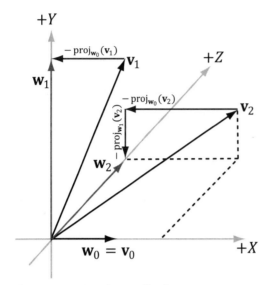

Figure 1.12. 3D orthogonalization.

modify $\mathbf{v}_1$ to make it orthogonal to $\mathbf{w}_0$; this is done by subtracting out the portion of $\mathbf{v}_1$ that acts in the $\mathbf{w}_0$ direction:

$$\mathbf{w}_1 = \mathbf{v}_1 - \text{proj}_{\mathbf{w}_0}\left(\mathbf{v}_1\right)$$

Next, we modify $\mathbf{v}_2$ to make it orthogonal to *both* $\mathbf{w}_0$ and $\mathbf{w}_1$. This is done by subtracting out the portion of $\mathbf{v}_2$ that acts in the $\mathbf{w}_0$ direction and the portion of $\mathbf{v}_2$ that acts in the $\mathbf{w}_1$ direction:

$$\mathbf{w}_2 = \mathbf{v}_2 - \text{proj}_{\mathbf{w}_0}\left(\mathbf{v}_2\right) - \text{proj}_{\mathbf{w}_1}\left(\mathbf{v}_2\right)$$

We now have a mutually orthogonal set of vectors $\{\mathbf{w}_0, \mathbf{w}_1, \mathbf{w}_2\}$; the last step to constructing the orthonormal set is to normalize $\mathbf{w}_0$, $\mathbf{w}_1$, and $\mathbf{w}_2$ to make them unit length.

For the general case of n vectors $\{\mathbf{v}_0,\dots,\mathbf{v}_{n-1}\}$ that we want to orthogonalize into an orthonormal set, we have the following procedure commonly called the *Gram-Schmidt Orthogonalization* process:

$$\text{Base Step} : \text{Set } \mathbf{w}_0 = \mathbf{v}_0$$

$$\text{For } 1 \leq i \leq n-1, \text{ Set } \mathbf{w}_i = \mathbf{v}_i - \sum_{j=0}^{i-1} \text{proj}_{\mathbf{w}_j}\left(\mathbf{v}_i\right)$$

$$\text{Normalization Step} : \text{Set } \mathbf{w}_i = \frac{\mathbf{w}_i}{\|\mathbf{w}_i\|}$$

Again, the intuitive idea is that when we pick a vector $\mathbf{v}_i$ from the input set to add to the orthonormal set, we need to subtract out the components of $\mathbf{v}_i$ that act in the directions of the other vectors ($\mathbf{w}_0$, $\mathbf{w}_1$,..., $\mathbf{w}_{i-1}$) that are already in the orthonormal set to ensure the new vector being added is orthogonal to the other vectors already in the orthonormal set.

1.4 THE CROSS PRODUCT

The second form of multiplication vector math defines is the cross product. Unlike the dot product, which evaluates to a scalar, the cross product evaluates to another vector; moreover, the cross product is only defined for 3D vectors (in particular, there is no 2D cross product). Taking the cross product of two 3D vectors $\mathbf{u}$ and $\mathbf{v}$ yields another vector, $\mathbf{w}$ that is mutually orthogonal to $\mathbf{u}$ and $\mathbf{v}$. By that we mean $\mathbf{w}$ is orthogonal to $\mathbf{u}$, and $\mathbf{w}$ is orthogonal to $\mathbf{v}$; see Figure 1.13. If $\mathbf{u} = (u_x, u_y, u_z)$ and $\mathbf{v} = (u_x, u_y, u_z)$, then the cross product is computed like so:

$$\mathbf{w} = \mathbf{u} \times \mathbf{v} = (u_y v_z - u_z v_y, u_z v_x - u_x v_z, u_x v_y - u_y v_x) \qquad \textbf{(eq. 1.5)}$$

Note: *If you are working in a right-handed coordinate system, then you use the right-hand-thumb rule: If you take your right hand and aim the fingers in the direction of the first vector, and then curl your fingers toward $\mathbf{v}$ along an angle $0 \le \theta \le \pi$, then your thumb roughly points in the direction of $\mathbf{w} = \mathbf{u} \times \mathbf{v}$.*

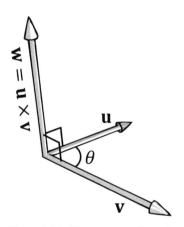

Figure 1.13. The cross product of two 3D vectors u and v yields another vector w that is mutually orthogonal to u and v. If you take your left hand and aim the fingers in the direction of the first vector u, and then curl your fingers toward v along an angle $0 \le \theta \le \pi$, then your thumb roughly points in the direction of $w = u \times v$; this is called the *left-hand-thumb rule*.

☞ Example 1.6

Let $\mathbf{u} = (2, 1, 3)$ and $\mathbf{v} = (2, 0, 0)$. Compute $\mathbf{w} = \mathbf{u} \times \mathbf{v}$ and $\mathbf{z} = \mathbf{v} \times \mathbf{u}$, and then verify that $\mathbf{w}$ is orthogonal to $\mathbf{u}$ and that $\mathbf{w}$ is orthogonal to $\mathbf{v}$. Applying Equation 1.5 we have,

$$\begin{aligned}
\mathbf{w} &= \mathbf{u} \times \mathbf{v} \\
&= (2, 1, 3) \times (2, 0, 0) \\
&= (1 \cdot 0 - 3 \cdot 0,\, 3 \cdot 2 - 2 \cdot 0,\, 2 \cdot 0 - 1 \cdot 2) \\
&= (0, 6, -2)
\end{aligned}$$

and

$$\begin{aligned}
\mathbf{z} &= \mathbf{v} \times \mathbf{u} \\
&= (2, 0, 0) \times (2, 1, 3) \\
&= (0 \cdot 3 - 0 \cdot 1,\, 0 \cdot 2 - 2 \cdot 3,\, 2 \cdot 1 - 0 \cdot 2) \\
&= (0, -6, 2)
\end{aligned}$$

This result makes one thing clear, generally speaking, $\mathbf{u} \times \mathbf{v} \neq \mathbf{v} \times \mathbf{u}$. Therefore, we say that the cross product is anti-commutative. In fact, it can be shown that $\mathbf{u} \times \mathbf{v} = -\mathbf{v} \times \mathbf{u}$. You can determine the vector returned by the cross product by the *left-hand-thumb* rule. If you first aim your fingers in the direction of the first vector, and then curl your fingers towards the second vector (always take the path with the smallest angle), your thumb points in the direction of the returned vector, as shown in Figure 1.13.

To show that $\mathbf{w}$ is orthogonal to $\mathbf{u}$ and that $\mathbf{w}$ is orthogonal to $\mathbf{v}$, we recall from §1.3 that if $\mathbf{u} \cdot \mathbf{v} = 0$, then $\mathbf{u} \perp \mathbf{v}$ (i.e., the vectors are orthogonal). Because

$$\mathbf{w} \cdot \mathbf{u} = (0, 6, -2) \cdot (2, 1, 3) = 0 \cdot 2 + 6 \cdot 1 + (-2) \cdot 3 = 0$$

and

$$\mathbf{w} \cdot \mathbf{v} = (0, 6, -2) \cdot (2, 0, 0) = 0 \cdot 2 + 6 \cdot 0 + (-2) \cdot 0 = 0$$

we conclude that $\mathbf{w}$ is orthogonal to $\mathbf{u}$ and that $\mathbf{w}$ is orthogonal to $\mathbf{v}$.

1.4.1 Pseudo 2D Cross Product

The cross product allows us to find a vector orthogonal to two given 3D vectors. In 2D we do not quite have the same situation, but given a 2D vector $\mathbf{u} = (u_x, u_y)$ it can be useful to find a vector $\mathbf{v}$ orthogonal to $\mathbf{u}$. Figure 1.14 shows the geometric setup from which it is suggested that $\mathbf{v} = (-u_y, u_x)$. The formal proof is straightforward:

$$\mathbf{u} \cdot \mathbf{v} = (u_x, u_y) \cdot (-u_y, u_x) = -u_x u_y + u_y u_x = 0$$

Thus $\mathbf{u} \perp \mathbf{v}$. Observe that $\mathbf{u} \cdot -\mathbf{v} = u_x u_y + u_y (-u_x) = 0$, too, so we also have that $\mathbf{u} \perp -\mathbf{v}$.

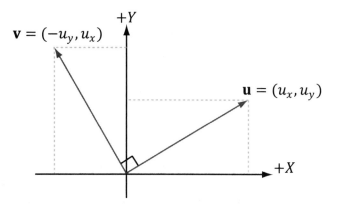

Figure 1.14. The 2D Pseudo Cross Product of a vector u evaluates to an orthogonal vector v.

1.4.2 Orthogonalization with the Cross Product

In §1.3.1, we looked at a way to orthogonalize a set of vectors using the *Gram-Schmidt* process. For 3D, there is another strategy to orthogonalize a set of vectors $\{\mathbf{v}_0, \mathbf{v}_1, \mathbf{v}_2\}$ that are almost orthonormal, but perhaps became un-orthonormal due to accumulated numerical precision errors, using the cross product. Refer to Figure 1.15 for the geometry of this process:

1. Set $\mathbf{w}_0 = \frac{\mathbf{v}_0}{\|\mathbf{v}_0\|}$.

2. Set $\mathbf{w}_2 = \frac{\mathbf{w}_0 \times \mathbf{v}_1}{\|\mathbf{w}_0 \times \mathbf{v}_1\|}$.

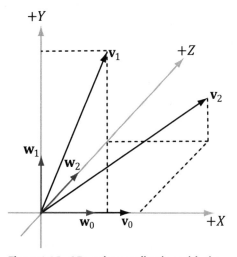

Figure 1.15. 3D orthogonalization with the cross product.

3. Set $\mathbf{w}_1 = \mathbf{w}_2 \times \mathbf{w}_0$. By Exercise 14, $\|\mathbf{w}_2 \times \mathbf{w}_0\| = 1$ because $\mathbf{w}_2 \perp \mathbf{w}_0$ and $\|\mathbf{w}_2\| = \|\mathbf{w}_0\| = 1$, so we do not need to do any normalization in this last step.

At this point, the set of vectors $\{\mathbf{w}_0, \mathbf{w}_1, \mathbf{w}_2\}$ is orthonormal.

Note: *In the previous example, we started with* $\mathbf{w}_0 = \frac{\mathbf{v}_0}{\|\mathbf{v}_0\|}$, *which means we did not change the direction when going from* $\mathbf{v}_0$ *to* $\mathbf{w}_0$; *we only changed the length. However, the directions of* $\mathbf{w}_1$ *and* $\mathbf{w}_2$ *could be different from* $\mathbf{v}_1$ *and* $\mathbf{v}_2$, *respectively. Depending on the specific application, the vector you choose not to change the direction of might be important. For example, later in this book we represent the orientation of the camera with three orthonormal vectors* $\{\mathbf{v}_0, \mathbf{v}_1, \mathbf{v}_2\}$ *where the third vector* $\mathbf{v}_2$ *describes the direction the camera is looking. When orthogonalizing these vectors, we often do not want to change the direction we are looking, and so we will start the previous algorithm with* $\mathbf{v}_2$ *and modify* $\mathbf{v}_0$ *and* $\mathbf{v}_1$ *to orthogonalize the vectors.*

1.5 POINTS

So far we have been discussing vectors, which do not describe positions. However, we will also need to specify positions in our 3D programs, for example, the position of 3D geometry and the position of the 3D virtual camera. Relative to a coordinate system, we can use a vector in standard position (Figure 1.16) to represent a 3D position in space; we call this a *position vector*. In this case, the location of the tip of the vector is the characteristic of interest, not the direction or magnitude. We will use the terms "position vector" and "point" interchangeably since a position vector is enough to identify a point.

One side effect of using vectors to represent points, especially in code, is that we can do vector operations that do not make sense for points; for instance, geometrically, what should the sum of two points mean? On the other hand, some

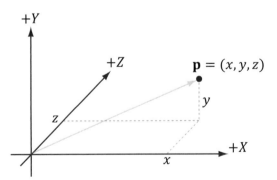

Figure 1.16. The position vector, which extends from the origin to the point, fully describes where the point is located relative to the coordinate system.

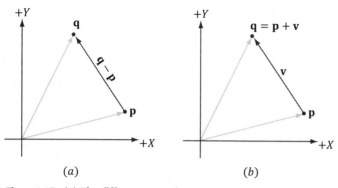

Figure 1.17. (a) The difference q − p between two points is defined as the vector from p to q.
(b) A point p plus the vector v is defined to be the point q obtained by displacing p by the vector v.

operations can be extended to points. For example, we define the difference of two points **q** − **p** to be the vector from **p** to **q**. Also, we define a point **p** plus a vector **v** to be the point **q** obtained by displacing **p** by the vector **v**. Conveniently, because we are using vectors to represent points relative to a coordinate system, no extra work needs to be done for the point operations just discussed, as the vector algebra framework already takes care of them; see Figure 1.17.

Aside: *Actually there is a geometric meaningful way to define a special sum of points, called an affine combination, which is like a weighted average of points.*

1.6 XNA MATH VECTORS

In Direct3D 9 and 10, the D3DX library shipped with a 3D math utility library that included support for vectors among other core 3D math types required for doing 3D graphics. The D3DX library for version 11 no longer ships with 3D math code. Instead it ships with the XNA Math library, which is a vector math library developed separately from Direct3D that takes advantages of special hardware registers on Windows and XBox 360. On Windows, the library uses the SSE2 (Streaming SIMD Extensions 2) instruction set. With 128-bit wide SIMD (single instruction multiple data) registers, SIMD instructions can operate on four 32-bit `floats` or `ints` with one instruction. This is very useful for vector calculations; for example, if you look at vector addition:

$$\mathbf{u} + \mathbf{v} = (u_x + v_x, u_y + v_y, u_z + v_z)$$

we see that we just add corresponding components. By using SIMD, we can do 4D vector addition with one SIMD instruction instead of 4 scalar instructions. If we are working in 3D, we can still use SIMD, but we would just set the 4th component to 0 and ignore it; likewise for 2D.

Our coverage of the XNA Math library is not comprehensive, and we only cover the key parts needed for this book. For all the details, we recommend the online documentation [XNAMath2010]. For readers wishing to understand how an SIMD vector library might be developed optimally, and, perhaps, to gain some insight into why the XNA Math library made some of the design decisions that it did, we recommend the article *Designing Fast Cross-Platform SIMD Vector Libraries* by [Oliveira2010].

To use the XNA Math library, you only need to #include <xnamath.h>. There are no additional library files, as all the code is implemented inline in the header file.

> Note: *There is nothing that stops you from including <d3dx10.h>, linking with d3dx10.lib, and using the D3DX10 Math functions instead of the XNA math library.*

1.6.1 Vector Types

In XNA Math, the core vector type is **XMVECTOR**, which maps to SIMD hardware registers. This is a 128-bit type that can process four 32-bit floats with a single SIMD instruction. When SSE2 is available, it is defined like so:

```
typedef __m128 XMVECTOR;
```

where **__m128** is a special SIMD type. When doing calculations, vectors must be of this type to take advantage of SIMD. As already mentioned, we still use this type for 2D and 3D vectors to take advantage of SIMD, but we just zero out the unused components and ignore them.

XMVECTOR needs to be 16-byte aligned, and this is done automatically for local and global variables. For class data members, it is recommended to use **XMFLOAT2** (2D), **XMFLOAT3** (3D), and **XMFLOAT4** (4D) instead; these structures are defined below:

```
typedef struct _XMFLOAT2 {
    FLOAT x;
    FLOAT y;
} XMFLOAT2;

typedef struct _XMFLOAT3 {
    FLOAT x;
    FLOAT y;
    FLOAT z;
} XMFLOAT3;

typedef struct _XMFLOAT4 {
    FLOAT x;
    FLOAT y;
    FLOAT z;
    FLOAT w;
} XMFLOAT4;
```

However, if we use these types directly for calculations, then we will not take advantage of SIMD. In order to use SIMD, we need to convert instances of these types into the **XMVECTOR** type. This is done with the XNA Math loading functions. Conversely, XNA Math provides storage functions which are used to convert data from **XMVECTOR** into the **XMFLOAT*** types described previously.

To summarize,

1. Use **XMVECTOR** for local or global variables.

2. Use **XMFLOAT2**, **XMFLOAT3**, and **XMFLOAT4** for class data members.

3. Use loading functions to convert from **XMFLOAT*** to **XMVECTOR** before doing calculations.

4. Do calculations with **XMVECTOR** instances.

5. Use storage functions to convert from **XMVECTOR** to **XMFLOAT***.

1.6.2 Loading and Storage Methods

We use the following methods to load data from **XMFLOAT*** into **XMVECTOR**:

```
// Loads XMFLOAT2 into XMVECTOR
XMVECTOR XMLoadFloat2(CONST XMFLOAT2 *pSource);

// Loads XMFLOAT3 into XMVECTOR
XMVECTOR XMLoadFloat3(CONST XMFLOAT3 *pSource);

// Loads XMFLOAT4 into XMVECTOR
XMVECTOR XMLoadFloat4(CONST XMFLOAT4 *pSource);
```

Note: *There are many more loading methods used to load other data types into an* **XMVECTOR***; the reader can view the XNA Math documentation for the complete list. Following are a few more examples:*

```
// Loads 3-element UINT array into XMVECTOR
XMVECTOR XMLoadInt3(CONST UINT* pSource);

// Loads XMCOLOR into XMVECTOR
XMVECTOR XMLoadColor(CONST XMCOLOR *pSource);

// Loads XMBYTE4 into XMVECTOR
XMVECTOR XMLoadByte4(CONST XMBYTE4 *pSource);
```

We use the following methods to store data from **XMVECTOR** into **XMFLOAT***:

```
// Loads XMVECTOR into XMFLOAT2
VOID XMStoreFloat2(XMFLOAT2 *pDestination, FXMVECTOR V);

// Loads XMVECTOR into XMFLOAT3
VOID XMStoreFloat3(XMFLOAT3 *pDestination, FXMVECTOR V);

// Loads XMVECTOR into XMFLOAT4
VOID XMStoreFloat4(XMFLOAT4 *pDestination, FXMVECTOR V);
```

There are many more storing methods used to store **XMVECTOR** *into other data types. Following is a small sampling; the reader can see the XNA Math documentation for the complete list.*

```
// Loads XMVECTOR into 3 element UINT array
VOID XMStoreInt3(UINT* pDestination, FXMVECTOR V);

// Loads XMVECTOR into XMCOLOR
VOID XMStoreColor(XMCOLOR* pDestination, FXMVECTOR V);

// Loads XMVECTOR into XMBYTE4
VOID XMStoreByte4(XMBYTE4 *pDestination, FXMVECTOR V);
```

Sometimes we just want to get or set one component of an **XMVECTOR**; the following getter and setter functions facilitate this:

```
FLOAT XMVectorGetX(FXMVECTOR V);
FLOAT XMVectorGetY(FXMVECTOR V);
FLOAT XMVectorGetZ(FXMVECTOR V);
FLOAT XMVectorGetW(FXMVECTOR V);

XMVECTOR XMVectorSetX(FXMVECTOR V, FLOAT x);
XMVECTOR XMVectorSetY(FXMVECTOR V, FLOAT y);
XMVECTOR XMVectorSetZ(FXMVECTOR V, FLOAT z);
XMVECTOR XMVectorSetW(FXMVECTOR V, FLOAT w);
```

1.6.3 Parameter Passing

To take advantage of SIMD, there are some rules for passing parameters to functions of type **XMVECTOR**. These rules differ based on the platform; in particular, they differ between 32-bit Windows, 64-bit Windows, and XBox 360. To be platform independent, we use the types **CXMVECTOR** and **FXMVECTOR** for passing **XMVECTOR** parameters; these are defined to the right type based on the platform. For Windows, these are defined as:

```
// 32-bit Windows
typedef const XMVECTOR FXMVECTOR;
typedef const XMVECTOR& CXMVECTOR;

// 64-bit Windows
typedef const XMVECTOR& FXMVECTOR;
typedef const XMVECTOR& CXMVECTOR;
```

The difference is whether we can pass a copy of **XMVECTOR** directly, or if we must pass a reference. Now the rule for passing **XMVECTOR** parameters is as follows:

The first 3 **XMVECTOR** parameters should be of type **FXMVECTOR**; any additional **XMVECTOR** parameters should be of type **CXMVECTOR**. Here is an example:

```
XMINLINE XMMATRIX XMMatrixTransformation(
    FXMVECTOR ScalingOrigin,
    FXMVECTOR ScalingOrientationQuaternion,
```

```
    FXMVECTOR Scaling,
    CXMVECTOR RotationOrigin,
    CXMVECTOR RotationQuaternion,
    CXMVECTOR Translation);
```

This function takes 6 **XMVECTOR** parameters, but following the parameter passing rules, it uses the **FXMVECTOR** and **CXMVECTOR** types. The first three **XMVECTOR** parameters are of type **FXMVECTOR** and the additional **XMVECTOR** parameters are of type **CXMVECTOR**. Note that you can have non-**XMVECTOR** parameters between **XMVECTOR** parameters; the first 3 **XMVECTOR** parameters are still typed as **XMVECTOR**, and additional **XMVECTOR** parameters are typed as **CXMVECTOR**:

```
XMINLINE XMMATRIX XMMatrixTransformation2D(
    FXMVECTOR ScalingOrigin,
    FLOAT     ScalingOrientation,
    FXMVECTOR Scaling,
    FXMVECTOR RotationOrigin,
    FLOAT     Rotation,
    CXMVECTOR Translation);
```

1.6.4 Constant Vectors

Constant **XMVECTOR** instances should use the **XMVECTORF32** type. Here are some examples from the DirectX SDK's CascadedShadowMaps11 sample:

```
static const XMVECTORF32 g_vHalfVector = { 0.5f, 0.5f, 0.5f, 0.5f };
static const XMVECTORF32 g_vZero = { 0.0f, 0.0f, 0.0f, 0.0f };

XMVECTORF32 vRightTop = {
    vViewFrust.RightSlope,
    vViewFrust.TopSlope,
    1.0f,1.0f
};

XMVECTORF32 vLeftBottom = {
    vViewFrust.LeftSlope,
    vViewFrust.BottomSlope,
    1.0f,1.0f
};
```

Essentially, we use **XMVECTORF32** whenever we want to use initialization syntax. **XMVECTORF32** is a 16-byte aligned structure with a **XMVECTOR** conversion operator; it is defined as follows:

```
// Conversion types for constants
typedef _DECLSPEC_ALIGN_16_ struct XMVECTORF32 {
    union {
      float f[4];
      XMVECTOR v;
    };

#if defined(__cplusplus)
    inline operator XMVECTOR() const { return v; }
```

```
#if !defined(_XM_NO_INTRINSICS_) && defined(_XM_SSE_INTRINSICS_)
    inline operator __m128i() const
      { return reinterpret_cast<const __m128i *>(&v)[0]; }
    inline operator __m128d() const
      { return reinterpret_cast<const __m128d *>(&v)[0]; }
#endif
#endif // __cplusplus
} XMVECTORF32;
```

You can also create a constant **xmvector** of integer data using **xmvectoru32**:

```
static const XMVECTORU32 vGrabY = {
    0x00000000,0xFFFFFFFF,0x00000000,0x00000000
};
```

1.6.5 Overloaded Operators

The **xmvector** has several overloaded operators for doing vector addition, subtraction, and scalar multiplication. Operator overloading can be disabled by defining **XM_NO_OPERATOR_OVERLOADS**. The reason some application would want to disable operator overloading is for performance, as the function versions can be faster when forming complex expressions (see [Oliveira2010]). We prefer the more intuitive syntax of operator overloading in this book and keep it enabled.

```
// Vector operators
#if defined(__cplusplus) && !defined(XM_NO_OPERATOR_OVERLOADS)

XMVECTOR    operator+ (FXMVECTOR V);
XMVECTOR    operator- (FXMVECTOR V);

XMVECTOR&   operator+= (XMVECTOR& V1, FXMVECTOR V2);
XMVECTOR&   operator-= (XMVECTOR& V1, FXMVECTOR V2);
XMVECTOR&   operator*= (XMVECTOR& V1, FXMVECTOR V2);
XMVECTOR&   operator/= (XMVECTOR& V1, FXMVECTOR V2);
XMVECTOR&   operator*= (XMVECTOR& V, FLOAT S);
XMVECTOR&   operator/= (XMVECTOR& V, FLOAT S);

XMVECTOR    operator+ (FXMVECTOR V1, FXMVECTOR V2);
XMVECTOR    operator- (FXMVECTOR V1, FXMVECTOR V2);
XMVECTOR    operator* (FXMVECTOR V1, FXMVECTOR V2);
XMVECTOR    operator/ (FXMVECTOR V1, FXMVECTOR V2);
XMVECTOR    operator* (FXMVECTOR V, FLOAT S);
XMVECTOR    operator* (FLOAT S, FXMVECTOR V);
XMVECTOR    operator/ (FXMVECTOR V, FLOAT S);

#endif // __cplusplus && !XM_NO_OPERATOR_OVERLOADS
```

1.6.6 Miscellaneous

The XNA Math library defined the following constants useful for approximating different expressions involving π:

```
#define XM_PI               3.141592654f
#define XM_2PI              6.283185307f
#define XM_1DIVPI           0.318309886f
#define XM_1DIV2PI          0.159154943f
#define XM_PIDIV2           1.570796327f
#define XM_PIDIV4           0.785398163f
```

In addition, it defines the following inline functions for converting between radians and degrees:

```
XMFINLINE FLOAT XMConvertToRadians(FLOAT fDegrees)
{
    return fDegrees * (XM_PI / 180.0f);
}


XMFINLINE FLOAT XMConvertToDegrees(FLOAT fRadians)
{
    return fRadians * (180.0f / XM_PI);
}
```

It also defines min/max macros:

```
#define XMMin(a, b) (((a) < (b)) ? (a) : (b))
#define XMMax(a, b) (((a) > (b)) ? (a) : (b))
```

1.6.7 Setter Functions

XNA Math provides the following functions to set the contents of an **XMVECTOR**:

```
XMVECTOR XMVectorZero();          // Returns the zero vector 0

XMVECTOR XMVectorSplatOne();      // Returns the vector (1, 1, 1, 1)

XMVECTOR XMVectorSet(             // Returns the vector (x, y, z, w)
    FLOAT x, FLOAT y, FLOAT z, FLOAT w);

XMVECTOR XMVectorReplicate(       // Returns the vector (s, s, s, s)
    FLOAT s);

XMVECTOR XMVectorSplatX(          // Returns the vector (v_x, v_x, v_x, v_x)
    FXMVECTOR V);

XMVECTOR XMVectorSplatY(          // Returns the vector (v_y, v_y, v_y, v_y)
    FXMVECTOR V);

XMVECTOR XMVectorSplatZ(          // Returns the vector (v_z, v_z, v_z, v_z)
    FXMVECTOR V);
```

The following program illustrates most of these functions:

```
#include <windows.h> // for FLOAT definition
#include <xnamath.h>
#include <iostream>
using namespace std;
```

```
// Overload the "<<" operators so that we can use cout to
// output XMVECTOR objects.
ostream& operator<<(ostream& os, FXMVECTOR v)
{
    XMFLOAT3 dest;
    XMStoreFloat3(&dest, v);

    os << "(" << dest.x << ", " << dest.y << ", " << dest.z << ")";
    return os;
}

int main()
{
    cout.setf(ios_base::boolalpha);

    // Check support for SSE2 (Pentium4, AMD K8, and above).
    if( !XMVerifyCPUSupport() )
    {
      cout << "xna math not supported" << endl;
      return 0;
    }

    XMVECTOR p = XMVectorZero();
    XMVECTOR q = XMVectorSplatOne();
    XMVECTOR u = XMVectorSet(1.0f, 2.0f, 3.0f, 0.0f);
    XMVECTOR v = XMVectorReplicate(-2.0f);
    XMVECTOR w = XMVectorSplatZ(u);

    cout << "p = " << p << endl;
    cout << "q = " << q << endl;
    cout << "u = " << u << endl;
    cout << "v = " << v << endl;
    cout << "w = " << w << endl;

    return 0;
}
```

1.6.8 Vector Functions

XNA Math provides the following functions to do various vector operations. We illustrate with the 3D versions, but there are analogous versions for 2D and 4D; the

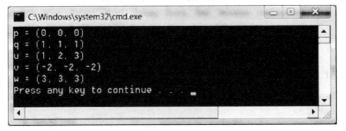

Figure 1.18. Output for the previous program.

2D and 4D versions have the same names as the 3D versions, with the exception of a 2 and 4 substituted for the 3, respectively.

```
XMVECTOR XMVector3Length(          // Returns ||v||
    FXMVECTOR V);                  // Input v

XMVECTOR XMVector3LengthSq(        // Returns ||v||²
    FXMVECTOR V);                  // Input v

XMVECTOR XMVector3Dot(             // Returns  v₁ · v₂
    FXMVECTOR V1,                  // Input v₁
    FXMVECTOR V2);                 // Input v₂

XMVECTOR XMVector3Cross(           // Returns v₁ × v₂
    FXMVECTOR V1,                  // Input  v₁
    FXMVECTOR V2);                 // Input  v₂

XMVECTOR XMVector3Normalize(       // Returns v/||v||
    FXMVECTOR V);                  // Input v

XMVECTOR XMVector3Orthogonal(      // Returns a vector orthogonal to v
    FXMVECTOR V);                  // Input v

XMVECTOR
XMVector3AngleBetweenVectors(      // Returns the angle between v₁ and v₂
    FXMVECTOR V1,                  // Input v₁
    FXMVECTOR V2);                 // Input v₂

VOID XMVector3ComponentsFromNormal(
    XMVECTOR* pParallel,           // Returns projₙ(v)
    XMVECTOR* pPerpendicular,      // Returns prepₙ(v)
    FXMVECTOR  V,                  // Input v
    FXMVECTOR  Normal);            // Input n

BOOL XMVector3Equal(               // Returns v₁ = v₂
    FXMVECTOR V1,                  // Input v₁
    FXMVECTOR V2);                 // Input v₂

BOOL XMVector3NotEqual(            // Returns v₁ ≠ v₂
    FXMVECTOR V1,                  // Input v₁
    FXMVECTOR V2);                 // Input v₂
```

The function listings above reflect the source code. The inline mathematical annotations are rendered as:

- $XMVector3Length$: Returns $\|\mathbf{v}\|$; Input $\mathbf{v}$
- $XMVector3LengthSq$: Returns $\|\mathbf{v}\|^2$; Input $\mathbf{v}$
- $XMVector3Dot$: Returns $\mathbf{v}_1 \cdot \mathbf{v}_2$; Input $\mathbf{v}_1$, $\mathbf{v}_2$
- $XMVector3Cross$: Returns $\mathbf{v}_1 \times \mathbf{v}_2$; Input $\mathbf{v}_1$, $\mathbf{v}_2$
- $XMVector3Normalize$: Returns $\mathbf{v}/\|\mathbf{v}\|$; Input $\mathbf{v}$
- $XMVector3Orthogonal$: Returns a vector orthogonal to $\mathbf{v}$; Input $\mathbf{v}$
- $XMVector3AngleBetweenVectors$: Returns the angle between $\mathbf{v}_1$ and $\mathbf{v}_2$; Input $\mathbf{v}_1$, $\mathbf{v}_2$
- $XMVector3ComponentsFromNormal$: Returns $\text{proj}_n(\mathbf{v})$, $\text{prep}_n(\mathbf{v})$; Input $\mathbf{v}$, $\mathbf{n}$
- $XMVector3Equal$: Returns $\mathbf{v}_1 = \mathbf{v}_2$; Input $\mathbf{v}_1$, $\mathbf{v}_2$
- $XMVector3NotEqual$: Returns $\mathbf{v}_1 \neq \mathbf{v}_2$; Input $\mathbf{v}_1$, $\mathbf{v}_2$

Note: *Observe that these functions return XMVECTORs even for operations that mathematically return a scalar (for example, the dot product $k = \mathbf{v}_1 \cdot \mathbf{v}_2$). The scalar result is replicated in each component of the XMVECTOR. For example, for the dot product, the returned vector would be $(\mathbf{v}_1 \cdot \mathbf{v}_2, \mathbf{v}_1 \cdot \mathbf{v}_2, \mathbf{v}_1 \cdot \mathbf{v}_2, \mathbf{v}_1 \cdot \mathbf{v}_2)$. One reason for this is to minimize mixing of scalar and SIMD vector operations; it is more efficient to keep everything SIMD until you are done with your calculations.*

The following demo program shows how to use most of these functions, as well as some of the overloaded operators:

```cpp
#include <windows.h> // for FLOAT definition
#include <xnamath.h>
#include <iostream>
using namespace std;

// Overload the  "<<" operators so that we can use cout to
// output XMVECTOR objects.
ostream& operator<<(ostream& os, FXMVECTOR v)
{
    XMFLOAT3 dest;
    XMStoreFloat3(&dest, v);

    os << "(" << dest.x << ", " << dest.y << ", " << dest.z << ")";
    return os;
}

int main()
{
    cout.setf(ios_base::boolalpha);

    // Check support for SSE2 (Pentium4, AMD K8, and above).
    if( !XMVerifyCPUSupport() )
    {
      cout << "xna math not supported" << endl;
      return 0;
    }

    XMVECTOR n = XMVectorSet(1.0f, 0.0f, 0.0f, 0.0f);
    XMVECTOR u = XMVectorSet(1.0f, 2.0f, 3.0f, 0.0f);
    XMVECTOR v = XMVectorSet(-2.0f, 1.0f, -3.0f, 0.0f);
    XMVECTOR w = XMVectorSet(0.707f, 0.707f, 0.0f, 0.0f);

    // Vector addition: XMVECTOR operator +
    XMVECTOR a = u + v;
    // Vector subtraction: XMVECTOR operator -
    XMVECTOR b = u - v;

    // Scalar multiplication: XMVECTOR operator *
    XMVECTOR c = 10.0f*u;

    // ||u||
    XMVECTOR L = XMVector3Length(u);

    // d = u / ||u||
    XMVECTOR d = XMVector3Normalize(u);

    // s = u dot v
    XMVECTOR s = XMVector3Dot(u, v);

    // e = u x v
    XMVECTOR e = XMVector3Cross(u, v);

    // Find proj_n(w) and perp_n(w)
    XMVECTOR projW;
```

```
XMVECTOR perpW;
XMVector3ComponentsFromNormal(&projW, &perpW, w, n);

// Does projW + perpW == w?
bool equal = XMVector3Equal(projW + perpW, w) != 0;
bool notEqual = XMVector3NotEqual(projW + perpW, w) != 0;

// The angle between projW and perpW should be 90 degrees.
XMVECTOR angleVec = XMVector3AngleBetweenVectors(projW, perpW);
float angleRadians = XMVectorGetX(angleVec);
float angleDegrees = XMConvertToDegrees(angleRadians);

cout << "u                  = " << u << endl;
cout << "v                  = " << v << endl;
cout << "w                  = " << w << endl;
cout << "n                  = " << n << endl;
cout << "a = u + v          = " << a << endl;
cout << "b = u - v          = " << b << endl;
cout << "c = 10 * u         = " << c << endl;
cout << "d = u / ||u||      = " << d << endl;
cout << "e = u x v          = " << e << endl;
cout << "L  = ||u||         = " << L << endl;
cout << "s = u.v            = " << s << endl;
cout << "projW              = " << projW << endl;
cout << "perpW              = " << perpW << endl;
cout << "projW + perpW == w = " << equal << endl;
cout << "projW + perpW != w = " << notEqual << endl;
cout << "angle              = " << angleDegrees << endl;

return 0;
}
```

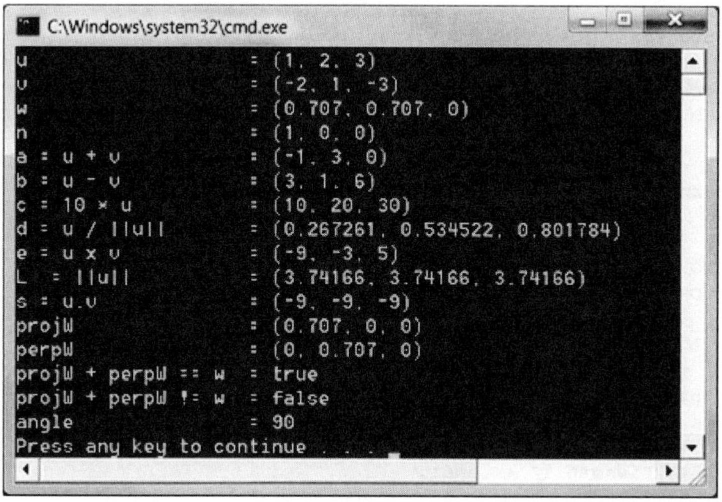

Figure 1.19. Output for the above program.

Note: *The XNA Math library also includes some estimation methods, which are less accurate but faster to compute. If you are willing to sacrifice some accuracy for speed, then use the estimate methods. Here are two examples of estimate functions:*

```
XMFINLINE XMVECTOR XMVector3LengthEst(      // Returns estimated ||v||
    FXMVECTOR V);                            // Input v


XMFINLINE XMVECTOR XMVector3NormalizeEst(   // Returns estimated v/||v||
    FXMVECTOR V);                            // Input v
```

1.6.9 Floating-Point Error

While on the subject of working with vectors on a computer, we should be aware of the following. When comparing floating-point numbers, care must be taken due to floating-point imprecision. Two floating-point numbers that we expect to be equal may differ slightly. For example, mathematically, we'd expect a normalized vector to have a length of one, but in a computer program, the length will only be approximately one. Moreover, mathematically, $1^p = 1$ for any real number p, but when we only have a numerical approximation for , we see that the approximation raised to the th power increases the error; thus, numerical error also accumulates. The following short program illustrates these ideas:

```cpp
#include <windows.h> // for FLOAT definition
#include <xnamath.h>
#include <iostream>
using namespace std;

int main()
{
    cout.precision(8);

    // Check support for SSE2 (Pentium4, AMD K8, and above).
    if( !XMVerifyCPUSupport() )
    {
        cout << "xna math not supported" << endl;
        return 0;
    }

    XMVECTOR u = XMVectorSet(1.0f, 1.0f, 1.0f, 0.0f);
    XMVECTOR n = XMVector3Normalize(u);

    float LU = XMVectorGetX(XMVector3Length(n));

    // Mathematically, the length should be 1.  Is it numerically?
    cout << LU << endl;
    if( LU == 1.0f )
        cout << "Length 1" << endl;
    else
        cout << "Length not 1" << endl;
```

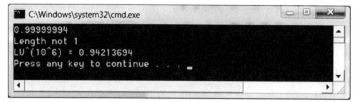

Figure 1.20. Output for the above program.

```
        // Raising 1 to any power should still be 1.  Is it?
        float powLU = powf(LU, 1.0e6f);
        cout << "LU^(10^6) = " << powLU << endl;
}
```

To compensate for floating-point imprecision, we test if two floating-point numbers are approximately equal. We do this by defining an Epsilon constant, which is a very small value we use as a "buffer." We say two values are approximately equal if their distance is less than Epsilon. In other words, Epsilon gives us some tolerance for floating-point imprecision. The following function illustrates how Epsilon can be used to test if two floating-point values are equal:

```
const float Epsilon = 0.001f;
bool Equals(float lhs, float rhs)
{
        // Is the distance between lhs and rhs less than EPSILON?
        return fabs(lhs - rhs) < Epsilon ? true : false;
}
```

The XNA Math library provides the XMVector3NearEqual function when testing the equality of vectors with an allowed tolerance Epsilon parameter:

```
// Returns
//      abs(U.x - V.x) <= Epsilon.x &&
//      abs(U.y - V.y) <= Epsilon.y &&
//      abs(U.z - V.z) <= Epsilon.z
XMFINLINE BOOL XMVector3NearEqual(
        FXMVECTOR U,
        FXMVECTOR V,
        FXMVECTOR Epsilon);
```

1.7 SUMMARY

1. Vectors are used to model physical quantities that possess both magnitude and direction. Geometrically, we represent a vector with a directed line segment. A vector is in standard position when it is translated parallel to itself so that its tail coincides with the origin of the coordinate system. A vector in standard

position can be described numerically by specifying the coordinates of its head relative to a coordinate system.

2.   If $\mathbf{u} = (u_x, u_y, u_z)$ and $\mathbf{v} = (v_x, v_y, v_z)$, then we have the following vector operations:

(a) Addition: $\mathbf{u} + \mathbf{v} = (u_x + v_x, u_y + v_y, u_z + v_z)$

(b) Subtraction: $\mathbf{u} - \mathbf{v} = (u_x - v_x, u_y - v_y, u_z - v_z)$

(c) Scalar Multiplication: $k\mathbf{u} = (ku_x, ku_y, ku_z)$

(d) Length: $\| \mathbf{u} \| = \sqrt{x^2 + y^2 + z^2}$

(e) Normalization: $\hat{\mathbf{u}} = \frac{\mathbf{u}}{\|\mathbf{u}\|} = \left(\frac{x}{\|\mathbf{u}\|}, \frac{y}{\|\mathbf{u}\|}, \frac{z}{\|\mathbf{u}\|} \right)$

(f) Dot Product: $\mathbf{u} \cdot \mathbf{v} = \| \mathbf{u} \| \| \mathbf{v} \| \cos \theta = u_x v_x + u_y v_y + u_z v_z$

(g) Cross Product: $\mathbf{u} \times \mathbf{v} = (u_y v_z - u_z v_y, u_z v_x - u_x v_z, u_x v_y - u_y v_x)$

3.   We use the XNA Math **XMVECTOR** class to describe vectors efficiently in code using SIMD operations. For class data members, we use the **XMFLOAT3** class, and then use the loading and storage methods to convert back and forth between **XMVECTOR** and **XMFLOAT3**. Constant vectors that require initialization syntax should use the **XMVECTORF32** type.

4.   To take advantage of SIMD, there are some rules for passing parameters to functions of type **XMVECTOR**. To be platform independent, we use the types **CXMVECTOR** and **FXMVECTOR** for passing **XMVECTOR** parameters; these are defined to the right type based on the platform. Then the rule for passing **XMVECTOR** parameters is that the first 3 **XMVECTOR** parameters should be of type **FXMVECTOR**; any additional **XMVECTOR** parameters should be of type **CXMVECTOR**.

5.   The **XMVECTOR** class overloads the arithmetic operators to do vector addition, subtraction, and scalar multiplication. Moreover, the XNA Math library provides the following useful functions for computing the length of a vector, the squared length of a vector, computing the dot product of two vectors, computing the cross product of two vectors, and normalizing a vector:

```
XMVECTOR XMVector3Length(FXMVECTOR V);
XMVECTOR XMVector3LengthSq(FXMVECTOR V);
XMVECTOR XMVector3Dot(FXMVECTOR V1, FXMVECTOR V2);
XMVECTOR XMVector3Cross(FXMVECTOR V1, FXMVECTOR V2);
XMVECTOR XMVector3Normalize(FXMVECTOR V);
```

1.8 EXERCISES

1.   Let $\mathbf{u} = (1, 2)$ and $\mathbf{v} = (3, -4)$. Perform the following computations and draw the vectors relative to a 2D coordinate system.

   (a) $\mathbf{u} + \mathbf{v}$

   (b) $\mathbf{u} - \mathbf{v}$

   (c) $2\mathbf{u} + \frac{1}{2}\mathbf{v}$

   (d) $-2\mathbf{u} + \mathbf{v}$

2. Let $\mathbf{u} = (-1, 3, 2)$ and $\mathbf{v} = (3, -4, 1)$ Perform the following computations.

   (a) $\mathbf{u} + \mathbf{v}$

   (b) $\mathbf{u} - \mathbf{v}$

   (c) $3\mathbf{u} + 2\mathbf{v}$

   (δ) $-2\mathbf{u} + \mathbf{v}$

3. This exercise shows that vector algebra shares many of the nice properties of real numbers (this is not an exhaustive list). Assume $\mathbf{u} = (u_x, u_y, u_z)$, $\mathbf{v} = (v_x, v_y, v_z)$, and $\mathbf{w} = (w_x, w_y, w_z)$. Also assume that c and k are scalars. Prove the following vector properties.

   (a) $\mathbf{u} + \mathbf{v} = \mathbf{v} + \mathbf{u}$ (Commutative Property of Addition)

   (b) $\mathbf{u} + (\mathbf{v} + \mathbf{w}) = (\mathbf{u} + \mathbf{v}) + \mathbf{w}$ (Associative Property of Addition)

   (c) $(ck)\mathbf{u} = c(k\mathbf{u})$ (Associative Property of Scalar Multiplication)

   (d) $k(\mathbf{u} + \mathbf{v}) = k\mathbf{u} + k\mathbf{v}$ (Distributive Property 1)

   (e) $\mathbf{u}(k + c) = k\mathbf{u} + c\mathbf{u}$ (Distributive Property 2)

Hint: *Just use the definition of the vector operations and the properties of real numbers. For example,*

$$(ck)\mathbf{u} = (ck)(u_x, u_y, u_z)$$
$$= ((ck)u_x, (ck)u_y, (ck)u_z)$$
$$= (c(ku_x), c(ku_y), c(ku_z))$$
$$= c(ku_x, ku_y, ku_z) = c(k\mathbf{u})$$

4. Solve the equation $2((1, 2, 3) - \mathbf{x}) - (-2, 0, 4) = -2(1, 2, 3)$ for $\mathbf{x}$.

5. Let $\mathbf{u} = (-1, 3, 2)$ and $\mathbf{v} = (3, -4, 1)$. Normalize $\mathbf{u}$ and $\mathbf{v}$.

6. Let k be a scalar and let $\mathbf{u} = (u_x, u_y, u_z)$. Prove that $\| k\mathbf{u} \| = |k| \, \| \mathbf{u} \|$.

7. Is the angle between $\mathbf{u}$ and $\mathbf{v}$ orthogonal, acute, or obtuse?

   (a) $\mathbf{u} = (1, 1, 1), \mathbf{v} = (2, 3, 4)$

   (b) $\mathbf{u} = (1, 1, 0), \mathbf{v} = (-2, 2, 0)$

   (c) $\mathbf{u} = (-1, -1, -1), \mathbf{v} = (3, 1, 0)$

8. Let $\mathbf{u} = (-1, 3, 2)$ and $\mathbf{v} = (3, -4, 1)$. Find the angle θ between $\mathbf{u}$ and $\mathbf{v}$.

9. Let $\mathbf{u} = (u_x, u_y, u_z)$, $\mathbf{v} = (v_x, v_y, v_z)$, and $\mathbf{w} = (w_x, w_y, w_z)$. Also let c and k be scalars. Prove the following dot product properties.

    (a) $\mathbf{u} \cdot \mathbf{v} = \mathbf{v} \cdot \mathbf{u}$

    (b) $\mathbf{u} \cdot (\mathbf{v} + \mathbf{w}) = \mathbf{u} \cdot \mathbf{v} + \mathbf{u} \cdot \mathbf{w}$

    (c) $k\,(\mathbf{u} \cdot \mathbf{v}) = (k\mathbf{u}) \cdot \mathbf{v} = \mathbf{u} \cdot (k\mathbf{v})$

    (d) $\mathbf{v} \cdot \mathbf{v} = \|\mathbf{v}\|^2$

    (e) $\mathbf{0} \cdot \mathbf{v} = 0$

 Just use the definitions, for example,

$$\mathbf{v} \cdot \mathbf{v} = v_x v_x + v_y v_y + v_z v_z$$
$$= v_x^2 + v_y^2 + v_z^2$$
$$= \left(\sqrt{v_x^2 + v_y^2 + v_z^2}\right)^2$$
$$= \|\mathbf{v}\|^2$$

10 . Use the law of cosines ($c^2 = a^2 + b^2 - 2ab \cos \theta$, where a, b, and c are the lengths of the sides of a triangle and θ is the angle between sides a and b) to show

$$u_x v_x + u_y v_y + u_z v_z = \|\mathbf{u}\| \|\mathbf{v}\| \cos \theta$$

 Consider Figure 1.9 and set $c^2 = \|\mathbf{u} - \mathbf{v}\|$, $a^2 = \|\mathbf{u}\|^2$, and $b^2 = \|\mathbf{v}\|^2$, and use the dot product properties from the previous exercise.

11 . Let $\mathbf{n} = (-2, 1)$. Decompose the vector $\mathbf{g} = (0, -9.8)$ into the sum of two orthogonal vectors, one parallel to $\mathbf{n}$ and the other orthogonal to $\mathbf{n}$. Also, draw the vectors relative to a 2D coordinate system.

12 . Let $\mathbf{u} = (-2, 1, 4)$ and $\mathbf{v} = (3, -4, 1)$. Find $\mathbf{w} = \mathbf{u} \times \mathbf{v}$, and show $\mathbf{w} \cdot \mathbf{u} = 0$ and $\mathbf{w} \cdot \mathbf{v} = 0$.

13 . Let the following points define a triangle relative to some coordinate system: $\mathbf{A} = (0,0,0)$, $\mathbf{B} = (0,1,3)$, and $\mathbf{C} = (5,1,0)$. Find a vector orthogonal to this triangle.

 Find two vectors on two of the triangle's edges and use the cross product.

14 . Prove that $\|\mathbf{u} \times \mathbf{v}\| = \|\mathbf{u}\| \|\mathbf{v}\| \sin \theta$.

 Start with $\|\mathbf{u}\| \|\mathbf{v}\| \sin \theta$ and use the trigonometric identity $\cos^2 \theta + \sin^2 \theta = 1 \Rightarrow \sin \theta = \sqrt{1 - \cos^2 \theta}$; then apply Equation 1.4.

15 . Prove that $\|\mathbf{u} \times \mathbf{v}\|$ gives the area of the parallelogram spanned by $\mathbf{u}$ and $\mathbf{v}$; see Figure 1.21.

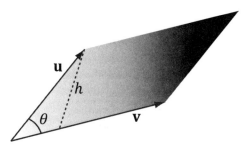

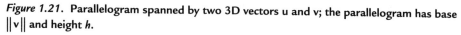

Figure 1.21. Parallelogram spanned by two 3D vectors u and v; the parallelogram has base $\|\mathbf{v}\|$ and height *h*.

16 . Give an example of 3D vectors **u**, **v**, and **w** such that $\mathbf{u} \times (\mathbf{v} \times \mathbf{w}) \neq (\mathbf{u} \times \mathbf{v}) \times \mathbf{w}$. This shows the cross product is generally not associative.

 Consider combinations of the simple vectors $\mathbf{i} = (1,0,0), \mathbf{j} = (0,1,0),$ *and* $\mathbf{k} = (0,0,1)$.

17 . Prove that the cross product of two nonzero parallel vectors results in the null vector; that is, $\mathbf{u} \times k\mathbf{u} = 0$.

Just use the cross product definition.

18 . Orthonormalize the set of vectors $\{(1,0,0),(1,5,0),(2,1,-4)\}$ using the *Gram-Schmidt* process.

19 . Consider the following program and output. Make a conjecture of what each **XMVector*** function does; then look up each function in the XNA Math documentation.

```
#include <windows.h> // for FLOAT definition
#include <xnamath.h>
#include <iostream>
using namespace std;

// Overload the  "<<" operators so that we can use cout to
// output XMVECTOR objects.
ostream& operator<<(ostream& os, FXMVECTOR v)
{
    XMFLOAT4 dest;
    XMStoreFloat4(&dest, v);

    os << "(" << dest.x << ", " << dest.y << ", "
      << dest.z <<  ", " << dest.w << ")";
    return os;
}

int main()
{
    cout.setf(ios_base::boolalpha);
```

```
// Check support for SSE2 (Pentium4, AMD K8, and above).
if( !XMVerifyCPUSupport() )
{
  cout << "xna math not supported" << endl;
  return 0;
}

XMVECTOR p = XMVectorSet(2.0f, 2.0f, 1.0f, 0.0f);
XMVECTOR q = XMVectorSet(2.0f, -0.5f, 0.5f, 0.1f);
XMVECTOR u = XMVectorSet(1.0f, 2.0f, 4.0f, 8.0f);
XMVECTOR v = XMVectorSet(-2.0f, 1.0f, -3.0f, 2.5f);
XMVECTOR w = XMVectorSet(0.0f, XM_PIDIV4, XM_PIDIV2, XM_PI);

cout << "XMVectorAbs(v)            = " << XMVectorAbs(v) << endl;
cout << "XMVectorCos(w)            = " << XMVectorCos(w) << endl;
cout << "XMVectorLog(u)            = " << XMVectorLog(u) << endl;
cout << "XMVectorExp(p)            = " << XMVectorExp(p) << endl;

cout << "XMVectorPow(u, p)         = " << XMVectorPow(u, p) << endl;
cout << "XMVectorSqrt(u)           = " << XMVectorSqrt(u) << endl;

cout << "XMVectorSwizzle(u, 2, 2, 1, 3) = "
  << XMVectorSwizzle(u, 2, 2, 1, 3) << endl;
cout << "XMVectorSwizzle(u, 2, 1, 0, 3) = "
  << XMVectorSwizzle(u, 2, 1, 0, 3) << endl;

cout << "XMVectorMultiply(u, v)  = "
  << XMVectorMultiply(u, v) << endl;
cout << "XMVectorSaturate(q)       = "
  << XMVectorSaturate(q) << endl;
cout << "XMVectorMin(p, v          = " << XMVectorMin(p, v) << endl;
cout << "XMVectorMax(p, v)         = " << XMVectorMax(p, v) << endl;

return 0;
}
```

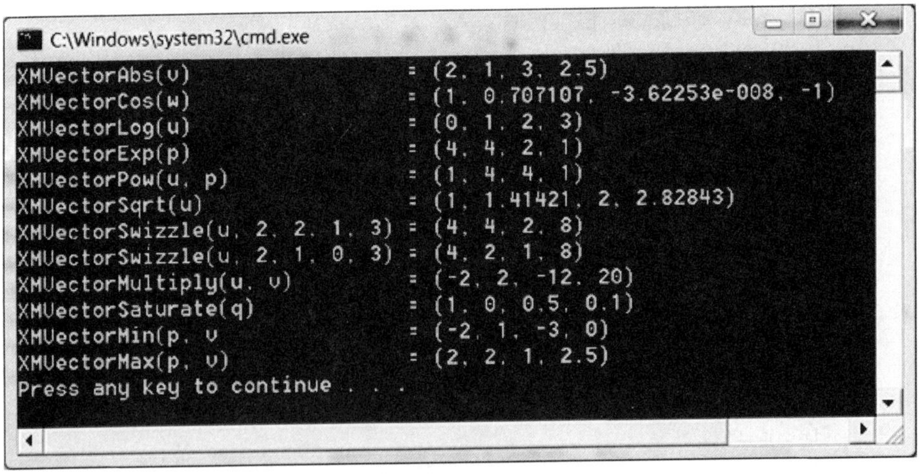

Figure 1.22. Output for the previous program.

Chapter 2 MATRIX ALGEBRA

In 3D computer graphics, we use matrices to compactly describe geometric transformations such as scaling, rotation, and translation, and also to change the coordinates of a point or vector from one frame to another. This chapter explores the mathematics of matrices.

Objectives:

1. To obtain an understanding of matrices and the operations defined on them.
2. To discover how a vector-matrix multiplication can be viewed as a linear combination.
3. To learn what the identity matrix is, and what the transpose, determinant, and inverse of a matrix are.
4. To become familiar with the subset of classes and functions provided by the XNA library used for matrix mathematics.

2.1 DEFINITION

An $m \times n$ *matrix* **M** is a rectangular array of real numbers with m rows and n columns. The product of the number of rows and columns gives the dimensions of the matrix. The numbers in a matrix are called *elements* or *entries*. We identify a matrix element by specifying the row and column of the element using a double subscript notation M_{ij}, where the first subscript identifies the row and the second subscript identifies the column.

☞ Example 2.1

Consider the following matrices:

$$\mathbf{A} = \begin{bmatrix} 3.5 & 0 & 0 & 0 \\ 0 & 1 & 0 & 0 \\ 0 & 0 & 0.5 & 0 \\ 2 & -5 & \sqrt{2} & 1 \end{bmatrix} \quad \mathbf{B} = \begin{bmatrix} B_{11} & B_{12} \\ B_{21} & B_{22} \\ B_{31} & B_{32} \end{bmatrix} \quad \mathbf{u} = \begin{bmatrix} u_1, u_2, u_3 \end{bmatrix} \quad \mathbf{v} = \begin{bmatrix} 1 \\ 2 \\ \sqrt{3} \\ \pi \end{bmatrix}$$

1. The matrix **A** is a 4×4 matrix; the matrix **B** is a 3×2 matrix; the matrix **u** is a 1×3 matrix; and the matrix **v** is a 4×1 matrix.

2. We identify the element in the fourth row and second column of the matrix **A** by $A_{42} = -5$. We identify the element in the second row and first column of the matrix **B** by B_{21}.

3. The matrices **u** and **v** are special matrices in the sense that they contain a single row or column, respectively. We sometimes call these kinds of matrices *row vectors* or *column vectors* because they are used to represent a vector in matrix form (e.g., we can freely interchange the vector notations (x, y, z) and $[x, y, z]$). Observe that for row and column vectors, it is unnecessary to use a double subscript to denote the elements of the matrix—we only need one subscript.

Occasionally we like to think of the rows of a matrix as vectors. For example, we might write:

$$\begin{bmatrix} A_{11} & A_{12} & A_{13} \\ A_{21} & A_{22} & A_{23} \\ A_{31} & A_{32} & A_{33} \end{bmatrix} = \begin{bmatrix} \leftarrow \mathbf{A}_{1,*} \rightarrow \\ \leftarrow \mathbf{A}_{2,*} \rightarrow \\ \leftarrow \mathbf{A}_{3,*} \rightarrow \end{bmatrix}$$

where $\mathbf{A}_{1,*} = [A_{11}, A_{12}, A_{13}]$, $\mathbf{A}_{2,*} = [A_{21}, A_{22}, A_{23}]$, and $\mathbf{A}_{3,*} = [A_{31}, A_{32}, A_{33}]$. In this notation, the first index specifies the row, and we put a '*' in the second index to indicate that we are referring to the entire row vector. Likewise, we like to do the same thing for the columns:

$$\begin{bmatrix} A_{11} & A_{12} & A_{13} \\ A_{21} & A_{22} & A_{23} \\ A_{31} & A_{32} & A_{33} \end{bmatrix} = \begin{bmatrix} \uparrow & \uparrow & \uparrow \\ \mathbf{A}_{*,1} & \mathbf{A}_{*,2} & \mathbf{A}_{*,3} \\ \downarrow & \downarrow & \downarrow \end{bmatrix}$$

where

$$\mathbf{A}_{*,1} = \begin{bmatrix} A_{11} \\ A_{21} \\ A_{31} \end{bmatrix}, \quad \mathbf{A}_{*,2} = \begin{bmatrix} A_{12} \\ A_{22} \\ A_{32} \end{bmatrix}, \quad \mathbf{A}_{*,3} = \begin{bmatrix} A_{13} \\ A_{23} \\ A_{33} \end{bmatrix}$$

In this notation, the second index specifies the column, and we put a '*' in the first index to indicate that we are referring to the entire column vector.

We now define equality, addition, scalar multiplication, and subtraction on matrices.

1. Two matrices are equal if and only if their corresponding elements are equal; as such, two matrices must have the same number of rows and columns in order to be compared.

2. We add two matrices by adding their corresponding elements; as such, it only makes sense to add matrices that have the same number of rows and columns.

3. We multiply a scalar and a matrix by multiplying the scalar with every element in the matrix.

4. We define subtraction in terms of matrix addition and scalar multiplication. That is, $\mathbf{A} - \mathbf{B} = \mathbf{A} + (-1 \cdot \mathbf{B}) = \mathbf{A} + (-\mathbf{B})$.

☞ Example 2.2

Let

$$A = \begin{bmatrix} 1 & 5 \\ -2 & 3 \end{bmatrix}, \quad B = \begin{bmatrix} 6 & 2 \\ 5 & -8 \end{bmatrix}, \quad C = \begin{bmatrix} 1 & 5 \\ -2 & 3 \end{bmatrix}, \quad D = \begin{bmatrix} 2 & 1 & -3 \\ -6 & 3 & 0 \end{bmatrix}$$

Then,

(i) $\mathbf{A} + \mathbf{B} = \begin{bmatrix} 1 & 5 \\ -2 & 3 \end{bmatrix} + \begin{bmatrix} 6 & 2 \\ 5 & -8 \end{bmatrix} = \begin{bmatrix} 1+6 & 5+2 \\ -2+5 & 3+(-8) \end{bmatrix} = \begin{bmatrix} 7 & 7 \\ 3 & -5 \end{bmatrix}$

(ii) $\mathbf{A} = \mathbf{C}$

(iii) $3\mathbf{D} = 3 \begin{bmatrix} 2 & 1 & -3 \\ -6 & 3 & 0 \end{bmatrix} = \begin{bmatrix} 3(2) & 3(1) & 3(-3) \\ 3(-6) & 3(3) & 3(0) \end{bmatrix} = \begin{bmatrix} 6 & 3 & -9 \\ -18 & 9 & 0 \end{bmatrix}$

(iv) $\mathbf{A} - \mathbf{B} = \begin{bmatrix} 1 & 5 \\ -2 & 3 \end{bmatrix} - \begin{bmatrix} 6 & 2 \\ 5 & -8 \end{bmatrix} = \begin{bmatrix} 1-6 & 5-2 \\ -2-5 & 3-(-8) \end{bmatrix} = \begin{bmatrix} -5 & 3 \\ -7 & 11 \end{bmatrix}$

Because addition and scalar multiplication is done element-wise, matrices essentially inherit the following addition and scalar multiplication properties from real numbers:

1. $\mathbf{A} + \mathbf{B} = \mathbf{B} + \mathbf{A}$ Commutative law of addition
2. $(\mathbf{A} + \mathbf{B}) + \mathbf{C} = \mathbf{A} + (\mathbf{B} + \mathbf{C})$ Associative law of addition
3. $r(\mathbf{A} + \mathbf{B}) = r\mathbf{A} + r\mathbf{B}$ Scalar distribution over matrices
4. $(r + s)\mathbf{A} = r\mathbf{A} + s\mathbf{A}$ Matrix distribution over scalars

2.2 MATRIX MULTIPLICATION

2.2.1 Definition

If $\mathbf{A}$ is a $m \times n$ matrix and $\mathbf{B}$ is a $n \times p$ matrix, then the product $\mathbf{AB}$ is defined and is a $m \times p$ matrix $\mathbf{C}$, where the ijth entry of the product $\mathbf{C}$ is given by taking the dot product of the ith row vector in $\mathbf{A}$ with the jth column vector in $\mathbf{B}$, that is,

$$\mathbf{C}_{ij} = \mathbf{A}_{i,*} \cdot \mathbf{B}_{*,j} \qquad\qquad \text{(eq. 2.1)}$$

So note that in order for the matrix product $\mathbf{AB}$ to be defined, we require that the number of columns in $\mathbf{A}$ equal the number of rows in $\mathbf{B}$, which is to say, we require that the dimension of the row vectors in $\mathbf{A}$ equal the dimension of the column vectors in $\mathbf{B}$. If these dimensions did not match, then the dot product in Equation 2.1 would not make sense.

☞ Example 2.3

Let

$$A = \begin{bmatrix} 1 & 5 \\ -2 & 3 \end{bmatrix} \quad \text{and} \quad B = \begin{bmatrix} 2 & -6 \\ 1 & 3 \\ -3 & 0 \end{bmatrix}$$

The product AB is not defined since the row vectors in A have dimension 2 and the column vectors in B have dimension 3. In particular, we cannot take the dot product of the first row vector in A with the first column vector in B because we cannot take the dot product of a 2D vector with a 3D vector.

☞ Example 2.4

Let

$$A = \begin{bmatrix} -1 & 5 & -4 \\ 3 & 2 & 1 \end{bmatrix} \quad \text{and} \quad B = \begin{bmatrix} 2 & 1 & 0 \\ 0 & -2 & 1 \\ -1 & 2 & 3 \end{bmatrix}$$

We first point out that the product AB is defined (and is a matrix) because the number of columns of A equals the number of rows of B. Applying Equation 2.1 yields:

$$
\begin{aligned}
AB &= \begin{bmatrix} -1 & 5 & -4 \\ 3 & 2 & 1 \end{bmatrix} \begin{bmatrix} 2 & 1 & 0 \\ 0 & -2 & 1 \\ -1 & 2 & 3 \end{bmatrix} \\
&= \begin{bmatrix} (-1,5,-4)\cdot(2,0,-1) & (-1,5,-4)\cdot(1,-2,2) & (-1,5,-4)\cdot(0,1,3) \\ (3,2,1)\cdot(2,0,-1) & (3,2,1)\cdot(1,-2,2) & (3,2,1)\cdot(0,1,3) \end{bmatrix} \\
&= \begin{bmatrix} 2 & -19 & -7 \\ 5 & 1 & 5 \end{bmatrix}
\end{aligned}
$$

Observe that the product BA is not defined because the number of columns in B does *not* equal the number of rows in A. This demonstrates that, in general, matrix multiplication is not commutative; that is, $AB \neq BA$.

2.2.2 Vector-Matrix Multiplication

Consider the following vector-matrix multiplication:

$$\mathbf{uA} = \begin{bmatrix} x,y,z \end{bmatrix} \begin{bmatrix} A_{11} & A_{12} & A_{13} \\ A_{21} & A_{22} & A_{23} \\ A_{31} & A_{32} & A_{33} \end{bmatrix} = \begin{bmatrix} x,y,z \end{bmatrix} \begin{bmatrix} \uparrow & \uparrow & \uparrow \\ \mathbf{A}_{*,1} & \mathbf{A}_{*,2} & \mathbf{A}_{*,3} \\ \downarrow & \downarrow & \downarrow \end{bmatrix}$$

Observe that $\mathbf{uA}$ evaluates to a 1×3 row vector in this case. Now, applying Equation 2.1 gives:

$$\begin{aligned}
\mathbf{uA} &= \begin{bmatrix} \mathbf{u} \cdot \mathbf{A}_{*,1} & \mathbf{u} \cdot \mathbf{A}_{*,2} & \mathbf{u} \cdot \mathbf{A}_{*,3} \end{bmatrix} \\
&= \begin{bmatrix} xA_{11} + yA_{21} + zA_{31}, & xA_{12} + yA_{22} + zA_{32}, & xA_{13} + yA_{23} + zA_{33} \end{bmatrix} \\
&= \begin{bmatrix} xA_{11}, xA_{12}, xA_{13} \end{bmatrix} + \begin{bmatrix} yA_{21}, yA_{22}, yA_{23} \end{bmatrix} + \begin{bmatrix} zA_{31}, zA_{32}, zA_{33} \end{bmatrix} \\
&= x \begin{bmatrix} A_{11}, A_{12}, A_{13} \end{bmatrix} + y \begin{bmatrix} A_{21}, A_{22}, A_{23} \end{bmatrix} + z \begin{bmatrix} A_{31}, A_{32}, A_{33} \end{bmatrix} \\
&= x\mathbf{A}_{1,*} + y\mathbf{A}_{2,*} + z\mathbf{A}_{3,*}
\end{aligned}$$

Thus,

$$\mathbf{uA} = x\mathbf{A}_{1,*} + y\mathbf{A}_{2,*} + z\mathbf{A}_{3,*} \qquad \text{(eq. 2.2)}$$

Equation 2.2 is an example of a *linear combination*, and it says that the vector-matrix product $\mathbf{uA}$ is equivalent to a linear combination of the row vectors of the matrix $\mathbf{A}$ with scalar coefficients x, y, and z given by the vector $\mathbf{u}$. Note that, although we showed this for a 1×3 row vector and a 3×3 matrix, the result is true in general. That is, for a $1 \times n$ row vector $\mathbf{u}$ and a $n \times m$ matrix $\mathbf{A}$, we have that $\mathbf{uA}$ is a linear combination of the row vectors in $\mathbf{A}$ with scalar coefficients given by $\mathbf{u}$:

$$\begin{bmatrix} u_1, \ldots, u_n \end{bmatrix} \begin{bmatrix} A_{11} & \cdots & A_{1m} \\ \vdots & \ddots & \vdots \\ A_{n1} & \cdots & A_{nm} \end{bmatrix} = u_1 \mathbf{A}_{1,*} + \ldots + u_n \mathbf{A}_{n,*}$$

$$\text{(eq. 2.3)}$$

2.2.3 Associativity

Matrix multiplication has some nice algebraic properties. For example, matrix multiplication distributes over addition: $\mathbf{A}(\mathbf{B} + \mathbf{C}) = \mathbf{AB} + \mathbf{AC}$ and $(\mathbf{A} + \mathbf{B})\mathbf{C} = \mathbf{AC} + \mathbf{BC}$. In particular, however, we will use the associative law of matrix multiplication from time to time, which allows us to choose the order we multiply matrices:

$$(\mathbf{AB})\mathbf{C} = \mathbf{A}(\mathbf{BC})$$

2.3 THE TRANSPOSE OF A MATRIX

The *transpose* of a matrix is found by interchanging the rows and columns of the matrix. Thus the transpose of an $m \times n$ matrix is an $n \times m$ matrix. We denote the transpose of a matrix $\mathbf{M}$ as $\mathbf{M}^T$.

☞ Example 2.5

Find the transpose for the following three matrices:

$$\mathbf{A} = \begin{bmatrix} 2 & -1 & 8 \\ 3 & 6 & -4 \end{bmatrix}, \qquad \mathbf{B} = \begin{bmatrix} a & b & c \\ d & e & f \\ g & h & i \end{bmatrix}, \qquad \mathbf{C} = \begin{bmatrix} 1 \\ 2 \\ 3 \\ 4 \end{bmatrix}$$

To reiterate, the transposes are found by interchanging the rows and columns, thus

$$\mathbf{A}^T = \begin{bmatrix} 2 & 3 \\ -1 & 6 \\ 8 & -4 \end{bmatrix}, \quad \mathbf{B}^T = \begin{bmatrix} a & d & g \\ b & e & h \\ c & f & i \end{bmatrix}, \quad \mathbf{C}^T = \begin{bmatrix} 1 & 2 & 3 & 4 \end{bmatrix}$$

The transpose has the following useful properties:

1. $(\mathbf{A} + \mathbf{B})^T = \mathbf{A}^T + \mathbf{B}^T$
2. $(c\mathbf{A})^T = c\mathbf{A}^T$
3. $(\mathbf{AB})^T = \mathbf{B}^T\mathbf{A}^T$
4. $(\mathbf{A}^T)^T = \mathbf{A}$
5. $(\mathbf{A}^{-1})^T = (\mathbf{A}^T)^{-1}$

2.4 THE IDENTITY MATRIX

There is a special matrix called the *identity matrix*. The identity matrix is a square matrix that has zeros for all elements except along the main diagonal; the elements along the main diagonal are all ones.

For example, below are 2×2, 3×3, and 4×4 identity matrices.

$$\begin{bmatrix} 1 & 0 \\ 0 & 1 \end{bmatrix}, \qquad \begin{bmatrix} 1 & 0 & 0 \\ 0 & 1 & 0 \\ 0 & 0 & 1 \end{bmatrix}, \qquad \begin{bmatrix} 1 & 0 & 0 & 0 \\ 0 & 1 & 0 & 0 \\ 0 & 0 & 1 & 0 \\ 0 & 0 & 0 & 1 \end{bmatrix}$$

The identity matrix acts as a multiplicative identity; that is, if $\mathbf{A}$ is an $m \times n$ matrix, $\mathbf{B}$ is an $n \times p$ matrix, and $\mathbf{I}$ is the $n \times n$ identity matrix, then

$$\mathbf{AI} = \mathbf{A} \quad \text{and} \quad \mathbf{IB} = \mathbf{B}$$

In other words, multiplying a matrix by the identity matrix does not change the matrix. The identity matrix can be thought of as the number 1 for matrices. In particular, if $\mathbf{M}$ is a square matrix, then multiplication with the identity matrix is commutative:

$$\mathbf{MI} = \mathbf{IM} = \mathbf{M}$$

☞ Example 2.6

Let $\mathbf{M} = \begin{bmatrix} 1 & 2 \\ 0 & 4 \end{bmatrix}$ and let $\mathbf{I} = \begin{bmatrix} 1 & 0 \\ 0 & 1 \end{bmatrix}$. Verify that $\mathbf{MI} = \mathbf{IM} = \mathbf{M}$.

Applying Equation 2.1 yields:

$$\mathbf{MI} = \begin{bmatrix} 1 & 2 \\ 0 & 4 \end{bmatrix}\begin{bmatrix} 1 & 0 \\ 0 & 1 \end{bmatrix} = \begin{bmatrix} (1,2) \cdot (1,0) & (1,2) \cdot (0,1) \\ (0,4) \cdot (1,0) & (0,4) \cdot (0,1) \end{bmatrix} = \begin{bmatrix} 1 & 2 \\ 0 & 4 \end{bmatrix}$$

and

$$\mathbf{IM} = \begin{bmatrix} 1 & 0 \\ 0 & 1 \end{bmatrix}\begin{bmatrix} 1 & 2 \\ 0 & 4 \end{bmatrix} = \begin{bmatrix} (1,0) \cdot (1,0) & (1,0) \cdot (2,4) \\ (0,1) \cdot (1,0) & (0,1) \cdot (2,4) \end{bmatrix} = \begin{bmatrix} 1 & 2 \\ 0 & 4 \end{bmatrix}$$

Thus it is true that $\mathbf{MI} = \mathbf{IM} = \mathbf{M}$.

☞ Example 2.7

Let $\mathbf{u} = \begin{bmatrix} -1, 2 \end{bmatrix}$ and let $\mathbf{I} = \begin{bmatrix} 1 & 0 \\ 0 & 1 \end{bmatrix}$. Verify that $\mathbf{uI} = \mathbf{u}$.

Applying Equation 2.1 yields:

$$\mathbf{uI} = \begin{bmatrix} -1, & 2 \end{bmatrix}\begin{bmatrix} 1 & 0 \\ 0 & 1 \end{bmatrix} = \begin{bmatrix} (-1,2) \cdot (1,0) & (-1,2) \cdot (0,1) \end{bmatrix} = \begin{bmatrix} -1, & 2 \end{bmatrix}$$

Note that we cannot take the product $\mathbf{Iu}$ because the matrix multiplication is not defined.

2.5 THE DETERMINANT OF A MATRIX

The determinant is a special function which inputs a square matrix and outputs a real number. The determinant of a square matrix $\mathbf{A}$ is commonly denoted by det $\mathbf{A}$. It can be shown that the determinant has a geometric interpretation related to volumes of boxes and that the determinant provides information on how volumes change under linear transformations. In addition, determinants are used to solve systems of linear equations using Cramer's Rule. However, for our purposes, we are mainly motivated to study the determinant because it gives us an explicit formula for finding the inverse of a matrix (the topic of §2.7). In addition, it can be proved that: *A square matrix* $\mathbf{A}$ *is invertible if and only if* det $\mathbf{A} \neq 0$. This fact is useful because it gives us a computational tool for determining if a matrix is invertible. Before we can define the determinant, we first introduce the concept of matrix minors.

2.5.1 Matrix Minors

Given an $n \times n$ matrix $\mathbf{A}$, the *minor matrix* $\overline{\mathbf{A}}_{ij}$ is the $(n-1) \times (n-1)$ matrix found by deleting the *i*th row and *j*th column of $\mathbf{A}$.

☞ Example 2.8

Find the minor matrices $\overline{\mathbf{A}}_{11}$, $\overline{\mathbf{A}}_{22}$, and $\overline{\mathbf{A}}_{13}$ of the following matrix:

$$\mathbf{A} = \begin{bmatrix} A_{11} & A_{12} & A_{13} \\ A_{21} & A_{22} & A_{23} \\ A_{31} & A_{32} & A_{33} \end{bmatrix}$$

For $\overline{\mathbf{A}}_{11}$ we eliminate the first row and first column to obtain:

$$\overline{\mathbf{A}}_{11} = \begin{bmatrix} A_{22} & A_{23} \\ A_{32} & A_{33} \end{bmatrix}$$

For $\overline{\mathbf{A}}_{22}$ we eliminate the second row and second column to obtain:

$$\overline{\mathbf{A}}_{22} = \begin{bmatrix} A_{11} & A_{13} \\ A_{31} & A_{33} \end{bmatrix}$$

For $\overline{\mathbf{A}}_{13}$ we eliminate the first row and third column to obtain:

$$\overline{\mathbf{A}}_{13} = \begin{bmatrix} A_{21} & A_{22} \\ A_{31} & A_{32} \end{bmatrix}$$

2.5.2 Definition

The determinant of a matrix is defined recursively; for instance, the determinant of a 4×4 matrix is defined in terms of the determinant of a 3×3 matrix, and the determinant of a 3×3 matrix is defined in terms of the determinant of a 2×2 matrix, and the determinant of a 2×2 matrix is defined in terms of the determinant of a 1×1 matrix (the determinant of a 1×1 matrix $\mathbf{A} = [A_{11}]$ is trivially defined to be $\det[A_{11}] = A_{11}$).

Let $\mathbf{A}$ be an $n \times n$ matrix. Then for $n > 1$ we define:

$$\det \mathbf{A} = \sum_{j=1}^{n} A_{1j} \left(-1\right)^{1+j} \det \overline{\mathbf{A}}_{1j}$$

(eq. 2.4)

Recalling the definition of the minor matrix $\overline{\mathbf{A}}_{ij}$, for 2×2 matrices, this gives the formula:

$$\det \begin{bmatrix} A_{11} & A_{12} \\ A_{21} & A_{22} \end{bmatrix} = A_{11} \det[A_{22}] - A_{12} \det[A_{21}] = A_{11}A_{22} - A_{12}A_{21}$$

For 3×3 matrices, this gives the formula:

$$\det \begin{bmatrix} A_{11} & A_{12} & A_{13} \\ A_{21} & A_{22} & A_{23} \\ A_{31} & A_{32} & A_{33} \end{bmatrix} = A_{11} \det \begin{bmatrix} A_{22} & A_{23} \\ A_{32} & A_{33} \end{bmatrix} - A_{12} \det \begin{bmatrix} A_{21} & A_{23} \\ A_{31} & A_{33} \end{bmatrix} + A_{13} \det \begin{bmatrix} A_{21} & A_{22} \\ A_{31} & A_{32} \end{bmatrix}$$

And for 4×4 matrices, this gives the formula:

$$\det \begin{bmatrix} A_{11} & A_{12} & A_{13} & A_{14} \\ A_{21} & A_{22} & A_{23} & A_{24} \\ A_{31} & A_{32} & A_{33} & A_{34} \\ A_{41} & A_{42} & A_{43} & A_{44} \end{bmatrix}$$

$$= A_{11} \det \begin{bmatrix} A_{22} & A_{23} & A_{24} \\ A_{32} & A_{33} & A_{34} \\ A_{42} & A_{43} & A_{44} \end{bmatrix} - A_{12} \det \begin{bmatrix} A_{21} & A_{23} & A_{24} \\ A_{31} & A_{33} & A_{34} \\ A_{41} & A_{43} & A_{44} \end{bmatrix}$$

$$+ A_{13} \det \begin{bmatrix} A_{21} & A_{22} & A_{24} \\ A_{31} & A_{32} & A_{34} \\ A_{41} & A_{42} & A_{44} \end{bmatrix} - A_{14} \det \begin{bmatrix} A_{21} & A_{22} & A_{23} \\ A_{31} & A_{32} & A_{33} \\ A_{41} & A_{42} & A_{43} \end{bmatrix}$$

In 3D graphics, we primarily work with 4×4 matrices, and so we do not need to continue generating explicit formulas for $n > 4$.

👉 Example 2.9

Find the determinant of the matrix

$$\mathbf{A} = \begin{bmatrix} 2 & -5 & 3 \\ 1 & 3 & 4 \\ -2 & 3 & 7 \end{bmatrix}$$

We have that:

$$\det \mathbf{A} = A_{11} \det \begin{bmatrix} A_{22} & A_{23} \\ A_{32} & A_{33} \end{bmatrix} - A_{12} \det \begin{bmatrix} A_{21} & A_{23} \\ A_{31} & A_{33} \end{bmatrix} + A_{13} \det \begin{bmatrix} A_{21} & A_{22} \\ A_{31} & A_{32} \end{bmatrix}$$

$$\det \mathbf{A} = 2 \det \begin{bmatrix} 3 & 4 \\ 3 & 7 \end{bmatrix} - (-5) \det \begin{bmatrix} 1 & 4 \\ -2 & 7 \end{bmatrix} + 3 \det \begin{bmatrix} 1 & 3 \\ -2 & 3 \end{bmatrix}$$

$$= 2(3 \cdot 7 - 4 \cdot 3) + 5(1 \cdot 7 - 4 \cdot (-2)) + 3(1 \cdot 3 - 3 \cdot (-2))$$

$$= 2(9) + 5(15) + 3(9)$$

$$= 18 + 75 + 27$$

$$= 120$$

2.6 THE ADJOINT OF A MATRIX

Let $\mathbf{A}$ be an $n \times n$ matrix. The product $C_{ij} = (-1)^{i+j} \det \overline{\mathbf{A}}_{ij}$ is called the *cofactor of A_{ij}*. If we compute C_{ij} and place it in the ijth position of a corresponding matrix $\mathbf{C_A}$ for every element in $\mathbf{A}$, we obtain the *cofactor matrix of* $\mathbf{A}$:

$$\mathbf{C_A} = \begin{bmatrix} C_{11} & C_{12} & \cdots & C_{1n} \\ C_{21} & C_{22} & \cdots & C_{2n} \\ \vdots & \vdots & \ddots & \vdots \\ C_{n1} & C_{n2} & \cdots & C_{nn} \end{bmatrix}$$

If we take the transpose of $\mathbf{C_A}$ we get a matrix that is called the *adjoint of* $\mathbf{A}$, which we denote by

$$\mathbf{A}^* = \mathbf{C_A}^T \qquad \qquad \textbf{(eq. 2.5)}$$

In the next section, we learn that the adjoint enables us to find an explicit formula for computing matrix inverses.

2.7 THE INVERSE OF A MATRIX

Matrix algebra does not define a division operation, but it does define a multiplicative inverse operation. The following list summarizes the important information about inverses:

1. Only square matrices have inverses; therefore, when we speak of matrix inverses, we assume we are dealing with a square matrix.

2. The inverse of an $n \times n$ matrix $\mathbf{M}$ is an $n \times n$ matrix denoted by $\mathbf{M}^{-1}$.

3. Not every square matrix has an inverse. A matrix that does have an inverse is said to be *invertible*, and a matrix that does not have an inverse is said to be *singular*.

4. The inverse is unique when it exists.

5. Multiplying a matrix with its inverse results in the identity matrix: $\mathbf{M}\mathbf{M}^{-1} = \mathbf{M}^{-1}\mathbf{M} = \mathbf{I}$. Note that multiplying a matrix with its own inverse is a case when matrix multiplication is commutative.

Matrix inverses are useful when solving for other matrices in a matrix equation. For example, suppose that we are given the matrix equation $\mathbf{p}' = \mathbf{p}\mathbf{M}$. Further suppose that we are given $\mathbf{p}'$ and $\mathbf{M}$, and want to solve for $\mathbf{p}$. Assuming that $\mathbf{M}$ is invertible (i.e., $\mathbf{M}^{-1}$ exists), we can solve for $\mathbf{p}$ like so:

$\mathbf{p}' = \mathbf{p}\mathbf{M}$	
$\mathbf{p}'\mathbf{M}^{-1} = \mathbf{p}\mathbf{M}\mathbf{M}^{-1}$	Multiplying both sides of the equation by $\mathbf{M}^{-1}$
$\mathbf{p}'\mathbf{M}^{-1} = \mathbf{p}\mathbf{I}$	$\mathbf{M}\mathbf{M}^{-1} = \mathbf{I}$, by definition of the inverse
$\mathbf{p}'\mathbf{M}^{-1} = \mathbf{p}$	$\mathbf{p}\mathbf{I} = \mathbf{p}$, by definition of the identity matrix

A formula for finding inverses, which we do not prove here but should be proved in any college level linear algebra text, can be given in terms of the adjoint and determinant:

$$\mathbf{A}^{-1} = \frac{\mathbf{A}^*}{\det \mathbf{A}}$$

(eq. 2.6)

☞ Example 2.10

Find a general formula for the inverse of a 2×2 matrix $\mathbf{A} = \begin{bmatrix} A_{11} & A_{12} \\ A_{21} & A_{22} \end{bmatrix}$, and use this formula to find the inverse of the matrix $\mathbf{M} = \begin{bmatrix} 3 & 0 \\ -1 & 2 \end{bmatrix}$.

We have that

$$\det \mathbf{A} = A_{11}A_{22} - A_{12}A_{21}$$

$$\mathbf{C}_{\mathbf{A}} = \begin{bmatrix} (-1)^{1+1} \det\overline{\mathbf{A}}_{11} & (-1)^{1+2} \det\overline{\mathbf{A}}_{12} \\ (-1)^{2+1} \det\overline{\mathbf{A}}_{21} & (-1)^{2+2} \det\overline{\mathbf{A}}_{22} \end{bmatrix} = \begin{bmatrix} A_{22} & -A_{21} \\ -A_{12} & A_{11} \end{bmatrix}$$

Therefore,

$$\mathbf{A}^{-1} = \frac{\mathbf{A}^{*}}{\det \mathbf{A}} = \frac{\mathbf{C}_{\mathbf{A}}^{T}}{\det \mathbf{A}} = \frac{1}{A_{11}A_{22} - A_{12}A_{21}} \begin{bmatrix} A_{22} & -A_{12} \\ -A_{21} & A_{11} \end{bmatrix}$$

Now we apply this formula to invert $\mathbf{M} = \begin{bmatrix} 3 & 0 \\ -1 & 2 \end{bmatrix}$:

$$\mathbf{M}^{-1} = \frac{1}{3 \cdot 2 - 0 \cdot (-1)} \begin{bmatrix} 2 & 0 \\ 1 & 3 \end{bmatrix} = \begin{bmatrix} 1/3 & 0 \\ 1/6 & 1/2 \end{bmatrix}$$

To check our work we verify $\mathbf{MM}^{-1} = \mathbf{M}^{-1}\mathbf{M} = \mathbf{I}$:

$$\begin{bmatrix} 3 & 0 \\ -1 & 2 \end{bmatrix}\begin{bmatrix} 1/3 & 0 \\ 1/6 & 1/2 \end{bmatrix} = \begin{bmatrix} 1 & 0 \\ 0 & 1 \end{bmatrix} = \begin{bmatrix} 1/3 & 0 \\ 1/6 & 1/2 \end{bmatrix}\begin{bmatrix} 3 & 0 \\ -1 & 2 \end{bmatrix}$$

Note: *For small matrices (sizes 4×4 and smaller), the adjoint method is computationally efficient. For larger matrices, other methods are used such as Gaussian elimination. However, the matrices we are concerned about in 3D computer graphics have special forms, which enable us to determine the inverse formulas ahead of time, so that we do not need to waste CPU cycles finding the inverse of a general matrix. Consequently, we rarely need to apply Equation 2.6 in code.*

To conclude this section on inverses, we present the following useful algebraic property for the inverse of a product:

$$(\mathbf{AB})^{-1} = \mathbf{B}^{-1}\mathbf{A}^{-1}$$

This property assumes both $\mathbf{A}$ and $\mathbf{B}$ are invertible and that they are both square matrices of the same dimension. To prove that $\mathbf{B}^{-1}\mathbf{A}^{-1}$ is the inverse of $\mathbf{AB}$, we must show $(\mathbf{AB})^{-1} (\mathbf{B}^{-1}\mathbf{A}^{-1}) = \mathbf{I}$ and $(\mathbf{B}^{-1}\mathbf{A}^{-1})(\mathbf{AB}) = \mathbf{I}$. This is done as follows:

$$(\mathbf{AB})(\mathbf{B}^{-1}\mathbf{A}^{-1}) = \mathbf{A}(\mathbf{BB}^{-1})\mathbf{A}^{-1} = \mathbf{AIA}^{-1} = \mathbf{AA}^{-1} = \mathbf{I}$$

$$(\mathbf{B}^{-1}\mathbf{A}^{-1})(\mathbf{AB}) = \mathbf{B}^{-1}(\mathbf{A}^{-1}\mathbf{A})\mathbf{B} = \mathbf{B}^{-1}\mathbf{IB} = \mathbf{B}^{-1}\mathbf{B} = \mathbf{I}$$

2.8 XNA MATRICES

For transforming points and vectors, we use 1×4 row vectors and 4×4 matrices. The reason for this will be explained in the next chapter. For now, we concentrate on the XNA math types used to represent 4×4 matrices.

2.8.1 Matrix Types

To represent 4×4 matrices in XNA math, we use the **XMMATRIX** class, which is defined as follows in the *xnamath.h* header file as follows (with some additional comments we have added):

```
// Matrix type: Sixteen 32 bit floating point components aligned on a
// 16 byte boundary and mapped to four hardware vector registers
#if (defined(_XM_X86_) || defined(_XM_X64_)) && defined(_XM_NO_
    INTRINSICS_)
typedef struct _XMMATRIX
#else
typedef _DECLSPEC_ALIGN_16_ struct _XMMATRIX
#endif
{
    union
    {
      // Use 4 XMVECTORs to represent the matrix for SIMD.
      XMVECTOR r[4];
      struct
      {
        FLOAT _11, _12, _13, _14;
        FLOAT _21, _22, _23, _24;
        FLOAT _31, _32, _33, _34;
        FLOAT _41, _42, _43, _44;
      };
      FLOAT m[4][4];
    };

#ifdef __cplusplus

    _XMMATRIX() {};

    // Initialize matrix by specifying 4 row vectors.
    _XMMATRIX(FXMVECTOR R0, FXMVECTOR R1, FXMVECTOR R2, CXMVECTOR R3);

    // Initialize matrix by specifying the 16 elements.
    _XMMATRIX(FLOAT m00, FLOAT m01, FLOAT m02, FLOAT m03,
        FLOAT m10, FLOAT m11, FLOAT m12, FLOAT m13,
        FLOAT m20, FLOAT m21, FLOAT m22, FLOAT m23,
        FLOAT m30, FLOAT m31, FLOAT m32, FLOAT m33);

    // Pass array of sixteen floats to construct matrix.
    _XMMATRIX(CONST FLOAT *pArray);
```

```
    FLOAT operator() (UINT Row, UINT Column) CONST { return m[Row]
    [Column]; }
    FLOAT& operator() (UINT Row, UINT Column) { return m[Row][Column]; }

    _XMMATRIX&  operator= (CONST _XMMATRIX& M);

#ifndef XM_NO_OPERATOR_OVERLOADS
    _XMMATRIX&  operator*= (CONST _XMMATRIX& M);
    _XMMATRIX   operator* (CONST _XMMATRIX& M) CONST;
#endif // !XM_NO_OPERATOR_OVERLOADS

#endif // __cplusplus

} XMMATRIX;
```

As you can see, XMMATRIX uses four XMVECTOR instances to use SIMD. Moreover, XMMATRIX provides overloaded operators for multiplying matrices and overloaded parenthesis operators for accessing/modifying the elements in a XMMATRIX by specifying its row and column (using zero-based indices).

In addition to using the various constructors, an XMMATRIX instance can be created using the XMMatrixSet function:

```
XMMATRIX XMMatrixSet(FLOAT m00, FLOAT m01, FLOAT m02, FLOAT m03,
    FLOAT m10, FLOAT m11, FLOAT m12, FLOAT m13,
    FLOAT m20, FLOAT m21, FLOAT m22, FLOAT m23,
    FLOAT m30, FLOAT m31, FLOAT m32, FLOAT m33);
```

Just as we use XMFLOAT2 (2D), XMFLOAT3 (3D), and XMFLOAT4 (4D) when storing vectors in a class, it is recommended, by the XNA math documentation, to use the XMFLOAT4X4 type to store matrices as class data members.

```
// 4x4 Matrix: 32 bit floating point components
typedef struct _XMFLOAT4X4
{
    union
    {
      struct
      {
        FLOAT _11, _12, _13, _14;
        FLOAT _21, _22, _23, _24;
        FLOAT _31, _32, _33, _34;
        FLOAT _41, _42, _43, _44;
      };
      FLOAT m[4][4];
    };

#ifdef __cplusplus

    _XMFLOAT4X4() {};
    _XMFLOAT4X4(FLOAT m00, FLOAT m01, FLOAT m02, FLOAT m03,
      FLOAT m10, FLOAT m11, FLOAT m12, FLOAT m13,
      FLOAT m20, FLOAT m21, FLOAT m22, FLOAT m23,
```

```
    FLOAT m30, FLOAT m31, FLOAT m32, FLOAT m33);
    _XMFLOAT4X4(CONST FLOAT *pArray);

    FLOAT operator() (UINT Row, UINT Column) CONST { return m[Row]
    [Column]; }
    FLOAT& operator() (UINT Row, UINT Column) { return m[Row][Column]; }

    _XMFLOAT4X4& operator= (CONST _XMFLOAT4X4& Float4x4);
#endif // __cplusplus

} XMFLOAT4X4;
```

2.8.2 Matrix Functions

The XNA Math library includes the following useful matrix related functions:

```
XMMATRIX XMMatrixIdentity();  // Returns the identity matrix I
```

```
BOOL XMMatrixIsIdentity(          // Returns true if M is the identity matrix
CXMMATRIX M);                     // Input M
```

```
XMMATRIX XMMatrixMultiply(        // Returns the matrix product AB
CXMMATRIX A,                      // Input A
CXMMATRIX B);                     // Input B
```

```
XMMATRIX XMMatrixTranspose(       // Returns M^T
CXMMATRIX M);                     // Input M
```

```
XMVECTOR XMMatrixDeterminant(     // Returns (det M,det M,det M,det M)
CXMMATRIX M);                     // Input M
```

```
XMMATRIX XMMatrixInverse(         // Returns M^{-1}
XMVECTOR* pDeterminant,           // Input (det M,det M,det M,det M)
CXMMATRIX  M);                    // Input M
```

> **Note:** **XMMATRIX** *parameters should be given the type* **CXMMATRIX**. *This ensures that* **XMMATRIX** *parameters are passed correctly on Xbox 360 and Windows platforms:*

```
// Fix-up for XMMATRIX parameters to pass in-register on Xbox 360,
// by reference otherwise
#if defined(_XM_VMX128_INTRINSICS_)
typedef const XMMATRIX CXMMATRIX;
#elif defined(__cplusplus)
typedef const XMMATRIX& CXMMATRIX;
```

2.8.3 XNA Matrix Sample Program

The following code provides some examples on how to use the **XMMATRIX** class and most of the functions listed in the previous section.

```
#include <windows.h> // for FLOAT definition
    #include <xnamath.h>
    #include <iostream>
    using namespace std;

    // Overload the  "<<" operators so that we can use cout to
    // output XMVECTOR and XMMATRIX objects.
    ostream& operator<<(ostream& os, FXMVECTOR v)
    {
    XMFLOAT4 dest;
    XMStoreFloat4(&dest, v);

    os << "(" << dest.x << ", " << dest.y << ", "
      << dest.z << ", " << dest.w << ")";
    return os;
}

ostream& operator<<(ostream& os, CXMMATRIX m)
{
    for(int i = 0; i < 4; ++i)
    {
      for(int j = 0; j < 4; ++j)
      os << m(i, j) << "\t";
    os << endl;
    }
    return os;
}

int main()
{
    // Check support for SSE2 (Pentium4, AMD K8, and above).
    if( !XMVerifyCPUSupport() )
    {
      cout << "xna math not supported" << endl;
      return 0;
    }

    XMMATRIX A(1.0f, 0.0f, 0.0f, 0.0f,
               0.0f, 2.0f, 0.0f, 0.0f,
               0.0f, 0.0f, 4.0f, 0.0f,
               1.0f, 2.0f, 3.0f, 1.0f);

    XMMATRIX B = XMMatrixIdentity();

    XMMATRIX C = A * B;

    XMMATRIX D = XMMatrixTranspose(A);

    XMVECTOR det = XMMatrixDeterminant(A);
    XMMATRIX E = XMMatrixInverse(&det, A);

    XMMATRIX F = A * E;

    cout << "A = "                        << endl << A << endl;
    cout << "B = "                        << endl << B << endl;
    cout << "C = A*B = "                  << endl << C << endl;
```

```
      cout << "D = transpose(A) = "        << endl << D << endl;
      cout << "det = determinant(A) = "    << det << endl << endl;
      cout << "E = inverse(A) = "          << endl << E << endl;
      cout << "F = A*E = "                 << endl << F << endl;

      return 0;
}
```

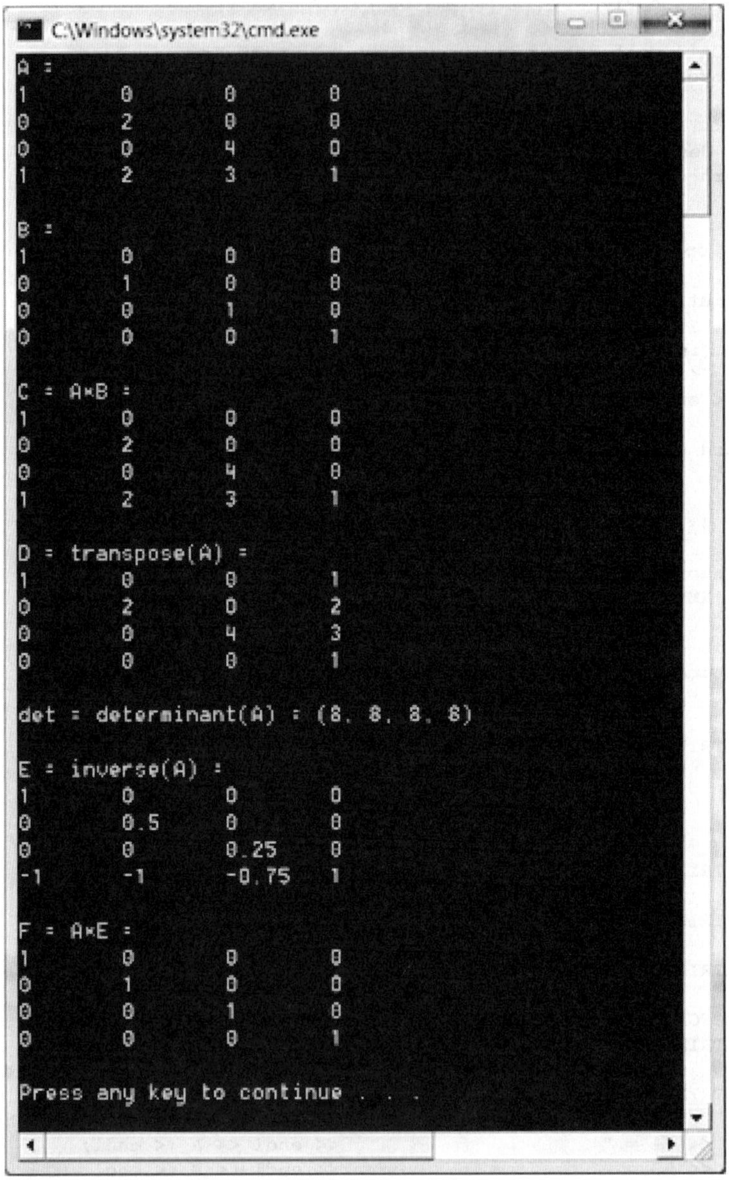

Figure 2.1. Output of the above program.

2.9 SUMMARY

1. An $m \times n$ matrix **M** is a rectangular array of real numbers with m rows and n columns. Two matrices of the same dimensions are equal if and only if their corresponding components are equal. We add two matrices of the same dimensions by adding their corresponding elements. We multiply a scalar and a matrix by multiplying the scalar with every element in the matrix.

2. If **A** is an $m \times n$ matrix and **B** is an $n \times p$ matrix, then the product **AB** is defined and is an $m \times p$ matrix **C**, where the ijth entry of the product **C** is given by taking the dot product of the ith row vector in **A** with the jth column vector in **B**, that is, $\mathbf{C}_{ij} = \mathbf{A}_{i,*} \cdot \mathbf{B}_{*,j}$.

3. Matrix multiplication is not commutative (i.e., $\mathbf{AB} \neq \mathbf{BA}$, in general). Matrix multiplication is associative: $(\mathbf{AB})\mathbf{C} = \mathbf{A}(\mathbf{BC})$.

4. The transpose of a matrix is found by interchanging the rows and columns of the matrix. Thus the transpose of an $m \times n$ matrix is an $n \times m$ matrix. We denote the transpose of a matrix **M** as $\mathbf{M}^T$.

5. The identity matrix is a square matrix that has zeros for all elements except along the main diagonal, and the elements along the main diagonal are all ones.

6. The determinant, det **A**, is a special function which inputs a square matrix and outputs a real number. A square matrix **A** is invertible if and only if det $\mathbf{A} \neq 0$. The determinant is used in the formula for computing the inverse of a matrix.

7. Multiplying a matrix with its inverse results in the identity matrix: $\mathbf{MM}^{-1} = \mathbf{M}^{-1}\mathbf{M} = \mathbf{I}$. The inverse of a matrix, if it exists, is unique. Only square matrices have inverses and even then, a square matrix may not be invertible. The inverse of a matrix can be computed with the formula: $\mathbf{A}^{-1} = \mathbf{A}^*/\det \mathbf{A}$, where $\mathbf{A}^*$ is the adjoint (transpose of the cofactor matrix of **A**).

2.10 EXERCISES

1. Solve the following matrix equation for **X**: $3\left(\begin{bmatrix} -2 & 0 \\ 1 & 3 \end{bmatrix} - 2\mathbf{X} \right) = 2\begin{bmatrix} -2 & 0 \\ 1 & 3 \end{bmatrix}$

2. Compute the following matrix products:

a) $\begin{bmatrix} -2 & 0 & 3 \\ 4 & 1 & -1 \end{bmatrix}\begin{bmatrix} 2 & -1 \\ 0 & 6 \\ 2 & -3 \end{bmatrix}$, b) $\begin{bmatrix} 1 & 2 \\ 3 & 4 \end{bmatrix}\begin{bmatrix} -2 & 0 \\ 1 & 1 \end{bmatrix}$, c) $\begin{bmatrix} 2 & 0 & 2 \\ 0 & -1 & -3 \\ 0 & 0 & 1 \end{bmatrix}\begin{bmatrix} 1 \\ 2 \\ 1 \end{bmatrix}$

3. Compute the transpose of the following matrices:

a) $\begin{bmatrix} 1, & 2, & 3 \end{bmatrix}$, b) $\begin{bmatrix} x & y \\ z & w \end{bmatrix}$, c) $\begin{bmatrix} 1 & 2 \\ 3 & 4 \\ 5 & 6 \\ 7 & 8 \end{bmatrix}$

4. Write the following linear combinations as vector-matrix products:
a) $\mathbf{v} = 2(1,2,3) - 4(-5,0,-1) + 3(2,-2,3)$
b) $\mathbf{v} = 3(2,-4) + 2(1,4) - 1(-2,-3) + 5(1,1)$

5. Show that

$$\mathbf{AB} = \begin{bmatrix} A_{11} & A_{12} & A_{13} \\ A_{21} & A_{22} & A_{23} \\ A_{31} & A_{32} & A_{33} \end{bmatrix} \begin{bmatrix} B_{11} & B_{12} & B_{13} \\ B_{21} & B_{22} & B_{23} \\ B_{31} & B_{32} & B_{33} \end{bmatrix} = \begin{bmatrix} \leftarrow A_{1,*}\mathbf{B} \rightarrow \\ \leftarrow A_{2,*}\mathbf{B} \rightarrow \\ \leftarrow A_{3,*}\mathbf{B} \rightarrow \end{bmatrix}$$

6. Show that

$$\mathbf{Au} = \begin{bmatrix} A_{11} & A_{12} & A_{13} \\ A_{21} & A_{22} & A_{23} \\ A_{31} & A_{32} & A_{33} \end{bmatrix} \begin{bmatrix} x \\ y \\ z \end{bmatrix} = x\mathbf{A}_{*,1} + y\mathbf{A}_{*,2} + z\mathbf{A}_{*,3}$$

7. Prove that the cross product can be expressed by the matrix product:

$$\mathbf{u} \times \mathbf{v} = \begin{bmatrix} v_x & v_y & v_z \end{bmatrix} \begin{bmatrix} 0 & u_z & -u_y \\ -u_z & 0 & u_x \\ u_y & -u_x & 0 \end{bmatrix}$$

8. Let $= \begin{bmatrix} 2 & 0 & 1 \\ 0 & -1 & -3 \\ 0 & 0 & 1 \end{bmatrix}$. Is $\mathbf{B} = \begin{bmatrix} 1/2 & 0 & -1/2 \\ 0 & -1 & -3 \\ 0 & 0 & 1 \end{bmatrix}$ the inverse of $\mathbf{A}$?

9. Let $\mathbf{A} = \begin{bmatrix} 1 & 2 \\ 3 & 4 \end{bmatrix}$. Is $\mathbf{B} = \begin{bmatrix} -2 & 1 \\ 3/2 & 1/2 \end{bmatrix}$ the inverse of $\mathbf{A}$?

10 . Find the determinants of the following matrices:

$\begin{bmatrix} 21 & -4 \\ 10 & 7 \end{bmatrix}$	$\begin{bmatrix} 2 & 0 & 0 \\ 0 & 3 & 0 \\ 0 & 0 & 7 \end{bmatrix}$

11 . Find the inverse of the following matrices:

$\begin{bmatrix} 21 & -4 \\ 10 & 7 \end{bmatrix}$	$\begin{bmatrix} 2 & 0 & 0 \\ 0 & 3 & 0 \\ 0 & 0 & 7 \end{bmatrix}$

12 . Is the following matrix invertible?

$$\begin{bmatrix} 1 & 2 & 3 \\ 0 & 4 & 5 \\ 0 & 0 & 0 \end{bmatrix}$$

13 . Show that $(\mathbf{A}^{-1})^T = (\mathbf{A}^T)^{-1}$, assuming $\mathbf{A}$ is invertible.

14 . Let $\mathbf{A}$ and $\mathbf{B}$ be $n \times n$ matrices. A fact proved in linear algebra books is that $\det(\mathbf{AB}) = \det \mathbf{A} \cdot \det \mathbf{B}$. Use this fact along with the fact that $\det\mathbf{I} = 1$ to prove $\det \mathbf{A}^{-1} = \frac{1}{\det \mathbf{A}}$, assuming $\mathbf{A}$ is invertible.

15 . Prove that the 2D determinant $\begin{bmatrix} u_x & u_y \\ v_x & v_y \end{bmatrix}$ gives the signed area of the parallelogram spanned by $\mathbf{u} = (u_x, u_y)$ and $\mathbf{v} = (v_x, v_y)$. The result is positive if $\mathbf{u}$ can be rotated counterclockwise to coincide with $\mathbf{v}$ by an angle $\theta \in (0, \pi)$, and negative otherwise.

16 . Find the area of the parallelogram spanned by:
a) $\mathbf{u} = (3, 0)$ and $\mathbf{v} = (1, 1)$
b) $\mathbf{u} = (-1, -1)$ and $\mathbf{v} = (0, 1)$

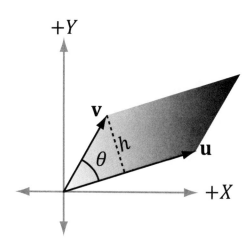

17 . Let $\mathbf{A} = \begin{bmatrix} A_{11} & A_{12} \\ A_{21} & A_{22} \end{bmatrix}$, $\mathbf{B} = \begin{bmatrix} B_{11} & B_{12} \\ B_{21} & B_{22} \end{bmatrix}$, and $\mathbf{C} = \begin{bmatrix} C_{11} & C_{12} \\ C_{21} & C_{22} \end{bmatrix}$. Show that $\mathbf{A}(\mathbf{BC}) = (\mathbf{AB})\mathbf{C}$. This shows that matrix multiplication is associative for matrices. (In fact, matrix multiplication is associative for general sized matrices, whenever the multiplication is defined.)

18 . Write a computer program that computes the transpose of an $m \times n$ matrix without using XNA math (just use an array of arrays in C++).

19 . Write a computer program that computes the determinant and inverse of 4×4 matrices without using XNA math (just use an array of arrays in C++).

Chapter **3** **TRANSFORMATIONS**

We describe objects in our 3D worlds geometrically; that is, as a collection of triangles that approximate the exterior surfaces of the objects. It would be an uninteresting world if our objects remained motionless. Thus we are interested in methods for transforming geometry; examples of geometric transformations are translation, rotation, and scaling. In this chapter, we develop matrix equations, which can be used to transform points and vectors in 3D space.

Objectives:

1. To understand how linear and affine transformations can be represented by matrices.

2. To learn the coordinate transformations for scaling, rotating, and translating geometry.

3. To discover how several transformation matrices can be combined into one net transformation matrix through matrix-matrix multiplication.

4. To find out how we can convert coordinates from one coordinate system to another, and how this change of coordinate transformation can be represented by a matrix.

5. To become familiar with the subset of functions provided by the XNA Math library used for constructing transformation matrices.

3.1 LINEAR TRANSFORMATIONS

3.1.1 Definition

Consider the mathematical function $\tau(\mathbf{v}) = \tau(x, y, z) = (x', y', z')$. This function inputs a 3D vector and outputs a 3D vector. We say that τ is a *linear transformation* if and only if the following properties hold:

$$
\begin{aligned}
&\textbf{1. } \tau(\mathbf{u} + \mathbf{v}) = \tau(\mathbf{u}) + \tau(\mathbf{v}) \\
&\textbf{2. } \tau(k\mathbf{u}) = k\tau(\mathbf{u})
\end{aligned}
\qquad \textbf{(eq. 3.1)}
$$

where $\mathbf{u} = (u_x, u_y, u_z)$ and $\mathbf{v} = (v_x, v_y, v_z)$ are any 3D vectors, and k is a scalar.

Note: *A linear transformation can consist of input and output values other than 3D vectors, but we do not need such generality in a 3D graphics book.*

☞ Example 3.1

Define the function $\tau(x, y, z) = (x^2, y^2, z^2)$; for example, $\tau(1, 2, 3) = (1, 4, 9)$. This function is not linear because, for $k = 2$ and $\mathbf{u} = (1, 2, 3)$, we have:

$$\tau(k\mathbf{u}) = \tau(2, 4, 6) = (4, 16, 36)$$

but

$$k\tau(\mathbf{u}) = 2(1, 4, 9) = (2, 8, 18)$$

So property 2 of Equation 3.1 is not satisfied.

If τ is linear, then it follows that:

$$
\begin{aligned}
\tau(a\mathbf{u} + b\mathbf{v} + c\mathbf{w}) &= \tau\left(a\mathbf{u} + (b\mathbf{v} + c\mathbf{w})\right) \\
&= a\tau(\mathbf{u}) + \tau(b\mathbf{v} + c\mathbf{w}) \\
&= a\tau(\mathbf{u}) + b\tau(\mathbf{v}) + c\tau(\mathbf{w})
\end{aligned}
\qquad \textbf{(eq. 3.2)}
$$

We will use this result in the next section.

3.1.2 Matrix Representation

Let $\mathbf{u} = (x, y, z)$. Observe that we can always write this as:

$$\mathbf{u} = (x, y, z) = x\mathbf{i} + y\mathbf{j} + z\mathbf{k} = x(1, 0, 0) + y(0, 1, 0) + z(0, 0, 1)$$

The vectors $\mathbf{i} = (1, 0, 0)$, $\mathbf{j} = (0, 1, 0)$, and $\mathbf{k} = (0, 0, 1)$, which are unit vectors that aim along the working coordinate axes, respectively, are called the *standard basis vectors* for $\mathbb{R}^3$. ($\mathbb{R}^3$ denotes the set of all 3D coordinate vectors (x, y, z)). Now let τ be a linear transformation; by linearity (i.e., Equation 3.2), we have:

$$\tau(\mathbf{u}) = \tau(x\mathbf{i} + y\mathbf{j} + z\mathbf{k}) = x\tau(\mathbf{i}) + y\,\tau(\mathbf{j}) + z\tau(\mathbf{k}) \qquad \textbf{(eq. 3.3)}$$

Observe that this is nothing more than a linear combination, which, as we learned in the previous chapter, can be written by vector-matrix multiplication. By Equation 2.2 we may rewrite Equation 3.3 as:

$$\tau(\mathbf{u}) = x\tau(\mathbf{i}) + y\tau(\mathbf{j}) + z\tau(\mathbf{k})$$

$$= \mathbf{u}\mathbf{A} = \begin{bmatrix} x, & y, & z \end{bmatrix} \begin{bmatrix} \leftarrow \tau(\mathbf{i}) \rightarrow \\ \leftarrow \tau(\mathbf{j}) \rightarrow \\ \leftarrow \tau(\mathbf{k}) \rightarrow \end{bmatrix} = \begin{bmatrix} x, & y, & z \end{bmatrix} \begin{bmatrix} A_{11} & A_{12} & A_{13} \\ A_{21} & A_{22} & A_{23} \\ A_{31} & A_{32} & A_{33} \end{bmatrix} \textbf{(eq. 3.4)}$$

where $\tau(\mathbf{i}) = (A_{11}, A_{12}, A_{13})$, $\tau(\mathbf{j}) = (A_{21}, A_{22}, A_{23})$, and $\tau(\mathbf{k}) = (A_{31}, A_{32}, A_{33})$. We call the matrix $\mathbf{A}$ the matrix representation of the linear transformation τ.

3.1.3 Scaling

Scaling refers to changing the size of an object as shown in Figure 3.1.

Figure 3.1. **The left pawn is the original object. The middle pawn is the original pawn scaled 2 units on the *y*-axis making it taller. The right pawn is the original pawn scaled 2 units on the *x*-axis making it fatter.**

We define the scaling transformation by:

$$S(x, y, z) = (s_x x, s_y y, s_z z)$$

This scales the vector by s_x units on the x-axis, s_y units on the y-axis, and s_z units on the z-axis, relative to the origin of the working coordinate system. We now show that S is indeed a linear transformation. We have that:

$$S(\mathbf{u} + \mathbf{v}) = \left(s_x \left(u_x + v_x \right), s_y \left(u_y + v_y \right), s_z \left(u_z + v_z \right) \right)$$
$$= \left(s_x u_x + s_x v_x, s_y u_y + s_y v_y, s_z u_z + s_z v_z \right)$$
$$= \left(s_x u_x, s_y u_y, s_z u_z \right) + \left(s_x v_x, s_y v_y, s_z v_z \right)$$
$$= S(\mathbf{u}) + S(\mathbf{v})$$
$$S(k\mathbf{u}) = \left(s_x k u_x, s_y k u_y, s_z k u_z \right)$$
$$= k \left(s_x u_x, s_y u_y, s_z u_z \right)$$
$$= k S(\mathbf{u})$$

Thus both properties of Equation 3.1 are satisfied, so S is linear, and there exists a matrix representation. To find the matrix representation, we just apply S to each of the standard basis vectors, as in Equation 3.3, and then place the resulting vectors into the rows of a matrix (as in Equation 3.4):

$$S(\mathbf{i}) = \left(s_x \cdot 1, s_y \cdot 0, s_z \cdot 0 \right) = \left(s_x, 0, 0 \right)$$
$$S(\mathbf{j}) = \left(s_x \cdot 0, s_y \cdot 1, s_z \cdot 0 \right) = \left(0, s_y, 0 \right)$$
$$S(\mathbf{k}) = \left(s_x \cdot 0, s_y \cdot 0, s_z \cdot 1 \right) = \left(0, 0, s_z \right)$$

Thus the matrix representation of S is:

$$\mathbf{S} = \begin{bmatrix} s_x & 0 & 0 \\ 0 & s_y & 0 \\ 0 & 0 & s_z \end{bmatrix}$$

We call this matrix the *scaling matrix*.

The inverse of the scaling matrix is given by:

$$\mathbf{S}^{-1} = \begin{bmatrix} 1/s_x & 0 & 0 \\ 0 & 1/s_y & 0 \\ 0 & 0 & 1/s_z \end{bmatrix}$$

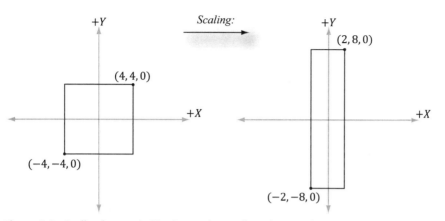

Figure 3.2. Scaling by one-half units on the x-axis and two units on the y-axis. Note that when looking down the negative z-axis, the geometry is basically 2D because z = 0.

☞ Example 3.2

Suppose we have a square defined by a minimum point $(-4, -4, 0)$ and a maximum point $(4, 4, 0)$. Suppose now that we wish to scale the square 0.5 units on the x-axis, 2.0 units on the y-axis, and leave the z-axis unchanged. The corresponding scaling matrix is:

$$S = \begin{bmatrix} 0.5 & 0 & 0 \\ 0 & 2 & 0 \\ 0 & 0 & 1 \end{bmatrix}$$

Now to actually scale (transform) the square, we multiply both the minimum point and maximum point by this matrix:

$$[-4,-4,0]\begin{bmatrix} 0.5 & 0 & 0 \\ 0 & 2 & 0 \\ 0 & 0 & 1 \end{bmatrix} = [-2,-8,0] \qquad [4,4,0]\begin{bmatrix} 0.5 & 0 & 0 \\ 0 & 2 & 0 \\ 0 & 0 & 1 \end{bmatrix} = [2,8,0]$$

The result is shown in Figure 3.2.

3.1.4 Rotation

In this section, we describe rotating a vector $\mathbf{v}$ about an axis $\mathbf{n}$ by an angle θ ; see Figure 3.3. Note that we measure the angle clockwise when looking down the axis $\mathbf{n}$; moreover, we assume $\|\mathbf{n}\| = 1$.

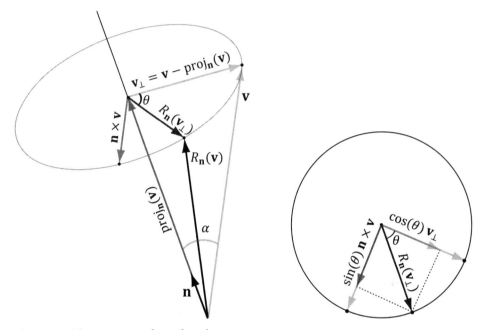

Figure 3.3. The geometry of rotation about a vector n.

First, decompose **v** into two parts: one part parallel to **n** and the other part orthogonal to **n**. The parallel part is just $\text{proj}_\mathbf{n}$ (**v**) (recall Example 1.5); the orthogonal part is given by $\mathbf{v}_\perp = \text{perp}_\mathbf{n}$ (**v**) = **v** − $\text{proj}_\mathbf{n}$ (**v**). (Recall, also from Example 1.5, that since **n** is a unit vector, we have $\text{proj}_\mathbf{n}$ (**v**) = (**n** · **v**)**n**.) The key observation is that the part $\text{proj}_\mathbf{n}$ (**v**) that is parallel to **n** is invariant under the rotation, so we only need to figure out how to rotate the orthogonal part. That is, the rotated vector $R_\mathbf{n}$ (**v**) = $\text{proj}_\mathbf{n}$ (**v**) + $R_\mathbf{n}$ ($\mathbf{v}_\perp$), by Figure 3.3.

To find $R_\mathbf{n}$ ($\mathbf{v}_\perp$), we set up a 2D coordinate system in the plane of rotation. We will use $\mathbf{v}_\perp$ as one reference vector. To get a second reference vector orthogonal to $\mathbf{v}_\perp$ and **n** we take the cross product **n** × **v** (left-hand-thumb rule). From the trigonometry of Figure 3.3 and Exercise 14 of Chapter 1, we see that

$$\|\mathbf{n} \times \mathbf{v}\| = \|\mathbf{n}\|\,\|\mathbf{v}\| \sin \alpha = \|\mathbf{v}\|\sin \alpha = \|\mathbf{v}_\perp\|$$

where α is the angle between **n** and **v**. So both reference vectors have the same length and lie on the circle of rotation. Now that we have set up these two reference vectors, we see from trigonometry that:

$$R_\mathbf{n}\,(\mathbf{v}_\perp) = \cos \theta\,\mathbf{v}_\perp + \sin \theta\,(\mathbf{n} \times \mathbf{v})$$

This gives us the following rotation formula:

$$R_{\mathbf{n}}(\mathbf{v}) = \text{proj}_{\mathbf{n}}(\mathbf{v}) + R_{\mathbf{n}}(\mathbf{v}_{\perp})$$
$$= (\mathbf{n} \cdot \mathbf{v})\mathbf{n} + \cos\theta\,\mathbf{v}_{\perp} + \sin\theta(\mathbf{n} \times \mathbf{v})$$
$$= (\mathbf{n} \cdot \mathbf{v})\mathbf{n} + \cos\theta(\mathbf{v} - (\mathbf{n} \cdot \mathbf{v})\mathbf{n}) + \sin\theta(\mathbf{n} \times \mathbf{v})$$
$$= \cos\theta\,\mathbf{v} + (1 - \cos\theta)(\mathbf{n} \cdot \mathbf{v})\mathbf{n} + \sin\theta(\mathbf{n} \times \mathbf{v}) \qquad \text{(eq. 3.5)}$$

We leave it as an exercise to show that this is a linear transformation. To find the matrix representation, we just apply $R_{\mathbf{n}}$ to each of the standard basis vectors, as in Equation 3.3, and then place the resulting vectors into the rows of a matrix (as in Equation 3.4). The final result is:

$$\mathbf{R_n} = \begin{bmatrix} c+(1-c)x^2 & (1-c)xy+sz & (1-c)xz-sy \\ (1-c)xy-sz & c+(1-c)y^2 & (1-c)yz+sx \\ (1-c)xz+sy & (1-c)yz-sx & c+(1-c)z^2 \end{bmatrix}$$

where we let $c = \cos\theta$ and $s = \sin\theta$.

The rotation matrices have an interesting property. Each row vector is unit length (verify) and the row vectors are mutually orthogonal (verify). Thus the row vectors are *orthonormal* (i.e., mutually orthogonal and unit length). A matrix whose rows are orthonormal is said to be an *orthogonal matrix*. An orthogonal matrix has the attractive property that its inverse is actually equal to its transpose. Thus, the inverse of $R_{\mathbf{n}}$ is:

$$\mathbf{R_n}^{-1} = \mathbf{R_n}^T = \begin{bmatrix} c+(1-c)x^2 & (1-c)xy-sz & (1-c)xz+sy \\ (1-c)xy+sz & c+(1-c)y^2 & (1-c)yz-sx \\ (1-c)xz-sy & (1-c)yz+sx & c+(1-c)z^2 \end{bmatrix}$$

In general, orthogonal matrices are desirable to work with because their inverses are easy and efficient to compute.

In particular, if we choose the x-, y-, and z-axes for rotation (i.e., $\mathbf{n} = (1, 0, 0)$, $\mathbf{n} = (0, 1, 0)$, and $\mathbf{n} = (0, 0, 1)$, respectively), then we get the following rotation matrices which rotate about the x-, y-, and z-axis, respectively:

$$\mathbf{R_x} = \begin{bmatrix} 1 & 0 & 0 & 0 \\ 0 & \cos\theta & \sin\theta & 0 \\ 0 & -\sin\theta & \cos\theta & 0 \\ 0 & 0 & 0 & 1 \end{bmatrix}, \mathbf{R_y} = \begin{bmatrix} \cos\theta & 0 & -\sin\theta & 0 \\ 0 & 1 & 0 & 0 \\ \sin\theta & 0 & \cos\theta & 0 \\ 0 & 0 & 0 & 1 \end{bmatrix}, \mathbf{R_z} = \begin{bmatrix} \cos\theta & \sin\theta & 0 & 0 \\ -\sin\theta & \cos\theta & 0 & 0 \\ 0 & 0 & 1 & 0 \\ 0 & 0 & 0 & 1 \end{bmatrix}$$

☞ Example 3.3

Suppose we have a square defined by a minimum point $(-1, 0, -1)$ and a maximum point $(1, 0, 1)$. Suppose now that we wish to rotate the square $-30°$ clockwise about the y-axis (i.e., $30°$ counterclockwise). In this case, $\mathbf{n} = (0, 1, 0)$, which simplifies $\mathbf{R_n}$ considerably; the corresponding y-axis rotation matrix is:

$$\mathbf{R}_y = \begin{bmatrix} \cos\theta & 0 & -\sin\theta \\ 0 & 1 & 0 \\ \sin\theta & 0 & \cos\theta \end{bmatrix} = \begin{bmatrix} \cos(-30°) & 0 & -\sin(-30°) \\ 0 & 1 & 0 \\ \sin(-30°) & 0 & \cos(-30°) \end{bmatrix} = \begin{bmatrix} \dfrac{\sqrt{3}}{2} & 0 & \dfrac{1}{2} \\ 0 & 1 & 0 \\ -\dfrac{1}{2} & 0 & \dfrac{\sqrt{3}}{2} \end{bmatrix}$$

Now to actually rotate (transform) the square, we multiply both the minimum point and maximum point by this matrix:

$$[-1,0,-1]\begin{bmatrix} \dfrac{\sqrt{3}}{2} & 0 & \dfrac{1}{2} \\ 0 & 1 & 0 \\ -\dfrac{1}{2} & 0 & \dfrac{\sqrt{3}}{2} \end{bmatrix} \approx [-0.36, 0, -1.36] \qquad [1,0,1]\begin{bmatrix} \dfrac{\sqrt{3}}{2} & 0 & \dfrac{1}{2} \\ 0 & 1 & 0 \\ -\dfrac{1}{2} & 0 & \dfrac{\sqrt{3}}{2} \end{bmatrix} \approx [0.36, 0, 1.36]$$

The result is shown in Figure 3.4.

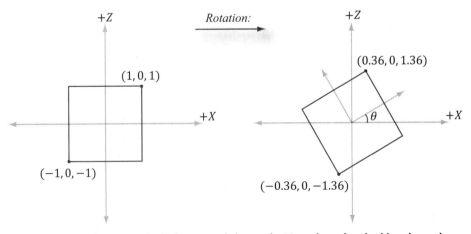

Figure 3.4. Rotating $-30°$ clockwise around the y-axis. Note that when looking down the positive y-axis, the geometry is basically 2D since $y = 0$.

3.2 AFFINE TRANSFORMATIONS

3.2.1 Homogeneous Coordinates

We will see in the next section that an affine transformation is a linear transformation combined with a translation. However, translation does not make sense for vectors because a vector only describes direction and magnitude, independent of location; in other words, vectors should be unchanged under translations. Translations should only be applied to points (i.e., position vectors). *Homogeneous coordinates* provide a convenient notational mechanism that enables us to handle points and vectors uniformly. With homogeneous coordinates, we augment to 4-tuples and what we place in the fourth w-coordinate depends on whether we are describing a point or vector. Specifically, we write:

1. $(x, y, z, 0)$ for vectors

2. $(x, y, z, 1)$ for points

We will see later that setting $w = 1$ for points allows translations of points to work correctly, and setting $w = 0$ for vectors prevents the coordinates of vectors from being modified by translations (we do not want to translate the coordinates of a vector, as that would change its direction and magnitude—translations should not alter the properties of vectors).

Note: *The notation of homogeneous coordinates is consistent with the ideas shown in Figure 1.17. That is, the difference between two points $\mathbf{q} - \mathbf{p} = (q_x, q_y, q_z, 1) - (p_x, p_y, p_z, 1) = (q_x - p_x, q_y - p_y, q_z - p_z, 0)$ results in a vector, and a point plus a vector $\mathbf{p} + \mathbf{v} = (p_x, p_y, p_z, 1) + (v_x, v_y, v_z, 0) = (p_x + v_x, p_y + v_y, p_z + v_z, 1)$ results in a point.*

3.2.2 Definition and Matrix Representation

A linear transformation cannot describe all the transformations we wish to do; therefore, we augment to a larger class of functions called affine transformations. An affine transformation is a linear transformation plus a translation vector $\mathbf{b}$; that is:

$$\alpha(\mathbf{u}) = \tau(\mathbf{u}) + \mathbf{b}$$

Or in matrix notation:

$$\alpha(\mathbf{u}) = \mathbf{u}\,\mathbf{A} + \mathbf{b} = \begin{bmatrix} x, & y, & z \end{bmatrix} \begin{bmatrix} A_{11} & A_{12} & A_{13} \\ A_{21} & A_{22} & A_{23} \\ A_{31} & A_{32} & A_{33} \end{bmatrix} + \begin{bmatrix} b_x, & b_y, & b_z \end{bmatrix} = \begin{bmatrix} x', & y', & z' \end{bmatrix}$$

where $\mathbf{A}$ is the matrix representation of a linear transformation.

If we augment to homogeneous coordinates with $w = 1$, then we can write this more compactly as:

$$[x, \quad y, \quad z, \quad 1] \begin{bmatrix} A_{11} & A_{12} & A_{13} & 0 \\ A_{21} & A_{22} & A_{23} & 0 \\ A_{31} & A_{32} & A_{33} & 0 \\ b_x & b_y & b_z & 1 \end{bmatrix} = [x', \quad y', \quad z', \quad 1]$$

(eq. 3.6)

The 4×4 matrix in Equation 3.6 is called the matrix representation of the affine transformation.

Observe that the addition by **b** is essentially a translation (i.e., change in position). We do not want to apply this to vectors because vectors have no position. However, we still want to apply the linear part of the affine transformation to vectors. If we set $w = 0$ in the fourth component for vectors, then the translation by **b** is *not* applied (verify by doing the matrix multiplication).

> **Note:** *Because the dot product of the row vector with the 4th column of the previous 4×4 affine transformation matrix is $[x, y, z, w] \cdot [0, 0, 0, 1] = w$, this matrix does not modify the w-coordinate of the input vector.*

3.2.2 Translation

The *identity transformation* is a linear transformation that just returns its argument; that is, $I(\mathbf{u}) = \mathbf{u}$. It can be shown that the matrix representation of this linear transformation is the identity matrix.

Now, we define the translation transformation to be the affine transformation whose linear transformation is the identity transformation; that is,

$$\tau(\mathbf{u}) = \mathbf{u} I + \mathbf{b} = \mathbf{u} + \mathbf{b}$$

As you can see, this simply translates (or displaces) point **u** by **b**. Figure 3.5 illustrates how this could be used to displace objects—we translate every point on the object by the same vector **b** to move it.

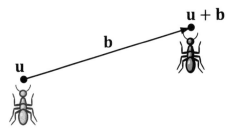

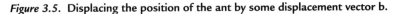

Figure 3.5. **Displacing the position of the ant by some displacement vector b.**

By Equation 3.6, τ has the matrix representation:

$$\mathbf{T} = \begin{bmatrix} 1 & 0 & 0 & 0 \\ 0 & 1 & 0 & 0 \\ 0 & 0 & 1 & 0 \\ b_x & b_y & b_z & 1 \end{bmatrix}$$

This is called the *translation matrix*.

The inverse of the translation matrix is given by:

$$\mathbf{T}^{-1} = \begin{bmatrix} 1 & 0 & 0 & 0 \\ 0 & 1 & 0 & 0 \\ 0 & 0 & 1 & 0 \\ -b_x & -b_y & -b_z & 1 \end{bmatrix}$$

☞ Example 3.4

Suppose we have a square defined by a minimum point $(-8, 2, 0)$ and a maximum point $(-2, 8, 0)$. Suppose now that we wish to translate the square 12 units on the x-axis, -10.0 units on the y-axis, and leave the z-axis unchanged. The corresponding translation matrix is:

$$\mathbf{T} = \begin{bmatrix} 1 & 0 & 0 & 0 \\ 0 & 1 & 0 & 0 \\ 0 & 0 & 1 & 0 \\ 12 & -10 & 0 & 1 \end{bmatrix}$$

Now to actually translate (transform) the square, we multiply both the minimum point and maximum point by this matrix:

$$\begin{bmatrix} -8, & 2, & 0, & 1 \end{bmatrix} \begin{bmatrix} 1 & 0 & 0 & 0 \\ 0 & 1 & 0 & 0 \\ 0 & 0 & 1 & 0 \\ 12 & -10 & 0 & 1 \end{bmatrix} = \begin{bmatrix} 4, & -8 & 0, & 1 \end{bmatrix}$$

$$\begin{bmatrix} -2, & 8, & 0, & 1 \end{bmatrix} \begin{bmatrix} 1 & 0 & 0 & 0 \\ 0 & 1 & 0 & 0 \\ 0 & 0 & 1 & 0 \\ 12 & -10 & 0 & 1 \end{bmatrix} = \begin{bmatrix} 10, & -2, & 0, & 1 \end{bmatrix}$$

The result is shown in Figure 3.6.

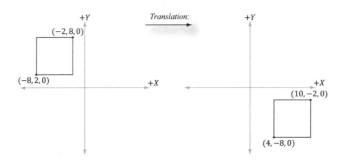

Figure 3.6. Translating 12 units on the x-axis and −10 units on the y-axis. Note that when looking down the negative z-axis, the geometry is basically 2D since z = 0.

Note: *Let **T** be a transformation matrix, and recall that we transform a point/vector by computing the product **vT** = **v′**. Observe that if we transform a point/vector by **T** and then transform it again by the inverse **T⁻¹** we end up with the original vector: **vTT⁻¹** = **vI** = **v**. In other words, the inverse transformation undoes the transformation. For example, if we translate a point 5 units on the x-axis, and then translate by the inverse −5 units on the x-axis, we end up where we started. Likewise, if we rotate a point 30° about the y-axis, and then rotate by the inverse −30° about the y-axis, then we end up with our original point. In summary, the inverse of a transformation matrix does the opposite transformation such that the composition of the two transformations leaves the geometry unchanged.*

3.2.3 Affine Matrices for Scaling and Rotation

Observe that if **b** = **0**, the affine transformation reduces to a linear transformation. We can express any linear transformation as an affine transformation with **b** = **0**. This, in turn, means we can represent any linear transformation by a 4 × 4 affine matrix. For example, the scaling and rotation matrices written using 4 × 4 matrices are given as follows:

$$
\mathbf{S} = \begin{bmatrix} s_x & 0 & 0 & 0 \\ 0 & s_y & 0 & 0 \\ 0 & 0 & s_z & 0 \\ 0 & 0 & 0 & 1 \end{bmatrix}
$$

$$
\mathbf{R_n} = \begin{bmatrix} c+(1-c)x^2 & (1-c)xy+sz & (1-c)xz-sy & 0 \\ (1-c)xy-sz & c+(1-c)y^2 & (1-c)yz+sx & 0 \\ (1-c)xz+sy & (1-c)yz-sx & c+(1-c)z^2 & 0 \\ 0 & 0 & 0 & 1 \end{bmatrix}
$$

In this way, we can express all of our transformations consistently using 4×4 matrices and points and vectors using 1×4 homogeneous row vectors.

3.2.4 Geometric Interpretation of an Affine Transformation Matrix

In this section, we develop some intuition of what the numbers inside an affine transformation matrix mean geometrically. First, let us consider a *rigid body transformation*, which is essentially a shape preserving transformation. A real-world example of a rigid body transformation might be picking a book off your desk and placing it on a bookshelf; during this process you are translating the book from your desk to the bookshelf, but also very likely changing the orientation of the book in the process (rotation). Let τ be a rotation transformation describing how we want to rotate an object and let **b** define a displacement vector describing how we want to translate an object. This rigid body transform can be described by the affine transformation:

$$\alpha(x, y, z) = \tau(x, y, z) + \mathbf{b} = x\tau(\mathbf{i}) + y\tau(\mathbf{j}) + z\tau(\mathbf{k}) + \mathbf{b}$$

In matrix notation, using homogeneous coordinates ($w = 1$ for points and $w = 0$ for vectors so that the translation is not applied to vectors), this is written as:

$$\begin{bmatrix} x, & y, & z, & w \end{bmatrix} \begin{bmatrix} \leftarrow \tau(\mathbf{i}) \rightarrow \\ \leftarrow \tau(\mathbf{j}) \rightarrow \\ \leftarrow \tau(\mathbf{k}) \rightarrow \\ \leftarrow \mathbf{b} \rightarrow \end{bmatrix} = \begin{bmatrix} x', & y', & z', & w \end{bmatrix}$$

(eq. 3.7)

Now, to see what this equation is doing geometrically, all we need to do is graph the row vectors in the matrix (see Figure 3.7). Because τ is a rotation transformation

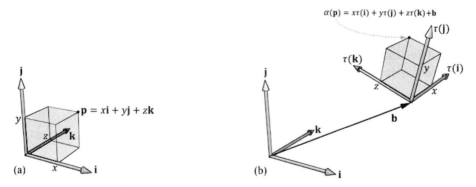

Figure 3.7. The geometry of the rows of an affine transformation matrix. The transformed point, α (**p**), is given as a linear combination of the transformed basis vectors τ (**i**), τ (**j**), τ (**k**), and the offset b.

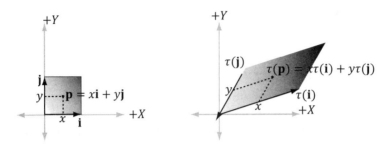

Figure 3.8. For a linear transformation that warps a square into a parallelogram, the transformed point $\tau(\mathbf{p}) = (x, y)$ is given as a linear combination of the transformed basis vectors $\tau(\mathbf{i})$, $\tau(\mathbf{j})$.

it preserves lengths and angles; in particular, we see that τ is just rotating the standard basis vectors $\mathbf{i}$, $\mathbf{j}$, and $\mathbf{k}$ into a new orientation $\tau(\mathbf{i})$, $\tau(\mathbf{j})$, and $\tau(\mathbf{k})$. The vector $\mathbf{b}$ is just a position vector denoting a displacement from the origin. Now Figure 3.7 shows how the transformed point is obtained geometrically when $\alpha(x, y, z) = x\tau(\mathbf{i}) + y\tau(\mathbf{j}) + z\tau(\mathbf{k}) + \mathbf{b}$ is computed.

The same idea applies to scaling or skew transformations. Consider the linear transformation τ that warps a square into a parallelogram as shown in Figure 3.8. The warped point is simply the linear combination of the warped basis vectors.

3.3 COMPOSITION OF TRANSFORMATIONS

Suppose $\mathbf{S}$ is a scaling matrix, $\mathbf{R}$ is a rotation matrix, and $\mathbf{T}$ is a translation matrix. Assume we have a cube made up of eight vertices $\mathbf{v}_i$ for $i = 0, 1, \ldots, 7$, and we wish to apply these three transformations to each vertex successively. The obvious way to do this is step-by-step:

$$((\mathbf{v}_i \mathbf{S})\mathbf{R})\,\mathbf{T} = (\mathbf{v}_i'\,\mathbf{R})\,\mathbf{T} = \mathbf{v}_i''\mathbf{T} = \mathbf{v}_i''' \qquad \text{for} \quad i = 0, 1, \ldots, 7$$

However, because matrix multiplication is associative, we can instead write this equivalently as:

$$\mathbf{v}_i\,(\mathbf{SRT}) = \mathbf{v}_i''' \qquad \text{for} \quad i = 0, 1, \ldots, 7$$

We can think of the matrix $\mathbf{C} = \mathbf{SRT}$ as a matrix that encapsulates all three transformations into one net transformation matrix. In other words, matrix-matrix multiplication allows us to concatenate transforms.

This has performance implications. To see this, assume that a 3D object is composed of 20,000 points and that we want to apply these three successive geometric transformations to the object. Using the step-by-step approach, we would require $20,000 \times 3$ vector-matrix multiplications. On the other hand, using the combined matrix approach requires 20,000 vector-matrix multiplications and 2 matrix-matrix multiplications. Clearly, 2 extra matrix-matrix multiplications is a cheap price to pay for the large savings in vector-matrix multiplications.

Note: *Again, we point out that matrix multiplication is not commutative. This is even seen geometrically. For example, a rotation followed by a translation, which we can describe by the matrix product **RT**, does not result in the same transformation as the same translation followed by the same rotation, that is, **TR**. Figure 3.9 demonstrates this.*

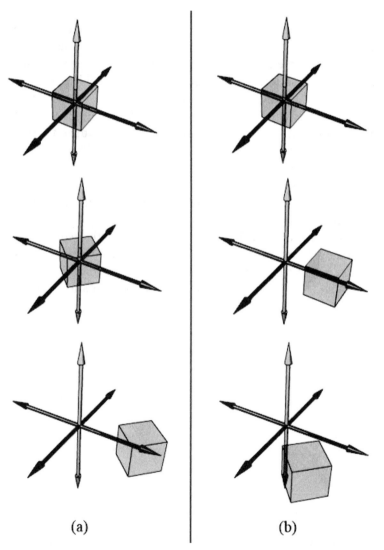

(a)   (b)

Figure 3.9. (a) Rotating first and then translating. (b) Translating first and then rotating.

3.4 CHANGE OF COORDINATE TRANSFORMATIONS

The scalar $100°\,C$ represents the temperature of boiling water relative to the Celsius scale. How do we describe the *same* temperature of boiling water relative to the Fahrenheit scale? In other words, what is the scalar, relative to the Fahrenheit scale, that represents the temperature of boiling water? To make this conversion (or change of frame), we need to know how the Celsius and Fahrenheit scales relate. They are related as follows: $T_F = \frac{9}{5}T_C + 32°$. Therefore, the temperature of boiling water relative to the Fahrenheit scale is given by $T_F = \frac{9}{5}(100)° + 32° = 212°\,F$.

This example illustrated that we can convert a scalar k that describes some quantity relative to a frame A into a new scalar k' that describes the *same* quantity relative to a different frame B, provided that we knew how frame A and B were related. In the following subsections, we look at a similar problem, but instead of scalars, we are interested in how to convert the coordinates of a point/vector relative to one frame into coordinates relative to a different frame (see Figure 3.10). We call the transformation that converts coordinates from one frame into coordinates of another frame a *change of coordinate transformation.*

It is worth emphasizing that in a change of coordinate transformation, we do not think of the geometry as changing; rather, we are changing the frame of reference, which thus changes the coordinate representation of the geometry. This is in contrast to how we usually think about rotations, translations, and scaling, where we think of actually physically moving or deforming the geometry.

In 3D computer graphics, we employ multiple coordinate systems, so we need to know how to convert from one to another. Because location is a property of points, but not of vectors, the change of coordinate transformation is different for points and vectors.

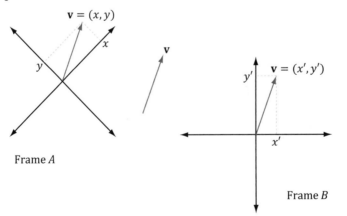

Figure 3.10. The *same* vector v has different coordinates when described relative to different frames. It has coordinates (x, y) relative to frame A and coordinates (x', y') relative to frame B.

3.4.1 Vectors

Consider Figure 3.11 in which we have two frames A and B and a vector **p**. Suppose we are given the coordinates $\mathbf{p}_A = (x, y)$ of **p** relative to frame A, and we wish to find the coordinates $\mathbf{p}_B = (x', y')$ of **p** relative to frame B. In other words, given the coordinates identifying a vector relative to one frame, how do we find the coordinates that identify the same vector relative to a different frame?

From Figure 3.11, it is clear that

$$\mathbf{p} = x\mathbf{u} + y\mathbf{v}$$

where **u** and **v** are unit vectors which aim, respectively, along the x- and y-axes of frame A. Expressing each vector in the previous equation in frame B coordinates we get:

$$\mathbf{p}_B = x\mathbf{u}_B + y\mathbf{v}_B$$

Thus, if we are given $\mathbf{p}_A = (x, y)$ and we know the coordinates of the vectors **u** and **v** relative to frame B, that is, if we know $\mathbf{u}_B = (u_x, u_y)$ and $\mathbf{v}_B = (v_x, v_y)$, then we can always find $\mathbf{p}_B = (x', y')$.

Generalizing to 3D, if $\mathbf{p}_A = (x, y, z)$, then

$$\mathbf{p}_B = x\mathbf{u}_B + y\mathbf{v}_B + z\mathbf{w}_B$$

where **u**, **v**, and **w** are unit vectors which aim, respectively, along the x-, y-, and z-axes of frame A.

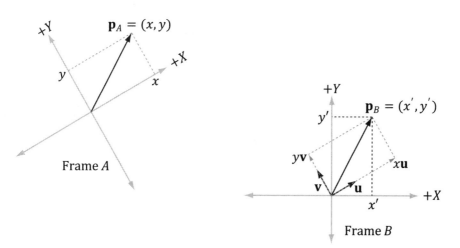

Figure 3.11. The geometry of finding the coordinates of p relative to frame B.

3.4.2 Points

The change of coordinate transformation for points is slightly different than it is for vectors; this is because location is important for points, so we cannot translate points as we translated the vectors in Figure 3.11.

Figure 3.12 shows the situation, and we see that the point **p** can be expressed by the equation:

$$\mathbf{p} = x\mathbf{u} + y\mathbf{v} + \mathbf{Q}$$

where **u** and **v** are unit vectors which aim, respectively, along the x- and y-axes of frame A, and **Q** is the origin of frame A. Expressing each vector/point in the previous equation in frame B coordinates we get:

$$\mathbf{p}_B = x\mathbf{u}_B + y\mathbf{v}_B + \mathbf{Q}_B$$

Thus, if we are given $\mathbf{p}_A = (x, y)$ and we know the coordinates of the vectors **u** and **v**, and origin **Q** relative to frame B, that is, if we know $\mathbf{u}_B = (u_x, u_y)$, $\mathbf{v}_B = (v_x, v_y)$, and $\mathbf{Q}_B = (Q_x, Q_y)$, then we can always find $\mathbf{p}_B = (x', y')$.

Generalizing to 3D, if $\mathbf{p}_A = (x, y, z)$, then

$$\mathbf{p}_B = x\mathbf{u}_B + y\mathbf{v}_B + z\mathbf{w}_B + \mathbf{Q}_B$$

where **u**, **v**, and **w** are unit vectors which aim, respectively, along the x-, y-, and z-axes of frame A, and **Q** is the origin of frame A.

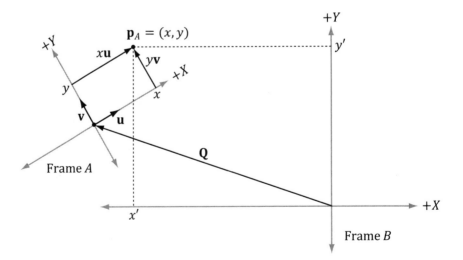

Figure 3.12. The geometry of finding the coordinates of p relative to frame B.

3.4.3 Matrix Representation

To review so far, the vector and point change of coordinate transformations are:

$(x', y', z') = x\mathbf{u}_B + y\mathbf{v}_B + z\mathbf{w}_B$ for vectors
$(x', y', z') = x\mathbf{u}_B + y\mathbf{v}_B + z\mathbf{w}_B + \mathbf{Q}_B$ for points

If we use homogeneous coordinates, then we can handle vectors and points by one equation:

$$(x', y', z', w) = x\mathbf{u}_B + y\mathbf{v}_B + z\mathbf{w}_B + w\mathbf{Q}_B \qquad \text{(eq. 3.8)}$$

If $w = 0$, then this equation reduces to the change of coordinate transformation for vectors; if $w = 1$, then this equation reduces to the change of coordinate transformation for points. The advantage of Equation 3.8 is that it works for both vectors and points, provided we set the w-coordinates correctly; we no longer need two equations (one for vectors and one for points). Equation 2.3 says that we can write Equation 3.8 in the language of matrices:

$$
\begin{bmatrix} x' & y' & z' & w \end{bmatrix} = \begin{bmatrix} x & y & z & w \end{bmatrix}
\begin{bmatrix}
\leftarrow \mathbf{u}_B \rightarrow \\
\leftarrow \mathbf{v}_B \rightarrow \\
\leftarrow \mathbf{w}_B \rightarrow \\
\leftarrow \mathbf{Q}_B \rightarrow
\end{bmatrix}
$$

$$
= \begin{bmatrix} x & y & z & w \end{bmatrix}
\begin{bmatrix}
u_x & u_y & u_z & 0 \\
v_x & v_y & v_z & 0 \\
w_x & w_y & w_z & 0 \\
Q_x & Q_y & Q_z & 1
\end{bmatrix}
$$

$$
= x\mathbf{u}_B + y\mathbf{v}_B + z\mathbf{w}_B + w\mathbf{Q}_B \qquad \text{(eq. 3.9)}
$$

where $\mathbf{Q}_B = (Q_x, Q_y, Q_z, 1)$, $\mathbf{u}_B = (u_x, u_y, u_z, 0)$, $\mathbf{v}_B = (v_x, v_y, v_z, 0)$, and $\mathbf{w}_B = (w_x, w_y, w_z, 0)$ describe the origin and axes of frame A with homogeneous coordinates relative to frame B. We call the 4×4 matrix in Equation 3.9 a *change of coordinate matrix or change of frame matrix*, and we say it converts (or maps) frame A coordinates into frame B coordinates.

3.4.4 Associativity and Change of Coordinate Matrices

Suppose now that we have three frames F, G, and H. Moreover, let $\mathbf{A}$ be the change of frame matrix from F to G, and let $\mathbf{B}$ be the change of frame matrix from G to H. Suppose we have the coordinates $\mathbf{p}_F$ of a vector relative to frame F and we want the coordinates of the same vector relative to frame H, that is, we want $\mathbf{p}_H$. One way to do this is step-by-step:

$$\left(\mathbf{p}_F \mathbf{A}\right)\mathbf{B} = \mathbf{p}_H$$

$$\left(\mathbf{p}_G\right)\mathbf{B} = \mathbf{p}_H$$

However, because matrix multiplication is associative, we can instead rewrite ($\mathbf{p}_F$ $\mathbf{A}$)$\mathbf{B} = \mathbf{p}_H$ as:

$$\mathbf{p}_F\left(\mathbf{A}\mathbf{B}\right) = \mathbf{p}_H$$

In this sense, the matrix product $\mathbf{C} = \mathbf{A}\mathbf{B}$ can be thought of as the change of frame matrix from F directly to H; it combines the effects of $\mathbf{A}$ and $\mathbf{B}$ into a net matrix. (The idea is like composition of functions.)

This has performance implications. To see this, assume that a 3D object is composed of 20,000 points and that we want to apply two successive change of frame transformations to the object. Using the step-by-step approach, we would require 20,000 × 2 vector-matrix multiplications. On the other hand, using the combined matrix approach requires 20,000 vector-matrix multiplications and 1 matrix-matrix multiplication to combine the two change of frame matrices. Clearly, 1 extra matrix-matrix multiplications is a cheap price to pay for the large savings in vector-matrix multiplications.

Note: *Again, matrix multiplication is not commutative, so we expect that* $\mathbf{AB}$ *and* $\mathbf{BA}$ *do not represent the same composite transformation. More specifically, the order in which you multiply the matrices is the order in which the transformations are applied, and in general, it is not a commutative process.*

3.4.5 Inverses and Change of Coordinate Matrices

Suppose that we are given $\mathbf{p}_B$ (the coordinates of a vector $\mathbf{p}$ relative to frame B), and we are given the change of coordinate matrix $\mathbf{M}$ from frame A to frame B; that is, $\mathbf{p}_B = \mathbf{p}_A\mathbf{M}$. We want to solve for $\mathbf{p}_A$. In other words, instead of mapping from frame A into frame B, we want the change of coordinate matrix that maps us from B into A. To find this matrix, suppose that $\mathbf{M}$ is invertible (i.e., $\mathbf{M}^{-1}$ exists). We can solve for $\mathbf{p}_A$ like so:

$\mathbf{p}_B = \mathbf{p}_A\mathbf{M}$	
$\mathbf{p}_B\mathbf{M}^{-1} = \mathbf{p}_A\mathbf{M}\mathbf{M}^{-1}$	Multiplying both sides of the equation by $\mathbf{M}^{-1}$.
$\mathbf{p}_B\mathbf{M}^{-1} = \mathbf{p}_A\mathbf{I}$	$\mathbf{M}\mathbf{M}^{-1} = \mathbf{I}$, by definition of inverse.
$\mathbf{p}_B\mathbf{M}^{-1} = \mathbf{p}_A$	$\mathbf{p}_A\mathbf{I} = \mathbf{p}_A$, by definition of the identity matrix.

Thus the matrix $\mathbf{M}^{-1}$ is the change of coordinate matrix from B into A.

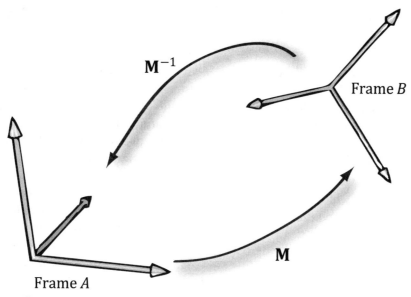

Figure 3.13. M maps *A* into *B* and M⁻¹ maps from *B* into *A*.

Figure 3.13 illustrates the relationship between a change of coordinate matrix and its inverse. Also note that all of the change of frame mappings that we do in this book will be invertible, so we won't have to worry about whether the inverse exists.

Figure 3.14 shows how the matrix inverse property $(\mathbf{AB})^{-1} = \mathbf{B}^{-1}\,\mathbf{A}^{-1})$ can be interpreted in terms of change of coordinate matrices.

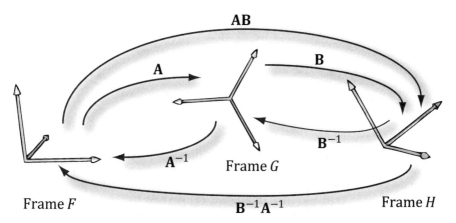

Figure 3.14. A maps from *F* into *G*, B maps from *G* into *H*, and AB maps from *F* directly into *H*. B⁻¹ maps from *H* into *G*, A⁻¹ maps from *G* into *F*, and B⁻¹A⁻¹ maps from *H* directly into *F*.

3.5 TRANSFORMATION MATRIX VERSUS CHANGE OF COORDINATE MATRIX

So far we have distinguished between "active" transformations (scaling, rotation, translation) and change of coordinate transformations. We will see in this section that mathematically, the two are equivalent, and an active transformation can be interpreted as a change of coordinate transformation, and conversely.

Figure 3.15 shows the geometric resemblance between the rows in Equation 3.7 (rotation followed by translation affine transformation matrix) and the rows in Equation 3.9 (change of coordinate matrix).

If we think about this, it makes sense. For with a change of coordinate transformation, the frames differ in position and orientation. Therefore, the mathematical conversion formula to go from one frame to the other would require rotating and translating the coordinates; and so we end up with the same mathematical form. In either case, we end up with the same numbers; the difference is the way we interpret the transformation. For some situations, it is more intuitive to work with multiple coordinate systems and convert between the systems where the object remains unchanged, but its coordinate representation changes since it is being described relative to a different frame of reference (this situation corresponds with Figure 3.15b). Other times, we want to transform an object inside a coordinate system without changing our frame of reference (this situation corresponds with Figure 3.15a).

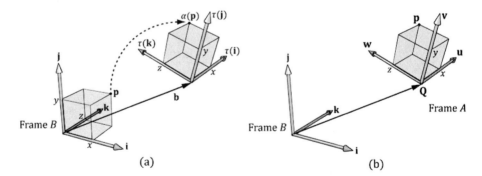

(a)   (b)

Figure 3.15. We see that $\mathbf{b} = \mathbf{Q}$, $\tau(\mathbf{i}) = \mathbf{u}$, $\tau(\mathbf{j}) = \mathbf{v}$, and $\tau(\mathbf{k}) = \mathbf{w}$. (a) We work with one coordinate system, call it frame B, and we apply an affine transformation to the cube to change its position and orientation relative to frame B:

$\alpha(x, y, z, w) = x\tau(\mathbf{i}) + y\tau(\mathbf{j}) + z\tau(\mathbf{k}) + w\mathbf{b}$. (b) We have two coordinate systems called frame A and frame B. The points of the cube relative to frame A can be converted to frame B coordinates by the formula $\mathbf{p}_B = x\mathbf{u}_B + y\mathbf{v}_B + z\mathbf{w}_B + w\mathbf{Q}_B$, where $\mathbf{p}_A = (x, y, z, w)$. In both cases, we have $\alpha(\mathbf{p}) = (x', y', z', w) = \mathbf{p}_B$ with coordinates relative to frame B.

Note: *In particular, this discussion shows that we can interpret a composition of active transformations (scaling, rotation, translation) as a change of coordinate transformation. This is important because we will often define our world space (Chapter 5) change of coordinate matrix as a composition of scaling, rotation, and translation transformations.*

3.6 XNA MATH TRANSFORMATION FUNCTIONS

We summarize the XNA Math related transformation functions for reference.

```
// Constructs a scaling matrix:
XMMATRIX XMMatrixScaling(
    FLOAT ScaleX,
    FLOAT ScaleY,
    FLOAT ScaleZ);                    // Scaling factors
```

```
// Constructs a scaling matrix from components in vector:
XMMATRIX XMMatrixScalingFromVector(
    FXMVECTOR Scale);                 // Scaling factors (s_x, s_y, s_z)
```

```
// Constructs a x-axis rotation matrix : R_x
XMMATRIX XMMatrixRotationX(
    FLOAT Angle);                     // Clockwise angle θ to rotate
```

```
// Constructs a y-axis rotation matrix : R_y
XMMATRIX XMMatrixRotationY(
    FLOAT Angle);                     // Clockwise angle θ to rotate
```

```
// Constructs a z-axis rotation matrix : R_z
XMMATRIX XMMatrixRotationZ(
    FLOAT Angle);                     // Clockwise angle θ to rotate
```

```
// Constructs an arbitrary axis rotation matrix : R_n
XMMATRIX XMMatrixRotationAxis(
    FXMVECTOR Axis,                   // Axis n to rotate about
    FLOAT Angle);                     // Clockwise angle θ to rotate
```

```
Constructs a translation matrix:
XMMATRIX XMMatrixTranslation(
    FLOAT OffsetX,
    FLOAT OffsetY,
    FLOAT OffsetZ);                   // Translation factors
```

```
Constructs a translation matrix from components in a vector:
XMMATRIX XMMatrixTranslationFromVector(
    FXMVECTOR Offset);                // Translation factors (t_x, t_y, t_z)
```

```
// Computes the vector-matrix product vM:
XMVECTOR XMVector3Transform(
        FXMVECTOR V,                                    // Input v
        CXMMATRIX M);                                   // Input M
```

```
// Computes the vector-matrix product vM where vw = 1 for transforming points:
XMVECTOR XMVector3TransformCoord(
        FXMVECTOR V,                                    // Input v
        CXMMATRIX M);                                   // Input M
```

```
// Computes the vector-matrix product vM where vw = 0 for transforming vectors:
XMVECTOR XMVector3TransformNormal(
        FXMVECTOR V,                                    // Input v
        CXMMATRIX M);                                   // Input M
```

Note: *For the last two functions* `XMVector3TransformCoord` *and* `XMVector3TransformNormal`, *you do not need to explicitly set the w coordinate. The functions will always use* $v_w = 1$ *and* $v_w = 0$ *for* `XMVector3TransformCoord` *and* `XMVector3TransformNormal`, *respectively.*

3.7 SUMMARY

1. The fundamental transformation matrices—scaling, rotation, and translation—are given by:

$$S = \begin{bmatrix} s_x & 0 & 0 & 0 \\ 0 & s_y & 0 & 0 \\ 0 & 0 & s_z & 0 \\ 0 & 0 & 0 & 1 \end{bmatrix} \qquad T = \begin{bmatrix} 1 & 0 & 0 & 0 \\ 0 & 1 & 0 & 0 \\ 0 & 0 & 1 & 0 \\ b_x & b_y & b_z & 1 \end{bmatrix}$$

$$R_n = \begin{bmatrix} c+(1-c)x^2 & (1-c)xy+sz & (1-c)xz-sy & 0 \\ (1-c)xy-sz & c+(1-c)y^2 & (1-c)yz+sx & 0 \\ (1-c)xz+sy & (1-c)yz-sx & c+(1-c)z^2 & 0 \\ 0 & 0 & 0 & 1 \end{bmatrix}$$

2. We use 4×4 matrices to represent transformations and 1×4 homogeneous coordinates to describe points and vectors, where we denote a point by setting the fourth component to $w = 1$ and a vector by setting $w = 0$. In this way, translations are applied to points but not to vectors.

3. A matrix is orthogonal if all of its row vectors are of unit length and mutually orthogonal. An orthogonal matrix has the special property that its inverse is equal to its transpose, thereby making the inverse easy and efficient to compute. All the rotation matrices are orthogonal.

4. From the associative property of matrix multiplication, we can combine several transformation matrices into one transformation matrix, which represents the net effect of applying the individual matrices sequentially.

5. Let $\mathbf{Q}_B$, $\mathbf{u}_B$, $\mathbf{v}_B$, and $\mathbf{w}_B$ describe the origin, x-, y-, and z-axes of frame A with coordinates relative to frame B, respectively. If a vector/point $\mathbf{p}$ has coordinates $\mathbf{p}_A = (x, y, z)$ relative to frame A, then the same vector/point relative to frame B has coordinates:

(a) $\mathbf{p}_B = (x', y', z') = x\mathbf{u}_B + y\mathbf{v}_B + z\mathbf{w}_B$ For vectors (direction and magnitude)

(b) $\mathbf{p}_B = (x', y', z') = \mathbf{Q}_B + x\mathbf{u}_B + y\mathbf{v}_B + z\mathbf{w}_B$ For position vectors (points)

These change of coordinate transformations can be written in terms of matrices using homogeneous coordinates.

6. Suppose we have three frames, F, G, and H, and let $\mathbf{A}$ be the change of frame matrix from F to G, and let $\mathbf{B}$ be the change of frame matrix from G to H. Using matrix-matrix multiplication, the matrix $\mathbf{C} = \mathbf{AB}$ can be thought of as the change of frame matrix F directly to H; that is, matrix-matrix multiplication combines the effects of $\mathbf{A}$ and $\mathbf{B}$ into one net matrix, and so we can write: $\mathbf{p}_F (\mathbf{AB}) = \mathbf{p}_H$.

7. If the matrix $\mathbf{M}$ maps frame A coordinates into frame B coordinates, then the matrix $\mathbf{M}^{-1}$ maps frame B coordinates into frame A coordinates.

8. An active transformation can be interpreted as a change of coordinate transformation, and conversely. For some situations, it is more intuitive to work with multiple coordinate systems and convert between the systems where the object remains unchanged, but its coordinate representation changes because it is being described relative to a different frame of reference. Other times, we want to transform an object inside a coordinate system without changing our frame of reference.

3.8 EXERCISES

1. Let $\tau{:}\mathbb{R}^3 \to \mathbb{R}^3$ be defined by $\tau(x, y, z) = (x+y, x-3, z)$. Is τ a linear transformation? If it is, find its standard matrix representation.

2. Let $\tau{:}\mathbb{R}^3 \to \mathbb{R}^3$ be defined by $\tau(x, y, z) = (3x + 4z, 2x - z, x+y+z)$. Is τ a linear transformation? If it is, find its standard matrix representation.

3. Assume that $\tau:\mathbb{R}^3 \rightarrow \mathbb{R}^3$ is a linear transformation. Further suppose that $\tau(1, 0, 0) = (3, 1, 2)$, $\tau(0, 1, 0) = (2, -1, 3)$, and $\tau(0, 0, 1) = (4, 0, 2)$. Find $\tau(1, 1, 1)$.

4. Build a scaling matrix that scales 2 units on the x-axis, -3 units on the y-axis, and keeps the z-dimension unchanged.

5. Build a rotation matrix that rotates 30° along the axis $(1, 1, 1)$.

6. Build a translation matrix that translates 4 units on the x-axis, no units on the y-axis, and -9 units on the z-axis.

7. Build a single transformation matrix that first scales 2 units on the x-axis, -3 units on the y-axis, and keeps the z-dimension unchanged, and then translates 4 units on the x-axis, no units on the y-axis, and -9 units on the z-axis.

8. Build a single transformation matrix that first rotates 45° about the y-axis and then translates -2 units on the x-axis, 5 units on the y-axis, and 1 unit on the z-axis.

9. Redo Example 3.2, but this time scale the square 1.5 units on the x-axis, 0.75 units on the y-axis, and leave the z-axis unchanged. Graph the geometry before and after the transformation to confirm your work.

10 . Redo Example 3.3, but this time rotate the square $-45°$ clockwise about the y-axis (i.e., 45° counterclockwise). Graph the geometry before and after the transformation to confirm your work.

11 . Redo Example 3.4, but this time translate the square -5 units on the x-axis, -3.0 units on the y-axis, and 4.0 units on the z-axis. Graph the geometry before and after the transformation to confirm your work.

12 . Show that $R_n(\mathbf{v}) = \cos\theta\,\mathbf{v} + (1-\cos\theta)(\mathbf{n}\cdot\mathbf{v})\mathbf{n} + \sin\theta\,(\mathbf{n}\times\mathbf{v})$ is a linear transformation and find its standard matrix representation.

13 . Prove that the rows of $\mathbf{R}_y$ are orthonormal. For a more computational intensive exercise, the reader can do this for the general rotation matrix (rotation matrix about an arbitrary axis), too.

14 . Prove the matrix $\mathbf{M}$ is orthogonal if and only if $\mathbf{M}^T = \mathbf{M}^{-1}$.

15 . Compute:

$$[x,y,z,1]\begin{bmatrix} 1 & 0 & 0 & 0 \\ 0 & 1 & 0 & 0 \\ 0 & 0 & 1 & 0 \\ b_x & b_y & b_z & 1 \end{bmatrix} \quad \text{and} \quad [x,y,z,0]\begin{bmatrix} 1 & 0 & 0 & 0 \\ 0 & 1 & 0 & 0 \\ 0 & 0 & 1 & 0 \\ b_x & b_y & b_z & 1 \end{bmatrix}$$

Does the translation translate points? Does the translation translate vectors? Why does it not make sense to translate the coordinates of a vector in standard position?

16 . Verify that the given scaling matrix inverse is indeed the inverse of the scaling matrix; that is, show, by directly doing the matrix multiplication, $SS^{-1} = S^{-1}S = I$. Similarly, verify that the given translation matrix inverse is indeed the inverse of the translation matrix; that is, show that $TT^{-1} = T^{-1}T = I$.

17 . Suppose that we have frames A and B. Let $\mathbf{p}_A = (1, -2, 0)$ and $\mathbf{q}_A = (1, 2, 0)$ represent a point and force, respectively, relative to frame A. Moreover, let $\mathbf{Q}_B = (-6, 2, 0)$, $\mathbf{u}_B = \left(\frac{1}{\sqrt{2}}, \frac{1}{\sqrt{2}}, 0\right)$, $\mathbf{v}_B = \left(-\frac{1}{\sqrt{2}}, \frac{1}{\sqrt{2}}, 0\right)$, and $\mathbf{w}_B = (0, 0, 1)$ describe frame A with coordinates relative to frame B. Build the change of coordinate matrix that maps frame A coordinates into frame B coordinates, and find $\mathbf{p}_B = (x, y, z)$ and $\mathbf{q}_B = (x, y, z)$. Draw a picture on graph paper to verify that your answer is reasonable.

18 . The analog for points to a linear combination of vectors is an *affine combination*: $\mathbf{p} = a_1 \mathbf{p}_1 + \ldots + a_n \mathbf{p}_n$ where $a_1 + \ldots + a_n = 1$ and $\mathbf{p}_1, \ldots, \mathbf{p}_n$ are points. The scalar coefficient a_k can be thought of as a "point" weight that describe how much influence the point $\mathbf{p}_k$ has in determining $\mathbf{p}$; loosely speaking, the closer a_k is to 1, the closer $\mathbf{p}$ will be to $\mathbf{p}_k$, and a negative a_k "repels" $\mathbf{p}$ from $\mathbf{p}_k$. (The next exercise will help you develop some intuition on this.) The weights are also known as *barycentric coordinates*. Show that an affine combination can be written as a point plus a vector:

$$\mathbf{p} = \mathbf{p}_1 + a_2 (\mathbf{p}_2 - \mathbf{p}_1) + \ldots + a_n (\mathbf{p}_n - \mathbf{p}_1)$$

19 . Consider the triangle defined by the points $\mathbf{p}_1 = (0, 0, 0)$, $\mathbf{p}_2 = (0, 1, 0)$, and $\mathbf{p}_3 = (2, 0, 0)$. Graph the following points:

(a) $\frac{1}{3}\mathbf{p}_1 + \frac{1}{3}\mathbf{p}_2 + \frac{1}{3}\mathbf{p}_3$

(b) $0.7\mathbf{p}_1 + 0.2\mathbf{p}_2 + 0.1\mathbf{p}_3$

(c) $0.0\mathbf{p}_1 + 0.5\mathbf{p}_2 + 0.5\mathbf{p}_3$

(d) $-0.2\mathbf{p}_1 + 0.6\mathbf{p}_2 + 0.6\mathbf{p}_3$

(e) $0.6\mathbf{p}_1 + 0.5\mathbf{p}_2 - 0.1\mathbf{p}_3$

(f) $0.8\mathbf{p}_1 - 0.3\mathbf{p}_2 + 0.5\mathbf{p}_3$

What is special about the point in part (a)? What would be the barycentric coordinates of $\mathbf{p}_2$ and the point $(1, 0, 0)$ in terms of $\mathbf{p}_1, \mathbf{p}_2, \mathbf{p}_3$? Can you make a conjecturer about where the point $\mathbf{p}$ will be located relative to the triangle if one of the barycentric coordinates is negative?

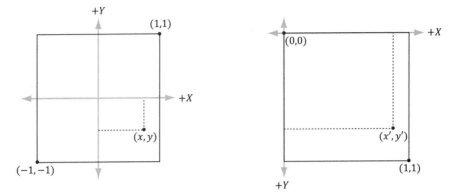

Figure 3.16. Change of coordinates from frame A (the square $[-1,1]^2$) to frame B (the square $[0,1]^2$ where the *y*-axis aims opposite to the one in Frame A).

20 . One of the defining factors of an affine transformation is that it preserves affine combinations. Prove that the affine transformation $\alpha(\mathbf{u})$ preserves affine transformations; that is, $\alpha(a_1\mathbf{p}_1 + \ldots + a_n\mathbf{p}_n) = a_1\,\alpha(\mathbf{p}_1) + \ldots + a_n\,\alpha(\mathbf{p}_n)$ where $a_1 + \ldots + a_n = 1$.

21 . Consider Figure 3.16. A common change of coordinate transformation in computer graphics is to map coordinates from frame A (the square $[-1, 1]^2$) to frame B (the square $[0, 1]^2$ where the *y*-axis aims opposite to the one in frame A). Prove that the change of coordinate transformation from frame A to frame B is given by:

$$\begin{bmatrix} x, & y, & 0 & 1 \end{bmatrix} \begin{bmatrix} 0.5 & 0 & 0 & 0 \\ 0 & -0.5 & 0 & 0 \\ 0 & 0 & 1 & 0 \\ 0.5 & 0.5 & 0 & 1 \end{bmatrix} = \begin{bmatrix} x', & y', & 0 & 1 \end{bmatrix}$$

22 . It was mentioned in the last chapter that the determinant was related to the change in volume of a box under a linear transformation. Find the determinant of the scaling matrix and interpret the result in terms of volume.

23 . Consider the transformation τ that warps a square into a parallelogram (See for example, Figure 3.17) given by:

$$\tau(x, y) = (3x + y, x + 2y)$$

Find the standard matrix representation of this transformation, and show that the determinant of the transformation matrix is equal to the area of the parallelogram spanned by $\tau(\mathbf{i})$ and $\tau(\mathbf{j})$.

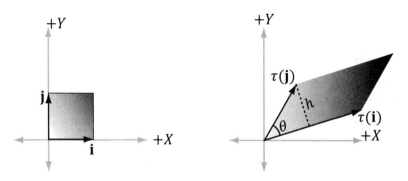

Figure 3.17. **Transformation that maps square into parallelogram.**

24 . Show that the determinant of the y-axis rotation matrix is 1. Based on the previous exercise, explain why it makes sense that it is 1. For a more computational intensive exercise, the reader can show the determinant of the general rotation matrix (rotation matrix about an arbitrary axis) is 1.

25 . A rotation matrix can be characterized algebraically as an orthogonal matrix with determinant equal to 1. If we reexamine Figure 3.7 along with Exercise 24 this makes sense; the rotated basis vectors $\tau(\mathbf{i})$, $\tau(\mathbf{j})$, and $\tau(\mathbf{k})$ are unit length and mutually orthogonal; moreover, rotation does not change the size of the object, so the determinant should be 1. Show that the product of two rotation matrices $\mathbf{R}_1 \mathbf{R}_2 = \mathbf{R}$ is a rotation matrix. That is, show $\mathbf{R}\mathbf{R}^T = \mathbf{R}^T\mathbf{R} = \mathbf{I}$ (to show $\mathbf{R}$ is orthogonal), and show $\det \mathbf{R} = 1$.

26 . Show that the following properties hold for a rotation matrix:

(a) $(\mathbf{u}\mathbf{R}) \cdot (\mathbf{v}\mathbf{R}) = \mathbf{u} \cdot \mathbf{v}$ Preservation of dot product

(b) $\|\mathbf{u}\mathbf{R}\| = \|\mathbf{u}\|$ Preservation of length

(c) $\theta(\mathbf{u}\mathbf{R}, \mathbf{v}\mathbf{R}) = \theta(\mathbf{u}, \mathbf{v})$ Preservation of angle, where $\theta(\mathbf{x}, \mathbf{y})$
          evaluates to the angle between $\mathbf{x}$ and $\mathbf{y}$:

$$\theta(\mathbf{x},\mathbf{y}) = \cos^{-1} \frac{\mathbf{x} \cdot \mathbf{y}}{\|\mathbf{x}\| \|\mathbf{y}\|}$$

Explain why all these properties make sense for a rotation transformation.

27 . Find a scaling, rotation, and translation matrix whose product transforms the line segment with start point $\mathbf{p} = (0, 0, 0)$ and endpoint $\mathbf{q} = (0, 0, 1)$ into the line segment with length 2, parallel to the vector $(1, 1, 1)$, with start point $(3, 1, 2)$.

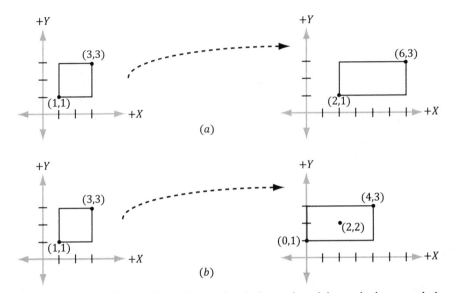

Figure 3.18. (a) Scaling 2-units on the *x*-axis relative to the origin results in a translation of the rectangle. (b) Scaling 2-units on the *x*-axis relative to the center of the rectangle does not result in a translation (the rectangle maintains its original center point).

28 . Suppose we have a box positioned at (x, y, z). The scaling transform we have defined uses the origin as a reference point for the scaling, so scaling this box (not centered about the origin) has the side effect of translating the box (Figure 3.18); this can be undesirable in some situations. Find a transformation that scales the box relative to its center point. (Hint: Change coordinates to the box coordinate system with the origin at the center of the box, scale the box, then transform back to the original coordinate system.)

Part 2 DIRECT3D FOUNDATIONS

In this part, we study fundamental Direct3D concepts and techniques that are used throughout the rest of this book. With these fundamentals mastered, we can move on to writing more interesting applications. A brief description of the chapters in this part follows.

Chapter 4, Direct3D Initialization: In this chapter, we learn what Direct3D is about and how to initialize it in preparation for 3D drawing. Basic Direct3D topics are also introduced, such as surfaces, pixel formats, page flipping, depth buffering, and multisampling. We also learn how to measure time with the performance counter, which we use to compute the frames rendered per second. In addition, we give some tips on debugging Direct3D applications. We develop and use our own application framework–not the SDK's framework.

Chapter 5, The Rendering Pipeline: In this long chapter, we provide a thorough introduction to the rendering pipeline, which is the sequence of steps necessary to generate a 2D image of the world based on what the virtual camera sees. We learn how to define 3D worlds, control the virtual camera, and project 3D geometry onto a 2D image plane.

Chapter 6, Drawing in Direct3D: This chapter focuses on the Direct3D API interfaces and methods needed to configure the rendering pipeline, define vertex and pixel shaders, and submit geometry to the rendering pipeline for drawing. The effects framework is also introduced. By the end of this chapter, you will be able to draw grids, boxes, spheres and cylinders.

Chapter 7, Lighting: This chapter shows how to create light sources and define the interaction between light and surfaces via materials. In particular, we show how to implement directional lights, point lights, and spotlights with vertex and pixel shaders.

Chapter 8, Texturing: This chapter describes texture mapping, which is a technique used to increase the realism of the scene by mapping 2D image data onto a 3D primitive. For example, using texture mapping, we can model a brick wall by applying a 2D brick wall image onto a 3D rectangle. Other key texturing topics covered include texture tiling and animated texture transformations.

Chapter 9, Blending: Blending allows us to implement a number of special effects like transparency. In addition, we discuss the intrinsic clip function, which enables us to mask out certain parts of an image from showing up; this can be used to implement fences and gates, for example. We also show how to implement a fog effect.

Chapter 10, Stenciling: This chapter describes the stencil buffer, which, like a stencil, allows us to block pixels from being drawn. Masking out pixels is a useful tool for a variety of situations. To illustrate the ideas of this chapter, we include a thorough discussion on implementing planar reflections and planar shadows using the stencil buffer.

Chapter 11, The Geometry Shader: This chapter shows how to program geometry shaders, which are special because they can create or destroy entire geometric primitives. Some applications include billboards, fur rendering, subdivisions, and particle systems. In addition, this chapter explains primitive IDs and texture arrays.

Chapter 12, The Compute Shader: The Compute Shader is a programmable shader Direct3D exposes that is not directly part of the rendering pipeline. It enables applications to use the graphics processing unit (GPU) for general purpose computation. For example, an imaging application can take advantage of the GPU to speed up image processing algorithms by implementing them with the compute shader. Because the Compute Shader is part of Direct3D, it reads from and writes to Direct3D resources, which enables us integrate results directly to the rendering pipeline. Therefore, in addition to general purpose computation, the compute shader is still applicable for 3D rendering.

Chapter 13, The Tessellation Stages: This chapter explores the tessellation stages of the rendering pipeline. Tessellation refers to subdividing geometry into smaller triangles and then offsetting the newly generated vertices in some way. The motivation to increase the triangle count is to add detail to the mesh. To illustrate the ideas of this chapter, we show how to tessellate a quad patch based on distance, and we show how to render cubic Bézier quad patch surfaces.

Chapter **4** # DIRECT3D INITIALIZATION

The initialization process of Direct3D requires us to be familiar with some basic Direct3D types and basic graphics concepts; the first section of this chapter addresses these requirements. We then detail the necessary steps to initialize Direct3D. After that, a small detour is taken to introduce accurate timing and the time measurements needed for real-time graphics applications. Finally, we explore the sample framework code, which is used to provide a consistent interface that all demo applications in this book follow.

Objectives:

1. To obtain a basic understanding of Direct3D's role in programming 3D hardware.
2. To understand the role COM plays with Direct3D.
3. To learn fundamental graphics concepts, such as how 2D images are stored, page flipping, depth buffering, and multisampling.
4. To learn how to use the performance counter functions for obtaining high-resolution timer readings.
5. To find out how to initialize Direct3D.
6. To become familiar with the general structure of the application framework that all the demos of this book employ.

4.1 PRELIMINARIES

The Direct3D initialization process requires us to be familiar with some basic graphics concepts and Direct3D types. We introduce these ideas and types in this section, so that we do not have to digress in the next section.

4.1.1 Direct3D Overview

Direct3D is a low-level graphics API (application programming interface) that enables us to render 3D worlds using 3D hardware acceleration. Essentially, Direct3D provides the software interfaces through which we control the graphics hardware. For example, to instruct the graphics hardware to clear the render target (e.g., the screen), we would call the Direct3D method `ID3D11DeviceContext::ClearRenderTargetView`. Having the Direct3D layer between the application and the graphics hardware means we do not have to worry about the specifics of the 3D hardware, so long as it is a Direct3D 11 capable device.

A Direct3D 11 capable graphics device must support the entire Direct3D 11 capability set, with few exceptions (some things like the multisampling count still need to be queried, as they can vary between Direct3D 11 hardware). This is in contrast to Direct3D 9, where a device only had to support a subset of Direct3D 9 capabilities; consequently, if a Direct3D 9 application wanted to use a certain feature, it was necessary to first check if the available hardware supported that feature, as calling a Direct3D function not implemented by the hardware resulted in failure. In Direct3D 11, device capability checking is no longer necessary because it is now a strict requirement that a Direct3D 11 device implement the entire Direct3D 11 capability set.

4.1.2 COM

Component Object Model (COM) is the technology that allows DirectX to be programming language independent and have backwards compatibility. We usually refer to a COM object as an interface, which for our purposes can be thought of and used as a C++ class. Most of the details of COM are hidden to us when programming DirectX with C++. The only thing that we must know is that we obtain pointers to COM interfaces through special functions or by the methods of another COM interface—we do not create a COM interface with the C++ `new` keyword. In addition, when we are done with an interface we call its `Release` method (all COM interfaces inherit functionality from the `IUnknown` COM interface, which provides the `Release` method) rather than `delete` it—COM objects perform their own memory management.

There is, of course, much more to COM, but more detail is not necessary for using DirectX effectively.

 COM interfaces are prefixed with a capital I. *For example, the COM interface that represents a 2D texture is called* ID3D11Texture2D.

4.1.3 Textures and Data Resource Formats

A 2D texture is a matrix of data elements. One use for 2D textures is to store 2D image data, where each element in the texture stores the color of a pixel. However, this is not the only usage; for example, in an advanced technique called normal mapping, each element in the texture stores a 3D vector instead of a color. Therefore, although it is common to think of textures as storing image data, they are really more general purpose than that. A 1D texture is like a 1D array of data elements, and a 3D texture is like a 3D array of data elements. As will be discussed in later chapters, textures are actually more than just arrays of data; they can have mipmap levels, and the GPU can do special operations on them, such as apply filters and multisampling. In addition, a texture cannot store arbitrary kinds of data; it can only store certain kinds of data formats, which are described by the DXGI_FORMAT enumerated type. Some example formats are:

1. DXGI_FORMAT_R32G32B32_FLOAT: Each element has three 32-bit floating-point components.

2. DXGI_FORMAT_R16G16B16A16_UNORM: Each element has four 16-bit components mapped to the [0, 1] range.

3. DXGI_FORMAT_R32G32_UINT: Each element has two 32-bit unsigned integer components.

4. DXGI_FORMAT_R8G8B8A8_UNORM: Each element has four 8-bit unsigned components mapped to the [0, 1] range.

5. DXGI_FORMAT_R8G8B8A8_SNORM: Each element has four 8-bit signed components mapped to the [−1, 1] range.

6. DXGI_FORMAT_R8G8B8A8_SINT: Each element has four 8-bit signed integer components mapped to the [−128, 127] range.

7. DXGI_FORMAT_R8G8B8A8_UINT: Each element has four 8-bit unsigned integer components mapped to the [0, 255] range.

Note that the R, G, B, A letters are used to stand for red, green, blue, and alpha, respectively. Colors are formed as combinations of the basis colors red, green, and blue (e.g., equal red and equal green makes yellow). The alpha channel or alpha component is generally used to control transparency. However, as we said earlier, textures need not store color information; for example, the format

```
DXGI_FORMAT_R32G32B32_FLOAT
```

has three floating-point components and can therefore store a 3D vector with floating-point coordinates. There are also *typeless* formats, where we just reserve memory and then specify how to reinterpret the data at a later time (sort of like a C++ reinterpret cast) when the texture is bound to the pipeline; for example, the following typeless format reserves elements with four 8-bit components, but does not specify the data type (e.g., integer, floating-point, unsigned integer):

```
DXGI_FORMAT_R8G8B8A8_TYPELESS
```

4.1.4 The Swap Chain and Page Flipping

To avoid flickering in animation, it is best to draw an entire frame of animation into an off screen texture called the back buffer. Once the entire scene has been drawn to the back buffer for the given frame of animation, it is presented to the screen as one complete frame; in this way, the viewer does not watch as the frame gets drawn—the viewer only sees complete frames. To implement this, two texture buffers are maintained by the hardware, one called the *front buffer* and a second called the *back buffer*. The front buffer stores the image data currently being displayed on the monitor, while the next frame of animation is being drawn to the back buffer. After the frame has been drawn to the back buffer, the roles of the back buffer and front buffer are reversed: the back buffer becomes the front buffer and the front buffer becomes the back buffer for the next frame of animation. Swapping the roles of the back and front buffers is called *presenting*. Presenting is an efficient operation, as the pointer to the current front buffer and the pointer to the current back buffer just need to be swapped. Figure 4.1 illustrates the process.

The front and back buffer form a *swap chain*. In Direct3D, a swap chain is represented by the `IDXGISwapChain` interface. This interface stores the front and back buffer textures, as well as provides methods for resizing the buffers (`IDXGISwapChain::ResizeBuffers`) and presenting (`IDXGISwapChain::Present`). We will discuss these methods in detail in §4.4.

Using two buffers (front and back) is called *double buffering*. More than two buffers can be employed; using three buffers is called *triple buffering*. Two buffers are usually sufficient, however.

Note: *Even though the back buffer is a texture (so an element should be called a texel), we often call an element a pixel because, in the case of the back buffer, it stores*

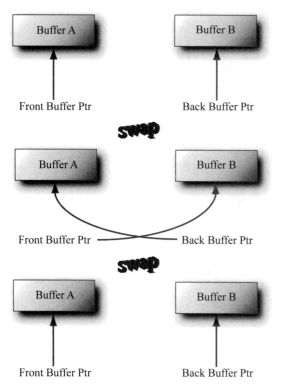

Figure 4.1. From top-to-bottom, we first render to Buffer B, which is serving as the current back buffer. Once the frame is completed, the pointers are swapped and Buffer B becomes the front buffer and Buffer A becomes the new back buffer. We then render the next frame to Buffer A. Once the frame is completed, the pointers are swapped and Buffer A becomes the front buffer and Buffer B becomes the back buffer again.

color information. Sometimes people will call an element of a texture a pixel, even if it doesn't store color information (e.g., "the pixels of a normal map").

4.1.5 Depth Buffering

The *depth buffer* is an example of a texture that does not contain image data, but rather depth information about a particular pixel. The possible depth values range from 0.0 to 1.0, where 0.0 denotes the closest an object can be to the viewer and 1.0 denotes the farthest an object can be from the viewer. There is a one-to-one correspondence between each element in the depth buffer and each pixel in the back buffer (i.e., the *ij*th element in the back buffer corresponds to the *ij*th element in the depth buffer). So if the back buffer had a resolution of 1280 × 1024, there would be 1280 × 1024 depth entries.

Figure 4.2. A group of objects that partially obscure each other.

Figure 4.2 shows a simple scene, where some objects partially obscure the objects behind them. In order for Direct3D to determine which pixels of an object are in front of another, it uses a technique called *depth buffering or z-buffering*. Let us emphasize that with depth buffering, the order in which we draw the objects does not matter.

> **Remark:** *To handle the depth problem, one might suggest drawing the objects in the scene in the order of farthest to nearest. In this way, near objects will be painted over far objects, and the correct results should be rendered. This is how a painter would draw a scene. However, this method has its own problems—sorting a large data set in back-to-front order and intersecting geometry. Besides, the graphics hardware gives us depth buffering for free.*

To illustrate how depth buffering works, let us look at an example. Consider Figure 4.3, which shows the volume the viewer sees and a 2D side view of that volume. From the figure, we observe that three different pixels compete to be rendered onto the pixel *P* on the view window. (Of course, we know the closest pixel should be rendered to *P* because it obscures the ones behind it, but the computer does not.) First, before any rendering takes place, the back buffer is cleared to a default color (like black or white), and the depth buffer is cleared to a default value—usually 1.0 (the farthest depth value a pixel can have). Now, suppose that the objects are rendered in the order of cylinder, sphere, and cone. The following table summarizes how the pixel P and its corresponding depth value d are updated as the objects are drawn; a similar process happens for the other pixels.

Operation	P	d	Description
Clear Operation	Black	1.0	Pixel and corresponding depth entry initialized.
Draw Cylinder	P_3	d_3	Since $d_3 \leq d = 1.0$ the depth test passes and we update the buffers by setting $P = P_3$ and $d = d_3$.
Draw Sphere	P_1	d_1	Since $d_1 \leq d = d_3$ the depth test passes and we update the buffers by setting $P = P_1$ and $d = d_1$.
Draw Cone	P_1	d_1	Since $d_2 > d = d_1$ the depth test fails and we do not update the buffers.

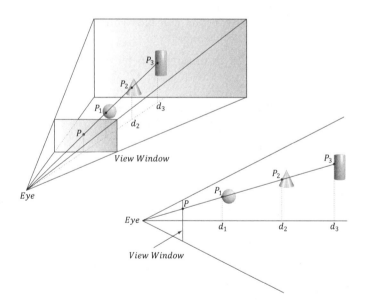

Figure 4.3. The view window corresponds to the 2D image (back buffer) we generate of the 3D scene. We see that three different pixels can be projected to the pixel *P*. Intuition tells us that *P1* should be written to *P* because it is closer to the viewer and blocks the other two pixels. The depth buffer algorithm provides a mechanical procedure for determining this on a computer. Note that we show the depth values relative to the 3D scene being viewed, but they are actually normalized to the range [0.0, 1.0] when stored in the depth buffer.

As you can see, we only update the pixel and its corresponding depth value in the depth buffer when we find a pixel with a smaller depth value. In this way, after all is said and done, the pixel that is closest to the viewer will be the one rendered. (You can try switching the drawing order around and working through this example again if you are still not convinced.)

To summarize, depth buffering works by computing a depth value for each pixel and performing a depth test. The depth test compares the depths of pixels competing to be written to a particular pixel location on the back buffer. The pixel with the depth value closest to the viewer wins, and that is the pixel that gets written to the back buffer. This makes sense because the pixel closest to the viewer obscures the pixels behind it.

The depth buffer is a texture, so it must be created with certain data formats. The formats used for depth buffering are as follows:

1. `DXGI_FORMAT_D32_FLOAT_S8X24_UINT`: Specifies a 32-bit floating-point depth buffer, with 8-bits (unsigned integer) reserved for the stencil buffer mapped to the $[0, 255]$ range and 24-bits not used for padding.

2. `DXGI_FORMAT_D32_FLOAT`: Specifies a 32-bit floating-point depth buffer.

3. `DXGI_FORMAT_D24_UNORM_S8_UINT`: Specifies an unsigned 24-bit depth buffer mapped to the $[0, 1]$ range with 8-bits (unsigned integer) reserved for the stencil buffer mapped to the $[0, 255]$ range.

4. `DXGI_FORMAT_D16_UNORM`: Specifies an unsigned 16-bit depth buffer mapped to the $[0, 1]$ range.

Note: *An application is not required to have a stencil buffer, but if it does, the stencil buffer is always attached to the depth buffer. For example, the 32-bit format*

`DXGI_FORMAT_D24_UNORM_S8_UINT`

uses 24-bits for the depth buffer and 8-bits for the stencil buffer. For this reason, the depth buffer is better called the depth/stencil buffer. Using the stencil buffer is a more advanced topic and will be explained in Chapter 10.

4.1.6 Texture Resource Views

A texture can be bound to different stages of the rendering pipeline; a common example is to use a texture as a render target (i.e., Direct3D draws into the texture) and as a shader resource (i.e., the texture will be sampled in a shader). A texture resource created for these two purposes would be given the bind flags:

`D3D11_BIND_RENDER_TARGET | D3D11_BIND_SHADER_RESOURCE`

indicating the two pipeline stages the texture will be bound to. Actually, resources are not directly bound to a pipeline stage; instead their associated resource views are bound to different pipeline stages. For each way we are going to use a texture, Direct3D requires that we create a *resource view* of that texture at initialization time. This is mostly for efficiency, as the SDK documentation points out: "This allows validation and mapping in the runtime and driver to occur at view creation, minimizing type checking at bind-time." So for the example of using a texture as a render target and shader resource, we would need to create two views: a render target view (`ID3D11RenderTargetView`) and a shader resource view (`ID3D11ShaderResourceView`). Resource views essentially do two things: they tell Direct3D how the resource will be used (i.e., what stage of the pipeline you will bind it to), and if the resource format was specified as typeless at creation time, then we must now state the type when creating a view. Thus, with typeless formats, it is possible for the elements of a texture to be viewed as floating-point values in one pipeline stage and as integers in another.

In order to create a specific view to a resource, the resource must be created with that specific bind flag. For instance, if the resource was not created with the `D3D11_BIND_DEPTH_STENCIL` bind flag (which indicates the texture will be bound to the pipeline as a depth/stencil buffer), then we cannot create an `ID3D11DepthStencilView` to that resource. If you try, you should get a Direct3D debug error like the following:

```
D3D11: ERROR: ID3D11Device::CreateDepthStencilView: A DepthStencilView
cannot be created of a Resource that did not specify
D3D11_BIND_DEPTH_STENCIL.
```

We will have a chance to see code for creating a render target view and a depth/stencil view in §4.2 of this chapter. Creating a shader resource view will be seen in Chapter **8**. Using a texture as a render target and shader resource will come much later in this book.

Note: *The August 2009 SDK documentation says: "Creating a fully-typed resource restricts the resource to the format it was created with. This enables the runtime to optimize access [...]." Therefore, you should only create a typeless resource if you really need the flexibility they provide (the ability to reinterpret the data in multiple ways with multiple views); otherwise, create a fully typed resource.*

4.1.7 Multisampling Theory

Because the pixels on a monitor are not infinitely small, an arbitrary line cannot be represented perfectly on the computer monitor. Figure 4.4 illustrates a "stair-step" (*aliasing*) effect, which can occur when approximating a line by a matrix of pixels. Similar aliasing effects occur with the edges of triangles.

Figure 4.4. On the top we observe aliasing (the stair-step effect when trying to represent a line by a matrix of pixels). On the bottom, we see an antialiased line, which generates the final color of a pixel by sampling and using its neighboring pixels; this results in a smoother image and dilutes the stair-step effect.

Shrinking the pixel sizes by increasing the monitor resolution can alleviate the problem significantly to where the stair-step effect goes largely unnoticed.

When increasing the monitor resolution is not possible or not enough, we can apply *antialiasing* techniques. One technique, called *supersampling*, works by making the back buffer and depth buffer 4X bigger than the screen resolution. The 3D scene is then rendered to the back buffer at this larger resolution. Then, when it comes time to present the back buffer to the screen, the back buffer is *resolved* (or downsampled) such that 4 pixel block colors are averaged together to get an averaged pixel color. In effect, supersampling works by increasing the resolution in software.

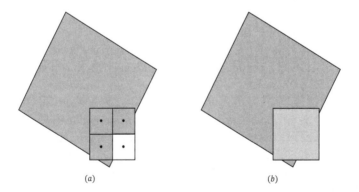

Figure 4.5. We consider one pixel that crosses the edge of a polygon. (a) The green color evaluated at the pixel center is stored in the three visible subpixels that are covered by the polygon. The subpixel in the 4th quadrant is not covered by the polygon and so does not get updated with the green color—it just keeps its previous color computed from previously drawn geometry or the Clear operation. (b) To compute the resolved pixel color, we average the four subpixels (three green pixels and one white pixel) to get a light green along the edge of the polygon. This results in a smoother looking image by diluting the stair-step effect along the edge of the polygon.

Supersampling is expensive because it increases the amount of pixel processing and memory by fourfold. Direct3D supports a compromising antialiasing technique called *multisampling*, which shares some computational information across subpixels making it less expensive than supersampling. Assuming we are using 4X multisampling (4 subpixels per pixel), multisampling also uses a back buffer and depth buffer 4X bigger than the screen resolution; however, instead of computing the image color for each subpixel, it computes it only once per pixel, at the pixel center, and then shares that color information with its subpixels based on visibility (the depth/stencil test is evaluated per subpixel) and coverage (does the subpixel center lie inside or outside the polygon?). Figure 4.5 shows an example.

Note: ▶ *Observe the key difference between supersampling and multisampling. With supersampling, the image color is computed per subpixel, and so each subpixel could potentially be a different color. With multisampling (Figure 4.5), the image color is computed once per pixel and that color is replicated into all visible subpixels that are covered by the polygon. Because computing the image color is one of the most expensive steps in the graphics pipeline, the savings from multisampling over supersampling is significant. On the other hand, supersampling is technically more accurate and handles texture and shader aliasing, which multisampling does not.*

Note: ▶ *In Figure 4.5, we show a pixel subdivided into four subpixels in a uniform grid pattern. The actual pattern used (the points where the subpixels are positioned) can vary across hardware vendors, as Direct3D does not define the placement of the subpixels. Some patterns do better than others in certain situations.*

4.1.8 Multisampling in Direct3D

In the next section, we will be required to fill out a DXGI_SAMPLE_DESC structure. This structure has two members and is defined as follows:

```
typedef struct DXGI_SAMPLE_DESC {
    UINT Count;
    UINT Quality;
} DXGI_SAMPLE_DESC, *LPDXGI_SAMPLE_DESC;
```

The Count member specifies the number of samples to take per pixel, and the Quality member is used to specify the desired quality level (what "quality level" means can vary across hardware manufacturers). Higher sample counts or higher quality is more expensive to render, so a tradeoff between quality and speed must be made. The range of quality levels depends on the texture format and the number of samples to take per pixel. Use the following method to query the number of quality levels for a given texture format and sample count:

```
HRESULT ID3D11Device::CheckMultisampleQualityLevels(
    DXGI_FORMAT Format, UINT SampleCount, UINT *pNumQualityLevels);
```

This method returns zero if the format and sample count combination is not supported by the device. Otherwise, the number of quality levels for the given combination will be returned through the `pNumQualityLevels` parameter. Valid quality levels for a texture format and sample count combination range from zero to `pNumQualityLevels -1`.

The maximum number of samples that can be taken per pixel is defined by:

```
#define D3D11_MAX_MULTISAMPLE_SAMPLE_COUNT    ( 32 )
```

However, a sample count of 4 or 8 is common in order to keep the performance and memory cost of multisampling reasonable. If you do not wish to use multisampling, set the sample count to one and the quality level to zero. All Direct3D 11 capable devices support 4X multisampling for all render target formats.

 Note: *A* `DXGI_SAMPLE_DESC` *structure needs to be filled out for both the swap chain buffers and the depth buffer. Both the back buffer and depth buffer must be created with the same multisampling settings; sample code illustrating this is given in the next section.*

4.1.9 Feature Levels

Direct3D 11 introduces the concept of *feature levels* (represented in code by the `D3D_FEATURE_LEVEL` enumerated type), which roughly correspond to various Direct3D versions from version 9 to 11:

```
typedef enum D3D_FEATURE_LEVEL
{
    D3D_FEATURE_LEVEL_9_1 = 0x9100,
    D3D_FEATURE_LEVEL_9_2 = 0x9200,
    D3D_FEATURE_LEVEL_9_3 = 0x9300,
    D3D_FEATURE_LEVEL_10_0 = 0xa000,
    D3D_FEATURE_LEVEL_10_1 = 0xa100,
    D3D_FEATURE_LEVEL_11_0 = 0xb000,
} D3D_FEATURE_LEVEL;
```

Feature levels define a strict set of functionality (see the SDK documentation for the specific capabilities each feature level supports). The idea is that if a user's hardware did not support a certain feature level, the application could fallback to an older feature level. For example, to support a wider audience, an application might support Direct3D 11, 10.1, 10, and 9.3 level hardware. The application would check feature level support from newest to oldest: That is, the application would first check if Direct3D 11 is supported, second Direct3D 10.1, then Direct3D 10, and finally Direct3D 9.3. To facilitate this order of testing, the following feature level array would be used (the element ordering the array implies the order of feature level testing):

```
D3D_FEATURE_LEVEL featureLevels[4] =
{
    D3D_FEATURE_LEVEL_11_0, // First check D3D 11 support
    D3D_FEATURE_LEVEL_10_1, // Second check D3D 10.1 support
    D3D_FEATURE_LEVEL_10_0, // Next, check D3D 10 support
    D3D_FEATURE_LEVEL_9_3   // Finally, check D3D 9.3 support
};
```

This array would be input into a Direct3D initialization function (§4.2.1), and the function would output the first supported feature level in the array. If, for example, Direct3D reported back that the first feature level in the array that was supported was D3D_FEATURE_LEVEL_10_0, then the application could disable Direct3D 11 and Direct3D 10.1 features and use the Direct3D 10 rendering path. In this book, we always require support for feature level D3D_FEATURE_LEVEL_11_0, as this is a Direct3D 11 book. However, real-world applications do need to worry about supporting older hardware to maximize their audience.

4.2 INITIALIZING DIRECT3D

The following subsections show how to initialize Direct3D. Our process of initializing Direct3D can be broken down into the following steps:

1. Create the ID3D11Device and ID3D11DeviceContext interfaces using the D3D11CreateDevice function.

2. Check 4X MSAA quality level support using the ID3D11Device::CheckMultisam pleQualityLevels method.

3. Describe the characteristics of the swap chain we are going to create by filling out an instance of the DXGI_SWAP_CHAIN_DESC structure.

4. Query the IDXGIFactory instance that was used to create the device, and create an IDXGISwapChain instance.

5. Create a render target view to the swap chain's back buffer.

6. Create the depth/stencil buffer and its associated depth/stencil view.

7. Bind the render target view and depth/stencil view to the output merger stage of the rendering pipeline so that they can be used by Direct3D.

8. Set the viewport.

4.2.1 Create the Device and Context

Initializing Direct3D begins by creating the Direct3D 11 device (`ID3D11Device`) and context (`ID3D11DeviceContext`). These two interfaces are the chief Direct3D interfaces and can be thought of as our software controller of the physical graphics device hardware; that is, through these interfaces we can interact with the hardware and instruct it to do things (such as allocate resource in GPU memory, clear the back buffer, bind resources to the various pipeline stages, and draw geometry). More specifically,

1. The `ID3D11Device` interface is used to check feature support, and allocate resources.

2. The `ID3D11DeviceContext` interface is used to set render states, bind resources to the graphics pipeline, and issue rendering commands.

The device and context can be created with the following function:

```
HRESULT D3D11CreateDevice(
    IDXGIAdapter *pAdapter,
    D3D_DRIVER_TYPE DriverType,
    HMODULE Software,
    UINT Flags,
    CONST D3D_FEATURE_LEVEL *pFeatureLevels,
    UINT FeatureLevels,
    UINT SDKVersion,
    ID3D11Device **ppDevice,
    D3D_FEATURE_LEVEL *pFeatureLevel,
    ID3D11DeviceContext **ppImmediateContext
);
```

1. `pAdapter`: Specifies the display adapter we want the create device to represent. Specifying null for this parameter uses the primary display adapter. We always use the primary adapter in the sample programs of this book. The chapter exercises have you investigate using other display adapters.

2. `DriverType`: In general, you will always specify `D3D_DRIVER_TYPE_HARDWARE` for this parameter to use 3D hardware acceleration for rendering. However, some additional options are:

   (a) `D3D_DRIVER_TYPE_REFERENCE`: Creates a so-called *reference device*. The reference device is a software implementation of Direct3D with the goal of correctness (it is extremely slow because it is a software implementation). The reference device is installed with the DirectX SDK and is available to developers only; it should not be used for shipping applications. There are two reasons to use the reference device:

      (i) To test code your hardware does not support; for example, to test Direct3D 11 code when you do not have a Direct3D 11 capable graphics card.

(i i) To test for driver bugs. If you have code that works correctly with the reference device, but not with the hardware, then there is probably a bug in the hardware drivers.

(c) `D3D_DRIVER_TYPE_SOFTWARE`: Creates a software driver used to emulate 3D hardware. To use a software driver, you must build your own, or use a 3rd party software driver. Other than the WARP driver described next, Direct3D does not provide a software driver.

(d) `D3D_DRIVER_TYPE_WARP`: Creates a high performance Direct3D 10.1 software driver. WARP stands for Windows Advanced Rasterization Platform. We are uninterested in this because it does not support Direct3D 11.

3. `Software`: This is used for supplying a software driver. We always specify null because we are using hardware for rendering. Moreover, one must have a software driver available to use one.

4. `Flags`: Optional device creation flags (that can be bitwise ORed together). Two common flags are:

(a) `D3D11_CREATE_DEVICE_DEBUG`: For debug mode builds, this flag should be set to enable the debug layer. When the debug flag is specified, Direct3D will send debug messages to the VC++ output window; Figure 4.6 shows an example of some of the error messages that can be output.

(b) `D3D11_CREATE_DEVICE_SINGLETHREADED`: Improves performance if you can guarantee that Direct3D will not be called from multiple threads. If this flag is enabled, then the `ID3D11Device::CreateDeferredContext` method will fail (see "Note" at the end of this section).

5. `pFeatureLevels`: An array of `D3D_FEATURE_LEVEL` elements, whose order indicates the order in which to test feature level support (see §4.1.9). Specifying null for this parameter indicates to choose the greatest feature level supported. In our framework, we check to make sure this is `D3D_FEATURE_LEVEL_11_0` (i.e., Direct3D 11 support), as we only target Direct3D 11 in this book.

6. `FeatureLevels`: The number of `D3D_FEATURE_LEVEL`s in the array `pFeatureLevels`. Specify 0 if you specified null for the previous parameter `pFeatureLevels`.

7. `SDKVersion`: Always specify `D3D11_SDK_VERSION`.

8. `ppDevice`: Returns the created device.

9. `pFeatureLevel`: Returns the first supported feature level in the `pFeatureLevels` array (or the greatest feature level supported, if `pFeatureLevels` was null).

10 . `ppImmediateContext`: Returns the created device context.

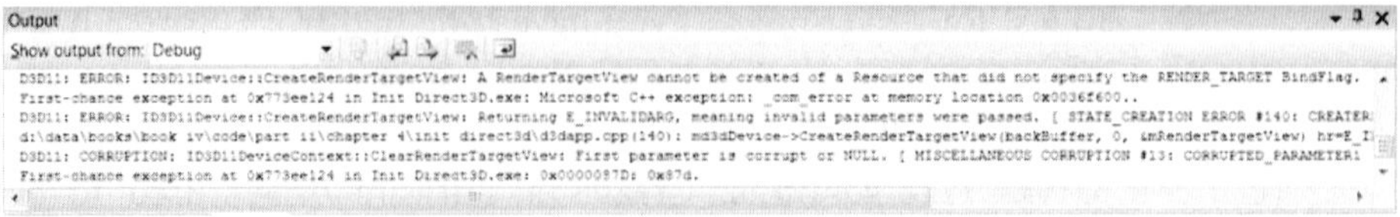

Figure 4.6. An example of Direct3D 11 debug output.

Here is an example call of this function:

```
UINT createDeviceFlags = 0;

#if defined(DEBUG) || defined(_DEBUG)
    createDeviceFlags |= D3D11_CREATE_DEVICE_DEBUG;
#endif

D3D_FEATURE_LEVEL featureLevel;
ID3D11Device* md3dDevice;
ID3D11DeviceContext* md3dImmediateContext;
HRESULT hr = D3D11CreateDevice(
        0,                      // default adapter
        D3D_DRIVER_TYPE_HARDWARE,
        0,                      // no software device
        createDeviceFlags,
        0, 0,                   // default feature level array
        D3D11_SDK_VERSION,
        &md3dDevice,
        &featureLevel,
        &md3dImmediateContext);

if( FAILED(hr) )
{
    MessageBox(0, L"D3D11CreateDevice Failed.", 0, 0);
    return false;
}

if( featureLevel != D3D_FEATURE_LEVEL_11_0 )
{
    MessageBox(0, L"Direct3D Feature Level 11 unsupported.", 0, 0);
    return false;
}
```

Note: *Observe that we call our pointer to the device context an immediate context:*

```
ID3D11DeviceContext* md3dImmediateContext;
```

There is also such a thing called a deferred context (ID3D11Device::CreateDef erredContext). This is part of the multithreading support in Direct3D 11. We consider multithreading an advance topic and do not cover it in this book, but the basic idea is as follows:

1. *Have the immediate context on the main rendering thread.*

2. *Have any additional deferred contexts on separate worker threads.*

(a) *Each worker thread can record graphics commands into a command list* (`ID3D11CommandList`).

(b) *The command list from each worker thread can then be executed on the main rendering thread.*

If the command lists take time to assemble, which they can for complicated rendering graphs, being able to assemble the command lists in parallel on multi-core systems is advantageous.

4.2.2 Check 4X MSAA Quality Support

Now that we have a created device, we can check the quality level support for 4X MSAA. Recall that all Direct3D 11 capable devices support 4X MSAA with all render target formats (however, the supported quality levels could be different).

```
UINT m4xMsaaQuality;
HR(md3dDevice->CheckMultisampleQualityLevels(
    DXGI_FORMAT_R8G8B8A8_UNORM, 4, & m4xMsaaQuality));
assert(m4xMsaaQuality > 0 );
```

Because 4X MSAA is always supported, the returned quality should always be greater than 0; therefore, we `assert` that this is the case.

4.2.3 Describe the Swap Chain

The next step in the initialization process is to create the swap chain. This is done by first filling out an instance of the `DXGI_SWAP_CHAIN_DESC` structure, which describes the characteristics of the swap chain we are going to create. This structure is defined as follows:

```
typedef struct DXGI_SWAP_CHAIN_DESC {
    DXGI_MODE_DESC BufferDesc;
    DXGI_SAMPLE_DESC SampleDesc;
    DXGI_USAGE BufferUsage;
    UINT BufferCount;
    HWND OutputWindow;
    BOOL Windowed;
    DXGI_SWAP_EFFECT SwapEffect;
    UINT Flags;
} DXGI_SWAP_CHAIN_DESC;
```

The `DXGI_MODE_DESC` type is another structure, defined as:

```
typedef struct DXGI_MODE_DESC
{
    UINT Width;      // desired back buffer width
    UINT Height;     // desired back buffer height
    DXGI_RATIONAL RefreshRate; // display mode refresh rate
```

```
    DXGI_FORMAT Format;           // back buffer pixel format
    DXGI_MODE_SCANLINE_ORDER ScanlineOrdering; // display scanline mode
    DXGI_MODE_SCALING Scaling; // display scaling mode
} DXGI_MODE_DESC;
```

Note: *In the following data member descriptions, we only cover the common flags and options that are most important to a beginner at this point. For a description of further flags and options, refer to the SDK documentation.*

1. `BufferDesc`: This structure describes the properties of the back buffer we want to create. The main properties we are concerned with are the width and height, and pixel format; see the SDK documentation for further details on the other members.

2. `SampleDesc`: The number of multisamples and quality level; see §4.1.8.

3. `BufferUsage`: Specify `DXGI_USAGE_RENDER_TARGET_OUTPUT` because we are going to be rendering to the back buffer (i.e., use it as a render target).

4. `BufferCount`: The number of back buffers to use in the swap chain; we usually only use one back buffer for double buffering, although you could use two for triple buffering.

5. `OutputWindow`: A handle to the window we are rendering into.

6. `Windowed`: Specify `true` to run in windowed mode or `false` for full-screen mode.

7. `SwapEffect`: Specify `DXGI_SWAP_EFFECT_DISCARD` in order to let the display driver select the most efficient presentation method.

8. `Flags`: Optional flags. If you specify `DXGI_SWAP_CHAIN_FLAG_ALLOW_MODE_SWITCH`, then when the application is switching to full-screen mode, it will choose a display mode that best matches the current back buffer settings. If this flag is not specified, then when the application is switching to full-screen mode, it will use the current desktop display mode. In our sample framework, we do not specify this flag, as using the current desktop display mode in full-screen mode works fine for our demos (most desktop displays are set to the optimal resolution of the monitor).

The following code shows how we fill out the `DXGI_SWAP_CHAIN_DESC` structure in our sample framework:

```
DXGI_SWAP_CHAIN_DESC sd;
sd.BufferDesc.Width  = mClientWidth;  // use window's client area dims
sd.BufferDesc.Height = mClientHeight;
sd.BufferDesc.RefreshRate.Numerator = 60;
sd.BufferDesc.RefreshRate.Denominator = 1;
sd.BufferDesc.Format = DXGI_FORMAT_R8G8B8A8_UNORM;
sd.BufferDesc.ScanlineOrdering = DXGI_MODE_SCANLINE_ORDER_UNSPECIFIED;
sd.BufferDesc.Scaling = DXGI_MODE_SCALING_UNSPECIFIED;

// Use 4X MSAA?
if( mEnable4xMsaa )
{
```

```
    sd.SampleDesc.Count   = 4;

    // m4xMsaaQuality is returned via CheckMultisampleQualityLevels().
    sd.SampleDesc.Quality = m4xMsaaQuality-1;
}
// No MSAA
else
{
    sd.SampleDesc.Count   = 1;
    sd.SampleDesc.Quality = 0;
}

sd.BufferUsage  = DXGI_USAGE_RENDER_TARGET_OUTPUT;
sd.BufferCount  = 1;
sd.OutputWindow = mhMainWnd;
sd.Windowed     = true;
sd.SwapEffect   = DXGI_SWAP_EFFECT_DISCARD;
sd.Flags        = 0;
```

Note: *If you wanted to change the multisampling settings at runtime, you would have to destroy and recreate the swap chain.*

Note: *We use the* `DXGI_FORMAT_R8G8B8A8_UNORM` *format (8-bits red, green, blue, and alpha) for the back buffer because monitors generally do not support more than 24-bit color, so the extra precision would be wasted. The extra 8-bits of alpha is not output by the monitor, but having an extra 8-bits in the back buffer can be used for certain special effects.*

4.2.4 Create the Swap Chain

A swap chain interface (`IDXGISwapChain`) is created through an `IDXGIFactory` instance with the `IDXGIFactory::CreateSwapChain` method:

```
HRESULT IDXGIFactory::CreateSwapChain(
    IUnknown *pDevice,            // Pointer to ID3D11Device.
    DXGI_SWAP_CHAIN_DESC *pDesc,  // Pointer to swap chain description.
    IDXGISwapChain **ppSwapChain);  // Returns created swap chain interface.
```

We can obtain a pointer to an `IDXGIFactory` instance with the `CreateDXGIFactory` (requires linking *dxgi.lib*). However, if we acquire an `IDXGIFactory` instance this way, and call `IDXGIFactory::CreateSwapChain`, then we will get the following error:

```
DXGI Warning: IDXGIFactory::CreateSwapChain: This function is being
called with a device from a different IDXGIFactory.
```

The necessary fix is to use the `IDXGIFactory` instance that was used to create the device. To get this instance, we have to proceed through the following series of COM queries (which is described in the documentation for `IDXGIFactory`):

```
IDXGIDevice* dxgiDevice = 0;
HR(md3dDevice->QueryInterface(__uuidof(IDXGIDevice),
    (void**)&dxgiDevice));

IDXGIAdapter* dxgiAdapter = 0;
HR(dxgiDevice->GetParent(__uuidof(IDXGIAdapter),
    (void**)&dxgiAdapter));

// Finally got the IDXGIFactory interface.
IDXGIFactory* dxgiFactory = 0;
HR(dxgiAdapter->GetParent(__uuidof(IDXGIFactory),
    (void**)&dxgiFactory));

// Now, create the swap chain.
IDXGISwapChain* mSwapChain;
HR(dxgiFactory->CreateSwapChain(md3dDevice, &sd, &mSwapChain));

// Release our acquired COM interfaces (because we are done with them).
ReleaseCOM(dxgiDevice);
ReleaseCOM(dxgiAdapter);
ReleaseCOM(dxgiFactory);
```

Note:
> *DXGI (DirectX Graphics Infrastructure) is a separate API from Direct3D that handles graphics related things like the swap chain, enumerating graphics hardware, and switching between windowed and full-screen mode. The idea for keeping it separate from Direct3D is that other graphics APIs (such as Direct2D) also require swap chains, enumerating graphics hardware, and switching between windowed and full-screen mode. In this way, multiple graphics APIs can use the DXGI API.*

4.2.5 Create the Render Target View

As said in §4.1.6, we do not bind a resource to a pipeline stage directly; instead, we must create a resource view to the resource and bind the view to the pipeline stage. In particular, in order to bind the back buffer to the output merger stage of the pipeline (so Direct3D can render onto it), we need to create a render target view to the back buffer. The following example code shows how this is done:

```
ID3D11RenderTargetView* mRenderTargetView;
ID3D11Texture2D* backBuffer;
mSwapChain->GetBuffer(0, __uuidof(ID3D11Texture2D),
    reinterpret_cast<void**>(&backBuffer));
md3dDevice->CreateRenderTargetView(backBuffer, 0, &mRenderTargetView);
ReleaseCOM(backBuffer);
```

1. A pointer to the swap chain's back buffer is obtained using the `IDXGISwapChain::GetBuffer` method. The first parameter of this method is an index identifying the particular back buffer we want to get (in case there is more than one). In our demos, we only use one back buffer, and it has index

zero. The second parameter is the interface type of the buffer, which is usually always a 2D texture (`ID3D11Texture2D`). The third parameter returns a pointer to the back buffer.

2. To create the render target view, we use the `ID3D11Device::CreateRenderT` `argetView` method. The first parameter specifies the resource that will be used as the render target, which, in the previous example, is the back buffer (i.e., we are creating a render target view to the back buffer). The second parameter is a pointer to a `D3D11_RENDER_TARGET_VIEW_DESC`. Among other things, this structure describes the data type (format) of the elements in the resource. If the resource was created with a typed format (i.e., not typeless), then this parameter can be null, which indicates to create a view to the first mipmap level of this resource (the back buffer only has one mipmap level) with the format the resource was created with. (Mipmaps are discussed in Chapter 8.) Because we specified the type of our back buffer, we specify null for this parameter. The third parameter returns a pointer to the create render target view object.

3. The call to `IDXGISwapChain::GetBuffer` increases the COM reference count to the back buffer, which is why we release it (`ReleaseCOM`) at the end of the code fragment when we are done with it.

4.2.6 Create the Depth/Stencil Buffer and View

We now need to create the depth/stencil buffer. As described in §4.1.5, the depth buffer is just a 2D texture that stores the depth information (and stencil information if using stenciling). To create a texture, we need to fill out a `D3D11_TEXTURE2D_DESC` structure describing the texture to create, and then call the `ID3D11Device::CreateTexture2D` method. The `D3D11_TEXTURE2D_DESC` structure is defined as follows:

```
typedef struct D3D11_TEXTURE2D_DESC {
    UINT Width;
    UINT Height;
    UINT MipLevels;
    UINT ArraySize;
    DXGI_FORMAT Format;
    DXGI_SAMPLE_DESC SampleDesc;
    D3D11_USAGE Usage;
    UINT BindFlags;
    UINT CPUAccessFlags;
    UINT MiscFlags;
} D3D11_TEXTURE2D_DESC;
```

1. `Width`: The width of the texture in texels.
2. `Height`: The height of the texture in texels.

3. **MipLevels:** The number of mipmap levels. Mipmaps are covered in the chapter on texturing. For creating the depth/stencil buffer, our texture only needs one mipmap level.

4. **ArraySize:** The number of textures in a texture array. For the depth/stencil buffer, we only need one texture.

5. **Format:** A member of the **DXGI_FORMAT** enumerated type specifying the format of the texels. For a depth/stencil buffer, this needs to be one of the formats shown in §4.1.5.

6. **SampleDesc:** The number of multisamples and quality level; see §4.1.7 and §4.1.8. Recall that 4X MSAA uses a back buffer and depth buffer 4X bigger than the screen resolution, in order to store color and depth/stencil information per subpixel. Therefore, *the multisampling settings used for the depth/stencil buffer must match the settings used for the render target.*

7. **Usage:** A member of the **D3D11_USAGE** enumerated type specifying how the texture will be used. The four usage values are:

    (a) **D3D11_USAGE_DEFAULT:** Specify this usage if the GPU (graphics processing unit) will be reading and writing to the resource. The CPU cannot read or write to a resource with this usage. For the depth/stencil buffer, we specify **D3D11_USAGE_DEFAULT** because the GPU will be doing all the reading and writing to the depth/stencil buffer.

    (b) **D3D11_USAGE_IMMUTABLE:** Specify this usage if the contents of a resource does not ever change after creation. This allows for some potential optimizations, as the resource will be read-only by the GPU. The CPU and GPU cannot write to an immutable resource, except at creation time to initialize the resource. The CPU cannot read from an immutable resource.

    (c) **D3D11_USAGE_DYNAMIC:** Specify this usage if the application (CPU) needs to update the data contents of the resource frequently (e.g., on a per frame basis). A resource with this usage can be read by the GPU and written to by the CPU. Updating a GPU resource dynamically from the CPU incurs a performance hit, as the new data must be transferred over from CPU memory (i.e., system RAM) to GPU memory (i.e., video RAM); therefore, dynamic usage should be avoided unless necessary.

    (d) **D3D11_USAGE_STAGING:** Specify this usage if the application (CPU) needs to be able to read a copy of the resource (i.e., the resource supports copying data from video memory to system memory). Copying from GPU to CPU memory is a slow operation and should be avoided unless necessary.

8. **BindFlags:** One or more flags ORed together specifying where the resource will be bound to the pipeline. For a depth/stencil buffer, this needs to be **D3D11_ BIND_DEPTH_STENCIL.** Some other bind flags for textures are:

(a) `D3D11_BIND_RENDER_TARGET`: The texture will be bound as a render target to the pipeline.

(b) `D3D11_BIND_SHADER_RESOURCE`: The texture will be bound as a shader resource to the pipeline.

9. `CPUAccessFlags`: Specifies how the CPU will access the resource. If the CPU needs to write to the resource, specify `D3D11_CPU_ACCESS_WRITE`. A resource with write access must have usage `D3D11_USAGE_DYNAMIC` or `D3D11_USAGE_STAGING`. If the CPU needs to read from the buffer, specify `D3D11_CPU_ACCESS_READ`. A buffer with read access must have usage `D3D11_USAGE_STAGING`. For the depth/stencil buffer, only the GPU writes and reads to the depth/buffer; therefore, we can specify zero for this value, as the CPU will not be reading or writing to the depth/stencil buffer.

10 . `MiscFlags`: Optional flags, which do not apply to the depth/stencil buffer, so are set to zero.

Note: *We commented that the usage flags `D3D11_USAGE_DYNAMIC` and `D3D11_USAGE_STAGING` should be avoided because there is a performance penalty. The common factor is that the CPU is involved with both of these flags. Going back and forth between CPU and GPU memory incurs a performance hit. For maximum speed, graphics hardware works best when we create all of our resources and upload the data to the GPU, and the resources stay on the GPU where only the GPU reads and writes to the resources. However, for some applications, these flags cannot be avoided and the CPU must get involved, but you should always try to minimize the usage of these flags.*

Throughout this book, we will see different examples of creating resources with different options; for example, different usage flags, different bind flags, and different CPU access flags. For now, just concentrate on the values we need to specify to create the depth/stencil buffer, and do not worry about every single option.

In addition, before using the depth/stencil buffer, we must create an associated depth/stencil view to be bound to the pipeline. This is done similarly to creating the render target view. The following code example shows how we create the depth/stencil texture and its corresponding depth/stencil view:

```
D3D11_TEXTURE2D_DESC depthStencilDesc;
depthStencilDesc.Width     = mClientWidth;
depthStencilDesc.Height    = mClientHeight;
depthStencilDesc.MipLevels = 1;
depthStencilDesc.ArraySize = 1;
depthStencilDesc.Format    = DXGI_FORMAT_D24_UNORM_S8_UINT;

// Use 4X MSAA? --must match swap chain MSAA values.
if( mEnable4xMsaa )
{
```

```
        depthStencilDesc.SampleDesc.Count   = 4;
        depthStencilDesc.SampleDesc.Quality = m4xMsaaQuality-1;
    }
    // No MSAA
    else
    {
        depthStencilDesc.SampleDesc.Count   = 1;
        depthStencilDesc.SampleDesc.Quality = 0;
    }

    depthStencilDesc.Usage         = D3D11_USAGE_DEFAULT;
    depthStencilDesc.BindFlags     = D3D11_BIND_DEPTH_STENCIL;
    depthStencilDesc.CPUAccessFlags = 0;
    depthStencilDesc.MiscFlags     = 0;

    ID3D11Texture2D* mDepthStencilBuffer;
    ID3D11DepthStencilView* mDepthStencilView;

    HR(md3dDevice->CreateTexture2D(
        &depthStencilDesc,      // Description of texture to create.
        0,
        &mDepthStencilBuffer)); // Return pointer to depth/stencil buffer.

    HR(md3dDevice->CreateDepthStencilView(
        mDepthStencilBuffer,  // Resource we want to create a view to.
        0,
    &mDepthStencilView)); // Return depth/stencil view
```

The second parameter of `CreateTexture2D` is a pointer to initial data to fill the texture with. However, because this texture is to be used as the depth/stencil buffer, we do not need to fill it ourselves with any data. Direct3D will write to the depth/stencil buffer directly when performing depth buffering and stencil operations. Thus, we specify null for the second parameter.

The second parameter of `CreateDepthStencilView` is a pointer to a `D3D11_DEPTH_STENCIL_VIEW_DESC`. Among other things, this structure describes the data type (format) of the elements in the resource. If the resource was created with a typed format (i.e., not typeless), then this parameter can be null, which indicates to create a view to the first mipmap level of this resource (the depth/stencil buffer was created with only one mipmap level) with the format the resource was created with. (Mipmaps are discussed in Chapter 8.) Because we specified the type of our depth/stencil buffer, we specify null for this parameter.

4.2.7 Bind the Views to the Output Merger Stage

Now that we have created views to the back buffer and depth buffer, we can bind these views to the output merger stage of the pipeline to make the resources the render target and depth/stencil buffer of the pipeline:

```
md3dImmediateContext->OMSetRenderTargets(
    1, &mRenderTargetView, mDepthStencilView);
```

The first parameter is the number of render targets we are binding; we bind only one here, but more can be bound to render simultaneously to several render targets (an advanced technique). The second parameter is a pointer to the first element in an array of render target view pointers to bind to the pipeline. The third parameter is a pointer to the depth/stencil view to bind to the pipeline.

Note: ▶ *We can set an array of render target views, but only one depth/stencil view. Using multiple render targets is an advanced technique covered in Part III of this book.*

4.2.8 Set the Viewport

Usually we like to draw the 3D scene to the entire back buffer. However, sometimes we only want to draw the 3D scene into a subrectangle of the back buffer; see Figure 4.7.

The subrectangle of the back buffer we draw into is called the *viewport* and it is described by the following structure:

```
typedef struct D3D11_VIEWPORT {
    FLOAT TopLeftX;
    FLOAT TopLeftY;
    FLOAT Width;
    FLOAT Height;
    FLOAT MinDepth;
    FLOAT MaxDepth;
} D3D11_VIEWPORT;
```

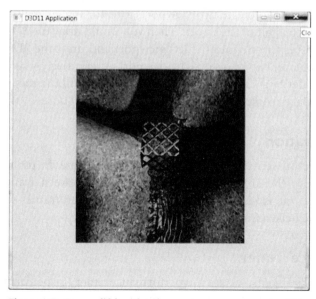

Figure 4.7. By modifying the viewport, we can draw the 3D scene into a subrectangle of the back buffer. The back buffer then gets presented to the client area of the window.

The first four data members define the viewport rectangle relative to the client area rectangle of the window we are drawing into (observe that we can specify fractional pixel coordinates because the data members are of type **float**). The **MinDepth** member specifies the minimum depth buffer value and **MaxDepth** specifies the maximum depth buffer value. Direct3D uses a depth buffer range of 0 to 1, so **MinDepth** and **MaxDepth** should be set to those values, respectively, unless a special effect is desired.

Once we have filled out the **D3D11_VIEWPORT** structure, we set the viewport with Direct3D with the **ID3D11DeviceContext::RSSetViewports** method. The following example creates and sets a viewport that draws onto the entire back buffer:

```
D3D11_VIEWPORT vp;
vp.TopLeftX = 0.0f;
vp.TopLeftY = 0.0f;
vp.Width    = static_cast<float>(mClientWidth);
vp.Height   = static_cast<float>(mClientHeight);
vp.MinDepth = 0.0f;
vp.MaxDepth = 1.0f;

md3dImmediateContext->RSSetViewports(1, &vp);
```

The first parameter is the number of viewports to bind (using more than one is for advanced effects), and the second parameter is a pointer to an array of viewports.

You could use the viewport to implement split screens for two player game modes, for example. You would create two viewports, one for the left-half of the screen and one for the right-half of the screen. Then you would draw the 3D scene from the perspective of player one into the left viewport and draw the 3D scene from the perspective of player two into the right viewport. Alternatively, you might use the viewport to render to a subrectangle of the screen, and fill the remaining area with UI (user interface) controls like buttons, sliders, and list boxes.

4.3 Timing and Animation

To do animation correctly, we will need to keep track of the time. In particular, we will need to measure the amount of time that elapses between frames of animation. If the frame rate is high, these time intervals between frames will be very short; therefore, we need a timer with a high level of accuracy.

4.3.1 The Performance Timer

For accurate time measurements, we use the performance timer (or performance counter). To use the Win32 functions for querying the performance timer, we must `#include <windows.h>`.

The performance timer measures time in units called *counts*. We obtain the current time value, measured in counts, of the performance timer with the `QueryPerformanceCounter` function like so:

```
__int64 currTime;
QueryPerformanceCounter((LARGE_INTEGER*)&currTime);
```

Observe that this function returns the current time value through its parameter, which is a 64-bit integer value.

To get the frequency (counts per second) of the performance timer, we use the `QueryPerformanceFrequency` function:

```
__int64 countsPerSec;
QueryPerformanceFrequency((LARGE_INTEGER*)&countsPerSec);
```

Then the number of seconds (or fractions of a second) per count is just the reciprocal of the counts per second:

```
mSecondsPerCount = 1.0 / (double)countsPerSec;
```

Thus, to convert a time reading `valueInCounts` to seconds, we just multiply it by the conversion factor `mSecondsPerCount`:

```
valueInSecs = valueInCounts * mSecondsPerCount;
```

The values returned by the `QueryPerformanceCounter` function are not particularly interesting in and of themselves. What we do is get the current time value using `QueryPerformanceCounter`, and then get the current time value a little later using `QueryPerformanceCounter` again. Then the time that elapsed between those two time calls is just the difference. That is, we always look at the relative difference between two time stamps to measure time, not the actual values returned by the performance counter. The following better illustrates the idea:

```
__int64 A = 0;
QueryPerformanceCounter((LARGE_INTEGER*)&A);

/* Do work */

__int64 B = 0;
QueryPerformanceCounter((LARGE_INTEGER*)&B);
```

So it took `(B-A)` counts to do the work, or `(B-A)*mSecondsPerCount` seconds to do the work.

Note:

MSDN has the following remark about `QueryPerformanceCounter`: *"On a multiprocessor computer, it should not matter which processor is called. However, you can get different results on different processors due to bugs in the basic input/output system (BIOS) or the hardware abstraction layer (HAL)." You can use the* `SetThreadAffinityMask` *function so that the main application thread does not get switched to another processor.*

4.3.2 Game Timer Class

In the next two sections, we will discuss the implementation of the following `GameTimer` class.

```
class GameTimer
{
public:
    GameTimer();

    float GameTime()const;   // in seconds
    float DeltaTime()const; // in seconds

    void Reset(); // Call before message loop.
    void Start(); // Call when unpaused.
    void Stop();  // Call when paused.
    void Tick();  // Call every frame.

private:
    double mSecondsPerCount;
    double mDeltaTime;

    __int64 mBaseTime;
    __int64 mPausedTime;
    __int64 mStopTime;
    __int64 mPrevTime;
    __int64 mCurrTime;

    bool mStopped;
};
```

The constructor, in particular, queries the frequency of the performance counter. The other member functions are discussed in the next two sections.

```
GameTimer::GameTimer()
: mSecondsPerCount(0.0), mDeltaTime(-1.0), mBaseTime(0),
  mPausedTime(0), mPrevTime(0), mCurrTime(0), mStopped(false)
{
    __int64 countsPerSec;
    QueryPerformanceFrequency((LARGE_INTEGER*)&countsPerSec);
    mSecondsPerCount = 1.0 / (double)countsPerSec;
}
```

> Note: *The* `GameTimer` *class and implementations are in the GameTimer.h and GameTimer.cpp files, which can be found in the Common directory of the sample code.*

4.3.3 Time Elapsed Between Frames

When we render our frames of animation, we will need to know how much time has elapsed between frames so that we can update our game objects based on how much time has passed. Computing the time elapsed between frames proceeds as follows. Let t_i be the time returned by the performance counter during the ith frame and let t_{i-1} be the time returned by the performance counter during the previous frame. Then the time elapsed between the t_{i-1} reading and the t_i reading is $\Delta t = t_i - t_{i-1}$. For real-time rendering, we typically require at least 30 frames per second for smooth animation (and we usually have much higher rates); thus, $\Delta t = t_i - t_{i-1}$ tends to be a relatively small number.

The following code shows how Δt is computed in code:

```
void GameTimer::Tick()
{
    if(mStopped)
    {
      mDeltaTime = 0.0;
      return;
    }

    // Get the time this frame.
    __int64 currTime;
    QueryPerformanceCounter((LARGE_INTEGER*)&currTime);
    mCurrTime = currTime;

    // Time difference between this frame and the previous.
    mDeltaTime = (mCurrTime - mPrevTime)*mSecondsPerCount;

    // Prepare for next frame.
    mPrevTime = mCurrTime;

    // Force nonnegative. The DXSDK's CDXUTTimer mentions that if the
    // processor goes into a power save mode or we get shuffled to another
    // processor, then mDeltaTime can be negative.
    if(mDeltaTime < 0.0)
    {
      mDeltaTime = 0.0;
    }
}

float GameTimer::DeltaTime()const
{
    return (float)mDeltaTime;
}
```

The function Tick is called in the application message loop as follows:

```
int D3DApp::Run()
{
    MSG msg = {0};

    mTimer.Reset();

    while(msg.message != WM_QUIT)
    {
      // If there are Window messages then process them.
      if(PeekMessage(&msg, 0, 0, 0, PM_REMOVE))
      {
```

```
          TranslateMessage(&msg);
          DispatchMessage(&msg);
      }
      // Otherwise, do animation/game stuff.
      else
  {
          mTimer.Tick();

          if(!mAppPaused)
          {
              CalculateFrameStats();
              UpdateScene(mTimer.DeltaTime());
              DrawScene();
          }
          else
          {
              Sleep(100);
          }
      }
  }

      return (int)msg.wParam;
}
```

In this way, Δt is computed every frame and fed into the `UpdateScene` method so that the scene can be updated based on how much time has passed since the previous frame of animation. The implementation of the `Reset` method is:

```
void GameTimer::Reset()
{
    __int64 currTime;
    QueryPerformanceCounter((LARGE_INTEGER*)&currTime);

    mBaseTime = currTime;
    mPrevTime = currTime;
    mStopTime = 0;
    mStopped  = false;
}
```

Some of the variables shown have not been discussed yet (see §4.3.4). However, we see that this initializes `mPrevTime` to the current time when `Reset` is called. It is important to do this because for the first frame of animation, there is no previous frame, and therefore, no previous time stamp t_{i-1}. Thus this value needs to be initialized in the `Reset` method before the message loop starts.

4.3.4 Total Time

Another time measurement that can be useful is the amount of time that has elapsed since the application start, not counting paused time; we will call this *total time*. The following situation shows how this could be useful. Suppose the player has 300 seconds to complete a level. When the level starts, we can get the time

t_{start} which is the time elapsed since the application started. Then after the level has started, we can check the time t since the application started every so often. If $t - t_{start} > 300$ s (see Figure 4.8) then the player has been in the level for over 300 seconds and loses. Obviously in this situation, we do not want to count any time the game was paused against the player.

Another application of total time is when we want to animate a quantity as a function of time. For instance, suppose we wish to have a light orbit the scene as a function of time. Its position can be described by the parametric equations:

$$\begin{cases} x = 10\cos t \\ y = 20 \\ z = 10\sin t \end{cases}$$

Here t represents time, and as t (time) increases, the coordinates of the light are updated so that the light moves in a circle with radius 10 in the $y = 20$ plane. For this kind of animation, we also do not want to count paused time; see Figure 4.9.

To implement total time, we use the following variables:

```
__int64 mBaseTime;
__int64 mPausedTime;
__int64 mStopTime;
```

As we saw in §4.3.3, mBaseTime is initialized to the current time when Reset was called. We can think of this as the time when the application started. In most cases, you will only call Reset once before the message loop, so mBaseTime stays constant throughout the application's lifetime. The variable mPausedTime accumulates all the time that passes while we are paused. We need to accumulate this time so we can subtract it from the total running time, in order to not count paused time. The mStopTime variable gives us the time when the timer is stopped (paused); this is used to help us keep track of paused time.

Two important methods of the GameTimer class are Stop and Start. They should be called when the application is paused and unpaused, respectively, so that the GameTimer can keep track of paused time. The code comments explain the details of these two methods.

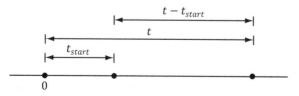

Figure 4.8. Computing the time since the level started. Note that we choose the application start time as the origin (zero), and measure time values relative to that frame of reference.

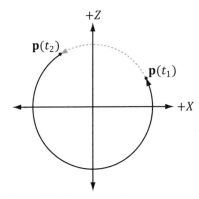

Figure 4.9. If we paused at t_1 and unpaused at t_2, and counted paused time, then when we unpause, the position will jump abruptly from $\mathbf{p}(t_1)$ to $\mathbf{p}(t_2)$.

```
void GameTimer::Stop()
{
    // If we are already stopped, then don't do anything.
    if(!mStopped)
    {
        __int64 currTime;
        QueryPerformanceCounter((LARGE_INTEGER*)&currTime);

        // Otherwise, save the time we stopped at, and set
        // the Boolean flag indicating the timer is stopped.
        mStopTime = currTime;
        mStopped  = true;
    }
}

void GameTimer::Start()
{
    __int64 startTime;
    QueryPerformanceCounter((LARGE_INTEGER*)&startTime);

    // Accumulate the time elapsed between stop and start pairs.
    //
    //                     |<-------d------->|
    // ---------------*-----------------*-----------> time
    //            mStopTime          startTime

    // If we are resuming the timer from a stopped state...
    if( mStopped )
    {
        // then accumulate the paused time.
        mPausedTime += (startTime - mStopTime);

        // since we are starting the timer back up, the current
        // previous time is not valid, as it occurred while paused.
        // So reset it to the current time.
        mPrevTime = startTime;
```

```
      // no longer stopped...
      mStopTime = 0;
      mStopped  = false;
   }
}
```

Finally, the `TotalTime` member function, which returns the time elapsed since
`Reset` was called not counting paused time, is implemented as follows:

```
float GameTimer::TotalTime()const
{
    // If we are stopped, do not count the time that has passed
    // since we stopped.  Moreover, if we previously already had
    // a pause, the distance mStopTime - mBaseTime includes paused
    // time,which we do not want to count.  To correct this, we can
    // subtract the paused time from mStopTime:
    //
    //                  previous paused time
    //                  |<---------->|
    // ---*------------*-------------*-------*-----------*------> time
    // mBaseTime                     mStopTime   mCurrTime

    if(mStopped)
    {
      return (float)(((mStopTime - mPausedTime)-
        mBaseTime)*mSecondsPerCount);
    }

    // The distance mCurrTime - mBaseTime includes paused time,
    // which we do not want to count.  To correct this, we can subtract
    // the paused time from mCurrTime:
    //
    //   (mCurrTime - mPausedTime) - mBaseTime
    //
    //                        |<--paused time-->|
    // ----*---------------*-----------------*-----------*------> time
    //   mBaseTime       mStopTime         startTime   mCurrTime

    else
    {
      return (float)(((mCurrTime-mPausedTime)-
        mBaseTime)*mSecondsPerCount);
    }
}
```

> **Note:** *Our demo framework creates an instance of `GameTimer` for measuring the
> total time since the application started, and the time elapsed between frames;
> however, you can also create additional instances and use them as generic
> "stopwatches." For example, when a bomb is ignited, you could start a new
> `GameTimer`, and when the `TotalTime` reaches 5 seconds, you could raise an
> event that the bomb exploded.*

4.4 THE DEMO APPLICATION FRAMEWORK

The demos in this book use code from the *d3dUtil.h, d3dApp.h,* and *d3dApp.cpp* files, which can be downloaded from the book's website. These common files, which are used in every demo application, reside in a *Common* directory for parts II and III of the book, so that the files are not duplicated in each project. The *d3dUtil.h* file contains useful utility code, and the *d3dApp.h* and *d3dApp.cpp* files contain the core Direct3D application class code that is used to encapsulate a Direct3D application. The reader is encouraged to study these files after reading this chapter, as we do not cover every line of code in these files (e.g., we do not show how to create a window, as basic Win32 programming is a prerequisite of this book). The goal of this framework was to hide the window creation code and Direct3D initialization code; by hiding this code, we feel it makes the demos less distracting, as you can focus only on the specific details the sample code is trying to illustrate.

4.4.1 D3DApp

The D3DApp class is the base Direct3D application class which provides functions for creating the main application window, running the application message loop, handling window messages, and initializing Direct3D. Moreover, the class defines the framework functions for the demo applications. Clients are to derive from D3DApp, override the virtual framework functions, and instantiate only a single instance of the derived D3DApp class. The D3DApp class is defined as follows:

```
class D3DApp
{
public:
    D3DApp(HINSTANCE hInstance);
    virtual ~D3DApp();

    HINSTANCE AppInst()const;
    HWND      MainWnd()const;
    float     AspectRatio()const;

    int Run();

    // Framework methods. Derived client class overrides these methods to
    // implement specific application requirements.

    virtual bool Init();
    virtual void OnResize();
    virtual void UpdateScene(float dt)=0;
    virtual void DrawScene()=0;
    virtual LRESULT MsgProc(HWND hwnd, UINT msg,
                            WPARAM wParam, LPARAM lParam);
```

```
      // Convenience overrides for handling mouse input.
      virtual void OnMouseDown(WPARAM btnState, int x, int y){ }
      virtual void OnMouseUp(WPARAM btnState, int x, int y){ }
      virtual void OnMouseMove(WPARAM btnState, int x, int y){ }

  protected:
      bool InitMainWindow();
      bool InitDirect3D();

      void CalculateFrameStats();

  protected:

      HINSTANCE mhAppInst;   // application instance handle
      HWND      mhMainWnd;    // main window handle
      bool      mAppPaused;   // is the application paused?
      bool      mMinimized;   // is the application minimized?
      bool      mMaximized;   // is the application maximized?
      bool      mResizing;    // are the resize bars being dragged?
      UINT      m4xMsaaQuality; // quality level of 4X MSAA

      // Used to keep track of the "delta-time" and game time (§4.3).
      GameTimer mTimer;

      // The D3D11 device (§4.2.1), the swap chain for page flipping
      // (§4.2.4), the 2D texture for the depth/stencil buffer (§4.2.6),
      // the render target (§4.2.5) and depth/stencil views (§4.2.6), and
      // the viewport (§4.2.8).

      ID3D11Device* md3dDevice;
      ID3D11DeviceContext* md3dImmediateContext;
      IDXGISwapChain* mSwapChain;
      ID3D11Texture2D* mDepthStencilBuffer;
      ID3D11RenderTargetView* mRenderTargetView;
      ID3D11DepthStencilView* mDepthStencilView;
      D3D11_VIEWPORT mScreenViewport;

      // The following variables are initialized in the D3DApp constructor
      // to default values.  However, you can override the values in the
      // derived class constructor to pick different defaults.

      // Window title/caption.  D3DApp defaults to "D3D11 Application".
      std::wstring mMainWndCaption;

      // Hardware device or reference device?  D3DApp defaults to
      // D3D_DRIVER_TYPE_HARDWARE.
      D3D_DRIVER_TYPE md3dDriverType;

      // Initial size of the window's client area.  D3DApp defaults to
      // 800x600.  Note, however, that these values change at runtime
      // to reflect the current client area size as the window is
      // resized.
      int mClientWidth;
      int mClientHeight;

      // True to use 4X MSAA (§4.1.8).  The default is false.
      bool mEnable4xMsaa;
  };
```

We have used comments in the previous code to describe some of the data members; the methods are discussed in the subsequent sections.

4.4.2 Non-Framework Methods

1. **D3DApp:** The constructor simply initializes the data members to default values.

2. **~D3DApp:** The destructor releases the COM interfaces the **D3DApp** acquires.

3. **AppInst:** Trivial access function returns a copy of the application instance handle.

4. **MainWnd:** Trivial access function returns a copy of the main window handle.

5. **AspectRatio:** The aspect ratio is defined as the ratio of the back buffer width to its height. The aspect ratio will be used in the next chapter. It is trivially implemented as:

```
float D3DApp::AspectRatio()const
{
    return static_cast<float>(mClientWidth) / mClientHeight;
}
```

6. **Run:** This method wraps the application message loop. It uses the Win32 **PeekMessage** function so that it can process our game logic when no messages are present. The implementation of this function was shown in §4.3.3.

7. **InitMainWindow:** Initializes the main application window; we assume the reader is familiar with basic Win32 window initialization.

8. **InitDirect3D:** Initializes Direct3D by implementing the steps discussed in §4.2.

9. **CalculateFrameStats:** Calculates the average frames per second and the average milliseconds per frame. The implementation of this method is discussed in §4.4.4.

4.4.3 Framework Methods

For each sample application in this book, we consistently override five virtual functions of **D3DApp**. These five functions are used to implement the code specific to the particular sample. The benefit of this setup is that the initialization code, message handling, etc., is implemented in the **D3DApp** class, so the derived class needs to only focus on the specific code of the demo application. Here is a description of the framework methods:

1. **Init:** Use this method to put initialization code for the application such as allocating resources, initializing objects, and setting up lights. The **D3DApp** implementation of this method calls **InitMainWindow** and **InitDirect3D**; therefore, you should call the **D3DApp** version of this method in your derived implementation first like this:

```
bool TestApp::Init()
{
    if(!D3DApp::Init())
        return false;

    /* Rest of initialization code goes here */
}
```

so that the ID3D11Device is available for the rest of your initialization code. (Direct3D resource acquisition requires a valid ID3D11Device.)

2. **OnResize:** This method is called by D3DApp::MsgProc when a WM_SIZE message is received. When the window is resized, some Direct3D properties need to be changed, as they depend on the client area dimensions. In particular, the back buffer and depth/stencil buffers need to be recreated to match the new client area of the window. The back buffer can be resized by calling the IDXGISwapChain::ResizeBuffers method. The depth/stencil buffer needs to be destroyed and then remade based on the new dimension. In addition, the render target and depth/stencil views need to be recreated. The D3DApp implementation of OnResize handles the code necessary to resize the back and depth/stencil buffers; see the source code for the straightforward details. In addition to the buffers, other properties depend on the size of the client area (e.g., the projection matrix), so this method is part of the framework because the client code may need to execute some of its own code when the window is resized.

3. **UpdateScene:** This abstract method is called every frame and should be used to update the 3D application over time (e.g., perform animations, move the camera, do collision detection, check for user input, etc.).

4. **DrawScene:** This abstract method is invoked every frame and is where we issue rendering commands to actually draw our current frame to the back buffer. When we are done drawing our frame, we call the IDXGISwapChain::Present method to present the back buffer to the screen.

5. **MsgProc:** This method implements the window procedure function for the main application window. Generally, you only need to override this method if there is a message you need to handle that D3DApp::MsgProc does not handle (or does not handle to your liking). The D3DApp implementation of this method is explored in §4.4.5. If you override this method, any message that you do not handle should be forwarded to D3DApp::MsgProc.

Note: *In addition to the previous five framework methods, we provide three other virtual functions for convenience to handle the events when a mouse button is pressed, released, and when the mouse moves:*

```
virtual void OnMouseDown(WPARAM btnState, int x, int y){ }
virtual void OnMouseUp(WPARAM btnState, int x, int y)   { }
virtual void OnMouseMove(WPARAM btnState, int x, int y){ }
```

In this way, if you want to handle mouse messages, you can override these methods instead of overriding the MsgProc method. The first parameter is the same as the WPARAM parameter for the various mouse messages, which stores the mouse button states (i.e., which mouse buttons were pressed when the event was raised). The second and third parameters are the client area (x, y) coordinates of the mouse cursor.

4.4.4 Frame Statistics

It is common for games and graphics applications to measure the number of frames being rendered per second (FPS). To do this, we simply count the number of frames processed (and store it in a variable n) over some specified time period t. Then, the average FPS over the time period t is $fps_{avg} = n/t$. If we set $t = 1$, then $fps_{avg} = n/1 = n$. In our code, we use $t = 1$ (second) because it avoids a division, and moreover, one second gives a pretty good average—it is not too long and not too short. The code to compute the FPS is provided by the D3DApp::CalculateFrameStats method:

```
void D3DApp::CalculateFrameStats()
{
    // Code computes the average frames per second, and also the
    // average time it takes to render one frame.  These stats
    // are appeneded to the window caption bar.

    static int frameCnt = 0;
    static float timeElapsed = 0.0f;

    frameCnt++;

    // Compute averages over one second period.
    if( (mTimer.TotalTime() - timeElapsed) >= 1.0f )
    {
      float fps = (float)frameCnt; // fps = frameCnt / 1
      float mspf = 1000.0f / fps;

      std::wostringstream outs;
      outs.precision(6);
      outs << mMainWndCaption << L"    "
        << L"FPS: " << fps << L"    "
        << L"Frame Time: " << mspf << L" (ms)";
      SetWindowText(mhMainWnd, outs.str().c_str());

      // Reset for next average.
      frameCnt = 0;
      timeElapsed += 1.0f;
    }
}
```

This method would be called every frame in order to count the frame.

In addition to computing the FPS, the previous code also computes the number of milliseconds it takes, on average, to process a frame:

```
float mspf = 1000.0f / fps;
```

The seconds per frame is just the reciprocal of the FPS, but we multiply by 1000 ms / 1 s to convert from seconds to milliseconds (recall there are 1000 ms per second).

The idea behind this line is to compute the time, in milliseconds, it takes to render a frame; this is a different quantity than FPS (but observe this value can be derived from the FPS). In actuality, the time it takes to render a frame is more useful than the FPS, as we may directly see the increase/decrease in time it takes to render a frame as we modify our scene. On the other hand, the FPS does not immediately tell us the increase/decrease in time as we modify our scene. Moreover, as [Dunlop03] points out in his article *FPS versus Frame Time*, due to the non-linearity of the FPS curve, using the FPS can give misleading results. For example, consider situation (1): Suppose our application is running at 1000 FPS, taking 1 ms (millisecond) to render a frame. If the frame rate drops to 250 FPS, then it takes 4 ms to render a frame. Now consider situation (2): Suppose that our application is running at 100 FPS, taking 10 ms to render a frame. If the frame rate drops to about 76.9 FPS, then it takes about 13 ms to render a frame. In both situations, the rendering per frame increased by 3 ms, and thus both represent the same increase in time it takes to render a frame. Reading the FPS is not as straightforward. The drop from 1000 FPS to 250 FPS seems much more drastic than the drop from 100 FPS to 76.9 FPS; however, as we have just showed, they actually represent the same increase in time it takes to render a frame.

4.4.5 The Message Handler

The window procedure we implement for our application framework does the bare minimum. In general, we won't be working very much with Win32 messages anyway. In fact, the core of our application code gets executed during idle processing (i.e., when no window messages are present). Still, there are some important messages we do need to process. However, because of the length of the window procedure, we do not embed all the code here; rather, we just explain the motivation behind each message we handle. We encourage the reader to download the source code files and spend some time getting familiar with the application framework code, as it is the foundation of every sample for this book.

The first message we handle is the **WM_ACTIVATE** message. This message is sent when an application becomes activated or deactivated. We implement it like so:

```
case WM_ACTIVATE:
  if(LOWORD(wParam) == WA_INACTIVE)
  {
    mAppPaused = true;
    mTimer.Stop();
  }
  else
  {
    mAppPaused = false;
    mTimer.Start();
  }
  return 0;
```

As you can see, when our application becomes deactivated, we set the data member mAppPaused to true, and when our application becomes active, we set the data member mAppPaused to false. In addition, when the application is paused, we stop the timer, and then resume the timer once the application becomes active again. If we look back at the implementation to D3DApp::Run (§4.3.3), we find that if our application is paused, we do not update our application code, but instead free some CPU cycles back to the OS; in this way, our application does not hog CPU cycles when it is inactive.

The next message we handle is the WM_SIZE message. Recall that this message is called when the window is resized. The main reason for handling this message is that we want the back buffer and depth/stencil dimensions to match the dimensions of the client area rectangle (so no stretching occurs). Thus, every time the window is resized, we want to resize the buffer dimensions. The code to resize the buffers is implemented in D3DApp::OnResize. As already stated, the back buffer can be resized by calling the IDXGISwapChain::ResizeBuffers method. The depth/stencil buffer needs to be destroyed and then remade based on the new dimensions. In addition, the render target and depth/stencil views need to be recreated. If the user is dragging the resize bars, we must be careful because dragging the resize bars sends continuous WM_SIZE messages, and we do not want to continuously resize the buffers. Therefore, if we determine that the user is resizing by dragging, we actually do nothing (except pause the application) until the user is done dragging the resize bars. We can do this by handling the WM_EXITSIZEMOVE message. This message is sent when the user releases the resize bars

```
// WM_ENTERSIZEMOVE is sent when the user grabs the resize bars.
case WM_ENTERSIZEMOVE:
    mAppPaused = true;
    mResizing  = true;
    mTimer.Stop();
    return 0;

// WM_EXITSIZEMOVE is sent when the user releases the resize bars.
// Here we reset everything based on the new window dimensions.
case WM_EXITSIZEMOVE:
```

```
    mAppPaused = false;
    mResizing  = false;
    mTimer.Start();
    OnResize();
    return 0;
```

The next three messages we handle are trivially implemented and so we just show the code:

```
// WM_DESTROY is sent when the window is being destroyed.
case WM_DESTROY:
    PostQuitMessage(0);
    return 0;

// The WM_MENUCHAR message is sent when a menu is active and the user presses
// a key that does not correspond to any mnemonic or accelerator key.
case WM_MENUCHAR:
    // Don't beep when we alt-enter.
    return MAKELRESULT(0, MNC_CLOSE);

// Catch this message to prevent the window from becoming too small.
case WM_GETMINMAXINFO:
    ((MINMAXINFO*)lParam)->ptMinTrackSize.x = 200;
    ((MINMAXINFO*)lParam)->ptMinTrackSize.y = 200;
    return 0;
```

Finally, to support our mouse input virtual functions, we handle the following mouse messages as follows:

```
case WM_LBUTTONDOWN:
case WM_MBUTTONDOWN:
case WM_RBUTTONDOWN:
    OnMouseDown(wParam, GET_X_LPARAM(lParam), GET_Y_LPARAM(lParam));
    return 0;

case WM_LBUTTONUP:
case WM_MBUTTONUP:
case WM_RBUTTONUP:
    OnMouseUp(wParam, GET_X_LPARAM(lParam), GET_Y_LPARAM(lParam));
    return 0;

case WM_MOUSEMOVE:
    OnMouseMove(wParam, GET_X_LPARAM(lParam), GET_Y_LPARAM(lParam));
    return 0;
```

> **Note:** *We must* #include <Windowsx.h> *for the* GET_X_LPARAM *and* GET_Y_LPARAM *macros.*

4.4.6 Going Full Screen

The IDXGISwapChain interface we created automatically catches the **ALT-ENTER** key combination and will switch the application to full-screen mode. Pressing **ALT-ENTER** while in full-screen mode will switch back to windowed mode. During the mode switch, the application window will be resized, and this sends a WM_SIZE message to the application; this gives the application a chance to resize

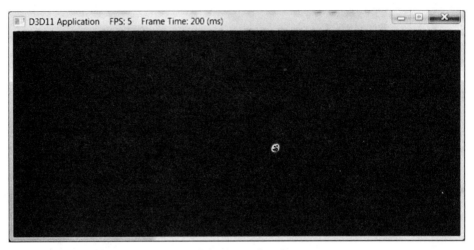

Figure 4.10. A screenshot of the sample program for Chapter 4.

the back and depth/stencil buffers to match the new screen dimensions. Also, if switching to full-screen mode, the window style will change to a full-screen friendly style. You can use the Visual Studio Spy++ tool to see what Windows messages are generated during **ALT-ENTER** for one the demo applications.

The exercises explore how you can disable the default **ALT-ENTER** functionality should you need to.

The reader may wish to review the DXGI_SWAP_CHAIN_DESC::Flags description in §4.2.3.

4.4.7 The "Init Direct3D" Demo

Now that we have discussed the application framework, let us make a small application using it. The program requires almost no real work on our part since the parent class D3DApp does most of the work required for this demo. The main thing to note is how we derive a class from D3DApp and implement the framework functions, where we will write our sample specific code. All of the programs in this book will follow the same template.

```
#include "d3dApp.h"

class InitDirect3DApp : public D3DApp
{
public:
    InitDirect3DApp(HINSTANCE hInstance);
    ~InitDirect3DApp();

    bool Init();
```

```cpp
    void OnResize();
    void UpdateScene(float dt);
    void DrawScene();
};

int WINAPI WinMain(HINSTANCE hInstance, HINSTANCE prevInstance,
          PSTR cmdLine, int showCmd)
{
    // Enable run-time memory check for debug builds.
#if defined(DEBUG) | defined(_DEBUG)
    _CrtSetDbgFlag( _CRTDBG_ALLOC_MEM_DF | _CRTDBG_LEAK_CHECK_DF );
#endif

    InitDirect3DApp theApp(hInstance);

    if( !theApp.Init() )
      return 0;

    return theApp.Run();
}

InitDirect3DApp::InitDirect3DApp(HINSTANCE hInstance)
: D3DApp(hInstance)
{

}

InitDirect3DApp::~InitDirect3DApp()
{
}

bool InitDirect3DApp::Init()
{
    if(!D3DApp::Init())
      return false;

    return true;
}

void InitDirect3DApp::OnResize()
{
    D3DApp::OnResize();
}

void InitDirect3DApp::UpdateScene(float dt)
{

}

void InitDirect3DApp::DrawScene()
{
    assert(md3dImmediateContext);
    assert(mSwapChain);

    // Clear the back buffer blue.  Colors::Blue is defined in d3dUtil.h.
```

```
md3dImmediateContext->ClearRenderTargetView(mRenderTargetView,
   reinterpret_cast<const float*>(&Colors::Blue));

// Clear the depth buffer to 1.0f and the stencil buffer to 0.
md3dImmediateContext->ClearDepthStencilView(mDepthStencilView,
   D3D11_CLEAR_DEPTH|D3D11_CLEAR_STENCIL, 1.0f, 0);

// Present the back buffer to the screen.
HR(mSwapChain->Present(0, 0));
}
```

4.5 DEBUGGING DIRECT3D APPLICATIONS

In order to shorten the code and minimize distractions, we mainly omit error handling in this book. However, we do implement a macro to check the **HRESULT** return codes returned by many Direct3D functions. Our macro is defined as follows in *d3dUtil.h*:

```
#if defined(DEBUG) | defined(_DEBUG)
    #ifndef HR
    #define HR(x)                                                    \
    {                                                                \
      HRESULT hr = (x);                                              \
      if(FAILED(hr))                                                 \
      {                                                              \
         DXTrace(__FILE__, (DWORD)__LINE__, hr, L#x, true);         \
      }                                                              \
    }
    #endif

#else
    #ifndef HR
    #define HR(x) (x)
    #endif
#endif
```

If the returned function's return code indicates failure, then we pass the return code into the **DXTrace** function (`#include <dxerr.h>` and *link dxerr.lib*):

```
HRESULT WINAPI DXTraceW(const char* strFile, DWORD dwLine,
    HRESULT hr, const WCHAR* strMsg, BOOL bPopMsgBox);
```

This function displays a nice message box indicating the file and line number where the error occurred, as well as a textual description of the error, and the name of the function that generated the error; Figure 4.11 shows an example. Note that if you specify **false** for the last parameter of **DXTrace**, then instead of a message box, the debug info will be output to the Visual C++ output window. Observe that the macro **HR** does nothing if we are not in debug mode. Also, **HR** must be a macro and not a function; otherwise **__FILE__** and **__LINE__** would refer to the file and line of the function implementation instead of the file and line where the function **HR** was called.

To use this macro, we just surround a Direct3D function that returns an **HRESULT** by it as this example shows:

```
HR(D3DX11CreateShaderResourceViewFromFile(md3dDevice,
    L"grass.dds", 0, 0, &mGrassTexRV, 0 ));
```

This works well for debugging our demos, but a real application needs to handle errors that can occur once an application has shipped (e.g., unsupported hardware, missing files, etc.).

Note: *The **L#x** turns the **HR** macro's argument token into a Unicode string. In this way, we can output the function call that caused the error to the message box.*

4.6 SUMMARY

1. Direct3D can be thought of as a mediator between the programmer and the graphics hardware. For example, the programmer calls Direct3D functions to bind resource views to the hardware rendering pipeline, to configure the output of the rendering pipeline, and to draw 3D geometry.

2. In Direct3D 11, a Direct3D 11 capable graphics device must support the entire Direct3D 11 capability set, with few exceptions.

3. Component Object Model (COM) is the technology that allows DirectX to be language independent and have backwards compatibility. Direct3D programmers don't need to know the details of COM and how it works; they need only to know how to acquire COM interfaces and how to release them.

4. A 1D texture is like a 1D array of data elements, a 2D texture is like a 2D array of data elements, and a 3D texture is like a 3D array of data elements. The elements of a texture must have a format described by a member of the **DXGI_FORMAT** enumerated type. Textures typically contain image data, but they can contain other data, too, such as depth information (e.g., the depth buffer). The GPU can do special operations on textures, such as filter and multisample them.

5. In Direct3D, resources are not bound to the pipeline directly. Instead, a resource view is bound to the pipeline. Different views of a single resource may be created. In this way, a single resource may be bound to different stages of the rendering pipeline. If a resource was created with a typeless format, then the type must be specified at view creation.

6. The **ID3D11Device** and **ID3D11DeviceContext** interfaces can be thought of as our software controller of the physical graphics device hardware; that is, with these

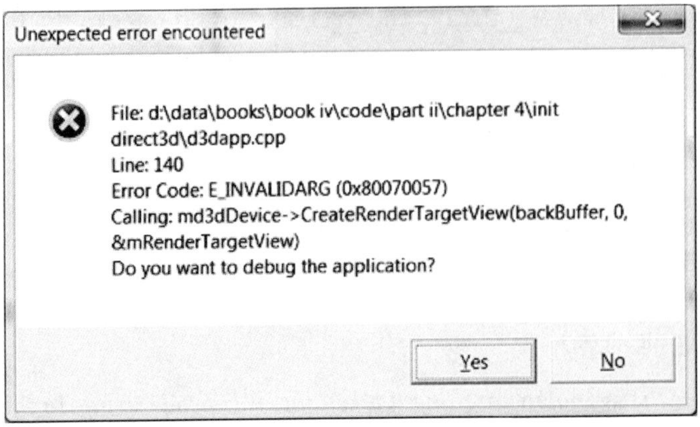

Figure 4.11. The message box displayed by the DXTrace function if a Direct3D function returns an error.

interfaces we can interact with the hardware and instruct it to do things. The ID3D11Device interface is responsible for checking feature support and allocate resources. The ID3D11DeviceContext interface is responsible for setting render states, binding resources to the graphics pipeline, and issuing rendering commands.

7. To avoid flickering in animation, it is best to draw an entire frame of animation into an off screen texture called the back buffer. Once the entire scene has been drawn to the back buffer for the given frame of animation, it is presented to the screen as one complete frame; in this way, the viewer does not watch as the frame gets drawn. After the frame has been drawn to the back buffer, the roles of the back buffer and front buffer are reversed: the back buffer becomes the front buffer and the front buffer becomes the back buffer for the next frame of animation. Swapping the roles of the back and front buffers is called presenting. The front and back buffer form a swap chain, represented by the IDXGISwapChain interface. Using two buffers (front and back) is called double buffering.

8. Assuming opaque scene objects, the points nearest to the camera occlude any points behind them. Depth buffering is a technique for determining the points in the scene nearest to the camera. In this way, we do not have to worry about the order in which we draw our scene objects.

9. The performance counter is a high-resolution timer that provides accurate timing measurements needed for measuring small time differentials, such as the time elapsed between frames. The performance timer works in time units called *counts*. The QueryPerformanceFrequency outputs the counts per second of the performance timer, which can then be used to convert from units of counts to seconds. The current time value of the performance timer (measured in counts) is obtained with the QueryPerformanceCounter function.

10 . To compute the average frames per second (FPS), we count the number of frames processed over some time interval Δt. Let n be the number of frames counted over time Δt, then the average frames per second over that time interval is $fps_{avg} = n/\Delta t$. The frame rate can give misleading conclusions about performance; the time it takes to process a frame is more informative. The amount of time, in seconds, spent processing a frame is the reciprocal of the frame rate (i.e., $1/fps_{avg}$).

11 . The sample framework is used to provide a consistent interface that all demo applications in this book follow. The code provided in the *d3dUtil.h*, *d3dApp.h*, and *d3dApp.cpp* files wrap standard initialization code that every application must implement. By wrapping this code up, we hide it, which allows the samples to be more focused on demonstrating the current topic.

12 . For debug mode builds, create the Direct3D device with the `D3D11_CREATE_DEVICE_DEBUG` flag to enable the debug layer. When the debug flag is specified, Direct3D will send debug messages to the VC++ output window. Also use the debug version of the D3DX library (i.e., *d3dx11d.lib*) for debug builds.

4.7 EXERCISES

1. Modify the previous exercise solution by disabling the **ALT-ENTER** functionality to switch between full screen and windowed mode; use the `IDXGIFactory::MakeWindowAssociation` method and specify the `DXGI_MWA_NO_WINDOW_CHANGES` flag so that DXGI does not monitor the message queue. Note that the `IDXGIFactory::MakeWindowAssociation` method needs to be called after `IDXGIFactory::CreateSwapChain` is called.

2. Some systems have more than one adapter (video card), and the application may wish to let the user choose which one to use, instead of always using the default adapter. Use the `IDXGIFactory::EnumAdapters` method to determine how many adapters are on your system.

3. For each adapter the system possesses, `IDXGIFactory::EnumAdapters` outputs a pointer to a filled out `IDXGIAdapter` interface. This interface can be used to query information about the adapter. Use the `IDXGIAdapter::CheckInterfaceSupport` method to see if the adapters on your system support Direct3D 11.

4. An adapter has outputs associated with it (e.g., a monitor). You can use the `IDXGIAdapter::EnumOutputs` method to enumerate the outputs for a particular adapter. Use this method to determine the number of outputs for the default adapter.

5. Each output has a list of supported display modes (`DXGI_MODE_DESC`) for a given pixel format. For each output (`IDXGIOutput`), show the width, height, and refresh

rate of each display mode the output supports for the DXGI_FORMAT_R8G8B8A8_ UNORM format using the IDXGIOutput::GetDisplayModeList method.

Example output for Exercises 2, 3, 4, and 5 is listed below. It is useful to use the OutputDebugString function for quick output to the VC++ output window.

```
*** NUM ADAPTERS = 1
*** D3D11 SUPPORTED FOR ADAPTER 0
*** NUM OUTPUTS FOR DEFAULT ADAPTER = 1
***WIDTH = 640  HEIGHT = 480  REFRESH = 60000/1000
***WIDTH = 640  HEIGHT = 480  REFRESH = 72000/1000
***WIDTH = 640  HEIGHT = 480  REFRESH = 75000/1000
***WIDTH = 720  HEIGHT = 480  REFRESH = 56250/1000
***WIDTH = 720  HEIGHT = 480  REFRESH = 56250/1000
***WIDTH = 720  HEIGHT = 480  REFRESH = 60000/1000
***WIDTH = 720  HEIGHT = 480  REFRESH = 60000/1000
***WIDTH = 720  HEIGHT = 480  REFRESH = 72188/1000
***WIDTH = 720  HEIGHT = 480  REFRESH = 72188/1000
***WIDTH = 720  HEIGHT = 480  REFRESH = 75000/1000
***WIDTH = 720  HEIGHT = 480  REFRESH = 75000/1000
***WIDTH = 720  HEIGHT = 576  REFRESH = 56250/1000
***WIDTH = 720  HEIGHT = 576  REFRESH = 56250/1000
***WIDTH = 720  HEIGHT = 576  REFRESH = 60000/1000
***WIDTH = 720  HEIGHT = 576  REFRESH = 60000/1000
***WIDTH = 720  HEIGHT = 576  REFRESH = 72188/1000
***WIDTH = 720  HEIGHT = 576  REFRESH = 72188/1000
***WIDTH = 720  HEIGHT = 576  REFRESH = 75000/1000
***WIDTH = 720  HEIGHT = 576  REFRESH = 75000/1000
***WIDTH = 800  HEIGHT = 600  REFRESH = 56250/1000
***WIDTH = 800  HEIGHT = 600  REFRESH = 60000/1000
***WIDTH = 800  HEIGHT = 600  REFRESH = 60000/1000
***WIDTH = 800  HEIGHT = 600  REFRESH = 72188/1000
***WIDTH = 800  HEIGHT = 600  REFRESH = 75000/1000
***WIDTH = 848  HEIGHT = 480  REFRESH = 60000/1000
***WIDTH = 848  HEIGHT = 480  REFRESH = 60000/1000
***WIDTH = 848  HEIGHT = 480  REFRESH = 70069/1000
***WIDTH = 848  HEIGHT = 480  REFRESH = 70069/1000
***WIDTH = 848  HEIGHT = 480  REFRESH = 75029/1000
***WIDTH = 848  HEIGHT = 480  REFRESH = 75029/1000
***WIDTH = 960  HEIGHT = 600  REFRESH = 60000/1000
***WIDTH = 960  HEIGHT = 600  REFRESH = 60000/1000
***WIDTH = 960  HEIGHT = 600  REFRESH = 70069/1000
***WIDTH = 960  HEIGHT = 600  REFRESH = 70069/1000
***WIDTH = 960  HEIGHT = 600  REFRESH = 75029/1000
***WIDTH = 960  HEIGHT = 600  REFRESH = 75029/1000
***WIDTH = 1024 HEIGHT = 768  REFRESH = 60000/1000
***WIDTH = 1024 HEIGHT = 768  REFRESH = 60000/1000
***WIDTH = 1024 HEIGHT = 768  REFRESH = 70069/1000
***WIDTH = 1024 HEIGHT = 768  REFRESH = 75029/1000
***WIDTH = 1152 HEIGHT = 864  REFRESH = 60000/1000
***WIDTH = 1152 HEIGHT = 864  REFRESH = 60000/1000
***WIDTH = 1152 HEIGHT = 864  REFRESH = 75000/1000
***WIDTH = 1280 HEIGHT = 720  REFRESH = 60000/1000
***WIDTH = 1280 HEIGHT = 720  REFRESH = 60000/1000
```

```
***WIDTH = 1280 HEIGHT =  720 REFRESH = 60000/1001
***WIDTH = 1280 HEIGHT =  768 REFRESH = 60000/1000
***WIDTH = 1280 HEIGHT =  768 REFRESH = 60000/1000
***WIDTH = 1280 HEIGHT =  800 REFRESH = 60000/1000
***WIDTH = 1280 HEIGHT =  800 REFRESH = 60000/1000
***WIDTH = 1280 HEIGHT =  960 REFRESH = 60000/1000
***WIDTH = 1280 HEIGHT =  960 REFRESH = 60000/1000
***WIDTH = 1280 HEIGHT = 1024 REFRESH = 60000/1000
***WIDTH = 1280 HEIGHT = 1024 REFRESH = 60000/1000
***WIDTH = 1280 HEIGHT = 1024 REFRESH = 75025/1000
***WIDTH = 1360 HEIGHT =  768 REFRESH = 60000/1000
***WIDTH = 1360 HEIGHT =  768 REFRESH = 60000/1000
***WIDTH = 1600 HEIGHT = 1200 REFRESH = 60000/1000
```

6. Experiment with modifying the viewport settings to draw the scene into a subrectangle of the back buffer. For example, try:

```
D3D11_VIEWPORT vp;
    vp.TopLeftX = 100.0f;
    vp.TopLeftY = 100.0f;
    vp.Width    = 500.0f;
    vp.Height   = 400.0f;
    vp.MinDepth = 0.0f;
    vp.MaxDepth = 1.0f;
```

Chapter 5

THE RENDERING PIPELINE

The primary theme of this chapter is the rendering pipeline. Given a geometric description of a 3D scene with a positioned and oriented virtual camera, the *rendering pipeline* refers to the entire sequence of steps necessary to generate a 2D image based on what the virtual camera sees (Figure 5.1). This chapter is mostly theoretical—the next chapter puts the theory into practice as we learn to draw with Direct3D. Before we begin coverage of the rendering pipeline, we have two short stops: First, we discuss some elements of the 3D illusion (i.e., the illusion that we are looking into a 3D world through a flat 2D monitor screen); and second, we explain how colors will be represented and worked with mathematically and in Direct3D code.

Objectives:

1. To discover several key signals used to convey a realistic sense of volume and spatial depth in a 2D image.
2. To find out how we represent 3D objects in Direct3D.
3. To learn how we model the virtual camera.
4. To understand the rendering pipeline—the process of taking a geometric description of a 3D scene and generating a 2D image from it.

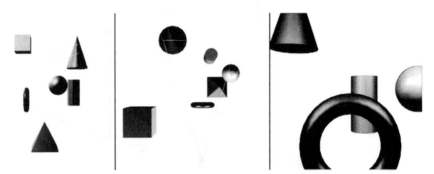

Figure 5.1. The left image shows a side view of some objects set up in the 3D world with a camera positioned and aimed; the middle image shows the same scene, but from a top-down view. The "pyramid" volume specifies the volume of space that the viewer can see; objects (and parts of objects) outside this volume are not seen. The image on the right shows the 2D image created based on what the camera "sees."

5.1 THE 3D ILLUSION

Before we embark on our journey of 3D computer graphics, a simple question remains outstanding: How do we display a 3D world with depth and volume on a flat 2D monitor screen? Fortunately for us, this problem has been well studied, as artists have been painting 3D scenes on 2D canvases for centuries. In this section, we outline several key techniques that make an image look 3D, even though it is actually drawn on a 2D plane.

Suppose that you have encountered a railroad track that doesn't curve, but goes along a straight line for a long distance. The railroad rails remain parallel to each other for the length of the track, but if you stand on the railroad and look down its path, you will observe that the two railroad rails get closer and closer together as their distance from you increases, and eventually they converge at an infinite distance. This is one observation that characterizes our human viewing system: parallel lines of vision converge to a *vanishing point*; see Figure 5.2.

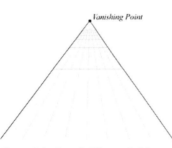

Figure 5.2. Parallel lines of vision converge to a vanishing point. Artists sometimes call this *linear perspective.*

Figure 5.3. Here, all the columns are of the same size, but a viewer observes a diminishing in size with respect to depth phenomenon.

Another simple observation of how humans see things is that the size of an object appears to diminish with depth; that is, objects near us look bigger than objects far away. For example, a house far away on a hill will look very small, while a tree near us will look very large in comparison. Figure 5.3 shows a simple scene where parallel rows of columns are placed behind each other, one after another. The columns are actually all the same size, but as their depths increase from the viewer, they appear to get smaller and smaller. Also notice how the columns are converging to the vanishing point at the horizon.

We all experience *object overlap* (Figure 5.4), which refers to the fact that opaque objects obscure parts (or all) of the objects behind them. This is an important

Figure 5.4. A group of objects that partially obscure each other because one is in front of the other, etc. (they overlap).

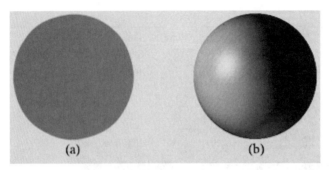

Figure 5.5. (a) An unlit sphere that looks 2D. (b) A lit sphere that looks 3D.

perception, as it conveys the depth ordering relationship of the objects in the scene. We already discussed (Chapter 4) how Direct3D uses a depth buffer to figure out which pixels are being obscured and thus should not be drawn.

Consider Figure 5.5. On the left we have an unlit sphere, and on the right, we have a lit sphere. As you can see, the sphere on the left looks rather flat—maybe it is not even a sphere at all, but just a textured 2D circle! Thus, lighting and shading play a very important role in depicting the solid form and volume of 3D objects.

Finally, Figure 5.6 shows a spaceship and its shadow. The shadow serves two key purposes. First, it tells us the origin of the light source in the scene. And secondly, it provides us with a rough idea of how high off the ground the spaceship is.

The observations just discussed, no doubt, are intuitively obvious from our day-to-day experiences. Nonetheless, it is helpful to explicitly state what we know and to keep these observations in mind as we study and work on 3D computer graphics.

Figure 5.6. A spaceship and its shadow. The shadow implies the location of the light source in the scene and also gives an idea of how high off the ground the spaceship is.

5.2 MODEL REPRESENTATION

A solid 3D *object* is represented by a *triangle mesh* approximation, and consequently, triangles form the basic building blocks of the objects we model. As Figure 5.7 implies, we can approximate any real-world 3D object by a triangle mesh. In general, the more triangles you use to approximate an object, the better the approximation, as you can model finer details. Of course, the more triangles we use, the more processing power is required, so a balance must be made based on the hardware power of the application's target audience. In addition to triangles, it is sometimes useful to draw lines or points. For example, a curve could be graphically drawn by a sequence of short line segments a pixel thick.

The large number of triangles used in Figure 5.7 makes one thing clear: It would be extremely cumbersome to manually list the triangles of a 3D model. For all but the simplest models, special 3D applications called *3D modelers* are used to generate and manipulate 3D objects. These modelers allow the user to build complex and realistic meshes in a visual and interactive environment with a rich tool set, thereby making the entire modeling process much easier. Examples of popular modelers used for game development are 3D Studio Max (http://usa.autodesk.com/3ds-max/), LightWave 3D (http://www.newtek.com/lightwave/), Maya (http://usa.autodesk.com/maya/), Softimage|XSI (http://www.softimage.com), and Blender (http://www.blender.org/). (Blender has the advantage for hobbyists of being open source and free.) Nevertheless, for the first part of this book, we will generate our 3D models manually by hand, or via a mathematical formula (the triangle list for cylinders and spheres, for example, can easily be generated with parametric formulas). In the third part of this book, we show how to load and display 3D models exported from 3D modeling programs.

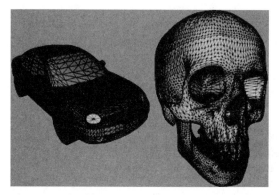

Figure 5.7. (Left) A car approximated by a triangle mesh. (Right) A skull approximated by a triangle mesh.

5.3 BASIC COMPUTER COLOR

Computer monitors emit a mixture of red, green, and blue light through each pixel. When the light mixture enters the eye and strikes an area of the retina, cone receptor cells are stimulated and neural impulses are sent down the optic nerve toward the brain. The brain interprets the signal and generates a color. As the light mixture varies, the cells are stimulated differently, which in turn generates a different color in the mind. Figure 5.8 shows some examples of mixing red, green, and blue to get different colors; it also shows different intensities of red. By using different intensities for each color component and mixing them together, we can describe all the colors we need to display realistic images.

The best way to get comfortable with describing colors by RGB (red, green, blue) values is to use a paint program like Adobe Photoshop, or even the Win32 `ChooseColor` dialog box (Figure 5.9), and experiment with different RGB combinations to see the colors they produce.

A monitor has a maximum intensity of red, green, and blue light it can emit. To describe the intensities of light, it is useful to use a normalized range from 0 to 1. Zero denotes no intensity and 1 denotes the full intensity. Intermediate values denote intermediate intensities. For example, the values (0.25, 0.67, 1.0) mean the light mixture consists of 25% intensity of red light, 67% intensity of green light, and 100% intensity of blue light. As the example just stated implies, we can represent a color by a 3D color vector (r, g, b), where $0 \leq r, g, b \leq 1$, and each color component describes the intensity of red, green, and blue light in the mixture.

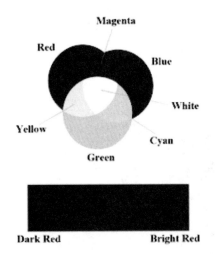

Figure 5.8. (Top) The mixing of pure red, green, and blue colors to get new colors. (Bottom) Different shades of red found by controlling the intensity of red light.

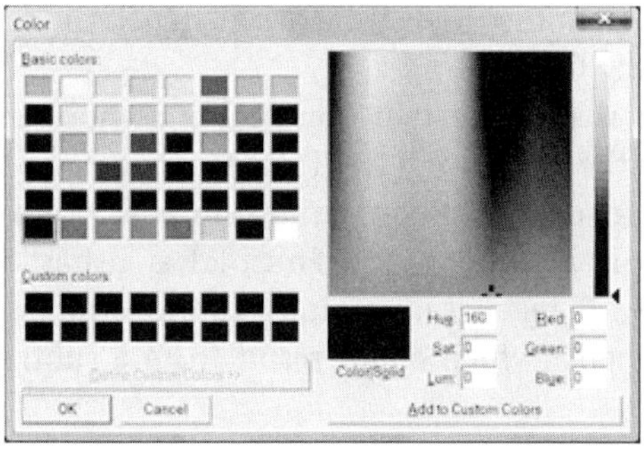

Figure 5.9. The `ChooseColor` dialog box.

5.3.1 Color Operations

Some vector operations also apply to color vectors. For example, we can add color vectors to get new colors:

$$(0.0, 0.5, 0) + (0, 0.0, 0.25) = (0.0, 0.5, 0.25)$$

By combining a medium intensity green color with a low intensity blue color, we get a dark-green color.

Colors can also be subtracted to get new colors:

$$(1, 1, 1) - (1, 1, 0) = (0, 0, 1)$$

That is, we start with white and subtract out the red and green parts, and we end up with blue.

Scalar multiplication also makes sense. Consider the following:

$$0.5\,(1, 1, 1) = (0.5, 0.5, 0.5)$$

That is, we start with white and multiply by 0.5, and we end up with a medium shade of gray. On the other hand, the operation $2(0.25, 0, 0) = (0.5, 0, 0)$ doubles the intensity of the red component.

Obviously expressions like the dot product and cross product do not make sense for color vectors. However, color vectors do get their own special color operation called *modulation* or *componentwise* multiplication. It is defined as:

$$(c_r, c_g, c_b) \otimes (k_r, k_g, k_b) = (c_r k_r, c_g k_g, c_b k_b)$$

This operation is mainly used in lighting equations. For example, suppose we have an incoming ray of light with color (r, g, b) and it strikes a surface which reflects 50% red light, 75% green light, and 25% blue light, and absorbs the rest. Then the color of the reflected light ray is given by:

$$(r, g, b) \otimes (0.5, 0.75, 0.25) = (0.5r, 0.75g, 0.25b)$$

So we can see that the light ray lost some intensity when it struck the surface, since the surface absorbed some of the light.

When doing color operation, it is possible that your color components go outside the [0, 1] interval; consider the equation, (1, 0.1, 0.6) + (0, 0.3, 0.5) = (1, 0.4, 1.1), for example. Because 1.0 represents the maximum intensity of a color component, you cannot become more intense than it. Thus, 1.1 is just as intense as 1.0. So what we do is clamp $1.1 \rightarrow 1.0$. Likewise, a monitor cannot emit negative light, so any negative color component (which could result from a subtraction operation) should be clamped to 0.0.

5.3.2 128-Bit Color

It is common to incorporate an additional color component, called the *alpha component*. The alpha component is often used to denote the opacity of a color, which is useful in blending (Chapter 9 Blending). (Since we are not using blending yet, just set the alpha component to 1 for now.)

Including the alpha component means we can represent a color by a 4D color vector (r, g, b, a) where $0 \le r, g, b, a \le 1$. To represent a color with 128-bits, we use a floating-point value for each component. Because mathematically a color is just a 4D vector, we can use the **XMVECTOR** type to represent a color in code, and we gain the benefit of SIMD operations whenever we use the XNA Math vector functions to do color operations (e.g., color addition, subtraction, scalar multiplication). For componentwise multiplication, the XNA Math library provides the following function:

```
XMVECTOR XMColorModulate(// Returns (c_r, c_g, c_b, c_a) ⊗ (k_r, k_g, k_b, k_a)
    FXMVECTOR C1,          // (c_r, c_g, c_b, c_a)
    FXMVECTOR C2);         // (k_r, k_g, k_b, k_a)
```

5.3.3 32-Bit Color

To represent a color with 32-bits, a byte is given to each component. Since each color is given an 8-bit byte, we can represent 256 different shades for each color component—0 being no intensity, 255 being full intensity, and intermediate values being intermediate intensities. A byte per color component may seem small, but when we look at all the combinations ($256 \times 256 \times 256 = 16,777,216$), we see millions of distinct colors can be represented. The XNA Math library provides the following structure for storing a 32-bit color:

```
// ARGB Color; 8-8-8-8 bit unsigned normalized integer components
// packed into a 32 bit integer.  The normalized color is packed into
// 32 bits using 8 bit unsigned, normalized integers for the alpha,
// red, green, and blue components.
// The alpha component is stored in the most significant bits and the
// blue component in the least significant bits (A8R8G8B8):
```

```
// [32] aaaaaaaa rrrrrrrr gggggggg bbbbbbbb [0]
typedef struct _XMCOLOR
{
    union
    {
      struct
        {
            UINT b     : 8;  // Blue:     0/255 to 255/255
            UINT g     : 8;  // Green:    0/255 to 255/255
            UINT r     : 8;  // Red:      0/255 to 255/255
            UINT a     : 8;  // Alpha:    0/255 to 255/255
        };
        UINT c;
    };

#ifdef __cplusplus

    _XMCOLOR() {};
    _XMCOLOR(UINT Color) : c(Color) {};
    _XMCOLOR(FLOAT _r, FLOAT _g, FLOAT _b, FLOAT _a);
    _XMCOLOR(CONST FLOAT *pArray);

    operator UINT () { return c; }

    _XMCOLOR& operator= (CONST _XMCOLOR& Color);
    _XMCOLOR& operator= (CONST UINT Color);

#endif // __cplusplus

} XMCOLOR;
```

A 32-bit color can be converted to a 128-bit color by mapping the integer range $[0, 255]$ onto the real-valued interval $[0, 1]$. This is done by dividing by 255. That is, if $0 \leq n \leq 255$ is an integer, then $0 \leq \frac{n}{255} \leq 1$ gives the intensity in the normalized range from 0 to 1. For example, the 32-bit color $(80, 140, 200, 255)$ becomes

$$(80, 140, 200, 255) \rightarrow \left(\frac{80}{255}, \frac{140}{255}, \frac{200}{255}, \frac{255}{255} \right) \approx (0.31, 0.55, 0.78, 1.0)$$

On the other hand, a 128-bit color can be converted to a 32-bit color by multiplying each component by 255 and rounding to the nearest integer. For example:

$(0.3, 0.6, 0.9, 1.0) \rightarrow (0.3 \cdot 255, 0.6 \cdot 255, 0.9 \cdot 255, 1.0 \cdot 255) = (77, 153, 230, 255)$

Additional bit operations must usually be done when converting a 32-bit color to a 128-bit color and conversely because the 8-bit color components are usually packed into a 32-bit integer value (e.g., an unsigned int), as it is in XMCOLOR. The XNA Math library defines the following function which takes a XMCOLOR and returns an XMVECTOR from it:

```
XMVECTOR XMLoadColor(CONST XMCOLOR* pSource);
```

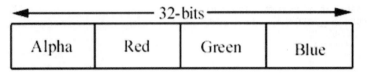

Figure 5.10. A 32-bit color, where a byte is allocated for each color component alpha, red, green, and blue.

Figure 5.10 shows how the 8-bit color components are packed into a UINT. Note that this is just one way to pack the color components. Another format might be ABGR or RGBA, instead of ARGB; however, the XMCOLOR class uses the ARGB layout. The XNA Math library also provides a function to convert an XMVECTOR color to a XMCOLOR:

```
VOID XMStoreColor(XMCOLOR* pDestination, FXMVECTOR V);
```

Typically, 128-bit colors values are used where many color operations will take place (e.g., in a pixel shader); in this way, we have many bits of accuracy for the calculations so arithmetic error does not accumulate too much. The final pixel color, however, is usually stored in a 32-bit color value in the back buffer; current physical display devices cannot take advantage of the higher resolution color [Verth04].

5.4 OVERVIEW OF THE RENDERING PIPELINE

Given a geometric description of a 3D scene with a positioned and oriented virtual camera, the *rendering pipeline* refers to the entire sequence of steps necessary to generate a 2D image based on what the virtual camera sees. Figure 5.11 shows a diagram of the stages that make up the rendering pipeline, as well as GPU memory resources off to the side. An arrow going from the resource memory pool to a stage means the stage can access the resources as input; for example, the pixel shader stage may need to read data from a texture resource stored in memory in order to do its work. An arrow going from a stage to memory means the stage writes to GPU resources; for example, the output merger stage writes data to textures such as the back buffer and depth/stencil buffer. Observe that the arrow for the output merger stage is bidirectional (it reads and writes to GPU resources). As we can see, most stages do not write to GPU resources. Instead, their output is just fed in as input to the next stage of the pipeline; for example, the Vertex Shader stage inputs data from the Input Assembler stage, does its own work, and then outputs its results to the Geometry Shader stage. The subsequent sections give an overview of each stage of the rendering pipeline.

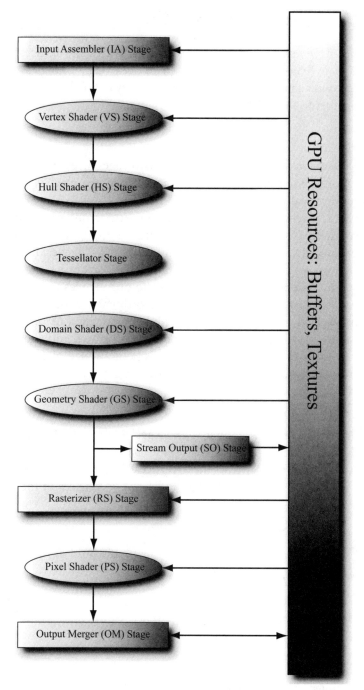

Figure 5.11. The stages of the rendering pipeline.

5.5 THE INPUT ASSEMBLER STAGE

The *input assembler* (IA) stage reads geometric data (vertices and indices) from memory and uses it to assemble geometric primitives (e.g., triangles, lines). (Indices are covered in a later subsection, but briefly, they define how the vertices should be put together to form the primitives.)

5.5.1 Vertices

Mathematically, the vertices of a triangle are where two edges meet; the vertices of a line are the endpoints; for a single point, the point itself is the vertex. Figure 5.12 illustrates vertices pictorially.

From Figure 5.12, it seems that a vertex is just a special point in a geometric primitive. However, in Direct3D, vertices are much more general than that. Essentially, a vertex in Direct3D can consist of additional data besides spatial location, which allows us to perform more sophisticated rendering effects. For example, in Chapter 7, we will add normal vectors to our vertices to implement lighting, and in Chapter 8, we will add texture coordinates to our vertices to implement texturing. Direct3D gives us the flexibility to define our own vertex formats (i.e., it allows us to define the components of a vertex), and we will see the code used to do this in the next chapter. In this book, we will define several different vertex formats based on the rendering effect we are doing.

5.5.2 Primitive Topology

Vertices are bound to the rendering pipeline in a special Direct3D data structure called a *vertex buffer*. A vertex buffer just stores a list of vertices in contiguous memory. However, it does not say how these vertices should be put together to form geometric primitives. For example, should every two vertices in the vertex

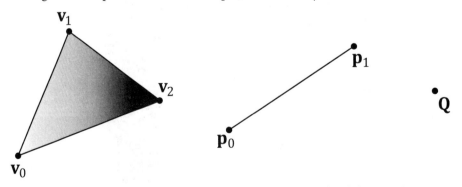

Figure 5.12. A triangle defined by the three vertices v_0, v_1, v_2; a line defined by the two vertices p_0, p_1; a point defined by the vertex Q.

buffer be interpreted as a line or should every three vertices in the vertex buffer be interpreted as a triangle? We tell Direct3D how to form geometric primitives from the vertex data by specifying the *primitive topology*:

```
void ID3D11DeviceContext::IASetPrimitiveTopology(
    D3D11_PRIMITIVE_TOPOLOGY Topology);

typedef enum D3D11_PRIMITIVE_TOPOLOGY
{
    D3D11_PRIMITIVE_TOPOLOGY_UNDEFINED = 0,
    D3D11_PRIMITIVE_TOPOLOGY_POINTLIST = 1,
    D3D11_PRIMITIVE_TOPOLOGY_LINELIST = 2,
    D3D11_PRIMITIVE_TOPOLOGY_LINESTRIP = 3,
    D3D11_PRIMITIVE_TOPOLOGY_TRIANGLELIST = 4,
    D3D11_PRIMITIVE_TOPOLOGY_TRIANGLESTRIP = 5,
    D3D11_PRIMITIVE_TOPOLOGY_LINELIST_ADJ = 10,
    D3D11_PRIMITIVE_TOPOLOGY_LINESTRIP_ADJ = 11,
    D3D11_PRIMITIVE_TOPOLOGY_TRIANGLELIST_ADJ = 12,
    D3D11_PRIMITIVE_TOPOLOGY_TRIANGLESTRIP_ADJ = 13,
    D3D11_PRIMITIVE_TOPOLOGY_1_CONTROL_POINT_PATCHLIST = 33,
    D3D11_PRIMITIVE_TOPOLOGY_2_CONTROL_POINT_PATCHLIST = 34,
                         .
                         .
                         .
    D3D11_PRIMITIVE_TOPOLOGY_32_CONTROL_POINT_PATCHLIST = 64,
} D3D11_PRIMITIVE_TOPOLOGY;
```

All subsequent drawing calls will use the currently set primitive topology until the topology is changed. The following code illustrates:

```
md3dImmediateContext->IASetPrimitiveTopology(
    D3D11_PRIMITIVE_TOPOLOGY_LINELIST);
/* ...draw objects using line list... */

md3dImmediateContext->IASetPrimitiveTopology(
    D3D11_PRIMITIVE_TOPOLOGY_TRIANGLELIST);
/* ...draw objects using triangle list... */

md3dImmediateContext->IASetPrimitiveTopology(
    D3D11_PRIMITIVE_TOPOLOGY_TRIANGLESTRIP);
/* ...draw objects using triangle strip... */
```

The following subsections elaborate on the different primitive topologies. In this book, we mainly use triangle lists exclusively with few exceptions.

5.5.2.1 Point List

A point list is specified by D3D11_PRIMITIVE_TOPOLOGY_POINTLIST. With a point list, every vertex in the draw call is drawn as an individual point, as shown in Figure 5.13a.

5.5.2.2 Line Strip

A line strip is specified by D3D11_PRIMITIVE_TOPOLOGY_LINESTRIP. With a line strip, the vertices in the draw call are connected to form lines (see Figure 5.13b); so $n + 1$ vertices induces n lines.

5.5.2.3 Line List

A line list is specified by D3D11_PRIMITIVE_TOPOLOGY_LINELIST. With a line list, every two vertices in the draw call forms an individual line (see Figure 5.13c); so $2n$ vertices induces n lines. The difference between a line list and strip is that the lines in the line list may be disconnected, whereas a line strip automatically assumes they are connected; by assuming connectivity, fewer vertices can be used because each interior vertex is shared by two lines.

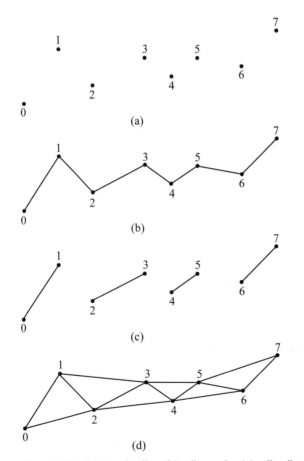

Figure 5.13. (a) A point list; (b) a line strip; (c) a line list; (d) a triangle strip.

5.5.2.4 Triangle Strip

A triangle strip is specified by D3D11_PRIMITIVE_TOPOLOGY_TRIANGLESTRIP. With a triangle strip, it is assumed the triangles are connected as shown in Figure 5.13d to form a strip. By assuming connectivity, we see that vertices are shared between adjacent triangles, and n vertices induce $n - 2$ triangles.

Note: *Observe that the winding order for even triangles in a triangle strip differs from the odd triangles, thereby causing culling issues (see §5.10.2). To fix this problem, the GPU internally swaps the order of the first two vertices of even triangles, so that they are consistently ordered like the odd triangles.*

5.5.2.5 Triangle List

A triangle list is specified by D3D11_PRIMITIVE_TOPOLOGY_TRIANGLELIST. With a triangle list, every three vertices in the draw call forms an individual triangle (see Figure 5.14a); so $3n$ vertices induces n triangles. The difference between a triangle list and strip is that the triangles in the triangle list may be disconnected, whereas a triangle strip assumes they are connected.

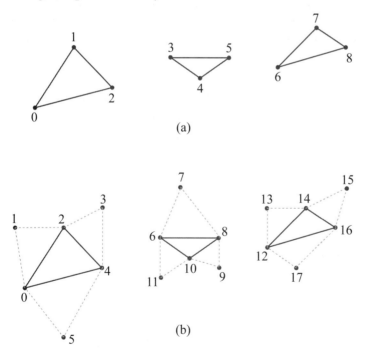

Figure 5.14. (a) A triangle list. (b) A triangle list with adjacency—observe that each triangle requires 6 vertices to describe it and its adjacent triangles. Thus *6n* vertices induces *n* triangles with adjacency info.

5.5.2.6 Primitives with Adjacency

A triangle list with adjacency is where, for each triangle, you also include its three neighboring triangles called *adjacent triangles*; see Figure 5.14*b* to observe how these triangles are defined. This is used for the geometry shader, where certain geometry shading algorithms need access to the adjacent triangles. In order for the geometry shader to get those adjacent triangles, the adjacent triangles need to be submitted to the pipeline in the vertex/index buffers along with the triangle itself, and the `D3D11_PRIMITIVE_TOPOLOGY_TRIANGLELIST_ADJ` topology must be specified so that the pipeline knows how construct the triangle and its adjacent triangles from the vertex buffer. Note that the vertices of adjacent primitives are only used as input into the geometry shader—they are not drawn. If there is no geometry shader, the adjacent primitives are still not drawn.

It is also possible to have a line list with adjacency, line strip with adjacency, and triangle with strip adjacency primitives; see the SDK documentation for details.

5.5.2.7 Control Point Patch List

The `D3D11_PRIMITIVE_TOPOLOGY_`N`_CONTROL_POINT_PATCHLIST` topology type indicates that the vertex data should be interpreted as a patch lists with N control points. These are used in the (optional) tessellation stage of the rendering pipeline, and therefore, we will postpone a discussion of them until Chapter 13, "The Tessellation Stages."

5.5.3 Indices

As already mentioned, triangles are the basic building blocks for solid 3D objects. The following code shows the vertex arrays used to construct a quad and octagon using triangle lists (i.e., every three vertices form a triangle).

```
Vertex quad[6] = {
    v0, v1, v2, // Triangle 0
    v0, v2, v3, // Triangle 1
};

Vertex octagon[24] = {
    v0, v1, v2, // Triangle 0
    v0, v2, v3, // Triangle 1
    v0, v3, v4, // Triangle 2
    v0, v4, v5, // Triangle 3
    v0, v5, v6, // Triangle 4
    v0, v6, v7, // Triangle 5
    v0, v7, v8, // Triangle 6
    v0, v8, v1  // Triangle 7
};
```

Note: ▶ *The order in which you specify the vertices of a triangle is important and is called the winding order; see §5.10.2 for details.*

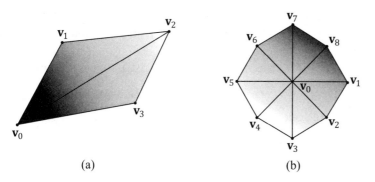

Figure 5.15. (a) A quad built from two triangles. (b) An octagon built from eight triangles.

As Figure 5.15 illustrates, the triangles that form a 3D object share many of the same vertices. More specifically, each triangle of the quad in Figure 5.15*a* shares the vertices v_0 and v_2. While duplicating two vertices is not too bad, the duplication is worse in the octagon example (Figure 5.15*b*), as every triangle duplicates the center vertex v_0, and each vertex on the perimeter of the octagon is shared by two triangles. In general, the number of duplicate vertices increases as the detail and complexity of the model increases.

There are two reasons why we do not want to duplicate vertices:

1. Increased memory requirements. (Why store the same vertex data more than once?)

2. Increased processing by the graphics hardware. (Why process the same vertex data more than once?)

Triangle strips can help the duplicate vertex problem in some situations, provided the geometry can be organized in a strip-like fashion. However, triangle lists are more flexible (the triangles need not be connected), and so it is worth devising a method to remove duplicate vertices for triangle lists. The solution is to use *indices*. It works like this: We create a vertex list and an index list. The vertex list consists of all the *unique* vertices and the index list contains values that index into the vertex list to define how the vertices are to be put together to form triangles. Returning to the shapes in Figure 5.16, the vertex list of the quad would be constructed as follows:

```
Vertex v[4] = {v0, v1, v2, v3};
```

Then the index list needs to define how the vertices in the vertex list are to be put together to form the two triangles.

```
UINT indexList[6] = {0, 1, 2,  // Triangle 0
                     0, 2, 3}; // Triangle 1
```

In the index list, every three elements define a triangle. So the previous index list says, "form triangle 0 by using the vertices v[0], v[1], and v[2], and form triangle 1 by using the vertices v[0], v[2], and v[3]."

Similarly, the vertex list for the circle would be constructed as follows:

```
Vertex v [9] = {v0, v1, v2, v3, v4, v5, v6, v7, v8};
```

and the index list would be:

```
UINT indexList[24] = {
    0, 1, 2,   // Triangle 0
    0, 2, 3,   // Triangle 1
    0, 3, 4,   // Triangle 2
    0, 4, 5,   // Triangle 3
    0, 5, 6,   // Triangle 4
    0, 6, 7,   // Triangle 5
    0, 7, 8,   // Triangle 6
    0, 8, 1    // Triangle 7
};
```

After the unique vertices in the vertex list are processed, the graphics card can use the index list to put the vertices together to form the triangles. Observe that we have moved the "duplication" over to the index list, but this is not bade because of the following:

1. Indices are simply integers and do not take up as much memory as a full vertex structure (and vertex structures can get big as we add more components to them).

2. With good vertex cache ordering, the graphics hardware won't have to process duplicate vertices (too often).

5.6 THE VERTEX SHADER STAGE

After the primitives have been assembled, the vertices are fed into the vertex shader stage. The vertex shader can be thought of as a function that inputs a vertex and outputs a vertex. Every vertex drawn will be pumped through the vertex shader; in fact, we can conceptually think of the following happening on the hardware:

```
for(UINT i = 0; i < numVertices; ++i)
    outputVertex[i] = VertexShader (inputVertex[i]);
```

The vertex shader function is something we implement, but it is executed by the GPU for each vertex, so it is very fast.

Many special effects can be done in the vertex shader such as transformations, lighting, and displacement mapping. Remember that not only do we have access to the input vertex data, but we also can access textures and other data stored in GPU memory such as transformation matrices and scene lights.

We will see many examples of different vertex shaders throughout this book; so by the end, you should have a good idea of what can be done with them. For our first code example, however, we will just use the vertex shader to transform vertices. The following subsections explain the kind of transformations that generally need to be done.

5.6.1 Local Space and World Space

Suppose for a moment that you are working on a film and your team has to construct a miniature version of a train scene for some special effect shots. In particular, suppose that you are tasked with making a small bridge. Now, you would not construct the bridge in the middle of the scene, where you would likely have to work from a difficult angle and be careful not to mess up the other miniatures that compose the scene. Instead, you would work on the bridge at your workbench away from the scene. Then, when it is all done, you would place the bridge at its correct position and angle in the scene.

3D artists do something similar when constructing 3D objects. Instead of building an object's geometry with coordinates relative to a global scene coordinate system (*world space*), they specify them relative to a local coordinate system (*local space*); the local coordinate system will usually be some convenient coordinate system located near the object and axis-aligned with the object. Once the vertices of the 3D model have been defined in local space, it is placed in the global scene. In order to do this, we must define how the local space and world space are related; this is done by specifying where we want the origin and axes of the local space coordinate system relative to the global scene coordinate system, and executing a change of coordinate transformation (see Figure 5.16 and recall §3.4). The process of changing coordinates relative to a local coordinate system into the global scene coordinate system is called the *world transform*, and the corresponding matrix is called the *world matrix*. Each object in the scene has its own world matrix. After each object has been transformed from its local space to the world space, then all the coordinates of all the objects are relative to the same coordinate system (the world space). If you want to define an object directly in the world space, then you can supply an identity world matrix.

Defining each model relative to its own local coordinate system has several advantages:

1. It is easier. For instance, usually in local space the object will be centered at the origin and symmetrical with respect to one of the major axes. As another example, the vertices of a cube are much easier to specify if we choose a local coordinate system with origin centered at the cube and with axes orthogonal to the cube faces; see Figure 5.17.

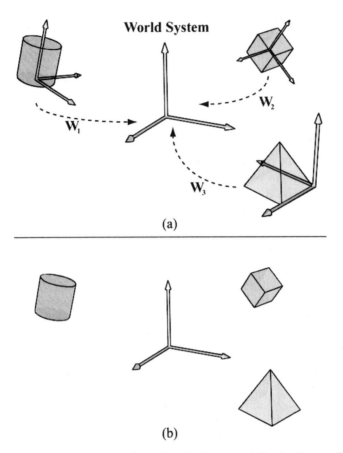

Figure 5.16. (a) The vertices of each object are defined with coordinates relative to their own local coordinate system. In addition, we define the position and orientation of each local coordinate system relative to the world space coordinate system based on where we want the object in the scene. Then we execute a change of coordinate transformation to make all coordinates relative to the world space system. (b) After the world transform, the objects' vertices have coordinates all relative to the same world system.

2. The object may be reused across multiple scenes, in which case it makes no sense to hardcode the object's coordinates relative to a particular scene. Instead, it is better to store its coordinates relative to a local coordinate system and then define, via a change of coordinate matrix, how the local coordinate system and world coordinate system are related for each scene.

3. Finally, sometimes we draw the same object more than once in a scene, but in different positions, orientations, and scales (e.g., a tree object may be reused several times to build a forest). It would be wasteful to duplicate the object's vertex and index data for each instance. Instead, we store a single copy of the

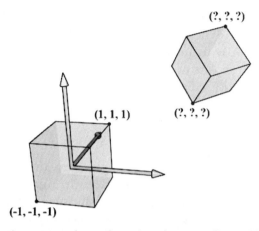

Figure 5.17. The vertices of a cube are easily specified when the cube is centered at the origin and axis-aligned with the coordinate system. It is not so easy to specify the coordinates when the cube is at an arbitrary position and orientation with respect to the coordinate system. Therefore, when we construct the geometry of an object, we usually always choose a convenient coordinate system near the object and aligned with the object, from which to build the object around.

geometry (i.e., vertex and index lists) relative to its local space. Then we draw the object several times, but each time with a different world matrix to specify the position, orientation, and scale of the instance in the world space. This is called *instancing*.

As §3.4.3 shows, the world matrix for an object is given by describing its local space with coordinates relative to the world space, and placing these coordinates in the rows of a matrix. If $\mathbf{Q}_w = (Q_x, Q_y, Q_z, 1)$, $\mathbf{u}_w = (u_x, u_y, u_z, 0)$, $\mathbf{v}_w = (v_x, v_y, v_z, 0)$, and $\mathbf{w}_w = (w_x, w_y, w_z, 0)$ describe, respectively, the origin, x-, y-, and z-axes of a local space with homogeneous coordinates relative to world space, then we know from §3.4.3 that the change of coordinate matrix from local space to world space is:

$$\mathbf{W} = \begin{bmatrix} u_x & u_y & u_z & 0 \\ v_x & v_y & v_z & 0 \\ w_x & w_y & w_z & 0 \\ Q_x & Q_y & Q_z & 1 \end{bmatrix}$$

We see that to construct a world matrix, we must directly figure out the coordinates of the local space origin and axes relative to the world space. This is sometimes not that easy or intuitive. A more common approach is to define $\mathbf{W}$ as a sequence of transformations, say $\mathbf{W} = \mathbf{SRT}$, the product of a scaling matrix $\mathbf{S}$ to scale the object into the world, followed by a rotation matrix $\mathbf{R}$ to define the orientation of the local space relative to the world space, followed by a translation matrix **T** to define the origin of the local space relative to the world space. From §3.5, we know that this sequence of transformations may be interpreted as a change of coordinate transformation, and that the row vectors of **W** = **SRT** store the homogeneous coordinates of the x-axis, y-axis, z-axis, and origin of the local space relative to the world space.

☞ Example

Suppose we have a unit square defined relative to some local space with minimum and maximum points $(-0.5, 0, -0.5)$ and $(0.5, 0, 0.5)$, respectively. Find the world matrix such that the square has a length of 2 in world space, the square is rotated 45° clockwise in the xz-plane of the world space, and the square is positioned at $(10, 0, 10)$ in world space. We construct **S**, **R**, **T**, and **W** as follows:

$$\mathbf{S} = \begin{bmatrix} 2 & 0 & 0 & 0 \\ 0 & 1 & 0 & 0 \\ 0 & 0 & 2 & 0 \\ 0 & 0 & 0 & 1 \end{bmatrix} \quad \mathbf{R} = \begin{bmatrix} \sqrt{2}/2 & 0 & -\sqrt{2}/2 & 0 \\ 0 & 1 & 0 & 0 \\ \sqrt{2}/2 & 0 & \sqrt{2}/2 & 0 \\ 0 & 0 & 0 & 1 \end{bmatrix} \quad \mathbf{T} = \begin{bmatrix} 1 & 0 & 0 & 0 \\ 0 & 1 & 0 & 0 \\ 0 & 0 & 1 & 0 \\ 10 & 0 & 10 & 1 \end{bmatrix}$$

$$\mathbf{W} = \mathbf{SRT} = \begin{bmatrix} \sqrt{2} & 0 & -\sqrt{2} & 0 \\ 0 & 1 & 0 & 0 \\ \sqrt{2} & 0 & \sqrt{2} & 0 \\ 10 & 0 & 10 & 1 \end{bmatrix}$$

Now from §3.5, the rows in **W** describe the local coordinate system relative to the world space; that is, $\mathbf{u}_W = \left(\sqrt{2}, 0, -\sqrt{2}, 0\right)$, $\mathbf{v}_W = (0, 1, 0, 0)$, $\mathbf{w}_W = \left(\sqrt{2}, 0, \sqrt{2}, 0\right)$, and $\mathbf{Q}_w = (10, 0, 10, 1)$. When we change coordinates from the local space to the world space with **W**, the square ends up in the desired place in world space (see Figure 5.18).

$$\begin{bmatrix} -0.5, & 0, & -0.5, & 1 \end{bmatrix} \mathbf{W} = \begin{bmatrix} 10 - \sqrt{2}, & 0, & 0, & 1 \end{bmatrix}$$

$$\begin{bmatrix} -0.5, & 0, & +0.5, & 1 \end{bmatrix} \mathbf{W} = \begin{bmatrix} 0, & 0, & 10 + \sqrt{2}, & 1 \end{bmatrix}$$

$$\begin{bmatrix} +0.5, & 0, & +0.5, & 1 \end{bmatrix} \mathbf{W} = \begin{bmatrix} 10 + \sqrt{2}, & 0, & 0, & 1 \end{bmatrix}$$

$$\begin{bmatrix} +0.5, & 0, & -0.5, & 1 \end{bmatrix} \mathbf{W} = \begin{bmatrix} 0, & 0, & 10 - \sqrt{2}, & 1 \end{bmatrix}$$

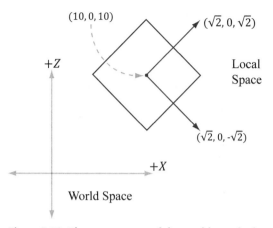

Figure 5.18. The row vectors of the world matrix describe the local coordinate system with coordinates relative to the world coordinate system.

The point of this example is that instead of figuring out $\mathbf{Q}_w$, $\mathbf{u}_w$, $\mathbf{v}_w$, and $\mathbf{w}_w$ directly to form the world matrix, we were able to construct the world matrix by compositing a sequence of simple transforms. This is often much easier than figuring out $\mathbf{Q}_w$, $\mathbf{u}_w$, $\mathbf{v}_w$, and $\mathbf{w}_w$ directly, as we need only ask: what size do we want the object in world space, at what orientation do we want the object in world space, and at what position do we want the object in world space.

Another way to consider the world transform is to just take the local space coordinates and treat them as world space coordinates (this is equivalent to using an identity matrix as the world transform). Thus if the object is modeled at the center of its local space, the object is just at the center of the world space. In general, the center of the world is probably not where we want to position all of our objects. So now, for each object, just apply a sequence of transformations to scale, rotation, and position the object where you want in the world space. Mathematically, this will give the same world transform as building the change of coordinate matrix from local space to world space.

5.6.2 View Space

In order to form a 2D image of the scene, we must place a virtual camera in the scene. The camera specifies what volume of the world the viewer can see and thus what volume of the world we need to generate a 2D image of. Let us attach a local coordinate system (called *view space*, *eye space*, or *camera space*) to the camera as shown in Figure 5.19; that is, the camera sits at the origin looking down the positive z-axis, the x-axis aims to the right of the camera, and the y-axis aims above the camera. Instead of describing our scene vertices relative to the world space, it

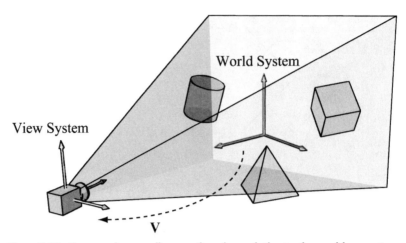

Figure 5.19. **Convert the coordinates of vertices relative to the world space to make them relative to the camera space.**

is convenient for later stages of the rendering pipeline to describe them relative to the camera coordinate system The change of coordinate transformation from world space to view space is called the *view transform*, and the corresponding matrix is called the *view matrix*.

If $\mathbf{Q}_w = (Q_x, Q_y, Q_z, 1)$, $\mathbf{u}_w = (u_x, u_y, u_z, 0)$, $\mathbf{v}_w = (v_x, v_y, v_z, 0)$, and $\mathbf{w}_w = (w_x, w_y, w_z, 0)$ describe, respectively, the origin, x-, y-, and z-axes of view space with homogeneous coordinates relative to world space, then we know from §3.4.3 that the change of coordinate matrix from view space to world space is:

$$\mathbf{W} = \begin{bmatrix} u_x & u_y & u_z & 0 \\ v_x & v_y & v_z & 0 \\ w_x & w_y & w_z & 0 \\ Q_x & Q_y & Q_z & 1 \end{bmatrix}$$

However, this is not the transformation we want. We want the reverse transformation from world space to view space. But recall from §3.4.5 that reverse transformation is just given by the inverse. Thus. $\mathbf{W}^{-1}$ transforms from world space to view space.

The world coordinate system and view coordinate system generally differ by position and orientation only, so it makes intuitive sense that $\mathbf{W} = \mathbf{RT}$ (i.e., the world matrix can be decomposed into a rotation followed by a translation). This form makes the inverse easier to compute:

$$\mathbf{V} = \mathbf{W}^{-1} = (\mathbf{RT})^{-1} = \mathbf{T}^{-1}\mathbf{R}^{-1} = \mathbf{T}^{-1}\mathbf{R}^{T}$$

$$
= \begin{bmatrix} 1 & 0 & 0 & 0 \\ 0 & 1 & 0 & 0 \\ 0 & 0 & 1 & 0 \\ -Q_x & -Q_y & -Q_z & 1 \end{bmatrix} \begin{bmatrix} u_x & v_x & w_x & 0 \\ u_y & v_y & w_y & 0 \\ u_z & v_z & w_z & 0 \\ 0 & 0 & 0 & 1 \end{bmatrix} = \begin{bmatrix} u_x & v_x & w_x & 0 \\ u_y & v_y & w_y & 0 \\ u_z & v_z & w_z & 0 \\ -Q \cdot u & -Q \cdot v & -Q \cdot w & 1 \end{bmatrix}
$$

So the view matrix has the form:

$$
V = \begin{bmatrix} u_x & v_x & w_x & 0 \\ u_y & v_y & w_y & 0 \\ u_z & v_z & w_z & 0 \\ -Q \cdot u & -Q \cdot v & -Q \cdot w & 1 \end{bmatrix}
$$

We now show an intuitive way to construct the vectors needed to build the view matrix. Let Q be the position of the camera and let T be the target point the camera is aimed at. Furthermore, let j be the unit vector that describes the "up" direction of the world space. (In this book, we use the world xz-plane as our world "ground plane" and the world y-axis describes the "up" direction; therefore, $j = (0,1,0)$ is just a unit vector parallel to the world y-axis. However, this is just a convention, and some applications might choose the xy-plane as the ground plane, and the z-axis as the "up" direction.) Referring to Figure 5.20, the direction the camera is looking is given by:

$$
w = \frac{T - Q}{\| T - Q \|}
$$

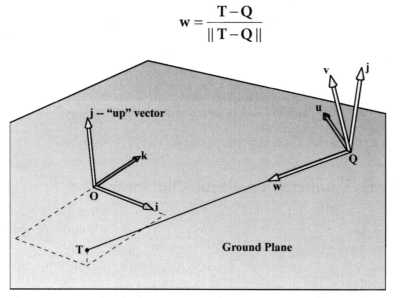

Figure 5.20. Constructing the camera coordinate system given the camera position, a target point, and a world "up" vector.

This vector describes the local z-axis of the camera. A unit vector that aims to the "right" of $\mathbf{w}$ is given by:

$$\mathbf{u} = \frac{\mathbf{j} \times \mathbf{w}}{\| \mathbf{j} \times \mathbf{w} \|}$$

This vector describes the local x-axis of the camera. Finally, a vector that describes the local y-axis of the camera is given by:

$$\mathbf{v} = \mathbf{w} \times \mathbf{u}$$

Since $\mathbf{w}$ and $\mathbf{u}$ are orthogonal unit vectors, $\mathbf{w} \times \mathbf{u}$ is necessarily a unit vector, and so it does not need to be normalized.

Thus, given the position of the camera, the target point, and the world "up" direction, we were able to derive the local coordinate system of the camera, which can be used to form the view matrix.

The XNA Math library provides the following function for computing the view matrix based on the just described process:

```
XMMATRIX XMMatrixLookAtLH(     // Outputs resulting view matrix V
    FXMVECTOR EyePosition,     // Input camera position Q
    FXMVECTOR FocusPosition,   // Input target point T
    FXMVECTOR UpDirection);    // Input world up vector j
```

Usually the world's y-axis corresponds to the "up" direction, so the "up" vector is almost always $\mathbf{j} = (0,1,0)$. As an example, suppose we want to position the camera at the point $(5, 3, -10)$ relative to the world space, and have the camera look at the origin of the world $(0, 0, 0)$. We can build the view matrix by writing:

```
XMVECTOR pos    = XMVectorSet(5, 3, -10, 1.0f);
XMVECTOR target = XMVectorZero();
XMVECTOR up     = XMVectorSet(0.0f, 1.0f, 0.0f, 0.0f);

XMMATRIX V = XMMatrixLookAtLH(pos, target, up);
```

5.6.3 Projection and Homogeneous Clip Space

So far we have described the position and orientation of the camera in the world, but there is another component to a camera, which is the volume of space the camera sees. This volume is described by a frustum (Figure 5.21).

Our next task is to project the 3D geometry inside the frustum onto a 2D projection window. The projection must be done in such a way that parallel lines converge to a vanishing point, and as the 3D depth of an object increases, the size of its projection diminishes; a perspective projection does this, and is illustrated in

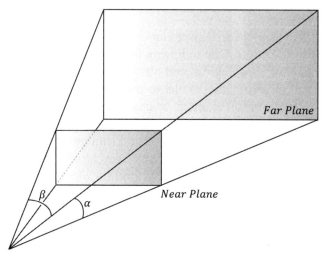

Figure 5.21. A frustum defines the volume of space that the camera "sees."

Figure 5.22. We call the line from a vertex to the eye point the *vertex's line of projection*. Then we define the *perspective projection transformation* as the transformation that transforms a 3D vertex **v** to the point **v′** where its line of projection intersects the 2D projection plane; we say that **v′** is the projection of **v**. The projection of a 3D object refers to the projection of all the vertices that make up the object.

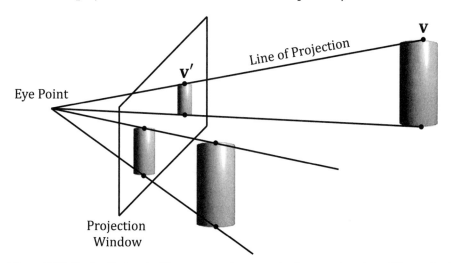

Figure 5.22. Both cylinders in 3D space are the same size but are placed at different depths. The projection of the cylinder closer to the eye is bigger than the projection of the farther cylinder. Geometry inside the frustum is projected onto a projection window; geometry outside the frustum gets projected onto the projection plane but will lie outside the projection window.

5.6.3.1 Defining a Frustum

We can define a frustum in view space, with center of projection at the origin and looking down the positive z-axis, by the following four quantities: a near plane n, far plane f, vertical field of view angle a, and aspect ratio r. Note that in view space, the near plane and far plane are parallel to the xy-plane; thus we simply specify their distance from the origin along the z-axis. The aspect ratio is defined by $r = w/h$ where w is the width of the projection window and h is the height of the projection window (units in view space). The projection window is essentially the 2D image of the scene in view space. The image here will eventually be mapped to the back buffer; therefore, we like the ratio of the projection window dimensions to be the same as the ratio of the back buffer dimensions. So the ratio of the back buffer dimensions is usually specified as the aspect ratio (it is a ratio so it has no units). For example, if the back buffer dimensions are 800×600, then we specify $r = \frac{800}{600} \approx 1.333$. If the aspect ratio of the projection window and the back buffer were not the same, then a nonuniform scaling would be necessary to map the projection window to the back buffer, which would cause distortion (e.g., a circle on the projection window might get stretched into an ellipse when mapped to the back buffer).

We label the horizontal field of view angle β, and it is determined by the vertical field of view angle α and aspect ratio r. To see how r helps us find β, consider Figure 5.23. Note that the actual dimensions of the projection window are not

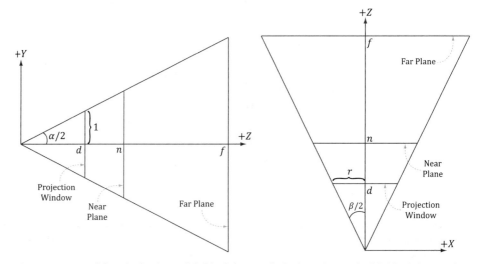

Figure 5.23. Deriving the horizontal field of view angle β given the vertical field of view angle α and the aspect ratio r.

important, just the aspect ratio needs to be maintained. Therefore, we will choose the convenient height of 2, and thus the width must be:

$$r = \frac{w}{h} = \frac{w}{2} \Rightarrow w = 2r$$

In order to have the specified vertical field of view α, the projection window must be placed a distance d from the origin:

$$\tan\left(\frac{\alpha}{2}\right) = \frac{1}{d} \Rightarrow d = \cot\left(\frac{\alpha}{2}\right)$$

We have now fixed the distance d of the projection window along the z-axis to have a vertical field of view α when the height of the projection window is 2. Now we can solve for β. Looking at the xz-plane in Figure 5.23, we now see that:

$$\tan\left(\frac{\beta}{2}\right) = \frac{r}{d} = \frac{r}{\cot\left(\frac{\alpha}{2}\right)}$$

$$= r \cdot \tan\left(\frac{\alpha}{2}\right)$$

So given the vertical field of view angle a and the aspect ratio r, we can always get the horizontal field of view angle β:

$$\beta = 2\tan^{-1}\left(r \cdot \tan\left(\frac{\alpha}{2}\right)\right)$$

5.6.3.2 Projecting Vertices

Refer to Figure 5.24. Given a point (x, y, z), we wish to find its projection (x', y', d) on the projection plane $z = d$. By considering the x- and y-coordinates separately and using similar triangles, we find:

$$\frac{x'}{d} = \frac{x}{z} \Rightarrow x' = \frac{xd}{z} = \frac{x\cot(\alpha/2)}{z} = \frac{x}{z\tan(\alpha/2)}$$

and

$$\frac{y'}{d} = \frac{y}{z} \Rightarrow y' = \frac{yd}{z} = \frac{y\cot(\alpha/2)}{z} = \frac{y}{z\tan(\alpha/2)}$$

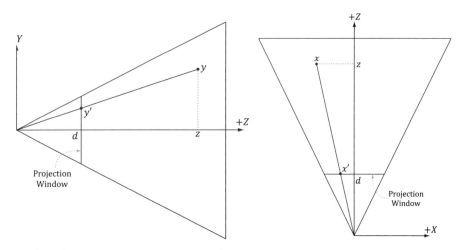

Figure 5.24. Similar triangles.

Observe that a point (x, y, z) is inside the frustum if and only if

$$-r \le x' \le r$$
$$-1 \le y' \le 1$$
$$n \le z \le f$$

5.6.3.3 Normalized Device Coordinates (NDC)

The coordinates of the projected points in the preceding section are computed in view space. In view space, the projection window has a height of 2 and a width of $2r$, where r is the aspect ratio. The problem with this is that the dimensions depend on the aspect ratio. This means we would need to tell the hardware the aspect ratio, since the hardware will later need to do some operations that involve the dimensions of the projection window (such as map it to the back buffer). It would be more convenient if we could remove this dependency on the aspect ratio. The solution is to scale the projected x-coordinate from the interval $[-r, r]$ to $[-1, 1]$ like so:

$$-r \le x' \le r$$
$$-1 \le x'/r \le 1$$

After this mapping, the x- and y-coordinates are said to be *normalized device coordinates* (NDC) (the z-coordinate has not yet been normalized), and a point (x, y, z) is inside the frustum if and only if

$$-1 \le x'/r \le 1$$
$$-1 \le y' \le 1$$
$$n \le z \le f$$

The transformation from view space to NDC space can be viewed as a unit conversion. We have the relationship that one NDC unit equals r units in view space (i.e., 1 ndc = r vs) on the x-axis. So given x view space units, we can use this relationship to convert units:

$$x\,\text{vs}\cdot\frac{1\,\text{ndc}}{r\,\text{vs}}=\frac{x}{r}\,\text{ndc}$$

We can modify our projection formulas to give us the projected x- and y-coordinates directly in NDC coordinates:

$$x'=\frac{x}{rz\tan(\alpha/2)}$$

$$y'=\frac{y}{z\tan(\alpha/2)} \qquad\qquad \text{(eq. 5.1)}$$

Note that in NDC coordinates, the projection window has a height of 2 and a width of 2. So now the dimensions are fixed, and the hardware need not know the aspect ratio, but it is our responsibility to always supply the projected coordinates in NDC space (the graphics hardware assumes we will).

5.6.3.4 Writing the Projection Equation with a Matrix

For uniformity, we would like to express the projection transformation by a matrix. However, Equation 5.1 is nonlinear, so it does not have a matrix representation. The "trick" is to separate it into two parts: a linear part and a nonlinear part. The nonlinear part is the divide by z. As will be discussed in the next section, we are going to normalize the z-coordinate; this means we will not have the original z-coordinate around for the divide. Therefore, we must save the input z-coordinate before it is transformed; to do this, we take advantage of homogeneous coordinates, and copy the input z-coordinate to the output w-coordinate. In terms of matrix multiplication, this is done by setting entry [2][3] = 1 and entry [3][3] = 0 (zero-based indices). Our projection matrix looks like this:

$$\mathbf{P}=\begin{bmatrix} \dfrac{1}{r\tan(\alpha/2)} & 0 & 0 & 0 \\[2mm] 0 & \dfrac{1}{\tan(\alpha/2)} & 0 & 0 \\[2mm] 0 & 0 & A & 1 \\[2mm] 0 & 0 & B & 0 \end{bmatrix}$$

Note that we have placed constants (to be determined in the next section) A and B into the matrix; these constants will be used to transform the input z-coordinate into the normalized range Multiplying an arbitrary point $(x, y, z, 1)$ by this matrix gives:

$$
[x, y, z, 1]
\begin{bmatrix}
\dfrac{1}{r\tan(\alpha/2)} & 0 & 0 & 0 \\
0 & \dfrac{1}{\tan(\alpha/2)} & 0 & 0 \\
0 & 0 & A & 1 \\
0 & 0 & B & 0
\end{bmatrix}
=
\left[\dfrac{x}{r\tan(\alpha/2)}, \dfrac{y}{\tan(\alpha/2)}, Az + B, z \right]
$$

(eq. 5.2)

After multiplying by the projection matrix (the linear part), we complete the transformation by dividing each coordinate by $w = z$ (the nonlinear part):

$$
\left[\dfrac{x}{r\tan(\alpha/2)}, \dfrac{y}{\tan(\alpha/2)}, Az + B, z \right] \xrightarrow{\text{divide by } w} \left[\dfrac{x}{rz\tan(\alpha/2)}, \dfrac{y}{z\tan(\alpha/2)}, A + \dfrac{B}{z}, 1 \right]
$$

(eq. 5.3)

Incidentally, you may wonder about a possible divide by zero; however, the near plane should be greater than zero, so such a point would be clipped (§5.9). The divide by w is sometimes called the *perspective divide* or *homogeneous divide*. We see that the projected x- and y-coordinates agree with Equation 5.1.

5.6.3.5 Normalized Depth Value

It may seem like after projection, we can discard the original 3D z-coordinate, as all the projected points now lay on the 2D projection window, which forms the 2D image seen by the eye. However, we still need 3D depth information around for the depth buffering algorithm. Just like Direct3D wants the projected x- and y-coordinates in a normalized range, Direct3D wants the depth coordinates in the normalized range $[0, 1]$. Therefore, we must construct an order preserving function $g(z)$ that maps the interval $[n, f]$ onto $[0, 1]$. Because the function is order preserving, if $z_1, z_2 \in [n, f]$ and $z_1 < z_2$, then $g(z_1) < g(z_2)$; so even though the depth values have been transformed, the relative depth relationships remain intact, so we can still correctly compare depths in the normalized interval, which is all we need for the depth buffering algorithm.

Mapping $[n, f]$ onto $[0, 1]$ can be done with a scaling and translation. However, this approach will not integrate into our current projection strategy. We see from Equation 5.3 that the z-coordinate undergoes the transformation:

$$g(z) = A + \frac{B}{z}$$

We now need to choose A and B subject to the constraints:

Condition 1: $g(n) = A + B/n = 0$ (the near plane gets mapped to zero)
Condition 2: $g(f) = A + B/f = 1$ (the far plane gets mapped to one)

Solving condition 1 for B yields: $B = -An$. Substituting this into condition 2 and solving for A gives:

$$A + \frac{-An}{f} = 1$$

$$\frac{Af - An}{f} = 1$$

$$Af - An = f$$

$$A = \frac{f}{f - n}$$

Therefore,

$$g(z) = \frac{f}{f - n} - \frac{nf}{(f - n)z}$$

A graph of g (Figure 5.25) shows it is strictly increasing (order preserving) and nonlinear. It also shows that most of the range is "used up" by depth values close to the near plane. Consequently, the majority of the depth values get mapped to a small subset of the range. This can lead to depth buffer precision problems (the computer can no longer distinguish between slightly different transformed depth values due to finite numerical representation). The general advice is to make the near and far planes as close as possible to minimize depth precision problems.

Now that we have solved for A and B, we can state the full *perspective projection matrix*:

$$\mathbf{P} = \begin{bmatrix} \dfrac{1}{r\tan(\alpha/2)} & 0 & 0 & 0 \\ 0 & \dfrac{1}{\tan(\alpha/2)} & 0 & 0 \\ 0 & 0 & \dfrac{f}{f-n} & 1 \\ 0 & 0 & \dfrac{-nf}{f-n} & 0 \end{bmatrix}$$

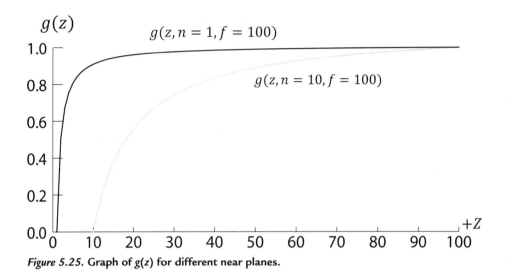

Figure 5.25. Graph of g(z) for different near planes.

After multiplying by the projection matrix, but before the perspective divide, geometry is said to be in *homogeneous clip space* or *projection space*. After the perspective divide, the geometry is said to be in normalized device coordinates (NDC).

5.6.3.6 **XMMatrixPerspectiveFovLH**

A perspective projection matrix can be built with the following XNA Math function:

```
XMMATRIX XMMatrixPerspectiveFovLH( // returns projection matrix
    FLOAT FovAngleY,    // vertical field of view angle in radians
    FLOAT AspectRatio, // aspect ratio = width / height
    FLOAT NearZ,        // distance to near plane
    FLOAT FarZ);        // distance to far plane
```

The following code snippet illustrates how to use **D3DXMatrixPerspectiveFovLH**. Here, we specify a 45° vertical field of view, a near plane at $z = 1$, and a far plane at $z = 1000$ (these lengths are in view space).

```
XMMATRIX P = XMMatrixPerspectiveFovLH(0.25f*MathX::Pi,
    AspectRatio(), 1.0f, 1000.0f);
```

The aspect ratio is taken to match our window aspect ratio:

```
float D3DApp::AspectRatio()const
{
    return static_cast<float>(mClientWidth) / mClientHeight;
}
```

5.7 THE TESSELLATION STAGES

Tessellation refers to subdividing the triangles of a mesh to add new triangles. These new triangles can then be offset into new positions to create finer mesh detail (see Figure 5.26).

There are a number of benefits to tessellations:

1. We can implement a level-of-detail (LOD) mechanism, where triangles near the camera are tessellated to add more detail, and triangles far away from the camera are not tessellated. In this way, we only use more triangles where the extra detail will be noticed.

2. We keep a simpler *low-poly* mesh (low-poly means low triangle count) in memory, and add the extra triangles on the fly, thus saving memory.

3. We do operations like animation and physics on a simpler low-poly mesh, and only use the tessellated high-poly mesh for rendering.

The tessellation stages are new to Direct3D 11, and they provide a way to tessellate geometry on the GPU. Before Direct3D 11, if you wanted to implement a form of tessellation, it would have to be done on the CPU, and then the new tessellated geometry would have to be uploaded back to the GPU for rendering. However, uploading new geometry from CPU memory to GPU memory is slow, and it also burdens the CPU with computing the tessellation. For this reason, tessellation methods have not been very popular for real-time graphics prior to Direct3D 11. Direct3D 11 provides an API to do tessellation completely in hardware with a Direct3D 11 capable video card. This makes tessellation a much more attractive technique. The tessellation stages are optional (you only need to use it if you want tessellation). We defer our coverage of tessellation until Chapter 13.

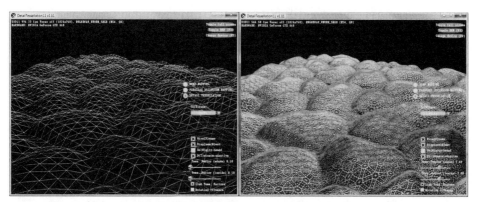

Figure 5.26. **The left image shows the original mesh. The right image shows the mesh after tessellation.**

5.8 THE GEOMETRY SHADER STAGE

The geometry shader stage is optional, and we do not use it until Chapter 11, so we will be brief here. The geometry shader inputs entire primitives. For example, if we were drawing triangle lists, then the input to the geometry shader would be the three vertices defining the triangle. (Note that the three vertices will have already passed through the vertex shader.) The main advantage of the geometry shader is that it can create or destroy geometry. For example, the input primitive can be expanded into one or more other primitives, or the geometry shader can choose not to output a primitive based on some condition. This is in contrast to a vertex shader, which cannot create vertices: it inputs one vertex and outputs one vertex. A common example of the geometry shader is to expand a point into a quad or to expand a line into a quad.

We also notice the "stream-out" arrow from Figure 5.11. That is, the geometry shader can stream-out vertex data into a buffer in memory, which can later be drawn. This is an advanced technique, and will be discussed in a later chapter.

Note: *Vertex positions leaving the geometry shader must be transformed to homogeneous clip space.*

5.9 CLIPPING

Geometry completely outside the viewing frustum needs to be discarded, and geometry that intersects the boundary of the frustum must be clipped, so that only the interior part remains; see Figure 5.27 for the idea illustrated in 2D.

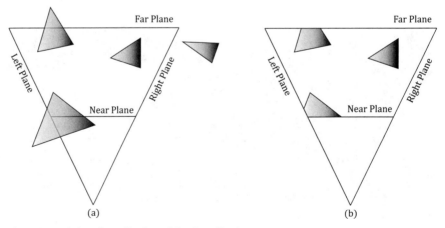

Figure 5.27. (a) Before clipping. (b) After clipping.

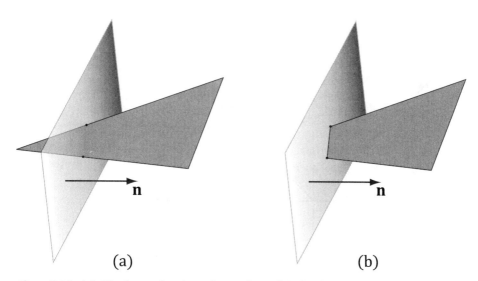

Figure 5.28. (a) Clipping a triangle against a plane. (b) The clipped triangle. Note that the clipped triangle is not a triangle, but a quad. Thus the hardware will need to triangulate the resulting quad, which is straightforward to do for convex polygons.

We can think of the frustum as being the region bounded by six planes: the top, bottom, left, right, near, and far planes. To clip a polygon against the frustum, we clip it against each frustum plane one by one. When clipping a polygon against a plane (Figure 5.28), the part in the positive half space of the plane is kept, and the part in the negative half space is discarded. Clipping a convex polygon against a plane will always result in a convex polygon. Because the hardware does clipping for us, we will not cover the details here; instead, we refer the reader to the popular Sutherland-Hodgeman clipping algorithm [Sutherland74]. It basically amounts to finding the intersection points between the plane and polygon edges, and then ordering the vertices to form the new clipped polygon.

[Blinn78] describes how clipping can be done in 4D homogeneous space (Figure 5.29). After the perspective divide, points $\left(\frac{x}{w}, \frac{y}{w}, \frac{z}{w}, 1\right)$ inside the view frustum are in normalized device coordinates and bounded as follows:

$$-1 \le x / w \le 1$$
$$-1 \le y / w \le 1$$
$$0 \le z / w \le 1$$

So in homogeneous clip space, before the divide, 4D points (x, y, z, w) inside the frustum are bounded as follows:

$$-w \le x \le w$$
$$-w \le y \le w$$
$$0 \le z \le w$$

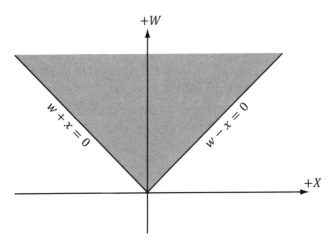

Figure 5.29. **The frustum boundaries in the *xw*-plane in homogeneous clip space.**

That is, the points are bounded by the simple 4D planes:

Left: $w = -x$
Right: $w = x$
Bottom: $w = -y$
Top: $w = y$
Near: $z = 0$
Far: $z = w$

Once we know the frustum plane equations in homogeneous space, we can apply a clipping algorithm (such as Sutherland-Hodgeman). Note that the mathematics of the segment/plane intersection test generalizes to $\mathbb{R}^4$, so we can do the test with 4D points and the 4D planes in homogeneous clip space.

5.10 THE RASTERIZATION STAGE

The main job of the rasterization stage is to compute pixel colors from the projected 3D triangles.

5.10.1 Viewport Transform

After clipping, the hardware can do the perspective divide to transform from homogeneous clip space to normalized device coordinates (NDC). Once vertices are in NDC space, the 2D x- and y- coordinates forming the 2D image are transformed to a rectangle on the back buffer called the viewport (recall §4.2.8). After this transform, the x- and y-coordinates are in units of pixels. Usually the viewport transformation does not modify the z-coordinate, as it is used for depth buffering, but it can by modifying the `MinDepth` and `MaxDepth` values of the `D3D11_VIEWPORT` structure. The `MinDepth` and `MaxDepth` values must be between 0 and 1.

5.10.2 Backface Culling

A triangle has two sides. To distinguish between the two sides we use the following convention. If the triangle vertices are ordered v_0, v_1, v_2 then we compute the triangle normal $\mathbf{n}$ like so:

$$\mathbf{e}_0 = \mathbf{v}_1 - \mathbf{v}_0$$
$$\mathbf{e}_1 = \mathbf{v}_2 - \mathbf{v}_0$$
$$\mathbf{n} = \frac{\mathbf{e}_0 \times \mathbf{e}_1}{\| \mathbf{e}_0 \times \mathbf{e}_1 \|}$$

The side the normal vector emanates from is the *front side* and the other side is the *back side*. Figure 5.30 illustrates this.

We say that a triangle is *front-facing* if the viewer sees the front side of a triangle, and we say a triangle is *back-facing* if the viewer sees the back side of a triangle. From our perspective of Figure 5.30, the left triangle is front-facing while the right triangle is back-facing. Moreover, from our perspective, the left triangle is ordered clockwise while the right triangle is ordered counterclockwise. This is no coincidence: with the convention we have chosen (i.e., the way we compute the triangle normal), a triangle ordered clockwise (with respect to that viewer) is front-facing, and a triangle ordered counterclockwise (with respect to that viewer) is back-facing.

Now, most objects in 3D worlds are enclosed solid objects. Suppose we agree to construct the triangles for each object in such a way that the normals are always

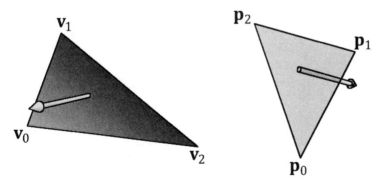

Figure 5.30. The left triangle is front-facing from our viewpoint, and the right triangle is back-facing from our viewpoint.

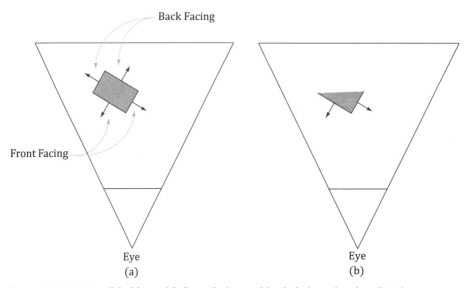

Figure 5.31. (a) A solid object with front-facing and back-facing triangles. (b) The scene after culling the back-facing triangles. Note that backface culling does not affect the final image since the back-facing triangles are occluded by the front-facing ones.

aimed outward. Then, the camera does not see the back-facing triangles of a solid object because the front-facing triangles occlude the back-facing triangles; Figure 5.31 illustrates this in 2D and 5.32 in 3D. Because the front-facing triangles occlude the back-facing triangles, it makes no sense to draw them. *Backface culling* refers to the process of discarding back-facing triangles from the pipeline. This can potentially reduce the amount of triangles that need to be processed by half.

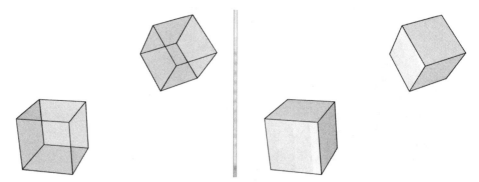

Figure 5.32. (Left) We draw the cubes with transparency so that you can see all six sides. (Right) We draw the cubes as solid blocks. Note that we do not see the three back-facing sides because the three front-facing sides occlude them—thus the back-facing triangles can actually be discarded from further processing and no one will notice.

By default, Direct3D treats triangles with a clockwise winding order (with respect to the viewer) as front-facing, and triangles with a counterclockwise winding order (with respect to the viewer) as back-facing. However, this convention can be reversed with a Direct3D render state setting.

5.10.3 Vertex Attribute Interpolation

Recall that we define a triangle by specifying its vertices. In addition to position, we can attach attributes to vertices such as colors, normal vectors, and texture coordinates. After the viewport transform, these attributes need to be interpolated for each pixel covering the triangle. In addition to vertex attributes, vertex depth values need to get interpolated so that each pixel has a depth value for the depth buffering algorithm. The vertex attributes are interpolated in screen space in such a way that the attributes are interpolated linearly across the triangle in 3D space (Figure 5.33); this requires the so-called *perspective correct interpolation*. Essentially, interpolation allows us to use the vertex values to compute values for the interior pixels.

The mathematical details of perspective correct attribute interpolation is not something we need to worry about since the hardware does it; the interested

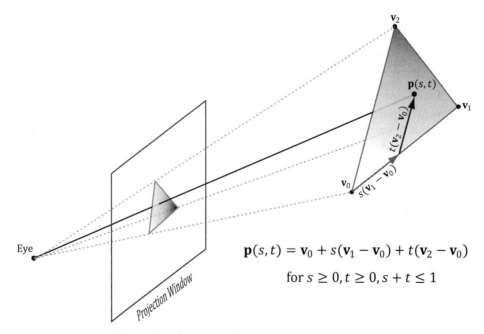

$$\mathbf{p}(s, t) = \mathbf{v}_0 + s(\mathbf{v}_1 - \mathbf{v}_0) + t(\mathbf{v}_2 - \mathbf{v}_0)$$

$$\text{for } s \geq 0, t \geq 0, s + t \leq 1$$

Figure 5.33. An attribute value *p(s, t)* on a triangle can be obtained by linearly interpolating between the attribute values at the vertices of the triangle.

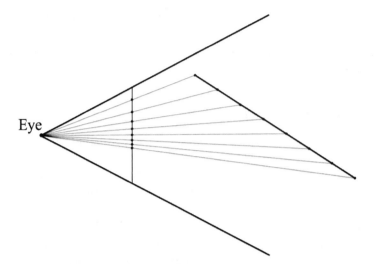

Figure 5.34. **A 3D line is being projected onto the projection window (the projection is a 2D line in screen space). We see that taking uniform step sizes along the 3D line corresponds to taking nonuniform step sizes in 2D screen space. Therefore, to do linear interpolation in 3D space, we need to do nonlinear interpolation in screen space.**

reader may find the mathematical derivation in [Eberly01]. However, Figure 5.34 gives the basic idea of what is going on.

5.11 THE PIXEL SHADER STAGE

Pixel shaders are programs we write that are executed on the GPU. A pixel shader is executed for each pixel fragment and uses the interpolated vertex attributes as input to compute a color. A pixel shader can be as simple as returning a constant color, to doing more complicated things like per-pixel lighting, reflections, and shadowing effects.

5.12 THE OUTPUT MERGER STAGE

After pixel fragments have been generated by the pixel shader, they move onto the output merger (OM) stage of the rendering pipeline. In this stage, some pixel fragments may be rejected (e.g., from the depth or stencil buffer tests). Pixel fragments that are not rejected are written to the back buffer. Blending is also done in this stage, where a pixel may be blended with the pixel currently on the back buffer instead of overriding it completely. Some special effects like transparency are implemented with blending; Chapter 9 is devoted to blending.

5.13 SUMMARY

1. We can simulate 3D scenes on 2D images by employing several techniques based on the way we see things in real life. We observe parallel lines converge to vanishing points, the size of objects diminish with depth, objects obscure the objects behind them, lighting and shading depict the solid form and volume of 3D objects, and shadows imply the location of light sources and indicate the position of objects relative to other objects in the scene.

2. We approximate objects with triangle meshes. We can define each triangle by specifying its three vertices. In many meshes, vertices are shared among triangles; indexed lists can be used to avoid vertex duplication.

3. Colors are described by specifying an intensity of red, green, and blue. The additive mixing of these three colors at different intensities allows us to describe millions of colors. To describe the intensities of red, green, and blue, it is useful to use a normalized range from 0 to 1. Zero denotes no intensity, 1 denotes the full intensity, and intermediate values denote intermediate intensities. It is common to incorporate an additional color component, called the *alpha component*. The alpha component is often used to denote the opacity of a color, which is useful in blending. Including the alpha component means we can represent a color by a 4D color vector (r, g, b, a) where $0 \le r, g, b, a \le 1$. Because the data needed to represent a color is a 4D vector, we can use the **XMVECTOR** type to represent a color in code, and we gain the benefit of SIMD operations whenever we use the XNA Math vector functions to do color operations. To represent a color with 32-bits, a byte is given to each component; the XNA Math library provides the **XMCOLOR** structure for storing a 32-bit color. Color vectors are added, subtracted, and scaled just like regular vectors, except that we must clamp their components to the $[0, 1]$ interval (or $[0, 255]$ for 32-bit colors). The other vector operations such as the dot product and cross product do not make sense for color vectors. The symbol $\otimes$ denotes component-wise multiplication and it is defined as: $(c_1, c_2, c_3, c_4) \otimes (k_1, k_2, k_3, k_4) = (c_1k_1, c_2k_2, c_3k_3, c_4k_4)$.

4. Given a geometric description of a 3D scene and a positioned and aimed virtual camera in that scene, the *rendering pipeline* refers to the entire sequence of steps necessary to generate a 2D image that can be displayed on a monitor screen based on what the virtual camera sees.

5. The rendering pipeline can be broken down into the following major stages. The input assembly (IA) stage; the vertex shader (VS) stage; the tessellation stages; the geometry shader (GS) stage; the clipping stage; the rasterization stage (RS); the pixel shader (PS) stage; and the output merger (OM) stage.

5.14 EXERCISES

1. Construct the vertex and index list of a pyramid, as shown in Figure 5.35.

2. Consider the two shapes shown in Figure 5.36. Merge the objects into one vertex and index list. (The idea here is that when you append the 2nd index list to the first, you will need to update the appended indices since they reference vertices in the original vertex list, not the merged vertex list.)

3. Relative to the world coordinate system, suppose that the camera is positioned at $(-20, 35, -50)$ and looking at the point $(10, 0, 30)$. Compute the view matrix assuming $(0, 1, 0)$ describes the "up" direction in the world.

4. Given that the view frustum has a vertical field of view angle $\theta = 45°$, the aspect ratio is $a = 4/3$, the near plane is $n = 1$, and the far plane is $f = 100$, find the corresponding perspective projection matrix.

5. Suppose that the view window has height 4. Find the distance d from the origin the view window must be to create a vertical field of view angle $\theta = 60°$.

6. Consider the following perspective projection matrix:

$$\begin{bmatrix} 1.86603 & 0 & 0 & 0 \\ 0 & 3.73205 & 0 & 0 \\ 0 & 0 & 1.02564 & 1 \\ 0 & 0 & -5.12821 & 0 \end{bmatrix}$$

Find the vertical field of view angle α, the aspect ratio r, and the near and far plane values that were used to build this matrix.

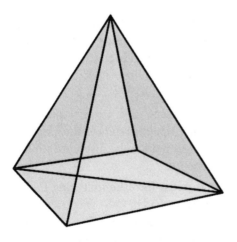

Figure 5.35. **The triangles of a pyramid.**

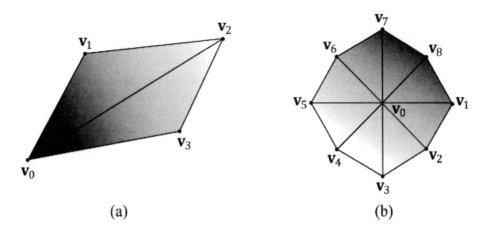

(a)

(b)

Figure 5.36. Shapes for Exercise 2.

7. Suppose that you are given the following perspective projection matrix with fixed A, B, C, D:

$$\begin{bmatrix} A & 0 & 0 & 0 \\ 0 & B & 0 & 0 \\ 0 & 0 & C & 1 \\ 0 & 0 & D & 0 \end{bmatrix}$$

Find the vertical field of view angle α, the aspect ratio r, and the near and far plane values that were used to build this matrix in terms of A, B, C, D. That is, solve the following equations:

$$A = \frac{1}{r\tan(\alpha/2)}$$

$$B = \frac{1}{\tan(\alpha/2)}$$

$$C = \frac{f}{f-n}$$

$$D = \frac{-nf}{f-n}$$

Solving these equations will give you formulas for extracting the vertical field of view angle α, the aspect ratio r, and the near and far plane values from any perspective projection matrix of the kind described in this book.

8. For projective texturing algorithms, we multiply an affine transformation matrix $\mathbf{T}$ after the projection matrix. Prove that it does not matter if we do the perspective divide before or after multiplying by **T**. Let **v** be a 4D vector, **P** be a projection matrix, **T** be a 4×4 affine transformation matrix, and let a w subscript denote the w-coordinate of a 4D vector, and prove:

$$\left(\frac{\mathbf{vP}}{(\mathbf{vP})_w} \right) \mathbf{T} = \frac{(\mathbf{vPT})}{(\mathbf{vPT})_w}$$

9. Prove that the inverse of the projection matrix is given by:

$$\mathbf{P}^{-1} = \begin{bmatrix} r\tan\left(\dfrac{\alpha}{2}\right) & 0 & 0 & 0 \\ 0 & \tan\left(\dfrac{\alpha}{2}\right) & 0 & 0 \\ 0 & 0 & 0 & -\dfrac{f-n}{nf} \\ 0 & 0 & 1 & \dfrac{1}{n} \end{bmatrix}$$

10. Let $[x, y, z, 1]$ be the coordinates of a point in view space, and let $[x_{ndc}, y_{ndc}, z_{ndc}, 1]$ be the coordinates of the same point in NDC space. Prove that you can transform from NDC space to view space in the following way:

$$[x_{ndc}, y_{ndc}, z_{ndc}, 1]\mathbf{P}^{-1} = \left[\frac{x}{z}, \frac{y}{z}, 1, \frac{1}{z}\right] \underline{\text{divide by } w} [x, y, z, 1]$$

Explain why you need the division by w. Would you need the division by w if you were transforming from homogeneous clip space to view space?

11. Another way to describe the view frustum is by specifying the width and height of the view volume at the near plane. Given the width w and height h of the view volume at the near plane, and given the near plane n and far plane f, show that the perspective projection matrix is given by:

$$\mathbf{P} = \begin{bmatrix} \dfrac{2n}{w} & 0 & 0 & 0 \\ 0 & \dfrac{2n}{h} & 0 & 0 \\ 0 & 0 & \dfrac{f}{f-n} & 1 \\ 0 & 0 & \dfrac{-nf}{f-n} & 0 \end{bmatrix}$$

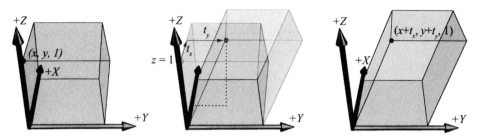

Figure 5.37. The x- and y-coordinates sheared by the z-coordinate. The top face of the box lies in the $z = 1$ plane. Observe that the shear transform translates points in this plane.

12 . Given a view frustum with vertical field of view angle θ, aspect ratio a, near plane n, and far plane f, find the 8 vertex corners of the frustum.

13 . Consider the 3D shear transform given by $S_{xy}(x, y, z) = (x + zt_x, y + zt_y, z)$. This transformation is illustrated in Figure 5.37. Prove that this is a linear transformation and has the following matrix representation:

$$\mathbf{S}_{xy} = \begin{bmatrix} 1 & 0 & 0 \\ 0 & 1 & 0 \\ t_x & t_y & 1 \end{bmatrix}$$

14 . Consider 3D points in the plane $z = 1$; that is, points of the form $(x, y, 1)$. Observe that transforming a point $(x, y, 1)$ by the shear transformation S_{xy} given in the previous exercise amounts to a 2D translation in the $z = 1$ plane:

$$\begin{bmatrix} x & y & 1 \end{bmatrix} \begin{bmatrix} 1 & 0 & 0 \\ 0 & 1 & 0 \\ t_x & t_y & 1 \end{bmatrix} = \begin{bmatrix} x + t_x, & y + t_y, & 1 \end{bmatrix}$$

If we are working on a 2D application, we could use 3D coordinates, but where our 2D universe always lies on the plane $z = 1$; then we could use S_{xy} to do translations in our 2D space.

Conclude the following generalizations:

(a) Just as a plane in 3D space is a 2D space, a plane in 4D space is a 3D space. When we write homogeneous points $(x, y, z, 1)$ we are working in the 3D space that lives in the 4D plane $w = 1$.

(b) The translation matrix is the matrix representation of the 4D shear transformation $S_{xyz}(x, y, z, w) = (x + wt_x, y + wt_y, z + wt_z, w)$. The 4D shear transformation has the effect of translating points in the plane $w = 1$.

Chapter 6 DRAWING IN DIRECT3D

In the previous chapter, we mostly focused on the conceptual and mathematical aspects of the rendering pipeline. This chapter, in turn, focuses on the Direct3D API interfaces and methods needed to configure the rendering pipeline, define vertex and pixel shaders, and submit geometry to the rendering pipeline for drawing. By the end of this chapter, you will be able to draw various geometric shapes with coloring or in wireframe mode.

Objectives:

1. To discover the Direct3D interfaces methods for defining, storing, and drawing geometric data.

2. To learn how to write basic vertex and pixel shaders.

3. To find out how to configure the rendering pipeline with render states.

4. To learn how the effects framework can be used to logically group shaders and render states into a rendering technique, and how to use the effects framework as a "shader generator."

6.1 VERTICES AND INPUT LAYOUTS

Recall from §5.5.1 that a vertex in Direct3D can consist of additional data besides spatial location. To create a custom vertex format, we first create a structure that holds the vertex data we choose. For instance, the following illustrates two different kinds of vertex formats; one consists of position and color, and the second consists of position, normal, and texture coordinates.

```
struct Vertex1
{
    XMFLOAT3 Pos;
    XMFLOAT4 Color;
};

struct Vertex2
{
    XMFLOAT3 Pos;
    XMFLOAT3 Normal;
    XMFLOAT2 Tex0;
    XMFLOAT2 Tex1;
};
```

Once we have defined a vertex structure, we need to provide Direct3D with a description of our vertex structure so that it knows what to do with each component. This description is provided to Direct3D in the form of an *input layout* (ID3D11InputLayout). An input layout is specified by an array of D3D11_INPUT_ELEMENT_DESC elements. Each element in the D3D11_INPUT_ELEMENT_DESC array describes and corresponds to one component in the vertex structure. So if the vertex structure has two components, then the corresponding D3D11_INPUT_ELEMENT_DESC array will have two elements. We refer to the D3D11_INPUT_ELEMENT_DESC array as the *input layout description*. The D3D11_INPUT_ELEMENT_DESC structure is defined as:

```
typedef struct D3D11_INPUT_ELEMENT_DESC {
    LPCSTR SemanticName;
    UINT SemanticIndex;
    DXGI_FORMAT Format;
    UINT InputSlot;
    UINT AlignedByteOffset;
    D3D11_INPUT_CLASSIFICATION InputSlotClass;
    UINT InstanceDataStepRate;
} D3D11_INPUT_ELEMENT_DESC;
```

1. SemanticName: A string to associate with the element. This can be any valid variable name. Semantics are used to map elements in the vertex structure to elements in the vertex shader input signature; see Figure 6.1.

2. SemanticIndex: An index to attach to a semantic. The motivation for this is also illustrated in Figure 6.1, where a vertex structure may have more than one set of

```
struct Vertex
{
    XMFLOAT3 Pos;  ───────────────────────────────
    XMFLOAT3 Normal;  ─────────────────────────────
    XMFLOAT2 Tex0;  ──────────────────────────────
    XMFLOAT2 Tex1;  ──────────────────────────────
};


D3D11_INPUT_ELEMENT_DESC vertexDesc[] =
{
    {"POSITION", 0, DXGI_FORMAT_R32G32B32_FLOAT, 0, 0,
        D3D11_INPUT_PER_VERTEX_DATA, 0},
    {"NORMAL", 0, DXGI_FORMAT_R32G32B32_FLOAT, 0, 12,
        D3D11_INPUT_PER_VERTEX_DATA, 0},
    {"TEXCOORD", 0, DXGI_FORMAT_R32G32_FLOAT, 0, 24,
        D3D11_INPUT_PER_VERTEX_DATA, 0},
    {"TEXCOORD", 1, DXGI_FORMAT_R32G32_FLOAT, 0, 32,
        D3D11_INPUT_PER_VERTEX_DATA, 0}
};


VertexOut VS(float3 iPos : POSITION,  ◄───────
             float3 iNormal : NORMAL,  ◄──────
             float2 iTex0 : TEXCOORD0,  ◄─────
             float2 iTex1 : TEXCOORD1)  ◄────
```

Figure 6.1. **Each element in the vertex structure is described by a corresponding element in
the** D3D11_INPUT_ELEMENT_DESC **array. The semantic name and index provides a way for
mapping vertex elements to the corresponding parameters of the vertex shader.**

texture coordinates; so rather than introducing a new semantic name, we can
attach an index to the end to distinguish the texture coordinates. A semantic
with no index specified in the shader code defaults to index zero; for instance,
POSITION is equivalent to POSITION0 in Figure 6.1.

3. **Format**: A member of the DXGI_FORMAT enumerated type specifying the format
   (i.e., the data type) of this vertex element to Direct3D; here are some common
   examples of formats used:

```
DXGI_FORMAT_R32_FLOAT              // 1D 32-bit float scalar
DXGI_FORMAT_R32G32_FLOAT          // 2D 32-bit float vector
DXGI_FORMAT_R32G32B32_FLOAT       // 3D 32-bit float vector
DXGI_FORMAT_R32G32B32A32_FLOAT    // 4D 32-bit float vector

DXGI_FORMAT_R8_UINT         // 1D 8-bit unsigned integer scalar
DXGI_FORMAT_R16G16_SINT     // 2D 16-bit signed integer vector
DXGI_FORMAT_R32G32B32_UINT  // 3D 32-bit unsigned integer vector
DXGI_FORMAT_R8G8B8A8_SINT   // 4D 8-bit signed integer vector
DXGI_FORMAT_R8G8B8A8_UINT   // 4D 8-bit unsigned integer vector
```

4. **InputSlot**: Specifies the input slot index this element will come from. Direct3D
   supports sixteen input slots (indexed from 0–15) through which you can feed
   vertex data. For instance, if a vertex consisted of position and color elements, you
   could either feed both elements through a single input slot, or you could split
   the elements up and feed the position elements through the first input slot and

feed the color elements through the second input slot. Direct3D will then use the elements from the different input slots to assemble the vertices. In this book, we only use one input slot, but Exercise 2 asks you to experiment with two.

5. **AlignedByteOffset**: For a single input slot, this is the offset, in bytes, from the start of the C++ vertex structure to the start of the vertex component. For example, in the following vertex structure, the element **Pos** has a 0-byte offset since its start coincides with the start of the vertex structure; the element **Normal** has a 12-byte offset because we have to skip over the bytes of **Pos** to get to the start of **Normal**; the element **Tex0** has a 24-byte offset because we need to skip over the bytes of **Pos** and **Normal** to get to the start of **Tex0**; the element **Tex1** has a 32-byte offset because we need to skip over the bytes of **Pos**, **Normal**, and **Tex0** to get to the start of **Tex1**.

```
struct Vertex2
{
    XMFLOAT3 Pos;        // 0-byte offset
    XMFLOAT3 Normal;     // 12-byte offset
    XMFLOAT2 Tex0;       // 24-byte offset
    XMFLOAT2 Tex1;       // 32-byte offset
};
```

6. **InputSlotClass**: Specify **D3D11_INPUT_PER_VERTEX_DATA** for now; the other option is used for the advanced technique of instancing.

7. **InstanceDataStepRate**: Specify 0 for now; other values are only used for the advanced technique of instancing.

For the previous two example vertex structures, **Vertex1** and **Vertex2**, the corresponding input layout descriptions would be:

```
D3D11_INPUT_ELEMENT_DESC desc1[] =
{
    {"POSITION", 0, DXGI_FORMAT_R32G32B32_FLOAT, 0, 0,
        D3D11_INPUT_PER_VERTEX_DATA, 0},
    {"COLOR", 0, DXGI_FORMAT_R32G32B32A32_FLOAT, 0, 12,
        D3D11_INPUT_PER_VERTEX_DATA, 0}
};

D3D11_INPUT_ELEMENT_DESC desc2[] =
{
    {"POSITION", 0, DXGI_FORMAT_R32G32B32_FLOAT, 0, 0,
        D3D11_INPUT_PER_VERTEX_DATA, 0},
    {"NORMAL",   0, DXGI_FORMAT_R32G32B32_FLOAT, 0, 12,
        D3D11_INPUT_PER_VERTEX_DATA, 0},
    {"TEXCOORD", 0, DXGI_FORMAT_R32G32_FLOAT,    0, 24,
        D3D11_INPUT_PER_VERTEX_DATA, 0},
    {"TEXCOORD", 1, DXGI_FORMAT_R32G32_FLOAT,    0, 32,
        D3D11_INPUT_PER_VERTEX_DATA, 0}
};
```

Once an input layout description has been specified, we can obtain a pointer to an `ID3D11InputLayout` interface, which represents an input layout, using the `ID3D11Device::CreateInputLayout` method:

```
HRESULT ID3D11Device::CreateInputLayout(
    const D3D11_INPUT_ELEMENT_DESC *pInputElementDescs,
    UINT NumElements,
    const void *pShaderBytecodeWithInputSignature,
    SIZE_T BytecodeLength,
    ID3D11InputLayout **ppInputLayout);
```

1. `pInputElementDescs`: An array of `D3D11_INPUT_ELEMENT_DESC` elements describing the vertex structure.

2. `NumElements`: The number of elements in the `D3D11_INPUT_ELEMENT_DESC` elements array.

3. `pShaderBytecodeWithInputSignature`: A pointer to the shader byte-code of the input signature of the vertex shader.

4. `BytecodeLength`: The byte size of the vertex shader signature data passed into the previous parameter.

5. `ppInputLayout`: Returns a pointer to the created input layout.

Parameter three needs some elaboration. A vertex shader takes a list of vertex elements as input parameters—the so-called *input signature*. The elements in the custom vertex structure need to be mapped to the corresponding inputs in the vertex shader; Figure 6.1 alludes to this. By passing in a description of the vertex shader input signature when the input layout is created, Direct3D can validate that the input layout matches the input signature and create the mapping from the vertex structure to the shader inputs at creation time. An input layout can be reused across different shaders, provided the input signatures are exactly the same.

Consider the case where you have the following input signature and vertex structure:

```
VertexOut VS(float3 Pos : POSITION, float4 Color : COLOR,
    float3 Normal : NORMAL) { }

struct Vertex
{
    XMFLOAT3 Pos;
    XMFLOAT4 Color;
};
```

This will generate an error, and the VC++ debug output window shows the following:

```
D3D11: ERROR: ID3D11Device::CreateInputLayout: The provided input
signature expects to read an element with SemanticName/Index: 'NORMAL'/0,
but the declaration doesn't provide a matching name.
```

Now consider the case where the vertex structure and input signature have matching vertex elements, but the types are different:

```
VertexOut VS(int3 Pos : POSITION, float4 Color : COLOR) { }

struct Vertex
{
    XMFLOAT3 Pos;
    XMFLOAT4 Color;
};
```

This is actually legal because Direct3D allows the bits in the input registers to be reinterpreted. However, the VC++ debug output window gives the following warning:

```
D3D11: WARNING: ID3D11Device::CreateInputLayout: The provided input
signature expects to read an element with SemanticName/Index:
'POSITION'/0 and component(s) of the type 'int32'. However, the
matching entry in the Input Layout declaration, element[0], specifies
mismatched format: 'R32G32B32_FLOAT'. This is not an error, since
behavior is well defined: The element format determines what data
conversion algorithm gets applied before it shows up in a shader
register. Independently, the shader input signature defines how the
shader will interpret the data that has been placed in its input
registers, with no change in the bits stored. It is valid for the
application to reinterpret data as a different type once it is in the
vertex shader, so this warning is issued just in case reinterpretation
was not intended by the author.
```

The following code provides an example to illustrate how the ID3D11Device::CreateInputLayout method is invoked. Note that the code involves some topics we have not discussed yet (such as ID3D11Effect). Essentially, an effect encapsulates one or more passes, and a vertex shader is associated with each pass. So from the effect, we can get a pass description (D3D11_PASS_DESC), from which we can get to the input signature of the vertex shader.

```
ID3DX11Effect* mFX;
ID3DX11EffectTechnique* mTech;
ID3D11InputLayout* mInputLayout;

/* ...create the effect... */

mTech = mFX->GetTechniqueByName("Tech");
D3DX11_PASS_DESC passDesc;
mTech->GetPassByIndex(0)->GetDesc(&passDesc);
HR(md3dDevice->CreateInputLayout(vertexDesc, 4, passDesc.
    pIAInputSignature, passDesc.IAInputSignatureSize, &mInputLayout));
```

After an input layout has been created, it is still not bound to the device yet. The last step is to bind the input layout you want to use to the device as the following code shows:

```
ID3D11InputLayout* mInputLayout;

/* ...create the input layout... */

md3dImmediateContext->IASetInputLayout(mInputLayout);
```

If some objects you are drawing use one input layout, and other objects you are drawing require a different layout, then you need to structure your code like this:

```
md3dImmediateContext->IASetInputLayout(mInputLayout1);
/* ...draw objects using input layout 1... */

md3dImmediateContext->IASetInputLayout(mInputLayout2);
/* ...draw objects using input layout 2... */
```

In other words, when an input layout is bound to the device, it does not change until you overwrite it.

6.2 VERTEX BUFFERS

In order for the GPU to access an array of vertices, they need to be placed in a special resource structure called a *buffer*, which is represented by the ID3D11Buffer interface.

A buffer that stores vertices is called a *vertex buffer*. Direct3D buffers not only store data, but also describe how the data will be accessed and where it will be bound to the rendering pipeline. To create a vertex buffer, we need to do the following steps:

1. Fill out a D3D11_BUFFER_DESC structure describing the buffer we are going to create.

2. Fill out a D3D11_SUBRESOURCE_DATA structure which specifies the data we want to initialize the buffer contents with.

3. Call ID3D11Device::CreateBuffer to create the buffer.

The D3D11_BUFFER_DESC structure is defined as follows:

```
typedef struct D3D11_BUFFER_DESC {
    UINT ByteWidth;
    D3D11_USAGE Usage;
    UINT BindFlags;
    UINT CPUAccessFlags;
    UINT MiscFlags;
    UINT StructureByteStride;
} D3D11_BUFFER_DESC;
```

1. **ByteWidth**: The size, in bytes, of the vertex buffer we are going to create.

2. **Usage**: A member of the **D3D11_USAGE** enumerated type specifying how the buffer will be used. The four usage values are:

    (a) **D3D11_USAGE_DEFAULT**: Specify this usage if the GPU will be reading and writing to the resource. The CPU cannot read or write to a resource with this usage using the mapping API (i.e., **ID3D11DeviceContext::Map**); however, it can use **ID3D11DeviceContext::UpdateSubresource**. The method **ID3D11DeviceContext::Map** is discussed in §6.14.

    (b) **D3D11_USAGE_IMMUTABLE**: Specify this usage if the contents of a resource do not ever change after creation. This allows for some potential optimizations, as the resource will be read-only by the GPU. The CPU cannot write to an immutable resource, except at creation time to initialize the resource. The CPU cannot read from an immutable resource. We cannot map or update an immutable resource.

    (c) **D3D11_USAGE_DYNAMIC**: Specify this usage if the application (CPU) needs to update the data contents of the resource frequently (e.g., on a per frame basis). A resource with this usage can be read by the GPU and written to by the CPU using the mapping API (i.e., **ID3D11DeviceContext::Map**). Updating a GPU resource dynamically from the CPU incurs a performance hit, as the new data must be transferred over from CPU memory (i.e., system RAM) to GPU memory (i.e., video RAM); therefore, dynamic usage should be avoided unless necessary.

    (d) **D3D11_USAGE_STAGING**: Specify this usage if the application (CPU) needs to be able to read a copy of the resource (i.e., the resource supports copying data from video memory to system memory). Copying from GPU to CPU memory is a slow operation and should be avoided unless necessary. Resources can be copied with the **ID3D11DeviceContext::CopyResource** and **ID3D11DeviceContext::CopySubresourceRegion** methods. §12.3.5 shows an example of **CopyResource**.

3. **BindFlags**: For a vertex buffer, specify **D3D11_BIND_VERTEX_BUFFER**.

4. **CPUAccessFlags**: Specifies how the CPU will access the buffer. Specify 0 if the CPU does not require read or write access after the buffer has been created. If the CPU needs to update the buffer by writing to it, specify **D3D11_CPU_ACCESS_WRITE**. A buffer with write access must have usage **D3D11_USAGE_DYNAMIC** or **D3D11_USAGE_STAGING**.

    If the CPU needs to read from the buffer, specify **D3D11_CPU_ACCESS_READ**. A buffer with read access must have usage **D3D11_USAGE_STAGING**. Only specify these flags if you need them. In general, the CPU reading from a Direct3D resource is slow (GPUs are optimized to pump data through the pipeline, but not read back) and can cause the GPU to stall (the GPU may need to wait for the resource being read from to finish before it can continue its work). The CPU writing to a resource is faster, but there is still the overhead of having to transfer the updated data back to video memory. It is best to not specify any of these flags (if possible), and let the resource sit in video memory where only the GPU writes and reads to it.

5. **MiscFlags:** We do not need any of the miscellaneous flags for vertex buffers; specify 0 and see the **D3D11_RESOURCE_MISC_FLAG** enumerated type in the SDK documentation for further info.

6. **StructureByteStride:** The size, in bytes, of a single element stored in the structured buffer. This property only applies for structured buffers and can be set to 0 for all other buffers. A structure buffer is a buffer that stores elements of equal size.

The **D3D11_SUBRESOURCE_DATA** structure is defined as follows:

```
typedef struct D3D11_SUBRESOURCE_DATA {
    const void *pSysMem;
    UINT SysMemPitch;
    UINT SysMemSlicePitch;
} D3D11_SUBRESOURCE_DATA;
```

1. **pSysMem:** A pointer to a system memory array which contains the data to initialize the vertex buffer. If the buffer can store *n* vertices, then the system array must contain at least *n* vertices so that the entire buffer can be initialized.

2. **SysMemPitch:** Not used for vertex buffers.

3. **SysMemSlicePitch:** Not used for vertex buffers.

The following code creates an immutable vertex buffer which is initialized with the eight vertices of a cube centered at the origin. The buffer is immutable because the cube geometry never needs to change once it is created—it always remains a cube. Moreover, we associate with each vertex a different color; these vertex colors will be used to color the cube, as we will see later in this chapter.

```
// Colors namespace defined in d3dUtil.h.
//
// #define XMGLOBALCONST extern CONST __declspec(selectany)
//    1. extern so there is only one copy of the variable, and not a
//       separate private copy in each .obj.
//    2. __declspec(selectany) so that the compiler does not complain
//       about multiple definitions in a .cpp file (it can pick anyone
//       and discard the rest because they are constant--all the same).
```

```
namespace Colors
{
    XMGLOBALCONST XMVECTORF32 White   = {1.0f, 1.0f, 1.0f, 1.0f};
    XMGLOBALCONST XMVECTORF32 Black   = {0.0f, 0.0f, 0.0f, 1.0f};
    XMGLOBALCONST XMVECTORF32 Red     = {1.0f, 0.0f, 0.0f, 1.0f};
    XMGLOBALCONST XMVECTORF32 Green   = {0.0f, 1.0f, 0.0f, 1.0f};
    XMGLOBALCONST XMVECTORF32 Blue    = {0.0f, 0.0f, 1.0f, 1.0f};
    XMGLOBALCONST XMVECTORF32 Yellow  = {1.0f, 1.0f, 0.0f, 1.0f};
    XMGLOBALCONST XMVECTORF32 Cyan    = {0.0f, 1.0f, 1.0f, 1.0f};
    XMGLOBALCONST XMVECTORF32 Magenta = {1.0f, 0.0f, 1.0f, 1.0f};
}

// define raw vertex data
Vertex vertices[] =
{
    { XMFLOAT3(-1.0f, -1.0f, -1.0f), (const float*)&Colors::White   },
    { XMFLOAT3(-1.0f, +1.0f, -1.0f), (const float*)&Colors::Black   },
    { XMFLOAT3(+1.0f, +1.0f, -1.0f), (const float*)&Colors::Red     },
    { XMFLOAT3(+1.0f, -1.0f, -1.0f), (const float*)&Colors::Green   },
    { XMFLOAT3(-1.0f, -1.0f, +1.0f), (const float*)&Colors::Blue    },
    { XMFLOAT3(-1.0f, +1.0f, +1.0f), (const float*)&Colors::Yellow  },
    { XMFLOAT3(+1.0f, +1.0f, +1.0f), (const float*)&Colors::Cyan    },
    { XMFLOAT3(+1.0f, -1.0f, +1.0f), (const float*)&Colors::Magenta }
};

D3D11_BUFFER_DESC vbd;
vbd.Usage = D3D11_USAGE_IMMUTABLE;
vbd.ByteWidth = sizeof(Vertex) * 8;
vbd.BindFlags = D3D11_BIND_VERTEX_BUFFER;
vbd.CPUAccessFlags = 0;
vbd.MiscFlags = 0;
vbd.StructureByteStride = 0;

D3D11_SUBRESOURCE_DATA vinitData;
vinitData.pSysMem = vertices;

ID3D11Buffer* mVB;
HR(md3dDevice->CreateBuffer(
    &vbd,       // description of buffer to create
    &vinitData, // data to initialize buffer with
    & mVB));    // return the created buffer
```

where the **Vertex** type and colors are defined as follows:

```
struct Vertex
{
    XMFLOAT3 Pos;
    XMFLOAT4 Color;
};
```

After a vertex buffer has been created, it needs to be bound to an input slot of the device in order to feed the vertices to the pipeline as input. This is done with the following method:

```
void ID3D11DeviceContext::IASetVertexBuffers(
    UINT StartSlot,
    UINT NumBuffers,
    ID3D11Buffer *const *ppVertexBuffers,
    const UINT *pStrides,
    const UINT *pOffsets);
```

1. `StartSlot`: The input slot in which to start binding vertex buffers. There are 16 input slots indexed from 0–15.

2. `NumBuffers`: The number of vertex buffers we are binding to the input slots. If the start slot has index k and we are binding n buffers, then we are binding buffers to input slots $I_k, I_{k+1}, \ldots, I_{k+n-1}$.

3. `ppVertexBuffers`: Pointer to the first element of an array of vertex buffers.

4. `pStrides`: Pointer to the first element of an array of strides (one for each vertex buffer where the ith stride corresponds to the ith vertex buffer). A stride is the size, in bytes, of an element in the corresponding vertex buffer.

5. `pOffsets`: Pointer to the first element of an array of offsets (one for each vertex buffer where the ith offset corresponds to the ith vertex buffer). This is an offset, in bytes, from the start of the vertex buffer to the position in the vertex buffer from which the input assembly should start reading the vertex data. You would use this if you wanted to skip over some vertex data at the front of the vertex buffer.

The `IASetVertexBuffers` method may seem a little complicated because it supports setting an array of vertex buffers to various input slots. However, most of the time we will only use one input slot. An end-of-chapter exercise gives you some experience working with two input slots.

A vertex buffer will stay bound to an input slot until you change it. So you may structure your code like this, if you are using more than one vertex buffers:

```
ID3D11Buffer* mVB1; // stores vertices of type Vertex1
ID3D11Buffer* mVB2; // stores vertices of type Vertex2

/*...Create the vertex buffers...*/

UINT stride = sizeof(Vertex1);
UINT offset = 0;
md3dImmediateContext->IASetVertexBuffers(0, 1, &mVB1, &stride, &offset);

/* ...draw objects using vertex buffer 1... */

stride = sizeof(Vertex2);
offset = 0;
md3dImmediateContext->IASetVertexBuffers(0, 1, &mVB2, &stride, &offset);
/* ...draw objects using vertex buffer 2... */
```

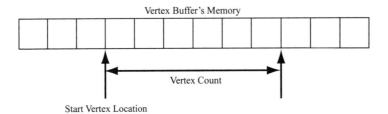

Figure 6.2. StartVertexLocation specifies the index (zero-based) of the first vertex in the vertex buffer to begin drawing. VertexCount specifies the number of vertices to draw.

Setting a vertex buffer to an input slot does not draw them; it only makes the vertices ready to be fed into the pipeline. The final step to actually draw the vertices is done with the ID3D11DeviceContext::Draw method:

```
void ID3D11DeviceContext::Draw(UINT VertexCount, UINT StartVertexLocation);
```

The two parameters define a contiguous subset of vertices in the vertex buffer to draw; see Figure 6.2.

6.3 INDICES AND INDEX BUFFERS

Because indices need to be accessed by the GPU, they need to be placed in a special resource structure: an *index buffer*. Creating an index buffer is very similar to creating a vertex buffer, except that the index buffer stores indices instead of vertices. Therefore, rather than repeating a discussion similar to the one carried out for vertex buffers, we just show an example of creating an index buffer:

```
UINT indices[24] = {
    0, 1, 2,  // Triangle 0
    0, 2, 3,  // Triangle 1
    0, 3, 4,  // Triangle 2
    0, 4, 5,  // Triangle 3
    0, 5, 6,  // Triangle 4
    0, 6, 7,  // Triangle 5
    0, 7, 8,  // Triangle 6
    0, 8, 1   // Triangle 7
};

// Describe the index buffer we are going to create.  Observe the
// D3D11_BIND_INDEX_BUFFER bind flag
D3D11_BUFFER_DESC ibd;
ibd.Usage = D3D11_USAGE_IMMUTABLE;
ibd.ByteWidth = sizeof(UINT) * 24;
ibd.BindFlags = D3D11_BIND_INDEX_BUFFER;
ibd.CPUAccessFlags = 0;
ibd.MiscFlags = 0;
ibd.StructureByteStride = 0;
```

```
// Specify the data to initialize the index buffer.
D3D11_SUBRESOURCE_DATA iinitData;
iinitData.pSysMem = indices;

// Create the index buffer.
ID3D11Buffer* mIB;
HR(md3dDevice->CreateBuffer(&ibd, &iinitData, &mIB));
```

As with vertex buffers, and other Direct3D resources for that matter, before we can use it, we need to bind it to the pipeline. An index buffer is bound to the input assembler stage with the `ID3D11DeviceContext::IASetIndexBuffer` method. Following is an example call:

```
md3dImmediateContext->IASetIndexBuffer(mIB, DXGI_FORMAT_R32_UINT, 0);
```

The second parameter specifies the format of the indices. In our example, we are using 32-bit unsigned integers (`DWORD`); therefore, we specified `DXGI_FORMAT_R32_UINT`. You could alternatively use 16-bit unsigned integers if you wanted to save memory and bandwidth, and did not need the extra range. Just remember that in addition to specifying the format in the `IASetIndexBuffer` method, the `D3D11_BUFFER_DESC::ByteWidth` data member depends on the format as well, so make sure they are consistent to avoid problems. Note that `DXGI_FORMAT_R16_UINT` and `DXGI_FORMAT_R32_UINT` are the only formats supported for index buffers. The third parameter is an offset, measured in bytes, from the start of the index buffer to the position in the index buffer the input assembly should start reading the data. You would use this if you wanted to skip over some data at the front of the index buffer.

Finally, when using indices, we must use the `DrawIndexed` method instead of `Draw`:

```
void ID3D11DeviceContext::DrawIndexed(
    UINT IndexCount,
    UINT StartIndexLocation,
    INT BaseVertexLocation);
```

1. `IndexCount`: The number of indices that will be used in this draw call. This need not be every index in the index buffer; that is, you can draw a contiguous subset of indices.

2. `StartIndexLocation`: Index to an element in the index buffer that marks the starting point from which to begin reading indices.

3. `BaseVertexLocation`: An integer value to be added to the indices used in this draw call before the vertices are fetched.

To illustrate these parameters, consider the following situation. Suppose we have three objects: a sphere, box, and cylinder. At first, each object has its own vertex buffer and its own index buffer. The indices in each local index buffer are relative to the corresponding local vertex buffer. Now suppose that we concatenate the vertices and indices of the sphere, box, and cylinder into one global vertex

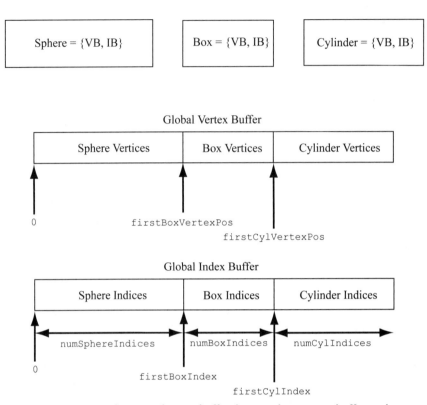

Figure 6.3. **Concatenating several vertex buffers into one large vertex buffer, and concatenating several index buffers into one large index buffer.**

and index buffer, as shown in Figure 6.3. (One might concatenate vertex and index buffers because there is some API overhead when changing the vertex and index buffers. Most likely this will not be a bottleneck, but if you have many small vertex and index buffers that could be easily merged, it may be worth doing so for performance reasons.) After this concatenation, the indices are no longer correct, as they store index locations relative to their corresponding local vertex buffers, not the global one; thus the indices need to be recomputed to index correctly into the global vertex buffer. The original box indices were computed with the assumption that the box's vertices ran through the indices

```
0, 1, ..., numBoxVertices-1
```

But after the merger, they run from

```
firstBoxVertexPos,
firstBoxVertexPos+1,
...,
firstBoxVertexPos+numBoxVertices-1
```

Therefore, to update the indices, we need to add **firstBoxVertexPos** to every box index. Likewise, we need to add **firstCylVertexPos** to every cylinder index. Note that the sphere's indices do not need to be changed (because the first sphere vertex position is zero). Let us call the position of an object's first vertex relative to the global vertex buffer its *base vertex location*. In general, the new indices of an object are computed by adding its base vertex location to each index. Instead of having to compute the new indices ourselves, we can let Direct3D do it by passing the base vertex location to the third parameter of **DrawIndexed**.

We can then draw the sphere, box, and cylinder one-by-one with the following three calls:

```
md3dImmediateContext->DrawIndexed(numSphereIndices, 0, 0);
md3dImmediateContext->DrawIndexed(numBoxIndices, firstBoxIndex, firstBoxVertexPos);
md3dImmediateContext->DrawIndexed(numCylIndices, firstCylIndex, firstCylVertexPos);
```

The "Shapes" demo project for this chapter uses this technique.

6.4 EXAMPLE VERTEX SHADER

Below in an implementation of the simple vertex shader:

```
cbuffer cbPerObject
{
    float4x4 gWorldViewProj;
};

void VS(float3 iPosL : POSITION,
    float4 iColor : COLOR,
    out float4 oPosH : SV_POSITION,
    out float4 oColor : COLOR)
{
    // Transform to homogeneous clip space.
    oPosH = mul(float4(iPosL, 1.0f), gWorldViewProj);

    // Just pass vertex color into the pixel shader.
    oColor = iColor;
}
```

Shaders are written in a language called the *high level shading language* (HLSL), which has similar syntax to C++, so it is easy to learn. Appendix B provides a concise reference to the HLSL. Our approach to teaching the HLSL and programming shaders will be example based. That is, as we progress through the book, we will introduce any new HLSL concepts we need in order to implement the demo at hand. Shaders are usually written in text-based files called *effect files* (.fx). We will discuss effect files later in this chapter, but for now, we will just concentrate on the vertex shader.

The vertex shader is the function called **vs**. Note that you can give the vertex shader any valid function name. This vertex shader has four parameters; the first two are *input* parameters, and the last two are output parameters (indicated by the **out** keyword). The HLSL does not have references or pointers, so to return multiple values from a function, you need to either use structures or out parameters.

The first two input parameters form the input signature of the vertex shader and correspond to data members in our custom vertex structure. The parameter semantics ":POSITION" and ":COLOR" are used for mapping the elements in the vertex structure to the vertex shader input parameters, as Figure 6.4 shows.

The output parameters also have attached semantics (":SV_POSITION" and ":COLOR"). These are used to map vertex shader outputs to the corresponding inputs of the next stage (either the geometry shader or pixel shader). Note that the SV_POSITION semantic is special (SV stands for system value). It is used to denote the vertex shader output element that holds the vertex position. The vertex position needs to be handled differently than other vertex attributes because it is involved in operations the other attributes are not involved in, such as clipping. The semantic name for output parameters that are not system values can be any valid semantic name.

```
struct Vertex
{
    XMFLOAT3 Pos;
    XMFLOAT4 Color;
};

D3D11_INPUT_ELEMENT_DESC vertexDesc[] =
{
    {"POSITION", 0, DXGI_FORMAT_R32G32B32_FLOAT, 0, 0,
        D3D11_INPUT_PER_VERTEX_DATA, 0},
    {"COLOR",    0, DXGI_FORMAT_R32G32B32A32_FLOAT, 0, 12,
        D3D11_INPUT_PER_VERTEX_DATA, 0}
};

void VS(float3 iPosL : POSITION,
        float4 iColor : COLOR,
        out float4 oPosH : SV_POSITION,
        out float4 oColor : COLOR)
{
    // Transform to homogeneous clip space.
    oPosH = mul(float4(iPosL, 1.0f), gWorldViewProj);

    // Just pass vertex color into the pixel shader.
    oColor = iColor;
}
```

Figure 6.4. **Each vertex element has an associated semantic specified by the D3D11_INPUT_ELEMENT_DESC array. Each parameter of the vertex shader also has an attached semantic. The semantics are used to match vertex elements with vertex shader parameters.**

The first line transforms the vertex position from local space to homogeneous clip space by multiplying by the 4×4 matrix `gWorldViewProj`:

```
// Transform to homogeneous clip space.
oPosH = mul(float4(iPosL, 1.0f), gWorldViewProj);
```

The constructor syntax `float4(iPosL, 1.0f)` constructs a 4D vector and is equivalent to `float4(iPosL.x, iPosL.y, iPosL.z, 1.0f)`; because we know the position of vertices are points and not vectors, we place a 1 in the fourth component ($w = 1$). The `float2` and `float3` types represent 2D and 3D vectors, respectively. The matrix variables `gWorldViewProj` lives in a constant buffer, which will be discussed in the next section. The built-in function `mul` is used for the vector-matrix multiplication. Incidentally, the `mul` function is overloaded for matrix multiplications of different sizes; for example, you can use it to multiply two 4×4 matrices, two 3×3 matrices, or a 1×3 vector and a 3×3 matrix. The last line in the shader body just copies the input color to the output parameter so that the color will be fed into the next stage of the pipeline:

```
oColor = iColor;
```

We can equivalently rewrite the previous vertex shader using structures for the return type and input signature (as opposed to a long parameter list):

```
cbuffer cbPerObject
{
    float4x4 gWorldViewProj;
};

struct VertexIn
{
    float3 PosL  : POSITION;
    float4 Color : COLOR;
};

struct VertexOut
{
    float4 PosH  : SV_POSITION;
    float4 Color : COLOR;
};

VertexOut VS(VertexIn vin)
{
    VertexOut vout;

    // Transform to homogeneous clip space.
    vout.PosH = mul(float4(vin.PosL, 1.0f), gWorldViewProj);

    // Just pass vertex color into the pixel shader.
    vout.Color = vin.Color;

    return vout;
}
```

If there is no geometry shader, then the vertex shader must at least do the projection transformation because this is the space the hardware expects the vertices to be in when leaving the vertex shader (if there is no geometry shader). If there is a geometry shader, the job of projection can be deferred to the geometry shader.

 A vertex shader (or geometry shader) does not do the perspective divide; it just does the projection matrix part. The perspective divide will be done later by the hardware.

6.5 CONSTANT BUFFERS

Above the example vertex shader in the previous section was the code:

```
cbuffer cbPerObject
{
    float4x4 gWorldViewProj;
};
```

This code defines a **cbuffer** object (constant buffer) called **cbPerObject**. Constant buffers are just blocks of data that can store different variables that may be accessed by a shader. In this example, the constant buffer stores a single 4 × 4 matrix called **gWorldViewProj**, representing the combined world, view, and projection matrices used to transform a point from local space to homogeneous clip space. In HLSL, a 4 × 4 matrix is declared by the built-in **float4x4** type; to declare a 3 × 4 matrix and 2 × 2 matrix, for example, you would use the **float3x4** and **float2x2** types, respectively. Data in constant buffers does not vary per vertex, but through the effects framework (§6.9), the C++ application code can update the contents of a constant buffer at runtime. This provides a means for the C++ application code and the effect code to communicate. For instance, because the world matrix varies per object, the combined world, view, and projection matrix varies per object; therefore, when using the previous vertex shader to draw multiple objects, we would need to update the **gWorldViewProj** variable appropriately before drawing each object.

The general advice is to create constant buffers based on the frequency in which you need to update their contents. For instance, you may create the following constant buffers:

```
cbuffer cbPerObject
{
    float4x4 gWVP;
};

cbuffer cbPerFrame
{
    float3 gLightDirection;
    float3 gLightPosition;
    float4 gLightColor;
};
```

```
cbuffer cbRarely
{
    float4 gFogColor;
    float gFogStart;
    float gFogEnd;
};
```

In this example, we use three constant buffers. The first constant buffer stores the combined world, view, and projection matrix. This variable depends on the object, so it must be updated on a per object basis. That is, if we are rendering 100 objects per frame, then we will be updating this variable 100 times per frame. The second constant buffer stores scene light variables. Here, we are assuming that the lights are animated and so need to be updated once every frame of animation. The last constant buffer stores variables used to control fog. Here, we are assuming that the scene fog rarely changes (e.g., maybe it only changes at certain times of day in the game).

The motivation for dividing the constant buffers up is efficiency. When a constant buffer is updated, all its variables must be updated; therefore, it is efficient to group them based on their update frequency to minimize redundant updates.

6.6 EXAMPLE PIXEL SHADER

As discussed in §5.10.3, during rasterization vertex attributes output from the vertex shader (or geometry shader) are interpolated across the pixels of a triangle. The interpolated values are then fed into the pixel shader as input. Assuming there is no geometry shader, Figure 6.5 illustrates the path vertex data takes up to now.

A pixel shader is like a vertex shader in that it is a function executed for each pixel fragment. Given the pixel shader input, the job of the pixel shader is to calculate a color value for the pixel fragment. We note that the pixel fragment may not survive and make it onto the back buffer; for example, it might be clipped in the pixel shader (the HLSL includes a `clip` function which can discard a pixel fragment from further processing), occluded by another pixel fragment with a smaller depth value, or the pixel fragment may be discarded by a later pipeline test like the stencil buffer test. Therefore, a pixel on the back buffer may have several pixel fragment candidates; this is the distinction between what is meant by "pixel fragment" and "pixel," although sometimes the terms are used interchangeably, but context usually makes it clear what is meant.

Note: *As a hardware optimization, it is possible that a pixel fragment is rejected by the pipeline before making it to the pixel shader (e.g., early-z rejection). This is where the depth test is done first, and if the pixel fragment is determined to be occluded by the depth test, then the pixel shader is skipped. However, there are*

```
struct Vertex
{
    XMFLOAT3 Pos;
    XMFLOAT3 Normal;
    XMFLOAT2 Tex0;
};


D3D11_INPUT_ELEMENT_DESC vertexDesc[] =
{
    {"POSITION", 0, DXGI_FORMAT_R32G32B32_FLOAT, 0, 0,
        D3D11_INPUT_PER_VERTEX_DATA, 0},
    {"NORMAL",   0, DXGI_FORMAT_R32G32B32_FLOAT, 0, 12,
        D3D11_INPUT_PER_VERTEX_DATA, 0},
    {"TEXCOORD", 0, DXGI_FORMAT_R32G32_FLOAT, 0, 24,
        D3D11_INPUT_PER_VERTEX_DATA, 0}
};

void VS(float3 iPosL        : POSITION,
        float3 iNormalL     : NORMAL,
        float2 iTex0        : TEXCOORD,
        out float4 oPosH    : SV_POSITION,
        out float3 oPosW    : POSITION,
        out float3 oNormalW : NORMAL,
        out float2 oTex0    : TEXCOORD0,
        out float  oFog     : TEXCOORD1)
{

}

void PS(float4 posH    : SV_POSITION,
        float3 posW    : POSITION,
        float3 normalW : NORMAL,
        float2 tex0    : TEXCOORD0,
        float  fog     : TEXCOORD1)
{

}
```

Figure 6.5. **Each vertex element has an associated semantic specified by the**
D3D11_INPUT_ELEMENT_DESC array. Each parameter of the vertex shader also has an
attached semantic. The semantics are used to match vertex elements with vertex shader
parameters. Likewise, each output from the vertex shader has an attached semantic, and
each pixel shader input parameter has an attached semantics. These semantics are used to
map vertex shader outputs into the pixel shader input parameters.

*some cases that can disable the early-z rejection optimization. For example, if
the pixel shader modifies the depth of the pixel, then the pixel shader has to be
executed because we do not really know what the depth of the pixel is before the
pixel shader if the pixel shader changes it.*

Below is a simple pixel shader which corresponds to the vertex shader given in
§6.4. For completeness, the vertex shader is shown again.

```
cbuffer cbPerObject
{
    float4x4 gWorldViewProj;
};

void VS(float3 iPos : POSITION, float4 iColor : COLOR,
    out float4 oPosH : SV_POSITION,
    out float4 oColor : COLOR)
{
    // Transform to homogeneous clip space.
    oPosH = mul(float4(iPos, 1.0f), gWorldViewProj);

    // Just pass vertex color into the pixel shader.
    oColor = iColor;
}

float4 PS(float4 posH : SV_POSITION, float4 color : COLOR) : SV_Target
{
    return pin.Color;
}
```

In this example, the pixel shader simply returns the interpolated color value. Notice that the pixel shader input exactly matches the vertex shader output; this is a requirement. The pixel shader returns a 4D color value, and the SV_TARGET semantic following the function parameter listing indicates the return value type should match the render target format.

We can equivalently rewrite the previous vertex and pixel shaders using input/output structures. The notation varies in that we attach the semantics to the members of the input/output structures, and that we use a return statement for output instead of output parameters.

```
cbuffer cbPerObject
{
    float4x4 gWorldViewProj;
};

struct VertexIn
{
    float3 Pos   : POSITION;
    float4 Color : COLOR;
};

struct VertexOut
{
    float4 PosH  : SV_POSITION;
    float4 Color : COLOR;
};

VertexOut VS(VertexIn vin)
{
    VertexOut vout;
```

```
    // Transform to homogeneous clip space.
    vout.PosH = mul(float4(vin.Pos, 1.0f), gWorldViewProj);

    // Just pass vertex color into the pixel shader.
    vout.Color = vin.Color;

    return vout;
}

float4 PS(VertexOut pin) : SV_Target
{
    return pin.Color;
}
```

6.7 RENDER STATES

Direct3D is basically a state machine. Things stay in their current state until we change them. For example, we saw in §6.1, §6.2, and §6.3 that the input layout, vertex buffer, and index buffer bound to the input assembler stage of the pipeline stay there until we bind different ones; likewise, the current set primitive topology stays in effect until it is changed. In addition, Direct3D has state groups which encapsulate settings that can be used to configure Direct3D:

1. **ID3D11RasterizerState**: This interface represents a state group used to configure the rasterization stage of the pipeline.

2. **ID3D11BlendState**: This interface represents a state group used to configure blending operations. We will discuss these states in the chapter on blending; by default, blending is disabled, so we do not need to worry about it for now.

3. **ID3D11DepthStencilState**: This interface represents a state group used to configure the depth and stencil tests. We will discuss these states in the chapter on the stencil buffer; by default, stenciling is disabled, so we do not need to worry about it for now. The default depth test settings are set to do the standard depth test as described in §4.1.5.

Right now, the only state block interface that concerns us is the ID3D11RasterizerState interface. We can create an interface of this type by filling out a D3D11_RASTERIZER_DESC structure and then calling the method:

```
HRESULT ID3D11Device::CreateRasterizerState(
    const D3D11_RASTERIZER_DESC *pRasterizerDesc,
    ID3D11RasterizerState **ppRasterizerState);
```

The first parameter is just the filled out D3D11_RASTERIZER_DESC structure describing the rasterizer state block to create; the second parameter is used to return a pointer to the created ID3D11RasterizerState interface.

The D3D11_RASTERIZER_DESC structure is defined as follows:

```
typedef struct D3D11_RASTERIZER_DESC {
    D3D11_FILL_MODE FillMode;        // Default: D3D11_FILL_SOLID
    D3D11_CULL_MODE CullMode;        // Default: D3D11_CULL_BACK
    BOOL FrontCounterClockwise;      // Default: false
    INT DepthBias;                   // Default: 0
    FLOAT DepthBiasClamp;            // Default: 0.0f
    FLOAT SlopeScaledDepthBias;      // Default: 0.0f
    BOOL DepthClipEnable;            // Default: true
    BOOL ScissorEnable;              // Default: false
    BOOL MultisampleEnable;          // Default: false
    BOOL AntialiasedLineEnable;      // Default: false
} D3D11_RASTERIZER_DESC;
```

Most of these members are advanced or not used very often; therefore, we refer you to the SDK documentation for the descriptions of each member. However, only the first three are worth discussing here.

1. **FillMode**: Specify D3D11_FILL_WIREFRAME for wireframe rendering or D3D11_FILL_SOLID for solid rendering. Solid rendering is the default.

2. **CullMode**: Specify D3D11_CULL_NONE to disable culling, D3D11_CULL_BACK to cull back-facing triangles, or D3D11_CULL_FRONT to cull front-facing triangles. Back-facing triangles are culled by default.

3. **FrontCounterClockwise**: Specify `false` if you want triangles ordered clockwise (with respect to the camera) to be treated as front-facing and triangles ordered counterclockwise (with respect to the camera) to be treated as back-facing. Specify `true` if you want triangles ordered counterclockwise (with respect to the camera) to be treated as front-facing and triangles ordered clockwise (with respect to the camera) to be treated as back-facing. This state is false by default.

Once an ID3D11RasterizerState object has been created, we can update the device with the new state block:

```
void ID3D11DeviceContext::RSSetState(
    ID3D11RasterizerState *pRasterizerState);
```

The following code shows how to create a rasterize state that disables backface culling:

```
D3D11_RASTERIZER_DESC rsDesc;
ZeroMemory(&rsDesc, sizeof(D3D11_RASTERIZER_DESC));
rsDesc.FillMode = D3D11_FILL_SOLID;
rsDesc.CullMode = D3D11_CULL_NONE;
rsDesc.FrontCounterClockwise = false;
rsDesc.DepthClipEnable = true;

HR(md3dDevice->CreateRasterizerState(&rsDesc, &mNoCullRS));
```

Note: *Using* `ZeroMemory` *works to initialize the other properties we do not set because their default values are zero or false. However, if a property had a nonzero or true default value, and you wanted the default value, then you would have to explicitly set the property.*

Note that for an application, you may need several different `ID3D11RasterizerState` objects. So what you would do is create them all at initialization time, and then switch between them as needed in the application update/draw code. For example, let's suppose you have two objects, and you wanted to draw the first one in wireframe mode and the second in solid mode. Then you would have two `ID3D11RasterizerState` objects and you would switch between them when drawing your objects:

```
// Create render state objects as initialization time.
ID3D11RasterizerState* mWireframeRS;
ID3D11RasterizerState* mSolidRS;
...

// Switch between the render state objects in the draw function.
md3dImmediateContext->RSSetState(mSolidRS);
DrawObject();

md3dImmediateContext->RSSetState(mWireframeRS);
DrawObject();
```

It should be noted that Direct3D never restores states to the previous setting. Therefore, you should always set the states you need when drawing an object. Making incorrect assumptions about the current state of the device will lead to incorrect output.

Each state block has a default state. We can revert back to the default state by calling the `RSSetState` method with null:

```
// Restore default state.
md3dImmediateContext->RSSetState( 0 );
```

Note: *Typically, an application will not need to create additional render state groups at runtime. Therefore, an application can define and create all the necessary render state groups at initialization time. Moreover, because the render state groups will not need to be modified at runtime, you can provide global read-only access to them to your rendering code. For example, you could put all of your render state group objects in a static class. This way, you do not create duplicate render state group objects, and various parts of your rendering code can share the render state group objects.*

6.8 EFFECTS

The *effects framework* is a set of utility code that provides a framework for organizing shader programs and render states that work together to implement a specific rendering effect. For example, you may have different effects for rendering water, clouds, metal objects, and animated characters. Each effect will consist of at least one vertex shader, one pixel shader, and render states that work to implement the effect.

In the previous version of Direct3D, the effects framework worked out of the box once you linked with the D3D 10 library. In Direct3D 11, the effects framework has been moved to the D3DX library, and you have to include a separate header file (`d3dx11Effect.h`) and link with a separate library (`D3DX11Effects.lib` for release builds and `D3DX11EffectsD.lib` for debug builds). Furthermore, in Direct3D 11, they give you the full source code for the effects library code (*DirectX SDK\Samples\C++ \Effects11*). Thus, you could modify the effects framework for your own needs. In this book, we will only be using the effects framework as is, without modification. In order to use the library, you need to first build the *Effects11* project in both release and debug mode to generate the `D3DX11Effects.lib` and `D3DX11EffectsD.lib` files; you will only need to do this once unless the effects framework is updated (e.g., a new version of the DirectX SDK may update these files, so you may want to rebuild the .lib files to get the latest version). The `d3dx11Effect.h` header file can be found in *DirectX SDK\Samples\C++\Effects11\Inc*. For our sample projects, we place the `d3dx11Effect.h`, `D3DX11EffectsD.lib`, and `D3DX11Effects.lib` files in the *Common* directory that all of our projects share code from (see the "Introduction" for a description of the sample project organization).

6.8.1 Effect Files

We have discussed vertex shaders, pixel shaders, and to a lesser extent, geometry and tessellation shaders. We have also discussed constant buffers, which can be used to store "global" variables accessible to the shaders. Such code is commonly written in an effect file (.fx), which is just a text file (just like C++ code is written in .h/.cpp files). In addition to housing shaders and constant buffers, an effect also contains at least one *technique*. In turn, a technique contains at least one *pass*.

1. `technique11`: A technique consists of one or more passes which are used to create a specific rendering technique. For each pass, the geometry is rendered in a different way, and the results of each pass are combined in some way to achieve the desired result. For example, a terrain rendering technique may use a multi-pass texturing technique. Note that multi-pass techniques are usually expensive because the geometry is redrawn for each pass; however, multi-pass techniques are required to implement some rendering techniques.

2. `pass`: A pass consists of a vertex shader, optional geometry shader, optional tessellation related shaders, a pixel shader, and render states. These components indicate how to process and shade the geometry for this pass. We note that a pixel shader can be optional as well (rarely). For instance, we may just want to

render to the depth buffer and not the back buffer; in this case we do not need to shade any pixels with a pixel shader.

Note: *Techniques can also be grouped together in what is called an effect group. If you do not explicitly define one, the compiler creates an anonymous one to contain all the techniques in the effect file. In this book, we do not explicitly define any effect groups.*

Below is the entire effect file for the demos of this chapter:

```
cbuffer cbPerObject
{
    float4x4 gWorldViewProj;
};

struct VertexIn
{
    float3 Pos   : POSITION;
    float4 Color : COLOR;
};

struct VertexOut
{
    float4 PosH  : SV_POSITION;
    float4 Color : COLOR;
};

VertexOut VS(VertexIn vin)
{
    VertexOut vout;

    // Transform to homogeneous clip space.
    vout.PosH = mul(float4(vin.Pos, 1.0f), gWorldViewProj);

    // Just pass vertex color into the pixel shader.
    vout.Color = vin.Color;

    return vout;
}

float4 PS(VertexOut pin) : SV_Target
{
    return pin.Color;
}

technique11 ColorTech
{
    pass P0
    {
      SetVertexShader( CompileShader( vs_5_0, VS() ) );
      SetPixelShader( CompileShader( ps_5_0, PS() ) );
    }
}
```

Note: *Point and vector coordinates are specified relative to many different spaces (e.g., local space, world space, view space, homogeneous space). When reading code, it might not be obvious which coordinate system the coordinates of the point/ vector are relative to. Therefore, we often use the following suffixes to denote the space: L (for local space), W (for world space), V (for view space), and H (for homogenous clip space). Here are some examples:*

```
float3 iPosL;      // local space
float3 gEyePosW;   // world space
float3 normalV;    // view space
float4 posH;       // homogeneous clip space
```

We mentioned that passes consist of render states. That is, state blocks can be created and set directly in an effect file. This is convenient when the effect requires specific render states to work; in contrast, some effects may work with variable render state settings, in which case we prefer to set the states at the application level in order to facilitate easy state switching. The following code shows how to create and set a rasterizer state block in an effect file.

```
RasterizerState WireframeRS
{
    FillMode = Wireframe;
    CullMode = Back;
    FrontCounterClockwise = false;

    // Default values used for any properties we do not set.
};

technique11 ColorTech
{
    pass P0
    {
      SetVertexShader( CompileShader( vs_5_0, VS() ) );
      SetPixelShader( CompileShader( ps_5_0, PS() ) );

      SetRasterizerState(WireframeRS);
    }
}
```

Observe that the right-hand values in the rasterizer state object definition are basically the same as in the C++ case, except the prefixes are omitted (e.g., D3D11_FILL_ and D3D11_CULL_ are omitted).

Note: *Because an effect is typically written in an external .fx file, it can be modified without having to recompile the source code.*

6.8.2 Compiling Shaders

The first step to creating an effect is to compile the shader programs that are defined inside the .fx file. This can be done with the following D3DX function.

```
HRESULT D3DX11CompileFromFile(
    LPCTSTR pSrcFile,
    CONST D3D10_SHADER_MACRO *pDefines,
    LPD3D10INCLUDE pInclude,
    LPCSTR pFunctionName,
    LPCSTR pProfile,
    UINT Flags1,
    UINT Flags2,
    ID3DX11ThreadPump *pPump,
    ID3D10Blob **ppShader,
    ID3D10Blob **ppErrorMsgs,
    HRESULT *pHResult);
```

1. **pFileName:** The name of the .fx file that contains the effect source code we want to compile.

2. **pDefines:** Advanced option we do not use; see the SDK documentation. We always specify null in this book.

3. **pInclude:** Advanced option we do not use; see the SDK documentation. We always specify null in this book.

4. **pFunctionName:** The shader function name entry point. This is only used when compiling shader programs individually. When using the effects framework, specify null, as the technique passes defined inside the effect file specify the shader entry points.

5. **pProfile:** A string specifying the shader version we are using. For Direct3D 11 effects, we use shader version 5.0 ("fx_5_0").

6. **Flags1:** Flags to specify how the shader code should be compiled. There are quite a few of these flags listed in the SDK documentation, but the only two we use in this book are:

   (a) **D3D10_SHADER_DEBUG:** Compiles the shaders in debug mode.

   (b) **D3D10_SHADER_SKIP_OPTIMIZATION:** Instructs the compiler to skip optimizations (useful for debugging).

7. **Flags2:** Advanced effect compilation options we do not use; see the SDK documentation.

8. **pPump:** Advanced option we do not use to compile the shader asynchronously; see the SDK documentation. We always specify null in this book.

9. **ppShader:** Returns a pointer to a **ID3D10Blob** data structure that stores the compiled shader.

10 . **ppErrorMsgs:** Returns a pointer to a **ID3D10Blob** data structure that stores a string containing the compilation errors, if any.

11 . **pHResult:** Used to obtain the returned error code if compiling asynchronously. Specify null if you specified null for **pPump**.

1. *In addition to compiling the shaders inside a .fx, this function can be used to compile individual shaders as well. Some programmers do not use the effects framework (or make their own), and so they define and compile their shaders separately.*

2. *The references to "D3D10" in the previous function are not typos. The D3D11 compiler is built on the D3D10 compiler, so the Direct3D 11 team did not bother renaming some of the identifiers.*

3. *The type* `ID3D10Blob` *is just a generic chunk of memory that has two methods:*

   (a) `LPVOID GetBufferPointer`: *Returns a void* to the data, so it must be casted to the appropriate type before use (see the example following).*

   (b) `SIZE_T GetBufferSize`: *Returns the byte size of the buffer.*

Once the effect shaders have been compiled, we can create an effect (represented by the `ID3DXEffect11` interface) with the following function:

```
HRESULT D3DX11CreateEffectFromMemory(
    void *pData,
    SIZE_T DataLength,
    UINT FXFlags,
    ID3D11Device *pDevice,
    ID3DX11Effect **ppEffect);
```

1. `pData`: Pointer to the compiled effect data.

2. `DataLength`: The byte size of the compiled effect data.

3. `FXFlags`: Effect flags should match the flags specified for `Flags2` in the `D3DX11CompileFromFile` function.

4. `pDevice`: Pointer to the Direct3D 11 device.

5. `ppEffect`: Returns a pointer to the created effect.

The following code shows how to compile and create an effect:

```
DWORD shaderFlags = 0;
#if defined(DEBUG) || defined(_DEBUG)
    shaderFlags |= D3D10_SHADER_DEBUG;
    shaderFlags |= D3D10_SHADER_SKIP_OPTIMIZATION;
#endif

    ID3D10Blob* compiledShader = 0;
    ID3D10Blob* compilationMsgs = 0;
    HRESULT hr = D3DX11CompileFromFile(L"color.fx", 0,
      0, 0, "fx_5_0", shaderFlags,
      0, 0, &compiledShader, &compilationMsgs, 0);

    // compilationMsgs can store errors or warnings.
```

```
if(compilationMsgs != 0)
{
  MessageBoxA(0, (char*)compilationMsgs->GetBufferPointer(), 0, 0);
  ReleaseCOM(compilationMsgs);
}

// Even if there are no compilationMsgs, check to make sure there
// were no other errors.
if(FAILED(hr))
{
  DXTrace(__FILE__, (DWORD)__LINE__, hr,
    L"D3DX11CompileFromFile", true);
}

ID3DX11Effect* mFX;
HR(D3DX11CreateEffectFromMemory(
  compiledShader->GetBufferPointer(),
  compiledShader->GetBufferSize(),
  0, md3dDevice, &mFX));

// Done with compiled shader.
ReleaseCOM(compiledShader);
```

Note: *Creating Direct3D resources is expensive and should always be done at initialization time, and never at runtime. That means creating input layouts, buffers, render state objects, and effects should always be done at initialization time.*

6.8.3 Interfacing with Effects from the C++ Application

The C++ application code typically needs to communicate with the effect; in particular, the C++ application usually needs to update variables in the constant buffers. For example, suppose that we had the following constant buffer defined in an effect file:

```
cbuffer cbPerObject
{
    float4x4 gWVP;
    float4 gColor;
    float gSize;
    int gIndex;
    bool gOptionOn;
};
```

Through the ID3DX11Effect interface, we can obtain pointers to the variables in the constant buffer:

```
ID3DX11EffectMatrixVariable* fxWVPVar;
ID3DX11EffectVectorVariable* fxColorVar;
ID3DX11EffectScalarVariable* fxSizeVar;
ID3DX11EffectScalarVariable* fxIndexVar;
ID3DX11EffectScalarVariable* fxOptionOnVar;
```

```
fxWVPVar     = mFX->GetVariableByName("gWVP")->AsMatrix();
fxColorVar   = mFX->GetVariableByName("gColor")->AsVector();
fxSizeVar    = mFX->GetVariableByName("gSize")->AsScalar();
fxIndexVar   = mFX->GetVariableByName("gIndex")->AsScalar();
fxOptionOnVar = mFX->GetVariableByName("gOptionOn")->AsScalar();
```

The `ID3DX11Effect::GetVariableByName` method returns a pointer of type `ID3DX11EffectVariable`. This is a generic effect variable type; to obtain a pointer to the specialized type (e.g., matrix, vector, scalar), you must use the appropriate `As-` method (e.g., `AsMatrix`, `AsVector`, `AsScalar`).

Once we have pointers to the variables, we can update them through the C++ interface. Here are some examples:

```
fxWVPVar->SetMatrix((float*)&M ); // assume M is of type XMMATRIX
fxColorVar->SetFloatVector( (float*)&v ); // assume v is of type XMVECTOR
fxSizeVar->SetFloat( 5.0f );
fxIndexVar->SetInt( 77 );
fxOptionOnVar->SetBool( true );
```

Note that these calls update an internal cache in the effect object, and are not transferred over to GPU memory until we apply the rendering pass (§6.8.4). This ensures one update to GPU memory instead of many small updates, which would be inefficient.

Note: ▶ *An effect variable need not be specialized. For example, you can write:*

```
ID3DX11EffectVariable* mfxEyePosVar;
mfxEyePosVar = mFX->GetVariableByName("gEyePosW");
...
mfxEyePosVar->SetRawValue(&mEyePos, 0, sizeof(XMFLOAT3));
```

This is useful for setting variables of arbitrary size (e.g., general structures). Note that the `ID3DX11EffectVectorVariable` *interface assumes 4D vectors, so you will need to use* `ID3DX11EffectVariable`, *as noted previously, if you want to use 3D vectors (like* `XMFLOAT3`).

In addition to constant buffer variables, it is necessary to obtain a pointer to the technique objects stored in the effect. This is done like so:

```
ID3DX11EffectTechnique* mTech;
mTech = mFX->GetTechniqueByName("ColorTech");
```

The single parameter this method takes is the string name of the technique you wish to obtain a pointer to.

6.8.4 Using Effects to Draw

To use a technique to draw geometry, we simply need to make sure the variables in the constant buffers are up to date. Then we just loop over each pass in the technique, apply the pass, and draw the geometry:

```
// Set constants
XMMATRIX world = XMLoadFloat4x4(&mWorld);
XMMATRIX view = XMLoadFloat4x4(&mView);
XMMATRIX proj = XMLoadFloat4x4(&mProj);
XMMATRIX worldViewProj = world*view*proj;

mfxWorldViewProj->SetMatrix(reinterpret_cast<float*>(&worldViewProj));

D3DX11_TECHNIQUE_DESC techDesc;
mTech->GetDesc(&techDesc);
for(UINT p = 0; p < techDesc.Passes; ++p)
{
    mTech->GetPassByIndex(p)->Apply(0, md3dImmediateContext);

    // Draw some geometry.
    md3dImmediateContext->DrawIndexed(36, 0, 0);
}
```

When the geometry is drawn in a pass, it will be drawn with the shaders and render states set by that pass. The `ID3DX11EffectTechnique::GetPassByIndex` method returns a pointer to an `ID3DX11EffectPass` interface, which represents the pass with the specified index. The `Apply` method updates the constant buffers stored in GPU memory, binds the shader programs to the pipeline, and applies any render states the pass sets. In the current version of Direct3D 11, the first parameter of `ID3DX11EffectPass::Apply` is unused, and zero should be specified; the second parameter is a pointer to the device context the pass will use.

If you need to change the values of variables in a constant buffer between draw calls, then you will have to call `Apply` to update the changes before drawing the geometry:

```
for(UINT i = 0; i < techDesc.Passes; ++i)
{
    ID3DX11EffectPass* pass = mTech->GetPassByIndex(i);

    // Set combined world-view-projection matrix for land geometry.
    worldViewProj = landWorld*view*proj;
    mfxWorldViewProj->SetMatrix(reinterpret_cast<float*>(&worldViewProj));
    pass->Apply(0, md3dImmediateContext);
    mLand.draw();

    // Set combined world-view-projection matrix for wave geometry.
    worldViewProj = wavesWorld*view*proj;
    mfxWorldViewProj->SetMatrix(reinterpret_cast<float*>(&worldViewProj));
    pass->Apply(0, md3dImmediateContext);
    mWaves.draw();
}
```

6.8.5 Compiling an Effect at Build Time

So far we have shown how to compile an effect at runtime via the `D3DX11CompileFromFile` function. Doing this is slightly irritating because if your effect file code has a compilation error, then you do not find out about it until you run the program. It is possible to compile your effects offline using the *fxc* tool that ships with the DirectX SDK (located in *DirectX SDK\Utilities\bin\x86*). Moreover, you can modify your VC++ project to invoke *fxc* to compile your effects as part of the normal build process. The following steps show how to do this:

1. Make sure the path to *DirectX SDK\Utilities\bin\x86* is listed under "Executable Directories" in your project's VC++ Directories tab, as described in the introduction.

2. Add the effect files to your project.

3. For each effect, right click on the effect file in Solution Explorer, select **Properties,** and add a custom build tool (see Figure 6.6).

(a) Debug mode:

```
fxc /Fc /Od /Zi /T fx_5_0 /Fo "%(RelativeDir)\%(Filename).fxo" "%(FullPath)"
```

(b) Release mode:

```
fxc /T fx_5_0 /Fo "%(RelativeDir)\%(Filename).fxo" "%(FullPath)"
```

You can see the SDK documentation for the complete list of compilation flags for *fxc*. The three flags we use for debug mode, "/Fc /Od /Zi" output the assembly listing, disable optimizations, and enable debug information, respectively.

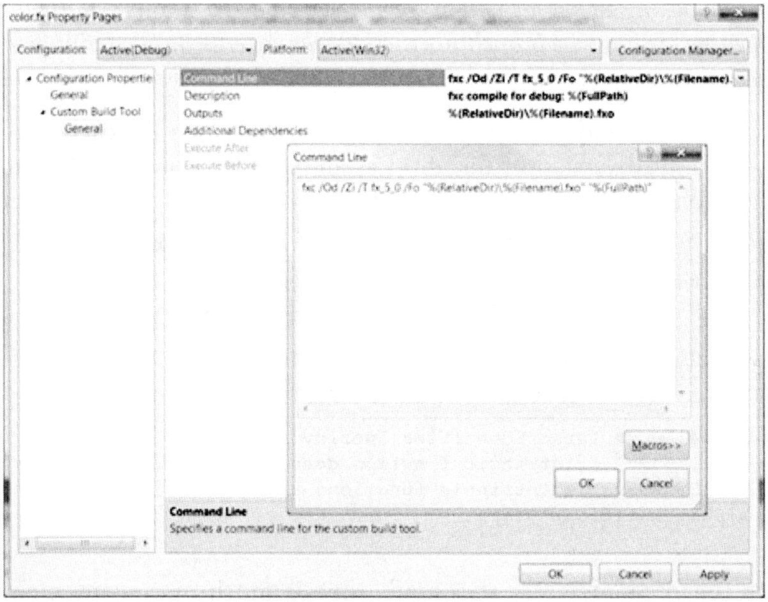

Figure 6.6. Adding a custom build tool to the project.

Note: *Looking at the assembly of your shaders from time to time is useful just to do a check that instructions are not being generated that you do not expect. For example, if you have a conditional statement in your HLSL code, then you might expect there to be a branching instruction in the assembly code. Branching on GPUs is quite expensive (or was not supported on some DirectX 9 hardware), and so sometimes the compiler will flatten a conditional statement by evaluating both branches and then interpolate between the two to pick the right answer. That is, the following codes will give the same answer:*

Conditional	Flattened

```float x = 0;```
 	
 ```// s == 1 (true) or s == 0 (false)```
 ```if(s)```
 ```{```
 ```   x = sqrt(y);```
 ```}```
 ```else```
 ```{```
 ```   x = 2*y;```
 ```}```
	```float a = 2*y;```
	 ```float b = sqrt(y);```
	 ```float x = a + s*(b-a);```
	
	 ```// s == 1:```
	 ```// x = a + b - a = b = sqrt(y)```
	
	 ```// s == 0:```
	 ```// x = a + 0*(b-a) = a = 2*y```

So the flattened method gives us the same result without any branching, but without looking at the assembly code, we would not know if flattening was happening, or if a true branch instruction was generated. The point being that sometimes you want to look at the assembly to see what is really going on.

Now when you build your project, *fxc* will be called on for each effect and generate a compiled version of the effect as an .fxo file. Moreover, if there were any compilation warnings or errors from *fxc*, they will be displayed in the debug output window. For example, if we misname a variable in the color.fx effect file:

```
// Should be gWorldViewProj, not worldViewProj!
vout.PosH = mul(float4(vin.Pos, 1.0f), worldViewProj);
```

Then we get quite a few errors from this one mistake (the top error being the key one to fix) listed in the debut output window:

```
error X3004: undeclared identifier 'worldViewProj'
error X3013: 'mul': intrinsic function does not take 2 parameters
error X3013: Possible intrinsic functions are:
error X3013: mul(float, float)
. . .
```

Getting the error messages at compile time is much more convenient than at runtime. We have now compiled our effect file (.fxo) as part of our build process, so we no longer need to do it at runtime (i.e., we do not need to call `D3DX11CompileFromFile`). However, we still need to load the compiled shader data from the .fxo file, and feed it into the `D3DX11CreateEffectFromMemory` function. This can done using standard C++ file input mechanisms like so:

```
std::ifstream fin("fx/color.fxo", std::ios::binary);

fin.seekg(0, std::ios_base::end);
int size = (int)fin.tellg();
fin.seekg(0, std::ios_base::beg);
std::vector<char> compiledShader(size);

fin.read(&compiledShader[0], size);
fin.close();

HR(D3DX11CreateEffectFromMemory(&compiledShader[0], size,
    0, md3dDevice, &mFX));
```

With the exception of the "Box" demo, which compiles the shader code at runtime, we compile all of our shaders as part of the build process.

6.8.6 The Effects Framework as a "Shader Generator"

We mentioned at the beginning of this section that an effect can have multiple techniques. So why would we have multiple techniques for a rendering effect? Let us use shadows as an example without getting into the details of how shadowing is done. Essentially, the higher the shadow quality, the more expensive the shadowing technique. In order to support users with both low-end and high-end graphics cards, we might implement a low, medium, and high quality shadowing technique. So even though we have one shadowing effect, we use multiple techniques to implement the effect. Our shadowing effect file might look like this:

```
// Omit constant buffers, vertex structures, etc...

VertexOut VS(VertexIn vin) {/* Omit implementation details */}

float4 LowQualityPS(VertexOut pin) : SV_Target
{
    /* Do work common to all quality levels */

    /* Do low quality specific stuff */

    /* Do more work common to all quality levels */
}

float4 MediumQualityPS(VertexOut pin) : SV_Target
{
    /* Do work common to all quality levels */
```

```
        /* Do medium quality specific stuff */

        /* Do more work common to all quality levels */
    }

    float4 HighQualityPS(VertexOut pin) : SV_Target
    {
        /* Do work common to all quality levels */

        /* Do high quality specific stuff */

        /* Do more work common to all quality levels */
    }

    technique11 ShadowsLow
    {
        pass P0
        {
          SetVertexShader(CompileShader(vs_5_0, VS()));
          SetPixelShader(CompileShader(ps_5_0, LowQualityPS()));
        }
    }

    technique11 ShadowsMedium
    {
        pass P0
        {
          SetVertexShader(CompileShader(vs_5_0, VS()));
          SetPixelShader( CompileShader(ps_5_0, MediumQualityPS()));
        }
    }

    technique11 ShadowsHigh
    {
        pass P0
        {
          SetVertexShader(CompileShader(vs_5_0, VS()));
          SetPixelShader( CompileShader(ps_5_0, HighQualityPS()));
        }
    }
```

Then the C++ application code could detect the power of the user's graphics card and select the appropriate technique to use for rendering.

Note: *The previous code assumes that only the pixel shaders differ between the three shadowing techniques, and so all the techniques share the same vertex shader. However, it is possible to also have different vertex shaders per technique if that is needed.*

One annoying problem with the previous implementation is that even though the pixel shaders differ in shadowing code, they still have code that is common to all of them that needs to be duplicated. One might suggest using conditional statements, and that is a step in the right direction. There is some overhead for dynamic branching statements in shaders, so we should only use them if we really need to. What we really want to do is a conditional compilation that will generate all the shader variations we need at compile time so that there is no branching instructions in the shader code. Fortunately, the effects framework provides a way to do that. Consider the new implementation:

```
// Omit constant buffers, vertex structures, etc...

VertexOut VS(VertexIn vin) {/* Omit implementation details */}

#define LowQuality 0
#define MediumQuality 1
#define HighQuality 2

float4 PS(VertexOut pin, uniform int gQuality) : SV_Target
{
    /* Do work common to all quality levels */

    if(gQuality == LowQuality)
    {
      /* Do low quality specific stuff */
    }
    else if(gQuality == MediumQuality)
    {
      /* Do medium quality specific stuff */
    }
    else
    {
      /* Do high quality specific stuff */
    }

    /* Do more work common to all quality levels */
}

technique11 ShadowsLow
{
    pass P0
    {
      SetVertexShader(CompileShader(vs_5_0, VS()));
      SetPixelShader(CompileShader(ps_5_0, PS(LowQuality)));
    }
}

technique11 ShadowsMedium
{
    pass P0
    {
      SetVertexShader(CompileShader(vs_5_0, VS()));
      SetPixelShader( CompileShader(ps_5_0, PS(MediumQuality)));
    }
}

technique11 ShadowsHigh
```

```
    {
        pass P0
        {
            SetVertexShader(CompileShader(vs_5_0, VS()));
            SetPixelShader(CompileShader(ps_5_0, PS(HighQuality)));
        }
    }
```

Observe that we have added an additional `uniform` parameter to the pixel shader that denotes the quality level. This parameter is different in that it does not vary per pixel, but is instead uniform/constant. Moreover, we do not change it at runtime either, like we change constant buffer variables. Instead we set it at compile time, and since the value is known at compile time, it allows the effects framework to generate different shader variations based on its value. This enables us to create our low, medium, and high quality pixel shaders without us duplicating code (the effects framework basically duplicates the code for us as a compile time process), and without using branching instructions.

Here are a couple other examples where shader generation is common:

1. Apply textures? An application may want to apply a texture to some objects but not to others. One solution would be to create two pixel shaders, one that applies textures and one that does not. Or we could use the shader generator mechanism to create the two pixel shaders for us, and then have the C++ application pick the desired technique.

```
float4 PS(VertexOut pin, uniform bool gApplyTexture) : SV_Target
{
    /* Do common work */

    if(gApplyTexture)
    {
        /* Apply texture */
    }

    /* Do more common work */
}

technique11 BasicTech
{
    pass P0
    {
        SetVertexShader(CompileShader(vs_5_0, VS()));
        SetPixelShader(CompileShader(ps_5_0, PS(false)));
    }
}

technique11 TextureTech
{
    pass P0
    {
```

```
        SetVertexShader(CompileShader(vs_5_0, VS()));
        SetPixelShader(CompileShader(ps_5_0, PS(true)));
    }
}
```

2. How many lights to use? A game level might support between 1 to 4 active lights at any given time. The more lights that are used the more expensive the lighting calculation is. We could implement separate vertex shaders based on the number of lights, or we could use the shader generator mechanism to create four vertex shaders for us, and then have the C++ application pick the desired technique based on the number of currently active lights:

```
VertexOut VS(VertexOut pin, uniform int gLightCount)
{
    /* Do common work */

    for(int i = 0; i < gLightCount; ++i)
    {
    /* do lighting work */
    }

    /* Do more common work */
}

technique11 Light1
{
    pass P0
    {
      SetVertexShader(CompileShader(vs_5_0, VS(1)));
      SetPixelShader(CompileShader(ps_5_0, PS()));
    }
}

technique11 Light2
{
    pass P0
    {
      SetVertexShader(CompileShader(vs_5_0, VS(2)));
      SetPixelShader( CompileShader(ps_5_0, PS()));
    }
}

technique11 Light3
{
    pass P0
    {
      SetVertexShader(CompileShader(vs_5_0, VS(3)));
      SetPixelShader(CompileShader(ps_5_0, PS()));
    }
}

technique11 Light4
```

```
{
    pass P0
    {
      SetVertexShader(CompileShader(vs_5_0, VS(4)));
      SetPixelShader(CompileShader(ps_5_0, PS()));
    }
}
```

There is nothing that limits us to one parameter. We will need to combine shadow quality, textures, and the number of lights all together so the vertex and pixel shaders would look like the following:

```
VertexOut VS(VertexOut pin, uniform int gLightCount)
{}

float4 PS(VertexOut pin,
    uniform int gQuality,
    uniform bool gApplyTexture) : SV_Target
{}
```

So for example, to create a technique that uses low quality shadows, two lights, and no textures, we would write:

```
technique11 LowShadowsTwoLightsNoTextures
{
    pass P0
    {
      SetVertexShader(CompileShader(vs_5_0, VS(2)));
      SetPixelShader(CompileShader(ps_5_0, PS(LowQuality, false)));
    }
}
```

6.8.7 What the Assembly Looks Like

In case you do not bother to ever look at the assembly output of one of your effect files, we show what one looks like in this section. We do not explain the assembly, however, but if you have studied assembly before, you might recognize the **mov** instruction, and maybe could guess that **dp4** does a 4D dot product. Even without understanding the assembly, the listing gives some useful information. It clearly identifies the input and output signatures, and gives the approximate instruction count, which is one useful metric to understand how expensive/complex your shader is. Moreover, we see that multiple versions of our shaders really were generated based on the compile time parameters with no branching instructions. The effect file we use is the same as the one shown in §6.8.1, except that we add a simple uniform **bool** parameter to generate two techniques:

```
float4 PS(VertexOut pin, uniform bool gUseColor) : SV_Target
{
    if(gUseColor)
    {
      return pin.Color;
    }
    else
    {
      return float4(0, 0, 0, 1);
    }
}

technique11 ColorTech
{
    pass P0
    {
      SetVertexShader(CompileShader(vs_5_0, VS()));
      SetPixelShader(CompileShader(ps_5_0, PS(true)));
    }
}

technique11 NoColorTech
{
    pass P0
    {
      SetVertexShader(CompileShader(vs_5_0, VS()));
      SetPixelShader(CompileShader(ps_5_0, PS(false)));
    }
}

//
// FX Version: fx_5_0
//
// 1 local buffer(s)
//
cbuffer cbPerObject
{
    float4x4 gWorldViewProj;              // Offset:    0, size:    64
}

//
// 1 groups(s)
//
fxgroup
{
    //
    // 2 technique(s)
    //
    technique11 ColorTech
    {
      pass P0
      {
        VertexShader = asm {
          //
          // Generated by Microsoft (R) HLSL Shader Compiler 9.29.952.3111
          //
          //
```

```
    // Buffer Definitions:
    //
    // cbuffer cbPerObject
    // {
    //
    //   float4x4 gWorldViewProj;      // Offset:   0 Size:   64
    //
    // }
    //
    //
    // Resource Bindings:
    //
    // Name                Type  Format         Dim Slot Elements
    // ------------------- ----- ------ ----------- ---- --------
    // cbPerObject         cbuffer  NA           NA    0        1
    //
    //
    //
    // Input signature:
    //
    // Name          Index  Mask Register SysValue Format   Used
    // ------------- ----- ------ -------- -------- ------ ------
    // POSITION          0   xyz        0     NONE  float    xyz
    // COLOR             0  xyzw        1     NONE  float   xyzw
    //
    //
    // Output signature:
    //
    // Name          Index  Mask Register SysValue Format   Used
    // ------------- ----- ------ -------- -------- ------ ------
    // SV_POSITION       0  xyzw        0      POS  float   xyzw
    // COLOR             0  xyzw        1     NONE  float   xyzw
    //
    vs_5_0
    dcl_globalFlags refactoringAllowed
    dcl_constantbuffer cb0[4], immediateIndexed
    dcl_input v0.xyz
    dcl_input v1.xyzw
    dcl_output_siv o0.xyzw, position
    dcl_output o1.xyzw
    dcl_temps 1
    mov r0.xyz, v0.xyzx
    mov r0.w, l(1.000000)
    dp4 o0.x, r0.xyzw, cb0[0].xyzw
    dp4 o0.y, r0.xyzw, cb0[1].xyzw
    dp4 o0.z, r0.xyzw, cb0[2].xyzw
    dp4 o0.w, r0.xyzw, cb0[3].xyzw
    mov o1.xyzw, v1.xyzw
    ret
    // Approximately 8 instruction slots used
};
PixelShader = asm {
    //
    // Generated by Microsoft (R) HLSL Shader Compiler 9.29.952.3111
    //
    //
    //
```

```
     // Input signature:
     //
     // Name          Index   Mask Register SysValue Format  Used
     // ------------- ----- ------ -------- -------- ------ ------
     // SV_POSITION       0  xyzw        0      POS   float
     // COLOR             0  xyzw        1     NONE   float   xyzw
     //
     //
     // Output signature:
     //
     // Name          Index   Mask Register SysValue Format  Used
     // ------------- ----- ------ -------- -------- ------ ------
     // SV_Target         0  xyzw        0   TARGET   float   xyzw
     //
     ps_5_0
     dcl_globalFlags refactoringAllowed
     dcl_input_ps linear v1.xyzw
     dcl_output o0.xyzw
     mov o0.xyzw, v1.xyzw
     ret
     // Approximately 2 instruction slots used
   };
 }
}

technique11 NoColorTech
{
  pass P0
  {
    VertexShader = asm {
      //
      // Generated by Microsoft (R) HLSL Shader Compiler 9.29.952.3111
      //
      //
      // Buffer Definitions:
      //
      // cbuffer cbPerObject
      // {
      //
      //   float4x4 gWorldViewProj;     // Offset:    0 Size:     64
      //
      // }
      //
      //
      // Resource Bindings:
      //
      // Name                 Type  Format        Dim Slot Elements
      // ------------------- ----- ------ ----------- ---- --------
      // cbPerObject         cbuffer    NA          NA    0        1
      //
      //
      //
      // Input signature:
      //
      // Name          Index   Mask Register SysValue Format  Used
      // ------------- ----- ------ -------- -------- ------ ------
      // POSITION          0   xyz        0     NONE   float   xyz
      // COLOR             0  xyzw        1     NONE   float   xyzw
      //
```

```
//
// Output signature:
//
// Name              Index   Mask Register SysValue Format   Used
// -------------     -----  ------ -------- -------- ------  ------
// SV_POSITION         0     xyzw      0      POS    float    xyzw
// COLOR               0     xyzw      1      NONE   float    xyzw
//
vs_5_0
dcl_globalFlags refactoringAllowed
dcl_constantbuffer cb0[4], immediateIndexed
dcl_input v0.xyz
dcl_input v1.xyzw
dcl_output_siv o0.xyzw, position
dcl_output o1.xyzw
dcl_temps 1
mov r0.xyz, v0.xyzx
mov r0.w, l(1.000000)
dp4 o0.x, r0.xyzw, cb0[0].xyzw
dp4 o0.y, r0.xyzw, cb0[1].xyzw
dp4 o0.z, r0.xyzw, cb0[2].xyzw
dp4 o0.w, r0.xyzw, cb0[3].xyzw
mov o1.xyzw, v1.xyzw
ret
// Approximately 8 instruction slots used

};
PixelShader = asm {
//
// Generated by Microsoft (R) HLSL Shader Compiler 9.29.952.3111
//
//
//
// Input signature:
//
// Name              Index   Mask Register SysValue Format   Used
// -------------     -----  ------ -------- -------- ------  ------
// SV_POSITION         0     xyzw      0      POS    float
// COLOR               0     xyzw      1      NONE   float
//
//
// Output signature:
//
// Name              Index   Mask Register SysValue Format   Used
// -------------     -----  ------ -------- -------- ------  ------
// SV_Target           0     xyzw      0      TARGET float    xyzw
//
ps_5_0
dcl_globalFlags refactoringAllowed
dcl_output o0.xyzw
mov o0.xyzw, l(0,0,0,1.000000)
ret
// Approximately 2 instruction slots used

};
}
}
}
```

6.9 BOX DEMO

At last, we have covered enough material to present a simple demo, which renders a colored box. This example essentially puts everything we have discussed in this chapter up to now into a single program. The reader should study the code and refer back to the previous sections of this chapter until every line is understood. Note that the program uses the "color.fx" effect, as written in §6.8.1.

```cpp
//***************************************************************************
// BoxDemo.cpp by Frank Luna (C) 2011 All Rights Reserved.
//
// Demonstrates rendering a colored box.
//
// Controls:
//     Hold the left mouse button down and move the mouse to rotate.
//     Hold the right mouse button down to zoom in and out.
//
//***************************************************************************

#include "d3dApp.h"
#include "d3dx11Effect.h"
#include "MathHelper.h"

struct Vertex
{
    XMFLOAT3 Pos;
    XMFLOAT4 Color;
};

class BoxApp : public D3DApp
{
public:
    BoxApp(HINSTANCE hInstance);
    ~BoxApp();

    bool Init();
    void OnResize();
    void UpdateScene(float dt);
    void DrawScene();

    void OnMouseDown(WPARAM btnState, int x, int y);
    void OnMouseUp(WPARAM btnState, int x, int y);
    void OnMouseMove(WPARAM btnState, int x, int y);

private:
    void BuildGeometryBuffers();
    void BuildFX();
    void BuildVertexLayout();
```

```
private:
    ID3D11Buffer* mBoxVB;
    ID3D11Buffer* mBoxIB;

    ID3DX11Effect* mFX;
    ID3DX11EffectTechnique* mTech;
    ID3DX11EffectMatrixVariable* mfxWorldViewProj;

    ID3D11InputLayout* mInputLayout;

    XMFLOAT4X4 mWorld;
    XMFLOAT4X4 mView;
    XMFLOAT4X4 mProj;

    float mTheta;
    float mPhi;
    float mRadius;

    POINT mLastMousePos;
};

int WINAPI WinMain(HINSTANCE hInstance, HINSTANCE prevInstance,
                   PSTR cmdLine, int showCmd)
{
    // Enable run-time memory check for debug builds.
#if defined(DEBUG) | defined(_DEBUG)
    _CrtSetDbgFlag(_CRTDBG_ALLOC_MEM_DF | _CRTDBG_LEAK_CHECK_DF);
#endif

    BoxApp theApp(hInstance);

    if(!theApp.Init())
      return 0;

    return theApp.Run();
}
BoxApp::BoxApp(HINSTANCE hInstance)
: D3DApp(hInstance), mBoxVB(0), mBoxIB(0), mFX(0), mTech(0),
  mfxWorldViewProj(0), mInputLayout(0),
  mTheta(1.5f*MathHelper::Pi), mPhi(0.25f*MathHelper::Pi), mRadius(5.0f)
{
    mMainWndCaption = L"Box Demo";

    mLastMousePos.x = 0;
    mLastMousePos.y = 0;

    XMMATRIX I = XMMatrixIdentity();
    XMStoreFloat4x4(&mWorld, I);
    XMStoreFloat4x4(&mView, I);
    XMStoreFloat4x4(&mProj, I);
}

BoxApp::~BoxApp()
{
    ReleaseCOM(mBoxVB);
    ReleaseCOM(mBoxIB);
```

```
    ReleaseCOM(mFX);
    ReleaseCOM(mInputLayout);
}

bool BoxApp::Init()
{
    if(!D3DApp::Init())
      return false;

    BuildGeometryBuffers();
    BuildFX();
    BuildVertexLayout();

    return true;
}

void BoxApp::OnResize()
{
    D3DApp::OnResize();

    // The window resized, so update the aspect ratio and recomputed
    // the projection matrix.
    XMMATRIX P = XMMatrixPerspectiveFovLH(0.25f*MathHelper::Pi,
    AspectRatio(), 1.0f, 1000.0f);
    XMStoreFloat4x4(&mProj, P);
}

void BoxApp::UpdateScene(float dt)
{
    // Convert Spherical to Cartesian coordinates.
    float x = mRadius*sinf(mPhi)*cosf(mTheta);
    float z = mRadius*sinf(mPhi)*sinf(mTheta);
    float y = mRadius*cosf(mPhi);

    // Build the view matrix.
    XMVECTOR pos    = XMVectorSet(x, y, z, 1.0f);
    XMVECTOR target = XMVectorZero();
    XMVECTOR up     = XMVectorSet(0.0f, 1.0f, 0.0f, 0.0f);

    XMMATRIX V = XMMatrixLookAtLH(pos, target, up);
    XMStoreFloat4x4(&mView, V);
}

void BoxApp::DrawScene()
{
    md3dImmediateContext->ClearRenderTargetView(mRenderTargetView,
            reinterpret_cast<const float*>(&Colors::Blue));
    md3dImmediateContext->ClearDepthStencilView(mDepthStencilView,
            D3D11_CLEAR_DEPTH|D3D11_CLEAR_STENCIL, 1.0f, 0);

    md3dImmediateContext->IASetInputLayout(mInputLayout);
    md3dImmediateContext->IASetPrimitiveTopology(
            D3D11_PRIMITIVE_TOPOLOGY_TRIANGLELIST);
```

```
    UINT stride = sizeof(Vertex);
    UINT offset = 0;
    md3dImmediateContext->IASetVertexBuffers(0, 1, &mBoxVB,
            &stride, &offset);
    md3dImmediateContext->IASetIndexBuffer(mBoxIB,
            DXGI_FORMAT_R32_UINT, 0);

    // Set constants
    XMMATRIX world = XMLoadFloat4x4(&mWorld);
    XMMATRIX view  = XMLoadFloat4x4(&mView);
    XMMATRIX proj  = XMLoadFloat4x4(&mProj);
    XMMATRIX worldViewProj = world*view*proj;

    mfxWorldViewProj->SetMatrix(reinterpret_cast<float*>(&worldViewProj));

    D3DX11_TECHNIQUE_DESC techDesc;
    mTech->GetDesc( &techDesc );
    for(UINT p = 0; p < techDesc.Passes; ++p)
    {
      mTech->GetPassByIndex(p)->Apply(0, md3dImmediateContext);

      // 36 indices for the box.
      md3dImmediateContext->DrawIndexed(36, 0, 0);
    }

    HR(mSwapChain->Present(0, 0));
}

void BoxApp::OnMouseDown(WPARAM btnState, int x, int y)
{
    mLastMousePos.x = x;
    mLastMousePos.y = y;

    SetCapture(mhMainWnd);
}

void BoxApp::OnMouseUp(WPARAM btnState, int x, int y)
{
    ReleaseCapture();
}

void BoxApp::OnMouseMove(WPARAM btnState, int x, int y)
{
    if( (btnState & MK_LBUTTON) != 0 )
    {
      // Make each pixel correspond to a quarter of a degree.
      float dx = XMConvertToRadians(
          0.25f*static_cast<float>(x - mLastMousePos.x));
      float dy = XMConvertToRadians(
          0.25f*static_cast<float>(y - mLastMousePos.y));

      // Update angles based on input to orbit camera around box.
      mTheta += dx;
      mPhi   += dy;
```

```
      // Restrict the angle mPhi.
      mPhi = MathHelper::Clamp(mPhi, 0.1f, MathHelper::Pi-0.1f);
   }
   else if( (btnState & MK_RBUTTON) != 0 )
   {
      // Make each pixel correspond to 0.005 unit in the scene.
      float dx = 0.005f*static_cast<float>(x - mLastMousePos.x);
      float dy = 0.005f*static_cast<float>(y - mLastMousePos.y);

      // Update the camera radius based on input.
      mRadius += dx - dy;

      // Restrict the radius.
      mRadius = MathHelper::Clamp(mRadius, 3.0f, 15.0f);
   }

   mLastMousePos.x = x;
   mLastMousePos.y = y;
}

void BoxApp::BuildGeometryBuffers()
{
   // Create vertex buffer
   Vertex vertices[] =
   {
      { XMFLOAT3(-1.0f, -1.0f, -1.0f), (const float*)&Colors::White   },
      { XMFLOAT3(-1.0f, +1.0f, -1.0f), (const float*)&Colors::Black   },
      { XMFLOAT3(+1.0f, +1.0f, -1.0f), (const float*)&Colors::Red     },
      { XMFLOAT3(+1.0f, -1.0f, -1.0f), (const float*)&Colors::Green   },
      { XMFLOAT3(-1.0f, -1.0f, +1.0f), (const float*)&Colors::Blue    },
      { XMFLOAT3(-1.0f, +1.0f, +1.0f), (const float*)&Colors::Yellow  },
      { XMFLOAT3(+1.0f, +1.0f, +1.0f), (const float*)&Colors::Cyan    },
      { XMFLOAT3(+1.0f, -1.0f, +1.0f), (const float*)&Colors::Magenta }
   };

   D3D11_BUFFER_DESC vbd;
   vbd.Usage = D3D11_USAGE_IMMUTABLE;
   vbd.ByteWidth = sizeof(Vertex) * 8;
   vbd.BindFlags = D3D11_BIND_VERTEX_BUFFER;
   vbd.CPUAccessFlags = 0;
   vbd.MiscFlags = 0;
   vbd.StructureByteStride = 0;
   D3D11_SUBRESOURCE_DATA vinitData;
   vinitData.pSysMem = vertices;
   HR(md3dDevice->CreateBuffer(&vbd, &vinitData, &mBoxVB));

   // Create the index buffer
   UINT indices[] = {
      // front face
      0, 1, 2,
      0, 2, 3,

      // back face
      4, 6, 5,
      4, 7, 6,
```

```
        // left face
        4, 5, 1,
        4, 1, 0,

        // right face
        3, 2, 6,
        3, 6, 7,

        // top face
        1, 5, 6,
        1, 6, 2,

        // bottom face
        4, 0, 3,
        4, 3, 7
    };

    D3D11_BUFFER_DESC ibd;
    ibd.Usage = D3D11_USAGE_IMMUTABLE;
    ibd.ByteWidth = sizeof(UINT) * 36;
    ibd.BindFlags = D3D11_BIND_INDEX_BUFFER;
    ibd.CPUAccessFlags = 0;
    ibd.MiscFlags = 0;
    ibd.StructureByteStride = 0;
    D3D11_SUBRESOURCE_DATA iinitData;
    iinitData.pSysMem = indices;
    HR(md3dDevice->CreateBuffer(&ibd, &iinitData, &mBoxIB));
}

void BoxApp::BuildFX()
{
    DWORD shaderFlags = 0;
#if defined(DEBUG) || defined(_DEBUG)
    shaderFlags |= D3D10_SHADER_DEBUG;
    shaderFlags |= D3D10_SHADER_SKIP_OPTIMIZATION;
#endif

    ID3D10Blob* compiledShader = 0;
    ID3D10Blob* compilationMsgs = 0;
    HRESULT hr = D3DX11CompileFromFile(L"FX/color.fx", 0, 0, 0,
      "fx_5_0", shaderFlags,
            0, 0, &compiledShader, &compilationMsgs, 0);

    // compilationMsgs can store errors or warnings.
    if(compilationMsgs != 0)
    {
      MessageBoxA(0, (char*)compilationMsgs->GetBufferPointer(), 0, 0);
      ReleaseCOM(compilationMsgs);
    }

    // Even if there are no compilationMsgs, check to make sure there
    // were no other errors.
    if(FAILED(hr))
    {
```

```
        DXTrace(__FILE__, (DWORD)__LINE__, hr,
            L"D3DX11CompileFromFile", true);
    }

    HR(D3DX11CreateEffectFromMemory(
        compiledShader->GetBufferPointer(),
        compiledShader->GetBufferSize(),
        0, md3dDevice, &mFX));

    // Done with compiled shader.
    ReleaseCOM(compiledShader);

    mTech          = mFX->GetTechniqueByName("ColorTech");
    mfxWorldViewProj = mFX->GetVariableByName(
            "gWorldViewProj")->AsMatrix();
}

void BoxApp::BuildVertexLayout()
{
    // Create the vertex input layout.
    D3D11_INPUT_ELEMENT_DESC vertexDesc[] =
    {
        {"POSITION", 0, DXGI_FORMAT_R32G32B32_FLOAT, 0, 0,
            D3D11_INPUT_PER_VERTEX_DATA, 0},
        {"COLOR",    0, DXGI_FORMAT_R32G32B32A32_FLOAT, 0, 12,
            D3D11_INPUT_PER_VERTEX_DATA, 0}
    };

    // Create the input layout
    D3DX11_PASS_DESC passDesc;
    mTech->GetPassByIndex(0)->GetDesc(&passDesc);
    HR(md3dDevice->CreateInputLayout(vertexDesc, 2,
        passDesc.pIAInputSignature,
        passDesc.IAInputSignatureSize, &mInputLayout));
}
```

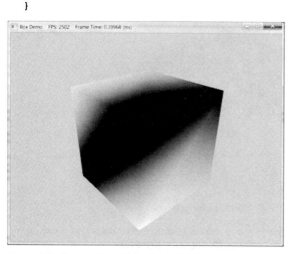

Figure 6.7. Screenshot of the "Box" demo.

6.10 HILLS DEMO

This chapter also includes a "Hills" demo. It uses the same Direct3D methods as the Box demo, except that is draws more complicated geometry. In particular, it shows how to construct a triangle grid mesh procedurally; such geometry turns out to be particularly useful for terrain and water rendering, among other things.

The graph of a "nice" real-valued function $y = f(x, z)$ is a surface. We can approximate the surface by constructing a grid in the xz-plane, where every quad is built from two triangles, and then applying the function to each grid point; see Figure 6.8.

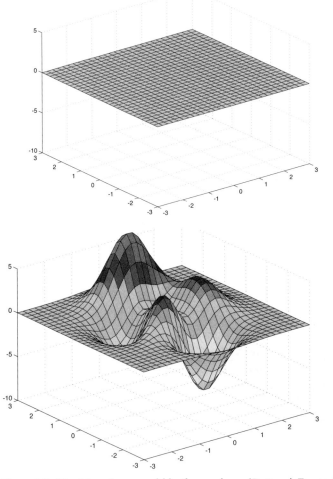

Figure 6.8. (Top) Lay down a grid in the xz-plane. (Bottom) For each grid point, apply the function $f(x, z)$ to obtain the y-coordinate. The plot of the points $(x, f(x, z), z)$ gives the graph of a surface.

6.10.1 Generating the Grid Vertices

So the main task is how to build the grid in the xz-plane. A grid of $m \times n$ vertices induces $(m-1) \times (n-1)$ quads (or cells), as shown in Figure 6.9. Each cell will be covered by two triangles, so there is a total of $2 \cdot (m-1) \times (n-1)$ triangles. If the grid has width w and depth d, the cell spacing along the x-axis is $dx = w/(n-1)$ and the cell spacing along the z-axis is $dz = d/(m-1)$. To generate the vertices, we start at the upper-left corner and incrementally compute the vertex coordinates row-by-row. The coordinates of the ijth grid vertex in the xz-plane are given by:

$$\mathbf{v}_{ij} = [-0.5w + j \cdot dx, \quad 0.0, \quad 0.5d - i \cdot dz)]$$

The following code generates the grid vertices:

```
void GeometryGenerator::CreateGrid(float width, float depth,
                                   UINT m, UINT n, MeshData& meshData)
{
    UINT vertexCount = m*n;
    UINT faceCount   = (m-1)*(n-1)*2;

    //
    // Create the vertices.
    //

    float halfWidth = 0.5f*width;
    float halfDepth = 0.5f*depth;

    float dx = width / (n-1);
    float dz = depth / (m-1);

    float du = 1.0f / (n-1);
    float dv = 1.0f / (m-1);

    meshData.Vertices.resize(vertexCount);
    for(UINT i = 0; i < m; ++i)
    {
    float z = halfDepth - i*dz;
    for(UINT j = 0; j < n; ++j)
    {
      float x = -halfWidth + j*dx;

      meshData.Vertices[i*n+j].Position = XMFLOAT3(x, 0.0f, z);

      // Ignore for now, used for lighting.
      meshData.Vertices[i*n+j].Normal   = XMFLOAT3(0.0f, 1.0f, 0.0f);
      meshData.Vertices[i*n+j].TangentU = XMFLOAT3(1.0f, 0.0f, 0.0f);

      // Ignore for now, used for texturing.
      meshData.Vertices[i*n+j].TexC.x = j*du;
      meshData.Vertices[i*n+j].TexC.y = i*dv;
    }
  }
}
```

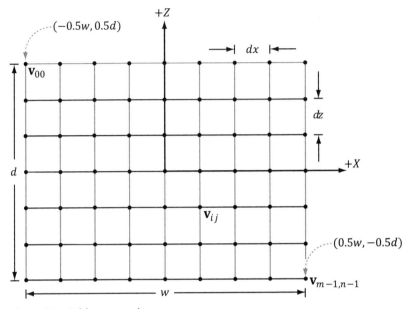

Figure 6.9. Grid construction.

GeometryGenerator is a utility class for generating simple geometric shapes like grids, spheres, cylinders, and boxes, which we use throughout this book for our demo programs. This class generates the data in system memory, and we must then copy the data we want to our vertex and index buffers. GeometryGenerator creates some vertex data that will be used in later chapters. We do not need this data in our current demos, and so we do *not* copy this data into our vertex buffers. The MeshData structure is a simple structure nested inside GeometryGenerator that stores a vertex and index list:

```
class GeometryGenerator
{
public:
    struct Vertex
    {
        Vertex(){}
        Vertex(const XMFLOAT3& p,
               const XMFLOAT3& n,
               const XMFLOAT3& t,
               const XMFLOAT2& uv)
          : Position(p), Normal(n), TangentU(t), TexC(uv){}
        Vertex(
            float px, float py, float pz,
            float nx, float ny, float nz,
            float tx, float ty, float tz,
            float u, float v)
          : Position(px,py,pz), Normal(nx,ny,nz),
            TangentU(tx, ty, tz), TexC(u,v){}
```

```
        XMFLOAT3 Position;
        XMFLOAT3 Normal;
        XMFLOAT3 TangentU;
        XMFLOAT2 TexC;
    };

    struct MeshData
    {
        std::vector<Vertex> Vertices;
        std::vector<UINT> Indices;
    };
    ...
};
```

6.10.2 Generating the Grid Indices

After we have computed the vertices, we need to define the grid triangles by specifying the indices. To do this, we iterate over each quad, again row-by-row starting at the top-left, and compute the indices to define the two triangles of the quad; referring to Figure 6.10, for an $m \times n$ vertex grid, the linear array indices of the two triangles are computed as follows:

$$\Delta ABC = (i \cdot n + j, \qquad i \cdot n + j + 1, \qquad (i+1) \cdot n + j)$$
$$\Delta CBD = ((i+1) \cdot n + j, \qquad i \cdot n + j + 1, \qquad (i+1) \cdot n + j + 1)$$

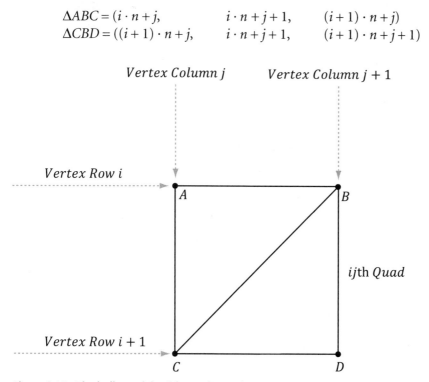

Figure 6.10. The indices of the *ij*th quad's vertices.

The corresponding code:

```
meshData.Indices.resize(faceCount*3); // 3 indices per face

    // Iterate over each quad and compute indices.
    UINT k = 0;
    for(UINT i = 0; i < m-1; ++i)
    {
      for(UINT j = 0; j < n-1; ++j)
      {
        meshData.Indices[k]   = i*n+j;
        meshData.Indices[k+1] = i*n+j+1;
        meshData.Indices[k+2] = (i+1)*n+j;
        meshData.Indices[k+3] = (i+1)*n+j;
        meshData.Indices[k+4] = i*n+j+1;
        meshData.Indices[k+5] = (i+1)*n+j+1;

        k += 6; // next quad
      }
    }
}
```

6.10.3 Applying the Height Function

After we have created the grid, we can extract the vertex elements we want from the `MeshData` grid, turn the flat grid into a surface representing hills, and generate a color for each vertex based on the vertex altitude (y-coordinate).

```
// Not to be confused with GeometryGenerator.Vertex.
struct Vertex
{
    XMFLOAT3 Pos;
    XMFLOAT4 Color;
};

void HillsApp::BuildGeometryBuffers()
{
    GeometryGenerator::MeshData grid;

    GeometryGenerator geoGen;

    geoGen.CreateGrid(160.0f, 160.0f, 50, 50, grid);

    mGridIndexCount = grid.Indices.size();

    //
    // Extract the vertex elements we are interested and apply the
    // height function to each vertex.  In addition, color the vertices
    // based on their height so we have sandy looking beaches, grassy low
    // hills, and snow mountain peaks.
    //

    std::vector<Vertex> vertices(grid.Vertices.size());
    for(size_t i = 0; i < grid.Vertices.size(); ++i)
    {
      XMFLOAT3 p = grid.Vertices[i].Position;
```

```
      p.y = GetHeight(p.x, p.z);

      vertices[i].Pos   = p;

      // Color the vertex based on its height.
      if( p.y < -10.0f )
      {
        // Sandy beach color.
        vertices[i].Color = XMFLOAT4(1.0f, 0.96f, 0.62f, 1.0f);
      }
      else if(p.y < 5.0f)
      {
        // Light yellow-green.
        vertices[i].Color = XMFLOAT4(0.48f, 0.77f, 0.46f, 1.0f);
      }
      else if(p.y < 12.0f)
      {
        // Dark yellow-green.
        vertices[i].Color = XMFLOAT4(0.1f, 0.48f, 0.19f, 1.0f);
      }
      else if(p.y < 20.0f)
      {
        // Dark brown.
        vertices[i].Color = XMFLOAT4(0.45f, 0.39f, 0.34f, 1.0f);
      }
      else
      {
        // White snow.
        vertices[i].Color = XMFLOAT4(1.0f, 1.0f, 1.0f, 1.0f);
      }
    }

    D3D11_BUFFER_DESC vbd;
    vbd.Usage = D3D11_USAGE_IMMUTABLE;
    vbd.ByteWidth = sizeof(Vertex) * grid.Vertices.size();
    vbd.BindFlags = D3D11_BIND_VERTEX_BUFFER;
    vbd.CPUAccessFlags = 0;
    vbd.MiscFlags = 0;
    D3D11_SUBRESOURCE_DATA vinitData;
    vinitData.pSysMem = &vertices[0];
    HR(md3dDevice->CreateBuffer(&vbd, &vinitData, &mVB));

    //
    // Pack the indices of all the meshes into one index buffer.
    //

    D3D11_BUFFER_DESC ibd;
    ibd.Usage = D3D11_USAGE_IMMUTABLE;
    ibd.ByteWidth = sizeof(UINT) * mGridIndexCount;
    ibd.BindFlags = D3D11_BIND_INDEX_BUFFER;
    ibd.CPUAccessFlags = 0;
    ibd.MiscFlags = 0;
    D3D11_SUBRESOURCE_DATA iinitData;
    iinitData.pSysMem = &grid.Indices[0];
    HR(md3dDevice->CreateBuffer(&ibd, &iinitData, &mIB));
}
```

Figure 6.11. **Screenshot of the "Hills Demo."**

The function $f(x, z)$ we have used in this demo is given by:

```
float HillsApp::GetHeight(float x, float z)const
{
    return 0.3f*(z*sinf(0.1f*x) + x*cosf(0.1f*z));
}
```

Its graph looks somewhat like a terrain with hills and valleys (see Figure 6.11). The rest of the demo program is very similar to the box demo.

6.11 SHAPES DEMO

In this section, we describe how to build the other two geometry shapes the `GeometryGenerator` class supports: spheres and cylinders. These shapes are useful for drawing sky domes, debugging, visualizing collision detection, and deferred rendering. For example, you might want to render all of your game characters as spheres for a debug test.

Figure 6.12 shows a screenshot of this section's demo. In addition to learning how to draw spheres and cylinders, you will also gain experience positioning and drawing multiple objects in a scene (i.e., creating multiple world transformation matrices). Furthermore, we place all of the scene geometry in one big vertex and index buffer. Then we will use the `DrawIndexed` method to draw one object at a time (as the world matrix needs to be changed between objects); so you will see an example of using the `StartIndexLocation` and `BaseVertexLocation` parameters of `DrawIndexed`.

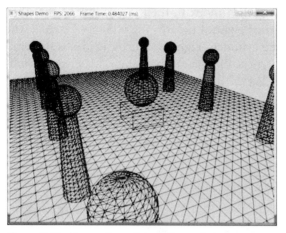

Figure 6.12. Screenshot of the "Shapes" demo.

6.11.1 Generating a Cylinder Mesh

We define a cylinder by specifying its bottom and top radii, its height, and the slice and stack count, as shown in Figure 6.13. We break the cylinder into three parts: 1) the side geometry, 2) the top cap geometry, and 3) the bottom cap geometry.

6.11.1.1 Cylinder Side Geometry

We generate the cylinder centered at the origin, parallel to the y-axis. From Figure 6.13, all the vertices lie on the "rings" of the cylinder, where there are *stackCount* + 1 rings, and each ring has *sliceCount* unique vertices. The difference in radius between consecutive rings is $\Delta r = (topRadius - bottomRadius)/stackCount$.

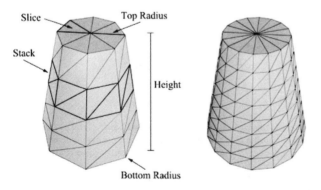

Figure 6.13. In this illustration, the cylinder on the left has 8 slices and 4 stacks, and the cylinder on the right has 16 slices and 8 stacks. The slices and stacks control the triangle density. Note that the top and bottom radii can differ so that we can create cone shaped objects, not just "pure" cylinders.

If we start at the bottom ring with index 0, then the radius of the ith ring is $r_i = bottomRadius + i\Delta r$ and the height of the ith ring is $h_i = -\frac{h}{2} + i\Delta h$, where Δh is the stack height and h is the cylinder height. So the basic idea is to iterate over each ring and generate the vertices that lie on that ring. This gives the following implementation (we have bolded the relevant code):

```
void GeometryGenerator::CreateCylinder(float bottomRadius, float topRadius,
float height, UINT sliceCount, UINT stackCount, MeshData& meshData)
{
    meshData.Vertices.clear();
    meshData.Indices.clear();

    //
    // Build Stacks.
    //

    float stackHeight = height / stackCount;

    // Amount to increment radius as we move up each stack
    // level from bottom to top.
    float radiusStep = (topRadius - bottomRadius) / stackCount;

    UINT ringCount = stackCount+1;

    // Compute vertices for each stack ring starting at
    // the bottom and moving up.
    for(UINT i = 0; i < ringCount; ++i)
    {
        float y = -0.5f*height + i*stackHeight;
        float r = bottomRadius + i*radiusStep;

        // vertices of ring
        float dTheta = 2.0f*XM_PI/sliceCount;
        for(UINT j = 0; j <= sliceCount; ++j)
        {
            Vertex vertex;

            float c = cosf(j*dTheta);
            float s = sinf(j*dTheta);

            vertex.Position = XMFLOAT3(r*c, y, r*s);

            vertex.TexC.x = (float)j/sliceCount;
            vertex.TexC.y = 1.0f - (float)i/stackCount;

            // Cylinder can be parameterized as follows, where we
            // introduce v parameter that goes in the same direction
            // as the v tex-coord so that the bitangent goes in the
            // same direction as the v tex-coord.
            //    Let r0 be the bottom radius and let r1 be the
            //    top radius.
            //    y(v) = h - hv for v in [0,1].
            //    r(v) = r1 + (r0-r1)v
            //
            //    x(t, v) = r(v)*cos(t)
```

```
//    y(t, v) = h - hv
//    z(t, v) = r(v)*sin(t)
//
//    dx/dt = -r(v)*sin(t)
//    dy/dt = 0
//    dz/dt = +r(v)*cos(t)
//
//    dx/dv = (r0-r1)*cos(t)
//    dy/dv = -h
//    dz/dv = (r0-r1)*sin(t)

//    TangentU us unit length.
vertex.TangentU = XMFLOAT3(-s, 0.0f, c);

float dr = bottomRadius-topRadius;
XMFLOAT3 bitangent(dr*c, -height, dr*s);

XMVECTOR T = XMLoadFloat3(&vertex.TangentU);
XMVECTOR B = XMLoadFloat3(&bitangent);
XMVECTOR N = XMVector3Normalize(XMVector3Cross(T, B));
XMStoreFloat3(&vertex.Normal, N);

meshData.Vertices.push_back(vertex);
    }
  }
```

Note: *Observe that the first and last vertex of each ring is duplicated in position, but the texture coordinates are not duplicated. We have to do this so that we can apply textures to cylinders correctly.*

Note: *The actual method* `GeometryGenerator::CreateCylinder` *creates additional vertex data such as normal vectors and texture coordinates that will be useful for future demos. Do not worry about these quantities for now.*

Observe from Figure 6.14 that there is a quad (two triangles) for each slice in every stack. Figure 6.14 shows that the indices for the ith stack and jth slice are given by:

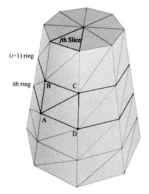

Figure 6.14. The vertices A, B, C, D contained in the ith and $i + 1$th ring, and jth slice.

$$\Delta ABC = (i \cdot n + j, \qquad (i+1) \cdot n + j), \qquad (i+1) \cdot n + j + 1)$$
$$\Delta ACD = (i \cdot n + j, \qquad (i+1) \cdot n + j + 1, \qquad i \cdot n + j + 1$$

where n is the number of vertices per ring. So the key idea is to loop over every slice in every stack, and apply the above formulas.

```
// Add one because we duplicate the first and last vertex per ring
// since the texture coordinates are different.
UINT ringVertexCount = sliceCount+1;

// Compute indices for each stack.
for(UINT i = 0; i < stackCount; ++i)
{
    for(UINT j = 0; j < sliceCount; ++j)
    {
      meshData.Indices.push_back(i*ringVertexCount + j);
      meshData.Indices.push_back((i+1)*ringVertexCount + j);
      meshData.Indices.push_back((i+1)*ringVertexCount + j+1);

      meshData.Indices.push_back(i*ringVertexCount + j);
      meshData.Indices.push_back((i+1)*ringVertexCount + j+1);
      meshData.Indices.push_back(i*ringVertexCount + j+1);
    }
}

    BuildCylinderTopCap(bottomRadius, topRadius,
        height, sliceCount, stackCount, meshData);
    BuildCylinderBottomCap(bottomRadius, topRadius,
        height, sliceCount, stackCount, meshData);
}
```

6.11.1.2 Cap Geometry

Generating the cap geometry amounts to generating the slice triangles of the top and bottom rings to approximate a circle:

```
void GeometryGenerator::BuildCylinderTopCap(float bottomRadius,
    float topRadius, float height, UINT sliceCount,
    UINT stackCount, MeshData& meshData)
{
    UINT baseIndex = (UINT)meshData.Vertices.size();

    float y = 0.5f*height;
    float dTheta = 2.0f*XM_PI/sliceCount;

    // Duplicate cap ring vertices because the texture coordinates
    // and normals differ.
    for(UINT i = 0; i <= sliceCount; ++i)
    {
      float x = topRadius*cosf(i*dTheta);
      float z = topRadius*sinf(i*dTheta);

      // Scale down by the height to try and make top cap
      // texture coord area proportional to base.
```

```
      float u = x/height + 0.5f;
      float v = z/height + 0.5f;

      meshData.Vertices.push_back(
        Vertex(x, y, z,
        0.0f, 1.0f, 0.0f,
        1.0f, 0.0f, 0.0f,
        u, v));
    }

    // Cap center vertex.
    meshData.Vertices.push_back(
        Vertex(0.0f, y, 0.0f,
        0.0f, 1.0f, 0.0f,
        1.0f, 0.0f, 0.0f,
        0.5f, 0.5f));

    // Index of center vertex.
    UINT centerIndex = (UINT)meshData.Vertices.size()-1;

    for(UINT i = 0; i < sliceCount; ++i)
    {
      meshData.Indices.push_back(centerIndex);
      meshData.Indices.push_back(baseIndex + i+1);
      meshData.Indices.push_back(baseIndex + i);
    }
  }
```

The bottom cap code is analogous.

6.11.2 Generating a Sphere Mesh

We define a sphere by specifying its radius, and the slice and stack count, as shown in Figure 6.15. The algorithm for generating the sphere is very similar to that of the cylinder, except that the radius per ring changes is a nonlinear way

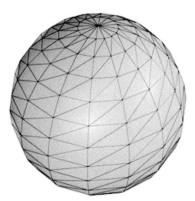

Figure 6.15. The idea of slices and stacks also apply to a sphere to control the level of tessellation.

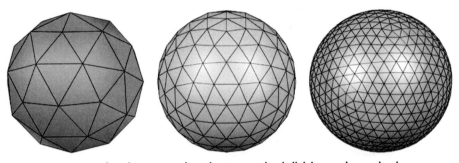

Figure 6.16. Approximating a geosphere by repeated subdivision and reprojection onto the sphere.

based on trigonometric functions. We will leave it to the reader to study the `GeometryGenerator::CreateSphere` code.

6.11.3 Generating a Geosphere Mesh

Observe from Figure 6.15 that the triangles of the sphere do not have equal areas. This can be undesirable for some situations. A geosphere approximates a sphere using triangles with almost equal areas as well as equal side lengths (see Figure 6.16).

To generate a geosphere, we start with an icosahedron, subdivide the triangles, and then project the new vertices onto the sphere with the given radius. We can repeat this process to improve the tessellation.

Figure 6.17 shows how a triangle can be subdivided into four equal sized triangles. The new vertices are found just by taking the midpoints along the edges of the original triangle. The new vertices can then be projected onto a sphere of radius r by projecting the vertices onto the unit sphere and then scalar multiplying by r : $\mathbf{v}' = r \frac{\mathbf{v}}{\|\mathbf{v}\|}$.

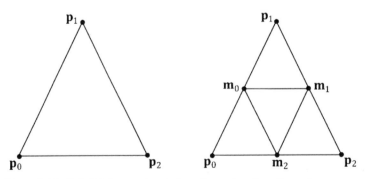

Figure 6.17. Subdividing a triangle into four triangles of equal area.

The code is given below:

```
void GeometryGenerator::CreateGeosphere(float radius,
UINT numSubdivisions, MeshData& meshData)
{
    // Put a cap on the number of subdivisions.
    numSubdivisions = MathHelper::Min(numSubdivisions, 5u);

    // Approximate a sphere by tessellating an icosahedron.

    const float X = 0.525731f;
    const float Z = 0.850651f;

    XMFLOAT3 pos[12] =
    {
      XMFLOAT3(-X, 0.0f, Z),   XMFLOAT3(X, 0.0f, Z),
      XMFLOAT3(-X, 0.0f, -Z),  XMFLOAT3(X, 0.0f, -Z),
      XMFLOAT3(0.0f, Z, X),    XMFLOAT3(0.0f, Z, -X),
      XMFLOAT3(0.0f, -Z, X),   XMFLOAT3(0.0f, -Z, -X),
      XMFLOAT3(Z, X, 0.0f),    XMFLOAT3(-Z, X, 0.0f),
      XMFLOAT3(Z, -X, 0.0f),   XMFLOAT3(-Z, -X, 0.0f)
    };

    DWORD k[60] =
    {
      1,4,0,   4,9,0,   4,5,9,   8,5,4,   1,8,4,
      1,10,8,  10,3,8,  8,3,5,   3,2,5,   3,7,2,
      3,10,7,  10,6,7,  6,11,7,  6,0,11,  6,1,0,
      10,1,6,  11,0,9,  2,11,9,  5,2,9,   11,2,7
    };

    meshData.Vertices.resize(12);
    meshData.Indices.resize(60);

    for(size_t i = 0; i < 12; ++i)
      meshData.Vertices[i].Position = pos[i];

    for(size_t i = 0; i < 60; ++i)
      meshData.Indices[i] = k[i];

    for(size_t i = 0; i < numSubdivisions; ++i)
      Subdivide(meshData);

    // Project vertices onto sphere and scale.
    for(size_t i = 0; i < meshData.Vertices.size(); ++i)
    {
      // Project onto unit sphere.
      XMVECTOR n = XMVector3Normalize(XMLoadFloat3(
        &meshData.Vertices[i].Position));

      // Project onto sphere.
      XMVECTOR p = radius*n;

      XMStoreFloat3(&meshData.Vertices[i].Position, p);
      XMStoreFloat3(&meshData.Vertices[i].Normal, n);
```

```
// Derive texture coordinates from spherical coordinates.
float theta = MathHelper::AngleFromXY(
  meshData.Vertices[i].Position.x,
  meshData.Vertices[i].Position.z);

float phi = acosf(meshData.Vertices[i].Position.y / radius);

meshData.Vertices[i].TexC.x = theta/XM_2PI;
meshData.Vertices[i].TexC.y = phi/XM_PI;

// Partial derivative of P with respect to theta
meshData.Vertices[i].TangentU.x = -radius*sinf(phi)*sinf(theta);
meshData.Vertices[i].TangentU.y = 0.0f;
meshData.Vertices[i].TangentU.z = +radius*sinf(phi)*cosf(theta);

XMVECTOR T = XMLoadFloat3(&meshData.Vertices[i].TangentU);
XMStoreFloat3(&meshData.Vertices[i].TangentU,
  XMVector3Normalize(T));
  }
}
```

6.11.4 Demo Code

In this section, we review the key differences between the "Shapes" demo and the previous two demos. Ignoring that we draw different geometry, the main difference is that we draw multiple objects. Each object has a world matrix that describes the object's local space relative to the world space, which specifies the placement of the object in the world. Note that even though we draw multiple spheres and cylinders in this demo, we only need one copy of the sphere and cylinder geometry. We simply redraw the same sphere and cylinder mesh multiple times, but with different world matrices; recall that this is called instancing. The matrices are created at initialization time like so:

```
// Define transformations from local spaces to world space.
XMFLOAT4X4 mSphereWorld[10];
XMFLOAT4X4 mCylWorld[10];
XMFLOAT4X4 mBoxWorld;
XMFLOAT4X4 mGridWorld;
XMFLOAT4X4 mCenterSphere;

XMMATRIX I = XMMatrixIdentity();
XMStoreFloat4x4(&mGridWorld, I);

XMMATRIX boxScale = XMMatrixScaling(2.0f, 1.0f, 2.0f);
XMMATRIX boxOffset = XMMatrixTranslation(0.0f, 0.5f, 0.0f);
XMStoreFloat4x4(&mBoxWorld, XMMatrixMultiply(boxScale, boxOffset));

XMMATRIX centerSphereScale = XMMatrixScaling(2.0f, 2.0f, 2.0f);
XMMATRIX centerSphereOffset = XMMatrixTranslation(0.0f, 2.0f, 0.0f);
XMStoreFloat4x4(&mCenterSphere, XMMatrixMultiply(centerSphereScale,
  centerSphereOffset));
```

```
// We create 5 rows of 2 cylinders and spheres per row.
for(int i = 0; i < 5; ++i)
{
    XMStoreFloat4x4(&mCylWorld[i*2+0],
        XMMatrixTranslation(-5.0f, 1.5f, -10.0f + i*5.0f));
    XMStoreFloat4x4(&mCylWorld[i*2+1],
        XMMatrixTranslation(+5.0f, 1.5f, -10.0f + i*5.0f));

    XMStoreFloat4x4(&mSphereWorld[i*2+0],
        XMMatrixTranslation(-5.0f, 3.5f, -10.0f + i*5.0f));
    XMStoreFloat4x4(&mSphereWorld[i*2+1],
        XMMatrixTranslation(+5.0f, 3.5f, -10.0f + i*5.0f));
}
```

We pack all the mesh vertices and indices into one vertex and index buffer. This is done by concatenating the vertex and index arrays. This means that when we draw an object, we are only drawing a subset of the vertex and index buffers. There are three quantities we need to know in order to draw only a subset of the geometry (recall Figure 6.3). We need to know the starting index to each object in the concatenated index buffer, and we need to know the index count per object. The third thing we need is the index offset to the first vertex of each object in the concatenated vertex buffer. This is because when we concatenated the vertex arrays, we did not offset the indices to compensate (recall Exercise 2 in Chapter 5); however, if we have the index offset to the first vertex for each object, we can pass it into the third parameter of ID3D11DeviceContext::DrawIndexed, and that offset will be added to all the indices in that draw call to do the offset for us.

The code following shows how the geometry buffers are created, how the necessary drawing quantities are cached, and how the objects are drawn.

```
void ShapesApp::BuildGeometryBuffers()
{
    GeometryGenerator::MeshData box;
    GeometryGenerator::MeshData grid;
    GeometryGenerator::MeshData sphere;
    GeometryGenerator::MeshData cylinder;

    GeometryGenerator geoGen;
    geoGen.CreateBox(1.0f, 1.0f, 1.0f, box);
    geoGen.CreateGrid(20.0f, 30.0f, 60, 40, grid);
    geoGen.CreateSphere(0.5f, 20, 20, sphere);
    geoGen.CreateCylinder(0.5f, 0.3f, 3.0f, 20, 20, cylinder);

    // Cache the vertex offsets to each object in the concatenated
    // vertex buffer.
    mBoxVertexOffset      = 0;
    mGridVertexOffset     = box.Vertices.size();
    mSphereVertexOffset   = mGridVertexOffset + grid.Vertices.size();
    mCylinderVertexOffset = mSphereVertexOffset + sphere.Vertices.size();

    // Cache the index count of each object.
    mBoxIndexCount        = box.Indices.size();
```

```
mGridIndexCount     = grid.Indices.size();
mSphereIndexCount   = sphere.Indices.size();
mCylinderIndexCount = cylinder.Indices.size();

// Cache the starting index for each object in the concatenated
// index buffer.
mBoxIndexOffset      = 0;
mGridIndexOffset     = mBoxIndexCount;
mSphereIndexOffset   = mGridIndexOffset + mGridIndexCount;
mCylinderIndexOffset = mSphereIndexOffset + mSphereIndexCount;

UINT totalVertexCount =
  box.Vertices.size() +
  grid.Vertices.size() +
  sphere.Vertices.size() +
  cylinder.Vertices.size();

UINT totalIndexCount =
  mBoxIndexCount +
  mGridIndexCount +
  mSphereIndexCount +
  mCylinderIndexCount;

//
// Extract the vertex elements we are interested in and pack the
// vertices of all the meshes into one vertex buffer.
//

std::vector<Vertex> vertices(totalVertexCount);

XMFLOAT4 black(0.0f, 0.0f, 0.0f, 1.0f);

UINT k = 0;
for(size_t i = 0; i < box.Vertices.size(); ++i, ++k)
{
  vertices[k].Pos   = box.Vertices[i].Position;
  vertices[k].Color = black;
}

for(size_t i = 0; i < grid.Vertices.size(); ++i, ++k)
{
  vertices[k].Pos   = grid.Vertices[i].Position;
  vertices[k].Color = black;
}

for(size_t i = 0; i < sphere.Vertices.size(); ++i, ++k)
{
  vertices[k].Pos   = sphere.Vertices[i].Position;
  vertices[k].Color = black;
}

for(size_t i = 0; i < cylinder.Vertices.size(); ++i, ++k)
{
  vertices[k].Pos   = cylinder.Vertices[i].Position;
  vertices[k].Color = black;
}
```

```
      D3D11_BUFFER_DESC vbd;
      vbd.Usage = D3D11_USAGE_IMMUTABLE;
      vbd.ByteWidth = sizeof(Vertex) * totalVertexCount;
      vbd.BindFlags = D3D11_BIND_VERTEX_BUFFER;
      vbd.CPUAccessFlags = 0;
      vbd.MiscFlags = 0;
      D3D11_SUBRESOURCE_DATA vinitData;
      vinitData.pSysMem = &vertices[0];
      HR(md3dDevice->CreateBuffer(&vbd, &vinitData, &mVB));

      //
      // Pack the indices of all the meshes into one index buffer.
      //

      std::vector<UINT> indices;
      indices.insert(indices.end(), box.Indices.begin(), box.Indices.end());
      indices.insert(indices.end(), grid.Indices.begin(), grid.Indices.end());
      indices.insert(indices.end(), sphere.Indices.begin(),
        sphere.Indices.end());
      indices.insert(indices.end(), cylinder.Indices.begin(),
        cylinder.Indices.end());

      D3D11_BUFFER_DESC ibd;
      ibd.Usage = D3D11_USAGE_IMMUTABLE;
      ibd.ByteWidth = sizeof(UINT) * totalIndexCount;
      ibd.BindFlags = D3D11_BIND_INDEX_BUFFER;
      ibd.CPUAccessFlags = 0;
      ibd.MiscFlags = 0;
      D3D11_SUBRESOURCE_DATA iinitData;
      iinitData.pSysMem = &indices[0];
      HR(md3dDevice->CreateBuffer(&ibd, &iinitData, &mIB));
}

void ShapesApp::DrawScene()
{
      md3dImmediateContext->ClearRenderTargetView(mRenderTargetView,
        reinterpret_cast<const float*>(&Colors::Blue));
      md3dImmediateContext->ClearDepthStencilView(mDepthStencilView,
        D3D11_CLEAR_DEPTH|D3D11_CLEAR_STENCIL, 1.0f, 0);

      md3dImmediateContext->IASetInputLayout(mInputLayout);
      md3dImmediateContext->IASetPrimitiveTopology(
        D3D11_PRIMITIVE_TOPOLOGY_TRIANGLELIST);

      md3dImmediateContext->RSSetState(mWireframeRS);

      UINT stride = sizeof(Vertex);
      UINT offset = 0;
      md3dImmediateContext->IASetVertexBuffers(0, 1, &mVB, &stride, &offset);
      md3dImmediateContext->IASetIndexBuffer(mIB, DXGI_FORMAT_R32_UINT, 0);

      // Set constants

      XMMATRIX view  = XMLoadFloat4x4(&mView);
      XMMATRIX proj  = XMLoadFloat4x4(&mProj);
      XMMATRIX viewProj = view*proj;
```

```
D3DX11_TECHNIQUE_DESC techDesc;
mTech->GetDesc(&techDesc);
for(UINT p = 0; p < techDesc.Passes; ++p)
{
  // Draw the grid.
  XMMATRIX world = XMLoadFloat4x4(&mGridWorld);
  mfxWorldViewProj->SetMatrix(
    reinterpret_cast<float*>(&(world*viewProj)));
  mTech->GetPassByIndex(p)->Apply(0, md3dImmediateContext);
  md3dImmediateContext->DrawIndexed(
    mGridIndexCount, mGridIndexOffset, mGridVertexOffset);

  // Draw the box.
  world = XMLoadFloat4x4(&mBoxWorld);
  mfxWorldViewProj->SetMatrix(
    reinterpret_cast<float*>(&(world*viewProj)));
  mTech->GetPassByIndex(p)->Apply(0, md3dImmediateContext);
  md3dImmediateContext->DrawIndexed(
    mBoxIndexCount, mBoxIndexOffset, mBoxVertexOffset);

  // Draw center sphere.
  world = XMLoadFloat4x4(&mCenterSphere);
  mfxWorldViewProj->SetMatrix(
    reinterpret_cast<float*>(&(world*viewProj)));
  mTech->GetPassByIndex(p)->Apply(0, md3dImmediateContext);
  md3dImmediateContext->DrawIndexed(
    mSphereIndexCount, mSphereIndexOffset, mSphereVertexOffset);

  // Draw the cylinders.
  for(int i = 0; i < 10; ++i)
  {
    world = XMLoadFloat4x4(&mCylWorld[i]);
    mfxWorldViewProj->SetMatrix(
      reinterpret_cast<float*>(&(world*viewProj)));
    mTech->GetPassByIndex(p)->Apply(0, md3dImmediateContext);
    md3dImmediateContext->DrawIndexed(mCylinderIndexCount,
      mCylinderIndexOffset, mCylinderVertexOffset);
  }

  // Draw the spheres.
  for(int i = 0; i < 10; ++i)
  {
    world = XMLoadFloat4x4(&mSphereWorld[i]);
    mfxWorldViewProj->SetMatrix(
      reinterpret_cast<float*>(&(world*viewProj)));
    mTech->GetPassByIndex(p)->Apply(0, md3dImmediateContext);
    md3dImmediateContext->DrawIndexed(mSphereIndexCount,
      mSphereIndexOffset, mSphereVertexOffset);
  }
}

HR(mSwapChain->Present(0, 0));
}
```

6.12 LOADING GEOMETRY FROM THE FILE

Although boxes, grids, spheres, and cylinders will suffice for some of the demos in this book, some demos will benefit by rendering more complicated geometry. Later we will describe how to load 3D meshes from a popular 3D modeling format. In the mean time, we have exported the geometry of a skull mesh (Figure 6.18) to a simple list of vertices (position and normal vectors only) and indices. We can simply read the vertices and indices from the file using standard C++ file I/O and copy them into our vertex and index buffers. The file format is a very simple text file:

```
VertexCount: 31076
TriangleCount: 60339
VertexList (pos, normal)
{
    0.592978 1.92413 -2.62486 0.572276 0.816877 0.0721907
    0.571224 1.94331 -2.66948 0.572276 0.816877 0.0721907
    0.609047 1.90942 -2.58578 0.572276 0.816877 0.0721907
    ...
}
TriangleList
{
    0 1 2
    3 4 5
    6 7 8
    ...
}
```

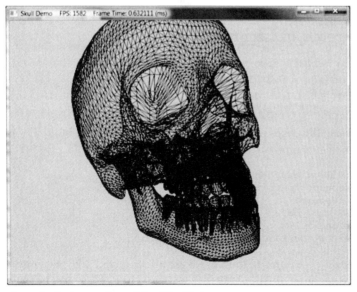

Figure 6.18. Screenshot of the "Skull" demo.

6.13 DYNAMIC VERTEX BUFFERS

So far we have worked with static buffers, which are fixed at initialization time. In contrast, the contents of a dynamic buffer change, usually per frame. Dynamic buffers are usually used when we need to animate something. For example, suppose we are doing a wave simulation, and we solve the wave equation for the solution function $f(x, z, t)$. This function represents the wave height at each point in the xz-plane at time t. If we were to use this function to draw the waves, we would use a triangle grid mesh like we did with the peaks and valleys, and apply $f(x, z, t)$ to each grid point in order to obtain the wave heights at the grid points. Because this function also depends on time t (i.e., the wave surface changes with time), we would need to reapply this function to the grid points a short time later (say every 1/30th of a second) to get a smooth animation. Thus, we need a dynamic vertex buffer in order to update the heights of the triangle grid mesh vertices as time passes. Another situation that leads to dynamic vertex buffers is particle systems with complex physics and collision detection. In each frame we will do the physics and collision detection on the CPU to find the new position of the particles. Because the particle positions are changing each frame, we need a dynamic vertex buffer in order to update the particle positions for drawing each frame.

Recall that in order to make a buffer dynamic, we must specify the usage D3D11_USAGE_DYNAMIC; in addition, because we will be writing to the buffer, we need the CPU access flag D3D11_CPU_ACCESS_WRITE:

```
D3D11_BUFFER_DESC vbd;
vbd.Usage = D3D11_USAGE_DYNAMIC;
vbd.ByteWidth = sizeof(Vertex) * mWaves.VertexCount();
vbd.BindFlags = D3D11_BIND_VERTEX_BUFFER;
vbd.CPUAccessFlags = D3D11_CPU_ACCESS_WRITE;
vbd.MiscFlags = 0;
HR(md3dDevice->CreateBuffer(&vbd, 0, &mWavesVB));
```

Then we can use the ID3D11DeviceContext::Map function to obtain a pointer to the start of the buffer memory block and write to it:

```
HRESULT ID3D11DeviceContext::Map(
    ID3D11Resource *pResource,
    UINT Subresource,
    D3D11_MAP MapType,
    UINT MapFlags,
    D3D11_MAPPED_SUBRESOURCE *pMappedResource);
```

1. **pResource**: Pointer to the resource we want to access for reading/writing. A buffer is one type of Direct3D 11 resource, but other resources can be accessed with this method as well, such as texture resources.

2. **Subresource**: An index to a subresource contained in the resource. We will see how this is used later; our buffers do not have subresources so specify 0.

3. **MapType**: Common flags are one of the following:

   (a) **D3D11_MAP_WRITE_DISCARD**: Instructs the hardware to discard the buffer and return a pointer to a newly allocated buffer; this prevents the hardware from stalling by allowing the hardware to continue rendering from the discarded buffer while we write to the newly allocated buffer.

   (b) **D3D11_MAP_WRITE_NO_OVERWRITE**: Tells the hardware we are only going to write to uninitialized parts of the buffer; this also prevents the hardware from stalling by allowing it to continue rendering previously written geometry at the same time we write to the uninitialized parts of the buffer.

   (c) **D3D11_MAP_READ**: Used with staging buffers, where you need to read a copy of the GPU buffer into system memory.

4. **MapFlags**: Optional flag we do not use and so specify as 0; see the SDK documentation for details.

5. **pMappedResource**: Returns a pointer to a **D3D11_MAPPED_SUBRESOURCE** from which we can access the resource data for reading/writing.

   The **D3D11_MAPPED_SUBRESOURCE** structure is defined like this:

```
typedef struct D3D11_MAPPED_SUBRESOURCE {
    void *pData;
    UINT RowPitch;
    UINT DepthPitch;
} D3D11_MAPPED_SUBRESOURCE;
```

1. **pData**: Pointer to the raw memory of the resource for reading/writing. You must cast this to the appropriate data format the resource stores.

2. **RowPitch**: The byte size of one row of data in a resource. For example, for a 2D texture, this is the byte size of one row.

3. **DepthPitch**: The byte size of a page of data in a resource. For example, for a 3D texture, this is the byte size of one 2D image subset of the 3D texture.

The difference between **RowPitch** and **DepthPitch** is to 2D and 3D resources (think 2D or 3D arrays). For vertex/index buffers that are essentially 1D arrays of data, the **RowPitch** and **DepthPitch** are given the same value, and it is equal to the byte size of the vertex/index buffer.

The following code shows how we update the vertex buffer in the "Waves" demo:

```
D3D11_MAPPED_SUBRESOURCE mappedData;
HR(md3dImmediateContext->Map(mWavesVB, 0,
    D3D11_MAP_WRITE_DISCARD, 0, &mappedData));
```

```
Vertex* v = reinterpret_cast<Vertex*>(mappedData.pData);
for(UINT i = 0; i < mWaves.VertexCount(); ++i)
{
    v[i].Pos = mWaves[i];
    v[i].Color = XMFLOAT4(0.0f, 0.0f, 0.0f, 1.0f);
}

md3dImmediateContext->Unmap(mWavesVB, 0);
```

The `ID3D11DeviceContext::Unmap` function must be called when you are done updating the buffer.

There is some overhead when using dynamic buffers, as the new data must be transferred from CPU memory back up to GPU memory. Therefore, static buffers should be preferred to dynamic buffers, provided static buffers will work. The latest versions of Direct3D have introduced new features to lessen the need for dynamic buffers. For instance,

1. simple animations may be done in a vertex shader.

2. through render to texture or compute shaders, and vertex texture fetch functionality, it is possible to implement a wave simulation like the one described previously that runs completely on the GPU.

3. the geometry shader provides the ability for the GPU to create or destroy primitives, a task that would normally need to be done on the CPU without a geometry shader.

Index buffers can be dynamic, too. However, in the "Waves" demo, the triangle topology remains constant and only the vertex heights change; therefore, only the vertex buffer needs to be dynamic.

The "Waves" demo for this chapter uses a dynamic vertex buffer to implement a simple wave simulation like the one described at the beginning of this section. For this book, we are not concerned with the actual algorithm details for the wave simulation (see [Lengyel02] for that), but more with the process so as to illustrate dynamic buffers: update the simulation on CPU and then update the vertex buffer accordingly using `Map`/`Unmap`.

 In the "Waves" demo, we render the waves in wireframe mode; this is because without lighting it is difficult to see the wave motion in solid fill mode.

 We mention again that this demo could be implemented on the GPU using more advanced methods such as render to texture functionality or the compute shader, and vertex texture fetch. Because we have not covered these topics yet, we do the wave simulation on the CPU and update the new vertices using dynamic vertex buffers.

6.14 SUMMARY

1. A vertex in Direct3D can consist of additional data besides spatial location. To create a custom vertex format, we first define a structure that holds the vertex data we choose. Once we have defined a vertex structure, we describe it to Direct3D by defining an input layout description—an array of `D3D11_INPUT_ELEMENT_DESC` elements, one per vertex component. With this array description, we create an `ID3D11InputLayout` object with `ID3D11Device::CreateInputLayout`, and we can bind the input layout to the IA stage via the `ID3D11DeviceContext::IASetInputLayout` method.

2. In order for the GPU to access an array of vertices/indices, they need to be placed in a special resource structure called a *buffer*, which is represented by the `ID3D11Buffer` interface.
   A buffer that stores vertices is called a *vertex buffer* and a buffer that stores indices is called an *index buffer*. Direct3D buffers not only store data, but also describe how the data will be accessed and where it will be bound to the rendering pipeline. A buffer is created by filling out a `D3D11_BUFFER_DESC` and `D3D11_SUBRESOURCE_DATA` instance, and calling `ID3D11Device::CreateBuffer`. A vertex buffer is bound to the IA stage with the `ID3D11DeviceContext::IASetVertexBuffers` method, and an index buffer is bound to the IA stage with the `ID3D11DeviceContext::IASetIndexBuffer` method. Nonindexed geometry can be drawn with `ID3D11DeviceContext::Draw`, and indexed geometry can be drawn with `ID3D11DeviceContext::DrawIndexed`.

3. A vertex shader is a program written in HLSL, executed on the GPU, which inputs a vertex and outputs a vertex. Every drawn vertex goes through the vertex shader. This enables the programmer to do specialized work on a per vertex basis to achieve various rendering effects. The values output from the vertex shader are passed on to the next stage in the pipeline.

4. Constant buffers are just blocks of data that can store different variables that may be accessed by both the C++ application code and a shader program. In this way, the C++ application can communicate with the shader and update the values in the constant buffers the shader uses; for example, the C++ application can change the world-view-projection matrix the shader uses.
   The general advice is to create constant buffers based on the frequency in which you need to update their contents. The motivation for dividing the constant buffers up is efficiency. When a constant buffer is updated, all its variables must be updated; therefore, it is efficient to group them based on their update frequency to minimize redundant updates.

5. A pixel shader is a program written in HLSL, executed on the GPU, which inputs interpolated vertex data and outputs a color value. As a hardware optimization,

it is possible that a pixel fragment is rejected by the pipeline before making it to the pixel shader (e.g., early-z rejection). Pixel shaders enable the programmer to do specialized work on a per pixel basis to achieve various rendering effects. The values output from the pixel shader are passed on to the next stage in the pipeline.

6. Render states are states the device maintains that affect how geometry is rendered. Render states remain in effect until changed, and the current values are applied to the geometry of any subsequent drawing operations. All render states have initial default states. Direct3D divides render states into three state blocks: the rasterizer state (`ID3D11RasterizerState`), the blend state (`ID3D11BlendState`), and the depth/stencil state (`ID3D11DepthStencilState`). Render states can be created and set at the C++ application level or in effect files.

7. A Direct3D effect (`ID3DX11Effect`) encapsulates at least one rendering technique. A rendering technique contains the code that specifies how to render 3D geometry in a particular way. A rendering technique consists of at least one rendering pass. For each rendering pass, the geometry is rendered. A multipass technique requires rendering the geometry several times to achieve the desired result. Each pass consists of the vertex shader, optional geometry shader, optional tessellation shaders, pixel shader, and the render states used to draw the geometry for that pass. The vertex, geometry, tessellation, and pixel shaders may access variables in the constant buffers defined in the effect file, as well as texture resources. We can use compile time parameters to use the effects framework to generate shader variations for us based on the given compile time arguments.

8. Dynamic buffers are used when the contents of the buffer needs to be updated frequently at runtime (e.g., every frame or every 1/30th of a second). A dynamic buffer must be created with the `D3D11_USAGE_DYNAMIC` usage and the `D3D11_CPU_ACCESS_WRITE` CPU access flag. Use the `ID3D11DeviceContext::Map` and `ID3D11DeviceContext::Unmap` methods to update the buffer.

6.15 EXERCISES

1. Write down the `D3D10_INPUT_ELEMENT_DESC` array for the following vertex structure:

```
struct Vertex
{
    XMFLOAT3 Pos;
    XMFLOAT3 Tangent;
    XMFLOAT3 Normal;
    XMFLOAT2 Tex0;
    XMFLOAT2 Tex1;
    XMCOLOR Color;
};
```

2. Redo the Colored Cube demo, but this time use two vertex buffers (and two input slots) to feed the pipeline with vertices, one that stores the position element and the other that stores the color element. Your D3D11_INPUT_ELEMENT_DESC array will look like this:

```
D3D11_INPUT_ELEMENT_DESC vertexDesc[] =
{
    {"POSITION", 0, DXGI_FORMAT_R32G32B32_FLOAT, 0, 0,
      D3D11_INPUT_PER_VERTEX_DATA, 0},
    {"COLOR",    0, DXGI_FORMAT_R32G32B32A32_FLOAT, 1, 0,
      D3D11_INPUT_PER_VERTEX_DATA, 0}
};
```

The position element is hooked up to input slot 0, and the color element is hooked up to input slot 1. Moreover note that the D3D11_INPUT_ELEMENT_DESC::AlignedByteOffset is 0 for both elements; this is because the position and color elements are no longer interleaved in a single input slot.

3. Draw
    (a) a point list like the one shown in Figure 5.13*a*.
    (b) a line strip like the one shown in Figure 5.13*b*.
    (c) a line list like the one shown in Figure 5.13*c*.
    (d) a triangle strip like the one shown in Figure 5.13*d*.
    (e) a triangle list like the one shown in Figure 5.14*a*.

4. Construct the vertex and index list of a pyramid, as shown in Figure 6.19, and draw it. Color the base vertices green and the tip vertex red.

5. Run the "Box" demo, and recall that we specified colors at the vertices only. Explain how pixel colors were obtained for each pixel on the triangle.

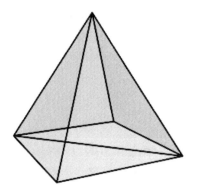

Figure 6.19. The triangles of a pyramid.

6. Modify the Colored Cube demo by applying the following transformation to each vertex in the vertex shader prior to transforming to world space.

```
vin.Pos.xy += 0.5f*sin(vin.Pos.x)*sin(3.0f*gTime);
vin.Pos.z  *= 0.6f + 0.4f*sin(2.0f*gTime);
```

The `gTime` constant buffer variable corresponds to the current `GameTimer::TotalTime()` value. This will animate the vertices as a function of time by distorting them periodically with the sine function.

7. Merge the vertices of a box and pyramid into one large vertex buffer. Also merge the indices of the box and pyramid into one large index buffer (but do not update the index values). Then draw the box and pyramid one-by-one using the parameters of `ID3D11DeviceContext::DrawIndexed`. Use the world transformation matrix so that the box and pyramid are disjoint in world space.

8. Modify the Colored Cube demo by rendering the cube in wireframe mode. Do this in two different ways: First, by setting the rasterization render state from the C++ code by calling `ID3D11DeviceContext::RSSetState`; second, by setting the rasterization render state from the effect file by calling `SetRasterizerState()` in the effect pass.

9. Modify the Colored Cube demo by disabling backface culling (`CullMode = None`); also try culling front faces instead of back faces (`CullMode = Front`). Do this in two different ways: First, by setting the rasterization render state from the C++ code by calling `ID3D11DeviceContext::RSSetState`; second, by setting the rasterization render state from the effect file by calling `SetRasterizerState()` in the effect pass. Output your results in wireframe mode so that you can see the difference.

10. If vertex memory is significant, then reducing from 128-bit color values to 32-bit color values may be worthwhile. Modify the "Box" demo by using a 32-bit color value instead of a 128-bit color value in the vertex structure. Your vertex structure and corresponding vertex input description will look like this:

```
struct Vertex
{
    XMFLOAT3 Pos;
    XMCOLOR  Color;
};

D3D11_INPUT_ELEMENT_DESC vertexDesc[] =
{
    {"POSITION", 0, DXGI_FORMAT_R32G32B32_FLOAT, 0, 0,
      D3D11_INPUT_PER_VERTEX_DATA, 0},
    {"COLOR",    0, DXGI_FORMAT_R8G8B8A8_UNORM, 0, 12,
      D3D11_INPUT_PER_VERTEX_DATA, 0}
};
```

The 8-bit color components need to be packed into a **UINT** *in the format ABGR, not RGBA; this is because the byte order is reversed in little-endian format (the bytes ABGR will actually be ordered RGBA in little-endian). For multi-byte data, big-endian stores the most significant byte at the lowest address in memory, and the least significant byte at the highest address, and little-endian stores the least significant byte at the lowest address in memory, and the most significant byte at the highest address in memory. The conversion from ARGB (which* **XMCOLOR** *uses) to ABGR can be done with a function like the following:*

```
static D3DX11INLINE UINT ArgbToAbgr(UINT argb)
{
    BYTE A = (argb >> 24) & 0xff;
    BYTE R = (argb >> 16) & 0xff;
    BYTE G = (argb >>  8) & 0xff;
    BYTE B = (argb >>  0) & 0xff;

    return (A << 24) | (B << 16) | (G << 8) | (R << 0);
}
```

11 . Modify the "Skull" demo by changing the viewport to only render to a subrectangle of the output window.

12 . Consider the following C++ vertex structure:

```
struct Vertex
{
    XMFLOAT3 Pos;
    XMFLOAT4 Color;
};
```

(a) Does the input layout description order need to match the vertex structure order? That is, is the following vertex declaration correct for this vertex structure? Do an experiment to find out. Then give reasoning for why you think it works or does not work.

```
D3D11_INPUT_ELEMENT_DESC vertexDesc[] =
{
  {"COLOR",    0, DXGI_FORMAT_R32G32B32A32_FLOAT, 0, 12,
    D3D11_INPUT_PER_VERTEX_DATA, 0},
  {"POSITION", 0, DXGI_FORMAT_R32G32B32_FLOAT, 0, 0,
    D3D11_INPUT_PER_VERTEX_DATA, 0},
};
```

(b) Does the corresponding vertex shader structure order need to match the C++ vertex structure order? That is, does the following vertex shader structure work with the previous C++ vertex structure? Do an experiment to find out. Then give reasoning for why you think it works or does not work.

```
struct VertexIn
{
  float4 Color : COLOR;
  float3 Pos   : POSITION;
};
```

13 . We can submit an array of screen rectangles to the Direct3D *scissor test*. The scissor test will discard all pixels outside the scissor rectangles. Modify the "Shapes" demo to use the scissor test. The scissor rectangles can be set with the following method:

```
void RSSetScissorRects(UINT NumRects, const D3D11_RECT *pRects);
```

Here is an example call:

```
D3D11_RECT rects = {100, 100, 400, 400};
md3dImmediateContext->RSSetScissorRects(1, &rects);
```

The previous call only sets the scissor rectangles, but it does not enable the scissor test. The scissor test is enabled/disabled via the D3D11_RASTERIZER_DESC::ScissorEnable.

14 . Modify the "Shape" demo to use GeometryGenerator::CreateGeosphere instead of GeometryGenerator::CreateSphere. Try with 0, 1, 2, and 3 subdivision levels.

Chapter 7   LIGHTING

Consider Figure 7.1. On the left we have an unlit sphere, and on the right, we have a lit sphere. As you can see, the sphere on the left looks rather flat—maybe it is not even a sphere at all, but just a 2D circle. On the other hand, the sphere on the right does look 3D—the lighting and shading aid in our perception of the solid form and volume of the object. In fact, our visual perception of the world depends on light and its interaction with materials, and consequently, much of the problem of generating photorealistic scenes has to do with physically accurate lighting models.

Of course, in general, the more accurate the model, the more computationally expensive it is; thus a balance must be reached between realism and speed. For example, 3D special FX scenes for films can be much more complex and utilize very realistic lighting models than a game because the frames for a film are pre-rendered, so they can afford to take hours or days to process a frame. Games, on the other hand, are real-time applications, and therefore, the frames need to be drawn at a rate of at least 30 frames per second.

Note that the lighting model explained and implemented in this book is largely based off the one described in [Möller02].

Objectives:

1. To gain a basic understanding of the interaction between lights and materials.
2. To understand the differences between local illumination and global illumination.

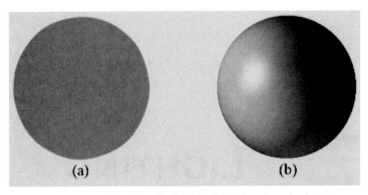

Figure 7.1. (a) An unlit sphere looks 2D. (b) A lit sphere looks 3D.

3. To find out how we can mathematically describe the direction a point on a surface is "facing" so that we can determine the angle at which incoming light strikes the surface.

4. To learn how to correctly transform normal vectors.

5. To be able to distinguish between ambient, diffuse, and specular light.

6. To learn how to implement directional lights, point lights, and spotlights.

7. To understand how to vary light intensity as a function of depth by controlling attenuation parameters.

7.1 LIGHT AND MATERIAL INTERACTION

When using lighting, we no longer specify vertex colors directly; rather, we specify materials and lights, and then apply a lighting equation, which computes the vertex colors for us based on light/material interaction. This leads to a much more realistic coloring of the object (compare Figure 7.1*a* and 7.1*b* again).

Materials can be thought of as the properties that determine how light interacts with a surface of an object. For example, the colors of light a surface reflects and absorbs, and also the reflectivity, transparency, and shininess are all parameters that make up the material of the surface. In this chapter, however, we only concern ourselves with the colors of light a surface reflects and absorbs, and shininess.

In our model, a light source can emit various intensities of red, green, and blue light; in this way, we can simulate many light colors. When light travels outwards from a source and collides with an object, some of that light may be absorbed and some may be reflected (for transparent objects, such as glass, some of the light passes through the medium, but we do not consider transparency here). The reflected light now travels along its new path and may strike other objects where some light

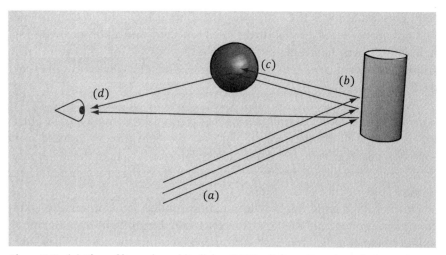

Figure 7.2. (a) Flux of incoming white light. (b) The light strikes the cylinder and some rays are absorbed and other rays are scatted toward the eye and sphere. (c) The light reflecting off the cylinder toward the sphere is absorbed or reflected again and travels into the eye. (d) The eye receives incoming light that determines what the eye sees.

is again absorbed and reflected. A light ray may strike many objects before it is fully absorbed. Presumably, some light rays eventually travel into the eye (see Figure 7.2) and strike the light receptor cells (named cones and rods) on the retina.

According to the *trichromatic* theory (see [Santrock03]), the retina contains three kinds of light receptors, each one sensitive to red, green, and blue light (with some overlap). The incoming RGB light stimulates its corresponding light receptors to varying intensities based on the strength of the light. As the light receptors are stimulated (or not), neural impulses are sent down the optic nerve toward the brain, where the brain generates an image in your head based on the stimulus of the light receptors. (Of course, if you close/cover your eyes, the receptor cells receive no stimulus and the brain registers this as black.)

For example, consider Figure 7.2 again. Suppose the material of the cylinder reflects 75% red light, 75% green light, and absorbs the rest, and the sphere reflects 25% red light and absorbs the rest. Also suppose that pure white light is being emitted from the light source. As the light rays strike the cylinder, all the blue light is absorbed and only 75% red and green light is reflected (i.e., a medium-high intensity yellow). This light is then scattered—some of it travels into the eye and some of it travels toward the sphere. The part that travels into the eye primarily stimulates the red and green cone cells to a semi-high degree; hence, the viewer sees the cylinder as a semi-bright shade of yellow. Now, the other light rays travel toward the sphere and strike it. The sphere reflects 25%

red light and absorbs the rest; thus, the diluted incoming red light (medium-high intensity red) is diluted further and reflected, and all of the incoming green light is absorbed. This remaining red light then travels into the eye and primarily stimulates the red cone cells to a low degree. Thus the viewer sees the sphere as a dark shade of red.

The lighting models we (and most real-time applications) adopt in this book are called *local illumination models*. With a local model, each object is lit independently of another object, and only the light directly emitted from light sources is taken into account in the lighting process (i.e., light that has bounced off other scene objects to strikes the object currently being lit is ignored). Figure 7.3 shows a consequence of this model.

On the other hand, global illumination models light objects by taking into consideration not only the light directly emitted from light sources, but also the indirect light that has bounced off other objects in the scene. These are called global illumination models because they take everything in the global scene into consideration when lighting an object. Global illumination models are generally prohibitively expensive for real-time games (but come very close to generating photorealistic scenes). There is research being done in real-time global illumination methods.

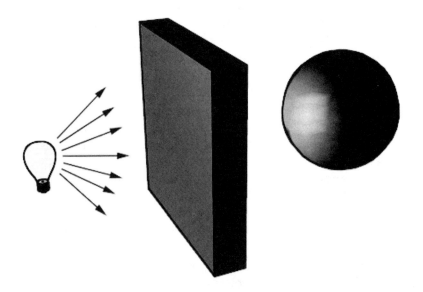

Figure 7.3. Physically, the wall blocks the light rays emitted by the light bulb and the sphere is in the shadow of the wall. However, in a local illumination model, the sphere is lit as if the wall were not there.

7.2 NORMAL VECTORS

A *face normal* is a unit vector that describes the direction a polygon is facing (i.e., it is orthogonal to all points on the polygon); see Figure 7.4*a*. A *surface normal* is a unit vector that is orthogonal to the tangent plane of a point on a surface; see Figure 7.4*b*. Observe that surface normals determine the direction a point on a surface is "facing."

For lighting calculations, we need the surface normal at each point on the surface of a triangle mesh so that we can determine the angle at which light strikes the point on the mesh surface. To obtain surface normals, we specify the surface normals only at the vertex points (so-called *vertex normals*). Then, in order to obtain a surface normal approximation at each point on the surface of a triangle mesh, these vertex normals will be interpolated across the triangle during rasterization (recall §5.10.3 and see Figure 7.5).

Note: *Interpolating the normal and doing lighting calculations per pixel is called pixel lighting or phong lighting. A less expensive, but less accurate, method is doing the lighting calculations per vertex. Then the result of the per vertex lighting calculation is output from the vertex shader and interpolated across the pixels of the triangle. Moving calculations from the pixel shader to the vertex shader is a common performance optimization at the sake of quality and sometimes the visual difference is very subtle making such optimizations very attractive.*

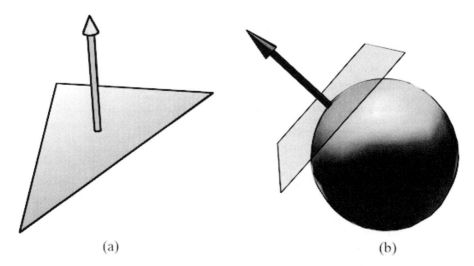

(a)   (b)

Figure 7.4. (a) The face normal is orthogonal to all points on the face. (b) The surface normal is the vector that is orthogonal to the tangent plane of a point on a surface.

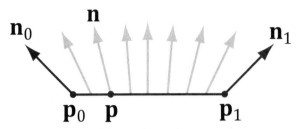

Figure 7.5. The vertex normals n_0 and n_1 are defined at the segment vertex points p_0 and p_1. A normal vector n for a point p in the interior of the line segment is found by linearly interpolating (weighted average) between the vertex normals; that is, $n = n_0 + t\,(n_1 - n_0)$, where t is such that $p = p_0 + t\,(p_1 - p_0)$. Although we illustrated normal interpolation over a line segment for simplicity, the idea straightforwardly generalizes to interpolating over a 3D triangle.

7.2.1 Computing Normal Vectors

To find the face normal of a triangle $\Delta p_0 p_1 p_2$, we first compute two vectors that lie on the triangle's edges:

$$u = p_1 - p_0$$
$$v = p_2 - p_0$$

Then the face normal is:

$$n = \frac{u \times v}{\| u \times v \|}$$

Following is a function that computes the face normal of the front side (§5.10.2) of a triangle from the three vertex points of the triangle.

```
void ComputeNormal(const D3DXVECTOR3& p0,
    const D3DXVECTOR3& p1,
    const D3DXVECTOR3& p2,
    D3DXVECTOR3& out)

{
    D3DXVECTOR3 u = p1 - p0;
    D3DXVECTOR3 v = p2 - p0;

    D3DXVec3Cross(&out, &u, &v);
    D3DXVec3Normalize(&out, &out);
}
```

For a differentiable surface, we can use calculus to find the normals of points on the surface. Unfortunately, a triangle mesh is not differentiable. The technique

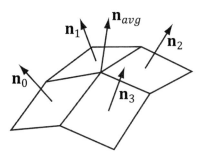

Figure 7.6. The middle vertex is shared by the neighboring four polygons, so we approximate the middle vertex normal by averaging the four polygon face normals.

that is generally applied to triangle meshes is called *vertex normal averaging*. The vertex normal $\mathbf{n}$ for an arbitrary vertex $\mathbf{v}$ in a mesh is found by averaging the face normals of every polygon in the mesh that shares the vertex $\mathbf{v}$. For example, in Figure 7.6, four polygons in the mesh share the vertex $\mathbf{v}$; thus, the vertex normal for $\mathbf{v}$ is given by:

$$\mathbf{n}_{avg} = \frac{\mathbf{n}_0 + \mathbf{n}_1 + \mathbf{n}_2 + \mathbf{n}_3}{\|\mathbf{n}_0 + \mathbf{n}_1 + \mathbf{n}_2 + \mathbf{n}_3\|}$$

In the previous example, we do not need to divide by 4, as we would in a typical average, because we normalize the result. Note also that more sophisticated averaging schemes can be constructed; for example, a weighted average might be used where the weights are determined by the areas of the polygons (e.g., polygons with larger areas have more weight than polygons with smaller areas).

The following pseudocode shows how this averaging can be implemented given the vertex and index list of a triangle mesh:

```
// Input:
// 1. An array of vertices (mVertices).  Each vertex has a
//    position component (pos) and a normal component (normal).
// 2. An array of indices (mIndices).

// For each triangle in the mesh:
for(UINT i = 0; i < mNumTriangles; ++i)
{
    // indices of the ith triangle
    UINT i0 = mIndices[i*3+0];
    UINT i1 = mIndices[i*3+1];
    UINT i2 = mIndices[i*3+2];

    // vertices of ith triangle
    Vertex v0 = mVertices[i0];
    Vertex v1 = mVertices[i1];
```

```
Vertex v2 = mVertices[i2];

// compute face normal
Vector3 e0 = v1.pos - v0.pos;
Vector3 e1 = v2.pos - v0.pos;
Vector3 faceNormal = Cross(e0, e1);

// This triangle shares the following three vertices,
// so add this face normal into the average of these
// vertex normals.
mVertices[i0].normal += faceNormal;
mVertices[i1].normal += faceNormal;
mVertices[i2].normal += faceNormal;
}

// For each vertex v, we have summed the face normals of all
// the triangles that share v, so now we just need to normalize.
for(UINT i = 0; i < mNumVertices; ++i)
    mVertices[i].normal = Normalize(&mVertices[i].normal));
```

7.2.2 Transforming Normal Vectors

Consider Figure 7.7a where we have a tangent vector $\mathbf{u} = \mathbf{v}_1 - \mathbf{v}_0$ orthogonal to a normal vector $\mathbf{n}$. If we apply a nonuniform scaling transformation $\mathbf{A}$, we see from Figure 7.7b that the transformed tangent vector $\mathbf{u}\mathbf{A} = \mathbf{v}_1\mathbf{A} - \mathbf{v}_0\mathbf{A}$ does not remain orthogonal to the transformed normal vector $\mathbf{n}\mathbf{A}$.

So our problem is this: Given a transformation matrix $\mathbf{A}$ that transforms points and vectors (non-normal), we want to find a transformation matrix $\mathbf{B}$ that transforms normal vectors such that the transformed tangent vector is orthogonal to the transformed normal vector (i.e., $\mathbf{u}\mathbf{A} \cdot \mathbf{n}\mathbf{B} = 0$). To do this, let us first start with something we know: we know that the normal vector $\mathbf{n}$ is orthogonal to the tangent vector $\mathbf{u}$:

$\mathbf{u} \cdot \mathbf{n} =$	Tangent vector orthogonal to normal vector
$\mathbf{u}\mathbf{n}^T = 0$	Rewriting the dot product as a matrix multiplication
$\mathbf{u}(\mathbf{A}\mathbf{A}^{-1})\,\mathbf{n}^T = 0$	Inserting the identity matrix $\mathbf{I} = \mathbf{A}\mathbf{A}^{-1}$
$(\mathbf{u}\mathbf{A})(\mathbf{A}^{-1}\,\mathbf{n}^T) = 0$	Associative property of matrix multiplication
$(\mathbf{u}\mathbf{A})\,((\mathbf{A}^{-1}\,\mathbf{n}^T)^T)^T = 0$	Transpose property $(\mathbf{A}^T)^T = \mathbf{A}$
$(\mathbf{u}\mathbf{A})\,(\mathbf{n}(\mathbf{A}^{-1})^T)^T = 0$	Transpose property $(\mathbf{A}\mathbf{B})^T = \mathbf{B}^T\mathbf{A}^T$
$\mathbf{u}\mathbf{A} \cdot \mathbf{n}(\mathbf{A}^{-1})^T = 0$	Rewriting the matrix multiplication as a dot product
$\mathbf{u}\mathbf{A} \cdot \mathbf{n}\mathbf{B} = 0$	Transformed tangent vector orthogonal to transformed normal vector

Thus $\mathbf{B} = (\mathbf{A}^{-1})^T$ (the inverse transpose of $\mathbf{A}$) does the job in transforming normal vectors so that they are perpendicular to its associated transformed tangent vector $\mathbf{u}\mathbf{A}$.

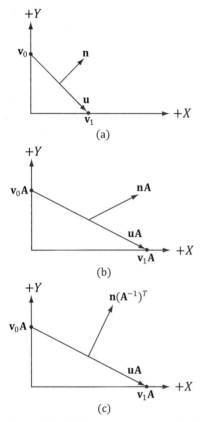

Figure 7.7. **(a) The surface normal before transformation. (b) After scaling by 2 units on the x-axis the normal is no longer orthogonal to the surface. (c) The surface normal correctly transformed by the inverse-transpose of the scaling transformation.**

Note that if the matrix is orthogonal ($\mathbf{A}^T = \mathbf{A}^{-1}$), then $\mathbf{B} = (\mathbf{A}^{-1})^T = (\mathbf{A}^T)^T = \mathbf{A}$; that is, we do not need to compute the inverse transpose, since $\mathbf{A}$ does the job in this case. In summary, when transforming a normal vector by a nonuniform or shear transformation, use the inverse-transpose.

We implement a helper function in *MathHelper.h* for computing the inverse-transpose:

```
static XMMATRIX InverseTranspose(CXMMATRIX M)
{
    XMMATRIX A = M;
    A.r[3] = XMVectorSet(0.0f, 0.0f, 0.0f, 1.0f);

    XMVECTOR det = XMMatrixDeterminant(A);
    return XMMatrixTranspose(XMMatrixInverse(&det, A));
}
```

We clear out any translation from the matrix because we use the inverse-transpose to transform vectors, and translations only apply to points. However, from §3.2.1 we know that setting $w = 0$ for vectors (using homogeneous coordinates) prevents vectors from being modified by translations. Therefore, we should not need to zero out the translation in the matrix. The problem is if we want to concatenate the inverse-transpose and another matrix that does not contain nonuniform scaling, say the view matrix $(\mathbf{A}^{-1})^T \mathbf{V}$, the transposed translation in the 4th column of $(\mathbf{A}^{-1})^T$ "leaks" into the product matrix causing errors. Hence, we zero out the translation as a precaution to avoid this error. The proper way would be to transform the normal by $((\mathbf{AV})^{-1})^T$. Following is an example of a scaling and translation matrix, and what the inverse-transpose looks like with a 4th column not $[0, 0, 0, 1]^T$:

$$\mathbf{A} = \begin{bmatrix} 1 & 0 & 0 & 0 \\ 0 & 0.5 & 0 & 0 \\ 0 & 0 & 0.5 & 0 \\ 1 & 1 & 1 & 1 \end{bmatrix}$$

$$\left(\mathbf{A}^{-1}\right)^T = \begin{bmatrix} 1 & 0 & 0 & -1 \\ 0 & 2 & 0 & -2 \\ 0 & 0 & 2 & -2 \\ 0 & 0 & 0 & 1 \end{bmatrix}$$

Note: *Even with the inverse-transpose transformation, normal vectors may lose their unit length; thus, they may need to be renormalized after the transformation.*

7.3 LAMBERT'S COSINE LAW

Light that strikes a surface point head-on is more intense than light that just glances a surface point; see Figure 7.8. Consider a small shaft of incoming light with cross-sectional area dA.

So the idea is to come up with a function that returns different intensities based on the alignment of the vertex normal and the *light vector*. (Observe that the light vector is the vector from the surface to the light source; that is, it is aimed in the opposite direction the light rays travel.) The function should return maximum intensity when the vertex normal and light vector are perfectly aligned (i.e., the angle θ between them is $0°$), and it should smoothly diminish in intensity as the angle between the vertex normal and light vector increases. If $\theta > 90°$, then the

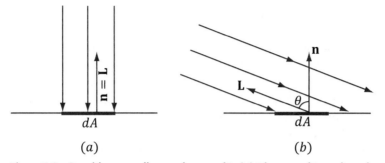

Figure 7.8. Consider a small area element *dA*. (a) The area *dA* receives the most light when the normal vector n and light vector L are aligned. (b) The area *dA* receives less light as the angle θ between n and L increases (as depicted by the light rays that miss the surface *dA*).

light strikes the back of a surface and so we set the intensity to zero. *Lambert's Cosine Law* gives the function we seek, which is given by

$$f(\theta) = \max(\cos\theta, 0) = \max(\mathbf{L} \cdot \mathbf{n}, 0)$$

where **L** and **n** are unit vectors. Figure 6.9 shows a plot of $f(\theta)$ to see how the intensity, ranging from 0.0 to 1.0 (i.e., 0% to 100%), varies with θ.

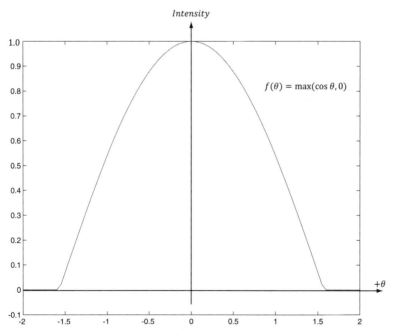

Figure 7.9. Plot of the function $f(\theta) = \max(\cos\theta, 0) = \max(\mathbf{L} \cdot \mathbf{n}, 0)$ for $-2 \leq \theta \leq 2$. Note that $\pi/2 \approx 1.57$.

7.4 DIFFUSE LIGHTING

Consider a rough surface, as in Figure 7.10. When light strikes a point on such a surface, the light rays scatter in various random directions; this is called a *diffuse reflection*. In our approximation for modeling this kind of light/surface interaction, we stipulate that the light scatters equally in all directions above the surface; consequently, the reflected light will reach the eye no matter the viewpoint (eye position). Therefore, we do not need to take the viewpoint into consideration (i.e., the diffuse lighting calculation is viewpoint independent), and the color of a point on the surface will always look the same no matter the viewpoint.

We break the calculation of diffuse lighting into two parts. For the first part, we specify a diffuse light color and a diffuse material color. The diffuse material specifies the amount of incoming diffuse light that the surface reflects and absorbs; this is handled with a component-wise color multiplication. For example, suppose some point on a surface reflects 50% incoming red light, 100% green light, and 75% blue light, and the incoming light color is 80% intensity white light. Hence the incoming diffuse light color is given by $\iota_d = (0.8, 0.8, 0.8)$ and the diffuse material color is given by $\mathbf{m}_d = (0.5, 1.0, 0.75)$; then the amount of light reflected off the point is given by:

$$\mathbf{D} = \iota_d \otimes \mathbf{m}_d = (0.8, 0.8, 0.8) \otimes (0.5, 1.0, 0.75) = (0.4, 0.8, 0.6)$$

To finish the diffuse lighting calculation, we simply include Lambert's cosine law (which controls how much of the original light the surface receives based on the angle between the surface normal and light vector). Let ι_d be the diffuse light color, $\mathbf{m}_d$ be the diffuse material color, and $k_d = \max(\mathbf{L} \cdot \mathbf{n}, 0)$, where $\mathbf{L}$ is the light vector, and $\mathbf{n}$ is the surface normal. Then the amount of diffuse light reflected off a point is given by:

$$\mathbf{c}_d = k_d \cdot \iota_d \otimes \mathbf{m}_d = k_d \mathbf{D} \qquad \qquad \textbf{(eq. 7.1)}$$

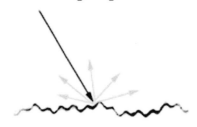

Figure 7.10. Incoming light scatters in random directions when striking a diffuse surface. The idea is that the surface is rough at a microscopic level.

7.5 AMBIENT LIGHTING

As stated earlier, our lighting model does not take into consideration indirect light that has bounced off other objects in the scenes. However, much light we see in the real world is indirect. For example, a hallway connected to a room might not be in the direct line of sight with a light source in the room, but the light bounces off the walls in the room and some of it may make it into the hallway, thereby lightening it up a bit. As a second example, suppose we are sitting in a room with a teapot on a desk and there is one light source in the room. Only one side of the teapot is in the direct line of sight of the light source; nevertheless, the backside of the teapot would not be pitch black. This is because some light scatters off the walls or other objects in the room and eventually strikes the backside of the teapot.

To sort of hack this indirect light, we introduce an ambient term to the lighting equation:

$$\mathbf{A} = \iota_a \otimes \mathbf{m}_a$$

The color ι_a specifies the total amount of indirect (ambient) light a surface receives from a light source. The ambient material color $\mathbf{m}_a$ specifies the amount of incoming ambient light that the surface reflects and absorbs. All ambient light does is uniformly brighten up the object a bit—there is no real physics calculation at all. The idea is that the indirect light has scattered and bounced around the scene so many times that it strikes the object equally in every direction.

Combining the ambient term with the diffuse term, our new lighting equations looks like this:

$$LitColor = \iota_a \otimes \mathbf{m}_a + k_d \cdot \iota_d \otimes \mathbf{m}_d$$
$$= \mathbf{A} + k_d \mathbf{D} \qquad\qquad \textbf{(eq. 7.2)}$$

7.6 SPECULAR LIGHTING

Consider a smooth surface, as in Figure 7.11. When light strikes such a surface, the light rays reflect sharply in a general direction through a *cone of reflectance*; this is called a *specular reflection*. In contrast to diffuse light, specular light might not travel into the eye because it reflects in a specific direction; the specular lighting calculation is viewpoint dependent. This means that as the eye moves about the scene, the amount of specular light it receives will change.

The cone the specular light reflects through is defined by an angle ϕ_{max} with respect to the reflection vector $\mathbf{r}$. Intuitively, it makes sense to vary the specular

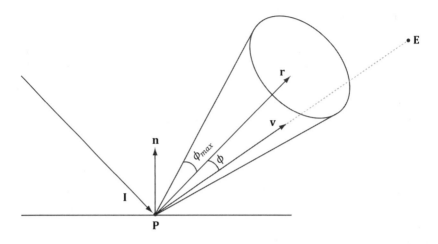

Figure 7.11. The incoming light ray is denoted by I. The specular reflection does not scatter in all directions, but instead reflects in a general cone of reflection whose size we can control with a parameter. If v is in the cone, the eye receives specular light; otherwise, it does not. The closer is aligned with the reflection vector r, the more specular light the eye receives.

light intensity based on the angle ϕ between the reflected vector $\mathbf{r}$ and the *view vector* $\mathbf{V} = \dfrac{\mathbf{E} - \mathbf{P}}{\|\mathbf{E} - \mathbf{P}\|}$ (i.e., the unit vector from the surface point $\mathbf{P}$ to the eye position $\mathbf{E}$) in the following way: We stipulate that the specular light intensity is maximized when $\phi = 0$ and smoothly decreases to zero as ϕ approaches ϕ_{max}. To model this mathematically, we modify the function used in Lambert's cosine law. Figure 7.12 shows the graph of the cosine function for different powers of $p \ge 1$. Essentially, by choosing different p, we indirectly control the cone angle ϕ_{max} where the light intensity drops to zero. The parameter p can be used to control the shininess of a surface; that is, highly polished surfaces will have a smaller cone of reflectance (the light reflects more sharply) than less shiny surfaces. So you would use a larger p for shiny surfaces than you would for matte surfaces.

Note that because $\mathbf{v}$ and $\mathbf{r}$ are unit vectors, we have that $\cos(\phi) = \mathbf{v} \cdot \mathbf{r}$.

The amount of specular light reflected off a point that makes it into the eye is given by:

$$\mathbf{c}_s = k_s \cdot \iota_s \otimes \mathbf{m}_s$$
$$= k_s \mathbf{S}$$

where

$$k_s = \begin{cases} \max(\mathbf{v} \cdot \mathbf{r}, 0)^p, & \mathbf{L} \cdot \mathbf{n} > 0 \\ 0, & \mathbf{L} \cdot \mathbf{n} \le 0 \end{cases}$$

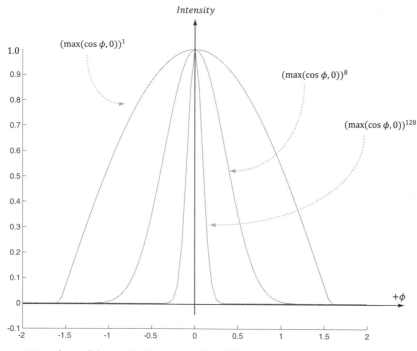

Figure 7.12. Plots of the cosine functions with different powers of $p \geq 1$.

The color ι_s specifies the amount of specular light the light source emits. The specular material color $\mathbf{m}_s$ specifies the amount of incoming specular light that the surface reflects. The factor k_s scales the intensity of the specular light based on the angle between $\mathbf{r}$ and $\mathbf{v}$. Figure 7.13 shows it is possible for a surface to receive no diffuse light ($\mathbf{L} \cdot \mathbf{n} < 0$),

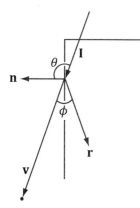

Figure 7.13. The eye can receive specular light even though the light strikes the back of a surface. This is incorrect, so we must detect this situation and set $k_S = 0$ in this case.

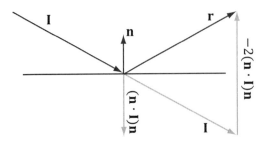

Figure 7.14. Geometry of reflection.

but to receive specular light. However, if the surface receives no diffuse light then it makes no sense for the surface to receive specular light, so we set $k_s = 0$ in this case.

Note: *The specular power p should always be greater than or equal to 1.*

Our new lighting model is:

$$LitColor = \iota_a \otimes \mathbf{m}_a + k_d \cdot \iota_d \otimes \mathbf{m}_d + k_s \cdot \iota_s \otimes \mathbf{m}_s$$
$$= \mathbf{A} + k_d \mathbf{D} + k_s \mathbf{S}$$

$$k_d = \max(\mathbf{L} \cdot \mathbf{n}, 0)$$

$$k_s = \begin{cases} \max(\mathbf{v} \cdot \mathbf{r}, 0)^p, & \mathbf{L} \cdot \mathbf{n} > 0 \\ 0, & \mathbf{L} \cdot \mathbf{n} \leq 0 \end{cases}$$

(eq. 7.3)

Note: *The reflection vector is given by:* $\mathbf{r} = \mathbf{I} - 2(\mathbf{n} \cdot \mathbf{I})\mathbf{n}$*; see Figure 7.14. (It is assumed that* $\mathbf{n}$ *is a unit vector.) However, we can actually use the HLSL intrinsic* `reflect` *function to compute* $\mathbf{r}$ *for us in a shader program.*

Observe that $\mathbf{I}$*, the incident vector, is the direction of the incoming light (i.e., opposite direction of the light vector* $\mathbf{L}$*).*

7.7 BRIEF RECAP

In our model, a light source emits three different kinds of light:

1. ambient light: to model indirect lighting.
2. diffuse light: to model the direct lighting of relatively rough surfaces.
3. specular light: to model the direct lighting of relatively smooth surfaces.

Figure 7.15. (a) Sphere colored with ambient light only, which uniformly brightens it. (b) Ambient and diffuse lighting combined. There is now a smooth transition from bright to dark due to Lambert's cosine law. (c) Ambient, diffuse, and specular lighting. The specular lighting yields a specular highlight.

Correspondingly, a surface point has the following material properties associated with it:

1. ambient material: the amount of ambient light the surface reflects and absorbs.

2. diffuse material: the amount of diffuse light the surface reflects and absorbs.

3. specular material: the amount of specular light the surface reflects and absorbs.

4. specular exponent: an exponent used in the specular lighting calculation which controls the cone of reflectance, and thus how shiny the surface is. The smaller the cone, the smoother/shinier the surface.

The reason for breaking lighting up into three components like this is for the flexibility; an artist has several degrees of freedom to tweak to obtain the desired output. Figure 7.15 shows how these three components work together.

7.8 SPECIFYING MATERIALS

How should we specify the material values? The material values may vary over the surface; that is, different points on the surface may have different material values (see Figure 7.16). For example, consider a car model, where the frame, windows, lights, and tires reflect and absorb light differently, and so the material values would need to vary over the car surface.

To approximately model this variation, one solution might be to specify material values on a per vertex basis. These per vertex materials would then interpolate across the triangle during rasterization, giving us material values for each point on the surface of the triangle mesh. However, as we saw from the "Hills" demo in Chapter 6, per vertex colors are still too coarse to realistically model fine details. Moreover, per vertex colors add additional data to our vertex structures, and we need to have tools to paint per vertex colors. Instead, the prevalent solution is to use

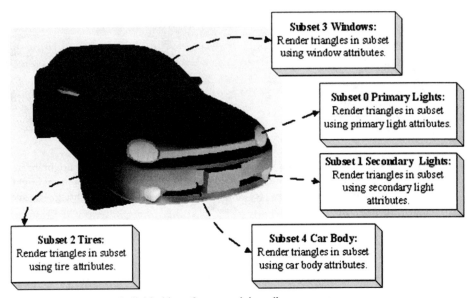

Figure 7.16. A car mesh divided into five material attribute groups.

texture mapping, which will have to wait until the next chapter. In the meantime, we allow material changes at the draw call frequency. That is, we set the material values to a member of a constant buffer, and all subsequently drawn geometry will use that material until it is changed between draw calls. The following pseudocode shows how we would draw the car:

```
Set Primary Lights material to constant buffer
Draw Primary Lights geometry

Set Secondary Lights material to constant buffer
Draw Secondary Lights geometry

Set Tire material to constant buffer
Draw Tire geometry

Set Window material to constant buffer
Draw Windows geometry

Set Car Body material to constant buffer
Draw car body geometry
```

Our material structure looks like this, and is defined in *LightHelper.h*:

```
struct Material
{
    Material() { ZeroMemory(this, sizeof(this)); }

    XMFLOAT4 Ambient;
```

```
    XMFLOAT4 Diffuse;
    XMFLOAT4 Specular; // w = SpecPower
    XMFLOAT4 Reflect;
};
```

Ignore the **Reflect** member for now; it will be used later when we model mirror like reflections and need to specify how much like a mirror a surface acts. Also, notice that we embed the specular power exponent p into the 4th component of the specular material color. This is because the alpha component is not needed for lighting, so we might as well use the empty slot to store something useful. The alpha component of the diffuse material will be used too, for alpha blending in a later chapter.

Finally, we remind the reader that we need normal vectors at each point on the surface of a triangle mesh so that we can determine the angle at which light strikes a point on the mesh surface (for Lambert's cosine law). In order to obtain a normal vector approximation at each point on the surface of the triangle mesh, we specify normals at the vertex level. These vertex normals will be interpolated across the triangle during rasterization.

So far we have discussed the components of light, but we have not discussed specific kinds of light sources. The next three sections describe how to implement parallel, point, and spot lights.

7.9 PARALLEL LIGHTS

A parallel light (or directional light) approximates a light source that is very far away. Consequently, we can approximate all incoming light rays as parallel to each other (Figure 7.17). A parallel light source is defined by a vector, which specifies the direction the light rays travel. Because the light rays are parallel, they all use the same direction vector. The light vector aims in the opposite direction the light rays travel. A common example of a real directional light source is the sun (Figure 7.18). The equation for a directional light is exactly Equation 7.3.

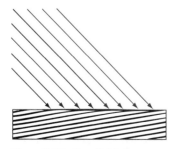

Figure 7.17. Parallel light rays striking a surface.

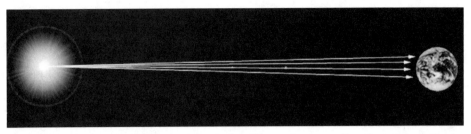

Figure 7.18. **The figure is not drawn to scale, but if you select a small surface area on the Earth, the light rays striking that area are approximately parallel.**

7.10 POINT LIGHTS

A good physical example of a point light is a lightbulb; it radiates spherically in all directions (Figure 7.19). In particular, for an arbitrary point **P**, there exists a light ray originating from the point light position **Q** traveling toward the point. As usual, we define the light vector to go in the opposite direction; that is, the direction from the point **P** to the point light source **Q**:

$$L = \frac{Q - P}{\|Q - P\|}$$

Essentially, the only difference between point lights and parallel lights is how the light vector is computed—it varies from point to point for point lights, but remains constant for parallel lights.

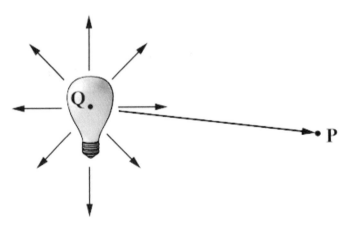

Figure 7.19. **Point lights radiate in every direction; in particular, for an arbitrary point there exists a light ray originating from the point source Q towards P.**

7.10.1 Attenuation

Physically, light intensity weakens as a function of distance based on the inverse squared law. That is to say, the light intensity at a point a distance d away from the light source is given by:

$$I(d) = \frac{I_0}{d^2}$$

where I_0 is the light intensity at a distance $d = 1$ from the light source. However, this formula does not always give aesthetically pleasing results. Thus, instead of worrying about physical accuracy, we make a more general function that gives the artist/programmer some parameters to control (i.e., the artist/programmer experiments with different parameter values until he is satisfied with the result). The typical formula used to scale light intensity is:

$$I(d) = \frac{I_0}{a_0 + a_1 d + a_2 d^2}$$

We call a_0, a_1, and a_2 *attenuation parameters*, and they are to be supplied by the artist or programmer. For example, if you actually want the light intensity to weaken with the inverse distance, then set $a_0 = 0$, $a_1 = 1$, and $a_2 = 0$. If you want the actual inverse square law, then set $a_0 = 0$, $a_1 = 0$, and $a_2 = 1$.

Incorporating attenuation into the lighting equation, we get:

$$LitColor = \mathbf{A} + \frac{k_d \mathbf{D} + k_s \mathbf{S}}{a_0 + a_1 d + a_2 d^2}$$

Notice that attenuation does not affect the ambient term, as the ambient term is used to model indirect light that has bounced around.

7.10.2 Range

For point lights, we include an additional *range* parameter. A point whose distance from the light source is greater than the range does not receive any light from that light source. This parameter is useful for localizing a light to a particular area. Even though the attenuation parameters weaken the light intensity with distance, it is still useful to be able to explicitly define the max range of the light source. The range parameter is also useful for shader optimization. As we will soon see, in our shader code if the point is out of range, then we can return early and skip the lighting calculations with dynamic branching. The range parameter does not affect parallel lights, which model light sources very far away.

7.11 SPOTLIGHTS

A good physical example of a spotlight is a flashlight. Essentially, a spotlight has a position $\mathbf{Q}$, is aimed in a direction $\mathbf{d}$, and radiates light through a cone (see Figure 7.20).

To implement a spotlight, we begin as we do with a point light: the light vector is given by:

$$L = \frac{Q - P}{\|Q - P\|}$$

where $\mathbf{P}$ is the position of the point being lit and $\mathbf{Q}$ is the position of the spotlight. Observe from Figure 7.20 that $\mathbf{P}$ is inside the spotlight's cone (and therefore receives light) if and only if the angle ϕ between $-\mathbf{L}$ and $\mathbf{d}$ is smaller than the cone angle ϕ_{max}. Moreover, all the light in the spotlight's cone should not be of equal intensity; the light at the center of the cone should be the most intense and the light intensity should fade to zero as ϕ increases from 0 to ϕ_{max}.

So how do we control the intensity falloff as a function of ϕ, and also how do we control the size of the spotlight's cone? Well, we can play the same game we did with the specular cone of reflectance. That is, we use the function:

$$k_{spot}(\phi) = \max(\cos\phi, 0)^s = \max(-\mathbf{L} \cdot \mathbf{d}, 0)^s$$

Refer back to Figure 7.12 for the graph of this function. As you can see, the intensity smoothly fades as ϕ increases, which is one of the characteristics we want; additionally, by altering the exponent s, we can indirectly control ϕ_{max} (the angle the intensity drops to 0); that is to say we can shrink or expand the spotlight cone by varying s. For example, if we set $s = 8$, the cone has approximately a 45° half angle.

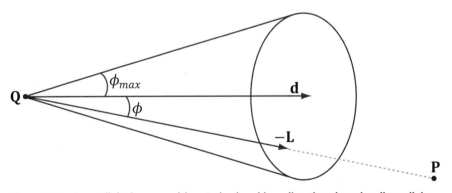

Figure 7.20. A spotlight has a position Q, is aimed in a direction d, and radiates light through a cone with angle ϕ_{max}.

So the spotlight equation is just like the point light equation, except that we multiply by the spotlight factor to scale the light intensity based on where the point is with respect to the spotlight cone:

$$LitColor = k_{spot}\left(\mathbf{A} + \frac{k_d\mathbf{D} + k_s\mathbf{S}}{a_0 + a_1d + a_2d^2}\right)$$

(eq. 7.5)

Note: *By comparing Equation 7.4 and 7.5, we see that a spotlight is more expensive than a point light because we need to compute the k_{spot} factor and multiply by it. Similarly, by comparing Equation 7.3 and 7.4, we see that a point light is more expensive than a directional light because the distance d needs to be computed (this is actually pretty expensive because distance involves a square root operation), and we need to divide by the attenuation expression. To summarize, directional lights are the least expensive light source, followed by point lights. Spotlights are the most expensive light source.*

7.12 IMPLEMENTATION

7.12.1 Lighting Structures

In *LightHelper.h*, we define the following structures to represent the three types of lights we support.

```
struct DirectionalLight
{
    DirectionalLight() { ZeroMemory(this, sizeof(this)); }

    XMFLOAT4 Ambient;
    XMFLOAT4 Diffuse;
    XMFLOAT4 Specular;
    XMFLOAT3 Direction;
    float Pad; // Pad the last float so we can set an
      // array of lights if we wanted.
};

struct PointLight
{
    PointLight() { ZeroMemory(this, sizeof(this)); }

    XMFLOAT4 Ambient;
    XMFLOAT4 Diffuse;
    XMFLOAT4 Specular;

    // Packed into 4D vector: (Position, Range)
    XMFLOAT3 Position;
    float Range;
```

```
    // Packed into 4D vector: (A0, A1, A2, Pad)
    XMFLOAT3 Att;
    float Pad; // Pad the last float so we can set an
        // array of lights if we wanted.
};

struct SpotLight
{
    SpotLight() { ZeroMemory(this, sizeof(this)); }

    XMFLOAT4 Ambient;
    XMFLOAT4 Diffuse;
    XMFLOAT4 Specular;

    // Packed into 4D vector: (Position, Range)
    XMFLOAT3 Position;
    float Range;

    // Packed into 4D vector: (Direction, Spot)
    XMFLOAT3 Direction;
    float Spot;

    // Packed into 4D vector: (Att, Pad)
    XMFLOAT3 Att;
    float Pad; // Pad the last float so we can set an
        // array of lights if we wanted.
};
```

Note:

1. **Ambient:** *The amount of ambient light emitted by the light source.*
2. **Diffuse:** *The amount of diffuse light emitted by the light source.*
3. **Specular:** *The amount of specular light emitted by the light source.*
4. **Direction:** *The direction of the light.*
5. **Position:** *The position of the light.*
6. **Range:** *The range of the light. A point whose distance from the light source is greater than the range is not lit.*
7. **Attenuation:** *Stores the three attenuation constants in the format (a_0, a_1, a_2) that control how light intensity falls off with distance.*
8. **Spot:** *The exponent used in the spotlight calculation to control the spotlight cone.*

We will discuss the necessity of the "pad" variables and "packing" format in the next section.

The *LightHelper.fx* file defines structures that mirror these:

```
struct DirectionalLight
{
    float4 Ambient;
    float4 Diffuse;
    float4 Specular;
    float3 Direction;
    float pad;
};
```

```
struct PointLight
{
      float4 Ambient;
      float4 Diffuse;
      float4 Specular;

      float3 Position;
      float Range;

      float3 Att;
      float pad;
};

struct SpotLight
{
    float4 Ambient;
    float4 Diffuse;
    float4 Specular;

    float3 Position;
    float Range;

    float3 Direction;
    float Spot;

    float3 Att;
    float pad;
};
```

7.12.2 Structure Packing

The previous section defined HLSL structures, which we instantiate in constant buffers like so:

```
cbuffer cbPerFrame
{
    DirectionalLight gDirLight;
    PointLight gPointLight;
    SpotLight gSpotLight;
    float3 gEyePosW;
};
```

At the application level, we instantiate the mirroring structures. We would like to set the light instances to the effect variables in one call, rather than setting each data member individually. A structure instance can be set to an effect variable instance using the following function:

```
ID3DX11EffectVariable::SetRawValue(void *pData,
    UINT Offset, UINT Count);

// Example call:
DirectionalLight mDirLight;
mfxDirLight->SetRawValue(&mDirLight, 0, sizeof(mDirLight));
```

However, because this function simply copies raw bytes over, it can lead to hard to find errors if we are not careful. Specifically, the thing that we need to be careful about is that C++ does not follow the same packing rules as HLSL.

In the HLSL, structure padding occurs so that elements are packed into 4D vectors, with the restriction that a single element cannot be split across two 4D vectors. Consider the following example:

```
// HLSL
struct S
{
    float3 Pos;
    float3 Dir;
};
```

If we have to pack the data into 4D vectors, you might think it is done like this:

```
vector 1: (Pos.x, Pos.y, Pos.z, Dir.x)
vector 2: (Dir.y, Dir.z, empty, empty)
```

However, this splits the element `dir` across two 4D vectors, which is not allowed by the HLSL rules—an element is not allowed to straddle a 4D vector boundary. Therefore, it has to be packed like this:

```
vector 1: (Pos.x, Pos.y, Pos.z, empty)
vector 2: (Dir.x, Dir.y, Dir.z, empty)
```

Now suppose our mirroring C++ structure was defined like so:

```
// C++
struct S
{
    XMFLOAT3 Pos;
    XMFLOAT3 Dir;
};
```

If we did not pay attention to these packing rules, and just blindly called and copied the bytes over, we would end up with the incorrect first situation:

```
vector 1: (Pos.x, Pos.y, Pos.z, Dir.x)
vector 2: (Dir.y, Dir.z, empty, empty)
```

Thus we must define our C++ structures so that the elements copy over correctly into the HLSL structures based on the HLSL packing rules; we use "pad" variables for this. Let us look at a few more examples of how HLSL are packed.

If we have a structure like this:

```
struct S
{
    float3 v;
    float  s;
    float2 p;
    float3 q;
};
```

The structure would be padded and the data will be packed into three 4D vectors like so:

```
vector 1: (v.x, v.y, v.z, s)
vector 2: (p.x, p.y, empty, empty)
vector 3: (q.x, q.y, q.z, empty)
```

Here we can put the scalar s in the 4th component of the first vector. However, we are not able to fit all of q in the remaining slots of vector 2, so q has to get its own vector. And a final example, the structure:

```
struct S
{
float2 u;
float2 v;
float a0;
float a1;
float a2;
};
```

would be padded and packed like so:

```
vector 1: (u.x, u.y, v.x, v.y)
vector 2: (a0, a1, a2, empty)
```

Note: *Arrays are handled differently. From the SDK documentation, "every element in an array is stored in a four-component vector." So, for example, if you have an array of* float2:

```
float2 TexOffsets[8];
```

you might assume that two float2 *elements will be packed into one* float4 *slot, as the examples above suggest. However, arrays are the exception, and the previous is equivalent to:*

```
float4 TexOffsets[8];
```

Therefore, from the C++ code you would need to set an array of 8 XMFLOAT4s, *not an array of 8* XMFLOAT2s *for things to work properly. Each element wastes two floats of storage because we really just wanted a* float2 *array. The SDK documentation points out that you can use casting and additional address computation instructions to make it more memory efficient:*

```
float4 array[4];
static float2 aggressivePackArray[8] = (float2[8])array;
```

7.12.3 Implementing Directional Lights

The following HLSL function outputs the lit color of a point given a material, directional light source, surface normal, and the unit vector from the surface point being lit to the eye:

```
// Defined in LightHelper.fx.
// Equation 7.3
void ComputeDirectionalLight(Material mat, DirectionalLight L,
                            float3 normal, float3 toEye,
                            out float4 ambient,
                            out float4 diffuse,
                            out float4 spec)
{
    // Initialize outputs.
    ambient = float4(0.0f, 0.0f, 0.0f, 0.0f);
    diffuse = float4(0.0f, 0.0f, 0.0f, 0.0f);
    spec    = float4(0.0f, 0.0f, 0.0f, 0.0f);

    // The light vector aims opposite the direction the light rays travel.
    float3 lightVec = -L.Direction;

    // Add ambient term.
    ambient = mat.Ambient * L.Ambient;

    // Add diffuse and specular term, provided the surface is in
    // the line of site of the light.

    float diffuseFactor = dot(lightVec, normal);

    // Flatten to avoid dynamic branching.
    [flatten]
    if(diffuseFactor > 0.0f)
    {
        float3 v         = reflect(-lightVec, normal);
        float specFactor = pow(max(dot(v, toEye), 0.0f), mat.Specular.w);

        diffuse = diffuseFactor * mat.Diffuse * L.Diffuse;
        spec    = specFactor * mat.Specular * L.Specular;
    }
}
```

The following intrinsic HLSL functions were used: dot, reflect, pow, and max, which are, respectively, the vector dot product function, vector reflection function, power function, and maximum function. Descriptions of most of the HLSL intrinsic functions can be found in Appendix B, along with a quick primer on other HLSL syntax. One thing to note, however, is that when two vectors are multiplied with operator*, the multiplication is done component-wise.

Note: ► *On the PC HLSL functions are always inlined; therefore, there is no performance overhead for functions or parameter passing.*

7.12.4 Implementing Point Lights

The following HLSL function outputs the lit color of a point given a material, point light source, surface position, surface normal, and the unit vector from the surface point being lit to the eye:

```
// Defined in LightHelper.fx.
// Equation 7.4
void ComputePointLight(Material mat, PointLight L, float3 pos,
float3 normal, float3 toEye,
    out float4 ambient, out float4 diffuse, out float4 spec)
{
    // Initialize outputs.
    ambient = float4(0.0f, 0.0f, 0.0f, 0.0f);
    diffuse = float4(0.0f, 0.0f, 0.0f, 0.0f);
    spec    = float4(0.0f, 0.0f, 0.0f, 0.0f);

    // The vector from the surface to the light.
    float3 lightVec = L.Position - pos;

    // The distance from surface to light.
    float d = length(lightVec);

    // Range test.
    if(d > L.Range)
      return;

    // Normalize the light vector.
    lightVec /= d;

    // Ambient term.
    ambient = mat.Ambient * L.Ambient;

    // Add diffuse and specular term, provided the surface is in
    // the line of site of the light.

    float diffuseFactor = dot(lightVec, normal);

    // Flatten to avoid dynamic branching.
    [flatten]
    if(diffuseFactor > 0.0f)
    {
      float3 v         = reflect(-lightVec, normal);
      float specFactor = pow(max(dot(v, toEye), 0.0f), mat.Specular.w);

      diffuse = diffuseFactor * mat.Diffuse * L.Diffuse;
      spec    = specFactor * mat.Specular * L.Specular;
    }
    // Attenuate
    float att = 1.0f / dot(L.Att, float3(1.0f, d, d*d));

    diffuse *= att;
    spec    *= att;
}
```

7.12.5 Implementing Spotlights

The following HLSL function outputs the lit color of a point given a material, spotlight source, surface position, surface normal, and the unit vector from the surface point being lit to the eye:

```
// Defined in LightHelper.fx.
// Equation 7.5
void ComputeSpotLight(Material mat, SpotLight L,
float3 pos, float3 normal, float3 toEye,
out float4 ambient, out float4 diffuse, out float4 spec)
{
    // Initialize outputs.
    ambient = float4(0.0f, 0.0f, 0.0f, 0.0f);
    diffuse = float4(0.0f, 0.0f, 0.0f, 0.0f);
    spec    = float4(0.0f, 0.0f, 0.0f, 0.0f);

    // The vector from the surface to the light.
    float3 lightVec = L.Position - pos;

    // The distance from surface to light.
    float d = length(lightVec);

    // Range test.
    if( d > L.Range )
      return;

    // Normalize the light vector.
    lightVec /= d;

    // Ambient term.
    ambient = mat.Ambient * L.Ambient;

    // Add diffuse and specular term, provided the surface is in
    // the line of site of the light.

    float diffuseFactor = dot(lightVec, normal);

    // Flatten to avoid dynamic branching.
    [flatten]
    if(diffuseFactor > 0.0f)
    {
      float3 v         = reflect(-lightVec, normal);
      float specFactor = pow(max(dot(v, toEye), 0.0f), mat.Specular.w);

      diffuse = diffuseFactor * mat.Diffuse * L.Diffuse;
      spec    = specFactor * mat.Specular * L.Specular;
    }

    // Scale by spotlight factor and attenuate.
    float spot = pow(max(dot(-lightVec, L.Direction), 0.0f), L.Spot);

    // Scale by spotlight factor and attenuate.
    float att = spot / dot(L.Att, float3(1.0f, d, d*d));

    ambient *= spot;
    diffuse *= att;
    spec    *= att;
}
```

7.13 LIGHTING DEMO

In our first lighting demo, we will have three lights active at once: a directional, point, and spot light. The directional light remains fixed, the point light circles about the terrain, and the spotlight moves with the camera and aims in the direction the camera is looking. The lighting demo builds off the "Waves" demo from the previous chapter. The effect file is given in the following section, which makes use of the structures and functions defined in §7.10.

7.13.1 Effect File

```
#include "LightHelper.fx"

cbuffer cbPerFrame
{
    DirectionalLight gDirLight;
    PointLight gPointLight;
    SpotLight gSpotLight;
    float3 gEyePosW;
};

cbuffer cbPerObject
{
    float4x4 gWorld;
    float4x4 gWorldInvTranspose;
    float4x4 gWorldViewProj;
    Material gMaterial;
};

struct VertexIn
{
    float3 PosL    : POSITION;
    float3 NormalL : NORMAL;
};

struct VertexOut
{
    float4 PosH    : SV_POSITION;
    float3 PosW    : POSITION;
    float3 NormalW : NORMAL;
};

VertexOut VS(VertexIn vin)
{
    VertexOut vout;

    // Transform to world space space.
    vout.PosW    = mul(float4(vin.PosL, 1.0f), gWorld).xyz;
    vout.NormalW = mul(vin.NormalL, (float3x3)gWorldInvTranspose);
```

```
    // Transform to homogeneous clip space.
    vout.PosH = mul(float4(vin.PosL, 1.0f), gWorldViewProj);

    return vout;
}

float4 PS(VertexOut pin) : SV_Target
{
    // Interpolating normal can unnormalize it, so normalize it.
    pin.NormalW = normalize(pin.NormalW);

    float3 toEyeW = normalize(gEyePosW - pin.PosW);

    // Start with a sum of zero.
    float4 ambient = float4(0.0f, 0.0f, 0.0f, 0.0f);
    float4 diffuse = float4(0.0f, 0.0f, 0.0f, 0.0f);
    float4 spec    = float4(0.0f, 0.0f, 0.0f, 0.0f);

    // Sum the light contribution from each light source.
    float4 A, D, S;

    ComputeDirectionalLight(gMaterial, gDirLight,
      pin.NormalW, toEyeW, A, D, S);
    ambient += A;
    diffuse += D;
    spec    += S;

    ComputePointLight(gMaterial, gPointLight,
      pin.PosW, pin.NormalW, toEyeW, A, D, S);
    ambient += A;
    diffuse += D;
    spec    += S;

    ComputeSpotLight(gMaterial, gSpotLight,
      pin.PosW, pin.NormalW, toEyeW, A, D, S);
    ambient += A;
    diffuse += D;
    spec    += S;

    float4 litColor = ambient + diffuse + spec;

    // Common to take alpha from diffuse material.
    litColor.a = gMaterial.Diffuse.a;

    return litColor;
}

technique11 LightTech
{
    pass P0
    {
      SetVertexShader(CompileShader(vs_5_0, VS()));
      SetGeometryShader(NULL);
      SetPixelShader(CompileShader(ps_5_0, PS()));
    }
}
```

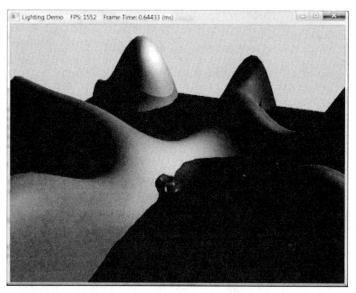

Figure 7.21. Screenshot of "Lighting" demo.

7.13.2 C++ Application Code

Lighting calculations require a surface normal. We define normals at the vertex level; these normals are then interpolated across the pixels of a triangle so that we may do the lighting calculations per pixel. Moreover, we no longer specify a vertex color. Instead, surface colors are generated by applying the lighting equation for each pixel. Our input layout description looks like this:

```
D3D11_INPUT_ELEMENT_DESC vertexDesc[] =
{
    {"POSITION", 0, DXGI_FORMAT_R32G32B32_FLOAT, 0, 0,
        D3D11_INPUT_PER_VERTEX_DATA, 0},
    {"COLOR",    0, DXGI_FORMAT_R32G32B32A32_FLOAT, 0, 12,
        D3D11_INPUT_PER_VERTEX_DATA, 0}
};
```

In the application class, we define three lights and two materials.

```
DirectionalLight mDirLight;
    PointLight mPointLight;
    SpotLight mSpotLight;
    Material mLandMat;
    Material mWavesMat;
```

They are initialized in the constructor:

```
LightingApp::LightingApp(HINSTANCE hInstance)
{
```

```
    /* ...Irrelevant code omitted... */

    // Directional light.
    mDirLight.Ambient   = XMFLOAT4(0.2f, 0.2f, 0.2f, 1.0f);
    mDirLight.Diffuse   = XMFLOAT4(0.5f, 0.5f, 0.5f, 1.0f);
    mDirLight.Specular  = XMFLOAT4(0.5f, 0.5f, 0.5f, 1.0f);
    mDirLight.Direction = XMFLOAT3(0.57735f, -0.57735f, 0.57735f);

    // Point light--position is changed every frame to animate
    // in UpdateScene function.
    mPointLight.Ambient  = XMFLOAT4(0.3f, 0.3f, 0.3f, 1.0f);
    mPointLight.Diffuse  = XMFLOAT4(0.7f, 0.7f, 0.7f, 1.0f);
    mPointLight.Specular = XMFLOAT4(0.7f, 0.7f, 0.7f, 1.0f);
    mPointLight.Att      = XMFLOAT3(0.0f, 0.1f, 0.0f);
    mPointLight.Range    = 25.0f;

    // Spot light--position and direction changed every frame to
    // animate in UpdateScene function.
    mSpotLight.Ambient  = XMFLOAT4(0.0f, 0.0f, 0.0f, 1.0f);
    mSpotLight.Diffuse  = XMFLOAT4(1.0f, 1.0f, 0.0f, 1.0f);
    mSpotLight.Specular = XMFLOAT4(1.0f, 1.0f, 1.0f, 1.0f);
    mSpotLight.Att      = XMFLOAT3(1.0f, 0.0f, 0.0f);
    mSpotLight.Spot     = 96.0f;
    mSpotLight.Range    = 10000.0f;

    mLandMat.Ambient  = XMFLOAT4(0.48f, 0.77f, 0.46f, 1.0f);
    mLandMat.Diffuse  = XMFLOAT4(0.48f, 0.77f, 0.46f, 1.0f);
    mLandMat.Specular = XMFLOAT4(0.2f, 0.2f, 0.2f, 16.0f);

    mWavesMat.Ambient  = XMFLOAT4(0.137f, 0.42f, 0.556f, 1.0f);
    mWavesMat.Diffuse  = XMFLOAT4(0.137f, 0.42f, 0.556f, 1.0f);
    mWavesMat.Specular = XMFLOAT4(0.8f, 0.8f, 0.8f, 96.0f);
}
```

When using multiple lights, one must be careful not to oversaturate the scene with light. So you will need to experiment with the ambient, diffuse, and specular numbers to get the right balance. Experimentation with the attenuation and range is also necessary. Observe that the spotlight emits yellow diffuse light. It is sometimes easy to forget about using colored lights, but they can be used for a variety of effects. For example, if you are using a directional light to model sunlight, and the sun is setting a bright orange, you may tweak your light color to emit orange lights, so that your scene objects have an orange tint to them. Subtle blue lights could work well for when exploring an alien ship and red lights could convey an emergency situation.

As mentioned, the point light and spotlight are animated; this is done in the **UpdateScene** method:

```
void LightingApp::UpdateScene(float dt)
{
    /* ...Irrelevant code omitted... */

    // Convert Spherical to Cartesian coordinates.
    float x = mRadius*sinf(mPhi)*cosf(mTheta);
```

```
    float z = mRadius*sinf(mPhi)*sinf(mTheta);
    float y = mRadius*cosf(mPhi);

    mEyePosW = XMFLOAT3(x, y, z);

    // Build the view matrix.
    XMVECTOR pos    = XMVectorSet(x, y, z, 1.0f);
    XMVECTOR target = XMVectorZero();
    XMVECTOR up     = XMVectorSet(0.0f, 1.0f, 0.0f, 0.0f);

    /* ...Irrelevant code omitted... */

    // Circle light over the land surface.
    mPointLight.Position.x = 70.0f*cosf(0.2f*mTimer.TotalTime());
    mPointLight.Position.z = 70.0f*sinf(0.2f*mTimer.TotalTime());
    mPointLight.Position.y = MathHelper::Max(
        GetHillHeight(mPointLight.Position.x,
            mPointLight.Position.z), -3.0f) + 10.0f;


    // The spotlight takes on the camera position and is aimed in the
    // same direction the camera is looking.  In this way, it looks
    // like we are holding a flashlight.
    mSpotLight.Position = mEyePosW;
    XMStoreFloat3(&mSpotLight.Direction,
        XMVector3Normalize(target - pos));
}
```

The point light basically follows a circular trajectory in the *xz*-plane, but always travels above the land or water. The spotlight is positioned at the eye and is aimed in the same direction the eye looks; this makes it look like the viewer is holding the light like a flashlight.

Finally, the lights and materials are set to the effect before rendering:

```
void LightingApp::DrawScene()
{
    /* ...Irrelevant code omitted... */

    // Set per frame constants.
    mfxDirLight->SetRawValue(&mDirLight, 0, sizeof(mDirLight));
    mfxPointLight->SetRawValue(&mPointLight, 0, sizeof(mPointLight));
    mfxSpotLight->SetRawValue(&mSpotLight, 0, sizeof(mSpotLight));
    mfxEyePosW->SetRawValue(&mEyePosW, 0, sizeof(mEyePosW));

    /* ...Irrelevant code omitted... */

    // Set land material (material varies per object).
    mfxMaterial->SetRawValue(&mLandMat, 0, sizeof(mLandMat));

    /* ...Render land... */

    // Set wave material (material varies per object).
    mfxMaterial->SetRawValue(&mWavesMat, 0, sizeof(mWavesMat));

    /* ...Render waves... */
}
```

7.13.3 Normal Computation

Because our terrain surface is given by a function $y = f(x, z)$, we can compute the normal vectors directly using calculus, rather than the normal averaging technique described in §7.2.1. To do this, for each point on the surface, we form two tangent vectors in the $+x$- and $+z$-directions by taking the partial derivatives:

$$\mathbf{T}_x = \left(1, \frac{\partial f}{\partial x}, 0\right)$$

$$\mathbf{T}_z = \left(0, \frac{\partial f}{\partial z}, 1\right)$$

These two vectors lie in the tangent plane of the surface point. Taking the cross product then gives the normal vector:

$$\mathbf{n} = \mathbf{T}_z \times \mathbf{T}_x = \begin{vmatrix} \mathbf{i} & \mathbf{j} & \mathbf{k} \\ 0 & \frac{\partial f}{\partial z} & 1 \\ 1 & \frac{\partial f}{\partial x} & 0 \end{vmatrix}$$

$$= \left(\begin{vmatrix} \frac{\partial f}{\partial z} & 1 \\ \frac{\partial f}{\partial x} & 0 \end{vmatrix}, -\begin{vmatrix} 0 & 1 \\ 1 & 0 \end{vmatrix}, \begin{vmatrix} 0 & \frac{\partial f}{\partial z} \\ 1 & \frac{\partial f}{\partial x} \end{vmatrix} \right)$$

$$= \left(-\frac{\partial f}{\partial x}, 1, -\frac{\partial f}{\partial z} \right)$$

The function we used to generate the land mesh is:

$$f(x, z) = 0.3z \cdot \sin(0.1x) + 0.3x \cdot \cos(0.1z)$$

The partial derivatives are:

$$\frac{\partial f}{\partial x} = 0.03z \cdot \cos(0.1x) + 0.3\cos(0.1z)$$

$$\frac{\partial f}{\partial z} = 0.3\sin(0.1x) - 0.03x \cdot \sin(0.1z)$$

The surface normal at a surface point $(x, f(x, z), z)$ is thus given by:

$$\mathbf{n}(x,z)=\left(-\frac{\partial f}{\partial x},1,-\frac{\partial f}{\partial z}\right)=\begin{bmatrix}-0.03z\cdot\cos(0.1x)-0.3\cos(0.1z)\\1\\-0.3\sin(0.1x)+0.03x\cdot\sin(0.1z)\end{bmatrix}^{T}$$

We note that this surface normal is not of unit length, so it needs to be normalized before lighting calculations.

In particular, we do the previous normal calculations at each vertex point to get the vertex normals:

```
XMFLOAT3 LightingApp::GetHillNormal(float x, float z)const
{
    // n = (-df/dx, 1, -df/dz)
    XMFLOAT3 n(
      -0.03f*z*cosf(0.1f*x) - 0.3f*cosf(0.1f*z),
      1.0f,
      -0.3f*sinf(0.1f*x) + 0.03f*x*sinf(0.1f*z));

    XMVECTOR unitNormal = XMVector3Normalize(XMLoadFloat3(&n));
    XMStoreFloat3(&n, unitNormal);

    return n;
}
```

The normal vectors for the water surface are done in a similar way, except that we do not have a formula for the water. However, tangent vectors at each vertex point can be approximated using a finite difference scheme (see [Lengyel02] or any numerical analysis book).

Note: ▶ *If your calculus is rusty, do not worry as it will not play a major role in this book. Right now it is useful because we are using mathematical surfaces to generate our geometry so that we have some interesting objects to draw. Eventually, we will load 3D meshes from files that were exported from 3D modeling programs.*

7.14 LIT SKULL DEMO

The "Lit Skull" demo (Figure 7.22) defines an effect we call *Basic.fx*, and it is generally inspired by XNA 4.0's effect class of the name **BasicEffect**. We will append functionality to this effect over the next few chapters as we learn more. When it is complete, this effect will become our default rendering effect; it will support common and basic operations like lighting, texturing, alpha testing, shadows, and fog. More specialized effects will be implemented by other effects.

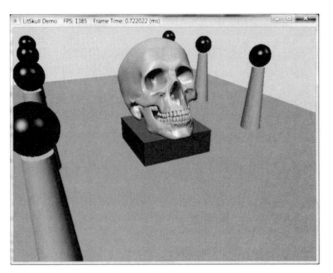

Figure 7.22. Screenshot of the "Lit Skull" demo.

One limitation we impose on the basic effect is that it only supports up to three directional lights. This is not really a necessary restriction, but for the sake of the demo applications it does keep some bookkeeping work simpler. In particular, it keeps the number of shader permutations down that need to be generated by the effects framework. Moreover, supporting a high number of lights starts to become very expensive. In Part III of this book, we show an alternative method of rendering called *deferred rendering* that can efficiently handle numerous light sources, and handles point and spot lights more uniformly.

The basic effect supports three directional lights to enable an implementation of a three-point lighting system. The three-point lighting system is commonly used in film and photography to get better lighting than just one light source can provide; it consists of a primary light source called the *key light*, a secondary *fill light* usually aiming in the side direction from the key light, and a *back light*.

In the "Lit Skull" demo, the user can press the '0', '1', '2', or '3' keys to activate 0, 1, 2, or 3 lights, respectively.

Another change to the "Lit Skull" demo from the previous demo is that we now encapsulate an ID3DX11Effect pointer with its corresponding effect variables into a class; this makes sense as the effect variables are tightly related to the effect they come from.

As our programs become larger, we will begin to divide the rendering code across different classes. Each class may need access to the effects we have implemented. An initial approach might be to have each class load the effect separately, but this creates duplicate effects which is wasteful. Because a single rendering effect can be shared for rendering geometry across an application, we create a single instance of each effect wrapper class and expose it globally by storing it as a public static variable in an `Effects` class. This avoids different parts of an application duplicating an effect from the same effect file. This organization is simple and sufficient for our demo projects and even medium sized projects, as we will only have a handful of effects. More sophisticated management may be needed for larger sized projects. The effect wrapper classes and `Effects` class are implemented in *Effects.h/.cpp*; because we will be appending to these files throughout the book, we do not put them in the *Common* directory.

As with effects, we will only have a handful of different vertex formats, and we would like to avoid duplicate input layouts being created (i.e., input layouts being created from the same input layout description). In *Vertex.h/.cpp*, we define our vertex format structures, the input layout descriptions, and create a single instance of each input layout and expose it globally by storing it as a public static variable in an `InputLayouts` class. We will be appending to *Vertex.h/.cpp* throughout the book; hence, we do not put them in the *Common* directory.

Render state objects can be handled similarly. A program will only use a handful of different render state objects, and the render state objects can be reused across the codebase. Therefore, in future demos we will create files *RenderState.h/.cpp* that define and provide global access to all of the render state objects we need.

The reader should study the "Lit Skull" demo until they are comfortable with the organizational changes going forward.

7.15 SUMMARY

1. With lighting, we no longer specify per-vertex colors but instead define scene lights and per-vertex materials. Materials can be thought of as the properties that determine how light interacts with a surface of an object. The per-vertex materials are interpolated across the face of the triangle to obtain material values at each surface point of the triangle mesh. The lighting equations then compute a surface color the eye sees based on the interaction between the light and surface materials; other parameters are also involved, such as the surface normal and eye position.

2. A *surface normal* is a unit vector that is orthogonal to the tangent plane of a point on a surface. Surface normals determine the direction a point on a surface is "facing." For lighting calculations, we need the surface normal at each point on the surface of a triangle mesh so that we can determine

the angle at which light strikes the point on the mesh surface. To obtain surface normals, we specify the surface normals only at the vertex points (so-called *vertex normals*). Then, in order to obtain a surface normal approximation at each point on the surface of a triangle mesh, these vertex normals will be interpolated across the triangle during rasterization. For arbitrary triangle meshes, vertex normals are typically approximated via a technique called normal averaging. If the matrix **A** is used to transform points and vectors (non-normal vectors), then $(\mathbf{A}^{-1})^T$ should be used to transform surface normals.

3. A parallel (directional) light approximates a light source that is very far away. Consequently, we can approximate all incoming light rays as parallel to each other. A physical example of a directional light is the sun relative to the earth. A point light emits light in *every* direction. A physical example of a point light is a lightbulb. A spotlight emits light through a cone. A physical example of a spotlight is a flashlight.

4. Ambient light models indirect light that has scattered and bounced around the scene so many times that it strikes the object equally in every direction, thereby uniformly brightening it up. Diffuse light travels in a particular direction, and when it strikes a surface, it reflects equally in all directions. Diffuse light should be used to model rough and/or matte surfaces. Specular light travels in a particular direction, and when it strikes a surface, it reflects sharply in one general direction, thereby causing a bright shine that can only be seen at some angles. Specular light should be used to model smooth and polished surfaces.

7.16 EXERCISES

1. Modify the lighting demo of this chapter so that the directional light only emits red light, the point light only emits green light, and the spotlight only emits blue light. Using colored lights can be useful for different game moods; for example, a red light might be used to signify emergency situations.

2. Modify the lighting demo of this chapter by changing the specular power material component, which controls the "shininess" of the surface. Try $p = 8$ $p = 32, p = 64, p = 128, p = 256,$ and $p = 512$.

3. One characteristic of toon lighting is the abrupt transition from one color shade to the next (in contrast with a smooth transition) as shown in Figure 7.23.

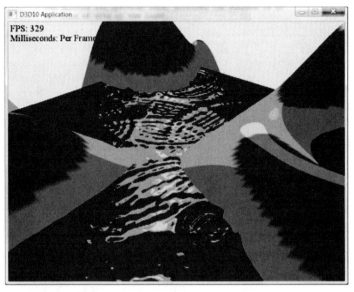

Figure 7.23. Screenshot of the toon shader.

This can be implemented by computing k_d and k_s in the usual way, but then transforming them by discrete functions like the following before using them in the pixel shader:

$$k_d' = f(k_d) = \begin{cases} 0.4 & \text{if} & -\infty < k_d \leq 0.0 \\ 0.6 & \text{if} & 0.0 < k_d \leq 0.5 \\ 1.0 & \text{if} & 0.5 < k_d \leq 1.0 \end{cases}$$

$$k_s' = g(k_s) = \begin{cases} 0.0 & \text{if} & 0.0 \leq k_s \leq 0.1 \\ 0.5 & \text{if} & 0.1 < k_s \leq 0.8 \\ 0.8 & \text{if} & 0.8 < k_s \leq 1.0 \end{cases}$$

Modify the lighting demo of this chapter to use this sort of toon shading. (Note: The functions f and g previously are just sample functions to start with, and can be tweaked until you get the results you want.)

4. Modify the lighting demo of this chapter so that the angle of the spotlight's cone can be increased or decreased based on user keyboard input.

Chapter 8 TEXTURING

Our demos are getting a little more interesting, but real-world objects typically have more details than per-vertex colors can capture. *Texture mapping* is a technique that allows us to map image data onto a triangle, thereby enabling us to increase the details and realism of our scene significantly. For instance, we can build a cube and turn it into a crate by mapping a crate texture on each side (Figure 8.1).

Objectives:

1. To learn how to specify the part of a texture that gets mapped to a triangle.
2. To find out how to create and enable textures.
3. To learn how textures can be filtered to create a smoother image.
4. To discover how to tile a texture several times with address modes.
5. To find out how multiple textures can be combined to create new textures and special effects.
6. To learn how to create some basic effects via texture animation.

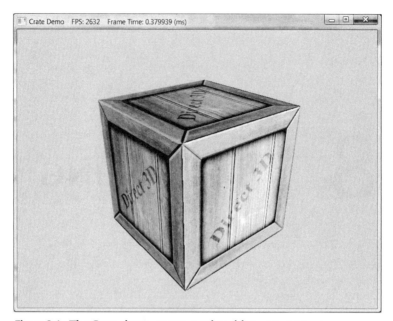

Figure 8.1. **The Crate demo creates a cube with a crate texture.**

8.1 TEXTURE AND RESOURCE RECAP

Recall that we have already been using textures since Chapter 4; in particular, the depth buffer and back buffer are 2D texture objects represented by the `ID3D11Texture2D` interface. For easy reference, in this first section we review much of the material on textures we have already covered in Chapter 4.

A 2D texture is a matrix of data elements. One use for 2D textures is to store 2D image data, where each element in the texture stores the color of a pixel. However, this is not the only usage; for example, in an advanced technique called normal mapping, each element in the texture stores a 3D vector instead of a color. Therefore, although it is common to think of textures as storing image data, they are really more general purpose than that. A 1D texture (`ID3D11Texture1D`) is like a 1D array of data elements, and a 3D texture (`ID3D11Texture3D`) is like a 3D array of data elements. The 1D, 2D, and 3D texture interfaces all inherit from `ID3D11Resource`.

As will be discussed later in this chapter, textures are more than just arrays of data; they can have mipmap levels, and the GPU can do special operations on them, such as apply filters and multisampling. However, textures are not arbitrary chunks of data; they can only store certain kinds of data formats, which are described by the `DXGI_FORMAT` enumerated type. Some example formats are:

1. `DXGI_FORMAT_R32G32B32_FLOAT`: Each element has three 32-bit floating-point components.

2. `DXGI_FORMAT_R16G16B16A16_UNORM`: Each element has four 16-bit components mapped to the [0, 1] range.

3. `DXGI_FORMAT_R32G32_UINT`: Each element has two 32-bit unsigned integer components.

4. `DXGI_FORMAT_R8G8B8A8_UNORM`: Each element has four 8-bit unsigned components mapped to the [0, 1] range.

5. `DXGI_FORMAT_R8G8B8A8_SNORM`: Each element has four 8-bit signed components mapped to the [−1, 1] range.

6. `DXGI_FORMAT_R8G8B8A8_SINT`: Each element has four 8-bit signed integer components mapped to the [−128, 127] range.

7. `DXGI_FORMAT_R8G8B8A8_UINT`: Each element has four 8-bit unsigned integer components mapped to the [0, 255] range.

Note that the R, G, B, A letters are used to stand for red, green, blue, and alpha, respectively. However, as we said earlier, textures need not store color information; for example, the format

`DXGI_FORMAT_R32G32B32_FLOAT`

has three floating-point components and can therefore store a 3D vector with floating-point coordinates (not necessarily a color vector). There are also *typeless* formats, where we just reserve memory and then specify how to reinterpret the data at a later time (sort of like a cast) when the texture is bound to the rendering pipeline; for example, the following typeless format reserves elements with four 8-bit components, but does not specify the data type (e.g., integer, floating-point, unsigned integer):

`DXGI_FORMAT_R8G8B8A8_TYPELESS`

A texture can be bound to different stages of the rendering pipeline; a common example is to use a texture as a render target (i.e., Direct3D draws into the texture) and as a shader resource (i.e., the texture will be sampled in a shader). A texture resource created for these two purposes would be given the bind flags:

`D3D11_BIND_RENDER_TARGET | D3D11_BIND_SHADER_RESOURCE`

indicating the two pipeline stages the texture will be bound to. Actually, resources are not directly bound to a pipeline stage; instead their associated resource views are bound to different pipeline stages. For each way we are going to use a texture, Direct3D requires that we create a *resource view* of that texture at initialization time. This is mostly for efficiency, as the SDK documentation points out: "This allows validation and mapping in the runtime and driver to occur at view creation, minimizing type checking at bind-time." So for the example of using a texture as a render target and shader resource, we would need to create two views: a render target view (`ID3D11RenderTargetView`) and a shader resource view (`ID3D11ShaderResourceView`). Resource views essentially do two things: they tell Direct3D how the resource will be used (i.e., what stage of the pipeline you will bind it to), and if the resource format was specified as typeless at creation time, then we must now state the type when creating a view. Thus, with typeless formats, it is possible for the elements of a texture to be viewed as floating-point values in one pipeline stage and as integers in another; this essentially amounts to a reinterpret cast of the data.

> **Note:** *The August SDK documentation says: "Creating a fully-typed resource restricts the resource to the format it was created with. This enables the runtime to optimize access [...]." Therefore, you should only create a typeless resource if you really need it; otherwise, create a fully typed resource.*

In order to create a specific view to a resource, the resource must be created with that specific bind flag. For instance, if the resource was not created with the `D3D11_BIND_SHADER_RESOURCE` bind flag (which indicates the texture will be bound to the pipeline as a depth/stencil buffer), then we cannot create an `ID3D11ShaderResourceView` to that resource. If you try, you should get a Direct3D debug error like the following:

```
D3D11: ERROR: ID3D11Device::CreateShaderResourceView: A
ShaderResourceView cannot be created of a Resource that did not specify
the D3D11_BIND_SHADER_RESOURCE BindFlag.
```

In this chapter, we will only be interested in binding textures as shader resources so that our pixel shaders can sample the textures and use them to color pixels.

8.2 TEXTURE COORDINATES

Direct3D uses a texture coordinate system that consists of a u-axis that runs horizontally to the image and a v-axis that runs vertically to the image. The coordinates, (u, v) such that $0 \leq u, v \leq 1$, identify an element on the texture called a *texel*. Notice that the v-axis is positive in the "down" direction (see Figure 8.2). Also, notice the normalized coordinate interval, $[0, 1]$, which is used because it gives Direct3D a dimension independent range to work with; for example, $(0.5, 0.5)$ always specifies the middle texel no matter if the actual texture dimensions is 256×256, 512×1024, or 2048×2048 in pixels. Likewise, $(0.25, 0.75)$ identifies the texel a quarter of the total width in the horizontal direction,

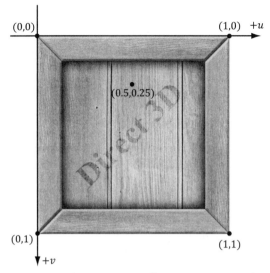

Figure 8.2. The texture coordinate system, sometimes called texture space.

and three-quarters of the total height in the vertical direction. For now, texture coordinates are always in the range $[0, 1]$, but later we explain what can happen when you go outside this range.

For each 3D triangle, we want to define a corresponding triangle on the texture that is to be mapped onto the 3D triangle (see Figure 8.3). Let $\mathbf{p}_0$, $\mathbf{p}_1$, and $\mathbf{p}_2$ be the vertices of a 3D triangle with respective texture coordinates $\mathbf{q}_0$, $\mathbf{q}_1$, and $\mathbf{q}_2$. For an arbitrary point (x, y, z) on the 3D triangle, its texture coordinates (u, v) are found

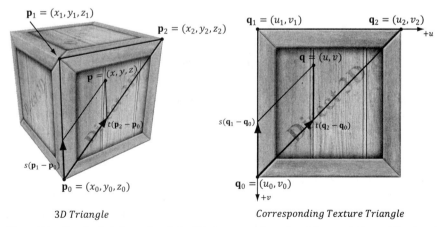

3D Triangle   Corresponding Texture Triangle

Figure 8.3. On the left is a triangle in 3D space, and on the right we define a 2D triangle on the texture that is going to be mapped onto the 3D triangle.

by linearly interpolating the vertex texture coordinates across the 3D triangle by the same s, t parameters; that is, if

$$(x, y, z) = \mathbf{p} = \mathbf{p}_0 + s\,(\mathbf{p}_1 - \mathbf{p}_0) + t\,(\mathbf{p}_2 - \mathbf{p}_0)$$

for $s \geq 0, t \geq 0, s + t \leq 1$ then,

$$(u, v) = \mathbf{q} = \mathbf{q}_0 + s(\mathbf{q}_1 - \mathbf{q}_0) + t(\mathbf{q}_2 - \mathbf{q}_0)$$

In this way, every point on the triangle has a corresponding texture coordinate.

To implement this, we modify our vertex structure once again and add a pair of texture coordinates that identify a point on the texture. Now every 3D vertex has a corresponding 2D texture vertex. Thus, every 3D triangle defined by three vertices also defines a 2D triangle in texture space (i.e., we have associated a 2D texture triangle for every 3D triangle).

```
// Basic 32-byte vertex structure.
struct Basic32
{
    XMFLOAT3 Pos;
    XMFLOAT3 Normal;
    XMFLOAT2 Tex;
};

const D3D11_INPUT_ELEMENT_DESC InputLayoutDesc::Basic32[3] =
{
    {"POSITION", 0, DXGI_FORMAT_R32G32B32_FLOAT, 0, 0,
D3D11_INPUT_PER_VERTEX_DATA, 0},
    {"NORMAL",   0, DXGI_FORMAT_R32G32B32_FLOAT, 0, 12,
D3D11_INPUT_PER_VERTEX_DATA, 0},
    {"TEXCOORD", 0, DXGI_FORMAT_R32G32_FLOAT, 0, 24,
D3D11_INPUT_PER_VERTEX_DATA, 0}
};
```

Note: *You can create "odd" texture mappings where the 2D texture triangle is much different than the 3D triangle. Thus, when the 2D texture is mapped onto the 3D triangle, a lot of stretching and distortion occurs making the results not look good. For example, mapping an acute angled triangle to a right angled triangle requires stretching. In general, texture distortion should be minimized, unless the texture artist desires the distortion look.*

Observe that in Figure 8.3, we map the entire texture image onto each face of the cube. This is by no means required. We can map only a subset of a texture onto geometry. In fact, we can play several unrelated images on one big texture map (this is called a *texture atlas*), and use it for several different objects (Figure 8.4). The texture coordinates are what will determine what part of the texture gets mapped on the triangles.

Figure 8.4. A texture atlas storing four subtextures on one large texture. The texture coordinates for each vertex are set so that the desired part of the texture gets mapped onto the geometry.

8.3 CREATING AND ENABLING A TEXTURE

Texture data is usually read from an image file stored on disk and loaded into an `ID3D11Texture2D` object (see `D3DX11CreateTextureFromFile`). However, texture resources are not bound directly to the rendering pipeline; instead, you create a shader resource view (`ID3D11ShaderResourceView`) to the texture, and then bind the view to the pipeline. So two steps need to be taken:

1. Call `D3DX11CreateTextureFromFile` to create the `ID3D11Texture2D` object from an image file stored on disk.

2. Call `ID3D11Device::CreateShaderResourceView` to create the corresponding shader resource view to the texture.

Both of these steps can be done at once with the following D3DX function:

```
HRESULT D3DX11CreateShaderResourceViewFromFile(
    ID3D11Device *pDevice,
    LPCTSTR pSrcFile,
    D3DX11_IMAGE_LOAD_INFO *pLoadInfo,
    ID3DX11ThreadPump *pPump,
    ID3D11ShaderResourceView **ppShaderResourceView,
    HRESULT *pHResult
);
```

1. **pDevice**: Pointer to the D3D device to create the texture with.

2. **pSrcFile**: Filename of the image to load.

3. **pLoadInfo**: Optional image info; specify null to use the information from the source image. For example, if we specify null here, then the source image dimensions will be used as the texture dimensions; also a full mipmap chain will be generated (§8.4.2). This is usually what we always want and a good default choice.

4. **pPump**: Used to spawn a new thread for loading the resource. To load the resource in the main thread, specify null. In this book, we will always specify null.

5. **ppShaderResourceView**: Returns a pointer to the created shader resource view to the texture loaded from file.

6. **pHResult**: Specify null if null was specified for **pPump**.

This function can load any of the following image formats: BMP, JPG, PNG, DDS, TIFF, GIF, and WMP (see **D3DX11_IMAGE_FILE_FORMAT**).

> **Note:** *Sometimes we will refer to a texture and its corresponding shader resource view as interchangeable. For example, we might say we are binding the texture to the pipeline, even though we are really binding its view.*

For example, to create a texture from an image called *WoodCreate01.dds*, we would write the following:

```
ID3D11ShaderResourceView* mDiffuseMapSRV;
HR(D3DX11CreateShaderResourceViewFromFile(md3dDevice,
    L"WoodCrate01.dds", 0, 0, &mDiffuseMapSRV, 0 ));
```

Once a texture is loaded, we need to set it to an effect variable so that it can be used in a pixel shader. A 2D texture object in an *.fx* file is represented by the **Texture2D** type; for example, we declare a texture variable in an effect file like so:

```
// Nonnumeric values cannot be added to a cbuffer.
Texture2D gDiffuseMap;
```

As the comment notes, texture objects are placed outside of constant buffers. We can obtain a pointer to an effect's **Texture2D** object (which is a shader resource variable) from our C++ application code as follows:

```
ID3DX11EffectShaderResourceVariable* DiffuseMap;
fxDiffuseMap = mFX->GetVariableByName("gDiffuseMap")->AsShaderResource();
```

Once we have obtained a pointer to an effect's **Texture2D** object, we can update it through the C++ interface like so:

```
// Set the C++ texture resource view to the effect texture variable.
fxDiffuseMap->SetResource(mDiffuseMapSRV);
```

As with other effect variables, if we need to change them between draw calls, we must call `Apply`:

```
// set crate texture
fxDiffuseMap->SetResource(mCrateMapSRV);
pass->Apply(0, md3dImmediateContext);
DrawCrate();

// set grass texture
fxDiffuseMap->SetResource(mGrassMapSRV);
pass->Apply(0, md3dImmediateContext);
DrawGrass();

// set brick texture
fxDiffuseMap->SetResource(mBrickMapSRV);
pass->Apply(0, md3dImmediateContext);
DrawBricks();
```

Texture atlases can improve performance because it can lead to drawing more geometry with one draw call. For example, suppose we used the texture atlas as in Figure 8.3 that contains the crate, grass, and brick textures. Then by adjusting the texture coordinates for each object to its corresponding subtexture, we could draw the geometry in one draw call (assuming no other parameters needed to be changed per object):

```
// set texture atlas
fxDiffuseMap->SetResource(mAtlasSRV);
pass->Apply(0, md3dImmediateContext);
DrawCrateGrassAndBricks();
```

There is overhead to draw calls, so it is desirable to minimize them with techniques like this.

Note: *A texture resource can actually be used by any shader (vertex, geometry, or pixel shader). For now, we will just be using them in pixel shaders. As we mentioned, textures are essentially special arrays, so it is not hard to imagine that array data could be useful in vertex and geometry shader programs, too.*

8.4 FILTERS

8.4.1 Magnification

The elements of a texture map should be thought of as discrete color samples from a continuous image; they should not be thought of as rectangles with areas. So the question is: What happens if we have texture coordinates (u, v) that do not coincide with one of the texel points? This can happen in the following situation.

Suppose the player zooms in on a wall in the scene so that the wall covers the entire screen. For the sake of example, suppose the monitor resolution is 1024×1024 and the wall's texture resolution is 256×256. This illustrates texture *magnification*— we are trying to cover many pixels with a few texels. In our example, between every texel point lies four pixels. Each pixel will be given a pair of unique texture coordinates when the vertex texture coordinates are interpolated across the triangle. Thus there will be pixels with texture coordinates that do not coincide with one of the texel points. Given the colors at the texels we can approximate the colors between texels using interpolation. There are two methods of interpolation graphics hardware supports: constant interpolation and linear interpolation. In practice, linear interpolation is almost always used.

Figure 8.5 illustrates these methods in 1D: Suppose we have a 1D texture with 256 samples and an interpolated texture coordinate $u = 0.126484375$. This normalized texture coordinate refers to the $0.126484375 \times 256 = 32.38$ texel. Of course, this value lies between two of our texel samples, so we must use interpolation to approximate it.

2D linear interpolation is called bilinear interpolation and is illustrated in Figure 8.6. Given a pair of texture coordinates between four texels, we do two 1D linear interpolations in the u-direction, followed by one 1D interpolation in the v-direction.

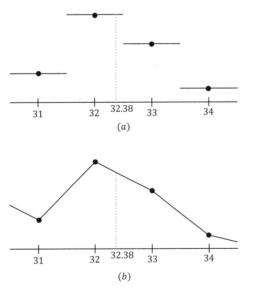

(a)

(b)

Figure 8.5. (a) Given the texel points, we construct a piecewise constant function to approximate values between the texel points; this is sometimes called *nearest neighbor point sampling,* as the value of the nearest texel point is used. (b) Given the texel points, we construct a piecewise linear function to approximate values between texel points.

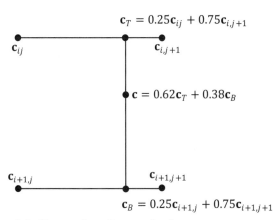

$$\mathbf{c}_T = 0.25\mathbf{c}_{ij} + 0.75\mathbf{c}_{i,j+1}$$

$\mathbf{c}_{ij}$ $\mathbf{c}_{i,j+1}$

$\mathbf{c} = 0.62\mathbf{c}_T + 0.38\mathbf{c}_B$

$\mathbf{c}_{i+1,j}$ $\mathbf{c}_{i+1,j+1}$

$$\mathbf{c}_B = 0.25\mathbf{c}_{i+1,j} + 0.75\mathbf{c}_{i+1,j+1}$$

Figure 8.6. Here we have four texel points c_{ij}, $c_{i,j+1}$, $c_{i+1,j}$, and $c_{i+1,j+1}$. We want to approximate the color of c, which lies between these four texel points using interpolation; in this example, c lies 0.75 units to the right of c_{ij} and 0.38 units below c_{ij}. We first do a 1D linear interpolation between the top two colors to get c_T. Likewise, we do a 1D linear interpolate between the bottom two colors to get c_B. Finally, we do a 1D linear interpolation between c_T and c_B to get c.

Figure 8.7 shows the difference between constant and linear interpolation. As you can see, constant interpolation has the characteristic of creating a blocky looking image. Linear interpolation is smoother, but still will not look as good as if we had real data (e.g., a higher resolution texture) instead of derived data via interpolation.

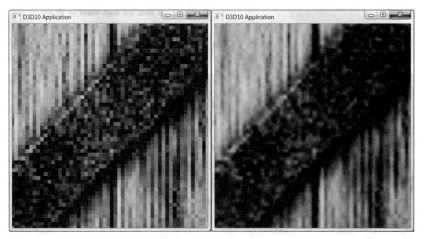

Figure 8.7. We zoom in on a cube with a crate texture so that magnification occurs. On the left we use constant interpolation, which results in a blocky appearance; this makes sense because the interpolating function has discontinuities (Figure 8.5a), which makes the changes abrupt rather than smooth. On the right we use linear filtering, which results in a smoother image due to the continuity of the interpolating function.

One thing to note about this discussion is that there is no real way to get around magnification in an interactive 3D program where the virtual eye is free to move around and explore. From some distances, the textures will look great, but will start to break down as the eye gets too close to them. Some games limit how close the virtual eye can get to a surface to avoid excessive magnification. Using higher resolution textures can help.

Note: *In the context of texturing, using constant interpolation to find texture values for texture coordinates between texels is also called point filtering. And using linear interpolation to find texture values for texture coordinates between texels is also called called linear filtering. Point and linear filtering is the terminology Direct3D uses.*

8.4.2 Minification

Minification is the opposite of magnification. In minification, too many texels are being mapped to too few pixels. For instance, consider the following situation where we have a wall with a 256 × 256 texture mapped over it. The eye, looking at the wall, keeps moving back so that the wall gets smaller and smaller until it only covers 64 × 64 pixels on screen. So now we have 256 × 256 texels getting mapped to 64 × 64 screen pixels. In this situation, texture coordinates for pixels will still generally not coincide with any of the texels of the texture map, so constant and linear interpolation filters still apply to the minification case. However, there is more that can be done with minification. Intuitively, a sort of average downsampling of the 256 × 256 texels should be taken to reduce it to 64 × 64. The technique of mipmapping offers an efficient approximation for this at the expense of some extra memory. At initialization time (or asset creation time), smaller versions of the texture are made by downsampling the image to create a mipmap chain (see Figure 8.8). Thus the averaging work is precomputed for the mipmap

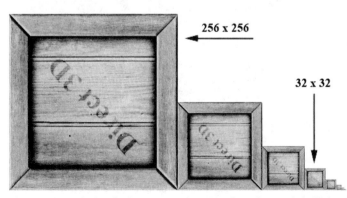

Figure 8.8. A chain of mipmaps; each successive mipmap is half the size, in each dimension, of the previous mipmap level of detail down to 1 × 1.

sizes. At runtime, the graphics hardware will do two different things based on the mipmap settings specified by the programmer:

1. Pick and use the mipmap level that best matches the projected screen geometry resolution for texturing, applying constant or linear interpolation as needed. This is called *point filtering* for mipmaps because it is like constant interpolation—you just choose the nearest mipmap level and use that for texturing.

2. Pick the two nearest mipmap levels that best match the projected screen geometry resolution for texturing (one will be bigger and one will be smaller than the screen geometry resolution). Next, apply constant or linear filtering to both of these mipmap levels to produce a texture color for each one. Finally, interpolate between these two texture color results. This is called *linear filtering* for mipmaps because it is like linear interpolation—you linearly interpolate between the two nearest mipmap levels.

By choosing the best texture levels of detail from the mipmap chain, the amount of minification is greatly reduced.

8.4.2.1 Creating of Mipmaps

Mipmap levels can be created by artists directly, or they can be created by filtering algorithms.

Some image file formats like .DDS (DirectDraw Surface format) can store mipmap levels directly in the data file; in this case, the data simply needs to be read—no runtime work is needed to compute the mipmap levels algorithmically. The DirectX Texture Tool can generate a mipmap chain for a texture and export it to a .DDS file. If an image file does not contain a complete mipmap chain, the `D3DX11CreateShaderResourceViewFromFile` or `D3DX11CreateTextureFromFile` will create a mipmap chain for you using some specified filtering algorithm (see `D3DX11_IMAGE_LOAD_INFO` and in particular the `MipFilter` data member in the SDK documentation). Thus we see that mipmapping is essentially automatic. The `D3DX11` functions will automatically generate a mipmap chain for us if the source file doesn't already contain one. And as long as mipmapping is enabled, the hardware will choose the right mipmap level to use at runtime.

Note: *Sometimes a general purpose filtering algorithm does not preserve the details we want when downsampling. For example, in Figure 8.8, the text "Direct 3D" written on the crate gets blurred away at the lower mip levels. If this is not acceptable, an artist can always manually create/adjust the mip levels to keep the important details.*

8.4.3 Anisotropic Filtering

Another type of filter that can be used is called *anisotropic filtering*. This filter helps alleviate the distortion that occurs when the angle between a polygon's normal vector and camera's look vector is wide (e.g., when a polygon is orthogonal to

Figure 8.9. The top face of the crate is nearly orthogonal to the view window. (Left) Using linear filtering the top of the crate is badly blurred. (Right) Anisotropic filtering does a better job at rendering the top face of the crate from this angle.

the view window). This filter is the most expensive, but can be worth the cost for correcting the distortion artifacts. Figure 8.9 shows a screenshot comparing anisotropic filtering with linear filtering.

8.5 SAMPLING TEXTURES

We saw that a `Texture2D` object represents a texture in an effect file. However, there is another object associated with a texture, called a `SamplerState` object (or sampler). A sampler object is where we define the filters to use with a texture. Here are some examples:

```
// Use linear filtering for minification, magnification, and mipmapping.
SamplerState mySampler0
{
    Filter = MIN_MAG_MIP_LINEAR;
};

// Use linear filtering for minification, point filtering for magnification,
// and point filtering for mipmapping.
SamplerState mySampler1
{
    Filter = MIN_LINEAR_MAG_MIP_POINT;
};

// Use point filtering for minification, linear filtering for magnification,
// and point filtering for mipmapping.
SamplerState mySampler2
{
    Filter = MIN_POINT_MAG_LINEAR_MIP_POINT;
};

// Use anisotropic interpolation for minification, magnification,
// and mipmapping.
SamplerState mySampler3
{
    Filter = ANISOTROPIC;
    MaxAnisotropy = 4;
};
```

Note that for anisotropic filtering, we must specify the maximum anisotropy, which is a number from 1 to 16. Larger values are more expensive, but can give better results. You can figure out the other possible permutations from these examples, or you can look up the D3D11_FILTER enumerated type in the SDK documentation. We will see shortly in the chapter that other properties are associated with a sampler, but for now this is all we need for our first demo.

Now, given a pair of texture coordinate for a pixel in the pixel shader, we actually sample a texture using the following syntax:

```
// Nonnumeric values cannot be added to a cbuffer.
Texture2D gDiffuseMap;

SamplerState samAnisotropic
{
    Filter = ANISOTROPIC;
    MaxAnisotropy = 4;
};

struct VertexOut
{
    float4 PosH    : SV_POSITION;
     float3 PosW    : POSITION;
     float3 NormalW : NORMAL;
    float2 Tex     : TEXCOORD;
};

float4 PS(VertexOut pin, uniform int gLightCount) : SV_Target
{
     float4 texColor = gDiffuseMap.Sample(samAnisotropic, pin.Tex);
     ...
```

As you can see, to sample a texture, we use the `Texture2D::Sample` method. We pass a `SamplerState` object for the first parameter, and we pass in the pixel's (u, v) texture coordinates for the second parameter. This method returns the interpolated color from the texture map at the specified (u, v) point using the filtering methods specified by the `SamplerState` object.

> **Note:** *The HLSL type* `SamplerState` *mirrors the interface* `ID3D11SamplerState`. *Sampler states can also be set at the application level using* `ID3DX11EffectSamplerVariable` `::SetSampler`. *See* `D3D11_SAMPLER_DESC` *and* `ID3D11Device::CreateSamplerState`. *As with render states, sampler states should be created at initialization time.*

8.6 TEXTURES AND MATERIALS

To integrate textures into our material/lighting system, it is common to modulate the texture color with the ambient and diffuse lighting terms, but not with the specular lighting term (this is often called "modulate with late add"):

```
// Modulate with late add.
litColor = texColor*(ambient + diffuse) + spec;
```

This modification gives per pixel ambient and diffuse material values, which offer finer resolution than per object materials since many texels generally cover a triangle. That is, every pixel will get interpolated texture coordinates (u, v); these texture coordinates are then used to sample the texture to get a color which contributes to the material description of that pixel.

8.7 CRATE DEMO

We now review the key points of adding a crate texture to a cube (as shown in Figure 8.1).

8.7.1 Specifying Texture Coordinates

The `GeometryGenerator::CreateBox` generates the texture coordinates for the box so that the entire texture image is mapped onto each face of the box. For brevity, we only show the vertex definitions for the front, back, and top face. Note also that we omit the coordinates for the normal and tangent vectors in the `Vertex` constructor (the texture coordinates are bolded).

```
void GeometryGenerator::CreateBox(float width, float height, float depth,
MeshData& meshData)
{
    Vertex v[24];

    float w2 = 0.5f*width;
    float h2 = 0.5f*height;
    float d2 = 0.5f*depth;

    // Fill in the front face vertex data.
    v[0] = Vertex(-w2, -h2, -d2, ..., 0.0f, 1.0f);
    v[1] = Vertex(-w2, +h2, -d2, ..., 0.0f, 0.0f);
    v[2] = Vertex(+w2, +h2, -d2, ..., 1.0f, 0.0f);
    v[3] = Vertex(+w2, -h2, -d2, ..., 1.0f, 1.0f);

    // Fill in the back face vertex data.
    v[4] = Vertex(-w2, -h2, +d2, ..., 1.0f, 1.0f);
    v[5] = Vertex(+w2, -h2, +d2, ..., 0.0f, 1.0f);
    v[6] = Vertex(+w2, +h2, +d2, ..., 0.0f, 0.0f);
    v[7] = Vertex(-w2, +h2, +d2, ..., 1.0f, 0.0f);

    // Fill in the top face vertex data.
    v[8]  = Vertex(-w2, +h2, -d2, ..., 0.0f, 1.0f);
    v[9]  = Vertex(-w2, +h2, +d2, ..., 0.0f, 0.0f);
    v[10] = Vertex(+w2, +h2, +d2, ..., 1.0f, 0.0f);
    v[11] = Vertex(+w2, +h2, -d2, ..., 1.0f, 1.0f);
```

Refer back to Figure 8.3 if you need help seeing why the texture coordinates are specified this way.

8.7.2 Creating the Texture

We create the texture from a file (technically the shader resource view to the textures) at initialization time as follows:

```
// CrateApp data members
ID3D11ShaderResourceView* mDiffuseMapSRV;

bool CrateApp::Init()
{
    if(!D3DApp::Init())
      return false;

    // Must init Effects first since InputLayouts depend
// on shader signatures.
    Effects::InitAll(md3dDevice);
    InputLayouts::InitAll(md3dDevice);

    HR(D3DX11CreateShaderResourceViewFromFile(md3dDevice,
      L"Textures/WoodCrate01.dds", 0, 0, &mDiffuseMapSRV, 0));

    BuildGeometryBuffers();

    return true;
}
```

8.7.3 Setting the Texture

Texture data is typically accessed in a pixel shader. In order for the pixel shader to access it, we need to set the texture view (`ID3D11ShaderResourceView`) to a `Texture2D` object in the .fx file. This is done as follows:

```
// Member of BasicEffect.
ID3DX11EffectShaderResourceVariable* DiffuseMap;

// Get pointers to effect file variables.
DiffuseMap = mFX->GetVariableByName("gDiffuseMap")->AsShaderResource();

void BasicEffect::SetDiffuseMap(ID3D11ShaderResourceView* tex)
{
DiffuseMap->SetResource(tex);
}

// [.FX code]
// Effect file texture variable.
Texture2D gDiffuseMap;
```

8.7.4 Updated Basic Effect

Below is the revised *Basic.fx* file that now supports texturing (texturing code has been bolded):

```
//=====================================================================
// Basic.fx by Frank Luna (C) 2011 All Rights Reserved.
//
// Basic effect that currently supports transformations, lighting,
// and texturing.
//=====================================================================

#include "LightHelper.fx"

cbuffer cbPerFrame
{
    DirectionalLight gDirLights[3];
    float3 gEyePosW;

    float  gFogStart;
    float  gFogRange;
    float4 gFogColor;
};

cbuffer cbPerObject
{
    float4x4 gWorld;
    float4x4 gWorldInvTranspose;
    float4x4 gWorldViewProj;
    float4x4 gTexTransform;
    Material gMaterial;
};

// Nonnumeric values cannot be added to a cbuffer.
Texture2D gDiffuseMap;

SamplerState samAnisotropic
{
    Filter = ANISOTROPIC;
    MaxAnisotropy = 4;

    AddressU = WRAP;
    AddressV = WRAP;
};

struct VertexIn
{
    float3 PosL    : POSITION;
    float3 NormalL : NORMAL;
    float2 Tex     : TEXCOORD;
};
```

```
struct VertexOut
{
    float4 PosH       : SV_POSITION;
    float3 PosW       : POSITION;
    float3 NormalW    : NORMAL;
    float2 Tex        : TEXCOORD;
};

VertexOut VS(VertexIn vin)
{
    VertexOut vout;

    // Transform to world space space.
    vout.PosW    = mul(float4(vin.PosL, 1.0f), gWorld).xyz;
    vout.NormalW = mul(vin.NormalL, (float3x3)gWorldInvTranspose);

    // Transform to homogeneous clip space.
    vout.PosH = mul(float4(vin.PosL, 1.0f), gWorldViewProj);

    // Output vertex attributes for interpolation across triangle.
    vout.Tex = mul(float4(vin.Tex, 0.0f, 1.0f), gTexTransform).xy;

    return vout;
}

float4 PS(VertexOut pin, uniform int gLightCount, uniform bool
    gUseTexure) : SV_Target
{
    // Interpolating normal can unnormalize it, so normalize it.
      pin.NormalW = normalize(pin.NormalW);

    // The toEye vector is used in lighting.
    float3 toEye = gEyePosW - pin.PosW;

    // Cache the distance to the eye from this surface point.
    float distToEye = length(toEye);

    // Normalize.
    toEye /= distToEye;

    // Default to multiplicative identity.
    float4 texColor = float4(1, 1, 1, 1);
    if(gUseTexure)
    {
      // Sample texture.
      texColor = gDiffuseMap.Sample(samAnisotropic, pin.Tex);
    }

    //
    // Lighting.
    //

    float4 litColor = texColor;
    if(gLightCount > 0)
    {
```

```
      // Start with a sum of zero.
      float4 ambient = float4(0.0f, 0.0f, 0.0f, 0.0f);
      float4 diffuse = float4(0.0f, 0.0f, 0.0f, 0.0f);
      float4 spec    = float4(0.0f, 0.0f, 0.0f, 0.0f);

      // Sum the light contribution from each light source.
      [unroll]
      for(int i = 0; i < gLightCount; ++i)
      {
        float4 A, D, S;
        ComputeDirectionalLight(gMaterial, gDirLights[i],
pin.NormalW, toEye,
          A, D, S);

        ambient += A;
        diffuse += D;
        spec    += S;
      }

      // Modulate with late add.
      litColor = texColor*(ambient + diffuse) + spec;
    }

    // Common to take alpha from diffuse material and texture.
    litColor.a = gMaterial.Diffuse.a * texColor.a;

    return litColor;
}

technique11 Light1
{
    pass P0
    {
      SetVertexShader(CompileShader(vs_5_0, VS()));
      SetGeometryShader(NULL);
      SetPixelShader(CompileShader(ps_5_0, PS(1, false)));
    }
}

technique11 Light2
{
    pass P0
    {
      SetVertexShader(CompileShader(vs_5_0, VS()));
      SetGeometryShader(NULL);
      SetPixelShader(CompileShader(ps_5_0, PS(2, false)));
    }
}

technique11 Light3
```

```
    {
        pass P0
        {
          SetVertexShader(CompileShader(vs_5_0, VS()));
          SetGeometryShader(NULL);
          SetPixelShader(CompileShader(ps_5_0, PS(3, false)));
        }
    }

technique11 Light0Tex
{
        pass P0
        {
          SetVertexShader(CompileShader(vs_5_0, VS()));
          SetGeometryShader(NULL);
          SetPixelShader(CompileShader(ps_5_0, PS(0, true)));
        }
}

technique11 Light1Tex
{
        pass P0
        {
          SetVertexShader(CompileShader(vs_5_0, VS()));
          SetGeometryShader(NULL);
          SetPixelShader(CompileShader(ps_5_0, PS(1, true)));
        }
}

technique11 Light2Tex
{
        pass P0
        {
          SetVertexShader(CompileShader(vs_5_0, VS()));
          SetGeometryShader(NULL);
          SetPixelShader(CompileShader(ps_5_0, PS(2, true)));
        }
}

technique11 Light3Tex
{
        pass P0
        {
          SetVertexShader(CompileShader(vs_5_0, VS()));
          SetGeometryShader(NULL);
          SetPixelShader(CompileShader(ps_5_0, PS(3, true)));
        }
}
```

Observe that *Basic.fx* has techniques with texturing and without, by using the uniform parameter gUseTexture. In this way, if we need to render something that does not need texturing, we select the technique without it, and therefore, do not have to pay the cost of texturing. Likewise, we select the technique with the number of lights we use, so that we do not pay the cost of additional lighting calculations that we do not need.

One constant buffer variable we have not discussed is `gTexTransform`. This variable is used in the vertex shader to transform the input texture coordinates:

```
vout.Tex = mul(float4(vin.Tex, 0.0f, 1.0f), gTexTransform).xy;
```

Texture coordinates are 2D points in texture plane. Thus, we can translate, rotate, and scale them like we could any other point. In this demo, we use an identity matrix transformation so that the input texture coordinates are left unmodified. However, as we will see in §8.9, some special effects can be obtained by transforming texture coordinates. Note that to transform the 2D texture coordinates by a 4×4 matrix, we augment it to a 4D vector:

```
vin.Tex ---> float4(vin.Tex, 0.0f, 1.0f)
```

After the multiplication is done, the resulting 4D vector is cast back to a 2D vector by throwing away the z- and w-components. That is,

```
vout.Tex = mul(float4(vin.Tex, 0.0f, 1.0f), gTexTransform).xy;
```

8.8 ADDRESS MODES

A texture, combined with constant or linear interpolation, defines a vector-valued function $T(u, v) = (r, g, b, a)$. That is, given the texture coordinates $(u, v) \in [0, 1]^2$ the texture function T returns a color (r, g, b, a). Direct3D allows us to extend the domain of this function in four different ways (called *address modes*): *wrap*, *border color*, *clamp*, and *mirror*.

1. *wrap* extends the texture function by repeating the image at every integer junction (see Figure 8.10).

2. *border color* extends the texture function by mapping each (u, v) not in $[0, 1]^2$ to some color specified by the programmer (see Figure 8.11).

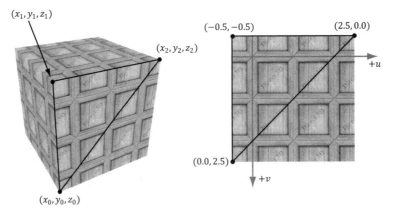

Figure 8.10. Wrap address mode.

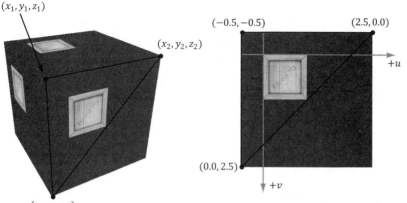

Figure 8.11. Border color address mode.

3. *clamp* extends the texture function by mapping each (u, v) not in $[0, 1]^2$ to the color $T(u_0, v_0)$, where (u_0, v_0) is the nearest point to (u, v) contained in $[0, 1]^2$ (see Figure 8.12).

4. *mirror* extends the texture function by mirroring the image at every integer junction (see Figure 8.13).

An address mode is always specified (wrap mode is the default), so therefore, texture coordinates outside the $[0, 1]$ range are always defined.

The wrap address mode is probably the most often employed; it allows us to tile a texture repeatedly over some surface. This effectively enables us to increase the texture resolution without supplying additional data (although the extra resolution is repetitive). With tiling, it is usually important that the texture is seamless. For

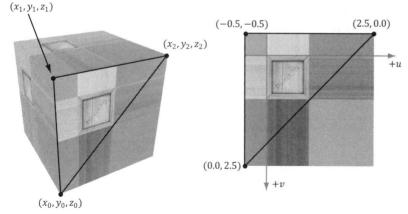

Figure 8.12. Clamp address mode.

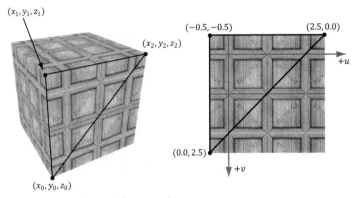

Figure 8.13. **Mirror address mode.**

example, the crate texture is not seamless, as you can see the repetition clearly. However, Figure 8.14 shows a seamless brick texture repeated 2 × 3 times.

Address modes are specified in sampler objects. The following examples were used to create Figures 8.10–8.13:

```
SamplerState samTriLinear
{
    Filter = MIN_MAG_MIP_LINEAR;
    AddressU = WRAP;
    AddressV = WRAP;
};

SamplerState samTriLinear
{
    Filter = MIN_MAG_MIP_LINEAR;
    AddressU = BORDER;
    AddressV = BORDER;

    // Blue border color
    BorderColor = float4(0.0f, 0.0f, 1.0f, 1.0f);
};

SamplerState samTriLinear
{
    Filter = MIN_MAG_MIP_LINEAR;
    AddressU = CLAMP;
    AddressV = CLAMP;
};

SamplerState samTriLinear
{
    Filter = MIN_MAG_MIP_LINEAR;
    AddressU = MIRROR;
    AddressV = MIRROR;
};
```

Tile 2 x 3

Figure 8.14. A brick texture tiled 2 × 3 times. Because the texture is seamless, the repetition pattern is harder to notice.

Note: *Observe that you can control the address modes in the u- and v-directions independently. The reader might try experimenting with this.*

8.9 TRANSFORMING TEXTURES

Texture coordinates represent 2D points in the texture plane. Thus, we can translate, rotate, and scale them like we could any other point. Here are some example uses for transforming textures:

1. A brick texture is stretched along a wall. The wall vertices currently have texture coordinates in the range [0, 1]. We scale the texture coordinates by 4 to scale them to the range [0, 4], so that the texture will be repeated four-by-four times across the wall.

2. We have cloud textures stretched over a clear blue sky. By translating the texture coordinates as a function of time, the clouds are animated over the sky.

3. Texture rotation is sometimes useful for particle-like effects, where we rotate a fireball texture over time, for example.

Texture coordinate transformations are done just like regular transformations. We specify a transformation matrix, and multiply the texture coordinate vector by the matrix. For example:

```
// Constant buffer variable
float4x4 gTexMtx;

// In shader program
vOut.texC = mul(float4(vIn.texC, 0.0f, 1.0f), gTexMtx);
```

Note that since we are working with 2D texture coordinates, we only care about transformations done to the first two coordinates. For instance, if the texture matrix translated the z-coordinate, it would have no effect on the resulting texture coordinates.

8.10 TEXTURED HILLS AND WAVES DEMO

In this demo, we add textures to our land and water scene. The first key issue is that we tile a grass texture over the land. Because the land mesh is a large surface, if we simply stretched a texture over it, then too few texels would cover each triangle. In other words, there is not enough texture resolution for the surface; we would thus get magnification artifacts. Therefore, we repeat the grass texture over the land mesh to get more resolution. The second key issue is that we scroll the water texture over the water geometry as a function of time. This added motion makes the water a bit more convincing. Figure 8.15 shows a screenshot of the demo.

Figure 8.15. **Screenshot of the "Land Tex" demo.**

8.10.1 Grid Texture Coordinate Generation

Figure 8.16 shows an $m \times n$ grid in the xz-plane and a corresponding grid in the normalized texture space domain $[0, 1]^2$. From the picture, it is clear that the texture coordinates of the ijth grid vertex in the xz-plane are the coordinates of the ijth grid vertex in the texture space. The texture space coordinates of the ijth vertex are:

$$u_{ij} = j \cdot \Delta u$$
$$v_{ij} = i \cdot \Delta v$$

where $\Delta u = \frac{1}{n-1}$ and $\Delta v = \frac{1}{m-1}$.

Thus, we use the following code to generate texture coordinates for a grid in the `GeometryGenerator::CreateGrid` method:

```
void GeometryGenerator::CreateGrid(float width, float depth, UINT m, UINT
    n, MeshData& meshData)
{
    UINT vertexCount = m*n;
    UINT faceCount   = (m-1)*(n-1)*2;

    //
    // Create the vertices.
    //

    float halfWidth = 0.5f*width;
    float halfDepth = 0.5f*depth;

    float dx = width / (n-1);
    float dz = depth / (m-1);

    float du = 1.0f / (n-1);
    float dv = 1.0f / (m-1);

    meshData.Vertices.resize(vertexCount);
    for(UINT i = 0; i < m; ++i)
    {
      float z = halfDepth - i*dz;
      for(UINT j = 0; j < n; ++j)
      {
        float x = -halfWidth + j*dx;

        meshData.Vertices[i*n+j].Position =
            XMFLOAT3(x, 0.0f, z);
        meshData.Vertices[i*n+j].Normal   =
            XMFLOAT3(0.0f, 1.0f, 0.0f);
        meshData.Vertices[i*n+j].TangentU =
            XMFLOAT3(1.0f, 0.0f, 0.0f);

        // Stretch texture over grid.
        meshData.Vertices[i*n+j].TexC.x = j*du;
        meshData.Vertices[i*n+j].TexC.y = i*dv;
      }
    }
```

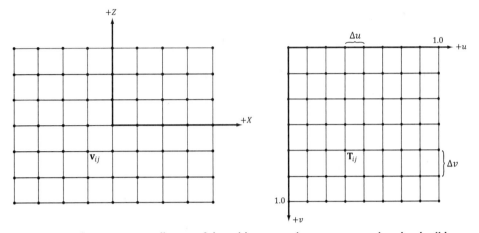

Figure 8.16. The texture coordinates of the grid vertex $\mathbf{v}_{ij}$ in *xz*-space are given by the *ij*th grid vertex $\mathbf{T}_{ij}$ in *uv*-space.

8.10.2 Texture Tiling

We said we wanted to tile a grass texture over the land mesh. But so far the texture coordinates we have computed lie in the unit domain $[0, 1]^2$; so no tiling will occur. To tile the texture, we specify the wrap address mode and scale the texture coordinates by 5 using a texture transformation matrix. Thus the texture coordinates are mapped to the domain $[0, 5]^2$ so that the texture is tiled 5×5 times across the land mesh surface:

```
XMMATRIX grassTexScale = XMMatrixScaling(5.0f, 5.0f, 0.0f);
XMStoreFloat4x4(&mGrassTexTransform, grassTexScale);
...
Effects::BasicFX->SetTexTransform(XMLoadFloat4x4(&mGrassTexTransform));
...
activeTech->GetPassByIndex(p)->Apply(0, md3dImmediateContext);
md3dImmediateContext->DrawIndexed(mLandIndexCount, 0, 0);
```

8.10.3 Texture Animation

To scroll a water texture over the water geometry, we translate the texture coordinates in the texture plane as a function of time in the **UpdateScene** method. Provided the displacement is small for each frame, this gives the illusion of a smooth animation. We use the wrap address mode along with a seamless texture so that we can seamlessly translate the texture coordinates around the texture space plane. The following code shows how we calculate the offset vector for the water texture, and how we build and set the water's texture matrix:

```
// Tile water texture.
XMMATRIX wavesScale = XMMatrixScaling(5.0f, 5.0f, 0.0f);

// Translate texture over time.
mWaterTexOffset.y += 0.05f*dt;
mWaterTexOffset.x += 0.1f*dt;
XMMATRIX wavesOffset = XMMatrixTranslation(mWaterTexOffset.x,
    mWaterTexOffset.y, 0.0f);

// Combine scale and translation.
XMStoreFloat4x4(&mWaterTexTransform, wavesScale*wavesOffset);


...

Effects::BasicFX->SetTexTransform(XMLoadFloat4x4(&mWaterTexTransform));
...
activeTech->GetPassByIndex(p)->Apply(0, md3dImmediateContext);
md3dImmediateContext->DrawIndexed(3*mWaves.TriangleCount(), 0, 0);
```

8.11 COMPRESSED TEXTURE FORMATS

The GPU memory requirements for textures add up quickly as your virtual worlds grow with hundreds of textures (remember we need to keep all these textures in GPU memory to apply them quickly). To help alleviate these memory requirements, Direct3D supports compressed texture formats: BC1, BC2, BC3, BC4, BC5, BC6, and BC7:

1. BC1 (DXGI_FORMAT_BC1_UNORM): Use this format if you need to compress a format that supports three color channels, and only a 1-bit (on/off) alpha component.

2. BC2 (DXGI_FORMAT_BC2_UNORM): Use this format if you need to compress a format that supports three color channels, and only a 4-bit alpha component.

3. BC3 (DXGI_FORMAT_BC3_UNORM): Use this format if you need to compress a format that supports three color channels, and an 8-bit alpha component.

4. BC4 (DXGI_FORMAT_BC4_UNORM): Use this format if you need to compress a format that contains one color channel (e.g., a grayscale image).

5. BC5 (DXGI_FORMAT_BC5_UNORM): Use this format if you need to compress a format that supports two color channels.

6. BC6 (DXGI_FORMAT_BC6_UF16): Use this format for compressed HDR (high dynamic range) image data.

7. BC7 (DXGI_FORMAT_BC7_UNORM): Use this format for high quality RGBA compression. In particular, this format significantly reduces the errors caused by compressing normal maps.

Note: *A compressed texture can only be used as an input to the shader stage of the rendering pipeline.*

Note: *Because the block compression algorithms work with 4 × 4 pixel blocks, the dimensions of the texture must be multiples of 4.*

The advantage of these formats is that they can be stored compressed in GPU memory, and then decompressed on the fly by the GPU when needed.

If you have a file that contains uncompressed image data, you can have Direct3D convert it to a compressed format at load time by using the `pLoadInfo` parameter of the `D3DX11CreateShaderResourceViewFromFile` function. For example, consider the following code, which loads a BMP file:

```
D3DX11_IMAGE_LOAD_INFO loadInfo;
loadInfo.Format = DXGI_FORMAT_BC3_UNORM;

HR(D3DX11CreateShaderResourceViewFromFile(md3dDevice,
    L"Textures/darkbrick.bmp", &loadInfo, 0, &mDiffuseMapSRV, 0));

// Get the actual 2D texture from the resource view.
ID3D11Texture2D* tex;
mDiffuseMapSRV->GetResource((ID3D11Resource**)&tex);

// Get the description of the 2D texture.
D3D11_TEXTURE2D_DESC texDesc;
tex->GetDesc(&texDesc);
```

Figure 8.17*a* shows what `texDesc` looks like in the debugger; we see that it has the desired compressed texture format. If instead we specified null for the `pLoadInfo` parameter, then the format from the source image is used (Figure 8.17*b*), which is the uncompressed `DXGI_FORMAT_R8G8B8A8_UNORM` format.

Alternatively, you can use the DDS (Direct Draw Surface) format, which can store compressed textures directly. To do this, load your image file into the DirectX Texture Tool (*DxTex.exe*) located in the SDK directory: *D:\Microsoft DirectX SDK (June 2010)\ Utilities\bin\x86*. Then go to **Menu->Format->Change Surface Format** and choose DXT1, DXT2, DXT3, DXT4, or DXT5. Save the file as a DDS file. These formats are actually Direct3D 9 compressed texture formats, but DXT1 is the same as BC1, DXT2 and DXT3 are the same as BC2, and DXT4 and DXT5 are the same as BC3. As an example, if we save a file as DXT1 and load it using `D3DX11CreateShaderResourceViewFromFile`, the texture will have format `DXGI_FORMAT_BC1_UNORM`:

```
HR(D3DX11CreateShaderResourceViewFromFile(md3dDevice,
    L"Textures/darkbrickdxt1.dds", 0, 0, &mDiffuseMapSRV, 0));

// Get the actual 2D texture from the resource view.
ID3D11Texture2D* tex;
mDiffuseMapSRV->GetResource((ID3D11Resource**)&tex);

// Get the description of the 2D texture.
D3D11_TEXTURE2D_DESC texDesc;
tex->GetDesc(&texDesc);
```

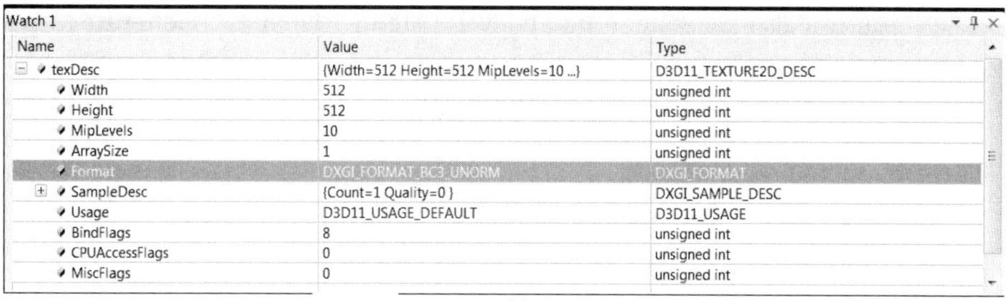

(a)

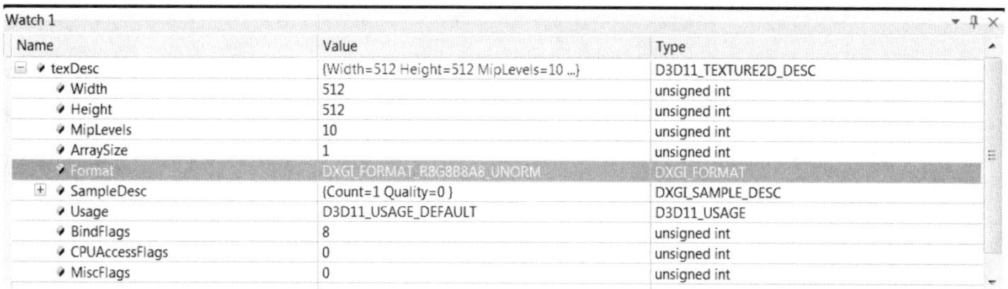

(b)

Figure 8.17. (a) The texture is created with the `DXGI_FORMAT_BC3_UNORM` compressed format. (b) The texture is created with the `DXGI_FORMAT_R8G8B8A8_UNORM` uncompressed format.

Note that if the DDS file uses one of the compressed formats, we can specify null for the `pLoadInfo` parameter, and `D3DX11CreateShaderResourceViewFromFile` will use the compressed format specified by the file.

For BC4 and BC5 formats, you can use NVIDIA Texture Tools (http://code. google.com/p/nvidia-texture-tools/). For BC6 and BC7 formats, the DirectX SDK has a sample called "BC6HBC7EncoderDecoder11." This program can be used to convert your texture files to BC6 or BC7. The sample includes full source code so that you can integrate it into your own art pipeline. Interestingly, the sample uses the GPU to do the conversion if the graphics hardware supports compute shaders; this gives a much faster conversion than a CPU implementation.

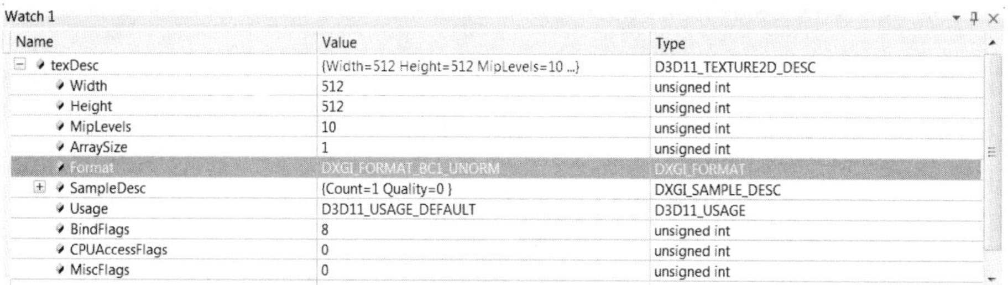

Figure 8.18. The texture is created with the `DXGI_FORMAT_BC1_UNORM` format.

You can also generate mipmap levels (**Menu->Format->Generate Mip Maps**) in the DirectX Texture Tool, and save them in a DDS file as well. In this way, the mipmap levels are precomputed and stored with the file so that they do not need to be computed at load time (they just need to be loaded).

Another advantage of storing your textures compressed in DDS files is that they also take up less disk space.

8.12 SUMMARY

1. Texture coordinates are used to define a triangle on the texture that gets mapped to the 3D triangle.

2. We can create textures from image files stored on disk using the `D3DX11CreateShaderResourceViewFromFile` function.

3. We can filter textures by using the minification, magnification, and mipmap filter sampler states.

4. Address modes define what Direct3D is supposed to do with texture coordinates outside the [0, 1] range. For example, should the texture be tiled, mirrored, clamped, etc.?

5. Texture coordinates can be scaled, rotated, and translated just like other points. By incrementally transforming the texture coordinates by a small amount each frame, we animate the texture.

6. By using compressed Direct3D texture formats BC1, BC2, BC3, BC4, BC5, BC6, or BC7, we can save a considerable amount of GPU memory. Use the DirectX Texture Tool to generate textures with formats BC1, BC2, and BC3. For BC4 and BC5, you can use NVIDIA Texture Tools (http://code.google.com/p/nvidia-texture-tools/). Use the SDK "BC6HBC7EncoderDecoder11" sample to generate textures with formats BC6 and BC7.

8.13 EXERCISES

1. Experiment with the "Crate" demo by changing the texture coordinates and using different address mode combinations and filtering options. In particular, reproduce the images in Figures 8.7, 8.9, 8.10, 8.11, 8.12, and 8.13.

2. Using the DirectX Texture Tool, we can manually specify each mipmap level (**File->Open Onto This Surface**). Create a DDS file with a mipmap chain like the one in Figure 8.19, with a different textual description or color on each level so that you can easily distinguish between each mipmap level. Modify the

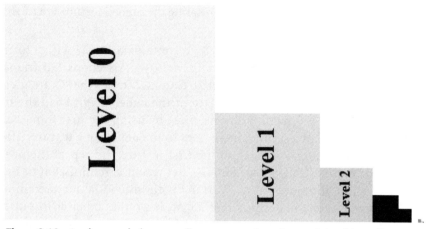

Figure 8.19. A mipmap chain manually constructed so that each level is easily distinguishable.

Crate demo by using this texture and have the camera zoom in and out so that you can explicitly see the mipmap levels changing. Try both point and linear mipmap filtering.

3.   Given two textures of the same size, we can combine them via different operations to obtain a new image. More generally, this is called *multitexturing*, where multiple textures are used to achieve a result. For example, we can add, subtract, or (component-wise) multiply the corresponding texels of two textures. Figure 8.20 shows the result of component-wise multiplying two textures to get a fireball-like result. For this exercise, modify the "Crate" demo by combining the two source textures in Figure 8.20 in a pixel shader to produce the fireball texture over each cube face. (The image files for this exercise may be downloaded from the book's website.) Note that you will have to modify the *Basic.fx* to support more than one texture.

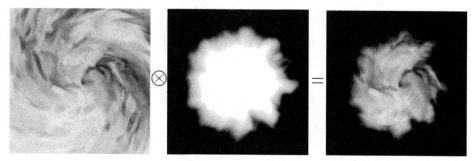

Figure 8.20. Component-wise multiplying corresponding texels of two textures to produce a new texture.

4. Modify the solution to Exercise 3 by rotating the fireball texture as a function of time over each cube face.

5. This chapter's downloadable directory contains a folder with 120 frames of a fire animation designed to be played over 4 seconds (30 frames per second). Figure 8.21 shows the first 30 frames. Modify the "Crate" demo by playing this animation over each face of the cube. (*Hint*: Load the images into an array of 120 texture objects. Start by using the first frame texture, and every 1/30th of a second, increment to the next frame texture. After the 120th frame texture, roll back to the first texture and repeat the process.) This is sometimes called *page flipping*, because it is reminiscent of flipping the pages in a flip book. *Note:* Working with individual texture animation frames one-by-one like this is inefficient. It would be better to put all the frames in one texture atlas, and then offset the texture coordinates every 1/30th of a second to the next frame of the animation. But for the sake of the exercise, the inefficient method is fine.

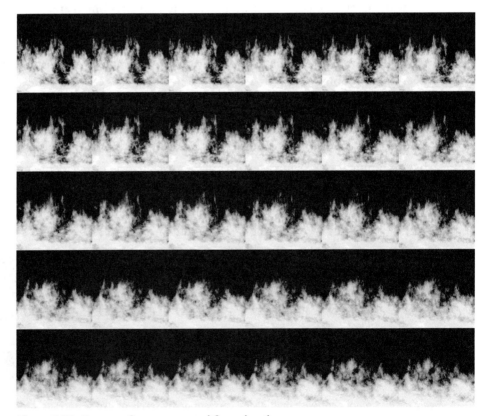

Figure 8.21. Frames of a precomputed fire animation.

6. Let $\mathbf{p}_0$, $\mathbf{p}_1$, and $\mathbf{p}_2$ be the vertices of a 3D triangle with respective texture coordinates $\mathbf{q}_0$, $\mathbf{q}_1$, and $\mathbf{q}_2$. Recall from §8.2 that for an arbitrary point on a 3D triangle $\mathbf{p}(s, t) = \mathbf{p}_0 + s(\mathbf{p}_1 - \mathbf{p}_0) + t(\mathbf{p}_2 - \mathbf{p}_0)$ where $s \geq 0$, $t \geq 0$, $s + t \leq 1$, its texture coordinates (u, v) are found by linearly interpolating the vertex texture coordinates across the 3D triangle by the same s, t parameters:

$$(u, v) = \mathbf{q}_0 + s(\mathbf{q}_1 - \mathbf{q}_0) + t(\mathbf{q}_2 - \mathbf{q}_0)$$

(a) Given (u, v) and $\mathbf{q}_0$, $\mathbf{q}_1$, and $\mathbf{q}_2$, solve for (s, t) in terms of u and v.

Hint: *Consider the vector equation* $(u, v) - \mathbf{q}_0 = s(\mathbf{q}_1 - \mathbf{q}_0) + t(\mathbf{q}_2 - \mathbf{q}_0)$.

(b) Express $\mathbf{p}$ as a function of u and v; that is, find a formula $\mathbf{p} = \mathbf{p}(u, v)$.

(c) Compute $\partial\mathbf{p}/\partial u$ and $\partial\mathbf{p}/\partial v$ and give a geometric interpretation of what these vectors mean.

7. Modify the "Lit Skull" demo from the previous chapter by adding textures to the ground, columns, and spheres (Figure 8.22). The textures can be found in this chapters code directory.

Figure 8.22. **Textured column scene.**

Chapter 9 BENDING

BLENDING

Consider Figure 9.1. We start rendering the frame by first drawing the terrain followed by the wooden crate, so that the terrain and crate pixels are on the back buffer. We then draw the water surface to the back buffer using *blending*, so that the water pixels get blended with the terrain and crate pixels on the back buffer in such a way that the terrain and crate shows through the water. In this chapter, we examine *blending* techniques which allow us to blend (combine) the pixels that we are currently rasterizing (so-called *source* pixels) with the pixels that were previously rasterized to the back buffer (so-called *destination* pixels). This technique enables us, among other things, to render semi-transparent objects such as water and glass.

> **Note:** For the sake of discussion, we specifically mention the back buffer as the render target. However, we will show later that we can render to "off screen" render targets as well. Blending applies to these render targets just the same, and the destination pixels are the pixel values that were previously rasterized to these off screen render targets.

Objectives:

1. To understand how blending works and how to use it with Direct3D.
2. To learn about the different blend modes that Direct3D supports.

347

Figure 9.1. **A semi-transparent water surface.**

3. To find out how the alpha component can be used to control the transparency of a primitive.

4. To learn how we can prevent a pixel from being drawn to the back buffer altogether by employing the HLSL `clip` function.

9.1 THE BLENDING EQUATION

Let $\mathbf{C}_{src}$ be the color output from the pixel shader for the ijth pixel we are currently rasterizing (source pixel), and let $\mathbf{C}_{dst}$ be the color of the ijth pixel currently on the back buffer (destination pixel). Without blending, $\mathbf{C}_{src}$ would overwrite $\mathbf{C}_{dst}$ (assuming it passes the depth/stencil test) and become the new color of the ijth back buffer pixel. But, with blending $\mathbf{C}_{src}$ and $\mathbf{C}_{dst}$ are blended together to get the new color $\mathbf{C}$ that will overwrite $\mathbf{C}_{dst}$ (i.e., the blended color $\mathbf{C}$ will be written to the ijth pixel of the back buffer). Direct3D uses the following blending equation to blend the source and destination pixel colors:

$$\mathbf{C} = \mathbf{C}_{src} \otimes \mathbf{F}_{src} \boxplus \mathbf{C}_{dst} \otimes \mathbf{F}_{dst}$$

The colors $\mathbf{F}_{src}$ (source blend factor) and $\mathbf{F}_{dst}$ (destination blend factor) may be any of the values described in §9.3, and they allow us modify the original source and destination pixels in a variety of ways, allowing for different effects to be achieved. The $\otimes$ operator means componentwise multiplication for color vectors as defined in §5.3.1; the $\boxplus$ operator may be any of the binary operators defined in §9.2.

The previous blending equation holds only for the RGB components of the colors. The alpha component is actually handled by a separate similar equation:

$$A = A_{src}F_{src} \boxplus A_{dst}F_{dst}$$

The equation is essentially the same, but it is possible that the blend factors and binary operation are different. The motivation for separating RGB from alpha is simply so that we can process them independently, and hence, differently.

Note: *Blending the alpha components is needed much less frequently than blending the RGB components. This is mainly because we do not care about the back buffer alpha values. Back buffer alpha values are only important if you have some algorithm that requires destination alpha values.*

9.2 BLEND OPERATIONS

The binary $\boxplus$ operator used in the blending equation may be one of the following:

```
typedef enum D3D11_BLEND_OP
{
    D3D11_BLEND_OP_ADD = 1,

    D3D11_BLEND_OP_SUBTRACT = 2,

    D3D11_BLEND_OP_REV_SUBTRACT = 3,

    D3D11_BLEND_OP_MIN = 4,

    D3D11_BLEND_OP_MAX = 5,
} D3D11_BLEND_OP;
```

$$\mathbf{C} = \mathbf{C}_{src} \otimes \mathbf{F}_{src} + \mathbf{C}_{dst} \otimes \mathbf{F}_{dst}$$
$$\mathbf{C} = \mathbf{C}_{dst} \otimes \mathbf{F}_{dst} - \mathbf{C}_{src} \otimes \mathbf{F}_{src}$$
$$\mathbf{C} = \mathbf{C}_{src} \otimes \mathbf{F}_{src} - \mathbf{C}_{dst} \otimes \mathbf{F}_{dst}$$
$$\mathbf{C} = \min\left(\mathbf{C}_{src}, \mathbf{C}_{dst}\right)$$
$$\mathbf{C} = \max\left(\mathbf{C}_{src}, \mathbf{C}_{dst}\right)$$

Note: *The blend factors are ignored in the min/max operation.*

These same operators also work for the alpha blending equation. Also, you can specify a different operator for RGB and alpha. For example, it is possible to add the two RGB terms, but subtract the two alpha terms:

$$\mathbf{C} = \mathbf{C}_{src} \otimes \mathbf{F}_{src} + \mathbf{C}_{dst} \otimes \mathbf{F}_{dst}$$
$$A = A_{dst}F_{dst} - A_{src}F_{src}$$

9.3 BLEND FACTORS

By setting different combinations for the source and destination blend factors along with different blend operators, dozens of different blending effects may be achieved. We will illustrate some combinations in §9.5, but you will need to experiment with others to get a feel of what they do. The following list describes the basic blend factors, which apply to both $\mathbf{F}_{src}$ and $\mathbf{F}_{dst}$. See the D3D11_BLEND enumerated type in the SDK documentation for some additional advanced blend factors. Letting $\mathbf{C}_{src} = (r_s, g_s, b_s)$, $A_{src} = a_s$ (the RGBA values output from the pixel shader), $\mathbf{C}_{dst} = (r_d, g_d, b_d)$, $A_{dst} = a_d$ (the RGBA values already stored in the render target), $\mathbf{F}$ being either $\mathbf{F}_{src}$ or $\mathbf{F}_{dst}$ and F being either F_{src} or F_{dst}, we have:

D3D11_BLEND_ZERO: $\mathbf{F} = (0,0,0)$ and $F = 0$

D3D11_BLEND_ONE: $\mathbf{F} = (1,1,1)$ and $F = 1$

D3D11_BLEND_SRC_COLOR: $\mathbf{F} = (r_s, g_s, b_s)$

D3D11_BLEND_INV_SRC_COLOR: $\mathbf{F} = (1 - r_s, 1 - g_s, 1 - b_s)$

D3D11_BLEND_SRC_ALPHA: $\mathbf{F} = (a_s, a_s, a_s)$ and $F = a_s$

D3D11_BLEND_INV_SRC_ALPHA: $\mathbf{F} = (1 - a_s, 1 - a_s, 1 - a_s)$ and $F = 1 - a_s$

D3D11_BLEND_DEST_ALPHA: $\mathbf{F} = (a_d, a_d, a_d)$ and $F = a_d$

D3D11_BLEND_INV_DEST_ALPHA: $\mathbf{F} = (1 - a_d, 1 - a_d, 1 - a_d)$ and $F = 1 - a_d$

D3D11_BLEND_DEST_COLOR: $\mathbf{F} = (r_d, g_d, b_d)$

D3D11_BLEND_INV_DEST_COLOR: $\mathbf{F} = (1 - r_d, 1 - g_d, 1 - b_d)$

D3D11_BLEND_SRC_ALPHA_SAT: $\mathbf{F} = (a'_s, a'_s, a'_s)$ and $F = a'_s$ where $a'_s = \text{clamp}(a_s, 0, 1)$

D3D11_BLEND_BLEND_FACTOR: $\mathbf{F} = (r, g, b)$ and $F = a$, where the color (r, g, b, a) is supplied to the second parameter of the ID3D11DeviceContext::OMSetBlendState method (§9.4). This allows you to specify the blend factor color to use directly; however, it is constant until you change the blend state.

D3D11_BLEND_INV_BLEND_FACTOR: $\mathbf{F} = (1 - r, 1 - g, 1 - b)$ and $F = 1 - a$, where the color (r, g, b, a) is supplied by the second parameter of the ID3D11DeviceContext::OMSetBlendState method (§9.4). This allows you to specify the blend factor color to use directly; however, it is constant until you change the blend state.

Note: ➤ *The* clamp *function is defined as:*

$$\text{clamp}(x, a, b) = \begin{cases} x, & a \le x \le b \\ a, & x < a \\ b, & x > b \end{cases}$$

All of the previous blend factors apply to the RGB blending equation. For the alpha blending equation, blend factors ending with _COLOR are *not allowed*.

9.4 BLEND STATE

We have talked about the blending operators and blend factors, but where do we set these values with Direct3D? These blend settings are controlled by the `ID3D11BlendState` interface. Such an interface is found by filling out a `D3D11_BLEND_DESC` structure and then calling `ID3D11Device::CreateBlendState`:

```
HRESULT ID3D11Device::CreateBlendState(
    const D3D11_BLEND_DESC *pBlendStateDesc,
    ID3D11BlendState **ppBlendState);
```

1. `pBlendStateDesc`: Pointer to the filled out `D3D11_BLEND_DESC` structure describing the blend state to create.

2. `ppBlendState`: Returns a pointer to the created blend state interface.

The `D3D11_BLEND_DESC`: Structure is defined like so:

```
typedef struct D3D11_BLEND_DESC {
    BOOL   AlphaToCoverageEnable;    // Default: False
    BOOL   IndependentBlendEnable;   // Default: False
    D3D11_RENDER_TARGET_BLEND_DESC RenderTarget[8];
} D3D11_BLEND_DESC;
```

1. `AlphaToCoverageEnable`: Specify true to enable alpha-to-coverage, which is a multisampling technique useful when rendering foliage or gate textures. Specify false to disable alpha-to-coverage. Alpha-to-coverage requires multisampling to be enabled (i.e., the back and depth buffer were created with multisampling). We will show a sample that uses alpha-to-coverage in Chapter 11.

2. `IndependentBlendEnable`: Direct3D 11 supports rendering to up to 8 render targets simultaneously. When this flag is set to true, it means blending can be performed for each render target differently (different blend factors, different blend operations, blending disabled/enabled, etc.). If this flag is set to false, it means all the render targets will be blended the same way as described by the first element in the `D3D11_BLEND_DESC::RenderTarget` array. Multiple render targets are used for advanced algorithms; for now, assume we only render to one render target at a time.

3. `RenderTarget`: An array of 8 `D3D11_RENDER_TARGET_BLEND_DESC` elements, where the ith element describes how blending is done for the ith simultaneous render target. If `IndependentBlendEnable` is set to false, then all the render targets use `RenderTarget[0]` for blending.

The `D3D11_RENDER_TARGET_BLEND_DESC` structure is defined like so:

```
typedef struct D3D11_RENDER_TARGET_BLEND_DESC {
    BOOL            BlendEnable;   // Default: False
    D3D11_BLEND     SrcBlend;      // Default: D3D11_BLEND_ONE
    D3D11_BLEND     DestBlend;     // Default: D3D11_BLEND_ZERO
    D3D11_BLEND_OP  BlendOp;       // Default: D3D11_BLEND_OP_ADD
```

```
D3D11_BLEND    SrcBlendAlpha;  // Default: D3D11_BLEND_ONE
D3D11_BLEND    DestBlendAlpha; // Default: D3D11_BLEND_ZERO
D3D11_BLEND_OP BlendOpAlpha;   // Default: D3D11_BLEND_OP_ADD
UINT8 RenderTargetWriteMask;   // Default: D3D11_COLOR_WRITE_ENABLE_ALL
} D3D11_RENDER_TARGET_BLEND_DESC;
```

1. `BlendEnable`: Specify true to enable blending and false to disable it.

2. `SrcBlend`: A member of the `D3D11_BLEND` enumerated type that specifies the source blend factor F_{src} for RGB blending.

3. `DestBlend`: A member of the `D3D11_BLEND` enumerated type that specifies the destination blend factor F_{dst} for RGB blending.

4. `BlendOp`: A member of the `D3D11_BLEND_OP` enumerated type that specifies the RGB blending operator.

5. `SrcBlendAlpha`: A member of the `D3D11_BLEND` enumerated type that specifies the destination blend factor F_{src} for alpha blending.

6. `DestBlendAlpha`: A member of the `D3D11_BLEND` enumerated type that specifies the destination blend factor F_{dst} for alpha blending.

7. `BlendOpAlpha`: A member of the `D3D11_BLEND_OP` enumerated type that specifies the alpha blending operator.

8. `RenderTargetWriteMask`: A combination of one or more of the following flags:

```
typedef enum D3D11_COLOR_WRITE_ENABLE {
    D3D11_COLOR_WRITE_ENABLE_RED     = 1,
    D3D11_COLOR_WRITE_ENABLE_GREEN   = 2,
    D3D11_COLOR_WRITE_ENABLE_BLUE    = 4,
    D3D11_COLOR_WRITE_ENABLE_ALPHA   = 8,
    D3D11_COLOR_WRITE_ENABLE_ALL     =
        (D3D11_COLOR_WRITE_ENABLE_RED | D3D11_COLOR_WRITE_ENABLE_GREEN |
         D3D11_COLOR_WRITE_ENABLE_BLUE | D3D11_COLOR_WRITE_ENABLE_ALPHA)
} D3D11_COLOR_WRITE_ENABLE;
```

These flags control which color channels in the back buffer are written to after blending. For example, you could disable writes to the RGB channels, and only write to the alpha channel, by specifying `D3D11_COLOR_WRITE_ENABLE_ALPHA`. This flexibility can be useful for advanced techniques. When blending is disabled, the color returned from the pixel shader is used with no write mask applied.

To bind a blend state object to the output merger stage of the pipeline, we call:

```
void ID3D11DeviceContext::OMSetBlendState(
    ID3D11BlendState *pBlendState,
    const FLOAT BlendFactor,
    UINT SampleMask);
```

1. `pBlendState`: A pointer to the blend state object to enable with the device.

2. `BlendFactor`: An array of four floats defining an RGBA color vector. This color vector is used as a blend factor when `D3D11_BLEND_BLEND_FACTOR` or `D3D11_BLEND_INV_BLEND_FACTOR` is specified.

3. `SampleMask`: Multisampling can take up to 32 samples. This 32-bit integer value is used to enable/disable the samples. For example, if you turn off the 5th bit, then the 5th sample will not be taken. Of course, disabling the 5th sample only has any consequence if you are actually using multisampling with at least 5 samples. If an application is using single sampling, then only the first bit of this parameter matters (see Exercise 1). Generally the default of 0xffffffff is used, which does not disable any samples an application might take from being taken.

As with the other state blocks, there is a default blend state (blending disabled); if you call `OMSetBlendState` with null, then it restores the default blend state. We note that blending does require additional per-pixel work, so only enable it if you need it, and turn it off when you are done.

The following code shows an example of creating and setting a blend state:

```
D3D11_BLEND_DESC transparentDesc = {0};
transparentDesc.AlphaToCoverageEnable = false;
transparentDesc.IndependentBlendEnable = false;

transparentDesc.RenderTarget[0].BlendEnable = true;
transparentDesc.RenderTarget[0].SrcBlend          = D3D11_BLEND_SRC_ALPHA;
transparentDesc.RenderTarget[0].DestBlend         = D3D11_BLEND_INV_SRC_ALPHA;
transparentDesc.RenderTarget[0].BlendOp           = D3D11_BLEND_OP_ADD;
transparentDesc.RenderTarget[0].SrcBlendAlpha     = D3D11_BLEND_ONE;
transparentDesc.RenderTarget[0].DestBlendAlpha    = D3D11_BLEND_ZERO;
transparentDesc.RenderTarget[0].BlendOpAlpha      = D3D11_BLEND_OP_ADD;
transparentDesc.RenderTarget[0].RenderTargetWriteMask =
D3D11_COLOR_WRITE_ENABLE_ALL;

ID3D11BlendState* TransparentBS;
HR(device->CreateBlendState(&transparentDesc, &TransparentBS));

...

float blendFactors[] = {0.0f, 0.0f, 0.0f, 0.0f};
md3dImmediateContext->OMSetBlendState(
    TransparentBS, blendFactor, 0xffffffff);
```

As with other state block interfaces, you should create them all at application initialization time, and then just switch between the state interfaces as needed.

A blend state object can also be set and defined in an effect file:

```
BlendState blend
{
    // Blending state for first render target.
    BlendEnable[0] = TRUE;
    SrcBlend[0] = SRC_COLOR;
    DestBlend[0] = INV_SRC_ALPHA;
    BlendOp[0] = ADD;
    SrcBlendAlpha[0] = ZERO;
    DestBlendAlpha[0] = ZERO;
    BlendOpAlpha[0] = ADD;
    RenderTargetWriteMask[0] = 0x0F;
```

```
            // Blending state for second simultaneous render target.
            BlendEnable[1] = True;
            SrcBlend[1] = One;
            DestBlend[1] = Zero;
            BlendOp[1] = Add;
            SrcBlendAlpha[1] = Zero;
            DestBlendAlpha[1] = Zero;
            BlendOpAlpha[1] = Add;
            RenderTargetWriteMask[1] = 0x0F;
    };

    technique11 Tech
    {
        pass P0
        {

            . . .

            // Use "blend" for this pass.
            SetBlendState(blend, float4(0.0f, 0.0f, 0.0f, 0.0f), 0xffffffff);
        }
    }
```

The values you assign to the blend state object are like those you assign to the C++ structure, except without the prefix. For example, instead of specifying D3D11_BLEND_SRC_COLOR we just specify SRC_COLOR in the effect code. Observe also that the value assignments to the state properties are not case sensitive.

9.5 EXAMPLES

In the following subsections, we look at some blend factor combinations used to get specific effects. In these examples, we only look at RGB blending. Alpha blending is handled analogously.

9.5.1 No Color Write

Suppose that we want to keep the original destination pixel exactly as it is and not overwrite it or blend it with the source pixel currently being rasterized. This can be useful, for example, if you just want to write to the depth/stencil buffer, and not the back buffer. To do this, set the source pixel blend factor to D3D11_BLEND_ZERO, the destination blend factor to D3D11_BLEND_ONE, and the blend operator to D3D11_BLEND_OP_ADD. With this setup, the blending equation reduces to:

$$\mathbf{C} = \mathbf{C}_{src} \otimes \mathbf{F}_{src} \boxplus \mathbf{C}_{dst} \otimes \mathbf{F}_{dst}$$
$$\mathbf{C} = \mathbf{C}_{src} \otimes (0,0,0) + \mathbf{C}_{dst} \otimes (1,1,1)$$
$$\mathbf{C} = \mathbf{C}_{dst}$$

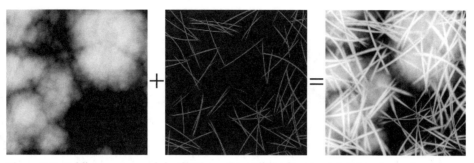

Figure 9.2. Adding source and destination color. Adding creates a brighter image because color is being added.

This is a contrived example; another way to implement the same thing would be to set the `D3D11_RENDER_TARGET_BLEND_DESC::RenderTargetWriteMask` member to 0, so that none of the color channels are written to.

9.5.2 Adding/Subtracting

Suppose that we want to add the source pixels with the destination pixels (see Figure 9.2). To do this, set the source blend factor to `D3D11_BLEND_ONE`, the destination blend factor to `D3D11_BLEND_ONE`, and the blend operator to `D3D11_BLEND_OP_ADD`. With this setup, the blending equation reduces to:

$$\mathbf{C} = \mathbf{C}_{src} \otimes \mathbf{F}_{src} \boxplus \mathbf{C}_{dst} \otimes \mathbf{F}_{dst}$$
$$\mathbf{C} = \mathbf{C}_{src} \otimes (1,1,1) + \mathbf{C}_{dst} \otimes (1,1,1)$$
$$\mathbf{C} = \mathbf{C}_{src} + \mathbf{C}_{dst}$$

We can subtract source pixels from destination pixels by using the previous blend factors and replacing the blend operation with `D3D11_BLEND_OP_SUBTRACT` (Figure 9.3).

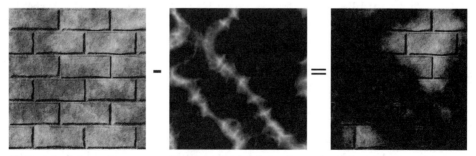

Figure 9.3. Subtracting source color from destination color. Subtraction creates a darker image because color is being removed.

Figure 9.4. Multiplying source color and destination color.

9.5.3 Multiplying

Suppose that we want to multiply a source pixel with its corresponding destination pixel (see Figure 9.4). To do this, we set the source blend factor to D3D11_BLEND_ZERO, the destination blend factor to D3D11_BLEND_SRC_COLOR, and the blend operator to D3D11_BLEND_OP_ADD. With this setup, the blending equation reduces to:

$$\mathbf{C} = \mathbf{C}_{src} \otimes \mathbf{F}_{src} \boxplus \mathbf{C}_{dst} \otimes \mathbf{F}_{dst}$$
$$\mathbf{C} = \mathbf{C}_{src} \otimes (0,0,0) + \mathbf{C}_{dst} \otimes \mathbf{C}_{src}$$
$$\mathbf{C} = \mathbf{C}_{dst} \otimes \mathbf{C}_{src}$$

9.5.4 Transparency

Let the source alpha component a_s be thought of as a percent that controls the opacity of the source pixel (e.g., 0 alpha means 0% opaque, 0.4 means 40% opaque, and 1.0 means 100% opaque). The relationship between opacity and transparency is simply $T = 1 - A$, where A is opacity and T is transparency. For instance, if something is 0.4 opaque, then it is $1 - 0.4 = 0.6$ transparent. Now suppose we want to blend the source and destination pixels based on the opacity of the source pixel. To do this, set the source blend factor to D3D11_BLEND_SRC_ALPHA and the destination blend factor to D3D11_BLEND_INV_SRC_ALPHA, and the blend operator to D3D11_BLEND_OP_ADD. With this setup, the blending equation reduces to:

$$\mathbf{C} = \mathbf{C}_{src} \otimes \mathbf{F}_{src} \boxplus \mathbf{C}_{dst} \otimes \mathbf{F}_{dst}$$
$$\mathbf{C} = \mathbf{C}_{src} \otimes (a_s, a_s, a_s) + \mathbf{C}_{dst} \otimes (1 - a_s, 1 - a_s, 1 - a_s)$$
$$\mathbf{C} = a_s \mathbf{C}_{dst} + (1 - a_s) \mathbf{C}_{src}$$

For example, suppose $a_s = 0.25$, which is to say the source pixel is only 25% opaque. Then when the source and destination pixels are blended together, we expect the final color will be a combination of 25% of the source pixel and 75% of the destination pixel (the pixel "behind" the source pixel), because the source pixel is 75% transparent. The equation above gives us precisely this:

$$\mathbf{C} = a_s \mathbf{C}_{dst} + (1 - a_s) \mathbf{C}_{src}$$
$$\mathbf{C} = 0.25 \mathbf{C}_{dst} + 0.75 \mathbf{C}_{src}$$

Using this blending method, we can draw transparent objects like the one in Figure 9.1. It should be noted that with this blending method, the order that you draw the objects matters. We use the following rule:

Draw objects that do not use blending first. Next, sort the objects that use blending by their distance from the camera. Finally, draw the objects that use blending in a back-to-front order.

The reason for the back-to-front draw order is so objects are blended with the objects spatially behind them. For if an object is transparent, we can see through it to see the scene behind it. So it is necessary that all the pixels behind the transparent object have already been written to the back buffer, so we can blend the transparent source pixels with the destination pixels of the scene behind it.

For the blending method in §9.5.1, draw order does not matter because it simply prevents source pixel writes to the back buffer. For the blending methods discussed in §9.5.2 and 9.5.3, we still draw non-blended objects first and blended objects last; this is because we want to first lay all the non-blended geometry onto the back buffer before we start blending. However, we do not need to sort the objects that use blending. This is because the operations are commutative. That is, if you start with a back buffer pixel color **B**, and then do n additive/subtractive/multiplicative blends to that pixel, the order does not matter:

$$\mathbf{B}' = \mathbf{B} + \mathbf{C}_0 + \mathbf{C}_1 + \ldots + \mathbf{C}_{n-1}$$
$$\mathbf{B}' = \mathbf{B} - \mathbf{C}_0 - \mathbf{C}_1 - \ldots - \mathbf{C}_{n-1}$$
$$\mathbf{B}' = \mathbf{B} \otimes \mathbf{C}_0 \otimes \mathbf{C}_1 \otimes \ldots \otimes \mathbf{C}_{n-1}$$

9.5.5 Blending and the Depth Buffer

When blending with additive/subtractive/multiplicative blending, an issue arises with the depth test. For the sake of example, we will explain only with additive blending, but the same idea holds for subtractive/multiplicative blending. If we are rendering a set S of objects with additive blending, the idea is that the objects in S do not obscure each other; instead, their colors are meant to simply accumulate (see Figure 9.5). Therefore, we do not want to perform the depth test between objects in S; for if we did, without a back-to-front draw ordering, one of the objects in S would obscure another object in S, thus causing the pixel fragments to be rejected due to the depth test, which means that object's pixel colors would

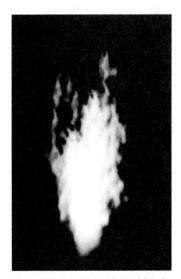

Figure 9.5. With additive blending, the intensity is greater near the source point where more particles are overlapping and being added together. As the particles spread out, the intensity weakens because there are less particles overlapping and being added together.

not be accumulated into the blend sum. We can disable the depth test between objects in S by disabling writes to the depth buffer while rendering objects in S. Because depth writes are disabled, the depths of an object in S drawn with additive blending will not be written to the depth buffer; hence, this object will not obscure any later drawn object in S behind it due to the depth test. Note that we only disable depth writes while drawing the objects in S (the set of objects drawn with additive blending). Depth reads and the depth test are still enabled. This is so that non-blended geometry (which is drawn before blended geometry) will still obscure blended geometry behind it. For example, if you have a set of additively blended objects behind a wall, you will not see the blended objects because the solid wall obscures them. How to disable depth writes and, more generally, configure the depth test settings will be covered in the next chapter.

9.6 ALPHA CHANNELS

The example from §9.5.4 showed that source alpha components can be used in RGB blending to control transparency. The source color used in the blending equation comes from the pixel shader. As we saw in the last chapter, we return the diffuse material's alpha value as the alpha output of the pixel shader. Thus the alpha channel of the diffuse map is used to control transparency.

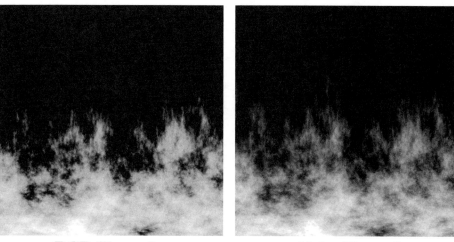

RGB Channels   **Alpha Channel**

Figure 9.6. An RGB image (left) and a grayscale image (right). The grayscale image will be inserted into the alpha channel of the texture.

```
float4 PS(VertexOut pin) : SV_Target
{
    . . .

    // Common to take alpha from diffuse material and texture.
    litColor.a = gMaterial.Diffuse.a * texColor.a;

return litColor;
}
```

You can generally add an alpha channel in any popular image editing software, such as Adobe Photoshop, and then save the image to a format that supports an alpha channel (e.g., 32-bit .bmp format or .dds format). However, here we show an alternative way to insert an alpha channel using the DXTex utility program that was discussed in the previous chapter.

We start by assuming we have two images—a color RGB image and a grayscale image that will be inserted into the alpha channel (see Figure 9.6).

Now, open the DXTex tool and open the *fire_rgb.bmp* file located in this chapter's sample folder on the web page. The fire texture is automatically loaded in as a 24-bit RGB texture (i.e., D3DFMT_R8G8B8), with 8-bits of red, 8-bits of green, and 8-bits of blue per pixel. We need to change the format to a format that supports an alpha channel, such as a 32-bit ARGB texture format D3DFMT_A8R8G8B8 or with a compressed format that supports alpha like D3DFMT_DXT5. Select **Format** from the menu and choose **Change Surface Format**. A dialog box pops up as shown in Figure 9.7, select the **DXT5** format and press **OK**.

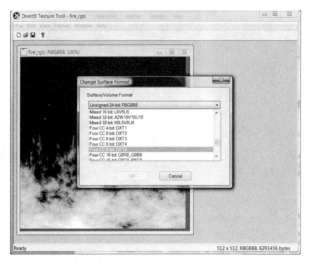

Figure 9.7. Changing the format of the texture.

This creates a compressed texture with an alpha channel. Our next task is to load data into the alpha channel. We will load the 8-bit grayscale map shown in Figure 9.6 into the alpha channel. Select **File** from the menu, and then choose **Open Onto Alpha Channel Of This Texture**, followed by **Format->Generate Mip Maps**. A dialog box will pop up asking you to locate the image file that contains the data you want to load into the alpha channel. Select the *fire_a.bmp* file that is located in this chapter's demo folder. Figure 9.8

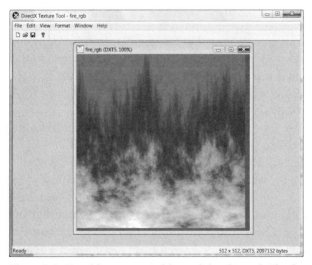

Figure 9.8. Resulting texture with an alpha channel. The fire texture is transparently blended against a blue background color.

shows the program after the alpha channel data has been inserted—the texture is transparently blended with a background color. The background color can be changed by choosing **View** from the menu bar, then **Change Background Color…**. You can also choose **View->Alpha Channel Only** to only view the alpha channel.

Now save the texture with the name of your choice (e.g., "fire.dds").

9.7 CLIPPING PIXELS

Sometimes we want to completely reject a source pixel from being further processed. This can be done with the intrinsic HLSL `clip(x)` function. This function can only be called in a pixel shader, and it discards the current pixel from further processing if `x` < `0`. This function is useful to render wire fence textures, for example, like the one shown in Figure 9.9. That is, it is useful for rendering pixels where a pixel is either completely opaque or completely transparent.

In the pixel shader, we grab the alpha component of the texture. If it is a small value close to 0, which indicates that the pixel is completely transparent, then we clip the pixel from further processing.

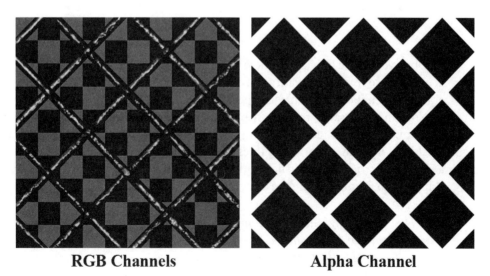

RGB Channels   **Alpha Channel**

Figure 9.9. A wire fence texture with its alpha channel. The pixels with black alpha values will be rejected by the `clip` function and not drawn; hence, only the wire fence remains. Essentially, the alpha channel is used to mask out the non-fence pixels from the texture.

```
float4 PS(VertexOut pin, uniform int gLightCount, uniform bool gUseTexure,
          uniform bool gAlphaClip, uniform bool gFogEnabled) : SV_Target
{
    // Interpolating normal can unnormalize it, so normalize it.
    pin.NormalW = normalize(pin.NormalW);

    // The toEye vector is used in lighting.
    float3 toEye = gEyePosW - pin.PosW;

    // Cache the distance to the eye from this surface point.
    float distToEye = length(toEye);

    // Normalize.
    toEye /= distToEye;

    // Default to multiplicative identity.
    float4 texColor = float4(1, 1, 1, 1);
    if(gUseTexure)
    {
      // Sample texture.
      texColor = gDiffuseMap.Sample(samAnisotropic, pin.Tex);

      if(gAlphaClip)
      {
        // Discard pixel if texture alpha < 0.1.  Note that
        // we do this test as soon as possible so that we can
        // potentially exit the shader early, thereby skipping the
        // rest of the shader code.
        clip(texColor.a - 0.1f);
      }
    }

    ...
```

Observe that we only clip if the uniform bool parameter gAlphaClip is true; this is because we might not want to invoke clip for some geometry, so we need to be able to switch it on/off by having specialized shaders.

Note that the same result can be obtained using blending, but this is more efficient. For one thing, no blending calculation needs to be done (blending can be disabled). Also, the draw order does not matter. And furthermore, by discarding a pixel early from the pixel shader, the remaining pixel shader instructions can be skipped (no point in doing the calculations for a discarded pixel).

Note: ▶ *Due to filtering, the alpha channel can get blurred a bit, so you should leave some buffer room when clipping pixels. For example, clip pixels with alpha values close to 0, but not necessarily exactly zero.*

Figure 9.10 shows a screenshot of the "Blend" demo. It renders semi-transparent water using transparency blending, and renders the wire fenced box using the clip

Figure 9.10. Screenshot of the "Blend" demo.

test. One other change worth mentioning is that, because we can now see through the box with the fence texture, we want to disable back face culling:

```
D3D11_RASTERIZER_DESC noCullDesc;
ZeroMemory(&noCullDesc, sizeof(D3D11_RASTERIZER_DESC));
noCullDesc.FillMode = D3D11_FILL_SOLID;
noCullDesc.CullMode = D3D11_CULL_NONE;
noCullDesc.FrontCounterClockwise = false;
noCullDesc.DepthClipEnable = true;

ID3D11RasterizerState* NoCullRS;
HR(device->CreateRasterizerState(&noCullDesc, &NoCullRS));

...

// Since the fence texture has transparent regions, we can
// see through it, and thus see the backsides of the triangles.
// Therefore, we don't want to backface culling in this case.
md3dImmediateContext->RSSetState(NoCullRS);
boxTech->GetPassByIndex(p)->Apply(0, md3dImmediateContext);
md3dImmediateContext->DrawIndexed(36, 0, 0);

// Restore default render state.
md3dImmediateContext->RSSetState(0);
```

9.8 FOG

To simulate certain types of weather conditions in our games, we need to be able to implement a fog effect; see Figure 9.11. In addition to the obvious purposes of fog, fog provides some fringe benefits. For example, it can mask distant rendering

Figure 9.11. **Screenshot of the "Blend" demo with fog enabled.**

artifacts and prevent *popping*. Popping refers to when an object that was previously behind the far plane all of a sudden comes in front of the frustum, due to camera movement, and thus becomes visible; so it seems to "pop" into the scene abruptly. By having a layer of fog in the distance, the popping is hidden. Note that if your scene takes place on a clear day, you may wish to still include a subtle amount of fog at far distances, because, even on clear days, distant objects such as mountains appear hazier and lose contrast as a function of depth, and we can use fog to simulate this *atmospheric perspective* phenomenon.

Our strategy for implementing fog works as follows: We specify a fog color, a fog start distance from the camera, and a fog range (i.e., the range from the fog start distance until the fog completely hides any objects). Then the color of a point on a triangle is a weighted average of its usual color and the fog color:

$$foggedColor = litColor + s\left(fogColor - litColor\right)$$
$$= \left(1 - s\right) \cdot litColor + s \cdot fogColor$$

The parameter *s* ranges from 0 to 1 and is a function of the distance between the camera position and the surface point. As the distance between a surface point and the eye increases, the point becomes more and more obscured by the fog. The parameter *s* is defined as follows:

$$s = \text{saturate}\left(\frac{\text{dist}\left(\mathbf{p}, \mathbf{E}\right) - fogStart}{fogRange}\right)$$

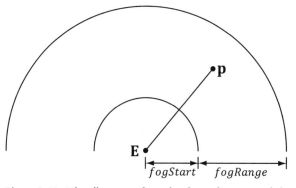

Figure 9.12. **The distance of a point from the eye, and the *fogStart* and *fogRange* parameters.**

where dist(**p**, **E**) is the distance between the surface point **p** and the camera position **E**. The `saturate` function clamps the argument to the range [0, 1]:

$$saturate(x) = \begin{cases} x, & 0 \le x \le 1 \\ 0, & x < 0 \\ 1, & x > 1 \end{cases}$$

Figure 9.13 shows a plot of s as a function of distance. We see that when dist(**p**, **E**) $\le fogStart$, $s = 0$ and the fogged color is given by:

$$foggedColor = litColor$$

In other words, the fog does not modify the color of vertices whose distance from the camera is less than *fogStart*. This makes sense based on the name "*fogStart*"; the fog does not start affecting the color until the distance from the camera is at least that of *fogStart*.

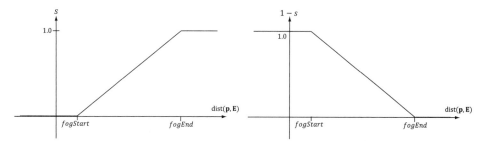

Figure 9.13. **(Left) A plot of s (the fog color weight) as a function of distance. (Right) A plot of $1 - s$ (the lit color weight) as a function of distance. As s increases, $(1 - s)$ decreases the same amount.**

Let *fogEnd* = *fogStart* + *fogRange*. When dist($\mathbf{p}$, $\mathbf{E}$) $\geq$ *fogEnd*, s = 1 and the fogged color is given by:

$$foggedColor = fogColor$$

In other words, the fog completely hides the surface point at distances greater than or equal to *fogEnd*—so all you see is the fog color.

When *fogStart* < dist($\mathbf{p}$, $\mathbf{E}$) < *fogEnd*, we see that s linearly ramps up from 0 to 1 as dist($\mathbf{p}$, $\mathbf{E}$) increases from *fogStart* to *fogEnd*. This means that as the distance increases, the fog color gets more and more weight while the original color gets less and less weight. This makes sense, of course, because as the distance increases, the fog obscures more and more of the surface point.

The following shader code shows how fog is implemented. We compute the distance and interpolation at the pixel level, after we have computed the lit color.

```
cbuffer cbPerFrame
{
    DirectionalLight gDirLights[3];
    float3 gEyePosW;

    // Allow application to change fog parameters once per frame.
    // For example, we may only use fog for certain times of day.
    float  gFogStart;
    float  gFogRange;
    float4 gFogColor;
};

struct VertexIn
{
    float3 PosL    : POSITION;
    float3 NormalL : NORMAL;
    float2 Tex     : TEXCOORD;
};

struct VertexOut
{
    float4 PosH    : SV_POSITION;
    float3 PosW    : POSITION;
    float3 NormalW : NORMAL;
    float2 Tex     : TEXCOORD;
};

VertexOut VS(VertexIn vin)
{
    VertexOut vout;

    // Transform to world space space.
    vout.PosW    = mul(float4(vin.PosL, 1.0f), gWorld).xyz;
    vout.NormalW = mul(vin.NormalL, (float3x3)gWorldInvTranspose);

    // Transform to homogeneous clip space.
    vout.PosH = mul(float4(vin.PosL, 1.0f), gWorldViewProj);
```

```
            // Output vertex attributes for interpolation across triangle.
            vout.Tex = mul(float4(vin.Tex, 0.0f, 1.0f), gTexTransform).xy;

            return vout;
        }

    float4 PS(VertexOut pin, uniform int gLightCount, uniform bool
            gUseTexure, uniform bool gAlphaClip, uniform bool gFogEnabled) : SV_Target
    {
            // Interpolating normal can unnormalize it, so normalize it.
            pin.NormalW = normalize(pin.NormalW);

            // The toEye vector is used in lighting.
            float3 toEye = gEyePosW - pin.PosW;

            // Cache the distance to the eye from this surface point.
            float distToEye = length(toEye);

            // Normalize.
            toEye /= distToEye;

            // Default to multiplicative identity.
            float4 texColor = float4(1, 1, 1, 1);
            if(gUseTexure)
            {
                // Sample texture.
                texColor = gDiffuseMap.Sample(samAnisotropic, pin.Tex);

                if(gAlphaClip)
                {
                    // Discard pixel if texture alpha < 0.1.  Note that
                    // we do this test as soon as possible so that we can
                    // potentially exit the shader early, thereby
                    // skipping the rest of the shader code.
                    clip(texColor.a - 0.1f);
                }
            }

            //
            // Lighting.
            //

            float4 litColor = texColor;
            if(gLightCount > 0)
            {
                // Start with a sum of zero.
                float4 ambient = float4(0.0f, 0.0f, 0.0f, 0.0f);
                float4 diffuse = float4(0.0f, 0.0f, 0.0f, 0.0f);
                float4 spec    = float4(0.0f, 0.0f, 0.0f, 0.0f);

                // Sum the light contribution from each light source.
                [unroll]
                for(int i = 0; i < gLightCount; ++i)
                {
                    float4 A, D, S;
                    ComputeDirectionalLight(gMaterial, gDirLights[i],
                        pin.NormalW, toEye,
                        A, D, S);
```

```
      ambient += A;
      diffuse += D;
      spec    += S;
   }

   // Modulate with late add.
   litColor = texColor*(ambient + diffuse) + spec;
}

//
// Fogging
//

if( gFogEnabled )
{
   float fogLerp = saturate((distToEye - gFogStart) / gFogRange);

   // Blend the fog color and the lit color.
   litColor = lerp(litColor, gFogColor, fogLerp);
}

// Common to take alpha from diffuse material and texture.
litColor.a = gMaterial.Diffuse.a * texColor.a;

return litColor;
}
```

 Observe that in the fog calculation, we use the `distToEye` *value, which we also computed to normalize the* `toEye` *vector. A less optimal implementation would have been to write:*

```
float3 toEye = normalize(gEyePosW - pin.PosW);
float distToEye = distance(gEyePosW, pin.PosW);
```

This essentially computes the length of the `toEye` *vector twice, once in the* `normalize` *function, and again in the* `distance` *function.*

The "Blend" demo supports three rendering modes, which can be toggled by pressing the '1', '2', and '3' keys. The first mode renders the scene using lighting only (see Figure 9.14). Lighting is a past topic, but it is useful to see what the scene looks like without textures. The second mode renders the scene with lighting and texturing (Figure 9.10). The third mode renders the scene with lighting, texturing, and fog (Figure 9.11). These rendering mode switches demonstrate how we use the uniform parameters in the effects framework to generate specialized shaders with functionality toggled on and off. The reader may wish to reexamine some of the assembly language outputs from our Basic. fx. It is also interesting to compare the frame rates between lighting, lighting and texturing, and lighting, texturing, and fog.

Figure 9.14. The "Blend" demo with only lighting enabled.

9.9 SUMMARY

1. Blending is a technique that allows us to blend (combine) the pixels we are currently rasterizing (so-called *source* pixels) with the pixels that were previously rasterized to the back buffer (so-called *destination* pixels). This technique enables us, among other things, to render semi-transparent objects such as water and glass.

2. The blending equation is:

$$\mathbf{C} = \mathbf{C}_{src} \otimes \mathbf{F}_{src} \boxplus \mathbf{C}_{dst} \otimes \mathbf{F}_{dst}$$
$$A = A_{src} F_{src} \boxplus A_{dst} F_{dst}$$

    Note that RGB components are blended independently to alpha components. The $\boxplus$ binary operator can be one of the operators defined by the `D3D11_BLEND_OP` enumerated type.

3. $\mathbf{F}_{src}, \mathbf{F}_{dst}, F_{src},$ and F_{dst} are called blend factors, and they provide a means for customizing the blending equation. They can be a member of the `D3D11_BLEND` enumerated type. For the alpha blending equation, blend factors ending with `_COLOR` are *not allowed*.

4. Source alpha information comes from the diffuse material. In our framework, the diffuse material is defined by a texture map, and the texture's alpha channel stores the alpha information.

5. Source pixels can be completely rejected from further processing using the intrinsic HLSL `clip(x)` function. This function can only be called in a pixel

shader, and it discards the current pixel from further processing if $x < 0$. Among other things, this function is useful for efficiently rendering pixels where a pixel is either completely opaque or completely transparent (it is used to reject completely transparent pixels—pixels with an alpha value near zero).

6. Use fog to model various weather effects and atmospheric perspective to hide distant rendering artifacts and to hide popping. In our linear fog model, we specify a fog color, a fog start distance from the camera, and a fog range. The color of a point on a triangle is a weighted average of its usual color and the fog color:

$$foggedColor = litColor + s\left(fogColor - litColor\right)$$
$$= \left(1 - s\right) \cdot litColor + s \cdot fogColor$$

The parameter s ranges from 0 to 1 and is a function of the distance between the camera position and the surface point. As the distance between a surface point and the eye increases, the point becomes more and more obscured by the fog.

9.10 EXERCISES

1. Modify the "Transparent Water" demo by using the following line before drawing the water:

```
md3dImmediateContext->OMSetBlendState(
    TransparentBS, blendFactors, 0xfffffffe);
```

This turns off the first bit which disables the first sample. Because we are not using multisampling (which is like using multisampling with one sample), this prevents the water pixels from being drawn.

2. Experiment with different blend operations and blend factor combinations.

3. Modify the "Blend" demo by drawing the water first. Explain the results.

4. Suppose $fogStart = 10$ and $fogRange = 200$. Compute $foggedColor$ for when

   (a) $dist(\mathbf{p}, \mathbf{E}) = 160$

   (b) $dist(\mathbf{p}, \mathbf{E}) = 110$

   (c) $dist(\mathbf{p}, \mathbf{E}) = 60$

   (d) $dist(\mathbf{p}, \mathbf{E}) = 30$

5. Verify the effect techniques with `gAlphaClip=false` which do not have a `discard` instruction, and the techniques with `gAlphaClip=true` which do, by looking at the generated shader assembly. The `discard` instruction corresponds to the HLSL `clip` instruction.

6. Modify the "Blend" demo by creating and applying a blend render state that disables color writes to the red and green color channels.

Chapter 10 STENCILING

The stencil buffer is an off-screen buffer we can use to achieve some special effects. The stencil buffer has the same resolution as the back buffer and depth buffer, such that the ijth pixel in the stencil buffer corresponds with the ijth pixel in the back buffer and depth buffer. Recall from §4.1.5 that when a stencil buffer is specified, it comes attached to the depth buffer. As the name suggests, the stencil buffer works as a stencil and allows us to block the rendering of certain pixel fragments to the back buffer.

For instance, when implementing a mirror, we need to reflect an object across the plane of the mirror; however, we only want to draw the reflection into the mirror. We can use the stencil buffer to block the rendering of the reflection unless it is being drawn into the mirror (see Figure 10.1).

The stencil buffer (and also the depth buffer) is controlled via the `ID3D11DepthStencilState` interface. Like blending, the interface offers a flexible and powerful set of capabilities. Learning to use the stencil buffer effectively comes best by studying an existing example application. Once you understand a few applications of the stencil buffer, you will have a better idea of how it can be used for your own specific needs.

Objectives:

1. To find out how to control the depth and stencil buffer settings with the `ID3D11DepthStencilState` interface.

371

Figure 10.1. (Left) The reflected skull shows properly in the mirror. The reflection does not show through the wall bricks because it fails the depth test in this area. However, looking behind the wall we are able to see the reflection, thus breaking the illusion (the reflection should only show up through the mirror). (Right) By using the stencil buffer, we can block the reflected skull from being rendered unless it is being drawn in the mirror.

2. To learn how to implement mirrors by using the stencil buffer to prevent reflections from being drawn to non-mirror surfaces.

3. To identify double blending and understand how the stencil buffer can prevent it.

4. To explain depth complexity and describe two ways the depth complexity of a scene can be measured.

10.1 DEPTH/STENCIL FORMATS AND CLEARING

Recalling that the depth/stencil buffer is a texture, it must be created with certain data formats. The formats used for depth/stencil buffering are as follows:

1. `DXGI_FORMAT_D32_FLOAT_S8X24_UINT`: Specifies a 32-bit floating-point depth buffer, with 8-bits (unsigned integer) reserved for the stencil buffer mapped to the [0, 255] range and 24-bits not used for padding.

2. `DXGI_FORMAT_D24_UNORM_S8_UINT`: Specifies an unsigned 24-bit depth buffer mapped to the [0, 1] range with 8-bits (unsigned integer) reserved for the stencil buffer mapped to the [0, 255] range.

In our `D3DApp` framework, when we create the depth buffer, we specify:

```
depthStencilDesc.Format = DXGI_FORMAT_D24_UNORM_S8_UINT;
```

Also, the stencil buffer should be reset to some value at the beginning of each frame. This is done with the following method (which also clears the depth buffer):

```
void ID3D11DeviceContext::ClearDepthStencilView(
    ID3D11DepthStencilView *pDepthStencilView,
    UINT ClearFlags, FLOAT Depth, UINT8 Stencil);
```

1. `pDepthStencilView`: Pointer to the view of the depth/stencil buffer we want to clear.

2. `ClearFlags`: Specify `D3D11_CLEAR_DEPTH` to clear the depth buffer only; specify `D3D11_CLEAR_STENCIL` to clear the stencil buffer only; specify `D3D11_CLEAR_DEPTH` | `D3D11_CLEAR_STENCIL` to clear both.

3. `Depth`: The float-value to set each pixel in the depth buffer to; it must be a floating point number x such that $0 \leq x \leq 1$.

4. `Stencil`: The integer-value to set each pixel of the stencil buffer to; it must be an integer n such that $0 \leq n \leq 255$.

We have already been calling this method every frame in our demos. For example:

```
void MirrorApp::DrawScene()
{
    md3dImmediateContext->ClearRenderTargetView(
      mRenderTargetView,
      reinterpret_cast<const float*>(&Colors::Black));

    md3dImmediateContext->ClearDepthStencilView(
      mDepthStencilView,
      D3D11_CLEAR_DEPTH|D3D11_CLEAR_STENCIL, 1.0f, 0);
}
```

10.2 THE STENCIL TEST

As previously stated, we can use the stencil buffer to block rendering to certain areas of the back buffer. The decision to block a particular pixel from being written is decided by the *stencil test*, which is given by the following:

```
if(StencilRef & StencilReadMask ⊴ Value & StencilReadMask)
    accept pixel
else
    reject pixel
```

The stencil test is performed as pixels get rasterized (i.e., during the output-merger stage), assuming stenciling is enabled, and takes two operands:

1. A left-hand-side (LHS) operand that is determined by ANDing an application-defined *stencil reference value* (`StencilRef`) with an application-defined *masking value* (`StencilReadMask`).

2. A right-hand-side (RHS) operand that is determined by ANDing the entry already in the stencil buffer of the particular pixel we are testing (`Value`) with an application-defined masking value (`StencilReadMask`).

Note that the `stencilReadMask` is the same for the LHS and the RHS. The stencil test then compares the LHS with the RHS as specified as an application-chosen *comparison function* ⊴, which returns a true or false value. We write the pixel to the back buffer if the test evaluates to true (assuming the depth test also passes). If the test evaluates to false, then we block the pixel from being written to the back buffer. And of course, if a pixel is rejected due to failing the stencil test, it is not written to the depth buffer either.

The ⊴ operator is any one of the functions defined in the `D3D11_COMPARISON_FUNC` enumerated type:

```
typedef enum D3D11_COMPARISON_FUNC
{
    D3D11_COMPARISON_NEVER = 1,
    D3D11_COMPARISON_LESS = 2,
    D3D11_COMPARISON_EQUAL = 3,
    D3D11_COMPARISON_LESS_EQUAL = 4,
    D3D11_COMPARISON_GREATER = 5,
    D3D11_COMPARISON_NOT_EQUAL = 6,
    D3D11_COMPARISON_GREATER_EQUAL = 7,
    D3D11_COMPARISON_ALWAYS = 8,
} D3D11_COMPARISON_FUNC;
```

1. `D3D11_COMPARISON_NEVER`: The function always returns false.

2. `D3D11_COMPARISON_LESS`: Replace ⊴ with the < operator.

3. `D3D11_COMPARISON_EQUAL`: Replace ⊴ with the == operator.

4. `D3D11_COMPARISON_LESS_EQUAL`: Replace ⊴ with the ≤ operator.

5. `D3D11_COMPARISON_GREATER`: Replace ⊴ with the > operator.

6. `D3D11_COMPARISON_NOT_EQUAL`: Replace ⊴ with the ! = operator.

7. `D3D11_COMPARISON_GREATER_EQUAL`: Replace ⊴ with the ≥ operator.

8. `D3D11_COMPARISON_ALWAYS`: The function always returns true.

10.3 THE DEPTH/STENCIL STATE BLOCK

The first step to creating an `ID3D11DepthStencilState` interface is to fill out a `D3D11_DEPTH_STENCIL_DESC` instance:

```
typedef struct D3D11_DEPTH_STENCIL_DESC {
    BOOL DepthEnable; // Default True

    // Default: D3D11_DEPTH_WRITE_MASK_ALL
    D3D11_DEPTH_WRITE_MASK DepthWriteMask;

    // Default: D3D11_COMPARISON_LESS
    D3D11_COMPARISON_FUNC DepthFunc;
```

```
      BOOL StencilEnable;              // Default: False
      UINT8 StencilReadMask;           // Default: 0xff
      UINT8 StencilWriteMask;          // Default: 0xff
      D3D11_DEPTH_STENCILOP_DESC FrontFace;
      D3D11_DEPTH_STENCILOP_DESC BackFace;
} D3D11_DEPTH_STENCIL_DESC;
```

10.3.1 Depth Settings

1. `DepthEnable`: Specify true to enable the depth buffering; specify false to disable it. When depth testing is disabled, the draw order matters, and a pixel fragment will be drawn even if it is behind an occluding object (review §4.1.5). If depth buffering is disabled, elements in the depth buffer are *not* updated either, regardless of the `DepthWriteMask` setting.

2. `DepthWriteMask`: This can be either `D3D11_DEPTH_WRITE_MASK_ZERO` or `D3D11_DEPTH_WRITE_MASK_ALL`, but not both. Assuming `DepthEnable` is set to true, `D3D11_DEPTH_WRITE_MASK_ZERO` disables writes to the depth buffer, but depth testing will still occur. `D3D11_DEPTH_WRITE_MASK_ALL` enables writes to the depth buffer; new depths will be written provided the depth and stencil test both pass. The ability to control depth reads and writes becomes necessary for implementing certain special effects.

3. `DepthFunc`: Specify one of the members of the `D3D11_COMPARISON_FUNC` enumerated type to define the depth test comparison function. Usually this is always `D3D11_COMPARISON_LESS` so that the usual depth test is performed, as described in §4.1.5. That is, a pixel fragment is accepted provided its depth value is less than the depth of the previous pixel written to the back buffer. But as you can see, Direct3D allows you to customize the depth test if necessary.

10.3.2 Stencil Settings

1. `StencilEnable`: Specify true to enable the stencil test; specify false to disable it.

2. `StencilReadMask`: The `StencilReadMask` used in the stencil test:

    ```
    if(StencilRef & StencilReadMask ⊴ Value & StencilReadMask)
        accept pixel
    else
        reject pixel
    ```

    The default does not mask any bits:

    ```
    #define D3D11_DEFAULT_STENCIL_READ_MASK      (0xff)
    ```

3. `StencilWriteMask`: When the stencil buffer is being updated, we can mask off certain bits from being written to with the write mask. For example, if you wanted to prevent the top 4 bits from being written to, you could use the write mask of 0x0f. The default value does not mask any bits:

    ```
    #define D3D11_DEFAULT_STENCIL_WRITE_MASK      (0xff)
    ```

4. **FrontFace**: A filled out `D3D11_DEPTH_STENCILOP_DESC` structure indicating how the stencil buffer works for front facing triangles.

5. **BackFace**: A filled out `D3D11_DEPTH_STENCILOP_DESC` structure indicating how the stencil buffer works for back facing triangles.

```
typedef struct D3D11_DEPTH_STENCILOP_DESC {

    D3D11_STENCIL_OP StencilFailOp;        // Default: D3D11_STENCIL_OP_KEEP
    D3D11_STENCIL_OP StencilDepthFailOp;   // Default: D3D11_STENCIL_OP_KEEP
    D3D11_STENCIL_OP StencilPassOp;        // Default: D3D11_STENCIL_OP_KEEP
    D3D11_COMPARISON_FUNC StencilFunc;     // Default: D3D11_COMPARISON_ALWAYS
} D3D11_DEPTH_STENCILOP_DESC;
```

1. **StencilFailOp**: A member of the `D3D11_STENCIL_OP` enumerated type describing how the stencil buffer should be updated when the stencil test fails for a pixel fragment.

2. **StencilDepthFailOp**: A member of the `D3D11_STENCIL_OP` enumerated type describing how the stencil buffer should be updated when the stencil test passes but the depth test fails for a pixel fragment.

3. **StencilPassOp**: A member of the `D3D11_STENCIL_OP` enumerated type describing how the stencil buffer should be updated when the stencil test and depth test both pass for a pixel fragment.

4. **StencilFunc**: A member of the `D3D11_COMPARISON_FUNC` enumerated type to define the stencil test comparison function.

```
typedef enum D3D11_STENCIL_OP {
    D3D11_STENCIL_OP_KEEP       = 1,
    D3D11_STENCIL_OP_ZERO       = 2,
    D3D11_STENCIL_OP_REPLACE    = 3,
    D3D11_STENCIL_OP_INCR_SAT   = 4,
    D3D11_STENCIL_OP_DECR_SAT   = 5,
    D3D11_STENCIL_OP_INVERT     = 6,
    D3D11_STENCIL_OP_INCR       = 7,
    D3D11_STENCIL_OP_DECR       = 8
} D3D11_STENCIL_OP;
```

1. **D3D11_STENCIL_OP_KEEP**: Specifies to not change the stencil buffer; that is, keep the value currently there.

2. **D3D11_STENCIL_OP_ZERO**: Specifies to set the stencil buffer entry to zero.

3. **D3D11_STENCIL_OP_REPLACE**: Specifies to replace the stencil buffer entry with the stencil-reference value (`StencilRef`) used in the stencil test. Note that the `StencilRef` value is set when we bind the depth/stencil state block to the rendering pipeline (§10.3.3).

4. **D3D11_STENCIL_OP_INCR_SAT**: Specifies to increment the stencil buffer entry. If the incremented value exceeds the maximum value (e.g., 255 for an 8-bit stencil buffer), then we clamp the entry to that maximum.

5. **D3D11_STENCIL_OP_DECR_SAT**: Specifies to decrement the stencil buffer entry. If the decremented value is less than zero, then we clamp the entry to zero.

6. **D3D11_STENCIL_OP_INVERT**: Specifies to invert the bits of the stencil buffer entry.

7. **D3D11_STENCIL_OP_INCR**: Specifies to increment the stencil buffer entry. If the incremented value exceeds the maximum value (e.g., 255 for an 8-bit stencil buffer), then we wrap to 0.

8. **D3D11_STENCIL_OP_DECR**: Specifies to decrement the stencil buffer entry. If the decremented value is less than zero, then we wrap to the maximum allowed value.

> **Note:** *Observe that the stenciling behavior for front facing and back facing triangles can be different. The* **BackFace** *settings are irrelevant in the case that we do not render back facing polygons due to back face culling. However, sometimes we do need to render back facing polygons for certain graphics algorithms, or for transparent geometry (like the wire fence box, where we could see through the box to see the back sides). In these cases, the* **BackFace** *settings are relevant.*

10.3.3 Creating and Binding a Depth/Stencil State

After we have filled out a **D3D11_DEPTH_STENCIL_DESC** structure, we can obtain a pointer to an **ID3D11DepthStencilState** interface with the following method:

```
HRESULT ID3D11Device::CreateDepthStencilState(
    const D3D11_DEPTH_STENCIL_DESC *pDepthStencilDesc,
    ID3D11DepthStencilState **ppDepthStencilState);
```

1. **pDepthStencilDesc**: Pointer to a filled out **D3D11_DEPTH_STENCIL_DESC** structure describing the depth/stencil state block we want to create.

2. **ppDepthStencilState**: Returns a pointer to the created **ID3D11DepthStencilState** interface.

Once an **ID3D11DepthStencilState** interface is created, we bind it to the output merger stage of the pipeline with the following method:

```
void ID3D11DeviceContext::OMSetDepthStencilState(
    ID3D11DepthStencilState *pDepthStencilState,
    UINT StencilRef);
```

1. **pDepthStencilState**: Pointer to the depth/stencil state block to set.

2. **StencilRef**: The 32-bit stencil reference value to use in the stencil test.

As with the other state groups, a default depth/stencil state exists (basically the usual depth test with stenciling disabled). The default depth/stencil state can be restored by passing null for the first parameter of **OMSetDepthStencilState**:

```
// restore default
md3dImmediateContext->OMSetDepthStencilState(0, 0);
```

10.3.4 Depth/Stencil States in Effect Files

A depth/stencil state can also be directly defined and set in an effect file:

```
DepthStencilState DSS
{
    DepthEnable     = true;
    DepthWriteMask = Zero;

    StencilEnable    = true;
    StencilReadMask  = 0xff;
    StencilWriteMask = 0xff;

    FrontFaceStencilFunc = Always;
    FrontFaceStencilPass = Incr;
    FrontFaceStencilFail = Keep;

    BackFaceStencilFunc = Always;
    BackFaceStencilPass = Incr;
    BackFaceStencilFail = Keep;
};

...

technique11 Tech
{
    pass P0
    {
      SetVertexShader(CompileShader(vs_5_0, VS()));
      SetGeometryShader(NULL);
      SetPixelShader(CompileShader(ps_5_0, PS()));

      SetDepthStencilState(DSS, 0);
    }
}
```

The values you assign to the depth/stencil state object are like those you assign to the C++ structure, except without the prefix. For example, instead of specifying D3D11_STENCIL_OP_INCR we just specify INCR in the effect code. Incidentally, the state values we specify are not case sensitive, so, for example, INCR is equivalent to Incr.

10.4 IMPLEMENTING PLANAR MIRRORS

Many surfaces in nature serve as mirrors and allow us to see the reflections of objects. This section describes how we can simulate mirrors for our 3D applications. Note that for simplicity, we reduce the task of implementing mirrors to planar surfaces only. For instance, a shiny car can display a reflection; however, a car's body is smooth, round, and not planar. Instead, we render reflections such as those that are displayed in a shiny marble floor or those that are displayed in a mirror hanging on a wall—in other words, mirrors that lie on a plane.

Implementing mirrors programmatically requires us to solve two problems. First, we must learn how to reflect an object about an arbitrary plane so that we can draw the reflection correctly. Second, we must only display the reflection in a mirror, that is, we must somehow "mark" a surface as a mirror and then, as we are rendering, only draw the reflected object if it is in a mirror. Refer back to Figure 10.1, which first introduced this concept.

The first problem is easily solved with some analytical geometry, and is discussed in Appendix C. The second problem can be solved using the stencil buffer.

10.4.1 Mirror Overview

Note: *When we draw the reflection, we also need to reflect the light source across the mirror plane. Otherwise, the lighting in the reflection would not be accurate.*

Figure 10.2 shows that to draw a reflection of an object, we just need to reflect it over the mirror plane. However, this introduces the problem shown in Figure 10.1. Namely, the reflection of the object (the skull in this case) is just another object in our scene, and if nothing is occluding it, then the eye will see it. However, the reflection should only be seen through the mirror. We can solve this problem using the stencil buffer because the stencil buffer allows us to block rendering to certain areas on the back buffer. Thus we can use the stencil buffer to block the rendering of the reflected skull if it is not being rendered into the mirror. The following outlines the steps to accomplish this:

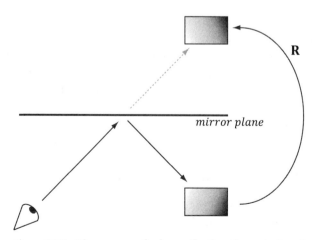

Figure 10.2. **The eye sees the box reflection through the mirror. To simulate this, we reflect the box across the mirror plane and render the reflected box as usual.**

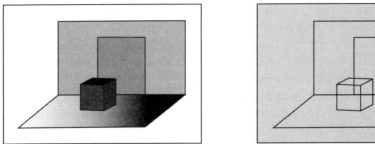

| **Back buffer** | **Stencil buffer** |

Figure 10.3. The floor, walls, and skull to the back buffer and the stencil buffer cleared to 0 (denoted by light gray color). The black outlines drawn on the stencil buffer illustrate the relationship between the back buffer pixels and the stencil buffer pixels—they do not indicate any data drawn on the stencil buffer.

1. Render the floor, walls, and skull to the back buffer as normal (but not the mirror). Note that this step does not modify the stencil buffer.

2. Clear the stencil buffer to 0. Figure 10.3 shows the back buffer and stencil buffer at this point (where we substitute a box for the skull to make the drawing simpler).

3. Render the mirror only to the stencil buffer. We can disable color writes to the back buffer by creating a blend state that sets

   `D3D11_RENDER_TARGET_BLEND_DESC::RenderTargetWriteMask = 0;`

   and we can disable writes to the depth buffer by setting

   `D3D11_DEPTH_STENCIL_DESC::DepthWriteMask = D3D11_DEPTH_WRITE_MASK_ZERO;`

   When rendering the mirror to the stencil buffer, we set the stencil test to always succeed (`D3D11_COMPARISON_ALWAYS`) and specify that the stencil buffer entry should be replaced (`D3D11_STENCIL_OP_REPLACE`) with 1 (`StencilRef`) if the test passes. If the depth test fails, we specify `D3D11_STENCIL_OP_KEEP` so that the stencil buffer is not changed if the depth test fails (this can happen, for example, if the skull obscures part of the mirror). Because we are only rendering the mirror to the stencil buffer, it follows that all the pixels in the stencil buffer will be 0 except for the pixels that correspond to the visible part of the mirror—they will have a 1. Figure 10.4 shows the updated stencil buffer. Essentially, we are marking the visible pixels of the mirror in the stencil buffer.

Note: *It is important to draw the mirror to the stencil buffer after we have drawn the skull so that pixels of the mirror occluded by the skull fail the depth test, and thus do not modify the stencil buffer. We do not want to turn on parts of the stencil buffer that are occluded; otherwise the reflection will show through the skull.*

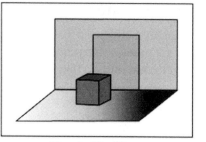 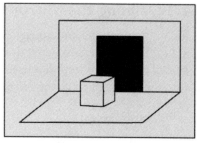

Back Buffer   **Stencil Buffer**

Figure 10.4. Rendering the mirror to the stencil buffer, essentially marking the pixels in the stencil buffer that correspond to the visible parts of the mirror. The solid black area on the stencil buffer denotes stencil entries set to 1. Note that the area on the stencil buffer occluded by the box does not get set to 1 because it fails the depth test (the box is in front of that part of the mirror).

4. Now we render the reflected skull to the back buffer and stencil buffer. But recall that we only will render to the back buffer if the stencil test passes. This time, we set the stencil test to only succeed if the value in the stencil buffer equals 1; this is done using a `StencilRef` of 1, and the stencil operator `D3D11_COMPARISON_EQUAL`. In this way, the reflected skull will only be rendered to areas that have a 1 in their corresponding stencil buffer entry. Because the areas in the stencil buffer that correspond to the visible parts of the mirror are the only entries that have a 1, it follows that the reflected skull will only be rendered into the visible parts of the mirror.

5. Finally, we render the mirror to the back buffer as normal. However, in order for the skull reflection to show through (which lies behind the mirror), we need to render the mirror with transparency blending. If we did not render the mirror with transparency, the mirror would simply occlude the reflection because its depth is less than that of the reflection. To implement this, we simply need to define a new material instance for the mirror; we set the alpha channel of the diffuse component to 0.5 to make the mirror 50% opaque, and we render the mirror with the transparency blend state as described in the last chapter (§9.5.4).

```
mMirrorMat.Ambient  = XMFLOAT4(0.5f, 0.5f, 0.5f, 1.0f);
mMirrorMat.Diffuse  = XMFLOAT4(1.0f, 1.0f, 1.0f, 0.5f);
mMirrorMat.Specular = XMFLOAT4(0.4f, 0.4f, 0.4f, 16.0f);
```

These settings give the following blending equation:

$$C = 0.5 \cdot C_{src} + 0.5 \cdot C_{dst}$$

Assuming we have laid down the reflected skull pixels to the back buffer, we see 50% of the color comes from the mirror (source) and 50% of the color comes from the skull (destination).

10.4.2 Defining the Mirror Depth/Stencil States

To implement the previously described algorithm, we need two depth/stencil states. The first is used when drawing the mirror to mark the mirror pixels on the stencil buffer. The second is used to draw the reflected skull so that it is only drawn into the visible parts of the mirror.

```
//
// MarkMirrorDSS
//

D3D11_DEPTH_STENCIL_DESC mirrorDesc;
mirrorDesc.DepthEnable      = true;
mirrorDesc.DepthWriteMask   = D3D11_DEPTH_WRITE_MASK_ZERO;
mirrorDesc.DepthFunc        = D3D11_COMPARISON_LESS;
mirrorDesc.StencilEnable    = true;
mirrorDesc.StencilReadMask  = 0xff;
mirrorDesc.StencilWriteMask = 0xff;

mirrorDesc.FrontFace.StencilFailOp      = D3D11_STENCIL_OP_KEEP;
mirrorDesc.FrontFace.StencilDepthFailOp = D3D11_STENCIL_OP_KEEP;
mirrorDesc.FrontFace.StencilPassOp      = D3D11_STENCIL_OP_REPLACE;
mirrorDesc.FrontFace.StencilFunc        = D3D11_COMPARISON_ALWAYS;

// We are not rendering backfacing polygons, so these settings do not matter.
mirrorDesc.BackFace.StencilFailOp       = D3D11_STENCIL_OP_KEEP;
mirrorDesc.BackFace.StencilDepthFailOp  = D3D11_STENCIL_OP_KEEP;
mirrorDesc.BackFace.StencilPassOp       = D3D11_STENCIL_OP_REPLACE;
mirrorDesc.BackFace.StencilFunc         = D3D11_COMPARISON_ALWAYS;

ID3D11DepthStencilState* MarkMirrorDSS;
HR(device->CreateDepthStencilState(&mirrorDesc, &MarkMirrorDSS));

//
// DrawReflectionDSS
//

D3D11_DEPTH_STENCIL_DESC drawReflectionDesc;
drawReflectionDesc.DepthEnable      = true;
drawReflectionDesc.DepthWriteMask   = D3D11_DEPTH_WRITE_MASK_ALL;
drawReflectionDesc.DepthFunc        = D3D11_COMPARISON_LESS;
drawReflectionDesc.StencilEnable    = true;
drawReflectionDesc.StencilReadMask  = 0xff;
drawReflectionDesc.StencilWriteMask = 0xff;

drawReflectionDesc.FrontFace.StencilFailOp      = D3D11_STENCIL_OP_KEEP;
drawReflectionDesc.FrontFace.StencilDepthFailOp = D3D11_STENCIL_OP_KEEP;
drawReflectionDesc.FrontFace.StencilPassOp      = D3D11_STENCIL_OP_KEEP;
drawReflectionDesc.FrontFace.StencilFunc        = D3D11_COMPARISON_EQUAL;

// We are not rendering backfacing polygons, so these settings do not matter.
drawReflectionDesc.BackFace.StencilFailOp      = D3D11_STENCIL_OP_KEEP;
drawReflectionDesc.BackFace.StencilDepthFailOp = D3D11_STENCIL_OP_KEEP;
drawReflectionDesc.BackFace.StencilPassOp = D3D11_STENCIL_OP_KEEP;
drawReflectionDesc.BackFace.StencilFunc   = D3D11_COMPARISON_EQUAL;

ID3D11DepthStencilState* DrawReflectionDSS;
HR(device->CreateDepthStencilState(&drawReflectionDesc, &DrawReflectionDSS));
```

10.4.3 Drawing the Scene

The following code outlines our draw method. We have omitted irrelevant details, such as setting constant buffer values, for brevity and clarity (see the example code for the full details).

```
//
// Draw the floor, walls and skull to the back buffer as normal.
//
...

//
// Draw the mirror to the stencil buffer.
// Here we set the stencil value of visible pixels of the mirror
// to 1, thereby marking "mirror pixels."
//
// Note that we have to draw the mirror last because we need to
// render the skull into the depth buffer first so that when we
// render the mirror, portions of the mirror that are occluded
// by the skull fail the depth test and do not get rendered
// into the stencil buffer.  We do not want to set pixels on
// the stencil buffer that are occluded.  Otherwise the reflection
// will show through the skull, too.
//

// Do not write to render target.
md3dImmediateContext->OMSetBlendState(
    RenderStates::NoRenderTargetWritesBS, blendFactor, 0xffffffff);

// Render visible mirror pixels to stencil buffer.
// Do not write mirror depth to depth buffer at this point, otherwise
// it will occlude the reflection.
md3dImmediateContext->OMSetDepthStencilState(
    RenderStates::MarkMirrorDSS, 1);

pass->Apply(0, md3dImmediateContext);

// Draw mirror.
md3dImmediateContext->Draw(6, 24);

//
// Draw the reflected skull.
//

// Build reflection matrix to reflect the skull.
XMVECTOR mirrorPlane = XMVectorSet(0.0f, 0.0f, 1.0f, 0.0f); // xy plane
XMMATRIX R = XMMatrixReflect(mirrorPlane);
XMMATRIX world = XMLoadFloat4x4(&mSkullWorld) * R;
...
// Reflect the light source as well.
// Cache the old light directions, and reflect the light directions.
XMFLOAT3 oldLightDirections[3];
for(int i = 0; i < 3; ++i)
```

```
    {
        oldLightDirections[i] = mDirLights[i].Direction;

        XMVECTOR lightDir = XMLoadFloat3(&mDirLights[i].Direction);
        XMVECTOR reflectedLightDir = XMVector3TransformNormal(lightDir, R);
        XMStoreFloat3(&mDirLights[i].Direction, reflectedLightDir);
    }

Effects::BasicFX->SetDirLights(mDirLights);

// Reflection changes winding order, so cull clockwise
// triangles instead (see §10.4.4).
md3dImmediateContext->RSSetState(RenderStates::CullClockwiseRS);

// Only render reflection to pixels with a stencil value equal to 1. Only
// visible mirror pixels have a stencil value of 1, hence the skull
// will only be rendered into the mirror.
md3dImmediateContext->OMSetDepthStencilState(
    RenderStates::DrawReflectionDSS, 1);
pass->Apply(0, md3dImmediateContext);
md3dImmediateContext->DrawIndexed(mSkullIndexCount, 0, 0);

// Restore default states.
md3dImmediateContext->RSSetState(0);
md3dImmediateContext->OMSetDepthStencilState(0, 0);


// Restore light directions.
for(int i = 0; i < 3; ++i)
{
    mDirLights[i].Direction = oldLightDirections[i];
}

Effects::BasicFX->SetDirLights(mDirLights);

//
// Draw the mirror to the back buffer as usual but with transparency
// blending so the reflection shows through.
//

// Mirror
md3dImmediateContext->OMSetBlendState(
    RenderStates::TransparentBS, blendFactor, 0xffffffff);
pass->Apply(0, md3dImmediateContext);
md3dImmediateContext->Draw(6, 24);
```

10.4.4 Winding Order and Reflections

When a triangle is reflected across a plane, its winding order does not reverse, and thus, its face normal does not reverse. Hence, outward facing normals become inward facing normals (see Figure 10.5), after reflection. To correct this, we tell Direct3D to interpret triangles with a counterclockwise winding order as front facing and triangles with a clockwise winding order as back facing (this is the

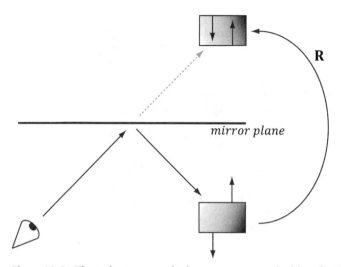

Figure 10.5. The polygon normals do not get reversed with reflection, which makes them inward facing after reflection.

opposite of our usual convention—§5.10.2). This effectively reflects the normal directions so that they are outward facing after reflection. We reverse the winding order convention by setting the following rasterizer state:

```
// Note: Define such that we still cull backfaces by making front faces CCW.
// If we did not cull backfaces, then we have to worry about the BackFace
// property in the D3D11_DEPTH_STENCIL_DESC.
D3D11_RASTERIZER_DESC cullClockwiseDesc;
ZeroMemory(&cullClockwiseDesc, sizeof(D3D11_RASTERIZER_DESC));
cullClockwiseDesc.FillMode = D3D11_FILL_SOLID;
cullClockwiseDesc.CullMode = D3D11_CULL_BACK;
cullClockwiseDesc.FrontCounterClockwise = true;
cullClockwiseDesc.DepthClipEnable = true;

ID3D11RasterizerState* CullClockwiseRS;
HR(device->CreateRasterizerState(&cullClockwiseDesc, &CullClockwiseRS));
```

10.5 IMPLEMENTING PLANAR SHADOWS

Portions of this section appeared in the book by Frank D. Luna, *Introduction to 3D Game Programming with DirectX 9.0c: A Shader Approach*, 2006: Jones and Bartlett Learning, Burlington, MA. www.jblearning.com. Reprinted with permission.

Shadows aid in our perception of where light is being emitted in a scene and ultimately makes the scene more realistic. In this section, we will show how to implement planar shadows; that is, shadows that lie on a plane (see Figure 10.6).

Figure 10.6. The main light source casts a planar shadow in the "Mirror" demo.

To implement planar shadows we must first find the shadow an object casts to a plane and model it geometrically so that we can render it. This can easily be done with some 3D math. We then render the triangles that describe the shadow with a black material at 50% transparency. Rendering the shadow like this can introduce some rendering artifacts called "double blending," which we explain in a few sections; we utilize the stencil buffer to prevent double blending from occurring.

10.5.1 Parallel Light Shadows

Figure 10.7 shows the shadow an object casts with respect to a parallel light source. Given a parallel light source with direction $\mathbf{L}$, the light ray that passes through a vertex $\mathbf{P}$ is given by $\mathbf{r}(t) = \mathbf{p} + t\mathbf{L}$. The intersection of the ray $\mathbf{r}(t)$ with the shadow plane $(\mathbf{n}, d)$ gives s. (The reader can read more about rays and planes in Appendix C.) The set of intersection points found by shooting a ray through each of the object's vertices with the plane defines the projected geometry of the shadow. For a vertex $\mathbf{p}$, its shadow projection is given by

$$\mathbf{s} = \mathbf{r}(t_s) = \mathbf{p} - \frac{\mathbf{n} \cdot \mathbf{p} + d}{\mathbf{n} \cdot \mathbf{L}} \mathbf{L}$$

(eq. 10.1)

The details of the ray/plane intersection test are given in Appendix C.

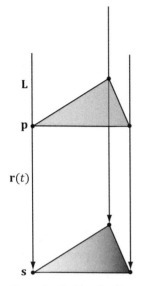

Figure 10.7. The shadow cast with respect to a parallel light source.

Equation 10.1 can be written in terms of matrices.

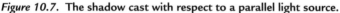

$$s' = \begin{bmatrix} p_x & p_y & p_z & 1 \end{bmatrix} \begin{bmatrix} \mathbf{n} \cdot \mathbf{L} - L_x n_x & -L_y n_x & -L_z n_x & 0 \\ -L_x n_y & \mathbf{n} \cdot \mathbf{L} - L_y n_y & -L_z n_y & 0 \\ -L_x n_z & -L_y n_z & \mathbf{n} \cdot \mathbf{L} - L_z n_z & 0 \\ -L_x d & -L_y d & -L_z d & \mathbf{n} \cdot \mathbf{L} \end{bmatrix}$$

We call the preceding 4×4 matrix the directional shadow matrix and denote it by S_{dir}. To see how this matrix is equivalent to Equation 10.1, we just need to perform the multiplication. First, however, observe that this equation modifies the w-component so that $s_w = \mathbf{n} \cdot \mathbf{L}$. Thus, when the perspective divide (§5.6.3.4) takes place, each coordinate of **s** will be divided by $\mathbf{n} \cdot \mathbf{L}$; this is how we get the division by $\mathbf{n} \cdot \mathbf{L}$ in Equation 10.1 using matrices. Now doing the matrix multiplication to obtain the ith coordinate s_i' for $i \in \{1, 2, 3\}$, followed by the perspective divide we obtain:

$$s_i' = \frac{(\mathbf{n} \cdot \mathbf{L}) p_i - L_i n_x p_x - L_i n_y p_y - L_i n_z p_z - L_i d}{\mathbf{n} \cdot \mathbf{L}}$$

$$= \frac{(\mathbf{n} \cdot \mathbf{L}) p_i - (\mathbf{n} \cdot \mathbf{p} + d) L_i}{\mathbf{n} \cdot \mathbf{L}}$$

$$= p_i - \frac{\mathbf{n} \cdot \mathbf{p} + d}{\mathbf{n} \cdot \mathbf{L}} L_i$$

This is exactly the ith coordinate of s in Equation 10.1, so $\mathbf{s} = \mathbf{s}'$.

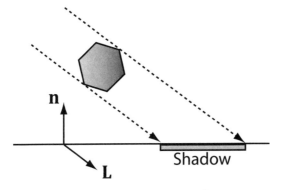

Figure 10.8. A situation where $\mathbf{n} \cdot \mathbf{L} < 0$.

To use the shadow matrix, we combine it with our world matrix. However, after the world transform, the geometry has not really been projected on to the shadow plane yet because the perspective divide has not occurred yet. A problem arises if $s_w = \mathbf{n} \cdot \mathbf{L} < 0$ because this makes the w-coordinate negative. Usually in the perspective projection process we copy the z-coordinate into the w-coordinate, and a negative w-coordinate would mean the point is not in the view volume and thus is clipped away (clipping is done in homogeneous space before the divide). This is a problem for planar shadows because we are now using the w-coordinate to implement shadows, in addition to the perspective divide. Figure 10.8 shows a valid situation where $\mathbf{n} \cdot \mathbf{L} < 0$, but the shadow will not show up.

To fix this, instead of using the light ray direction $\mathbf{L}$, we should use the vector towards the infinitely far away light source $\tilde{\mathbf{L}} = -\mathbf{L}$. Observe that $\mathbf{r}(t) = \mathbf{p} + t\mathbf{L}$ and $\mathbf{r}(t) = \mathbf{p} + t\tilde{\mathbf{L}}$ define the same 3D line, and the intersection point between the line and the plane will be the same (the intersection parameter t_s will be different to compensate for the sign difference between $\tilde{\mathbf{L}}$ and $\mathbf{L}$). So using $\tilde{\mathbf{L}} = -\mathbf{L}$ gives us the same answer, but with $\mathbf{n} \cdot \mathbf{L} > 0$, which avoids the negative w-coordinate.

10.5.2 Point Light Shadows

Figure 10.9 shows the shadow an object casts with respect to a point light source whose position is described by the point $\mathbf{L}$. The light ray from a point light through any vertex $\mathbf{p}$ is given by $\mathbf{r}(t) = \mathbf{p} + t(\mathbf{p} - \mathbf{L})$. The intersection of the ray $\mathbf{r}(t)$ with the shadow plane $(\mathbf{n}, d)$ gives $\mathbf{s}$. The set of intersection points found by shooting a ray through each of the object's vertices with the plane defines the projected geometry of the shadow. For a vertex $\mathbf{p}$, its shadow projection is given by

$$\mathbf{s} = \mathbf{r}(t_s) = \mathbf{p} - \frac{\mathbf{n} \cdot \mathbf{p} + d}{\mathbf{n} \cdot (\mathbf{p} - \mathbf{L})}(\mathbf{p} - \mathbf{L})$$

(eq. 10.2)

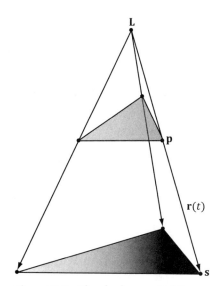

Figure 10.9. The shadow cast with respect to a point light source.

Equation 10.2 can also be written by a matrix equation:

$$
\mathbf{S}_{point} =
\begin{bmatrix}
\mathbf{n}\cdot\mathbf{L}+d-L_x n_x & -L_y n_x & -L_z n_x & -n_x \\
-L_x n_y & \mathbf{n}\cdot\mathbf{L}+d-L_y n_y & -L_z n_y & -n_y \\
-L_x n_z & -L_y n_z & \mathbf{n}\cdot\mathbf{L}+d-L_z n_z & -n_z \\
-L_x d & -L_y d & -L_z d & \mathbf{n}\cdot\mathbf{L}
\end{bmatrix}
$$

To see how this matrix is equivalent to Equation 10.2, we just need to perform the multiplication the same way we did in the previous section. Note that the last column has no zeros and gives:

$$
\begin{aligned}
s_w &= -p_x n_x - p_y n_y - p_z n_z + \mathbf{n}\cdot\mathbf{L} \\
&= -\mathbf{p}\cdot\mathbf{n} + \mathbf{n}\cdot\mathbf{L} \\
&= -\mathbf{n}\cdot(\mathbf{p}-\mathbf{L})
\end{aligned}
$$

This is the negative of the denominator in Equation 10.2, but we can negate the denominator if we also negate the numerator.

Note: *Notice that* **L** *serves different purposes for point and parallel lights. For point lights we use* **L** *to define the position of the point light. For parallel lights we use* **L** *to define the direction towards the infinitely far away light source (i.e., the opposite direction the parallel light rays travel).*

10.5.3 General Shadow Matrix

Using homogeneous coordinates, it is possible to create a general shadow matrix that works for both point and directional lights.

1. If $L_W = 0$ then $\mathbf{L}$ describes the direction towards the infinitely far away light source (i.e., the opposite direction the parallel light rays travel).

2. If $L_W = 1$ then $\mathbf{L}$ describes the location of the point light.

Then we represent the transformation from a vertex $\mathbf{p}$ to its projection s with the following *shadow matrix*:

$$\mathbf{S} = \begin{bmatrix} \mathbf{n} \cdot \mathbf{L} + dL_w - L_x n_x & -L_y n_x & -L_z n_x & -L_w n_x \\ -L_x n_y & \mathbf{n} \cdot \mathbf{L} + dL_w - L_y n_y & -L_z n_y & -L_w n_y \\ -L_x n_z & -L_y n_z & \mathbf{n} \cdot \mathbf{L} + dL_w - L_z n_z & -L_w n_z \\ -L_x d & -L_y d & -L_z d & \mathbf{n} \cdot \mathbf{L} \end{bmatrix}$$

It is easy to see that $\mathbf{S}$ reduced to $\mathbf{S}_{dir}$ if $L_W = 0$ and $\mathbf{S}$ reduces to $\mathbf{S}_{point}$ for $L_W = 1$.

The XNA math library provides the following function to build the shadow matrix given the plane we wish to project the shadow into and a vector describing a parallel light if $w = 0$ or a point light if $w = 1$:

```
XMFINLINE XMMATRIX XMMatrixShadow(
    FXMVECTOR ShadowPlane,
    FXMVECTOR LightPosition);
```

For further reading, both [Blinn96] and [Möller02] discuss planar shadows.

10.5.4 Using the Stencil Buffer to Prevent Double Blending

When we flatten out the geometry of an object onto the plane to describe its shadow, it is possible (and in fact likely) that two or more of the flattened triangles will overlap. When we render the shadow with transparency (using blending), these areas that have overlapping triangles will get blended multiple times and thus appear darker. Figure 10.10 shows this.

We can solve this problem using the stencil buffer.

1. Assume the stencil buffer pixels where the shadow will be rendered have been cleared to 0. This is true in our mirror demo because we are only casting a shadow onto the ground plane, and we only modified the mirror stencil buffer pixels.

2. Set the stencil test to only accept pixels if the stencil buffer has an entry of 0. If the stencil test passes, then we increment the stencil buffer value to 1.

The first time we render a shadow pixel, the stencil test will pass because the stencil buffer entry is 0. However, when we render this pixel, we also increment the

Figure 10.10. Notice the darker "acne" areas of the shadow in the left image; these correspond to areas where parts of the flattened skull overlapped, thus causing a "double blend." The image on the right shows the shadow rendered correctly, without double blending.

corresponding stencil buffer entry to 1. Thus, if we attempt to *overwrite* to an area that has already been rendered to (marked in the stencil buffer with a value of 1), the stencil test will fail. This prevents drawing over the same pixel more than once, and thus prevents double blending.

10.5.5 Shadow Code

We define a shadow material used to color the shadow that is just a 50% transparent black material:

```
mShadowMat.Ambient  = XMFLOAT4(0.0f, 0.0f, 0.0f, 1.0f);
mShadowMat.Diffuse  = XMFLOAT4(0.0f, 0.0f, 0.0f, 0.5f);
mShadowMat.Specular = XMFLOAT4(0.0f, 0.0f, 0.0f, 16.0f);
```

In order to prevent double blending we set up the following depth/stencil state object:

```
D3D11_DEPTH_STENCIL_DESC noDoubleBlendDesc;
noDoubleBlendDesc.DepthEnable      = true;
noDoubleBlendDesc.DepthWriteMask   = D3D11_DEPTH_WRITE_MASK_ALL;
noDoubleBlendDesc.DepthFunc        = D3D11_COMPARISON_LESS;
noDoubleBlendDesc.StencilEnable    = true;
noDoubleBlendDesc.StencilReadMask  = 0xff;
noDoubleBlendDesc.StencilWriteMask = 0xff;

noDoubleBlendDesc.FrontFace.StencilFailOp      = D3D11_STENCIL_OP_KEEP;
noDoubleBlendDesc.FrontFace.StencilDepthFailOp = D3D11_STENCIL_OP_KEEP;
noDoubleBlendDesc.FrontFace.StencilPassOp = D3D11_STENCIL_OP_INCR;
noDoubleBlendDesc.FrontFace.StencilFunc   = D3D11_COMPARISON_EQUAL;

// We are not rendering backfacing polygons, so these settings do not matter.
noDoubleBlendDesc.BackFace.StencilFailOp      = D3D11_STENCIL_OP_KEEP;
noDoubleBlendDesc.BackFace.StencilDepthFailOp = D3D11_STENCIL_OP_KEEP;
```

```
noDoubleBlendDesc.BackFace.StencilPassOp = D3D11_STENCIL_OP_INCR;
noDoubleBlendDesc.BackFace.StencilFunc   = D3D11_COMPARISON_EQUAL;

ID3D11DepthStencilState* NoDoubleBlendDSS;
HR(device->CreateDepthStencilState(&noDoubleBlendDesc, &NoDoubleBlendDSS));
```

We then draw the skull shadow as follows: building the shadow matrix and rendering with the "no-double-blend" depth/stencil state with a `StencilRef` value of 0:

```
XMVECTOR shadowPlane = XMVectorSet(0.0f, 1.0f, 0.0f, 0.0f); // xz plane
XMVECTOR toMainLight = -XMLoadFloat3(&mDirLights[0].Direction);
XMMATRIX S = XMMatrixShadow(shadowPlane, toMainLight);
XMMATRIX shadowOffsetY = XMMatrixTranslation(0.0f, 0.001f, 0.0f);

// Set per object constants.
XMMATRIX world = XMLoadFloat4x4(&mSkullWorld)*S*shadowOffsetY;
XMMATRIX worldInvTranspose = MathHelper::InverseTranspose(world);
XMMATRIX worldViewProj = world*view*proj;

Effects::BasicFX->SetWorld(world);
Effects::BasicFX->SetWorldInvTranspose(worldInvTranspose);
Effects::BasicFX->SetWorldViewProj(worldViewProj);
Effects::BasicFX->SetMaterial(mShadowMat);

md3dImmediateContext->OMSetDepthStencilState(
    RenderStates::NoDoubleBlendDSS, 0);
pass->Apply(0, md3dImmediateContext);
md3dImmediateContext->DrawIndexed(mSkullIndexCount, 0, 0);
```

10.6 SUMMARY

1. The stencil buffer is an off-screen buffer we can use to block the rendering of certain pixel fragments to the back buffer. The stencil buffer is shared with the depth buffer and thus has the same resolution as the depth buffer. Valid depth/stencil buffer formats are `DXGI_FORMAT_D32_FLOAT_S8X24_UINT` and `DXGI_FORMAT_D24_UNORM_S8_UINT`.

2. The decision to block a particular pixel from being written is decided by the *stencil test*, which is given by the following:

```
if(StencilRef & StencilReadMask ⊴ Value & StencilReadMask)
    accept pixel
else
    reject pixel
```

where the ⊴ operator is any one of the functions defined in the `D3D11_COMPARISON_FUNC` enumerated type. The `StencilRef`, `StencilReadMask`, `StencilReadMask`, and comparison operator ⊴ are all application-defined quantities set with the Direct3D depth/stencil API. The `Value` quantity is the current value in the stencil buffer.

3. The first step to creating an `ID3D11DepthStencilState` interface is to fill out a `D3D11_DEPTH_STENCIL_DESC` instance, which describes the depth/stencil state we want to create. After we have filled out a `D3D11_DEPTH_STENCIL_DESC` structure, we can obtain a pointer to an `ID3D11DepthStencilState` interface with the `ID3D11Device::CreateDepthStencilState` method. Finally, we bind a depth/stencil state block to the output merger stage of the pipeline with the `ID3D11Device::OMSetDepthStencilState` method.

10.7 EXERCISES

1. Prove that the general shadow matrix $\mathbf{S}$ reduced to $\mathbf{S}_{dir}$ if $L_w = 0$ and $\mathbf{S}$ reduces to $\mathbf{S}_{point}$ for $L_w = 1$.

2. Prove that $\mathbf{s} = \mathbf{p} - \frac{\mathbf{n} \cdot \mathbf{p} + d}{\mathbf{n} \cdot (\mathbf{p} - \mathbf{L})}(\mathbf{p} - \mathbf{L}) = \mathbf{p}\mathbf{S}_{point}$ by doing the matrix multiplication for each component, as was done in §10.5.1 for directional lights.

3. Modify the "Mirror" demo to produce the "Left" image in Figure 10.1.

4. Modify the "Mirror" demo to produce the "Left" image in Figure 10.10.

5. Modify the "Mirror" demo in the following way.
   First, draw a wall with the following depth settings:

   ```
   depthStencilDesc.DepthEnable     = false;
   depthStencilDesc.DepthWriteMask  = D3D11_DEPTH_WRITE_MASK_ALL;
   depthStencilDesc.DepthFunc       = D3D11_COMPARISON_LESS;
   ```

   Next, draw the skull behind the wall with the depth settings:

   ```
   depthStencilDesc.DepthEnable     = true;
   depthStencilDesc.DepthWriteMask  = D3D11_DEPTH_WRITE_MASK_ALL;
   depthStencilDesc.DepthFunc       = D3D11_COMPARISON_LESS;
   ```

   Does the wall occlude the skull? Explain. What happens if you use the following to draw the wall instead?

   ```
   depthStencilDesc.DepthEnable     = true;
   depthStencilDesc.DepthWriteMask  = D3D11_DEPTH_WRITE_MASK_ALL;
   depthStencilDesc.DepthFunc       = D3D11_COMPARISON_LESS;
   ```

   Note that this exercise does not use the stencil buffer, so that should be disabled.

6. Modify the "Mirror" demo by not reversing the triangle winding order convention. Does the reflected teapot render correctly?

7. Modify the "Blend" demo from Chapter 9 to draw a cylinder (with no caps) at the center of the scene. Texture the cylinder with the 60 frame animated electric bolt animation found in this chapter's directory using additive blending. Figure 10.11 shows an example of the output. (Hint: Refer back to §9.5.5 for the depth states to use when rendering additive blending geometry.)

Figure 10.11. **Sample screenshot of the solution to Exercise 7.**

8. *Depth complexity* refers to the number of pixel fragments that compete, via the depth test, to be written to a particular entry in the back buffer. For example, a pixel we have drawn may be overwritten by a pixel that is closer to the camera (and this can happen several times before the closest pixel is actually figured out once the entire scene has been drawn). The pixel in Figure 10.12 has a depth complexity of 3 since three pixel fragments compete for the pixel.

Potentially, the graphics card could fill a pixel several times each frame. This *overdraw* has performance implications, as the graphics card is wasting time processing pixels that eventually get overridden and are never seen. Consequently, it is useful to measure the depth complexity in a scene for performance analysis.

We can measure the depth complexity as follows: Render the scene and use the stencil buffer as a counter; that is, each pixel in the stencil buffer is originally cleared to zero, and every time a pixel fragment is processed, we increment its count with D3D11_STENCIL_OP_INCR. The corresponding stencil buffer entry should always be incremented for every pixel fragment no matter what, so use the stencil comparison function D3D11_COMPARISON_ALWAYS. Then, for example, after the frame has been drawn, if the *ij*th pixel has a corresponding entry of five in the stencil buffer, then we know that those five pixel fragments were processed for that pixel during that frame (i.e., the pixel has a depth complexity

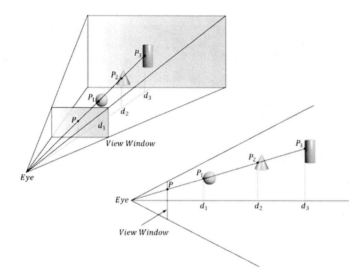

Figure 10.12. Multiple pixel fragments competing to be rendered to a single pixel on the projection window. In this scene, the pixel *P* has a depth complexity of 3.

of five). Note that when counting the depth complexity, technically you only need to render the scene to the stencil buffer.

To visualize the depth complexity (stored in the stencil buffer), proceed as follows:

(a) Associate a color c_k for each level of depth complexity k. For example, blue for a depth complexity of one, green for a depth complexity of two, red for a depth complexity of three, and so on. (In very complex scenes where the depth complexity for a pixel could get very large, you probably do not want to associate a color for each level. Instead, you could associate a color for a range of disjoint levels. For example, pixels with depth complexity 1–5 are colored blue, pixels with depth complexity 6–10 are colored green, and so on.)

(b) Set the stencil buffer operation to D3D11_STENCIL_OP_KEEP so that we do not modify it anymore. (We modify the stencil buffer with D3DSTENCILOP_INCR when we are counting the depth complexity as the scene is rendered, but when writing the code to visualize the stencil buffer, we only need to *read* from the stencil buffer and we should not *write* to it.)

(c) For each level of depth complexity k:

  (i) Set the stencil comparison function to D3D11_COMPARISON_EQUAL and set the stencil reference value to k.

  (i i) Draw a quad of color c_k that covers the entire projection window. Note that this will only color the pixels that have a depth complexity of k because of the preceding set stencil comparison function and reference value.

Figure 10.13. **Sample screenshot of the solution to Exercise 8.**

With this setup, we have colored each pixel based on its depth complexity uniquely, and so we can easily study the depth complexity of the scene. For this exercise, render the depth complexity of the scene used in the "Blend" demo from Chapter 9. Figure 10.13 shows a sample screenshot.

Note: *The depth test occurs in the output merger stage of the pipeline, which occurs after the pixel shader stage. This means that a pixel fragment is processed through the pixel shader, even if it may ultimately be rejected by the depth test. However, modern hardware does an "early z-test" where the depth test is performed before the pixel shader. This way, a rejected pixel fragment will be discarded before being processed by a potentially expensive pixel shader. To take advantage of this optimization, you should try to render your non-blended game objects in front-to-back order with respect to the camera; in this way, the nearest objects will be drawn first, and objects behind them will fail the early z-test and not be processed further. This can be a significant performance benefit if your scene suffers from lots overdraw due to a high depth complexity. We are not able to control the early z-test through the Direct3D API; the graphics driver is the one that decides if it is possible to perform the early z-test. For example, if a pixel shader modifies the pixel fragment's depth value, then the early z-test is not possible, as the pixel shader must be executed before the depth test since the pixel shader modifies depth values.*

Note: *We mentioned the ability to modify the depth of a pixel in the pixel shader. How does that work? A pixel shader can actually output a structure, not just a single color vector as we have been doing thus far:*

```
struct PixelOut
{
    float4 color : SV_Target;
    float depth  : SV_Depth;
};
```

```
PixelOut PS(VertexOut pin)
{
    PixelOut pout;

    // ... usual pixel work

    pout.Color = float4(litColor, alpha);

    // set pixel depth in normalized [0, 1] range
    pout.depth = pin.PosH.z - 0.05f;

    return pout;
}
```

The z-coordinate of the `SV_Position` *element (*`pin.PosH.z`*) gives the unmodified pixel depth value. Using the special system value semantic* `SV_Depth`*, the pixel shader can output a modified depth value.*

9. Another way to implement depth complexity visualization is to use additive blending. First, clear the back buffer black and disable the depth test. Next, set the source and destination blend factors both to `D3D11_BLEND_ONE`, and the blend operation to `D3D11_BLEND_OP_ADD` so that the blending equation looks like $C = C_{src} + C_{dst}$. Observe that with this formula, for each pixel, we are accumulating the colors of all the pixel fragments written to it. Now render all the objects in the scene with a pixel shader that outputs a low intensity color like (0.05, 0.05, 0.05). The more overdraw a pixel has, the more of these low intensity colors will be summed in, thus increasing the brightness of the pixel. If a pixel was overdrawn 10 times, for example, then it will have a color intensity of (0.5, 0.5, 0.5). Thus by looking at the intensity of each pixel after rendering the scene, we obtain an idea of the scene depth complexity. Implement this version of depth complexity measurement using the "Blend" demo from Chapter 9 as a test scene.

10 . Explain how you can count the number of pixels that pass the depth test. Explain how you can count the number of pixels that fail the depth test.

11 . Modify the "Mirror" demo to reflect the floor into the mirror in addition to the skull.

Chapter 11 THE GEOMETRY SHADER

Assuming we are not using the tessellation stages, the geometry shader stage is an optional stage that sits between the vertex and pixel shader stages. While the vertex shader inputs vertices, the geometry shader inputs entire primitives. For example, if we were drawing triangle lists, then the geometry shader program would be executed for each triangle T in the list:

```
for(UINT i = 0; i < numTriangles; ++i)
    OutputPrimitiveList = GeometryShader(T[i].vertexList);
```

Notice the three vertices of each triangle are input into the geometry shader, and the geometry shader outputs a list of primitives. Unlike vertex shaders which cannot destroy or create vertices, the main advantage of the geometry shader is that it can create or destroy geometry; this enables some interesting effects to be implemented on the GPU. For example, the input primitive can be expanded into one or more other primitives, or the geometry shader can choose not to output a primitive based on some condition. Note that the output primitives need not be the same type as the input primitive; for instance, a common application of the geometry shader is to expand a point into a quad (two triangles).

The primitives output from the geometry shader are defined by a vertex list. Vertex positions leaving the geometry shader must be transformed to homogeneous clip space. After the geometry shader stage, we have a list of vertices defining primitives in homogeneous clip space. These vertices are projected (homogeneous divide), and then rasterization occurs as usual.

Objectives:

1. To learn how to program geometry shaders.

2. To discover how billboards can be implemented efficiently using the geometry shader.

3. To recognize auto generated primitive IDs and some of their applications.

4. To find out how to create and use texture arrays, and understand why they are useful.

5. To understand how alpha-to-coverage helps with the aliasing problem of alpha cutouts.

11.1 PROGRAMMING GEOMETRY SHADERS

Programming geometry shaders is a lot like programming vertex or pixel shaders, but there are some differences. The following code shows the general form:

```
[maxvertexcount(N)]
void ShaderName (
    PrimitiveType InputVertexType InputName [NumElements],
    inout StreamOutputObject<OutputVertexType> OutputName)
{
    // Geometry shader body...
}
```

We must first specify the maximum number of vertices the geometry shader will output for a single invocation (the geometry shader is invoked per primitive). This is done by setting the max vertex count before the shader definition using the following *attribute* syntax:

```
[maxvertexcount(N)]
```

where N is the maximum number of vertices the geometry shader will output for a single invocation. The number of vertices a geometry shader can output per invocation is variable, but it cannot exceed the defined maximum. For performance purposes, `maxvertexcount` should be as small as possible; [NVIDIA08] states that peak performance of the GS is achieved when the GS outputs between 1–20 scalars, and performance drops to 50% if the GS outputs between 27–40 scalars. The number of scalars output per invocation is the product of `maxvertexcount` *and* the number of scalars in the output vertex type structure. Working with such restrictions is difficult in practice, so we can either accept lower than peak performance as good enough, or choose an alternative implementation that does not use the geometry shader; however, we must also consider that an alternative implementation may have other drawbacks, which can still make the geometry shader implementation a better choice. Furthermore, the recommendations in [NVIDIA08] are from 2008 (first generation geometry shaders), so things should have improved.

The geometry shader takes two parameters: an input parameter and an output parameter. (Actually, it can take more, but that is a special topic; see §11.2.4.) The input parameter is always an array of vertices that define the primitive—one vertex for a point, two for a line, three for a triangle, four for a line with adjacency, and six for a triangle with adjacency. The vertex type of the input vertices is the vertex type returned by the vertex shader (e.g., `VertexOut`). The input parameter must be prefixed by a primitive type, describing the type of primitives being input into the geometry shader. This can be any one of the following:

1. `point`: The input primitives are points.

2. `line`: The input primitives are lines (lists or strips).

3. `triangle`: The input primitives are triangles (lists or strips).

4. `lineadj`: The input primitives are lines with adjacency (lists or strips).

5. `triangleadj`: The input primitives are triangles with adjacency (lists or strips).

Note: ▶ *The input primitive into a geometry shader is always a complete primitive (e.g., two vertices for a line, and three vertices for a triangle). Thus the geometry shader does not need to distinguish between lists and strips. For example, if you are drawing triangle strips, the geometry shader is still executed for every triangle in the strip, and the three vertices of each triangle are passed into the geometry shader as input. This entails additional overhead, as vertices that are shared by multiple primitives are processed multiple times in the geometry shader.*

The output parameter always has the `inout` modifier. Additionally, the output parameter is always a stream type. A stream type stores a list of vertices which defines the geometry the geometry shader is outputting. A geometry shader adds a vertex to the outgoing stream list using the intrinsic `Append` method:

```
void StreamOutputObject<OutputVertexType>::Append(OutputVertexType v);
```

A stream type is a template type, where the template argument is used to specify the vertex type of the outgoing vertices (e.g., `GeoOut`). There are three possible stream types:

1. `PointStream<OutputVertexType>`: A list of vertices defining a point list.

2. `LineStream<OutputVertexType>`: A list of vertices defining a line strip.

3. `TriangleStream<OutputVertexType>`: A list of vertices defining a triangle strip.

The vertices output by a geometry shader form primitives; the type of output primitive is indicated by the stream type (`PointStream`, `LineStream`, `TriangleStream`). For lines and triangles, the output primitive is always a strip. Line and triangle lists, however, can be simulated by using the intrinsic `RestartStrip` method:

```
void StreamOutputObject<OutputVertexType>::RestartStrip();
```

For example, if you wanted to output triangle lists, then you would call `RestartStrip` every time after three vertices were appended to the output stream.

Following are some specific examples of geometry shader signatures:

```
// EXAMPLE 1: GS ouputs at most 4 vertices.  The input primitive is a line.
// The output is a triangle strip.
//
[maxvertexcount(4)]
void GS(line VertexOut gin[2],
    inout TriangleStream<GeoOut> triStream)
{
    // Geometry shader body...
}
//
// EXAMPLE 2: GS outputs at most 32 vertices.  The input primitive is
// a triangle.  The output is a triangle strip.
//
[maxvertexcount(32)]
void GS(triangle VertexOut gin[3],
    inout TriangleStream<GeoOut> triStream)
{
    // Geometry shader body...
}
//
// EXAMPLE 3: GS outputs at most 4 vertices.  The input primitive
// is a point.  The output is a triangle strip.
//
[maxvertexcount(4)]
void GS(point VertexOut gin[1],
    inout TriangleStream<GeoOut> triStream)
{
    // Geometry shader body...
}
```

The following geometry shader illustrates the `Append` and `RestartStrip` methods; it inputs a triangle, subdivides it (Figure 11.1), and outputs the four subdivided triangles:

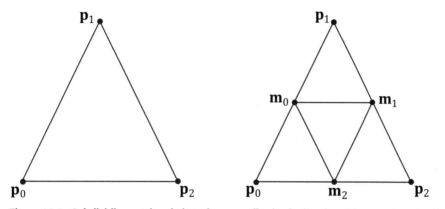

Figure 11.1. Subdividing a triangle into four equally sized triangles. Observe that the three new vertices are the midpoints along the edges of the original triangle.

```
struct VertexOut
{
    float3 PosL    : POSITION;
    float3 NormalL : NORMAL;
    float2 Tex     : TEXCOORD;
};

struct GeoOut
{
    float4 PosH    : SV_POSITION;
    float3 PosW    : POSITION;
    float3 NormalW : NORMAL;
    float2 Tex     : TEXCOORD;
    float  FogLerp : FOG;
};

void Subdivide(VertexOut inVerts[3], out VertexOut outVerts[6])
{
    //          1
    //          *
    //         / \
    //        /   \
    //   m0*-----*m1
    //    / \   / \
    //   /   \ /   \
    //  *-----*-----*
    //  0    m2     2

    VertexOut m[3];

    // Compute edge midpoints.
    m[0].PosL = 0.5f*(inVerts[0].PosL+inVerts[1].PosL);
    m[1].PosL = 0.5f*(inVerts[1].PosL+inVerts[2].PosL);
    m[2].PosL = 0.5f*(inVerts[2].PosL+inVerts[0].PosL);
```

```
    // Project onto unit sphere
    m[0].PosL = normalize(m[0].PosL);
    m[1].PosL = normalize(m[1].PosL);
    m[2].PosL = normalize(m[2].PosL);

    // Derive normals.
    m[0].NormalL = m[0].PosL;
    m[1].NormalL = m[1].PosL;
    m[2].NormalL = m[2].PosL;

    // Interpolate texture coordinates.
    m[0].Tex = 0.5f*(inVerts[0].Tex+inVerts[1].Tex);
    m[1].Tex = 0.5f*(inVerts[1].Tex+inVerts[2].Tex);
    m[2].Tex = 0.5f*(inVerts[2].Tex+inVerts[0].Tex);

    outVerts[0] = inVerts[0];
    outVerts[1] = m[0];
    outVerts[2] = m[2];
    outVerts[3] = m[1];
    outVerts[4] = inVerts[2];
    outVerts[5] = inVerts[1];
};

void OutputSubdivision(VertexOut v[6],
    inout TriangleStream<GeoOut> triStream)
{
    GeoOut gout[6];

    [unroll]
    for(int i = 0; i < 6; ++i)
    {
      // Transform to world space space.
      gout[i].PosW    = mul(float4(v[i].PosL, 1.0f), gWorld).xyz;
      gout[i].NormalW = mul(v[i].NormalL,
        (float3x3)gWorldInvTranspose);

      // Transform to homogeneous clip space.
      gout[i].PosH = mul(float4(v[i].PosL, 1.0f), gWorldViewProj);

      gout[i].Tex     = v[i].Tex;
    }

    //
    //          1
    //          *
    //         / \
    //        /   \
    //    m0*-----*m1
    //     / \   / \
    //    /   \ /   \
    //   *-----*-----*
    //   0    m2     2
```

```
    // We can draw the subdivision in two strips:
    //     Strip 1: bottom three triangles
    //     Strip 2: top triangle

    [unroll]
    for(int j = 0; j < 5; ++j)
    {
      triStream.Append(gout[j]);
    }
    triStream.RestartStrip();

    triStream.Append(gout[1]);
    triStream.Append(gout[5]);
    triStream.Append(gout[3]);
}

[maxvertexcount(8)]
void GS(triangle VertexOut gin[3], inout TriangleStream<GeoOut>)
{
    VertexOut v[6];
    Subdivide(gin, v);
    OutputSubdivision(v, triStream);
}
```

Once a geometry shader has been implemented, we must bind it to an effect pass if it is to be used when rendering:

```
technique11 Tech
{
    pass P0
    {
      SetVertexShader(CompileShader(vs_5_0, VS()));
      SetGeometryShader(CompileShader(gs_5_0, GS()));
      SetPixelShader(CompileShader(ps_5_0, PS()));
    }
}
```

Note: *Given an input primitive, the geometry shader can choose not to output it based on some condition. In this way, geometry is "destroyed" by the geometry shader, which can be useful for some algorithms.*

Note: *If you do not output enough vertices to complete a primitive in a geometry shader, then the partial primitive is discarded.*

11.2 TREE BILLBOARDS DEMO

11.2.1 Overview

When trees are far away, a *billboarding* technique is used for efficiency. That is, instead of rendering the geometry for a fully 3D tree, a quad with a picture of a 3D tree is painted on it (see Figure 11.2). From a distance, you cannot tell that a

RGB Channel   **Alpha Channel**

Figure 11.2. A tree billboard texture with alpha channel.

billboard is being used. However, the trick is to make sure that the billboard always faces the camera (otherwise the illusion would break).

Assuming the *y*-axis is up and the *xz*-plane is the ground plane, the tree billboards will generally be aligned with the *y*-axis and just face the camera in the *xz*-plane. Figure 11.3 shows the local coordinate systems of several billboards from a bird's eye view—notice that the billboards are "looking" at the camera.

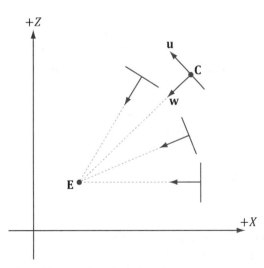

Figure 11.3. Billboards facing the camera.

So given the center position $\mathbf{C} = (C_x, C_y, C_z)$ of a billboard in world space and the position of the camera $\mathbf{E} = (E_x, E_y, E_z)$ in world space, we have enough information to describe the local coordinate system of the billboard relative to the world space:

$$\mathbf{w} = \frac{(E_x - C_x, 0, E_z - C_z)}{\|(E_x - C_x, 0, E_z - C_z)\|}$$

$$\mathbf{v} = (0, 1, 0)$$

$$\mathbf{u} = \mathbf{v} \times \mathbf{w}$$

Given the local coordinate system of the billboard relative to the world space, and the world size of the billboard, the billboard quad vertices can be obtained as follows (see Figure 114.):

```
v[0] = float4(gin[0].CenterW + halfWidth*right - halfHeight*up, 1.0f);
v[1] = float4(gin[0].CenterW + halfWidth*right + halfHeight*up, 1.0f);
v[2] = float4(gin[0].CenterW - halfWidth*right - halfHeight*up, 1.0f);
v[3] = float4(gin[0].CenterW - halfWidth*right + halfHeight*up, 1.0f);
```

Note that the local coordinate system of a billboard differs for each billboard, so it must be computed for each billboard.

For this demo, we will construct a list of point primitives (**D3D11_PRIMITIVE_ TOPOLOGY_POINTLIST**) that lie slightly above a land mass. These points represent the centers of the billboards we want to draw. In the geometry shader, we will expand these points into billboard quads. In addition, we will compute the world matrix of the billboard in the geometry shader. Figure 11.5 shows a screenshot of the demo.

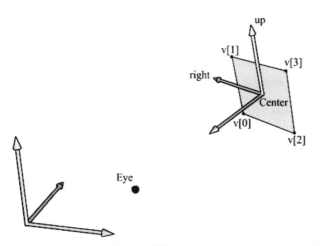

Figure 11.4. **Computing the billboard quad vertices from the local coordinate system and world size of the billboard.**

Figure 11.5. Screenshot of the "Tree Billboard" demo.

As Figure 11.5 shows, this sample builds off the "Blend" demo from Chapter 9.

Note: *A common CPU implementation of billboards would be to use four vertices per billboard in a dynamic vertex buffer. Then every time the camera moved, the vertices would be updated on the CPU using the* `ID3D11DeviceContext::Map` *method so that the billboards face the camera. This approach must submit four vertices per billboard to the IA stage, and requires updating dynamic vertex buffers, which has overhead. With the geometry shader approach, we can use static vertex buffers because the geometry shader does the billboard expansion and makes the billboards face the camera. Moreover, the memory footprint of the billboards is quite small, as we only have to submit one vertex per billboard to the IA stage.*

11.2.2 Vertex Structure

We use the following vertex structure for our billboard points:

```
struct TreePointSprite
{
    XMFLOAT3 Pos;
    XMFLOAT2 Size;
};

const D3D11_INPUT_ELEMENT_DESC InputLayoutDesc::TreePointSprite[2] =
{
    {"POSITION", 0, DXGI_FORMAT_R32G32B32_FLOAT, 0, 0,
D3D11_INPUT_PER_VERTEX_DATA, 0},
    {"SIZE", 0, DXGI_FORMAT_R32G32_FLOAT, 0, 12,
D3D11_INPUT_PER_VERTEX_DATA, 0}
};
```

The vertex stores a point which represents the center position of the billboard in world space. It also includes a size member, which stores the width/height of the billboard (scaled to world space units); this is so the geometry shader knows how large the billboard should be after expansion (Figure 11.6). By having the size vary per vertex, we can easily allow for billboards of different sizes.

Excepting texture arrays (§11.2.4), the other C++ code in the "Tree Billboard" demo should be routine Direct3D code by now (creating vertex buffers, effects, invoking draw methods, etc.). Thus we will now turn our attention to the *TreeSprite.fx* file.

11.2.3 The Effect File

Because this is our first demo with a geometry shader, we will show the entire effect file here so that you can see how it fits together with the vertex and pixel shaders, and the other effect objects. This effect also introduces some new objects that we have not discussed yet (**SV_PrimitiveID** and **Texture2DArray**); these items will be discussed next. For now, mainly focus on the geometry shader program **GS**; this shader expands a point into a quad aligned with the world's *y*-axis that faces the camera, as described in §11.2.1.

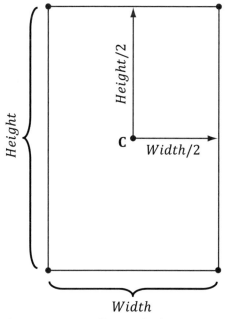

Figure 11.6. **Expanding a point into a quad.**

```
//***************************************************************
// TreeSprite.fx by Frank Luna (C) 2011 All Rights Reserved.
//
// Uses the geometry shader to expand a point sprite into a y-axis aligned
// billboard that faces the camera.
//***************************************************************

#include "LightHelper.fx"

cbuffer cbPerFrame
{
    DirectionalLight gDirLights[3];
    float3 gEyePosW;

    float  gFogStart;
    float  gFogRange;
    float4 gFogColor;
};

cbuffer cbPerObject
{
    float4x4 gViewProj;
    Material gMaterial;
};

cbuffer cbFixed
{
    //
    // Compute texture coordinates to stretch texture over quad.
    //

    float2 gTexC[4] =
    {
      float2(0.0f, 1.0f),
      float2(0.0f, 0.0f),
      float2(1.0f, 1.0f),
      float2(1.0f, 0.0f)
    };
};

// Nonnumeric values cannot be added to a cbuffer.
Texture2DArray gTreeMapArray;

SamplerState samLinear
{
    Filter  = MIN_MAG_MIP_LINEAR;
    AddressU = WRAP;
    AddressV = WRAP;
};

struct VertexIn
{
    float3 PosW  : POSITION;
    float2 SizeW : SIZE;
};
```

```
struct VertexOut
{
    float3 CenterW : POSITION;
    float2 SizeW   : SIZE;
};

struct GeoOut
{
    float4 PosH    : SV_POSITION;
    float3 PosW    : POSITION;
    float3 NormalW : NORMAL;
    float2 Tex     : TEXCOORD;
    uint   PrimID  : SV_PrimitiveID;
};

VertexOut VS(VertexIn vin)
{
    VertexOut vout;

    // Just pass data over to geometry shader.
    vout.CenterW = vin.PosW;
    vout.SizeW   = vin.SizeW;

    return vout;
}

 // We expand each point into a quad (4 vertices), so the maximum number
 // of vertices we output per geometry shader invocation is 4.
[maxvertexcount(4)]
void GS(point VertexOut gin[1],
    uint primID : SV_PrimitiveID,
    inout TriangleStream<GeoOut> triStream)
{
    //
    // Compute the local coordinate system of the sprite relative to the
    // world space such that the billboard is aligned with the y-axis
    // and faces the eye.
    //

    float3 up = float3(0.0f, 1.0f, 0.0f);
    float3 look = gEyePosW - gin[0].CenterW;
    look.y = 0.0f; // y-axis aligned, so project to xz-plane
    look = normalize(look);
    float3 right = cross(up, look);

    //
    // Compute triangle strip vertices (quad) in world space.
    //
    float halfWidth  = 0.5f*gin[0].SizeW.x;
    float halfHeight = 0.5f*gin[0].SizeW.y;

    float4 v[4];
    v[0] = float4(gin[0].CenterW + halfWidth*right - halfHeight*up, 1.0f);
    v[1] = float4(gin[0].CenterW + halfWidth*right + halfHeight*up, 1.0f);
```

```
  v[2] = float4(gin[0].CenterW - halfWidth*right - halfHeight*up, 1.0f);
  v[3] = float4(gin[0].CenterW - halfWidth*right + halfHeight*up, 1.0f);

  //
  // Transform quad vertices to world space and output
  // them as a triangle strip.
  //
  GeoOut gout;
  [unroll]
  for(int i = 0; i < 4; ++i)
  {
    gout.PosH    = mul(v[i], gViewProj);
    gout.PosW    = v[i].xyz;
    gout.NormalW = look;
    gout.Tex     = gTexC[i];
    gout.PrimID  = primID;

    triStream.Append(gout);
  }
}

float4 PS(GeoOut pin, uniform int gLightCount, uniform bool gUseTexure,
    uniform bool gAlphaClip, uniform bool gFogEnabled) : SV_Target
{
    // Interpolating normal can unnormalize it, so normalize it.
    pin.NormalW = normalize(pin.NormalW);

    // The toEye vector is used in lighting.
    float3 toEye = gEyePosW - pin.PosW;

    // Cache the distance to the eye from this surface point.
    float distToEye = length(toEye);

    // Normalize.
    toEye /= distToEye;

    // Default to multiplicative identity.
    float4 texColor = float4(1, 1, 1, 1);
    if(gUseTexture)
    {
      // Sample texture.
      float3 uvw = float3(pin.Tex, pin.PrimID%4);
      texColor = gTreeMapArray.Sample(samLinear, uvw);

      if(gAlphaClip)
      {
        // Discard pixel if texture alpha < 0.05.  Note that
        // we do this test as soon as possible so that we can
        // potentially exit the shader early, thereby skipping
        // the rest of the shader code.
        clip(texColor.a - 0.05f);
      }
    }
```

```
//
// Lighting.
//

float4 litColor = texColor;
if(gLightCount > 0)
{
  // Start with a sum of zero.
  float4 ambient = float4(0.0f, 0.0f, 0.0f, 0.0f);
  float4 diffuse = float4(0.0f, 0.0f, 0.0f, 0.0f);
  float4 spec    = float4(0.0f, 0.0f, 0.0f, 0.0f);

  // Sum the light contribution from each light source.
  [unroll]
  for(int i = 0; i < gLightCount; ++i)
  {
    float4 A, D, S;
    ComputeDirectionalLight(gMaterial, gDirLights[i],
      pin.NormalW, toEye,
      A, D, S);

    ambient += A;
    diffuse += D;
    spec    += S;
  }

  // Modulate with late add.
  litColor = texColor*(ambient + diffuse) + spec;
}

//
// Fogging
//

if(gFogEnabled)
{
  float fogLerp = saturate((distToEye - gFogStart) / gFogRange);

  // Blend the fog color and the lit color.
  litColor = lerp(litColor, gFogColor, fogLerp);
}

// Common to take alpha from diffuse material and texture.
litColor.a = gMaterial.Diffuse.a * texColor.a;

return litColor;
}

//-----------------------------------------------------------------------
// Techniques--just define the ones our demo needs; you can define the other
//   variations as needed.
//-----------------------------------------------------------------------
technique11 Light3
{
```

```
    pass P0
    {
      SetVertexShader(CompileShader(vs_5_0, VS()));
      SetGeometryShader(CompileShader(gs_5_0, GS()));
      SetPixelShader(CompileShader(ps_5_0, PS(3, false, false, false)));
    }
}

technique11 Light3TexAlphaClip
{
    pass P0
    {
      SetVertexShader(CompileShader(vs_5_0, VS()));
      SetGeometryShader(CompileShader(gs_5_0, GS()));
      SetPixelShader(CompileShader(ps_5_0, PS(3, true, true, false)));
    }
}

technique11 Light3TexAlphaClipFog
{
    pass P0
    {
      SetVertexShader(CompileShader(vs_5_0, VS()));
      SetGeometryShader(CompileShader(gs_5_0, GS()));
      SetPixelShader(CompileShader(ps_5_0, PS(3, true, true, true)));
    }
}
```

11.2.4 SV_PrimitiveID

The geometry shader in this example takes a special unsigned integer parameter with semantic SV_PrimitiveID.

```
[maxvertexcount(4)]
void GS(point VertexOut gin[1],
    uint primID : SV_PrimitiveID,
    inout TriangleStream<GeoOut> triStream)
```

When this semantic is specified, it tells the input assembler stage to automatically generate a primitive ID for each primitive. When a draw call is executed to draw n primitives, the first primitive is labeled 0; the second primitive is labeled 1; and so on, until the last primitive in the draw call is labeled $n-1$. The primitive IDs are only unique for a single draw call. In our billboard example, the geometry shader does not use this ID (although a geometry shader could); instead, the geometry shader writes the primitive ID to the outgoing vertices, thereby passing it on to the pixel shader stage. The pixel shader uses the primitive ID to index into a texture array, which leads us to the next section.

Note: *If a geometry shader is not present, the primitive ID parameter can be added to the parameter list of the pixel shader:*

```
float4 PS(VertexOut pin, uint primID : SV_PrimitiveID) : SV_Target
{
    // Pixel shader body...
}
```

However, if a geometry shader is present, then the primitive ID parameter must occur in the geometry shader signature. Then the geometry shader can use the primitive ID or pass it on to the pixel shader stage (or both).

Note: *It is also possible to have the input assembler generate a vertex ID. To do this, add an additional parameter of type* uint *to the vertex shader signature with semantic* SV_VertexID.

The following vertex shader signature shows how this is done.

```
VertexOut VS(VertexIn vin, uint vertID : SV_VertexID)
{
    // vertex shader body...
}
```

For a Draw *call, the vertices in the draw call will be labeled with IDs from 0, 1, ..., n–1, where n is the number of vertices in the draw call. For a* DrawIndexed *call, the vertex IDs correspond to the vertex index values.*

11.3 TEXTURE ARRAYS

11.3.1 Overview

A texture array stores an array of textures. In C++ code, a texture array is represented by the ID3D11Texture2D interface (the same one used for single textures). When creating an ID3D11Texture2D object, there is actually a property called ArraySize that can be set to specify the number of texture elements the texture stores. However, because we have been relying on D3DX for creating textures, we haven't explicitly set this data member. In an effect file, a texture array is represented by the Texture2DArray type:

```
Texture2DArray gTreeMapArray;
```

Now, you have to be wondering why we need texture arrays. Why not just do this:

```
Texture2D TexArray[4];
```

```
...
```

```
float4 PS(GeoOut pin) : SV_Target
{
    float4 c = TexArray[pin.PrimID%4].Sample(samLinear, pin.Tex);
```

This will give an error saying that the "sampler array index must be a literal expression." In other words, it does not like how the array index varies per pixel. This code would work if we specified a literal array index:

```
float4 c = TexArray[2].Sample(samLinear, pin.Tex);
```

But this is less powerful than the first scenario.

11.3.2 Sampling a Texture Array

In the Billboards demo, we sample a texture array with the following code:

```
float3 uvw = float3(pin.Tex, pin.PrimID%4);
texColor = gTreeMapArray.Sample(samLinear, uvw);
```

When using a texture array, three texture coordinates are required. The first two texture coordinates are the usual 2D texture coordinates; the third texture coordinate is an index into the texture array. For example, 0 is the index to the first texture in the array, 1 is the index to the second texture in the array, 2 is the index to the third texture in the array, and so on.

In the "Billboards" demo, we use a texture array with four texture elements, each with a different tree texture (Figure 11.7). However, because we are drawing more than four trees per draw call, the primitive IDs will become greater than three. Thus, we take the primitive ID modulo 4 (`pin.PrimID % 4`) to map the primitive ID to 0, 1, 2, or 3, which are valid array indices for an array with four elements.

Figure 11.7. Tree billboard images.

One of the advantages of texture arrays is that we were able to draw a collection of primitives, with different textures, in one draw call. Normally, we would have to do something like this (pseudocode):

```
SetTextureA();
DrawPrimitivesWithTextureA();

SetTextureB();
DrawPrimitivesWithTextureB();

...

SetTextureZ();
DrawPrimitivesWithTextureZ();
```

Each set and draw call has some overhead associated with it. With texture arrays, we could reduce this to one set and one draw call:

```
SetTextureArray();
DrawPrimitivesWithTextureArray();
```

11.3.3 Loading Texture Arrays

At the time of this writing, there is no D3DX function to load a set of images from the file into a texture array. Thus, we have to do this task ourselves. The process is summarized as follows:

1. Create each texture from the file individually one-by-one in system memory.
2. Create the texture array.
3. Copy each individual texture into the elements of the texture array.
4. Create a shader resource view to the texture array.

We have implemented a helper function in *d3dUtil.h/.cpp* to help with creating texture arrays from a list of filenames. The textures should all be of the same size.

```
ID3D11ShaderResourceView* d3dHelper::CreateTexture2DArraySRV(
    ID3D11Device* device, ID3D11DeviceContext* context,
    std::vector<std::wstring>& filenames,
    DXGI_FORMAT format,
    UINT filter,
    UINT mipFilter)
{
    //
    // Load the texture elements individually from file.  These textures
    // won't be used by the GPU (0 bind flags), they are just used to
    // load the image data from file.  We use the STAGING usage so the
    // CPU can read the resource.
    //

    UINT size = filenames.size();
```

```
std::vector<ID3D11Texture2D*> srcTex(size);
for(UINT i = 0; i < size; ++i)
{
  D3DX11_IMAGE_LOAD_INFO loadInfo;

  loadInfo.Width  = D3DX11_FROM_FILE;
  loadInfo.Height = D3DX11_FROM_FILE;
  loadInfo.Depth  = D3DX11_FROM_FILE;
  loadInfo.FirstMipLevel = 0;
  loadInfo.MipLevels = D3DX11_FROM_FILE;
  loadInfo.Usage = D3D11_USAGE_STAGING;
  loadInfo.BindFlags = 0;
  loadInfo.CpuAccessFlags = D3D11_CPU_ACCESS_WRITE | D3D11_CPU_
    ACCESS_READ;
  loadInfo.MiscFlags = 0;
  loadInfo.Format = format;
  loadInfo.Filter = filter;
  loadInfo.MipFilter = mipFilter;
  loadInfo.pSrcInfo  = 0;

  HR(D3DX11CreateTextureFromFile(device, filenames[i].c_str(),
    &loadInfo, 0, (ID3D11Resource**)&srcTex[i], 0));
}

//
// Create the texture array.  Each element in the texture
// array has the same format/dimensions.
//

D3D11_TEXTURE2D_DESC texElementDesc;
srcTex[0]->GetDesc(&texElementDesc);

D3D11_TEXTURE2D_DESC texArrayDesc;
texArrayDesc.Width              = texElementDesc.Width;
texArrayDesc.Height             = texElementDesc.Height;
texArrayDesc.MipLevels          = texElementDesc.MipLevels;
texArrayDesc.ArraySize          = size;
texArrayDesc.Format             = texElementDesc.Format;
texArrayDesc.SampleDesc.Count   = 1;
texArrayDesc.SampleDesc.Quality = 0;
texArrayDesc.Usage              = D3D11_USAGE_DEFAULT;
texArrayDesc.BindFlags          = D3D11_BIND_SHADER_RESOURCE;
texArrayDesc.CPUAccessFlags     = 0;
texArrayDesc.MiscFlags          = 0;

ID3D11Texture2D* texArray = 0;
HR(device->CreateTexture2D( &texArrayDesc, 0, &texArray));

//
// Copy individual texture elements into texture array.
//

// for each texture element...
for(UINT texElement = 0; texElement < size; ++texElement)
{
```

```
      // for each mipmap level...
      for(UINT mipLevel = 0; mipLevel < texElementDesc.MipLevels; ++mipLevel)
      {
        D3D11_MAPPED_SUBRESOURCE mappedTex2D;
        HR(context->Map(srcTex[texElement],
          mipLevel, D3D11_MAP_READ, 0, &mappedTex2D));

        context->UpdateSubresource(
          texArray,
          D3D11CalcSubresource(
            mipLevel,
            texElement,
            texElementDesc.MipLevels),
          0,
          mappedTex2D.pData,
          mappedTex2D.RowPitch,
          mappedTex2D.DepthPitch);

        context->Unmap(srcTex[texElement], mipLevel);
      }
    }

    //
    // Create a resource view to the texture array.
    //

    D3D11_SHADER_RESOURCE_VIEW_DESC viewDesc;
    viewDesc.Format = texArrayDesc.Format;
    viewDesc.ViewDimension = D3D11_SRV_DIMENSION_TEXTURE2DARRAY;
    viewDesc.Texture2DArray.MostDetailedMip = 0;
    viewDesc.Texture2DArray.MipLevels = texArrayDesc.MipLevels;
    viewDesc.Texture2DArray.FirstArraySlice = 0;
    viewDesc.Texture2DArray.ArraySize = size;

    ID3D11ShaderResourceView* texArraySRV = 0;
    HR(device->CreateShaderResourceView(texArray, &viewDesc, &texArraySRV));

    //
    // Cleanup--we only need the resource view.
    //

    ReleaseCOM(texArray);

    for(UINT i = 0; i < size; ++i)
      ReleaseCOM(srcTex[i]);

    return texArraySRV;
  }
```

The `ID3D11DeviceContext::UpdateSubresource` method copies memory from one subresource to another (see the SDK documentation for a description of the parameters).

```
void ID3D11DeviceContext::UpdateSubresource(
    ID3D11Resource *pDstResource,
    UINT DstSubresource,
    const D3D11_BOX *pDstBox,
    const void *pSrcData,
    UINT SrcRowPitch,
    UINT SrcDepthPitch);
```

1. `pDstResource`: The destination resource object.

2. `DstSubresource`: Index identifying the subresource we are updating in the destination resource (see §11.3.4).

3. `pDstBox`: Pointer to a `D3D11_BOX` instance that specifies the volume in the destination subresource we are updating; specify null to update the entire subresource.

4. `pSrcData`: Pointer to the source data.

5. `SrcRowPitch`: The byte size of one row of the source data.

6. `SrcDepthPitch`: The byte size of one depth slice of the source data.

Note that for 2D textures, the `SrcDepthPitch` parameter seems unnecessary, but this same method is used for updating 3D textures, which can be visualized as a stack of 2D textures.

We invoke the previous function at initialization time to create the texture array of our tree sprites:

```
ID3D11ShaderResourceView* mTreeTextureMapArraySRV;
mTreeTextureMapArraySRV = d3dHelper::CreateTexture2DArraySRV(
    md3dDevice, md3dImmediateContext, treeFilenames, DXGI_FORMAT_
    R8G8B8A8_UNORM);
```

11.3.4 Texture Subresources

Now that we have discussed texture arrays, we can talk about subresources. Figure 11.8 shows an example of a texture array with several textures. In turn, each texture has its own mipmap chain. The Direct3D API uses the term *array slice* to refer to an element in a texture along with its complete mipmap chain. The Direct3D API uses the term *mip slice* to refer to all the mipmaps at a particular level in the texture array. A subresource refers to a single mipmap level in a texture array element.

Given the texture array index, and a mipmap level, we can access a subresource in a texture array. However, the subresources can also be labeled by a linear index; Direct3D uses a linear index ordered as shown in Figure 11.9.

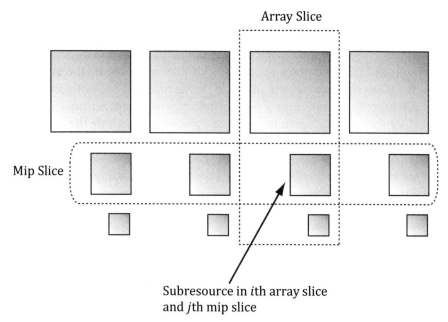

Figure 11.8. A texture array with four textures. Each texture has three mipmap levels.

The following utility function is used to compute the linear subresource index given the mip level, array index, and the number of mipmap levels:

```
inline UINT D3D11CalcSubresource(
    UINT MipSlice, UINT ArraySlice, UINT MipLevels);
```

The formula is simply: $k = ArraySlice * MipLevels + MipSlice$.

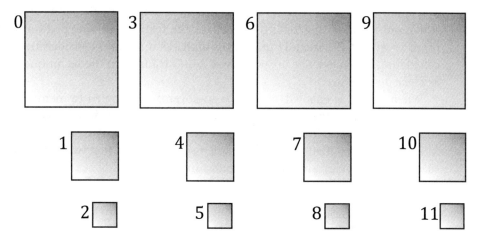

Figure 11.9. Subresources in a texture array labeled with a linear index.

11.4 ALPHA-TO-COVERAGE

When the "Tree Billboard" demo is run, notice that at some distances the edges of the tree billboard cutouts appear blocky. This is caused by the `clip` function, which we use to mask out the pixels of the texture that are not part of the tree; the clip function either keeps a pixel or rejects it—there is no smooth transition. The distance from the eye to the billboard plays a role because the short distances result in magnification, which makes the block artifacts larger, and short distances result in a lower resolution mipmap level being used.

One way to fix this problem is to use transparency blending instead of the alpha test. Due to linear texture filtering, the edge pixels will be blurred slightly making a smooth transition from white (opaque pixels) to black (masked out pixels). The transparency blending will consequently cause a smooth fade out along the edges from opaque pixels to masked pixels. Unfortunately, transparency blending requires sorting and rendering in back-to-front order. The overhead for sorting a small number of tree billboards is not high, but if we are rendering a forest or grass prairie, the sorting can be expensive as it must be done every frame; worse is that rendering in back-to-front order results in massive overdraw (see Exercise 8 in Chapter 10), which can kill performance.

One might suggest that MSAA (multisampling antialiasing—see §4.1.7) can help, as MSAA is used to smooth out blocky edges of polygons. Indeed it should be able to help, but there is a problem. MSAA executes the pixel shader once per pixel, at the pixel center, and then shares that color information with its subpixels based on visibility (the depth/stencil test is evaluated per subpixel) and coverage (does the subpixel center lie inside or outside the polygon?). The key here is that *coverage is determined at the polygon level*. Therefore, MSAA is not going to detect the edges of the tree billboard cutouts as defined by the alpha channel—it will only look at the edges of the quads the textures are mapped onto. So is there a way to tell Direct3D to take the alpha channel into consideration when calculating coverage? The answer is yes, and it leads us to the technique known as *alpha-to-coverage*.

When MSAA is enabled, and alpha-to-coverage is enabled (a member of the `ID3D11BlendState`), the hardware will look at the alpha value returned by the pixel shader and use that to determine coverage [NVIDIA05]. For example, with 4X MSAA, if the pixel shader alpha is 0.5, then we can assume that two out of the four subpixels are covered and this will create a smooth edge.

An alpha-to-coverage blend state object is created like so:

```
D3D11_BLEND_DESC a2CDesc = {0};
a2CDesc.AlphaToCoverageEnable = true;
a2CDesc.IndependentBlendEnable = false;
```

```
a2CDesc.RenderTarget[0].BlendEnable = false;
a2CDesc.RenderTarget[0].RenderTargetWriteMask =
    D3D11_COLOR_WRITE_ENABLE_ALL;

ID3D11BlendState* AlphaToCoverageBS;
HR(device->CreateBlendState(&a2CDesc, &AlphaToCoverageBS));
```

The general advice is that you always want to use alpha-to-coverage for alpha masked cut out textures like foliage and fences. However, it does require that MSAA is enabled. Note that in the constructor of our demo application, we set:

```
mEnable4xMsaa = true;
```

This causes our sample framework to create the back and depth buffers with 4X MSAA support.

 Note: *In the "Tree Billboard" demo, alpha-to-coverage can be toggled on and off by pressing the 'r' and 't' keys, respectively.*

11.5 SUMMARY

1. Assuming we are not using the tessellation stages, the geometry shader stage is an optional stage that sits between the vertex and pixel shader stages. The geometry shader is invoked for each primitive sent through the input assembler. The geometry shader can output zero, one, or more primitives. The output primitive type may be different from the input primitive type. The vertices of the output primitives should be transformed to homogeneous clip space before leaving the geometry shader. The primitives output from the geometry shader next enter the rasterization stage of the rendering pipeline. Geometry shaders are programmed in effect files, side-by-side vertex, and pixel shaders.

2. The billboard technique is where a quad textured with an image of an object is used instead of a true 3D model of the object. For objects far away, the viewer cannot tell a billboard is being used. The advantage of billboards is that the GPU does not have to waste processing time rendering a full 3D object, when a textured quad will suffice. This technique can be useful for rendering forests of trees, where true 3D geometry is used for trees near the camera, and billboards are used for trees in the distance. In order for the billboard trick to work, the billboard must always face the camera. The billboard technique can be implemented efficiently in a geometry shader.

3. A special parameter of type `uint` and semantic `SV_PrimitiveID` can be added to the parameter list of a geometry shader as the following example shows:

```
[maxvertexcount(4)]
void GS(point VertexOut gin[1],
  uint primID : SV_PrimitiveID,
  inout TriangleStream<GeoOut> triStream);
```

When this semantic is specified, it tells the input assembler stage to automatically generate a primitive ID for each primitive. When a draw call is executed to draw n primitives, the first primitive is labeled 0; the second primitive is labeled 1; and so on, until the last primitive in the draw call is labeled $n-1$. If a geometry shader is not present, the primitive ID parameter can be added to the parameter list of the pixel shader. However, if a geometry shader is present, then the primitive ID parameter must occur in the geometry shader signature. Then the geometry shader can use the primitive ID or pass it on to the pixel shader stage (or both).

4. The input assembler stage can generate a vertex ID. To do this, add an additional parameter of type `uint` to the vertex shader signature with semantic `SV_VertexID`. For a `Draw` call, the vertices in the draw call will be labeled with IDs from 0, 1, ..., $n-1$, where n is the number of vertices in the draw call. For a `DrawIndexed` call, the vertex IDs correspond to the vertex index values.

5. A texture array stores an array of textures. In C++ code, a texture array is represented by the `ID3D11Texture2D` interface (the same one used for single textures). In an effect file, a texture array is represented by the `Texture2DArray` type. When using a texture array, three texture coordinates are required. The first two texture coordinates are the usual 2D texture coordinates; the third texture coordinate is an index into the texture array. For example, 0 is the index to the first texture in the array, 1 is the index to the second texture in the array, 2 is the index to the third texture in the array, and so on. One of the advantages of texture arrays is that we were able to draw a collection of primitives, with different textures, in one draw call. Each primitive will have an index into the texture array which indicates which texture to apply to the primitive.

6. Alpha-to-coverage instructs the hardware to look at the alpha value returned by the pixel shader when determining subpixel coverage. This enables smooth edges for alpha masked cutout textures like foliage and fences. Alpha-to-coverage is controlled by the `ID3D11BlendState`. Set the `AlphaToCoverageEnable` property to true when filling out the `D3D11_BLEND_DESC` structure.

11.6 EXERCISES

1. Consider a circle, drawn with a line strip, in the xz-plane. Expand the line strip into a cylinder with no caps using the geometry shader.

2. An icosahedron is a rough approximation of a sphere. By subdividing each triangle (Figure 11.1), and projecting the new vertices onto the sphere, a better

approximation is obtained. (Projecting a vertex onto a unit sphere simply amounts to normalizing the position vector, as the heads of all unit vectors coincide with the surface of the unit sphere.) For this exercise, build and render an icosahedron. Use a geometry shader to subdivide the icosahedron based on its distance d from the camera. For example, if $d < 15$, then subdivide the original icosahedron twice; if $15 \leq d < 30$, then subdivide the original icosahedron once; if $d \geq 30$, then just render the original icosahedron. The idea of this is to only use a high number of polygons if the object is close to the camera; if the object is far away, then a coarser mesh will suffice, and we need not waste GPU power processing more polygons than needed. Figure 11.10 shows the three LOD levels side-by-side in wireframe and solid (lit) mode. Refer back to §6.12.3 for a discussion on tessellating an icosahedron.

3. A simple explosion effect can be simulated by translating triangles in the direction of their face normal as a function of time. This simulation can be implemented in a geometry shader. For each triangle input into the geometry shader, the geometry shader computes the face normal $\mathbf{n}$, and then translates the three triangle vertices, $\mathbf{p}_0$, $\mathbf{p}_1$, and $\mathbf{p}_2$, in the direction $\mathbf{n}$ based on the time t since the explosion started:

$$\mathbf{p}_i' = \mathbf{p}_i + t\mathbf{n} \quad \text{for} \quad i = 0,1,2$$

The face normal $\mathbf{n}$ need not be unit length, and can be scaled accordingly to control the speed of the explosion. One could even make the scale depend

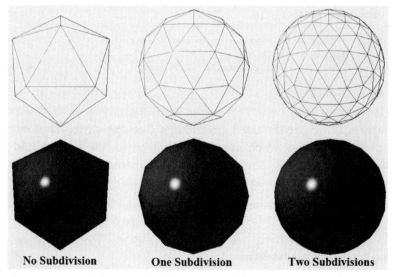

| No Subdivision | One Subdivision | Two Subdivisions |

Figure 11.10. Subdivision of an icosahedron with vertices projected onto the unit sphere.

on the primitive ID, so that each primitive travels at a different speed. Use an icosahedron (not subdivided) as a sample mesh for implementing this effect.

4. It can be useful for debugging to visualize the vertex normals of a mesh. Write an effect that renders the vertex normals of a mesh as short line segments. To do this, implement a geometry shader that inputs the point primitives of the mesh (i.e., its vertices with topology `D3D11_PRIMITIVE_TOPOLOGY_POINTLIST`), so that each vertex gets pumped through the geometry shader. Now the geometry shader can expand each point into a line segment of some length L. If the vertex has position **p** and normal **n**, then the two endpoints of the line segment representing the vertex normal are **p** and **p** + L**n**. After this is implemented, draw the mesh as normal, and then draw the scene again with the normal vector visualization technique so that the normals are rendered on top of the scene. Use the "Blend" demo as a test scene.

5. Similar to the previous exercise, write an effect that renders the face normals of a mesh as short line segments. For this effect, the geometry shader will input a triangle, calculate its normal, and output a line segment.

6. This exercise shows that for a `Draw` call, the vertices in the draw call will be labeled with IDs from 0, 1, …, $n-1$, where n is the number of vertices in the draw call, and that for a `DrawIndexed` call, the vertex IDs correspond to the vertex index values.

   Modify the "Tree Billboards" demo in the following way. First, change the vertex shader to the following:

```
VertexOut VS(VertexIn vin, uint vertID : SV_VertexID)
{
  VertexOut vout;

  // Just pass data over to geometry shader.
  vout.CenterW = vin.PosW;
  vout.SizeW   = float2(2+vertID, 2+vertID);

  return vout;
}
```

   In other words, we size the tree billboard based on the vertex ID of its center. Now run the program; when drawing 16 billboards, the sizes should range from 2 to 17. Now modify the drawing like so: Instead of using a single draw call to draw all 16 points at once, use four like so:

```
md3dImmediateContext->Draw(4, 0);

md3dImmediateContext->Draw(4, 4);

md3dImmediateContext->Draw(4, 8);

md3dImmediateContext->Draw(4, 12);
```

Now run the program. This time, the sizes should range from 2 to 5. Because each draw call draws 4 vertices, the vertex IDs range from 0–3 for each draw call. Now use an index buffer and four DrawIndexed calls. After running the program, the sizes should return back to the range of 2 to 17. This is because when using DrawIndexed, the vertex IDs correspond to the vertex index values.

7. Modify the "Tree Billboards" demo in the following way. First, remove the "modulo 4" from the pixel shader:

```
float3 uvw = float3(pin.Tex, pin.PrimID);
```

Now run the program. Because we are drawing 16 primitives, with primitive IDs ranging from 0–15, these IDs go outside the array bounds. However, this does not cause an error, as the out-of-bounds index will be clamped to the highest valid index (3 in this case). Now instead of using a single draw call to draw all 16 points at once, use four like so:

```
md3dImmediateContext->Draw(4, 0);

md3dImmediateContext->Draw(4, 4);

md3dImmediateContext->Draw(4, 8);

md3dImmediateContext->Draw(4, 12);
```

Run the program again. This time there is no clamping. Because each draw call draws 4 primitives, the primitive IDs range from 0–3 for each draw call. Thus the primitive IDs can be used as indices without going out of bounds. This shows that the primitive ID "count" resets to zero with each draw call.

12 THE COMPUTE SHADER

Chapter

GPUs have been optimized to process a large amount of memory from a single location or sequential locations (so-called "streaming operation"); this is in contrast to a CPU designed for random memory accesses [Boyd10]. Moreover, because vertices and pixels are independently processed, GPUs have been architected to be massively parallel; for example, the NVIDIA "Fermi" architecture supports up to 16 streaming multiprocessors of 32 CUDA cores for a total of 512 CUDA cores [NVIDIA09].

Obviously graphics benefit from this GPU architecture, as the architecture was designed for graphics. However, some non-graphical applications benefit from the massive amount of computational power a GPU can provide with its parallel architecture. Using the GPU for non-graphical applications is called *general purpose GPU* (GPGPU) *programming*. Not all algorithms are ideal for a GPU implementation; GPUs need data-parallel algorithms to take advantage of the parallel architecture of the GPU. That is, we need a large amount of data elements that will have similar operations performed on them so that the elements can be processed in parallel. Graphical operations like shading pixels is a good example, as each pixel fragment being drawn is operated on by the pixel shader. As another example, if you look at the code for our wave simulation from the previous chapters, you will see that in the update step, we perform a calculation on each grid element. So this, too, is a good candidate for a GPU implementation, as each grid element can be updated in parallel by the GPU. Particle systems provide yet another example, where the physics of each particle can be computed

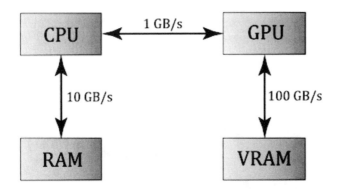

Figure 12.1. Image has been redrawn from [Boyd10]. The relative memory bandwidth speeds between CPU and RAM, CPU and GPU, and GPU and VRAM. These numbers are just illustrative numbers to show the order of magnitude difference between the bandwidths. Observe that transferring memory between CPU and GPU is the bottleneck.

independently provided we take the simplification that the particles do not interact with each other.

For GPGPU programming, the user generally needs to access the computation results back on the CPU. This requires copying the result from video memory to system memory, which is slow (see Figure 12.1), but may be a negligible issue compared to the speed up from doing the computation on the GPU. For graphics, we typically use the computation result as an input to the rendering pipeline, so no transfer from GPU to CPU is needed. For example, we can blur a texture with the compute shader, and then bind a shader resource view to that blurred texture to a shader as input.

The compute shader is a programmable shader Direct3D exposes that is not directly part of the rendering pipeline. Instead, it sits off to the side and can read from GPU resources and write to GPU resources (Figure 12.2). Essentially, the compute shader allows us to access the GPU to implement data-parallel algorithms without drawing anything. As mentioned, this is useful for GPGPU programming, but there are still many graphical effects that can be implemented on the compute shader as well—so it is still very relevant for a graphics programmer. And as already mentioned, because the compute shader is part of Direct3D, it reads from and writes to Direct3D resources, which enables us to bind the output of a compute shader directly to the rendering pipeline.

Objectives:

1. To learn how to program compute shaders.
2. To obtain a basic high-level understanding of how the hardware processes thread groups, and the threads within them.

3. To discover which Direct3D resources can be set as an input to a compute shader and which Direct3D resources can be set as an output to a compute shader.

4. To understand the various thread IDs and their uses.

5. To learn about shared memory and how it can be used for performance optimizations.

6. To find out where to obtain more detailed information about GPGPU programming.

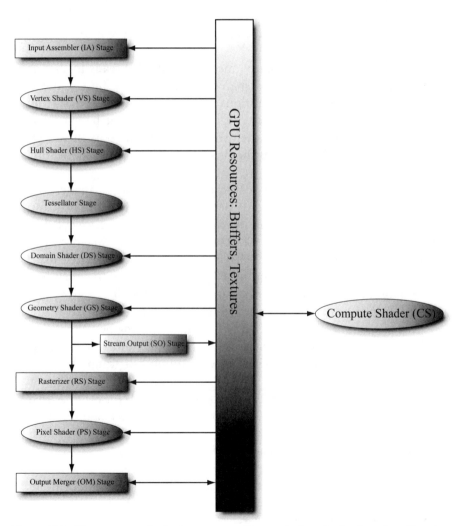

Figure 12.2. The compute shader is not part of the rendering pipeline but sits off to the side. The compute shader can read and write to GPU resources. The compute shader can be mixed with graphics rendering, or used alone for GPGPU programming.

12.1 THREADS AND THREAD GROUPS

In GPU programming, the number of threads desired for execution is divided up into a grid of *thread groups*. A thread group is executed on a single multiprocessor. Therefore, if you had a GPU with 16 multiprocessors, you would want to break up your problem into at least 16 thread groups so that each multiprocessor has work to do. For better performance, you would want at least two thread groups per multiprocessor since a multiprocessor can switch to processing the threads in a different group to hide stalls [Fung10] (a stall can occur, for example, if a shader needs to wait for a texture operation result before it can continue to the next instruction).

Each thread group gets shared memory that all threads in that group can access; a thread cannot access shared memory in a different thread group. Thread synchronization operations can take place amongst the threads in a thread group, but different thread groups cannot be synchronized. In fact, we have no control over the order in which different thread groups are processed. This makes sense as the thread groups can be executed on different multiprocessors.

A thread group consists of n threads. The hardware actually divides these threads up into *warps* (32 threads per warp), and a warp is processed by the multiprocessor in SIMD32 (i.e., the same instructions are executed for the 32 threads simultaneously). Each CUDA core processes a thread and recall that a "Fermi" multiprocessor has 32 CUDA cores (so a CUDA core is like an SIMD "lane"). In Direct3D, you can specify a thread group size with dimensions that are not multiples of 32, but for performance reasons, the thread group dimensions should always be multiples of the warp size [Fung10].

Thread group sizes of 256 seem to be a good starting point that should work well for various hardware. Then experiment with other sizes. Changing the number of threads per group will change the number of groups dispatched.

> Note: *NVIDIA hardware uses warp sizes of 32 threads. ATI uses "wavefront" sizes of 64 threads and recommends the thread group size should always be a multiple of the wavefront size [Bilodeau10]. Also, the warp size or wavefront size can change in future generations of hardware.*

In Direct3D, thread groups are launched via the following method call:

```
void ID3D11DeviceContext::Dispatch(
    UINT ThreadGroupCountX,
    UINT ThreadGroupCountY,
    UINT ThreadGroupCountZ);
```

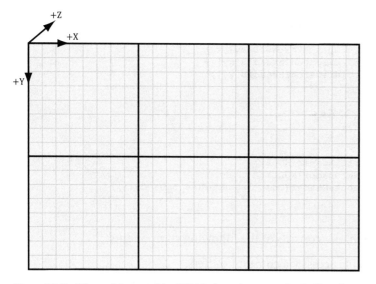

Figure 12.3. **Dispatching a grid of 3 × 2 thread groups. Each thread group has 8 × 8 threads.**

This enables you to launch a 3D grid of thread groups; however, in this book we will only be concerned with 2D grids of thread groups. The following example call launches three groups in the x direction and two groups in the y direction for a total of $3 \times 2 = 6$ thread groups (see Figure 12.3).

12.2 A SIMPLE COMPUTE SHADER

Following is a simple compute shader that sums two textures, assuming all the textures are the same size. This shader is not very interesting, but it illustrates the basic syntax of writing a compute shader.

```
cbuffer cbSettings
{
    // Compute shader can access values in constant buffers.
};

// Data sources and outputs.
Texture2D gInputA;
Texture2D gInputB;
RWTexture2D<float4> gOutput;

// The number of threads in the thread group.  The threads in a group can
// be arranged in a 1D, 2D, or 3D grid layout.
[numthreads(16, 16, 1)]
void CS(int3 dispatchThreadID : SV_DispatchThreadID) // Thread ID
```

```
    {
        // Sum the xyth texels and store the result in the xyth texel of
        // gOutput.
        gOutput[dispatchThreadID.xy] =
          gInputA[dispatchThreadID.xy] +
          gInputB[dispatchThreadID.xy];
    }

    technique11 AddTextures
    {
        pass P0
        {
          SetVertexShader(NULL);
          SetPixelShader(NULL);
          SetComputeShader(CompileShader(cs_5_0, CS()));
        }
    }
```

A compute shader consists of the following components:

1. Global variable access via constant buffers.

2. Input and output resources, which are discussed in the next section.

3. The [numthreads(X, Y, Z)] attribute, which specifies the number of threads in the thread group as a 3D grid of threads.

4. The shader body that has the instructions to execute for each thread.

5. Thread identification system value parameters (discussed in §12.4).

Observe that we can define different topologies of the thread group; for example, a thread group could be a single line of X threads [numthreads(X, 1, 1)] or a single column of Y threads [numthreads(1, Y, 1)]. 2D thread groups of $X \times Y$ threads can be made by setting the z-dimension to 1 like this, [numthreads(X, Y, 1)]. The topology you choose will be dictated by the problem you are working on. As mentioned in the previous section, the total thread count per group should be a multiple of the warp size (32 for NVIDIA cards) or a multiple of the wavefront size (64 for ATI cards). A multiple of the wavefront size is also a multiple of the warp size, so choosing a multiple of the wavefront size works for both types of cards.

12.3 DATA INPUT AND OUTPUT RESOURCES

Two types of resources can be bound to a compute shader: buffers and textures. We have worked with buffers already such as vertex and index buffers, and constant buffers. Although we use the effects framework to set constant buffers, they are just ID3D11Buffer instances with the D3D11_BIND_CONSTANT_BUFFER flag. We are also familiar with texture resources from Chapter 8.

12.3.1 Texture Inputs

The compute shader defined in the previous section defined two input texture resources:

```
Texture2D gInputA;
Texture2D gInputB;
```

The input textures `gInputA` and `gInputB` are bound as inputs to the shader by creating `ID3D11ShaderResourceView`s (SRVs) to the textures and setting them to the compute shader via `ID3DX11EffectShaderResourceVariable` variables. This is exactly the same way we bind shader resource views to pixel shaders. Note that SRVs are read-only.

12.3.2 Texture Outputs and Unordered Access Views (UAVs)

The compute shader defined in the previous section defined one output resource:

```
RWTexture2D<float4> gOutput;
```

Outputs are treated special and have the special prefix to their type "RW," which stands for read-write, and as the name implies, you can read and write to elements in this resource in the compute shader. In contrast, the textures `gInputA` and `gInputB` are read-only. Also, it is necessary to specify the type and dimensions of the output with the template angle brackets syntax <float4>. If our output was a 2D integer like `DXGI_FORMAT_R8G8_SINT`, then we would have instead written:

```
RWTexture2D<int2> gOutput;
```

Binding an output resource is different than an input, however. To bind a resource that we will write to in a compute shader, we need to bind it using a new view type called an *unordered access view* (UAV), which is represented in code by the `ID3D11UnorderedAccessView` interface. This is created in a similar way to a shader resource view. Here is an example:

```
// Note, compressed formats cannot be used for UAV.  We get error like:
// ERROR: ID3D11Device::CreateTexture2D: The format (0x4d, BC3_UNORM)
// cannot be bound as an UnorderedAccessView, or cast to a format that
// could be bound as an UnorderedAccessView.  Therefore this format
// does not support D3D11_BIND_UNORDERED_ACCESS.

D3D11_TEXTURE2D_DESC blurredTexDesc;
blurredTexDesc.Width     = width;
blurredTexDesc.Height    = height;
blurredTexDesc.MipLevels = 1;
blurredTexDesc.ArraySize = 1;
blurredTexDesc.Format    = format;
blurredTexDesc.SampleDesc.Count   = 1;
blurredTexDesc.SampleDesc.Quality = 0;
```

```
blurredTexDesc.Usage      = D3D11_USAGE_DEFAULT;
blurredTexDesc.BindFlags = D3D11_BIND_SHADER_RESOURCE |
    D3D11_BIND_UNORDERED_ACCESS;
blurredTexDesc.CPUAccessFlags = 0;
blurredTexDesc.MiscFlags      = 0;

ID3D11Texture2D* blurredTex = 0;
HR(device->CreateTexture2D(&blurredTexDesc, 0, &blurredTex));

D3D11_SHADER_RESOURCE_VIEW_DESC srvDesc;
srvDesc.Format = format;
srvDesc.ViewDimension = D3D11_SRV_DIMENSION_TEXTURE2D;
srvDesc.Texture2D.MostDetailedMip = 0;
srvDesc.Texture2D.MipLevels = 1;

ID3D11ShaderResourceView* mBlurredOutputTexSRV;
HR(device->CreateShaderResourceView(blurredTex,
    &srvDesc, &mBlurredOutputTexSRV));

D3D11_UNORDERED_ACCESS_VIEW_DESC uavDesc;
uavDesc.Format = format;
uavDesc.ViewDimension = D3D11_UAV_DIMENSION_TEXTURE2D;
uavDesc.Texture2D.MipSlice = 0;

ID3D11UnorderedAccessView* mBlurredOutputTexUAV;
HR(device->CreateUnorderedAccessView(blurredTex,
&uavDesc, &mBlurredOutputTexUAV));

// Views save a reference to the texture so we can release our reference.
ReleaseCOM(blurredTex);
```

Observe that if a texture is going to be bound as UAV, then it must be created with the D3D11_BIND_UNORDERED_ACCESS flag; in the previous example, the texture will be bound as a UAV and as a SRV (but not simultaneously), and therefore, it has the combined flags D3D11_BIND_SHADER_RESOURCE | D3D11_BIND_UNORDERED_ACCESS. This is common, as we often use the compute shader to perform some operation on a texture (so the texture will be bound to the compute shader as a UAV), and then after, we want to texture geometry with it, so it will be bound to the vertex or pixel shader as a SRV.

Once an ID3D11UnorderedAccessView object is created, we can bind it to a "RW" compute shader variable using the SetUnorderedAccessView method of the ID3DX11EffectUnorderedAccessViewVariable interface:

```
// HLSL variables.
Texture2D gInputA;
Texture2D gInputB;
RWTexture2D<float4> gOutput;

// C++ Code.
ID3DX11EffectShaderResourceVariable* InputA;
ID3DX11EffectShaderResourceVariable* InputB;
```

```
ID3DX11EffectUnorderedAccessViewVariable* Output;

InputA    = mFX->GetVariableByName("gInputA")->AsShaderResource();
InputB    = mFX->GetVariableByName("gInputB")->AsShaderResource();
Output    = mFX->GetVariableByName("gOutput")->AsUnorderedAccessView();

void SetInputA(ID3D11ShaderResourceView* tex)
{
    InputA->SetResource(tex);
}

void SetInputB(ID3D11ShaderResourceView* tex)
{
    InputB->SetResource(tex);
}

void SetOutput(ID3D11UnorderedAccessView* tex)
{
    Output->SetUnorderedAccessView(tex);
}
```

12.3.3 Indexing and Sampling Textures

The elements of the textures can be accessed using 2D indices. In the compute shader defined in §12.2, we index the texture based on the dispatch thread ID (thread IDs are discussed in §12.4). Each thread is given a unique dispatch ID.

```
[numthreads(16, 16, 1)]
void CS(int3 dispatchThreadID : SV_DispatchThreadID)
{
    // Sum the xyth texels and store the result in the xyth texel of
    // gOutput.
    gOutput[dispatchThreadID.xy] =
      gInputA[dispatchThreadID.xy] +
      gInputB[dispatchThreadID.xy];
}
```

Assuming that we dispatched enough thread groups to cover the texture (i.e., so there is one thread being executed for one texel), then this code sums the texture images and stores the result in the texture gOutput.

> Note: *The behavior of out-of-bounds indices are well defined in a compute shader. Out-of-bounds reads return 0, and out-of-bounds writes result in no-ops [Boyd08].*

Because the compute shader is executed on the GPU, it has access to the usual GPU tools. In particular, we can sample textures using texture filtering. There are two issues, however. First, we cannot use the **Sample** method, but instead must use the **SampleLevel** method. **SampleLevel** takes an additional third parameter that specifies the mipmap level of the texture; 0 takes the top most level, 1 takes the second mip level, etc., and fractional values are used to interpolate between two mip levels if linear mip filtering is enabled. On the other hand, `Sample` automatically selects the best mipmap level to use based on how many pixels on the screen the texture will cover. Because compute shaders are not used for rendering directly, it does not know how to automatically select a mipmap level like this, and therefore, we must explicitly specify the level with `SampleLevel` in a compute shader. The second issue is that when we sample a texture, we use normalized texture-coordinates in the range $[0, 1]^2$ instead of integer indices. However, the texture size (*width,height*) can be set to a constant buffer variable, and then normalized texture coordinates can be derived from the integer indices (x, y):

$$u = \frac{x}{width}$$

$$v = \frac{y}{height}$$

The following code shows a compute shader using integer indices, and a second equivalent version using texture coordinates and `SampleLevel`, where it is assumed the texture size is 512×512 and we only need the top level mip:

```
//
// VERSION 1: Using integer indices.
//

cbuffer cbUpdateSettings
{
      float gWaveConstants[3];
};

Texture2D gPrevSolInput;
Texture2D gCurrSolInput;
RWTexture2D<float> gNextSolOutput;

[numthreads(16, 16, 1)]
void CS(int3 dispatchThreadID : SV_DispatchThreadID)
{
    int x = dispatchThreadID.x;
    int y = dispatchThreadID.y;

    gNextSolOutput[int2(x,y)] =
      gWaveConstants[0]* gPrevSolInput[int2(x,y)].r +
      gWaveConstants[1]* gCurrSolInput[int2(x,y)].r +
      gWaveConstants[2]*(
        gCurrSolInput[int2(x,y+1)].r +
        gCurrSolInput[int2(x,y-1)].r +
        gCurrSolInput[int2(x+1,y)].r +
        gCurrSolInput[int2(x-1,y)].r);
}
```

```
//
// VERSION 2: Using SampleLevel and texture coordinates.
//

cbuffer cbUpdateSettings
{
    float gWaveConstants[3];
};

SamplerState samPoint
{
    Filter = MIN_MAG_MIP_POINT;

    AddressU = CLAMP;
    AddressV = CLAMP;
};

Texture2D gPrevSolInput;
Texture2D gCurrSolInput;
RWTexture2D<float> gNextSolOutput;

[numthreads(16, 16, 1)]
void CS(int3 dispatchThreadID : SV_DispatchThreadID)
{
    // Equivalently using SampleLevel() instead of operator [].
    int x = dispatchThreadID.x;
    int y = dispatchThreadID.y;

    float2 c = float2(x,y)/512.0f;
    float2 t = float2(x,y-1)/512.0;
    float2 b = float2(x,y+1)/512.0;
    float2 l = float2(x-1,y)/512.0;
    float2 r = float2(x+1,y)/512.0;

    gNextSolOutput[int2(x,y)] =
      gWaveConstants[0]*gPrevSolInput.SampleLevel(samPoint, c, 0.0f).r +
      gWaveConstants[1]*gCurrSolInput.SampleLevel(samPoint, c, 0.0f).r +
      gWaveConstants[2]*(
        gCurrSolInput.SampleLevel(samPoint, b, 0.0f).r +
        gCurrSolInput.SampleLevel(samPoint, t, 0.0f).r +
        gCurrSolInput.SampleLevel(samPoint, r, 0.0f).r +
        gCurrSolInput.SampleLevel(samPoint, l, 0.0f).r);
}
```

12.3.4 Structured Buffer Resources

The following examples show how *structured buffers* are defined in the HLSL:

```
struct Data
{
    float3 v1;
    float2 v2;
};

StructuredBuffer<Data> gInputA;
StructuredBuffer<Data> gInputB;

RWStructuredBuffer<Data> gOutput;
```

A structured buffer is simply a buffer of elements of the same type—essentially an array. As you can see, the type can be a user-defined structure in the HLSL. A structured buffer is created like a normal buffer, except that we specify the structured buffer flag and we must specify the byte size of the elements we are storing:

```
struct Data
{
    XMFLOAT3 v1;
    XMFLOAT2 v2;
};

// Create a buffer to be bound as a shader
// input (D3D11_BIND_SHADER_RESOURCE).

D3D11_BUFFER_DESC inputDesc;
inputDesc.Usage = D3D11_USAGE_DEFAULT;
inputDesc.ByteWidth = sizeof(Data) * mNumElements;
inputDesc.BindFlags = D3D11_BIND_SHADER_RESOURCE;
inputDesc.CPUAccessFlags = 0;
inputDesc.StructureByteStride = sizeof(Data);
inputDesc.MiscFlags = D3D11_RESOURCE_MISC_BUFFER_STRUCTURED;

D3D11_SUBRESOURCE_DATA vinitDataA;
vinitDataA.pSysMem = &dataA[0];

ID3D11Buffer* bufferA = 0;
HR(md3dDevice->CreateBuffer(&inputDesc, &vinitDataA, &bufferA));

// Create a read-write buffer the compute shader can
// write to (D3D11_BIND_UNORDERED_ACCESS).

D3D11_BUFFER_DESC outputDesc;
outputDesc.Usage = D3D11_USAGE_DEFAULT;
outputDesc.ByteWidth = sizeof(Data) * mNumElements;
outputDesc.BindFlags = D3D11_BIND_UNORDERED_ACCESS;
outputDesc.CPUAccessFlags = 0;
outputDesc.StructureByteStride = sizeof(Data);
outputDesc.MiscFlags = D3D11_RESOURCE_MISC_BUFFER_STRUCTURED;

ID3D11Buffer* mOutputBuffer;
HR(md3dDevice->CreateBuffer(&outputDesc, 0, &mOutputBuffer));
```

To bind a structured buffer to a compute shader as an input, we just created a SRV to it, and set it to the compute shader through an `ID3DX11EffectShaderResourceVariable` variable. Likewise, to bind a structured buffer as a RW output, we just create a UAV to it, and set it to the compute shader through an `ID3DX11EffectUnorderedAccessViewVariable` variable. The following code shows how to create a SRV and UAV to a structured buffer:

```
D3D11_SHADER_RESOURCE_VIEW_DESC srvDesc;
srvDesc.Format = DXGI_FORMAT_UNKNOWN;
srvDesc.ViewDimension = D3D11_SRV_DIMENSION_BUFFEREX;
```

```
srvDesc.BufferEx.FirstElement = 0;
srvDesc.BufferEx.Flags = 0;
srvDesc.BufferEx.NumElements = mNumElements;

md3dDevice->CreateShaderResourceView(bufferA, &srvDesc, &mInputASRV);
md3dDevice->CreateShaderResourceView(bufferB, &srvDesc, &mInputBSRV);

D3D11_UNORDERED_ACCESS_VIEW_DESC uavDesc;
uavDesc.Format = DXGI_FORMAT_UNKNOWN;
uavDesc.ViewDimension = D3D11_UAV_DIMENSION_BUFFER;
uavDesc.Buffer.FirstElement = 0;
uavDesc.Buffer.Flags = 0;
uavDesc.Buffer.NumElements = mNumElements;

md3dDevice->CreateUnorderedAccessView(mOutputBuffer, &uavDesc, &mOutputUAV);
```

This next section of code shows how to set the SRVs and UAVs to a compute shader through the effects framework:

```
// HLSL variables.
struct Data
{
    float3 v1;
    float2 v2;
};

StructuredBuffer<Data> gInputA;
StructuredBuffer<Data> gInputB;
RWStructuredBuffer<Data> gOutput;

// C++ Code.
ID3DX11EffectShaderResourceVariable* InputA;
ID3DX11EffectShaderResourceVariable* InputB;
ID3DX11EffectUnorderedAccessViewVariable* Output;

InputA = mFX->GetVariableByName("gInputA")->AsShaderResource();
InputB = mFX->GetVariableByName("gInputB")->AsShaderResource();
Output = mFX->GetVariableByName("gOutput")->AsUnorderedAccessView();

void SetInputA(ID3D11ShaderResourceView* srv)
{
    InputA->SetResource(srv);
}

void SetInputB(ID3D11ShaderResourceView* srv)
{
    InputB->SetResource(srv);
}

void SetOutput(ID3D11UnorderedAccessView* uav)
{
    Output->SetUnorderedAccessView(uav);
}
```

Observe that when creating a SRV or UAV to a structured buffer, for the `Format` property we specify `DXGI_FORMAT_UNKNOWN`. This is because, in general, a structured buffer uses a user-defined type, so the structure will not correspond directly to one of the `DXGI_FORMAT` members. There is such a thing as a *typed buffer*, which has the HLSL syntax:

```
Buffer<float4> typedBuffer1;
Buffer<float> typedBuffer2;
Buffer<int2> typedBuffer3;
```

When you create these buffers, do not specify the `D3D11_RESOURCE_MISC_BUFFER_STRUCTURED` flag, and when you create the views, you must specify the proper `DXGI_FORMAT` for the `Format` property. Note that the HLSL syntax just defines a type and the number of components, but there are many `DXGI_FORMAT` members that can correspond to a HLSL type. For example, possible formats for `typedBuffer1` are any floating-point formats with four components: `DXGI_FORMAT_R32G32B32A32_FLOAT`, `DXGI_FORMAT_R16G16B16A16_FLOAT`, and `DXGI_FORMAT_R8G8B8A8_UNORM`. Likewise, possible formats for `typedBuffer3` are `DXGI_FORMAT_R32G32_SINT`, `DXGI_FORMAT_R16G16_SINT`, and `DXGI_FORMAT_R8G8_SINT`.

> **Note:** *There is also such a thing called a raw buffer, which is basically a byte array of data. Byte offsets are used and the data can then be casted to the proper type. This could be useful for storing different data types in the same buffer, for example. We do not use raw buffers in this book; see the SDK documentation for details. The SDK sample "BasicCompute11" shows how to create raw buffers and work with them.*

12.3.5 Copying CS Results to System Memory

Typically when we use the compute shader to process a texture, we will display that processed texture on the screen; therefore, we visually see the result to verify the accuracy of our compute shader. With structured buffer calculations, and GPGPU computing in general, we might not display our results at all. So the question is how do we get our results from GPU memory (remember when we write to a structured buffer via a UAV, that buffer is stored in GPU memory) back to system memory. The common pattern is to create a system memory buffer with the staging flag `D3D11_USAGE_STAGING` and the CPU access flag `D3D11_CPU_ACCESS_READ`. Then we can use the `ID3D11DeviceContext::CopyResource` method to copy the GPU resource to the system memory resource. The system memory resource must be the same type and size as the resource we want to copy. Finally, we can map the system memory buffer with the mapping API to read it on the CPU. From there we can then copy the data into a system memory array for further processing on the CPU side, save the data to file, or what have you.

We have included a structured buffer demo for this chapter called "VecAdd," which simply sums the corresponding vector components stored in two structured buffers:

```
struct Data
{
    float3 v1;
    float2 v2;
};

StructuredBuffer<Data> gInputA;
StructuredBuffer<Data> gInputB;
RWStructuredBuffer<Data> gOutput;

[numthreads(32, 1, 1)]
void CS(int3 dtid : SV_DispatchThreadID)
{
    gOutput[dtid.x].v1 = gInputA[dtid.x].v1 + gInputB[dtid.x].v1;
    gOutput[dtid.x].v2 = gInputA[dtid.x].v2 + gInputB[dtid.x].v2;
}
```

For simplicity, the structured buffers only contain 32 elements; therefore, we only have to dispatch one thread group (because one thread group processes 32 elements). After the compute shader completes its work for all threads in this demo, we copy the results to system memory and save them to file. The following code shows how to create the system memory buffer and how to copy the GPU results to CPU memory:

```
// Create a system memory version of the buffer to read the
// results back from.
D3D11_BUFFER_DESC outputDesc;
outputDesc.Usage = D3D11_USAGE_STAGING;
outputDesc.BindFlags = 0;
outputDesc.ByteWidth = sizeof(Data) * mNumElements;
outputDesc.CPUAccessFlags = D3D11_CPU_ACCESS_READ;
outputDesc.StructureByteStride = sizeof(Data);
outputDesc.MiscFlags = D3D11_RESOURCE_MISC_BUFFER_STRUCTURED;

ID3D11Buffer* mOutputDebugBuffer;
HR(md3dDevice->CreateBuffer(&outputDesc, 0, &mOutputDebugBuffer));

// ...
//
// Compute shader finished!

struct Data
{
    XMFLOAT3 v1;
    XMFLOAT2 v2;
};

// Copy the output buffer to system memory.
md3dImmediateContext->CopyResource(mOutputDebugBuffer, mOutputBuffer);
```

```
// Map the data for reading.
D3D11_MAPPED_SUBRESOURCE mappedData;
md3dImmediateContext->Map(mOutputDebugBuffer, 0, D3D11_MAP_READ, 0,
    &mappedData);

Data* dataView = reinterpret_cast<Data*>(mappedData.pData);

for(int i = 0; i < mNumElements; ++i)
{
    fout << "(" << dataView[i].v1.x << ", " <<
      dataView[i].v1.y << ", " <<
      dataView[i].v1.z << ", " <<
      dataView[i].v2.x << ", " <<
      dataView[i].v2.y << ")" << std::endl;
}

md3dImmediateContext->Unmap(mOutputDebugBuffer, 0);

fout.close();
```

In the demo, we fill the two input buffers with the following initial data:

```
std::vector<Data> dataA(mNumElements);
std::vector<Data> dataB(mNumElements);
for(int i = 0; i < mNumElements; ++i)
{
    dataA[i].v1 = XMFLOAT3(i, i, i);
    dataA[i].v2 = XMFLOAT2(i, 0);

    dataB[i].v1 = XMFLOAT3(-i, i, 0.0f);
    dataB[i].v2 = XMFLOAT2(0, -i);
}
```

The resulting text file contains the following data, which confirms that the compute shader is working as expected.

```
(0, 0, 0, 0, 0)
(0, 2, 1, 1, -1)
(0, 4, 2, 2, -2)
(0, 6, 3, 3, -3)
(0, 8, 4, 4, -4)
(0, 10, 5, 5, -5)
(0, 12, 6, 6, -6)
(0, 14, 7, 7, -7)
(0, 16, 8, 8, -8)
(0, 18, 9, 9, -9)
(0, 20, 10, 10, -10)
(0, 22, 11, 11, -11)
(0, 24, 12, 12, -12)
(0, 26, 13, 13, -13)
(0, 28, 14, 14, -14)
(0, 30, 15, 15, -15)
(0, 32, 16, 16, -16)
(0, 34, 17, 17, -17)
```

```
(0, 36, 18, 18, -18)
(0, 38, 19, 19, -19)
(0, 40, 20, 20, -20)
(0, 42, 21, 21, -21)
(0, 44, 22, 22, -22)
(0, 46, 23, 23, -23)
(0, 48, 24, 24, -24)
(0, 50, 25, 25, -25)
(0, 52, 26, 26, -26)
(0, 54, 27, 27, -27)
(0, 56, 28, 28, -28)
(0, 58, 29, 29, -29)
(0, 60, 30, 30, -30)
(0, 62, 31, 31, -31)
```

> **Note:** *From Figure 12.1, we see that copying between CPU and GPU memory is the slowest. For graphics, we never want to do this copy per frame, as it will kill performance. For GPGPU programming, it is generally required to get the results back on the CPU; however, this is usually not a big deal for GPGPU programming, as the gains of using a GPU outweigh the copy cost from GPU to CPU—moreover, for GPGPU, the copy will be less frequent than "per frame." For example, suppose an application uses GPGPU programming to implement a costly image processing calculation. After the calculation is done the result is copied to the CPU. The GPU is not used again until the user requests another calculation.*

12.4 THREAD IDENTIFICATION SYSTEM VALUES

Consider Figure 12.4.

1. Each thread group is assigned an ID by the system; this is called the *group ID* and has the system value semantic `SV_GroupID`. If $G_x \times G_y \times G_z$ are the number of thread groups dispatched, then the group ID ranges from $(0,0,0)$ to $(G_x - 1, G_y - 1, G_z - 1)$.

2. Inside a thread group, each thread is given a unique ID relative to its group. If the thread group has size $X \times Y \times Z$, then the *group thread IDs* will range from $(0, 0, 0)$ to $(X - 1, Y - 1, Z - 1)$. The system value semantic for the group thread ID is `SV_GroupThreadID`.

3. A `Dispatch` call dispatches a grid of thread groups. The *dispatch thread ID* uniquely identifies a thread relative to *all* the threads generated by a `Dispatch` call. In other words, whereas the group thread ID uniquely identifies a thread relative to its thread group, the dispatch thread ID uniquely identifies a thread relative to the union of all the threads from all the thread groups dispatched by a `Dispatch` call. Let `ThreadGroupSize = (X,Y,Z)` be the thread group size, then

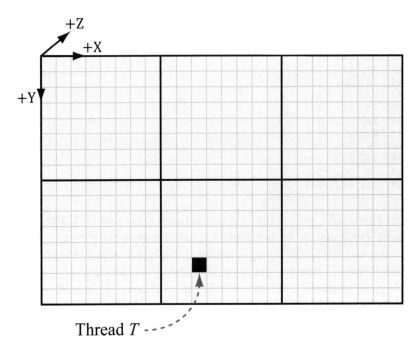

Figure 12.4. Consider the marked thread T. Thread T has thread group ID (1, 1, 0). It has group thread ID (2, 5, 0). It has dispatch thread ID (1, 1, 0) $\otimes$ (8, 8, 0) + (2, 5, 0) = (10, 13, 0). It has group index ID $5 \cdot 8 + 2 = 42$.

the dispatch thread ID can be derived from the group ID and the group thread ID as follows:

```
dispatchThreadID.xyz = groupID.xyz * ThreadGroupSize.xyz +
    groupThreadID.xyz;
```

The dispatch thread ID has the system value semantic `SV_DispatchThreadID`. If 3×2 thread groups are dispatched, where each thread group is 10×10, then a total of 60 threads are dispatched and the dispatch thread IDs will range from $(0, 0, 0)$ to $(29, 19, 0)$.

4. A linear index version of the group thread ID is given to us by Direct3D through the `SV_GroupIndex` system value; it is computed as:

```
groupIndex = groupThreadID.z*ThreadGroupSize.x*ThreadGroupSize.y +
             groupThreadID.y*ThreadGroupSize.x +
             groupThreadID.x;
```

 Regarding the indexing coordinate order, the first coordinate gives the x-position (or column) and the second coordinate gives the y-position (or row). This is in contrast to common matrix notation, where M_{ij} denotes the element in the ith row and jth column.

So why do we need these thread ID values. Well, a compute shader generally takes some input data structure and outputs to some data structure. We can use the thread ID values as indexes into these data structures:

```
Texture2D gInputA;
Texture2D gInputB;
RWTexture2D<float4> gOutput;

[numthreads(16, 16, 1)]
void CS(int3 dispatchThreadID : SV_DispatchThreadID)
{
    // Use dispatch thread ID to index into output and input textures.
    gOutput[dispatchThreadID.xy] =
      gInputA[dispatchThreadID.xy] +
      gInputB[dispatchThreadID.xy];
}
```

The sv_GroupThreadID is useful for indexing into thread local storage memory (§12.6).

12.5 APPEND AND CONSUME BUFFERS

Suppose we have a buffer of particles defined by the structure:

```
struct Particle
{
    float3 Position;
    float3 Velocity;
    float3 Acceleration;
};
```

and we want to update the particle positions based on their constant acceleration and velocity in the compute shader. Moreover, suppose that we do not care about the order the particles are updated nor the order they are written to the output buffer. Consume and append structured buffers are ideal for this scenario, and they provide the convenience that we do not have to worry about indexing:

```
struct Particle
{
    float3 Position;
    float3 Velocity;
    float3 Acceleration;
};

float TimeStep = 1.0f / 60.0f;

ConsumeStructuredBuffer<Particle> gInput;
AppendStructuredBuffer<Particle> gOutput;
[numthreads(16, 16, 1)]
void CS()
{
```

```
// Consume a data element from the input buffer.
Particle p = gInput.Consume();

p.Velocity += p.Acceleration*TimeStep;
p.Position += p.Velocity*TimeStep;

// Append normalized vector to output buffer.
gOutput.Append(p);
}
```

Once a data element is consumed, it cannot be consumed again by a different thread; one thread will consume exactly one data element. And again, we emphasize that the order elements consumed and appended are unknown; therefore, it is generally not the case that the *i*th element in the input buffer gets written to the *i*th element in the output buffer.

Note: *Append structured buffers do not dynamically grow. They must still be large enough to store all the elements you will append to them.*

The only step necessary on the application side is that when creating the UAV, we must specify the D3D11_BUFFER_UAV_FLAG_APPEND flag:

```
D3D11_UNORDERED_ACCESS_VIEW_DESC uavDesc;
uavDesc.Format = DXGI_FORMAT_UNKNOWN;
uavDesc.ViewDimension = D3D11_UAV_DIMENSION_BUFFER;
uavDesc.Buffer.FirstElement = 0;
uavDesc.Buffer.Flags = D3D11_BUFFER_UAV_FLAG_APPEND;
uavDesc.Buffer.NumElements = mNumElements;
```

12.6 SHARED MEMORY AND SYNCHRONIZATION

Thread groups are given a section of so-called *shared memory* or *thread local storage*. Accessing this memory is fast and can be thought of being as fast as a hardware cache. In the compute shader code, shared memory is declared like so:

```
groupshared float4 gCache[256];
```

The array size can be whatever you want, but the maximum size of group shared memory is 32kb. Because the shared memory is local to the thread group, it is indexed with the sv_ThreadGroupID; so, for example, you might give each thread in the group access to one slot in the shared memory.

Using too much shared memory can lead to performance issues [Fung10], as the following example illustrates. Suppose a multiprocessor supports 32kb of shared memory, and your compute shader requires 20kb of shared memory. This means that only one thread group will fit on the multiprocessor because there is not enough memory left for another thread group [Fung10], as 20kb + 20kb = 40kb > 32kb. This limits the parallelism of the GPU, as a multiprocessor cannot switch off between thread groups to hide latency (recall from §12.1 that at least two thread groups per multiprocessor is recommended). Thus, even though the hardware technically supports 32kb of shared memory, performance improvements can be achieved by using less.

A common application of shared memory is to store texture values in it. Certain algorithms, such as blurs, require fetching the same texel multiple times. Sampling textures is actually one of the slower GPU operations because memory bandwidth and memory latency have not improved as much as the raw computational power of GPUs [Möller08]. A thread group can avoid redundant texture fetches by preloading all the needed texture samples into the shared memory array. The algorithm then proceeds to look up the texture samples in the shared memory array, which is very fast. Suppose we implement this strategy with the following *erroneous* code:

```
Texture2D gInput;
RWTexture2D<float4> gOutput;

groupshared float4 gCache[256];

[numthreads(256, 1, 1)]
void CS(int3 groupThreadID : SV_GroupThreadID,
    int3 dispatchThreadID : SV_DispatchThreadID)
{
    // Each thread samples the texture and stores the
    // value in shared memory.
    gCache[groupThreadID.x] = gInput[dispatchThreadID.xy];

    // Do computation work: Access elements in shared memory
    // that other threads stored:

    // BAD!!!  Left and right neighbor threads might not have
    // finished sampling the texture and storing it in shared memory.
    float4 left  = gCache[groupThreadID.x - 1];
    float4 right = gCache[groupThreadID.x + 1];

    ...
}
```

A problem arises with this scenario because we have no guarantee that all the threads in the thread group finish at the same time. Thus a thread could go to access a shared memory element that is not yet initialized because the neighboring threads responsible for initializing those elements have not finished yet. To fix this problem, before the compute shader can continue, it must wait until all the threads have done their texture loading into shared memory. This is accomplished by a synchronization command:

```
Texture2D gInput;
RWTexture2D<float4> gOutput;

groupshared float4 gCache[256];

[numthreads(256, 1, 1)]
void CS(int3 groupThreadID : SV_GroupThreadID,
    int3 dispatchThreadID : SV_DispatchThreadID)
{
    // Each thread samples the texture and stores the
    // value in shared memory.
    gCache[groupThreadID.x] = gInput[dispatchThreadID.xy];

    // Wait for all threads in group to finish.
    GroupMemoryBarrierWithGroupSync();

    // Safe now to read any element in the shared memory
    //and do computation work.

    float4 left  = gCache[groupThreadID.x - 1];
    float4 right = gCache[groupThreadID.x + 1];

    . . .
}
```

12.7 BLUR DEMO

In this section, we explain how to implement a blur algorithm on the compute
shader. We begin by describing the mathematical theory of blurring. Then we
discuss the technique of render-to-texture, which our demo uses to generate a source
image to blur. Finally, we review the code for a compute shader implementation
and discuss how to handle certain details that make the implementation a
little tricky.

12.7.1 Blurring Theory

The blurring algorithm we use is described as follows: For each pixel P_{ij} in the
source image, compute the weighted average of the $m \times n$ matrix of pixels centered
about the pixel P_{ij} (see Figure 12.5); this weighted average becomes the ijth pixel in
the blurred image. Mathematically,

$$Blur\left(P_{ij}\right) = \sum_{r=-a}^{a} \sum_{c=-b}^{b} w_{rc} P_{i+r,j+c} \quad \text{for} \sum_{r=-a}^{a} \sum_{c=-b}^{b} w_{rc} = 1$$

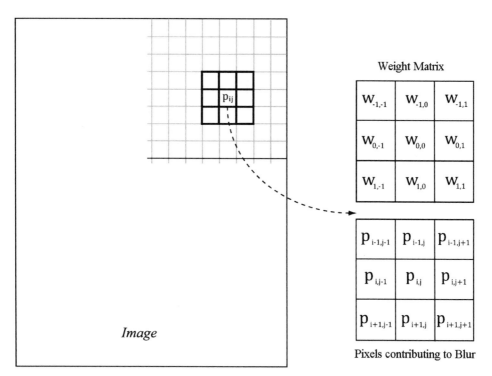

Figure 12.5. To blur the pixel P_{ij} we compute the weighted average of the $m \times n$ matrix of pixels centered about the pixel. In this example, the matrix is a square 3×3 matrix, with blur radius $a = b = 1$. Observe that the center weight w_{00} aligns with the pixel P_{ij}.

where $m = 2a + 1$ and $n = 2b + 1$. By forcing m and n to be odd, we ensure that the $m \times n$ matrix always has a natural "center." We call a the vertical blur radius and b the horizontal blur radius. If $a = b$, then we just refer to the *blur radius* without having to specify the dimension. The $m \times n$ matrix of weights is called the *blur kernel*. Observe also that the weights must sum to 1. If the sum of the weights is less than one, the blurred image will appear darker as color has been removed. If the sum of the weights is greater than one, the blurred image will appear brighter as color has been added.

There are various ways to compute the weights so long as they sum to 1. A well-known blur operator found in many image editing programs is the Gaussian blur, which obtains its weights from the Gaussian function $G(x) = \exp\left(-\frac{x^2}{2\sigma^2}\right)$. A graph of this function is shown in Figure 12.6 for different σ.

Let us suppose we are doing a 1×5 Gaussian blur (i.e., a 1D blur in the horizontal direction), and let $\sigma = 1$. Evaluating $G(x)$ for $x = -2, -1, 0, 1, 2$ we have:

$$G(-2) = \exp\left(-\frac{(-2)^2}{2}\right) = e^{-2}$$

$$G(-1) = \exp\left(-\frac{(-1)^2}{2}\right) = e^{-\frac{1}{2}}$$

$$G(0) = \exp(0) = 1$$

$$G(1) = \exp\left(-\frac{1^2}{2}\right) = e^{-\frac{1}{2}}$$

$$G(2) = \exp\left(-\frac{2^2}{2}\right) = e^{-2}$$

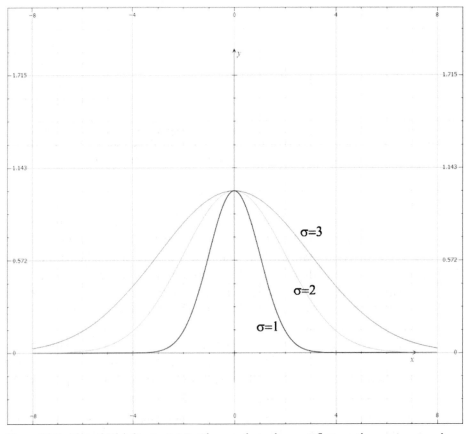

Figure 12.6. Plot of $G(x)$ for $\sigma = 1,2,3$. Observe that a larger σ flattens the curve out and gives more weight to the neighboring points.

However, these values are not the weights because they do not sum to 1:

$$\sum_{x=-2}^{x=2} G(x) = G(-2) + G(-1) + G(0) + G(1) + G(2)$$

$$= 1 + 2e^{-\frac{1}{2}} + 2e^{-2}$$

$$\approx 2.48373$$

If we normalize the previous equation by dividing by the sum $\sum_{x=2}^{x=-2} G(x)$, then we obtain weights based on the Gaussian function that sum to 1:

$$\frac{G(-2) + G(-1) + G(0) + G(1) + G(2)}{\sum_{x=-2}^{x=2} G(x)} = 1$$

Therefore, the Gaussian blur weights are:

$$w_{-2} = \frac{G(-2)}{\sum_{x=-2}^{x=2} G(x)} = \frac{e^{-2}}{1 + 2e^{-\frac{1}{2}} + 2e^{-2}} \approx 0.0545$$

$$w_{-1} = \frac{G(-1)}{\sum_{x=-2}^{x=2} G(x)} = \frac{e^{-\frac{1}{2}}}{1 + 2e^{-\frac{1}{2}} + 2e^{-2}} \approx 0.2442$$

$$w_0 = \frac{G(0)}{\sum_{x=-2}^{x=2} G(x)} = \frac{1}{1 + 2e^{-\frac{1}{2}} + 2e^{-2}} \approx 0.4026$$

$$w_1 = \frac{G(1)}{\sum_{x=-2}^{x=2} G(x)} = \frac{e^{-\frac{1}{2}}}{1 + 2e^{-\frac{1}{2}} + 2e^{-2}} \approx 0.2442$$

$$w_2 = \frac{G(2)}{\sum_{x=-2}^{x=2} G(x)} = \frac{e^{-2}}{1 + 2e^{-\frac{1}{2}} + 2e^{-2}} \approx 0.0545$$

The Gaussian blur is known to be *separable*, which means it can be broken up into two 1D blurs as follows.

1. Blur the input image I using a 1D horizontal blur: $I_H = Blur_H(I)$.
2. Blur the output from the previous step using a 1D vertical blur: $Blur(I) = Blur_V(I_H)$.

    Written more succinctly, we have:

$$Blur(I) = Blur_V(Blur_H(I))$$

Suppose that the blur kernel is a 9×9 matrix, so that we needed a total of 81 samples to do the 2D blur. By separating the blur into two 1D blurs, we only need $9 + 9 = 18$ samples. Typically we will be blurring textures; as mentioned in this chapter, fetching texture samples is expensive, so reducing texture samples by separating a blur is a welcome improvement. Even if a blur is not separable (some blur operators are not), we can often make the simplification and assume it is for the sake of performance, as long as the final image looks accurate enough.

12.7.2 Render-to-Texture

So far in our programs, we have been rendering to the back buffer. But what is the back buffer? If we review our D3DApp code, we see that the back buffer is just a texture in the swap chain:

```
ID3D11Texture2D* backBuffer;
HR(mSwapChain->GetBuffer(0, __uuidof(ID3D11Texture2D),
    reinterpret_cast<void**>(&backBuffer)));
HR(md3dDevice->CreateRenderTargetView(backBuffer, 0,
    &mRenderTargetView));
```

We instruct Direct3D to render to the back buffer by binding a render target view of the back buffer to the OM stage of the rendering pipeline:

```
md3dImmediateContext->OMSetRenderTargets(1,
    &mRenderTargetView, mDepthStencilView);
```

The contents of the back buffer are eventually displayed on the screen when the back buffer is presented via the IDXGISwapChain::Present method.

If we think about this code, there is nothing that stops us from creating another texture, creating a render target view to it, and binding it to the OM stage of the rendering pipeline. Thus we will be drawing to this different "off-screen" texture (possible with a different camera) instead of the back buffer. This technique is known as *render-to-off-screen-texture* or simply *render-to-texture*. The only difference is that because this texture is not the back buffer, it does not get displayed to the screen during presentation.

Consequently, render-to-texture might seem worthless at first as it does not get presented to the screen. But, after we have rendered-to-texture, we can bind the back buffer back to the OM stage, and resume drawing geometry to the back buffer. We can texture the geometry with the texture we generated during the render-to-texture period. This strategy is used to implement a variety of special effects. For example, you can render-to-texture the scene from a bird's eye view to a texture. Then, when drawing to the back buffer, you can draw a quad in the lower-right corner of the screen with the bird's eye view texture to simulate a radar system (see Figure 12.7). Other render-to-texture techniques include:

Figure 12.7. A camera is placed above the player from a bird's eye view and renders the scene into an off-screen texture. When we draw the scene from the player's eye to the back buffer, we map the texture onto a quad in the bottom-right corner of the screen to display the radar map.

1. Shadow mapping
2. Screen Space Ambient Occlusion
3. Dynamic reflections with cube maps

In this demo, we are going to render our normal demo scene of land and waves to an off-screen texture. This texture will be the input into our blurring algorithm that executes on the compute shader. After the texture is blurred, we will draw a full screen quad to the back buffer with the blurred texture applied so that we can see the blurred result to test our blur implementation. The steps are outlined as follows:

1. Draw scene of land and waves to an off-screen texture.
2. Blur the off-screen texture using a compute shader program.
3. Restore the back buffer as the render target, and draw a full screen quad with the blurred texture applied.

Note: *The previous process requires us to draw with the usual rendering pipeline, switch to the compute shader and do compute work, and finally switch back to the usual rendering pipeline. In general, try to avoid switching back and* *forth between rendering and doing compute work, as there is overhead due to a context switch [NVIDIA10]. For each frame, try to do all compute work, and then do all rendering work. Sometimes it is impossible; for example, in the process described previously, we need to render the scene to a texture, blur it with the compute shader, and then render the blurred results. However, try to minimize the number of switches.*

12.7.3 Blur Implementation Overview

We assume that the blur is separable, so we break the blur down into computing two 1D blurs—a horizontal one and a vertical one. Implementing this requires two texture buffers where we can read and write to both; therefore, we need a SRV and UAV to both textures. Let us call one of the textures **A** and the other texture **B**. The blurring algorithm proceeds as follows:

1. Bind the SRV to **A** as an input to the compute shader (this is the input image that will be horizontally blurred).

2. Bind the UAV to **B** as an output to the compute shader (this is the output image that will store the blurred result).

3. Dispatch the thread groups to perform the *horizontal* blur operation. After this, texture **B** stores the horizontally blurred result $Blur_H(I)$, where I is the image to blur.

4. Bind the SRV to **B** as an input to the compute shader (this is the horizontally blurred image that will next be vertically blurred).

5. Bind the UAV to **A** as an output to the compute shader (this is the output image that will store the final blurred result).

6. Dispatch the thread groups to perform the *vertical* blur operation. After this, texture **A** stores the final blurred result $Blur(I)$, where I is the image to blur.

This logic implements the separable blur formula $Blur(I) = Blur_V(Blur_H(I))$. Observe that both texture **A** and texture **B** serve as an input and an output to the compute shader at some point, but not simultaneously. (It is Direct3D error to bind a resource as an input and output at the same time.) The combined horizontal and vertical blur passes constitute one complete blur pass. The resulting image can be blurred further by performing another blur pass on it. We can repeatedly blur an image until the image is blurred to the desired level.

In our implementation, we use the input texture (the texture to blur) as texture **A** in the previous steps. That is, we blur *in-place*, which means that we ultimately blur the input texture. Sometimes this is not desired; that is, you may want both the original non-blurred image and the blurred image. In this case, you need to make a copy of the input texture and blur the copy.

The texture we render the scene to has the same resolution as the window client area. Therefore, we need to rebuild the off-screen texture, as well as the second texture buffer **B** used in the blur algorithm. We do this on the `OnResize` method:

```
void BlurApp::OnResize()
{
    D3DApp::OnResize();

    XMMATRIX P = XMMatrixPerspectiveFovLH(0.25f*MathHelper::Pi,
        AspectRatio(), 1.0f, 1000.0f);
    XMStoreFloat4x4(&mProj, P);

    //
    // Recreate the resources that depend on the client area size.
    //

    // Resize off-screen texture and rebuild views:
    // Render Targer View, SRV, UAV
    BuildOffscreenViews();

    // Resize texture B and rebuild views: SRV, UAV.
    mBlur.Init(md3dDevice, mClientWidth, mClientHeight,
        DXGI_FORMAT_R8G8B8A8_UNORM);
}
```

We will omit the implementation of these methods here, as we have already seen examples of creating textures, SRVs, and UAVs in this chapter. One thing to note is that the off-screen texture has the additional `D3D11_BIND_RENDER_TARGET` bind flag:

```
D3D11_BIND_RENDER_TARGET |
D3D11_BIND_SHADER_RESOURCE |
D3D11_BIND_UNORDERED_ACCESS
```

This is because we render to the off-screen texture, so we must create a render target view to it. The `mBlur` variable is an instance of a `BlurFilter` helper class we make. This class encapsulates the views to texture **B** and provides a method that kicks off the actual blur operation on the compute shader, the implementation of which we will see in a moment.

Note: *Blurring is an expensive operation and the time it takes is a function of the image size being blurred. Often, when rendering the scene to an off-screen texture, the off-screen texture will be made a quarter of the size of the back buffer. For example, if the back buffer is 800 × 600, the off-screen texture will be 400 × 300. This speeds up the drawing to the off-screen texture (less pixels to fill); moreover, it speeds up the blur (less pixels to blur), and there is additional blurring performed by the magnification texture filter when the texture is stretched from a quarter of the screen resolution to the full screen resolution.*

Suppose our image has width w and height h. As we will see in the next section when we look at the compute shader, for the horizontal 1D blur, our thread group is a horizontal line segment of 256 threads, and each thread is responsible for blurring one pixel in the image. Therefore, we need to dispatch $ceil\left(\frac{w}{256}\right)$ thread groups in the x-direction and h thread groups in the y-direction in order for each pixel in the image to be blurred. If 256 does not divide evenly into w, the last horizontal thread group will have extraneous threads (see Figure 12.8). There is

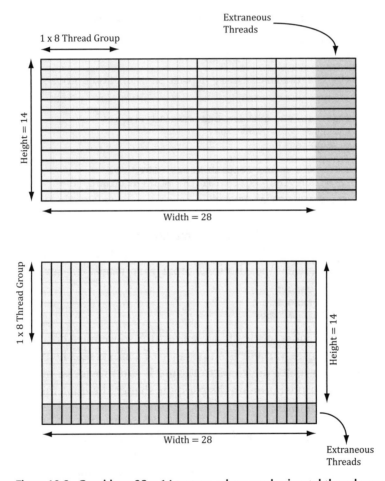

Figure 12.8. Consider a 28×14 texture, where our horizontal thread groups are 8×1 and our vertical thread groups are 1×8 ($X \times Y$ format). For the horizontal pass, in order to cover all the pixels we need to dispatch $ceil\left(\frac{w}{8}\right)=ceil\left(\frac{28}{8}\right)=4$ thread groups in the x-direction and 14 thread groups in the y-direction. Because 28 is not a multiple of 8, we end up with extraneous threads that do not do any work in the right-most thread groups. For the vertical pass, in order to cover all the pixels we need to dispatch $ceil\left(\frac{h}{8}\right)=ceil\left(\frac{14}{8}\right)=2$ thread groups in the y-direction and 28 thread groups in the x-direction. Because 14 is not a multiple of 8, we end up with extraneous threads that do not do any work in the bottom-most thread groups. The same concepts apply to a larger texture with thread groups of size 256.

not really anything we can do about this because the thread group size is fixed. We take care of out-of-bounds with clamping checks in the shader code.

The situation is similar for the vertical 1D blur. Again, our thread group is a vertical line segment of 256 threads, and each thread is responsible for blurring one pixel in the image. Therefore, we need to dispatch $ceil\left(\frac{h}{256}\right)$ thread groups in the y-direction and w thread groups in the x-direction in order for each pixel in the image to be blurred.

The code below figures out how many thread groups to dispatch in each direction, and kicks off the actual blur operation on the compute shader:

```
void BlurFilter::BlurInPlace(ID3D11DeviceContext* dc,
    ID3D11ShaderResourceView* inputSRV,
    ID3D11UnorderedAccessView* inputUAV,
    int blurCount)
{
    //
    // Run the compute shader to blur the offscreen texture.
    //

    for(int i = 0; i < blurCount; ++i)
    {
      // HORIZONTAL blur pass.
      D3DX11_TECHNIQUE_DESC techDesc;
      Effects::BlurFX->HorzBlurTech->GetDesc(&techDesc);
      for(UINT p = 0; p < techDesc.Passes; ++p)
      {
          Effects::BlurFX->SetInputMap(inputSRV);
          Effects::BlurFX->SetOutputMap(mBlurredOutputTexUAV);
          Effects::BlurFX->HorzBlurTech->GetPassByIndex(p)->Apply(0, dc);

          // How many groups do we need to dispatch to cover a
          // row of pixels, where each group covers 256 pixels
          // (the 256 is defined in the ComputeShader).
          UINT numGroupsX = (UINT)ceilf(mWidth / 256.0f);
          dc->Dispatch(numGroupsX, mHeight, 1);
      }

      // Unbind the input texture from the CS for good housekeeping.
      ID3D11ShaderResourceView* nullSRV[1] = { 0 };
      dc->CSSetShaderResources(0, 1, nullSRV);

      // Unbind output from compute shader (we are going to use
      // this output as an input in the next pass), and a resource
      // cannot be both an output and input at the same time.
      ID3D11UnorderedAccessView* nullUAV[1] = { 0 };
      dc->CSSetUnorderedAccessViews(0, 1, nullUAV, 0);

      // VERTICAL blur pass.
      Effects::BlurFX->VertBlurTech->GetDesc(&techDesc);
      for(UINT p = 0; p < techDesc.Passes; ++p)
```

```
  {
    Effects::BlurFX->SetInputMap(mBlurredOutputTexSRV);
    Effects::BlurFX->SetOutputMap(inputUAV);
    Effects::BlurFX->VertBlurTech->GetPassByIndex(p)->Apply(0, dc);

    // How many groups do we need to dispatch to cover a
    // column of pixels, where each group covers 256 pixels
    // (the 256 is defined in the ComputeShader).
    UINT numGroupsY = (UINT)ceilf(mHeight / 256.0f);
    dc->Dispatch(mWidth, numGroupsY, 1);
  }

  dc->CSSetShaderResources(0, 1, nullSRV);
  dc->CSSetUnorderedAccessViews(0, 1, nullUAV, 0);
}

// Disable compute shader.
dc->CSSetShader(0, 0, 0);
}
```

12.7.4 Compute Shader Program

In this section, we look at the compute shader program that actually does the blurring. We will only discuss the horizontal blur case. The vertical blur case is analogous, but the situation transposed.

As mentioned in the previous section, our thread group is a horizontal line segment of 256 threads, and each thread is responsible for blurring one pixel in the image. An inefficient first approach is to just implement the blur algorithm directly. That is, each thread simply performs the weighted average of the row matrix (row matrix because we are doing the 1D horizontal pass) of pixels centered

Figure 12.9. (Left) A screenshot of the "Blur" demo where the image has been blurred 2 times. (Right) A screenshot of the "Blur" demo where the image has been blurred 8 times.

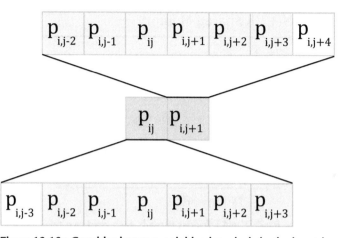

Figure 12.10. Consider just two neighboring pixels in the input image, and suppose that the blur kernel is 1 × 7. Observe that 6 out of the 8 unique pixels are sampled twice—once for each pixel.

about the pixel the thread is processing. The problem with this approach is that it requires fetching the same texel multiple times (see Figure 12.10).

We can optimize by following the strategy described in §12.6 and take advantage of shared memory. Each thread can read in a texel value and store it in shared memory. After all the threads are done reading their texel values into shared memory, the threads can proceed to perform the blur, but where it reads the texels from the shared memory, which is fast to access. The only tricky thing about this is that a thread group of $n = 256$ threads requires $n + 2R$ texels to perform the blur, where R is the blur radius (Figure 12.11).

The solution is simple; we allocate $n + 2R$ elements of shared memory, and have $2R$ threads look up two texel values. The only thing that is tricky about this is that it requires a little more bookkeeping when indexing into the shared memory; we no longer have the ith group thread ID corresponding to the ith element in the shared memory. Figure 12.12 shows the mapping from threads to shared memory for $R = 4$.

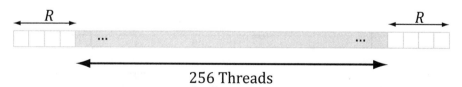

256 Threads

Figure 12.11. Pixels near the boundaries of the thread group will read pixels outside the thread group due to the blur radius.

N + 2R Shared Memory

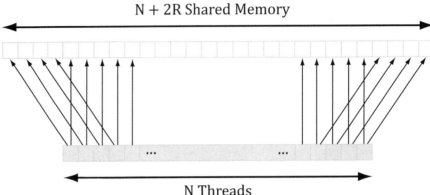

N Threads

Figure 12.12. In this example, $R = 4$. The 4 leftmost threads each read two texel values and store them into shared memory. The 4 rightmost threads each read two texel values and store them into shared memory. Every other thread just reads one texel value and stores it in shared memory. This gives us all the texel values we need to blur *N* pixels with blur radius *R*.

Finally, the last situation to discuss is that the leftmost thread group and the rightmost thread group can index the input image out-of-bounds, as shown in Figure 12.13.

Reading from an out-of-bounds index is not illegal—it is defined to return 0 (and writing to an out-of-bounds index results in a no-op). However, we do not want to read 0 when we go out-of-bounds, as it means 0 colors (i.e., black) will make their way into the blur at the boundaries. Instead, we want to implement

Leftmost threads of leftmost thread block will sample outside the image due to blur radius.

Extraneous threads are still executed and write to shared memory.

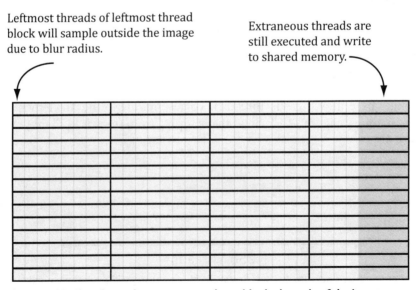

Figure 12.13. Situations where we can read outside the bounds of the image.

something analogous to the *clamp* texture address mode, where if we read an out-of-bounds value, it returns the same value as the boundary texel. This can be implemented by clamping the indices:

```
// Clamp out of bound samples that occur at left image borders.
int x = max(dispatchThreadID.x - gBlurRadius, 0);
gCache[groupThreadID.x] = gInput[int2(x, dispatchThreadID.y)];

// Clamp out of bound samples that occur at right image borders.
int x = min(dispatchThreadID.x + gBlurRadius, gInput.Length.x-1);
gCache[groupThreadID.x+2*gBlurRadius] =
    gInput[int2(x, dispatchThreadID.y)];

// Clamp out of bound samples that occur at image borders.
gCache[groupThreadID.x+gBlurRadius] =
    gInput[min(dispatchThreadID.xy, gInput.Length.xy-1)];
```

The full shader code is shown below:

```
//=====================================================================
// Blur.fx by Frank Luna (C) 2011 All Rights Reserved.
//
// Performs a separable blur with a blur radius of 5.
//=====================================================================

cbuffer cbSettings
{
    float gWeights[11] =
    {
      0.05f, 0.05f, 0.1f, 0.1f, 0.1f, 0.2f, 0.1f, 0.1f, 0.1f, 0.05f, 0.05f,
    };
};

cbuffer cbFixed
{
    static const int gBlurRadius = 5;
};

Texture2D gInput;
RWTexture2D<float4> gOutput;

#define N 256
#define CacheSize (N + 2*gBlurRadius)
groupshared float4 gCache[CacheSize];

[numthreads(N, 1, 1)]
void HorzBlurCS(int3 groupThreadID : SV_GroupThreadID,
    int3 dispatchThreadID : SV_DispatchThreadID)
{
    //
    // Fill local thread storage to reduce bandwidth.  To blur
    // N pixels, we will need to load N + 2*BlurRadius pixels
    // due to the blur radius.
    //
```

```
   // This thread group runs N threads.  To get the extra 2*BlurRadius
   // pixels, have 2*BlurRadius threads sample an extra pixel.
   if(groupThreadID.x < gBlurRadius)
   {
     // Clamp out of bound samples that occur at image borders.
     int x = max(dispatchThreadID.x - gBlurRadius, 0);
     gCache[groupThreadID.x] = gInput[int2(x, dispatchThreadID.y)];
   }
   if(groupThreadID.x >= N-gBlurRadius)
   {
     // Clamp out of bound samples that occur at image borders.
     int x = min(dispatchThreadID.x + gBlurRadius, gInput.Length.x-1);
     gCache[groupThreadID.x+2*gBlurRadius] =
       gInput[int2(x, dispatchThreadID.y)];
   }

   // Clamp out of bound samples that occur at image borders.
   gCache[groupThreadID.x+gBlurRadius] =
     gInput[min(dispatchThreadID.xy, gInput.Length.xy-1)];

   // Wait for all threads to finish.
   GroupMemoryBarrierWithGroupSync();

   //
   // Now blur each pixel.
   //

   float4 blurColor = float4(0, 0, 0, 0);

   [unroll]
   for(int i = -gBlurRadius; i <= gBlurRadius; ++i)
   {
     int k = groupThreadID.x + gBlurRadius + i;

     blurColor += gWeights[i+gBlurRadius]*gCache[k];
   }

   gOutput[dispatchThreadID.xy] = blurColor;
}

[numthreads(1, N, 1)]
void VertBlurCS(int3 groupThreadID : SV_GroupThreadID,
    int3 dispatchThreadID : SV_DispatchThreadID)
{
   //
   // Fill local thread storage to reduce bandwidth.  To blur
   // N pixels, we will need to load N + 2*BlurRadius pixels
   // due to the blur radius.
   //

   // This thread group runs N threads.  To get the extra 2*BlurRadius
   // pixels, have 2*BlurRadius threads sample an extra pixel.
   if(groupThreadID.y < gBlurRadius)
```

```
    {
      // Clamp out of bound samples that occur at image borders.
      int y = max(dispatchThreadID.y - gBlurRadius, 0);
      gCache[groupThreadID.y] = gInput[int2(dispatchThreadID.x, y)];
    }
    if(groupThreadID.y >= N-gBlurRadius)
    {
      // Clamp out of bound samples that occur at image borders.
      int y = min(dispatchThreadID.y + gBlurRadius, gInput.Length.y-1);
      gCache[groupThreadID.y+2*gBlurRadius] =
        gInput[int2(dispatchThreadID.x, y)];
    }

    // Clamp out of bound samples that occur at image borders.
    gCache[groupThreadID.y+gBlurRadius] =
      gInput[min(dispatchThreadID.xy, gInput.Length.xy-1)];


    // Wait for all threads to finish.
    GroupMemoryBarrierWithGroupSync();

    //
    // Now blur each pixel.
    //

    float4 blurColor = float4(0, 0, 0, 0);

    [unroll]
    for(int i = -gBlurRadius; i <= gBlurRadius; ++i)
    {
      int k = groupThreadID.y + gBlurRadius + i;

      blurColor += gWeights[i+gBlurRadius]*gCache[k];
    }

    gOutput[dispatchThreadID.xy] = blurColor;
}

technique11 HorzBlur
{
    pass P0
    {
      SetVertexShader(NULL);
      SetPixelShader(NULL);
      SetComputeShader(CompileShader(cs_5_0, HorzBlurCS()));
    }
}

technique11 VertBlur
{
    pass P0
    {
      SetVertexShader(NULL);
      SetPixelShader(NULL);
      SetComputeShader(CompileShader(cs_5_0, VertBlurCS()));
    }
}
```

For the last line

```
gOutput[dispatchThreadID.xy] = blurColor;
```

it is possible in the rightmost thread group to have extraneous threads that do not correspond to an element in the output texture (Figure 12.13). That is, the `dispatchThreadID.xy` will be an out-of-bounds index for the output texture. However, we do not need to worry about handling this case, as an out-of-bound write results in a no-op.

12.8 FURTHER RESOURCES

Compute shader programming is a subject in its own right, and there are several books on using GPUs for compute programs:

1. *Programming Massively Parallel Processors: A Hands-on Approach* by David B. Kirk and Wen-mei W. Hwu.

2. *OpenCL Programming Guide* by Aaftab Munshi, Benedict R. Gaster, Timothy G. Mattson, James Fung, and Dan Ginsburg.

Technologies like CUDA and OpenCL are just different APIs for accessing the GPU for writing compute programs. Best practices for CUDA and OpenCL programs are also best practices for Direct Compute programs, as the programs are all executed on the same hardware. In this chapter, we have shown the majority of Direct Compute syntax, and so you should have no trouble porting a CUDA or OpenCL program to Direct Compute.

Chuck Walbourn has posted a blog page consisting of links to many Direct Compute presentations:

http://blogs.msdn.com/b/chuckw/archive/2010/07/14/directcompute.aspx

In addition, Microsoft's Channel 9 has a series of lecture videos on Direct Compute programming:

http://channel9.msdn.com/tags/DirectCompute-Lecture-Series/

Finally, NVIDIA has a whole section on CUDA training:

http://developer.nvidia.com/cuda-training

In particular, there are full video lectures on CUDA programming from the University of Illinois, which we highly recommend. Again, we emphasize that CUDA is just another API for accessing the compute functionality of the GPU. Once you understand the syntax, the hard part about GPU computing is learning how to write efficient programs for it. By studying these lectures on CUDA, you will get a better idea of how GPU hardware works so that you can write optimal code.

12.9 SUMMARY

1. The `ID3D11DeviceContext::Dispatch` API call dispatches a grid of thread groups. Each thread group is a 3D grid of threads; the number of threads per thread group is specified by the `[numthreads(x,y,z)]` attribute in the compute shader. For performance reasons, the total number of threads should be a multiple of the warp size (32 for NVIDIA hardware) or a multiple of the wavefront size (64 ATI hardware).

2. To ensure parallelism, at least two thread groups should be dispatched per multiprocessor. So if your hardware has 16 multiprocessors, then at least 32 thread groups should be dispatched so a multiprocessor always has work to do. Future hardware will likely have more multiprocessors, so the number of thread groups should be even higher to ensure your program scales well to future hardware.

3. Once thread groups are assigned to a multiprocessor, the threads in the thread groups are divided into warps of 32 threads on NVIDIA hardware. The multiprocessor then works on a warp of threads at a time in an SIMD fashion (i.e., the same instruction is executed for each thread in the warp). If a warp becomes stalled, say to fetch texture memory, the multiprocessor can quickly switch and execute instructions for another warp to hide this latency. This keeps the multiprocessor always busy. You can see why there is the recommendation of the thread group size being a multiple of the warp size; if it were not then when the thread group is divided into warps, there will be warps with threads that are not doing anything.

4. Texture resources can be accessed by the compute shader for input by creating a SRV to the texture and binding it to the compute shader. A read-write texture (`RWTexture`) is a texture the compute shader can read and write output to. To set a texture for reading and writing to the compute shader, a UAV (unordered access view) to the texture is created and bound to the compute shader. Texture elements can be indexed with operator [] notation, or sampled via texture coordinates and sampler state with the `SampleLevel` method.

5. A structured buffer is a buffer of elements that are all the same type, like an array. The type can be a user-defined type defined by a `struct`, for example. Read-only structured buffers are defined in the HLSL like this:

```
StructuredBuffer<DataType> gInputA;
```

Read-write structured buffers are defined in the HLSL like this:

```
RWStructuredBuffer<DataType> gOutput;
```

Read-only buffer resources can be accessed by the compute shader for input by creating a SRV to a structured buffer and binding it to the compute shader. Read-write buffer resources can be accessed by the compute shader for reading and writing by creating a UAV to a structured buffer and binding it to the compute shader.

6. Various thread IDs are passed into the compute shader via the system values. These IDs are often used to index into resources and shared memory.

7. Consume and append structured buffers are defined in the HLSL like this:

```
ConsumeStructuredBuffer<DataType> gInput;
AppendStructuredBuffer<DataType> gOutput;
```

Consume and append structured buffers are useful if you do not care about the order in which data elements are processed and written to the output buffer, as it allows you to avoid indexing syntax. Note that append buffers do not automatically grow, and they must be large enough to store all the data elements you will append to it.

8. Thread groups are given a section of so-called shared memory or thread local storage. Accessing this memory is fast and can be thought of as being as fast as a hardware cache. This shared memory cache can be useful for optimizations or needed for algorithm implementations. In the compute shader code, shared memory is declared like so:

```
groupshared float4 gCache[N];
```

The array size **N** can be whatever you want, but the maximum size of group shared memory is 32kb. Assuming a multiprocessor supports the maximum of 32kb for shared memory, for performance, a thread group should not use more than 16kb of shared memory; otherwise it is impossible to fit two thread groups on a single multiprocessor.

9. Avoid switching between compute processing and rendering when possible, as there is overhead required to make the switch. In general, for each frame try to do all of your compute work first, then do all of your rendering work.

12.10 EXERCISES

1. Write a compute shader that inputs a structured buffer of 64 3D vectors with random magnitudes contained in [1,10]. The compute shader computes the length of the vectors and outputs the result into a floating-point buffer. Copy

the results to CPU memory and save the results to file. Verify that all the lengths are contained in [1,10].

2. Redo the previous exercise using typed buffers; that is, `Buffer<float3>` for the input buffer and `Buffer<float>` for the output buffer.

3. Assume that in the previous exercises that we do not care the order in which the vectors are normalized. Redo Exercise 1 using Append and Consume buffers.

4. Research the bilateral blur technique and implement it on the compute shader. Redo the "Blur" demo using the bilateral blur.

5. So far in our demos we have done a 2D wave equation on the CPU with the `Waves` class in *Waves.h/.cpp*. Port this to a GPU implementation. Use textures of `float`s to store the previous, current, and next height solutions:

```
Texture2D gPrevSolInput;
Texture2D gCurrSolInput;
RWTexture2D<float> gCurrSolOutput;
RWTexture2D<float> gNextSolOutput;
```

Use the compute shader to perform the wave update computations. A separate compute shader can be used to disturb the water to generate waves. After you have updated the grid heights, you can render a triangle grid with the same vertex resolution as the wave textures (so there is a texel corresponding to each grid vertex), and bind the current wave solution texture to a new "waves" vertex shader. Then in the vertex shader, you can sample the solution texture to offset the heights (this is called *displacement mapping*) and estimate the normal.

```
VertexOut VS(VertexIn vin)
{
    VertexOut vout;

    // Sample the displacement map using non-transformed
    // [0,1]^2 tex-coords.
    vin.PosL.y = gDisplacementMap.SampleLevel(
      samDisplacement, vin.Tex, 0.0f).r;

    // Estimate normal using finite difference.
    float du = gDisplacementMapTexelSize.x;
    float dv = gDisplacementMapTexelSize.y;
    float l = gDisplacementMap.SampleLevel(
      samDisplacement, vin.Tex-float2(du, 0.0f), 0.0f ).r;
    float r = gDisplacementMap.SampleLevel(
      samDisplacement, vin.Tex+float2(du, 0.0f), 0.0f ).r;
    float t = gDisplacementMap.SampleLevel(
      samDisplacement, vin.Tex-float2(0.0f, dv), 0.0f ).r;
    float b = gDisplacementMap.SampleLevel(
      samDisplacement, vin.Tex+float2(0.0f, dv), 0.0f ).r;
    vin.NormalL = normalize(float3(-r+l, 2.0f*gGridSpatialStep, b-t));
```

```
// Transform to world space space.
vout.PosW    = mul(float4(vin.PosL, 1.0f), gWorld).xyz;
vout.NormalW = mul(vin.NormalL, (float3x3)gWorldInvTranspose);

// Transform to homogeneous clip space.
vout.PosH = mul(float4(vin.PosL, 1.0f), gWorldViewProj);

// Output vertex attributes for interpolation across triangle.
vout.Tex = mul(float4(vin.Tex, 0.0f, 1.0f), gTexTransform).xy;

return vout;
}
```

Compare your performance results (time per frame) to a CPU implementation with 512×512 grid points in release mode.

Chapter 13 THE TESSELLATION STAGES

The tessellation stages refer to three stages in the rendering pipeline involved in tessellating geometry. Simply put, tessellation refers to subdividing geometry into smaller triangles and then offsetting the newly generated vertices in some way. The motivation to increase the triangle count is to add detail to the mesh. But why not just create a detailed high-poly mesh to start with and be done? Following are three reasons for tessellation.

1. Dynamic LOD on the GPU. We can dynamically adjust the detail of a mesh based on its distance from the camera and other factors. For example, if a mesh is very far away, it would be wasteful to render a high-poly version of it, as we would not be able to see all that detail anyway. As the object gets closer to the camera, we can continuously increase tessellation to increase the detail of the object.

2. Physics and animation efficiency. We can perform physics and animation calculations on the low-poly mesh, and then tessellate to the higher polygon version. This saves computation power by performing the physics and animation calculations at a lower frequency.

3. Memory savings. We can store lower polygon meshes in memory (on disk, RAM, and VRAM), and then have the GPU tessellate to the higher polygon version on the fly.

Figure 13.1 shows that the tessellation stages sit between the vertex shader and geometry shader. These stages are optional, as we have not been using them in this book so far.

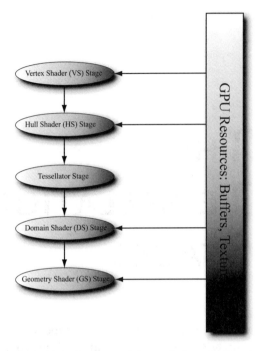

Figure 13.1. A subset of the rendering pipeline showing the tessellation stages.

Objectives:

1. To discover the patch primitive types used for tessellation.

2. To obtain an understanding of what each tessellation stage does, and what the expected inputs and outputs are for each stage.

3. To be able to tessellate geometry by writing hull and domain shader programs.

4. To become familiar with different strategies for determining when to tessellate and to become familiar with performance considerations regarding hardware tessellation.

5. To learn the mathematics of Bézier curves and surfaces and how to implement them in the tessellation stages.

13.1 TESSELLATION PRIMITIVE TYPES

When we render for tessellation, we do not submit triangles to the IA stage. Instead, we submit *patches* with a number of *control points*. Direct3D supports patches with 1–32 control points, and these are described by the following primitive types:

```
D3D11_PRIMITIVE_1_CONTROL_POINT_PATCH    = 8,
D3D11_PRIMITIVE_2_CONTROL_POINT_PATCH    = 9,
D3D11_PRIMITIVE_3_CONTROL_POINT_PATCH    = 10,
D3D11_PRIMITIVE_4_CONTROL_POINT_PATCH    = 11,
    .
    .
    .
D3D11_PRIMITIVE_31_CONTROL_POINT_PATCH   = 38,
D3D11_PRIMITIVE_32_CONTROL_POINT_PATCH   = 39
```

A triangle can be thought of as a triangle patch with three control points (D3D11_PRIMITIVE_3_CONTROL_POINT_PATCH), so you can still submit your usual triangle meshes to be tessellated. A simple quad patch can be submitted with four control points (D3D11_PRIMITIVE_4_CONTROL_POINT_PATCH). These patches are eventually tessellated into triangles by the tessellation stages.

So what about the patches with a higher number of control points? The idea of control points comes from the construction of certain kinds of mathematical curves and surfaces. If you have ever worked with Bézier curves in a drawing program like Adobe Illustrator, then you know that you mold the shape of the curve via control points. The mathematics of Bézier curves can be generalized to Bézier surfaces. For example, you can create a Bézier quad patch that uses 9 control points to shape it or 16 control points; increasing the number of control points gives you more degrees of freedom in shaping the patch. So the motivation for all these control type primitives is to provide support for these kinds of curved surfaces. We give an explanation and demo of Bézier quad patches in this chapter.

13.1.1 Tessellation and the Vertex Shader

Because we submit patch control points to the rendering pipeline, the control points are what get pumped through the vertex shader. Thus, when tessellation is enabled, the vertex shader is really a "vertex shader for control points," and we can do any control point work we need before tessellation starts. Typically, animation or physics calculations are done in the vertex shader at the lower frequency before the geometry is tessellated.

13.2 THE HULL SHADER

In the following subsections, we explore the hull shader, which actually consists of two shaders:

1. Constant Hull Shader
2. Control Point Hull Shader

13.2.1 Constant Hull Shader

This *constant hull shader* is evaluated per patch, and is tasked with outputting the so-called *tessellation factors* of the mesh. The tessellation factors instruct the tessellation stage how much to tessellate the patch. Here is an example of a *quad patch* with 4 control points, where we tessellate it uniformly 3 times.

```
struct PatchTess
{
    float EdgeTess[4]    : SV_TessFactor;
    float InsideTess[2]  : SV_InsideTessFactor;

    // Additional info you want associated per patch.
};

PatchTess ConstantHS(InputPatch<VertexOut, 4> patch,
                     uint patchID : SV_PrimitiveID)
{
    PatchTess pt;

    // Uniformly tessellate the patch 3 times.

    pt.EdgeTess[0] = 3; // Left edge
    pt.EdgeTess[1] = 3; // Top edge
    pt.EdgeTess[2] = 3; // Right edge
    pt.EdgeTess[3] = 3; // Bottom edge

    pt.InsideTess[0] = 3; // u-axis (columns)
    pt.InsideTess[1] = 3; // v-axis (rows)

    return pt;
}
```

The constant hull shader inputs all the control points of the patch, which is defined by the type `InputPatch<VertexOut, 4>`. Recall that the control points are first pumped through the vertex shader, so their type is determined by the output type of the vertex shader `VertexOut`. In this example, our patch has four control points, so we specify 4 for the second template parameter of `InputPatch`. The system also provides a patch ID value via the `SV_PrimitiveID` semantic that can be used if needed; the ID uniquely identifies the patches in a draw call. The constant hull shader must output the tessellation factors; the tessellation factors depend on the topology of the patch.

Note: *Besides the tessellation factors (`SV_TessFactor` and `SV_InsideTessFactor`), you can output other patch information from the constant hull shader. The domain shader receives the output from the constant hull shader as input, and could make use of this extra patch information.*

Tessellating a quad patch consists of two parts:

1. Four edge tessellation factors control how much to tessellate along each edge.

2. Two interior tessellation factors indicate how to tessellate the quad patch (one tessellation factor for the horizontal dimension of the quad, and one tessellation factor for the vertical dimension of the quad).

Figure 13.2 shows examples of different quad patch configurations we can get when the tessellation factors are not the same. Study these figures until you are comfortable with how the edge and interior tessellation factors work.

Tessellating a *triangle patch* also consists of two parts:

1. Three edge tessellation factors control how much to tessellate along each edge.

2. One interior tessellation factor indicates how much to tessellate the triangle patch.

Figure 13.3 shows examples of different triangle patch configurations we can get when the tessellation factors are not the same.

The maximum tessellation factor supported by Direct3D 11 hardware is 64. If all the tessellation factors are zero, the patch is rejected from further processing. This allows us to implement optimizations such as frustum culling and backface culling on a per patch basis.

1. If a patch is not visible by the frustum, then we can reject the patch from further processing (if we did tessellate it, the tessellated triangles would be rejected during triangle clipping).

2. If a patch is backfacing, then we can reject the patch from further processing (if we did tessellate it, the tessellated triangles would be rejected in the backface culling part of rasterization).

A natural question to ask is how much should you tessellate. So remember that the basic idea of tessellation is to add detail to your meshes. However, we do not want to unnecessarily add details if they cannot be appreciated by the user. The following are some common metrics used to determine the amount to tessellate:

1. Distance from the camera: The further an object is from the eye, the less we will notice fine details; therefore, we can render a low-poly version of the object when it is far away, and tessellate more as it gets closer to the eye.

2. Screen area coverage: We can estimate the number of pixels an object covers on the screen. If this number is small, then we can render a low-poly version of the object. As its screen area coverage increases, we can tessellate more.

3. Orientation: The orientation of the triangle with respect to the eye is taken into consideration with the idea that triangles along silhouette edges will be more refined than other triangles.

4. Roughness: Rough surfaces with lots of details will need more tessellation than smooth surfaces. A roughness value can be precomputed by examining the surface textures, which can be used to decide how much to tessellate.

[Story10] gives the following performance advice:

1. If the tessellation factors are 1 (which basically means we are not really tessellating), consider rendering the patch without tessellation, as we will be wasting GPU overhead going through the tessellation stages when they are not doing anything.

2. For performance reasons related to GPU implementations, do not tessellate such that the triangles are so small they cover less than 8 pixels.

3. Batch draw calls that use tessellation (i.e., turning tessellation on and off between draw calls is expensive).

13.2.2 Control Point Hull Shader

The control point hull shader inputs a number of control points and outputs a number of control points. The control point hull shader is invoked once per control point output. One application of the hull shader is to change surface representations, say from an ordinary triangle (submitted to the pipeline with 3 control points) to a cubic Bézier triangle patch (a patch with 10 control points). For example, suppose your mesh is modeled as usual by triangles (3 control points); you can use the hull shader to augment the triangle to a higher order cubic Bézier triangle patch with 10 control points, then detail can be added with the additional control points and the triangle patch tessellated to the desired amount. This strategy is the so-called *N-patches scheme* or *PN triangles* scheme [Vlachos01]; it is convenient because it uses tessellation to improve existing triangle meshes with no modification to the art pipeline. For our first demo, it will be a simple *pass-through* shader, where we just pass the control point through unmodified.

Note: *Drivers can detect and optimize pass-through shaders [Bilodeau10b].*

```
struct HullOut
{
    float3 PosL : POSITION;
};

[domain("quad")]
[partitioning("integer")]
[outputtopology("triangle_cw")]
[outputcontrolpoints(4)]
```

```
[patchconstantfunc("ConstantHS")]
[maxtessfactor(64.0f)]
HullOut HS(InputPatch<VertexOut, 4> p,
           uint i : SV_OutputControlPointID,
           uint patchId : SV_PrimitiveID)
{
    HullOut hout;

    hout.PosL = p[i].PosL;

    return hout;
}
```

The hull shader inputs all of the control points of the patch via the `InputPatch` parameter. The system value `SV_OutputControlPointID` gives an index identifying the output control point the hull shader is working on. Note that the input patch control point count does *not* need to match the output control point count; for example, the input patch could have 4 control points and the output patch could have 16 control points; the additional control points could be derived from the 4 input control points.

The control point hull shader introduces a number of attributes:

1. `domain`: The patch type. Valid arguments are `tri`, `quad`, or `isoline`.

2. `partitioning`: Specifies the subdivision mode of the tessellation.

    (a) `integer`: New vertices are added/removed only at integer tessellation factor values. The fractional part of a tessellation factor is ignored. This creates a noticeable "popping" when a mesh changes in tessellation level.

    (b) Fractional tessellation (`fractional_even`/`fractional_odd`): New vertices are added/removed at integer tessellation factor values, but "slide" in gradually based on the fractional part of the tessellation factor. This is useful when you want to smoothly transition from a coarser version of the mesh to a finer version through tessellation, rather than abruptly at integer steps. The difference between integer and fractional tessellation is best understood by an animation, so the exercises at the end of this chapter will have you experiment to see the difference first hand.

3. `outputtopology`: The winding order of the triangles created via subdivision.

    (a) `triangle_cw`: Clockwise winding order.

    (b) `triangle_ccw`: Counterclockwise winding order.

    (c) `line`: For line tessellation.

4. `outputcontrolpoints`: The number of times the hull shader executes, outputting one control point each time. The system value `SV_OutputControlPointID` gives an index identifying the output control point the hull shader is working on.

5. **patchconstantfunc**: A string specifying the constant hull shader function name.

6. **maxtessfactor**: A hint to the driver specifying the maximum tessellation factor your shader uses. This can potentially enable optimizations by the hardware if it knows this upper bound, as it will know how many resources are needed for the tessellation. The maximum tessellation factor supported by Direct3D 11 hardware is 64.

13.3 THE TESSELLATION STAGE

As programmers, we do not have control of the tessellation stage. This stage is all done by the hardware, which tessellates the patches based on the tessellation factors output from the constant hull shader program. The following figures illustrate different subdivisions based on the tessellation factors.

13.3.1 Quad Patch Tessellation Examples

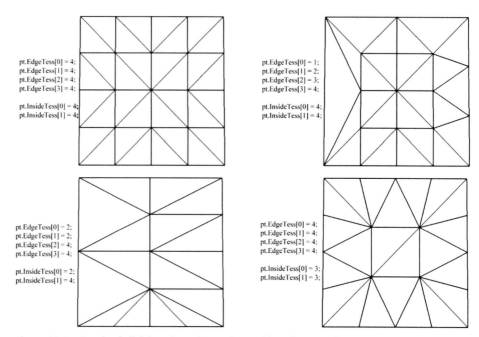

Figure 13.2. Quad subdivisions based on edge and interior tessellation factors.

13.3.2 Triangle Patch Tessellation Examples

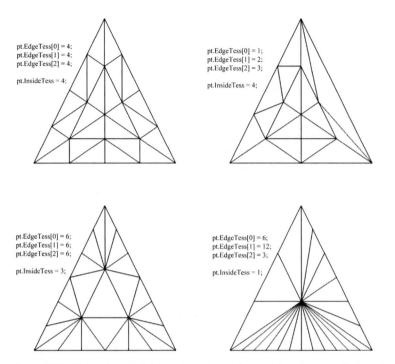

Figure 13.3. Triangle subdivisions based on edge and interior tessellation factors.

13.4 THE DOMAIN SHADER

The tessellation stage outputs all of our newly created vertices and triangles. The domain shader is invoked for each vertex created by the tessellation stage. With tessellation enabled, whereas the vertex shader acts as a vertex shader for each control point, the hull shader is essentially the vertex shader for the tessellated patch. In particular, it is here that we project the vertices of the tessellated patch to homogeneous clip space.

For a quad patch, the domain shader inputs the tessellation factors (and any other per patch information you output from the constant hull shader), the parametric (u, v) coordinates of the tessellated vertex positions, and all the patch control points output from the control point hull shader. Note that the domain shader does not give you the actual tessellated vertex positions; instead it gives you the parametric (u, v) coordinates (Figure 13.4) of these points in the patch domain space. It is up to you to use these parametric coordinates and the control

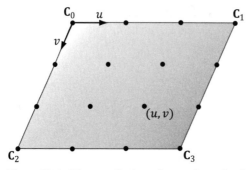

Figure 13.4. **The tessellation of a quad patch with 4 control points generating 16 vertices in the normalized *uv-space*, with coordinates in $[0, 1]^2$.**

points to derive the actual 3D vertex positions; in the following code, we do this via bilinear interpolation (which works just like texture linear filtering).

```
struct DomainOut
{
    float4 PosH : SV_POSITION;
};

// The domain shader is called for every vertex created by the
    tessellator.
// It is like the vertex shader after tessellation.
[domain("quad")]
DomainOut DS(PatchTess patchTess,
             float2 uv : SV_DomainLocation,
             const OutputPatch<HullOut, 4> quad)
{
    DomainOut dout;

    // Bilinear interpolation.
    float3 v1 = lerp(quad[0].PosL, quad[1].PosL, uv.x);
    float3 v2 = lerp(quad[2].PosL, quad[3].PosL, uv.x);
    float3 p = lerp(v1, v2, uv.y);

    dout.PosH = mul(float4(p, 1.0f), gWorldViewProj);

    return dout;
}
```

Note: *As shown in Figure 13.4, the ordering of the quad patch control points are row-by-row.*

The domain shader for a triangle patch is similar, except that instead of the parametric (u, v) values being input, the **float3** barycentric (u, v, w) coordinates of the vertex are input (see "Appendix C.," §C.3) for an explanation of barycentric coordinates. The reason for outputting barycentric coordinates for triangle patches is probably due to the fact that Bézier triangle patches are defined in terms of barycentric coordinates.

13.5 TESSELLATING A QUAD

For one of the demos in this chapter, we submit a quad patch to the rendering pipeline, tessellate it based on the distance from the camera, and displace the generated vertices by a mathematic function that is similar to the one we have been using for the "hills" in our past demos.

Our vertex buffer storing the 4 control points is created like so:

```
void BasicTessellation::BuildQuadPatchBuffer()
{
    D3D11_BUFFER_DESC vbd;
    vbd.Usage = D3D11_USAGE_IMMUTABLE;
    vbd.ByteWidth = sizeof(XMFLOAT3) * 4;
    vbd.BindFlags = D3D11_BIND_VERTEX_BUFFER;
    vbd.CPUAccessFlags = 0;
    vbd.MiscFlags = 0;

    XMFLOAT3 vertices[4] =
    {
      XMFLOAT3(-10.0f, 0.0f, +10.0f),
      XMFLOAT3(+10.0f, 0.0f, +10.0f),
      XMFLOAT3(-10.0f, 0.0f, -10.0f),
      XMFLOAT3(+10.0f, 0.0f, -10.0f)
    };

    D3D11_SUBRESOURCE_DATA vinitData;
    vinitData.pSysMem = vertices;
    HR(md3dDevice->CreateBuffer(&vbd, &vinitData, &mQuadPatchVB));
}
```

Submitting the quad patch to the IA stage is simply done as follows:

```
md3dImmediateContext->IASetPrimitiveTopology(
    D3D11_PRIMITIVE_TOPOLOGY_4_CONTROL_POINT_PATCHLIST);

UINT stride = sizeof(Vertex::Pos);
UINT offset = 0;

md3dImmediateContext->IASetVertexBuffers(
    0, 1, &mQuadPatchVB, &stride, &offset);

md3dImmediateContext->Draw(4, 0);
```

We will now turn attention to the hull shader. The hull shader is similar to what we showed in §13.2.1 and §13.2.2, except that we now determine the tessellation factors based on the distance from the eye. The idea behind this is to use a low-poly mesh in the distance, and increase the tessellation (and hence triangle count) as the mesh approaches the eye (see Figure 13.5). The hull shader is simply a pass-through shader.

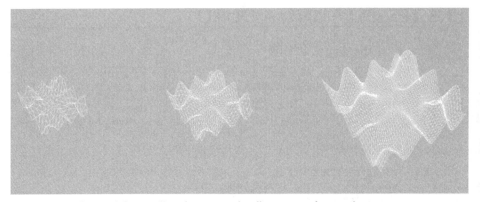

Figure 13.5. The mesh is tessellated more as the distance to the eye decreases.

```
struct VertexIn
{
    float3 PosL    : POSITION;
};

struct VertexOut
{
    float3 PosL    : POSITION;
};

VertexOut VS(VertexIn vin)
{
    VertexOut vout;

    vout.PosL = vin.PosL;

    return vout;
}

struct PatchTess
{
    float EdgeTess[4]    : SV_TessFactor;
    float InsideTess[2]  : SV_InsideTessFactor;
};

PatchTess ConstantHS(InputPatch<VertexOut, 4> patch, uint patchID :
    SV_PrimitiveID)
{
    PatchTess pt;

    // Find center of patch in world space.
    float3 centerL = 0.25f*(patch[0].PosL + patch[1].PosL +
                            patch[2].PosL + patch[3].PosL);
    float3 centerW = mul(float4(centerL, 1.0f), gWorld).xyz;

    float d = distance(centerW, gEyePosW);
```

```
// Tessellate the patch based on distance from the eye such that
// the tessellation is 0 if d >= d1 and 64 if d <= d0.  The interval
// [d0, d1] defines the range we tessellate in.

const float d0 = 20.0f;
const float d1 = 100.0f;
float tess = 64.0f*saturate((d1-d)/(d1-d0));

// Uniformly tessellate the patch.

pt.EdgeTess[0] = tess;
pt.EdgeTess[1] = tess;
pt.EdgeTess[2] = tess;
pt.EdgeTess[3] = tess;

pt.InsideTess[0] = tess;
pt.InsideTess[1] = tess;

return pt;
}

struct HullOut
{
    float3 PosL : POSITION;
};

[domain("quad")]
[partitioning("integer")]
[outputtopology("triangle_cw")]
[outputcontrolpoints(4)]
[patchconstantfunc("ConstantHS")]
[maxtessfactor(64.0f)]
HullOut HS(InputPatch<VertexOut, 4> p,
           uint i : SV_OutputControlPointID,
           uint patchId : SV_PrimitiveID)
{
    HullOut hout;

    hout.PosL = p[i].PosL;

    return hout;
}
```

Simply tessellating is not enough to add detail, as the new triangles just lie on the patch that was subdivided. We must offset those extra vertices in some way to better approximate the shape of the object we are modeling. This is done in the domain shader. In this demo, we offset the y-coordinates by the "hills" function we introduced in §6.10.

```
struct DomainOut
{
    float4 PosH : SV_POSITION;
};
```

```
// The domain shader is called for every vertex created by the tessellator.
// It is like the vertex shader after tessellation.
[domain("quad")]
DomainOut DS(PatchTess patchTess,
             float2 uv : SV_DomainLocation,
             const OutputPatch<HullOut, 4> quad)
{
    DomainOut dout;

    // Bilinear interpolation.
    float3 v1 = lerp(quad[0].PosL, quad[1].PosL, 1-uv.y);
    float3 v2 = lerp(quad[3].PosL, quad[2].PosL, 1-uv.y);
    float3 p  = lerp(v1, v2, uv.x);

    // Displacement mapping
    p.y = 0.3f*(p.z*sin(p.x) + p.x*cos(p.z));

    dout.PosH = mul(float4(p, 1.0f), gWorldViewProj);

    return dout;
}

float4 PS(DomainOut pin) : SV_Target
{
    return float4(1.0f, 1.0f, 1.0f, 1.0f);
}

technique11 Tess
{
    pass P0
    {
      SetVertexShader(CompileShader(vs_5_0, VS()));
      SetHullShader(CompileShader(hs_5_0, HS()));
      SetDomainShader(CompileShader(ds_5_0, DS()));
      SetPixelShader(CompileShader(ps_5_0, PS()));
    }
}
```

13.6 CUBIC BÉZIER QUAD PATCHES

In this section, we describe cubic Bézier quad patches to show how surfaces are constructed via a higher number of control points. Before we get to surfaces, however, it helps to first start with Bézier curves.

13.6.1 Bézier Curves

Consider three noncollinear points $\mathbf{p}_0$, $\mathbf{p}_1$, and $\mathbf{p}_2$ which we will call the control points. These three control points define a Bézier curve in the following way. A point $\mathbf{p}(t)$ on the curve is first found by linearly interpolating between $\mathbf{p}_0$ and $\mathbf{p}_1$ by t and $\mathbf{p}_1$ and $\mathbf{p}_2$ by t to get the intermediate points:

$$\mathbf{p}_0^1 = (1-t)\mathbf{p}_0 + t\mathbf{p}_1$$

$$\mathbf{p}_1^1 = (1-t)\mathbf{p}_1 + t\mathbf{p}_2$$

Then $\mathbf{p}(t)$ is found by linearly interpolating between $\mathbf{p}_0^1$ and $\mathbf{p}_1^1$ by t:

$$\begin{aligned}
\mathbf{p}(t) &= (1-t)\mathbf{p}_0^1 + t\mathbf{p}_1^1 \\
&= (1-t)\big((1-t)\mathbf{p}_0 + t\mathbf{p}_1\big) + t\big((1-t)\mathbf{p}_1 + t\mathbf{p}_2\big) \\
&= (1-t)^2\,\mathbf{p}_0 + 2(1-t)t\mathbf{p}_1 + t^2\mathbf{p}_2
\end{aligned}$$

In other words, this construction by repeated interpolation leads to the parametric formula for a quadratic (degree 2) Bézier curve:

$$\mathbf{p}(t) = (1-t)^2\,\mathbf{p}_0 + 2(1-t)t\mathbf{p}_1 + t^2\mathbf{p}_2$$

In a similar manner, four control points $\mathbf{p}_0$, $\mathbf{p}_1$, $\mathbf{p}_2$, and $\mathbf{p}_3$ define a cubic (degree 3) Bézier curve, and a point $\mathbf{p}(t)$ on the curve is found again by repeated interpolation. Figure 13.6 shows the situation. First, linearly interpolate along each line segment the four given control points defined to get three first generation intermediate points:

$$\mathbf{p}_0^1 = (1-t)\mathbf{p}_0 + t\mathbf{p}_1$$

$$\mathbf{p}_1^1 = (1-t)\mathbf{p}_1 + t\mathbf{p}_2$$

$$\mathbf{p}_2^1 = (1-t)\mathbf{p}_2 + t\mathbf{p}_3$$

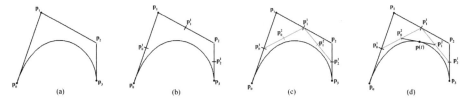

Figure 13.6. Repeated linear interpolation defined points on the cubic Bézier curve. The figure uses $t = 0.5$. (a) The 4 control points and the curve they define. (b) Linearly interpolate between the control points to calculate the first generation of intermediate points. (c) Linearly interpolate between the first generation intermediate points to get the second generation intermediate points. (d) Linearly interpolate between the second generation intermediate points to get the point on the curve.

Next, linearly interpolate along each line segment these first generation intermediate points defined to get two second generation intermediate points:

$$\mathbf{p}_0^2 = (1-t)\mathbf{p}_0^1 + t\mathbf{p}_1^1$$
$$= (1-t)^2 \mathbf{p}_0 + 2(1-t)t\mathbf{p}_1 + t^2\mathbf{p}_2$$
$$\mathbf{p}_1^2 = (1-t)\mathbf{p}_1^1 + t\mathbf{p}_2^1$$
$$= (1-t)^2 \mathbf{p}_1 + 2(1-t)t\mathbf{p}_2 + t^2\mathbf{p}_3$$

Finally, $\mathbf{p}(t)$ is found by linearly interpolating between these last generation intermediate points:

$$\mathbf{p}(t) = (1-t)\mathbf{p}_0^2 + t\mathbf{p}_1^2$$
$$= (1-t)\left((1-t)^2 \mathbf{p}_0 + 2(1-t)t\mathbf{p}_1 + t^2\mathbf{p}_2\right) + t\left((1-t)^2 \mathbf{p}_1 + 2(1-t)t\mathbf{p}_2 + t^2\mathbf{p}_3\right)$$

which simplifies to the parametric formula for a cubic (degree 3) Bézier curve:

$$\mathbf{p}(t) = (1 - t)^3\mathbf{p}_0 + 3t(1 - t)^2\mathbf{p}_1 + 3t^2(1 - t)\mathbf{p}_2 + t^3\mathbf{p}_3 \qquad \text{(eq. 13.1)}$$

Generally people stop at cubic curves, as they give enough smoothness and degrees of freedom for controlling the curve, but you can keep going to higher-order curves with the same recursive pattern of repeated interpolation.

It turns out that the formula for Bézier curves of degree n can be written in terms of the *Bernstein basis functions*, which are defined by:

$$B_i^n(t) = \frac{n!}{i!(n-i)!}t^i(1-t)^{n-i}$$

For degree 3 curves, the Bernstein basis functions are:

$$B_0^3(t) = \frac{3!}{0!(3-0)!}t^0(1-t)^{3-0} = (1-t)^3$$

$$B_1^3(t) = \frac{3!}{1!(3-1)!}t^1(1-t)^{3-1} = 3t(1-t)^2$$

$$B_2^3(t) = \frac{3!}{2!(3-2)!}t^2(1-t)^{3-2} = 3t^2(1-t)$$

$$B_3^3(t) = \frac{3!}{3!(3-3)!}t^3(1-t)^{3-3} = t^3$$

Compare these values to the factors in Equation 13.1. Therefore, we can write a cubic Bézier curve as:

$$\mathbf{p}(t) = \sum_{j=0}^{3} B_j^3(t)\mathbf{p}_j = B_0^3(t)\mathbf{p}_0 + B_1^3(t)\mathbf{p}_1 + B_2^3(t)\mathbf{p}_2 + B_3^3(t)\mathbf{p}_3$$

The derivatives of the cubic Bernstein basis functions can be found by application of the power and product rules:

$$B_0^{3'}(t) = -3(1-t)^2$$

$$B_1^{3'}(t) = 3(1-t)^2 - 6t(1-t)$$

$$B_2^{3'}(t) = 6t(1-t) - 3t^2$$

$$B_3^{3'}(t) = 3t^2$$

And the derivative of the cubic Bézier curve is:

$$\mathbf{p}'(t) = \sum_{j=0}^{3} B_j^3(t)\mathbf{p}_j = B_0^3(t)\mathbf{p}_0 + B_1^3(t)\mathbf{p}_1 + B_2^{3'}(t)\mathbf{p}_2 + B_3^{3'}(t)\mathbf{p}_3$$

Derivatives are useful for computing the tangent vector along the curve.

Note: *There are Bézier curve applets online that allow you to set and manipulate the control points to see how the curves are shaped interactively.*

13.6.2 Cubic Bézier Surfaces

Refer to Figure 13.7 throughout this section. Consider a patch of 4 × 4 control points. Each row, therefore, contains 4 control points that can be used to define the cubic Bézier curve; the Bézier curve of the ith row is given by:

$$\mathbf{q}_i(u) = \sum_{j=0}^{3} B_j^3(u)\mathbf{p}_{i,j}$$

If we evaluate each of these Bézier curves at say u_0, then we get a "column" of 4 points, one along each curve. We can use these 4 points to define another Bézier curve that lies on the *Bézier surface* at u_0:

$$\mathbf{p}(v) = \sum_{i=0}^{3} B_i^3(v)\mathbf{q}_i(u_0)$$

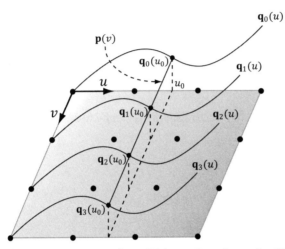

Figure 13.7. Constructing a Bézier surface. Some simplifications were made to make the figure easier to understand—the control points do not all lie in the plane, all the q_i (*u*) need not be the same as the figure suggests (they would only be the same if the control points were the same for each row to give the same curves), and p(*v*) generally would not be a straight line but a cubic Bézier curve.

Now, if we let *u* vary as well, we sweep out a family of cubic Bézier curves that form the *cubic Bézier surface*:

$$\mathbf{p}(u,v) = \sum_{i=0}^{3} B_i^3(v)\mathbf{q}_i(u)$$

$$= \sum_{i=0}^{3} B_i^3(v) \sum_{j=0}^{3} B_j^3(u)\mathbf{p}_{i,j}$$

The partial derivatives of a Bézier surface are useful for computing tangent and normal vectors:

$$\frac{\partial \mathbf{p}}{\partial u}(u,v) = \sum_{i=0}^{3} B_i^3(v) \sum_{j=0}^{3} \frac{\partial B_j^3}{\partial u}(u)\mathbf{p}_{i,j}$$

$$\frac{\partial \mathbf{p}}{\partial v}(u,v) = \sum_{i=0}^{3} \frac{\partial B_j^3}{\partial v}(v) \sum_{j=0}^{3} B_j^3(u)\mathbf{p}_{i,j}$$

13.6.3 Cubic Bézier Surface Evaluation Code

In this section, we give code to evaluate a cubic Bézier surface. To help understand the code that follows, we expand out the summation notation:

$$\mathbf{q}_0(u) = B_0^3(u)\mathbf{p}_{0,0} + B_1^3(u)\mathbf{p}_{0,1} + B_2^3(u)\mathbf{p}_{0,2} + B_3^3(u)\mathbf{p}_{0,3}$$

$$\mathbf{q}_1(u) = B_0^3(u)\mathbf{p}_{1,0} + B_1^3(u)\mathbf{p}_{1,1} + B_2^3(u)\mathbf{p}_{1,2} + B_3^3(u)\mathbf{p}_{1,3}$$

$$\mathbf{q}_2(u) = B_0^3(u)\mathbf{p}_{2,0} + B_1^3(u)\mathbf{p}_{2,1} + B_2^3(u)\mathbf{p}_{2,2} + B_3^3(u)\mathbf{p}_{2,3}$$

$$\mathbf{q}_3(u) = B_0^3(u)\mathbf{p}_{3,0} + B_1^3(u)\mathbf{p}_{3,1} + B_2^3(u)\mathbf{p}_{3,2} + B_3^3(u)\mathbf{p}_{3,3}$$

$$\begin{aligned}
\mathbf{p}(u,v) &= B_0^3(v)\mathbf{q}_0(u) + B_1^3(v)\mathbf{q}_1(u) + B_2^3(v)\mathbf{q}_2(u) + B_3^3(v)\mathbf{q}_3(u) \\
&= B_0^3(v)\left[B_0^3(u)\mathbf{p}_{0,0} + B_1^3(u)\mathbf{p}_{0,1} + B_2^3(u)\mathbf{p}_{0,2} + B_3^3(u)\mathbf{p}_{0,3} \right] \\
&\quad + B_1^3(v)\left[B_0^3(u)\mathbf{p}_{1,0} + B_1^3(u)\mathbf{p}_{1,1} + B_2^3(u)\mathbf{p}_{1,2} + B_3^3(u)\mathbf{p}_{1,3} \right] \\
&\quad + B_2^3(v)\left[B_0^3(u)\mathbf{p}_{2,0} + B_1^3(u)\mathbf{p}_{2,1} + B_2^3(u)\mathbf{p}_{2,2} + B_3^3(u)\mathbf{p}_{2,3} \right] \\
&\quad + B_3^3(v)\left[B_0^3(u)\mathbf{p}_{3,0} + B_1^3(u)\mathbf{p}_{3,1} + B_2^3(u)\mathbf{p}_{3,2} + B_3^3(u)\mathbf{p}_{3,3} \right]
\end{aligned}$$

The following code maps directly to the formulas just given:

```
float4 BernsteinBasis(float t)
{
    float invT = 1.0f - t;

    return float4(invT * invT * invT,      //  B_0^3(t) = (1-t)^3
                  3.0f * t * invT * invT,   //  B_1^3(t) = 3t(1-t)^2
                  3.0f * t * t * invT,      //  B_2^3(t) = 3t^2(1-t)
                  t * t * t);               //  B_3^3(t) = t^3
}


float4 dBernsteinBasis(float t)
{
    float invT = 1.0f - t;

    return float4(
        -3 * invT * invT,                  //  B_0^{3'}(t) = -3(1-t)^2
        3 * invT * invT - 6 * t * invT,    //  B_1^{3'}(t) = 3(1-t)^2 - 6t(1-t)
        6 * t * invT - 3 * t * t,          //  B_2^{3'}(t) = 6t(1-t) - 3t^2
        3 * t * t);                        //  B_3^{3'}(t) = 3t^2
}


float3 CubicBezierSum(const OutputPatch<HullOut, 16> bezpatch,
                      float4 basisU, float4 basisV)
```

```
{
    float3 sum = float3(0.0f, 0.0f, 0.0f);
    sum  = basisV.x * (basisU.x*bezpatch[0].PosL  +
                       basisU.y*bezpatch[1].PosL  +
                       basisU.z*bezpatch[2].PosL  +
                       basisU.w*bezpatch[3].PosL);

    sum += basisV.y * (basisU.x*bezpatch[4].PosL  +
                       basisU.y*bezpatch[5].PosL  +
                       basisU.z*bezpatch[6].PosL  +
                       basisU.w*bezpatch[7].PosL);

    sum += basisV.z * (basisU.x*bezpatch[8].PosL  +
                       basisU.y*bezpatch[9].PosL  +
                       basisU.z*bezpatch[10].PosL +
                       basisU.w*bezpatch[11].PosL);

    sum += basisV.w * (basisU.x*bezpatch[12].PosL +
                       basisU.y*bezpatch[13].PosL +
                       basisU.z*bezpatch[14].PosL +
                       basisU.w*bezpatch[15].PosL);

    return sum;
}
```

The previous functions can be utilized like so to evaluate $\mathbf{p}(u, v)$ and compute the partial derivatives:

```
float4 basisU = BernsteinBasis(uv.x);
float4 basisV = BernsteinBasis(uv.y);

// p(u, v)
float3 p  = CubicBezierSum(bezPatch, basisU, basisV);

float4 dBasisU = dBernsteinBasis(uv.x);
float4 dBasisV = dBernsteinBasis(uv.y);

// ∂p/∂v (u, v)
float3 dpdu  = CubicBezierSum(bezPatch, dbasisU, basisV);

// ∂p/∂v (u, v)
float3 dpdv  = CubicBezierSum(bezPatch, basisU, dbasisV);
```

Note: *Observe that we pass the evaluated basis function values to* CubicBezierSum. *This enables us to use* CubicBezierSum *for evaluating both* $\mathbf{p}(u, v)$ *and the partial derivatives, as the summation form is the same, the only difference being the basis functions.*

13.6.4 Defining the Patch Geometry

Our vertex buffer storing the 16 control points is created like so:

```
void BasicTessellation::BuildQuadPatchBuffer()
{
    D3D11_BUFFER_DESC vbd;
    vbd.Usage = D3D11_USAGE_IMMUTABLE;
    vbd.ByteWidth = sizeof(XMFLOAT3) * 16;
    vbd.BindFlags = D3D11_BIND_VERTEX_BUFFER;
    vbd.CPUAccessFlags = 0;
    vbd.MiscFlags = 0;

    XMFLOAT3 vertices[16] =
    {
      // Row 0
      XMFLOAT3(-10.0f, -10.0f, +15.0f),
      XMFLOAT3(-5.0f,   0.0f, +15.0f),
      XMFLOAT3(+5.0f,   0.0f, +15.0f),
      XMFLOAT3(+10.0f,  0.0f, +15.0f),

      // Row 1
      XMFLOAT3(-15.0f,  0.0f, +5.0f),
      XMFLOAT3(-5.0f,   0.0f, +5.0f),
      XMFLOAT3(+5.0f,  20.0f, +5.0f),
      XMFLOAT3(+15.0f,  0.0f, +5.0f),

      // Row 2
      XMFLOAT3(-15.0f,  0.0f, -5.0f),
      XMFLOAT3(-5.0f,   0.0f, -5.0f),
      XMFLOAT3(+5.0f,   0.0f, -5.0f),
      XMFLOAT3(+15.0f,  0.0f, -5.0f),

      // Row 3
      XMFLOAT3(-10.0f, 10.0f, -15.0f),
      XMFLOAT3(-5.0f,   0.0f, -15.0f),
      XMFLOAT3(+5.0f,   0.0f, -15.0f),
      XMFLOAT3(+25.0f, 10.0f, -15.0f)
    };

    D3D11_SUBRESOURCE_DATA vinitData;
    vinitData.pSysMem = vertices;
    HR(md3dDevice->CreateBuffer(&vbd, &vinitData, &mQuadPatchVB));
}
```

Note: *There is no restriction that the control points need to be equidistant to form a uniform grid.*

Submitting the quad patch to the IA stage is simply done as follows:

```
md3dImmediateContext->IASetPrimitiveTopology(
    D3D11_PRIMITIVE_TOPOLOGY_16_CONTROL_POINT_PATCHLIST);

UINT stride = sizeof(Vertex::Pos);
UINT offset = 0;

md3dImmediateContext->IASetVertexBuffers(
    0, 1, &mQuadPatchVB, &stride, &offset);

md3dImmediateContext->Draw(16, 0);
```

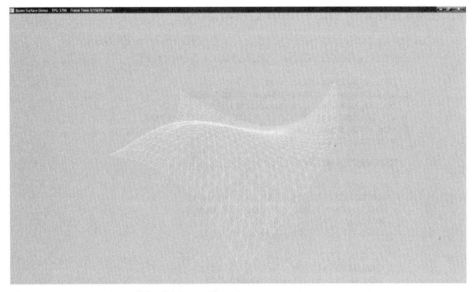

Figure 13.8. Screenshot of the Bézier surface demo.

13.7 SUMMARY

1. The tessellation stages are optional stages of the rendering pipeline. They consist of the hull shader, the tessellator, and the domain shader. The hull and domain shaders are programmable, and the tessellator is completely controlled by the hardware.

2. Hardware tessellation provides memory benefits, as a low-poly asset can be stored and then detail can be added on the fly via tessellation. Additionally, computations such as animation and physics can be done on the low-poly mesh frequency before tessellation. Finally, continuous LOD algorithms can now be implemented completely on the GPU, which always had to be implemented on the CPU before hardware tessellation was available.

3. New primitive types are used only with tessellation to submit control points to the rendering pipeline. Direct3D 11 supports between 1 and 32 control points, which are represented by the enumerated types `D3D11_PRIMITIVE_1_CONTROL_POINT_PATCH`... `D3D11_PRIMITIVE_32_CONTROL_POINT_PATCH`.

4. With tessellation, the vertex shader inputs control points and generally animates or performs physics computations per control point. The hull shader consists of the constant hull shader and the control point hull shader. The constant hull shader operates per patch and outputs the tessellation factors of the patch, which instruct the tessellator how much to tessellate the patch, as

well as any other optional per patch data. The control point hull shader inputs a number of control points and outputs a number of control points. The control point hull shader is invoked once per control point output. Typically the control point hull shader changes the surface representation of the input patch. For example, this stage might input a triangle with three control points and output a Bézier triangle surface patch with ten control points.

5. The domain shader is invoked for each vertex created by the tessellation stage. Whereas the vertex shader acts as a vertex shader for each control point, with tessellation enabled the hull shader is essentially the vertex shader for the tessellated patch vertices. In particular, it is here that we project the vertices of the tessellated patch to homogeneous clip space and do other per vertex work.

6. If you are not going to tessellate an object (e.g., tessellation factors are close to 1), then do not render the object with the tessellation stages enabled, as there is overhead. Avoid tessellating so much that triangles are smaller than eight pixels. Draw all your tessellated objects together to avoid turning tessellation on and off during a frame. Use back face culling and frustum culling in the hull shader to discard patches that are not seen from being tessellated.

7. Bézier curves and surfaces are parametric equations used to describe smooth surfaces. They are "shaped" via control points. In addition to allowing us to draw smooth surfaces directly, Bézier surfaces are used in many popular hardware tessellation algorithms such as PN Triangles and Catmull-Clark approximations.

13.8 EXERCISES

1. Redo the "Basic Tessellation" demo, but tessellate a triangle patch instead of a quad patch.

2. Tessellate an iscoahedron into a sphere based on distance.

3. Modify the "Basic Tessellation" demo so that it does fixed tessellation of a flat quad. Experiment with different edge/interior tessellation factors until you are comfortable with how the tessellation factors work.

4. Explore fractional tessellation. That is, try the "Basic Tessellation" demo with:

```
[partitioning("fractional_even")]
[partitioning("fractional_odd")]
```

5. Compute the Bernstein basis functions $B_0^2(t), B_1^2(t), B_2^2(t)$ for a quadratic Bézier curve, and compute the derivatives $B_0^{2'}(t), B_1^{2'}(t), B_2^{2'}(t)$. Derive the parametric equation for a quadratic Bézier surface.

6. Experiment with the "Bézier Patch" demo by changing the control points to change the Bézier surface.

7. Redo the "Bézier Patch" demo to use a quadratic Bézier surface with nine control points.

8. Modify the "Bézier Patch" demo to light and shade the Bézier surface. You will need to compute vertex normals in the domain shader. A normal at a vertex position can be found by taking the cross product of the partial derivatives at the position.

9. Research and implement Bézier triangle patches.

Part **3** TOPICS

In this part, we focus on applying Direct3D to implement several 3D applications, demonstrating techniques such as terrain rendering, sky rendering, working with meshes, character animation, particle systems, picking, environment mapping and normal mapping, and shadow mapping. A brief description of the chapters in this part follows.

Chapter 14, Building a First Person Camera: In this chapter, we show how to design a camera system that behaves more as you would expect in a first person game. We show how to control the camera via keyboard and mouse input.

Chapter 15, Instancing and Frustum Culling: Instancing is a hardware supported technique that optimizes the drawing of the same geometry multiple times with different properties (say at different positions in the scene and with different colors). Frustum culling is an optimization technique where we discard an entire object from being submitted to the rendering pipeline if it lies completely outside the virtual camera's field of view. We also show how to compute the bounding box and sphere of a mesh.

Chapter 16, Picking: This chapter shows how to determine the particular 3D object (or 3D primitive) that the user has selected with the mouse. Picking is often a necessity in 3D games and applications where the user interacts with the 3D world with the mouse.

Chapter 17, Cube Mapping: In this chapter, we show how to reflect environments onto arbitrary meshes with environment mapping; in addition, we use an environment map to texture a sky-sphere.

Chapter 18, Normal Mapping and Displacement Mapping: This chapter shows how to get detailed real-time lighting results using normal maps. In addition, we show how to combine tessellation with displacement maps to increase the geometry detail of our objects.

Chapter 19, Terrain Rendering: This chapter shows how to create, texture,and light, and render 3D terrains using heightmaps, tessellation, and a multi-texturing technique. Furthermore, we show how to smoothly "walk" " the camera over the terrain.

Chapter 20, Particle Systems and Stream-Out: In this chapter, we learn how to model systems that consist of many small particles that all behave in a similar manner. For example, particle systems can be used to model falling snow and rain, fire and smoke, rocket trails, sprinklers, and fountains.

Chapter 21, Shadow Mapping: Shadow mapping is a real-time shadowing technique, which shadows arbitrary geometry (it is not limited to planar shadows). In addition, we learn how projective texturing works.

Chapter 22, Ambient Occlusion: Lighting plays an important role in making our scenes look realistic. In this chapter, we improve the ambient term of our lighting equation by estimating how occluded a point in our scene is from incoming light.

Chapter 23, Meshes: This chapter shows how to load complex models from files and shows how to design a simple set of classes for working with meshes.

Chapter 24, Quaternions: In this chapter, we study mathematical objects called quaternions. We show that unit quaternions represent rotations and can be interpolated in a simple way, thereby giving us a way to interpolate rotations. Once we can interpolate rotations, we can create 3D animations.

Chapter 25, Character Animation: This chapter extends the "Meshes" chapter by loading complicated models from file, but with animation data. We cover the theory of character animation and show how to animate a typical human game character with a complex walking animation.

Chapter 14

14 BUILDING A FIRST PERSON CAMERA

In this short chapter, we design a camera system that behaves more as you would expect in a first person game. This camera system will replace the orbiting camera system we have been using thus far in the demos.

Objectives:

1. To review the mathematics of the view space transformation.
2. To be able to identify the typical functionality of a first person camera.
3. To learn how to implement a first person camera.

14.1 VIEW TRANSFORM REVIEW

View space is the coordinate system attached to the camera as shown in Figure 14.1. The camera sits at the origin looking down the positive z-axis, the x-axis aims to the right of the camera, and the y-axis aims above the camera. Instead of describing our scene vertices relative to the world space, it is convenient for later stages of the rendering pipeline to describe them relative to the camera coordinate system. The change of coordinate transformation from world space to view space is called the *view transform*, and the corresponding matrix is called the *view matrix*.

If $\mathbf{Q}_w = (Q_x, Q_y, Q_z, 1)$, $\mathbf{u}_w = (u_x, u_y, u_z, 0)$, $\mathbf{v}_w = (v_x, v_y, v_z, 0)$, and $\mathbf{w}_w = (w_x, w_y, w_z, 0)$ describe, respectively, the origin, x-, y-, and z-axes of view space with homogeneous coordinates relative to world space, then we know from §3.4.3 that the change of coordinate matrix from view space to world space is:

$$
\mathbf{W} = \begin{bmatrix}
u_x & u_y & u_z & 0 \\
v_x & v_y & v_z & 0 \\
w_x & w_y & w_z & 0 \\
Q_x & Q_y & Q_z & 1
\end{bmatrix}
$$

However, this is not the transformation we want. We want the reverse transformation from world space to view space. But recall from §3.4.5 that reverse transformation is just given by the inverse. Thus $\mathbf{W}^{-1}$ transforms from world space to view space.

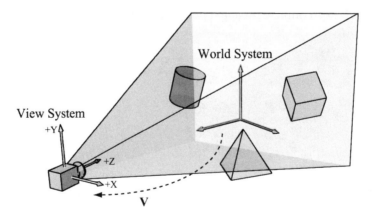

Figure 14.1. The camera coordinate system. Relative to its own coordinate system, the camera sits at the origin looking down the positive z-axis.

The world coordinate system and view coordinate system generally differ by position and orientation only, so it makes intuitive sense that $\mathbf{W} = \mathbf{RT}$ (i.e., the world matrix can be decomposed into a rotation followed by a translation). This form makes the inverse easier to compute:

$$\mathbf{V} = \mathbf{W}^{-1} = (\mathbf{RT})^{-1} = \mathbf{T}^{-1}\mathbf{R}^{-1} = \mathbf{T}^{-1}\mathbf{R}^{T}$$

$$= \begin{bmatrix} 1 & 0 & 0 & 0 \\ 0 & 1 & 0 & 0 \\ 0 & 0 & 1 & 0 \\ -Q_x & -Q_y & -Q_z & 1 \end{bmatrix} \begin{bmatrix} u_x & v_x & w_x & 0 \\ u_y & v_y & w_y & 0 \\ u_z & v_z & w_z & 0 \\ 0 & 0 & 0 & 1 \end{bmatrix} = \begin{bmatrix} u_x & v_x & w_x & 0 \\ u_y & v_y & w_y & 0 \\ u_z & v_z & w_z & 0 \\ -Q \cdot u & -Q \cdot v & -Q \cdot w & 1 \end{bmatrix}$$

So the view matrix has the form:

$$\mathbf{V} = \begin{bmatrix} u_x & v_x & w_x & 0 \\ u_y & v_y & w_y & 0 \\ u_z & v_z & w_z & 0 \\ -Q \cdot u & -Q \cdot v & -Q \cdot w & 1 \end{bmatrix}$$

(eq. 14.1)

As with all change-of-coordinate transformations, we are not moving anything in the scene. The coordinates change because we are using the camera space frame of reference instead of the world space frame of reference.

14.2 THE CAMERA CLASS

To encapsulate our camera related code, we define and implement a `Camera` class. The data of the camera class stores two key pieces of information. The *position*, *right*, *up*, and *look* vectors of the camera defining, respectively, the origin, *x*-axis, *y*-axis, and *z*-axis of the view space coordinate system in world coordinates, and the properties of the frustum. You can think of the lens of the camera as defining the frustum (its field of view and near and far planes). Most of the methods are trivial (e.g., simple access methods). See the following comments for an overview of the methods and data members. We review selected methods in the next section.

```
class Camera
{
public:
    Camera();
    ~Camera();

    // Get/Set world camera position.
    XMVECTOR GetPositionXM()const;
```

```
        XMFLOAT3 GetPosition()const;
        void SetPosition(float x, float y, float z);
        void SetPosition(const XMFLOAT3& v);

        // Get camera basis vectors.
        XMVECTOR GetRightXM()const;
        XMFLOAT3 GetRight()const;
        XMVECTOR GetUpXM()const;
        XMFLOAT3 GetUp()const;
        XMVECTOR GetLookXM()const;
        XMFLOAT3 GetLook()const;

        // Get frustum properties.
        float GetNearZ()const;
        float GetFarZ()const;
        float GetAspect()const;
        float GetFovY()const;
        float GetFovX()const;

        // Get near and far plane dimensions in view space coordinates.
        float GetNearWindowWidth()const;
        float GetNearWindowHeight()const;
        float GetFarWindowWidth()const;
        float GetFarWindowHeight()const;

        // Set frustum.
        void SetLens(float fovY, float aspect, float zn, float zf);

        // Define camera space via LookAt parameters.
        void LookAt(FXMVECTOR pos, FXMVECTOR target, FXMVECTOR worldUp);
        void LookAt(const XMFLOAT3& pos, const XMFLOAT3& target,
             const XMFLOAT3& up);

        // Get View/Proj matrices.
        XMMATRIX View()const;
        XMMATRIX Proj()const;
        XMMATRIX ViewProj()const;

        // Strafe/Walk the camera a distance d.
        void Strafe(float d);
        void Walk(float d);

        // Rotate the camera.
        void Pitch(float angle);
        void RotateY(float angle);

        // After modifying camera position/orientation, call
        // to rebuild the view matrix once per frame.
        void UpdateViewMatrix();

private:

        // Camera coordinate system with coordinates relative to world space.
        XMFLOAT3 mPosition; // view space origin
        XMFLOAT3 mRight;    // view space x-axis
```

```
    XMFLOAT3 mUp;        // view space y-axis
    XMFLOAT3 mLook;      // view space z-axis

    // Cache frustum properties.
    float mNearZ;
    float mFarZ;
    float mAspect;
    float mFovY;
    float mNearWindowHeight;
    float mFarWindowHeight;

    // Cache View/Proj matrices.
    XMFLOAT4X4 mView;
    XMFLOAT4X4 mProj;
};
```

Note: *The Camera.h/Camera.cpp files are in the Common directory.*

14.3 SELECTED METHOD IMPLEMENTATIONS

Many of the camera class methods are trivial get/set methods that we will omit here. However, we will review a few of the important ones in this section.

14.3.1 XMVECTOR Return Variations

First, we want to remark that we provide XMVECTOR return variations for many of the "get" methods; this is just for convenience so that the client code does not need to convert if they need an XMVECTOR:

```
XMVECTOR Camera::GetPositionXM()const
{
    return XMLoadFloat3(&mPosition);
}

XMFLOAT3 Camera::GetPosition()const
{
    return mPosition;
}
```

14.3.2 SetLens

We can think of the frustum as the lens of our camera, for it controls our view. We cache the frustum properties and build the projection matrix using the SetLens method:

```
void Camera::SetLens(float fovY, float aspect, float zn, float zf)
{
    // cache properties
    mFovY = fovY;
    mAspect = aspect;
```

```
mNearZ = zn;
mFarZ = zf;

mNearWindowHeight = 2.0f * mNearZ * tanf(0.5f*mFovY);
mFarWindowHeight  = 2.0f * mFarZ * tanf(0.5f*mFovY);

XMMATRIX P = XMMatrixPerspectiveFovLH(mFovY, mAspect, mNearZ, mFarZ);
XMStoreFloat4x4(&mProj, P);
}
```

14.3.3 Derived Frustum Info

As we just saw, we cache the vertical field of view angle, but additionally provide a method that derives the horizontal field of view angle. Moreover, we provide methods to return the width and height of the frustum at the near and far planes, which are sometimes useful to know. The implementations of these methods are just trigonometry, and if you have trouble following the equations, then review §5.6.3:

```
float Camera::GetFovX()const
{
    float halfWidth = 0.5f*GetNearWindowWidth();
    return 2.0f*atan(halfWidth / mNearZ);
}

float Camera::GetNearWindowWidth()const
{
    return mAspect * mNearWindowHeight;
}

float Camera::GetNearWindowHeight()const
{
    return mNearWindowHeight;
}

float Camera::GetFarWindowWidth()const
{
    return mAspect * mFarWindowHeight;
}

float Camera::GetFarWindowHeight()const
{
    return mFarWindowHeight;
}
```

14.3.4 Transforming the Camera

For a first person camera, ignoring collision detection, we want to be able to:

1. Move the camera along its look vector to move forwards and backwards. This can be implemented by translating the camera position along its look vector.

2. Move the camera along its right vector to strafe right and left. This can be implemented by translating the camera position along its right vector.

3. Rotate the camera around its right vector to look up and down. This can be implemented by rotating the camera's look and up vectors around its right vector using the `XMMatrixRotationAxis` function.

4. Rotate the camera around the world's y-axis (assuming the y-axis corresponds to the world's "up" direction) vector to look right and left. This can be implemented by rotating all the basis vectors around the world's y-axis using the `XMMatrixRotationY` function.

```
void Camera::Walk(float d)
{
    // mPosition += d*mLook
    XMVECTOR s = XMVectorReplicate(d);
    XMVECTOR l = XMLoadFloat3(&mLook);
    XMVECTOR p = XMLoadFloat3(&mPosition);
    XMStoreFloat3(&mPosition, XMVectorMultiplyAdd(s, l, p));}

void Camera::Strafe(float d)
{
    // mPosition += d*mRight
    XMVECTOR s = XMVectorReplicate(d);
    XMVECTOR r = XMLoadFloat3(&mRight);
    XMVECTOR p = XMLoadFloat3(&mPosition);
    XMStoreFloat3(&mPosition, XMVectorMultiplyAdd(s, r, p));
}

void Camera::Pitch(float angle)
{
    // Rotate up and look vector about the right vector.

    XMMATRIX R = XMMatrixRotationAxis(XMLoadFloat3(&mRight), angle);

    XMStoreFloat3(&mUp,   XMVector3TransformNormal(XMLoadFloat3(&mUp), R));
    XMStoreFloat3(&mLook, XMVector3TransformNormal(XMLoadFloat3(&mLook), R));
}

void Camera::RotateY(float angle)
{
    // Rotate the basis vectors about the world y-axis.

    XMMATRIX R = XMMatrixRotationY(angle);

    XMStoreFloat3(&mRight,   XMVector3TransformNormal(
                            XMLoadFloat3(&mRight), R));
    XMStoreFloat3(&mUp, XMVector3TransformNormal(XMLoadFloat3(&mUp), R));
    XMStoreFloat3(&mLook, XMVector3TransformNormal(XMLoadFloat3(&mLook), R));
}
```

14.3.5 Building the View Matrix

The first part of the `UpdateViewMatrix` method *reorthonormalizes* the camera's right, up, and look vectors. That is to say, it makes sure they are mutually orthogonal to each other and unit length. This is necessary because after several rotations, numerical errors can accumulate and cause these vectors to become non-orthonormal. When this happens, the vectors no longer represent a rectangular coordinate system, but a skewed coordinate system, which is not what we want. The second part of this method just plugs the camera vectors into Equation 14.1 to compute the view transformation matrix.

```cpp
void Camera:: UpdateViewMatrix()
{
    XMVECTOR R = XMLoadFloat3(&mRight);
    XMVECTOR U = XMLoadFloat3(&mUp);
    XMVECTOR L = XMLoadFloat3(&mLook);
    XMVECTOR P = XMLoadFloat3(&mPosition);

    //
    // Orthonormalize the right, up and look vectors.
    //

    // Make look vector unit length.
    L = XMVector3Normalize(L);

    // Compute a new corrected "up" vector and normalize it.
    U = XMVector3Normalize(XMVector3Cross(L, R));

    // Compute a new corrected "right" vector.  U and L are
    // already ortho-normal, so no need to normalize cross product.
    // ||up × look|| = ||up|| ||look|| sin90° = 1
    R = XMVector3Cross(U, L);

    //
    // Fill in the view matrix entries.
    //
    float x = -XMVectorGetX(XMVector3Dot(P, R));
    float y = -XMVectorGetX(XMVector3Dot(P, U));
    float z = -XMVectorGetX(XMVector3Dot(P, L));

    XMStoreFloat3(&mRight, R);
    XMStoreFloat3(&mUp, U);
    XMStoreFloat3(&mLook, L);

    mView(0,0) = mRight.x;
    mView(1,0) = mRight.y;
    mView(2,0) = mRight.z;
    mView(3,0) = x;

    mView(0,1) = mUp.x;
    mView(1,1) = mUp.y;
    mView(2,1) = mUp.z;
    mView(3,1) = y;

    mView(0,2) = mLook.x;
    mView(1,2) = mLook.y;
```

```
    mView(2,2) = mLook.z;
    mView(3,2) = z;

    mView(0,3) = 0.0f;
    mView(1,3) = 0.0f;
    mView(2,3) = 0.0f;
    mView(3,3) = 1.0f;
}
```

14.4 CAMERA DEMO COMMENTS

We can now remove all the old variables from our application class that were related to the orbital camera system such as mPhi, mTheta, mRadius, mView, and mProj. We will add a member variable:

```
Camera mCam;
```

When the window is resized, we no longer rebuild the projection matrix explicitly, and instead delegate the work to the Camera class with SetLens:

```
void CameraApp::OnResize()
{
    D3DApp::OnResize();

    mCam.SetLens(0.25f*MathHelper::Pi, AspectRatio(), 1.0f, 1000.0f);
}
```

In the UpdateScene method, we handle keyboard input to move the camera:

```
void CameraApp::UpdateScene(float dt)
{
    //
    // Control the camera.
    //
    if(GetAsyncKeyState('W') & 0x8000)
        mCam.Walk(10.0f*dt);

    if(GetAsyncKeyState('S') & 0x8000)
        mCam.Walk(-10.0f*dt);

    if(GetAsyncKeyState('A') & 0x8000)
        mCam.Strafe(-10.0f*dt);

    if(GetAsyncKeyState('D') & 0x8000)
        mCam.Strafe(10.0f*dt);
```

In the OnMouseMove method, we rotate the camera's look direction:

```
void CameraApp::OnMouseMove(WPARAM btnState, int x, int y)
{
    if((btnState & MK_LBUTTON) != 0)
    {
        // Make each pixel correspond to a quarter of a degree.
```

```
    float dx = XMConvertToRadians(
0.25f*static_cast<float>(x - mLastMousePos.x));
    float dy = XMConvertToRadians(
0.25f*static_cast<float>(y - mLastMousePos.y));

    mCam.Pitch(dy);
    mCam.RotateY(dx);
  }

  mLastMousePos.x = x;
  mLastMousePos.y = y;
}
```

Finally, for rendering, the view and projection matrices can be accessed from the camera instance:

```
mCam.UpdateViewMatrix();

XMMATRIX view     = mCam.View();
XMMATRIX proj     = mCam.Proj();
XMMATRIX viewProj = mCam.ViewProj();
```

14.5 SUMMARY

1. We define the camera coordinate system by specifying its position and orientation. The position is specified by a position vector relative to the world

Figure 14.2. Screenshot of the camera demo. Use the 'W', 'S', 'A', and 'D' keys to move forward, backward, strafe left, and strafe right, respectively. Hold the left mouse button down and move the mouse to "look" in different directions.

coordinate system, and the orientation is specified by three orthonormal vectors relative to the world coordinate system: a right, up, and look vector. Moving the camera amounts to moving the camera coordinate system relative to the world coordinate system.

2. We included projection related quantities in the camera class, as the perspective projection matrix can be thought of as the "lens" of the camera by controlling the field of view, and near and far planes.

3. Moving forward and backward can be implemented simply by translating the camera position along its look vector. Strafing right and left can be implemented simply by translating the camera position along its right vector. Looking up and down can be achieved by rotating the camera's look and up vectors around its right vector. Looking left and right can be implemented by rotating all the basis vectors around the world's y-axis.

14.6 EXERCISES

1. Given the world space axes and origin in world coordinates: $\mathbf{i} = (1,0,0), \mathbf{j} = (0,1,0), \mathbf{k} = (0,0,1)$, and $\mathbf{O} = (0,0,0)$, and the view space axes and origin in world coordinates: $\mathbf{u} = (u_x, u_y, u_z), \mathbf{v} = (v_x, v_y, v_z), \mathbf{w} = (w_x, w_y, w_z)$, and $\mathbf{Q} = (Q_x, Q_y, Q_z)$, derive the view matrix form

$$
\mathbf{V} = \begin{bmatrix} u_x & v_x & w_x & 0 \\ u_y & v_y & w_y & 0 \\ u_z & v_z & w_z & 0 \\ -\mathbf{Q}\cdot\mathbf{u} & -\mathbf{Q}\cdot\mathbf{v} & -\mathbf{Q}\cdot\mathbf{w} & 1 \end{bmatrix}
$$

using the dot product. (Remember, to find the change of coordinate matrix from world space to view space, you just need to describe the world space axes and origin with coordinates relative to view space. Then these coordinates become the rows of the view matrix.)

2. Modify the camera demo to support "roll." This is where the camera rotates around its look vector. This could be useful for an aircraft game.

Chapter 15

INSTANCING AND FRUSTUM CULLING

In this chapter, we study two brief topics: instancing and frustum culling. Instancing refers to drawing the same object more than once in a scene. We describe Direct3D features that allow us to implement instancing with minimal API overhead. Frustum culling refers to rejecting entire groups of triangles from further processing that are outside the viewing frustum with a simple test.

Objectives:

1. To learn how to implement hardware instancing.
2. To become familiar with bounding volumes, why they are useful, how to create them, and how to use them.
3. To discover how to implement frustum culling.

509

15.1 HARDWARE INSTANCING

Instancing refers to drawing the same object more than once in a scene, but in different positions, orientations, scales, materials, and textures (e.g., a tree object may be reused several times to build a forest). It would be wasteful to duplicate the vertex and index data for each instance. Instead, we store a single copy of the geometry (i.e., vertex and index lists) relative to the object's local space. Then we draw the object several times, but each time with a different world matrix and different material if variety is desired.

Although this strategy saves memory, it still requires per-object API overhead. That is, for each object, we must set its unique material, its world matrix, and invoke a draw command. Although Direct3D 10 and later was redesigned to minimize a lot of the API overhead that existed in Direct3D 9, there is still some overhead. Consequently, Direct3D provides a mechanism to implement instancing without this extra API overhead, which we call *hardware instancing*.

> Note: *Why the concern about API overhead? It was common for Direct3D 9 applications to be CPU bound due to the API overhead (this means the CPU was the bottleneck, not the GPU). The reason for this is that level designers like to draw many objects with unique materials and textures, and this requires state changes and draw calls for each object. When there is a high-level of CPU overhead for each API call, scenes would be limited to a few thousand draw calls in order to still maintain real-time rendering speeds. Graphics engines would then employ batching techniques (see [Wloka03]) to minimize the number of draw calls. Hardware instancing, often combined with texture arrays, is one aspect where the API helps perform batching.*

15.1.1 The Vertex Shader

Hardware instancing works by streaming instanced data to the input assembler, in addition to vertex and index data. We then tell the hardware to draw N instances of the mesh. As each instance is drawn, the vertex shader will have access to the input vertex *and* the instanced data of the current instance being drawn:

```
struct VertexIn
{
    float3 PosL       : POSITION;
    float3 NormalL    : NORMAL;
    float2 Tex        : TEXCOORD;
    row_major float4x4 World : WORLD;
    float4 Color      : COLOR;
    uint InstanceId   : SV_InstanceID;
};
```

We have bolded the instanced data: A world matrix per instance, so that each instance is uniquely positioned in the scene, and a color per instance, so that each instance is uniquely colored. The system also provides a system value identifier SV_InstanceID. For example, vertices of the first instance will have id 0, vertices of the second instance will have id 1, and so on. One application of the instance id is to use it as an index into a texture array so that each instance can be uniquely textured. The vertex shader uses the instanced world matrix for the world transform instead of the world matrix in the constant buffer; it also passes on the instance color to the pixel shader to give each instance a unique color:

```
struct VertexOut
{
    float4 PosH     : SV_POSITION;
    float3 PosW     : POSITION;
    float3 NormalW  : NORMAL;
    float2 Tex      : TEXCOORD;
    float4 Color    : COLOR;
};

VertexOut VS(VertexIn vin)
{
    VertexOut vout;

    // Transform to world space space.
    vout.PosW = mul(float4(vin.PosL, 1.0f), vin.World).xyz;
    vout.NormalW = mul(vin.NormalL, (float3x3)vin.World);

    // Transform to homogeneous clip space.
    vout.PosH = mul(float4(vout.PosW, 1.0f), gViewProj);

    // Output vertex attributes for interpolation across triangle.
    vout.Tex    = mul(float4(vin.Tex, 0.0f, 1.0f), gTexTransform).xy;
    vout.Color = vin.Color;

    return vout;
}
```

The pixel shader is like the one we used in the last chapter, except that we modulate the ambient and diffuse term with the instance color:

```
ambient += A*pin.Color;
diffuse += D*pin.Color;
```

15.1.2 Streaming Instanced Data

So how do we stream instanced data to the input assembler stage? We stream in vertex data via the input layout, so Direct3D uses the same mechanism to stream in instanced data. Recall the D3D11_INPUT_ELEMENT_DESC structure we first described in Chapter 6:

```
typedef struct D3D11_INPUT_ELEMENT_DESC {
    LPCSTR SemanticName;
    UINT SemanticIndex;
    DXGI_FORMAT Format;
    UINT InputSlot;
    UINT AlignedByteOffset;
    D3D11_INPUT_CLASSIFICATION InputSlotClass;
    UINT InstanceDataStepRate;
} D3D11_INPUT_ELEMENT_DESC;
```

The last two members are related to instancing:

1. `InputSlotClass`: Specifies whether the input element is streamed as a vertex element or an instanced element. Specify one of the following two values:

   (a) `D3D11_INPUT_PER_VERTEX_DATA`: The input element is streamed per-vertex.

   (b) `D3D11_INPUT_PER_INSTANCE_DATA`: The input element is streamed per-instance.

2. `InstanceDataStepRate`: Specifies how many instances to draw per-instanced data element. For example, suppose you want to draw 6 instances, but only supply an array of 3 instanced colors: red, green, and blue; then we set the step rate to 2 and the first 2 instances will be drawn with red, the second two instances will be drawn with green, and the last 2 instances will be drawn with blue. If there is a one-to-one correspondence between each instanced data element and each instance, then the step rate would be 1. For vertex data, specify 0 for the step rate.

In our demo, we stream a world matrix and color per-instance; this is how our input layout is defined:

```
const D3D11_INPUT_ELEMENT_DESC InputLayoutDesc::InstancedBasic32[8] =
{
    {"POSITION", 0, DXGI_FORMAT_R32G32B32_FLOAT, 0, 0,
      D3D11_INPUT_PER_VERTEX_DATA, 0},
    {"NORMAL",   0, DXGI_FORMAT_R32G32B32_FLOAT, 0, 12,
      D3D11_INPUT_PER_VERTEX_DATA, 0},
    {"TEXCOORD", 0, DXGI_FORMAT_R32G32_FLOAT, 0, 24,
      D3D11_INPUT_PER_VERTEX_DATA, 0},
    {"WORLD", 0, DXGI_FORMAT_R32G32B32A32_FLOAT, 1, 0,
      D3D11_INPUT_PER_INSTANCE_DATA, 1},
    {"WORLD", 1, DXGI_FORMAT_R32G32B32A32_FLOAT, 1, 16,
      D3D11_INPUT_PER_INSTANCE_DATA, 1},
    {"WORLD", 2, DXGI_FORMAT_R32G32B32A32_FLOAT, 1, 32,
      D3D11_INPUT_PER_INSTANCE_DATA, 1},
    {"WORLD", 3, DXGI_FORMAT_R32G32B32A32_FLOAT, 1, 48,
      D3D11_INPUT_PER_INSTANCE_DATA, 1},
    {"COLOR", 0, DXGI_FORMAT_R32G32B32A32_FLOAT, 1, 64,
      D3D11_INPUT_PER_INSTANCE_DATA, 1}
};
```

Observe that the vertex data comes from input slot 0, and the instanced data comes from input slot 1. We use two buffers: the first is the usual vertex buffer that contains the vertex data; the second is the instanced buffer that contains the instanced data. We then bind both buffers to the IA stage:

```
struct Basic32
{
    XMFLOAT3 Pos;
    XMFLOAT3 Normal;
    XMFLOAT2 Tex;
};

struct InstancedData
{
    XMFLOAT4X4 World;
    XMFLOAT4 Color;
};

UINT stride[2] = {sizeof(Vertex::Basic32), sizeof(InstancedData)};
UINT offset[2] = {0,0};

ID3D11Buffer* vbs[2] = {mSkullVB, mInstancedBuffer};
md3dImmediateContext->IASetVertexBuffers(0, 2, vbs, stride, offset);
md3dImmediateContext->IASetInputLayout(InputLayouts::InstancedBasic32);
```

15.1.3 Drawing Instanced Data

To draw instanced data, we use the `DrawIndexedInstanced` draw call:

```
void ID3D11DeviceContext::DrawIndexedInstanced(
    UINT IndexCountPerInstance,
    UINT InstanceCount,
    UINT StartIndexLocation,
    INT BaseVertexLocation,
    UINT StartInstanceLocation
);
```

1. `IndexCountPerInstance`: The number of indices that will be used in this draw call that defines one instance. This need not be every index in the index buffer; that is, you can draw a contiguous subset of indices.

2. `InstanceCount`: The number of instances to draw.

3. `StartIndexLocation`: Index to an element in the index buffer that marks the starting point from which to begin reading indices.

4. `BaseVertexLocation`: An integer value to be added to the indices used in this draw call before the vertices are fetched.

5. `StartInstanceLocation`: Index to an element in the instance buffer that marks the starting point from which to begin reading instanced data.

Here is an example call:

```
md3dImmediateContext->DrawIndexedInstanced(
    mSkullIndexCount, // number of indices in the skull mesh
    mVisibleObjectCount, // number of instances to draw
    0, 0, 0);
```

We can draw instanced data that does not use index buffers using the following variation:

```
void ID3D11DeviceContext::DrawInstanced(
    UINT VertexCountPerInstance,
    UINT InstanceCount,
    UINT StartVertexLocation,
    UINT StartInstanceLocation
);
```

15.1.4 Creating the Instanced Buffer

A buffer containing instanced data is created just like any other ID3D11Buffer. In our demo, we store a system memory copy of all the instanced data, and make the instanced buffer dynamic. Then every frame, we copy the instanced data of the *visible* instances into the buffer (this is related to frustum culling, see §15.3). Instanced data is often put in a dynamic buffer so that it can change. For example, if you wanted to move the objects around, you would need to update the world matrices, which you can do easily with a dynamic buffer.

```
void InstancingAndCullingApp::BuildInstancedBuffer()
{
    const int n = 5;
    mInstancedData.resize(n*n*n);

    float width = 200.0f;
    float height = 200.0f;
    float depth = 200.0f;

    float x = -0.5f*width;
    float y = -0.5f*height;
    float z = -0.5f*depth;
    float dx = width / (n-1);
    float dy = height / (n-1);
    float dz = depth / (n-1);
    for(int k = 0; k < n; ++k)
    {
      for(int i = 0; i < n; ++i)
      {
        for(int j = 0; j < n; ++j)
        {
          // Position instanced along a 3D grid.
            mInstancedData[k*n*n + i*n + j].World = XMFLOAT4X4(
              1.0f, 0.0f, 0.0f, 0.0f,
              0.0f, 1.0f, 0.0f, 0.0f,
```

```
                0.0f, 0.0f, 1.0f, 0.0f,
                x+j*dx, y+i*dy, z+k*dz, 1.0f);

        // Random color.
        mInstancedData[k*n*n + i*n + j].Color.x =
          MathHelper::RandF(0.0f, 1.0f);
        mInstancedData[k*n*n + i*n + j].Color.y =
          MathHelper::RandF(0.0f, 1.0f);
        mInstancedData[k*n*n + i*n + j].Color.z =
          MathHelper::RandF(0.0f, 1.0f);
        mInstancedData[k*n*n + i*n + j].Color.w = 1.0f;
      }
    }
  }

  D3D11_BUFFER_DESC vbd;
  vbd.Usage = D3D11_USAGE_DYNAMIC;
  vbd.ByteWidth = sizeof(InstancedData) * mInstancedData.size();
  vbd.BindFlags = D3D11_BIND_VERTEX_BUFFER;
  vbd.CPUAccessFlags = D3D11_CPU_ACCESS_WRITE;
  vbd.MiscFlags = 0;
  vbd.StructureByteStride = 0;

  HR(md3dDevice->CreateBuffer(&vbd, 0, &mInstancedBuffer));
}
```

15.2 BOUNDING VOLUMES AND FRUSTUMS

In order to implement frustum culling, we need to become familiar with the mathematical representation of a frustum and various bounding volumes. Bounding volumes are primitive geometric objects that approximate the volume of an object—see Figure 15.1. The tradeoff is that although the bounding volume

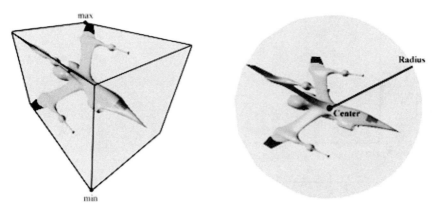

Figure 15.1. A mesh rendered with its AABB and bounding sphere.

only approximates the object, its form has a simple mathematical representation, which makes it easy to work with.

15.2.1 XNA Collision

We use the *xnacollision.h/.cpp* utility library. These files are located at *Microsoft DirectX SDK (June 2010)\Samples\C++\Misc\Collision*. They provide fast XNA math implementations to common geometric primitive intersection tests such as ray/triangle intersection, ray/box intersection, box/box intersection, box/plane intersection, box/frustum, sphere/frustum, and much more. Exercise 3 asks you to explore these files to get familiar with what they offer.

15.2.2 Boxes

The *axis-aligned bounding box* (AABB) of a mesh is a box that tightly surrounds the mesh and its faces are parallel to the major axes. An AABB can be described by a minimum point $\mathbf{v}_{min}$ and a maximum point $\mathbf{v}_{max}$ (see Figure 15.2). The minimum point $\mathbf{v}_{min}$ is found by searching through all the vertices of the mesh and finding the minimum x-, y-, and z-coordinates, and the maximum point $\mathbf{v}_{max}$ is found by searching through all the vertices of the mesh and finding the maximum x-, y-, and z-coordinates.

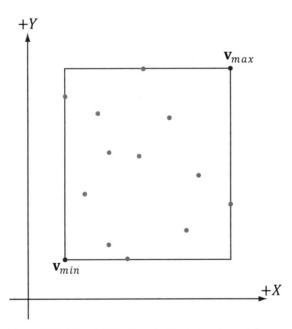

Figure 15.2. The AABB of a set of points using minimum and maximum point representation.

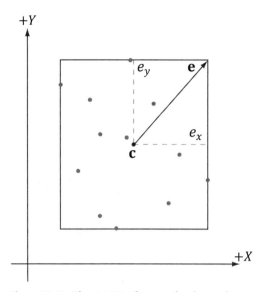

Figure 15.3. **The AABB of a set of points using center and extents representation.**

Alternatively, an AABB can be represented with the box center point **c** and *extents* vector **e**, which stores the distance from the center point to the sides of the box along the coordinate axes (see Figure 15.3).

The XNA collision library uses the center/extents representation:

```
_DECLSPEC_ALIGN_16_ struct AxisAlignedBox
{
    XMFLOAT3 Center;          // Center of the box.
    XMFLOAT3 Extents;         // Distance from the center to each side.
};
```

It is easy to convert from one representation to the other. For example, given a bounding box defined by $\mathbf{v}_{min}$ and $\mathbf{v}_{max}$, the center/extents representation is given by:

$$\mathbf{c} = 0.5(\mathbf{v}_{min} + \mathbf{v}_{max})$$
$$\mathbf{e} = 0.5(\mathbf{v}_{max} - \mathbf{v}_{min})$$

The following code shows how we compute the bounding box of the skull mesh in this chapter's demo:

```
XMFLOAT3 vMinf3(+MathHelper::Infinity, +MathHelper::Infinity,
+MathHelper::Infinity);
XMFLOAT3 vMaxf3(-MathHelper::Infinity, -MathHelper::Infinity,
    -MathHelper::Infinity);

XMVECTOR vMin = XMLoadFloat3(&vMinf3);
XMVECTOR vMax = XMLoadFloat3(&vMaxf3);
std::vector<Vertex::Basic32> vertices(vcount);
```

```
for(UINT i = 0; i < vcount; ++i)
{
    fin >> vertices[i].Pos.x >> vertices[i].Pos.y >>
        vertices[i].Pos.z;
    fin >> vertices[i].Normal.x >> vertices[i].Normal.y >>
        vertices[i].Normal.z;

    XMVECTOR P = XMLoadFloat3(&vertices[i].Pos);

    vMin = XMVectorMin(vMin, P);
    vMax = XMVectorMax(vMax, P);
}

// Convert min/max representation to center and extents representation.
XMStoreFloat3(&mSkullBox.Center, 0.5f*(vMin+vMax));
XMStoreFloat3(&mSkullBox.Extents, 0.5f*(vMax-vMin));
```

The `XMVectorMin` and `XMVectorMax` functions return the vectors:

$$\mathbf{min}(\mathbf{u}, \mathbf{v}) = (\min(u_x, v_x), \min(u_y, v_y), \min(u_z, v_z), \min(u_w, v_w))$$
$$\mathbf{max}(\mathbf{u}, \mathbf{v}) = (\max(u_x, v_x), \max(u_y, v_y), \max(u_z, v_z), \max(u_w, v_w))$$

15.2.2.1 Rotations and Axis-Aligned Bounding Boxes

Figure 15.4 shows that a box axis-aligned in one coordinate system may not be axis-aligned with a different coordinate system. In particular, if we compute the AABB of a mesh in local space, it gets transformed to an *oriented bounding box* (OBB) in world space. However, we can always transform into the local space of the mesh and do the intersection there where the box is axis-aligned.

Alternatively, we can recompute the AABB in the world space, but this can result in a "fatter" box that is a poorer approximation to the actual volume (see Figure 15.5).

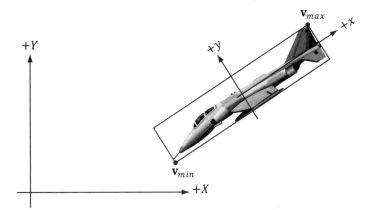

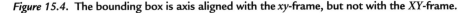

Figure 15.4. The bounding box is axis aligned with the *xy*-frame, but not with the *XY*-frame.

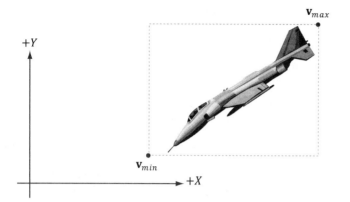

Figure 15.5. **The bounding box is axis aligned with the XY-frame.**

Yet another alternative is to abandon axis-aligned bounding boxes, and just work with oriented bounding boxes, where we maintain the orientation of the box relative to the world space. The XNA collision library provides the following structure for representing an oriented bounding box.

```
_DECLSPEC_ALIGN_16_ struct OrientedBox
{
    XMFLOAT3 Center;         // Center of the box.
    XMFLOAT3 Extents;        // Distance from the center to each side.
    XMFLOAT4 Orientation;    // Unit quaternion representing rotation
                             // (box -> world).
};
```

> **Note:** *In this chapter, you will see mention of quaternions for representing rotations/ orientations. Briefly, a unit quaternion can represent a rotation just like a rotation matrix can. We cover quaternions in Chapter 24. For now, just think of it as representing a rotation like a rotation matrix.*

An AABB and OBB can also be constructed using the XNA collision library functions:

```
VOID ComputeBoundingAxisAlignedBoxFromPoints(AxisAlignedBox* pOut,
    UINT Count, const XMFLOAT3* pPoints, UINT Stride);
VOID ComputeBoundingOrientedBoxFromPoints(OrientedBox* pOut,
    UINT Count, const XMFLOAT3* pPoints, UINT Stride);
```

If your vertex structure looks like this:

```
struct Basic32
{
    XMFLOAT3 Pos;
    XMFLOAT3 Normal;
    XMFLOAT2 Tex;
};
```

And you have an array of vertices forming your mesh:

```
std::vector<Vertex::Basic32> vertices;
```

Then you call this function like so:

```
AxisAlignedBox box;
ComputeBoundingAxisAlignedBoxFromPoints(&box,
    vertices.size(), &vertices[0].Pos, sizeof(Vertex::Basic32));
```

The stride indicates how many bytes to skip to get to the next position element.

Note: *In order to compute bounding volumes of your meshes, you need to have a system memory copy of your vertex list available, such as one stored in* `std::vector`. *This is because the CPU cannot read from a vertex buffer created for rendering—the CPU can only read* `D3D11_USAGE_STAGING` *resources. Therefore, it is common for applications to keep a system memory copy around for things like this, as well as picking (Chapter 16), and collision detection.*

15.2.3 Spheres

The bounding sphere of a mesh is a sphere that tightly surrounds the mesh. A bounding sphere can be described with a center point and radius. One way to compute the bounding sphere of a mesh is to first compute its AABB. We then take the center of the AABB as the center of the bounding sphere:

$$\mathbf{c} = 0.5(\mathbf{v}_{min} + \mathbf{v}_{max})$$

The radius is then taken to be the maximum distance between any vertex $\mathbf{p}$ in the mesh from the center $\mathbf{c}$:

$$r = \max\{\|\mathbf{c} - \mathbf{p}\| : \mathbf{p} \in mesh\}$$

Suppose we compute the bounding sphere of a mesh in local space. After the world transform, the bounding sphere may not tightly surround the mesh due to scaling. Thus the radius needs to be rescaled accordingly. To compensate for non-uniform scaling, we must scale the radius by the largest scaling component so that the sphere encapsulates the transformed mesh. Another possible strategy is to avoid scaling all together by having all your meshes modeled to the same scale of the game world. This way, models will not need to be rescaled once loaded into the application.

A bounding sphere can also be computed using the XNA collision library function:

```
VOID ComputeBoundingSphereFromPoints(Sphere* pOut,
    UINT Count, const XMFLOAT3* pPoints, UINT Stride);
```

15.2.4 Frustums

We are well familiar with frustums from Chapter 5. One way to specify a frustum mathematically is as the intersection of six planes: the left/right planes, the top/bottom planes, and the near/far planes. We assume the six frustum planes are "inward" facing—see Figure 15.6.

This six plane representation makes it easy to do frustum and bounding volume intersection tests.

15.2.4.1 Constructing the Frustum Planes

One easy way to construct the frustum planes is in view space, where the frustum takes on a canonical form centered at the origin looking down the positive z-axis. Here, the near and far planes are trivially specified by their distances along the z-axis, the left and right planes are symmetric and pass through the origin (see Figure 15.6 again), and the top and bottom planes are symmetric and pass through the origin. Consequently, we do not even need to store the full plane equations to represent the frustum in view space, we just need the plane slopes for the top/bottom/left/right planes, and the z distances for the near and far plane. The XNA collision library provides the following structure for representing a frustum:

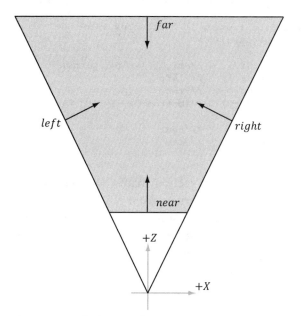

Figure 15.6. The intersection of the positive half spaces of the frustum planes defines the frustum volume.

```
_DECLSPEC_ALIGN_16_ struct Frustum
{
    XMFLOAT3 Origin;                // Origin of the frustum (and
    projection).
    XMFLOAT4 Orientation;           // Unit quaternion representing
    rotation.

    FLOAT RightSlope;               // Positive X slope (X/Z).
    FLOAT LeftSlope;                // Negative X slope.
    FLOAT TopSlope;                 // Positive Y slope (Y/Z).
    FLOAT BottomSlope;              // Negative Y slope.
    FLOAT Near, Far;                // Z of the near plane and far plane.
};
```

In the local space of the frustum (e.g., view space for the camera), the `Origin`
would be zero, and the `Orientation` would represent an identity transform (no
rotation). We can position and orientate the frustum somewhere in the world by
specifying an `Origin` position and `Orientation` quaternion.

If we cached the frustum vertical field of view, aspect ratio, near and far planes
of our camera, then we can determine the frustum plane equations in view space
with a little mathematical effort. However, it is also possible to derive the frustum
plane equations in view space from the projection matrix in a number of ways (see
[Lengyel02] or [Möller08] for two different ways). The XNA collision library takes
the following strategy. In NDC space, the view frustum has been warped into the
box $[-1,1] \times [-1,1] \times [0,1]$. So the 8 corners of the view frustum are simply:

```
// Corners of the projection frustum in homogenous space.
static XMVECTOR HomogenousPoints[6] =
{
    {  1.0f,  0.0f, 1.0f, 1.0f },    // right (at far plane)
    { -1.0f,  0.0f, 1.0f, 1.0f },    // left
    {  0.0f,  1.0f, 1.0f, 1.0f },    // top
    {  0.0f, -1.0f, 1.0f, 1.0f },    // bottom

    { 0.0f, 0.0f, 0.0f, 1.0f },      // near
    { 0.0f, 0.0f, 1.0f, 1.0f }       // far
};
```

We can compute the inverse of the projection matrix (as well as invert the
homogeneous divide) to transform the 8 corners from NDC space back to view
space. One we have the 8 corners of the frustum in view space, some simple
mathematics is used to compute the plane equations (again, this is simple
because in view space, the frustum is positioned at the origin, and axis aligned).
The following XNA collision code computes the frustum in view space from a
projection matrix:

```
//-----------------------------------------------------------------------
// Build a frustum from a persepective projection matrix.  The matrix
// may only contain a projection; any rotation, translation or scale
```

```
    // will cause the constructed frustum to be incorrect.
    //----------------------------------------------------------------------
    VOID ComputeFrustumFromProjection(Frustum* pOut, XMMATRIX* pProjection)
    {
        XMASSERT(pOut);
        XMASSERT(pProjection);

        // Corners of the projection frustum in homogenous space.
        static XMVECTOR HomogenousPoints[6] =
        {
          {  1.0f,  0.0f, 1.0f, 1.0f },   // right (at far plane)
          { -1.0f,  0.0f, 1.0f, 1.0f },   // left
          {  0.0f,  1.0f, 1.0f, 1.0f },   // top
          {  0.0f, -1.0f, 1.0f, 1.0f },   // bottom

          { 0.0f, 0.0f, 0.0f, 1.0f },     // near
          { 0.0f, 0.0f, 1.0f, 1.0f }      // far
        };

        XMVECTOR Determinant;
        XMMATRIX matInverse = XMMatrixInverse(&Determinant, *pProjection);

        // Compute the frustum corners in world space.
        XMVECTOR Points[6];

        for(INT i = 0; i < 6; i++)
        {
          // Transform point.
          Points[i] = XMVector4Transform(HomogenousPoints[i], matInverse);
        }

        pOut->Origin = XMFLOAT3(0.0f, 0.0f, 0.0f);
        pOut->Orientation = XMFLOAT4(0.0f, 0.0f, 0.0f, 1.0f);

        // Compute the slopes.
        Points[0] = Points[0] * XMVectorReciprocal(XMVectorSplatZ(Points[0]));
        Points[1] = Points[1] * XMVectorReciprocal(XMVectorSplatZ(Points[1]));
        Points[2] = Points[2] * XMVectorReciprocal(XMVectorSplatZ(Points[2]));
        Points[3] = Points[3] * XMVectorReciprocal(XMVectorSplatZ(Points[3]));

        pOut->RightSlope = XMVectorGetX(Points[0]);
        pOut->LeftSlope = XMVectorGetX(Points[1]);
        pOut->TopSlope = XMVectorGetY(Points[2]);
        pOut->BottomSlope = XMVectorGetY(Points[3]);

        // Compute near and far.
        Points[4] = Points[4] * XMVectorReciprocal(XMVectorSplatW(Points[4]));
        Points[5] = Points[5] * XMVectorReciprocal(XMVectorSplatW(Points[5]));

        pOut->Near = XMVectorGetZ(Points[4]);
        pOut->Far = XMVectorGetZ(Points[5]);

        return;
    }
```

15.2.4.2 Frustum/Sphere Intersection

For frustum culling, one test we will want to perform is a frustum/sphere intersection test. This tells us whether a sphere intersects the frustum. Note that a sphere completely inside the frustum counts as an intersection because we treat the frustum as a volume, not just a boundary. Because we model a frustum as six inward facing planes, a frustum/sphere test can be stated as follows: If there exists a frustum plane L such that the sphere is in the negative half-space of L, then we can conclude that the sphere is completely outside the frustum. If such a plane does not exist, then we conclude that the sphere intersects the frustum.

So a frustum/sphere intersection test reduces to six sphere/plane tests. Figure 15.7 shows the setup of a sphere/plane intersection test. Let the sphere have center point $\mathbf{c}$ and radius r. Then the signed distance from the center of the sphere to the plane is $k = \mathbf{n} \cdot \mathbf{c} + d$ (Appendix C). If $|k| \leq r$ then the sphere intersects the plane. If $k < -r$ then the sphere is behind the plane. If $k > r$ then the sphere is in front of the plane and the sphere intersects the positive half-space of the plane. For the purposes of the frustum/sphere intersection test, if the sphere is in front of the plane, then we count it as an intersection because it intersects the positive half-space the plane defines.

The XNA collision library provides the following function to test if a sphere intersects a frustum. Note that the sphere and frustum must be in the same coordinate system for the test to make sense.

```
// Return values: 0 = no intersection,
//                1 = intersection,
//                2 = A is completely inside B
INT IntersectSphereFrustum(
    const Sphere* pVolumeA,
    const Frustum* pVolumeB);
```

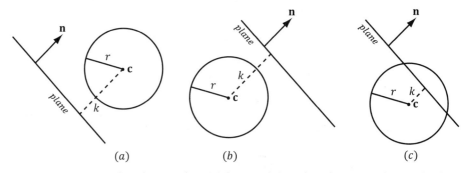

Figure 15.7. Sphere/plane intersection. (a) $k > r$ and the sphere intersects the positive half-space of the plane. (b) $k < -r$ and the sphere is completely behind the plane in the negative half-space. (c) $|k| \leq r$ and the sphere intersects the plane.

15.2.4.3 Frustum/AABB Intersection

The frustum/AABB intersection test follows the same strategy as the frustum/ sphere test. Because we model a frustum as six inward facing planes, a frustum/ AABB test can be stated as follows: If there exists a frustum plane L such that the box is in the negative half-space of L, then we can conclude that the box is completely outside the frustum. If such a plane does not exist, then we conclude that the box intersects the frustum.

So a frustum/AABB intersection test reduces to six AABB/plane tests. The algorithm for an AABB/plane test is as follows. Find the box diagonal vector $\mathbf{v} = \overrightarrow{PQ}$, passing through the center of the box, that is most aligned with the plane normal $\mathbf{n}$. From Figure 15.8, (a) if P is in front of the plane, then Q must be also in front of the plane; (b) if Q is behind the plane, then P must also be behind the plane; (c) if P is behind the plane and Q is in front of the plane, then the box intersects the plane.

Finding PQ most aligned with the plane normal vector $\mathbf{n}$ can be done with the following code:

```
// For each coordinate axis x, y, z...
for(int j = 0; j < 3; ++j)
{
    // Make PQ point in the same direction as
    // the plane normal on this axis.
    if(planeNormal[j] >= 0.0f)
    {
      P[j] = box.minPt[j];
      Q[j] = box.maxPt[j];
    }
    else
    {
      P[j] = box.maxPt[j];
      Q[j] = box.minPt[j];
    }
}
```

Figure 15.8. AABB/plane intersection test. The diagonal $\overrightarrow{PQ}$ is always the diagonal most directed with the plane normal.

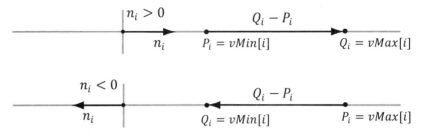

Figure 15.9. (Top) The normal component along the *i*th axis is positive, so we choose $P_i = vMin[i]$ and $Q_i = vMax[i]$ so that $Q_i - P_i$ has the same sign as the plane normal coordinate n_i. (Bottom) The normal component along the *i*th axis is negative, so we choose $P_i = vMax[i]$ and $Q_i = vMin[i]$ so that $Q_i - P_i$ has the same sign as the plane normal coordinate n_i.

This code just looks at one dimension at a time, and chooses P_i and Q_i such that $Q_i - P_i$ has the same sign as the plane normal coordinate n_i (Figure 15.9).

The XNA collision library provides the following function to test if an AABB intersects a frustum. Note that the AABB and frustum must be in the same coordinate system for the test to make sense.

```
// Return values: 0 = no intersection,
//                1 = intersection,
//                2 = A is completely inside B
INT IntersectAxisAlignedBoxFrustum(
    const AxisAlignedBox* pVolumeA,
    const Frustum* pVolumeB);
```

15.3 FRUSTUM CULLING

Recall from Chapter 5 that the hardware automatically discards triangles that are outside the viewing frustum in the clipping stage. However, if we have millions of triangles, all the triangles are still submitted to the rendering pipeline via draw calls (which has API overhead), and all the triangles go through the vertex shader, possibly through the tessellation stages, and possibly through the geometry shader, only to be discarded during the clipping stage. Clearly, this is wasteful inefficiency.

The idea of frustum culling is for the application code to cull groups of triangles at a higher level than on a per-triangle basis. Figure 15.10 shows a simple example. We build a bounding volume, such as a sphere or box, around each object in the scene. If the bounding volume does not intersect the frustum, then we do not need to submit the object (which could contain thousands of triangles) to Direct3D for drawing. This saves the GPU from having to do wasteful computations on invisible geometry, at the cost of an inexpensive

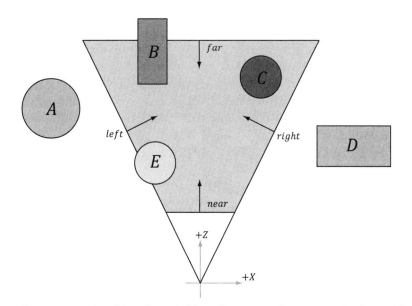

Figure 15.10. The objects bounded by volumes A and D are completely outside the frustum, and so do not need to be drawn. The object corresponding to volume C is completely inside the frustum, and needs to be drawn. The objects bounded by volumes B and E are partially outside the frustum and partially inside the frustum; we must draw these objects and let the hardware clip and triangles outside the frustum.

CPU test. Assuming a camera with a 90° field of view and infinitely far away far plane, the camera frustum only occupies 1/6th of the world volume, so 5/6th of the world objects can be frustum culled, assuming objects are evenly distributed throughout the scene. In practice, cameras use smaller field of view angles than 90° and a finite far plane, which means we could cull even more than 5/6th of the scene objects.

In our demo, we render a $5 \times 5 \times 5$ grid of skull meshes (see Figure 15.11) using instancing. We compute the AABB of the skull mesh in local space. In the **UpdateScene** method, we perform frustum culling on all of our instances. If the instance intersects the frustum, then we add it to the next available slot in our dynamic instanced buffer and increment the **mVisibleObjectCount** counter. This way, the front of the dynamic instanced buffer contains the data for all the visible instanced. (Of course, the instanced buffer is sized to match the number of instances in case all the instances are visible.) Because the AABB of the skull mesh is in local space, we must transform the view frustum into the local space of each instance in order to perform the intersection test; we could use alternative spaces, like transform the AABB to world space and the frustum to world space, for example. The frustum culling update code follows:

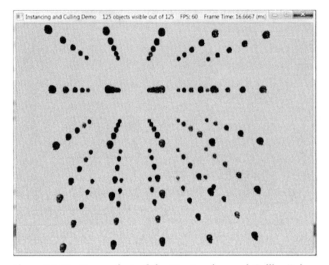

Figure 15.11. Screenshot of the "Instancing and Culling" demo.

```
mCam.UpdateViewMatrix();
mVisibleObjectCount = 0;

XMVECTOR detView = XMMatrixDeterminant(mCam.View());
XMMATRIX invView = XMMatrixInverse(&detView, mCam.View());

// Map the instanced buffer to write to it.
D3D11_MAPPED_SUBRESOURCE mappedData;
md3dImmediateContext->Map(mInstancedBuffer, 0,
    D3D11_MAP_WRITE_DISCARD, 0, &mappedData);

InstancedData* dataView =
    reinterpret_cast<InstancedData*>(mappedData.pData);

for(UINT i = 0; i < mInstancedData.size(); ++i)
{
    XMMATRIX W = XMLoadFloat4x4(&mInstancedData[i].World);
    XMMATRIX invWorld = XMMatrixInverse(&XMMatrixDeterminant(W), W);

    // View space to the object's local space.
    XMMATRIX toLocal = XMMatrixMultiply(invView, invWorld);

    // Decompose the matrix into its individual parts.
    XMVECTOR scale;
    XMVECTOR rotQuat;
    XMVECTOR translation;
    XMMatrixDecompose(&scale, &rotQuat, &translation, toLocal);

    // Transform the camera frustum from view space to the object's
    // local space.
    XNA::Frustum localspaceFrustum;
    XNA::TransformFrustum(&localspaceFrustum, &mCamFrustum,
```

```
      XMVectorGetX(scale), rotQuat, translation);

   // Perform the box/frustum intersection test in local space.
   if(XNA::IntersectAxisAlignedBoxFrustum(&mSkullBox,
   &localspaceFrustum) != 0)
   {
      // Write the instance data to dynamic VB of the visible objects.
      dataView[mVisibleObjectCount++] = mInstancedData[i];
   }
}

md3dImmediateContext->Unmap(mInstancedBuffer, 0);
```

Even though our instanced buffer has room for every instance, we only draw the visible instances which correspond to instances from 0 to mVisibleObjectCount-1:

```
md3dImmediateContext->DrawIndexedInstanced(
   mSkullIndexCount, // number of indices in the skull mesh
   mVisibleObjectCount, // number of instances to draw
   0, 0, 0);
```

Figure 15.12 shows the performance difference between having frustum culling enabled and not. With frustum culling, we only submit 11 instances to the rendering pipeline for processing. Without frustum culling, we submit all 125 instances to the rendering pipeline for processing. Even though the visible scene is the same, with frustum culling disabled, we waste computation power drawing over 100 skull meshes whose geometry is eventually discarded during the clipping stage. Each skull has about 60K triangles, so that is a lot of vertices to process and a lot of triangles to clip per skull. By doing one frustum/AABB test, we can reject 60K triangles from even being sent to the graphics pipeline—this is the advantage of frustum culling and we see the difference in the frames per second.

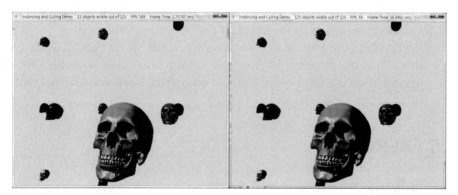

Figure 15.12. (Left) Frustum culling is turned on, and we see that 11 out of 125 instances are visible, and it takes about 1.75 ms to render a frame. (Right) Frustum culling is turned off, and we are rendering all 125 instances, and it takes about 16.94 ms to render a frame—9.68 times longer than when frustum culling is enabled.

15.4 SUMMARY

1. Instancing refers to drawing the same object more than once in a scene, but in different positions, orientations, scales, materials, and textures. To save memory, we only create one mesh, and submit multiple draw calls to Direct3D with a different world matrix, material, and texture. To avoid the API overhead of issuing resource changes, we can stream per-instance data to the input assembler, and have Direct3D draw several instances with the `ID3D11DeviceContext::DrawIndexedInstanced` method. Each instance will obtain its associated instanced data from the instanced buffer bound to the input assembler stage.

2. Bounding volumes are primitive geometric objects that approximate the volume of an object. The tradeoff is that although the bounding volume only approximates the object, its form has a simple mathematical representation, which makes it easy to work with. Examples of bounding volumes are spheres, axis-aligned bounding boxes (AABB), and oriented bounding boxes (OBB). The *xnacollision.h/.cpp* library has structures representing bounding volumes, and functions for transforming them and computing various intersection tests.

3. The GPU automatically discards triangles that are outside the viewing frustum in the clipping stage. However, clipped triangles are still submitted to the rendering pipeline via draw calls (which has API overhead), and all the triangles go through the vertex shader, possibly through the tessellation stages, and possibly through the geometry shader, only to be discarded during the clipping stage. To fix this inefficiency, we can implement frustum culling. The idea is to build a bounding volume, such as a sphere or box, around each object in the scene. If the bounding volume does not intersect the frustum, then we do not need to submit the object (which could contain thousands of triangles) to Direct3D for drawing. This saves the GPU from having to do wasteful computations on invisible geometry, at the cost of an inexpensive CPU test.

15.5 EXERCISES

1. Modify the "Instancing and Culling" demo to use bounding spheres instead of bounding boxes.

2. The plane equations in NDC space take on a very simple form. All points inside the view frustum are bounded as follows:

$$-1 \le x_{ndc} \le 1$$
$$-1 \le y_{ndc} \le 1$$
$$0 \le z_{ndc} \le 1$$

In particular, the left plane equation is given by $x = -1$ and the right plane equation is given by $x = 1$ in NDC space. In homogeneous clip space before the perspective divide, all points inside the view frustum are bounded as follows:

$$-w \le x_h \le w$$
$$-w \le y_h \le w$$
$$0 \le z_h \le w$$

Here, the left plane is defined by $w = -x_h$ and the right plane is defined by $w = x_h$. Let $\mathbf{M} = \mathbf{VP}$ be the view-projection matrix product, and let $\mathbf{v} = (x, y, z, 1)$ be a point in world space inside the frustum. Consider $(x_h, y_h, z_h, w) = \mathbf{vM} = (\mathbf{v} \cdot \mathbf{M}_{*,1}, \mathbf{v} \cdot \mathbf{M}_{*,2}, \mathbf{v} \cdot \mathbf{M}_{*,3}, \mathbf{v} \cdot \mathbf{M}_{*,4})$ to show that the inward facing frustum planes in world space are given by:

Left	$0 = \mathbf{p} \cdot (\mathbf{M}_{*,1} + \mathbf{M}_{*,4})$
Right	$0 = \mathbf{p} \cdot (\mathbf{M}_{*,4} - \mathbf{M}_{*,1})$
Bottom	$0 = \mathbf{p} \cdot (\mathbf{M}_{*,2} + \mathbf{M}_{*,4})$
Top	$0 = \mathbf{p} \cdot (\mathbf{M}_{*,4} - \mathbf{M}_{*,2})$
Near	$0 = \mathbf{p} \cdot \mathbf{M}_{*,3}$
Far	$0 = \mathbf{p} \cdot (\mathbf{M}_{*,4} - \mathbf{M}_{*,3})$

Note:

(a) *We ask for inward facing normals. That means a point inside the frustum has a positive distance from the plane; in other words, $\mathbf{n} \cdot \mathbf{p} + d \ge 0$ for a point $\mathbf{p}$ inside the frustum.*

(b) *Note that $v_w = 1$, so the previous dot product formulas do yield plane equations of the form $A_x + B_y + C_z + D = 0$.*

(c) *The calculated plane normal vectors are not unit length; see Appendix C for how to normalize a plane.*

3. Examine the *xnacollision.h* header file to get familiar with the functions it provides for intersection tests using the XNA math library.

4. An OBB can be defined by a center point $\mathbf{C}$, three orthonormal axis vectors $\mathbf{r}_0$, $\mathbf{r}_1$, and $\mathbf{r}_2$ defining the box orientation, and three extent lengths a_0, a_1, and a_2 along the box axes $\mathbf{r}_0$, $\mathbf{r}_1$, and $\mathbf{r}_2$, respectivey, that give the distance from the box center to the box sides.

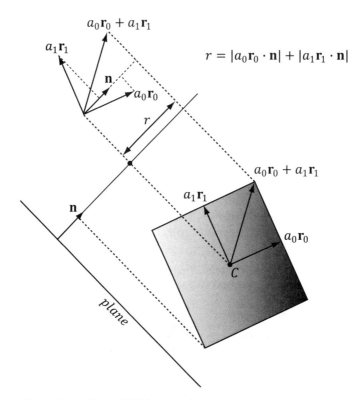

Figure 15.13. Plane/OBB intersection setup.

(a) Consider Figure 15.13 (which shows the situation in 2D) and conclude the projected "shadow" of the OBB onto the axis defined by the normal vector is $2r$, where

$$r = |a_0\mathbf{r}_0 \cdot \mathbf{n}| + |a_1\mathbf{r}_1 \cdot \mathbf{n}| + |a_2\mathbf{r}_2 \cdot \mathbf{n}|$$

(b) In the previous formula for r, explain why we must take the absolute values instead of just computing $r = (a_0\mathbf{r}_0 + a_1\mathbf{r}_1 + a_2\mathbf{r}_2) \cdot \mathbf{n}$.

(c) Derive a plane/OBB intersection test that determines if the OBB is in front of the plane, behind the plane, or intersecting the plane.

(d) An AABB is a special case of an OBB, so this test also works for an AABB. However, the formula for r simplifies in the case of an AABB. Find the simplified formula for r for the AABB case.

Chapter 16 Picking

In this chapter, we have the problem of determining the 3D object (or primitive) the user picked with the mouse cursor (see Figure 16.1). In other words, given the 2D screen coordinates of the mouse cursor, can we determine the 3D object that was projected onto that point? To solve this problem, in some sense, we must work backwards; that is to say, we typically transform from 3D space to screen space, but here we transform from screen space back to 3D space. Of course, we already have a slight problem: a 2D screen point does not correspond to a unique 3D point (i.e., more than one 3D point could be projected onto the same 2D projection window point—see Figure 16.2). Thus, there is some ambiguity in determining which object is really picked. However, this is not such a big problem, as the closest object to the camera is usually the one we want.

Consider Figure 16.3, which shows the viewing frustum. Here **p** is the point on the projection window that corresponds to the clicked screen point **s**. Now, we see that if we shoot a *picking ray*, originating at the eye position, through **p**, we will intersect the object whose projection surrounds **p**, namely the cylinder in this example. Therefore, our strategy is as follows: Once we compute the picking ray, we can iterate through each object in the scene and test if the ray intersects it. The object that the ray intersects is the object that was picked by the user. As mentioned, the ray may intersect several scene objects (or none at all—if nothing was picked), if the objects are along the ray's path but with different depth values, for example. In this case, we can just take the intersected object nearest to the camera as the picked object.

533

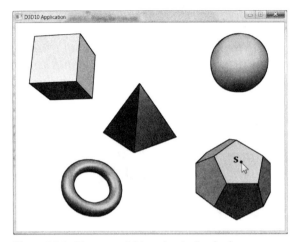

Figure 16.1. The user picking the dodecahedron.

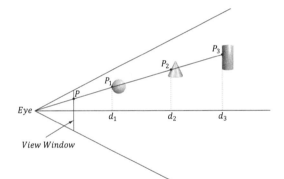

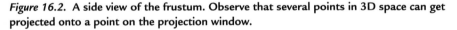

Figure 16.2. A side view of the frustum. Observe that several points in 3D space can get projected onto a point on the projection window.

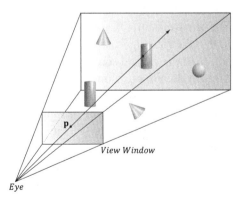

Figure 16.3. A ray shooting through p will intersect the object whose projection surrounds p. Note that the projected point p on the projection window corresponds to the clicked screen point s.

Objectives:

1. To learn how to implement the picking algorithm and to understand how it works. We break picking down into the following four steps:

   (a) Given the clicked screen point **s**, find its corresponding point on the projection window and call it **p**.

   (b) Compute the picking ray in view space. That is, the ray originating at the origin, in view space, which shoots through **p**.

   (c) Transform the picking ray and the models to be tested with the ray into the same space.

   (d) Determine the object the picking ray intersects. The nearest (from the camera) intersected object corresponds to the picked screen object.

16.1 SCREEN TO PROJECTION WINDOW TRANSFORM

The first task is to transform the clicked screen point to normalized device coordinates (see §5.4.3.3). Recall that the viewport matrix transforms vertices from normalized device coordinates to screen space; it is given below:

$$
\mathbf{M} = \begin{bmatrix}
\dfrac{Width}{2} & 0 & 0 & 0 \\
0 & -\dfrac{Height}{2} & 0 & 0 \\
0 & 0 & MaxDepth - MinDepth & 0 \\
TopLeftX + \dfrac{Width}{2} & TopLeftY + \dfrac{Height}{2} & MinDepth & 1
\end{bmatrix}
$$

The variables of the viewport matrix refer to those of the **D3D11_VIEWPORT** structure:

```
typedef struct D3D11_VIEWPORT {
    FLOAT TopLeftX;
    FLOAT TopLeftY;
    FLOAT Width;
    FLOAT Height;
    FLOAT MinDepth;
    FLOAT MaxDepth;
} D3D11_VIEWPORT;
```

Generally, for a game, the viewport is the entire backbuffer and the depth buffer range is 0 to 1. Thus, $TopLeftX = 0$, $TopLeftY = 0$, $MinDepth = 0$, $MaxDepth = 1$, $Width = w$, and $Height = h$, where w and h, are the width and height of the backbuffer, respectively. Assuming this is indeed the case, the viewport matrix simplifies to:

$$\mathbf{M} = \begin{bmatrix} w/2 & 0 & 0 & 0 \\ 0 & -h/2 & 0 & 0 \\ 0 & 0 & 1 & 0 \\ w/2 & h/2 & 0 & 1 \end{bmatrix}$$

Now let $\mathbf{p}_{ndc} = (x_{ndc}, y_{ndc}, z_{ndc}, 1)$ be a point in normalized device space (i.e., $-1 \le x_{ndc} \le 1, -1 \le y_{ndc} \le 1$, and $0 \le z_{ndc} \le 1$). Transforming $\mathbf{p}_{ndc}$ to screen space yields:

$$\begin{bmatrix} x_{ndc}, y_{ndc}, z_{ndc}, 1 \end{bmatrix} \begin{bmatrix} w/2 & 0 & 0 & 0 \\ 0 & -h/2 & 0 & 0 \\ 0 & 0 & 1 & 0 \\ w/2 & h/2 & 0 & 1 \end{bmatrix} = \begin{bmatrix} \dfrac{x_{ndc}w + w}{2}, \dfrac{-y_{ndc}h + h}{2}, z_{ndc}, 1 \end{bmatrix}$$

The coordinate z_{ndc} is just used by the depth buffer and we are not concerned with any depth coordinates for picking. The 2D screen point $\mathbf{p}_s = (x_s, y_s)$ corresponding to $\mathbf{p}_{ndc}$ is just the transformed x- and y-coordinates:

$$x_s = \frac{x_{ndc}w + w}{2}$$

$$y_s = \frac{-y_{ndc}h + h}{2}$$

The previous equation gives us the screen point $\mathbf{p}_s$ in terms of the normalized device point $\mathbf{p}_{ndc}$ and the viewport dimensions. However, in our picking situation, we are initially given the screen point $\mathbf{p}_s$ and the viewport dimensions, and we want to find $\mathbf{p}_{ndc}$. Solving the previous equations for $\mathbf{p}_{ndc}$ yields:

$$x_{ndc} = \frac{2x_s}{w} - 1$$

$$y_{ndc} = -\frac{2y_s}{h} + 1$$

We now have the clicked point in NDC space. But to shoot the picking ray, we really want the screen point in view space. Recall from §5.6.3.3 that we mapped the projected point from view space to NDC space by dividing the x-coordinate by the aspect ratio r:

$$-r \le x' \le r$$

$$-1 \le x'/r \le 1$$

Thus, to get back to view space, we just need to multiply the x-coordinate in NDC space by the aspect ratio. The clicked point in view space is thus:

$$x_v = r\left(\frac{2s_x}{w} - 1\right)$$

$$y_v = -\frac{2s_y}{h} + 1$$

Note: *The projected y-coordinate in view space is the same in NDC space. This is because we chose the height of the projection window in view space to cover the interval $[-1, 1]$.*

Now recall from §5.6.3.1 that the projection window lies at a distance $d = \cot\left(\frac{\alpha}{2}\right)$ from the origin, where α is the vertical field of view angle. So we could shoot the picking ray through the point (x_v, y_v, d) on the projection window. However, this requires that we compute $d = \cot\left(\frac{\alpha}{2}\right)$. A simpler way is to observe from Figure 16.4 that:

$$x_v' = \frac{x_v}{d} = \frac{x_v}{\cot\left(\frac{\alpha}{2}\right)} = x_v \cdot \tan\left(\frac{\alpha}{2}\right) = \left(\frac{2s_x}{w} - 1\right) r \tan\left(\frac{\alpha}{2}\right)$$

$$y_v' = \frac{y_v}{d} = \frac{y_v}{\cot\left(\frac{\alpha}{2}\right)} = y_v \cdot \tan\left(\frac{\alpha}{2}\right) = \left(-\frac{2s_y}{h} + 1\right) \tan\left(\frac{\alpha}{2}\right)$$

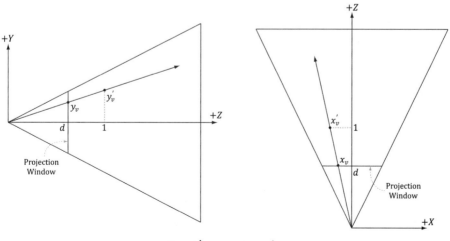

Figure 16.4. By similar triangles, $\frac{y_v}{d} = \frac{y_v'}{1}$ and $\frac{x_v}{d} = \frac{x_v'}{1}$.

Recalling that $\mathbf{P}_{00} = \frac{1}{r\tan\left(\frac{\alpha}{2}\right)}$ and $\mathbf{P}_{11} = \frac{1}{\tan\left(\frac{\alpha}{2}\right)}$ in the projection matrix, we can rewrite this as:

$$x'_v = \left(\frac{2s_x}{w} - 1\right) / \mathbf{P}_{00}$$

$$y'_v = \left(-\frac{2s_y}{h} + 1\right) / \mathbf{P}_{11}$$

Thus, we can shoot our picking ray through the point $\left(x'_v, y'_v, 1\right)$ instead. Note that this yields the same picking ray as the one shot through the point (x_v, y_v, d). The code that computes the picking ray in view space is given below:

```
void PickingApp::Pick(int sx, int sy)
{
    XMMATRIX P = mCam.Proj();

    // Compute picking ray in view space.
    float vx = (+2.0f*sx/mClientWidth  - 1.0f)/P(0,0);
    float vy = (-2.0f*sy/mClientHeight + 1.0f)/P(1,1);

    // Ray definition in view space.
    XMVECTOR rayOrigin = XMVectorSet(0.0f, 0.0f, 0.0f, 1.0f);
    XMVECTOR rayDir    = XMVectorSet(vx, vy, 1.0f, 0.0f);
```

Note that the ray originates from the origin in view space because the eye sits at the origin in view space.

16.2 WORLD/LOCAL SPACE PICKING RAY

So far we have the picking ray in view space, but this is only useful if our objects are in view space as well. Because the view matrix transforms geometry from world space to view space, the inverse of the view matrix transforms geometry from view space to world space. If $\mathbf{r}_v(t) = \mathbf{q} + t\mathbf{u}$ is the view space picking ray and $\mathbf{V}$ is the view matrix, then the world space picking ray is given by:

$$\mathbf{r}_w(t) = \mathbf{q}\mathbf{V}^{-1} + t\mathbf{u}\mathbf{V}^{-1}$$
$$= \mathbf{q}_w + t\mathbf{u}_w$$

Note that the ray origin $\mathbf{q}$ is transformed as a point (i.e., $q_w = 1$) and the ray direction $\mathbf{u}$ is transformed as a vector (i.e., $u_w = 0$).

A world space picking ray can be useful in some situations where you have some objects defined in world space. However, most of the time, the geometry of an object is defined relative to the object's own local space. Therefore, to perform the ray/object intersection test, we must transform the ray into the local space of the object. If **W** is the world matrix of an object, the matrix $\mathbf{W}^{-1}$ transforms geometry from world space to the local space of the object. Thus the local space picking ray is:

$$\mathbf{r}_L(t) = \mathbf{q}_w\mathbf{W}^{-1} + t\,\mathbf{u}_w\mathbf{W}^{-1}$$

Generally, each object in the scene has its own local space. Therefore, the ray must be transformed to the local space of each scene object to do the intersection test.

One might suggest transforming the meshes to world space and doing the intersection test there. However, this is too expensive. A mesh may contain thousands of vertices, and all those vertices would need to be transformed to world space. It is much more efficient to just transform the ray to the local spaces of the objects.

The following code shows how the picking ray is transformed from view space to the local space of an object:

```
// Tranform ray to local space of Mesh.
XMMATRIX V = mCam.View();
XMMATRIX invView = XMMatrixInverse(&XMMatrixDeterminant(V), V);

XMMATRIX W = XMLoadFloat4x4(&mMeshWorld);
XMMATRIX invWorld = XMMatrixInverse(&XMMatrixDeterminant(W), W);

XMMATRIX toLocal = XMMatrixMultiply(invView, invWorld);

rayOrigin = XMVector3TransformCoord(rayOrigin, toLocal);
rayDir = XMVector3TransformNormal(rayDir, toLocal);

// Make the ray direction unit length for the intersection tests.
rayDir = XMVector3Normalize(rayDir);
```

The `XMVector3TransformCoord` and `XMVector3TransformNormal` functions take 3D vectors as parameters, but note that with the `XMVector3TransformCoord` function there is an understood $w = 1$ for the 4th component. On the other hand, with the `XMVector3TransformNormal` function there is an understood $w = 0$ for the 4th component. Thus we can use `XMVector3TransformCoord` to transform points and we can use `XMVector3TransformNormal` to transform vectors.

16.3 RAY/MESH INTERSECTION

Once we have the picking ray and a mesh in the same space, we can perform the intersection test to see if the picking ray intersects the mesh. The following code iterates through each triangle in the mesh and does a ray/triangle intersection test. If the ray intersects one of the triangles, then it must have hit the mesh the triangle belongs to. Otherwise, the ray misses the mesh. Typically, we want the nearest triangle intersection, as it is possible for a ray to intersect several mesh triangles if the triangles overlap with respect to the ray.

```
// If we hit the bounding box of the Mesh, then we might have picked
// a Mesh triangle, so do the ray/triangle tests.
//
// If we did not hit the bounding box, then it is impossible that we
// hit the Mesh, so do not waste effort doing ray/triangle tests.

// Assume we have not picked anything yet, so init to -1.
mPickedTriangle = -1;
float tmin = 0.0f;
if(XNA::IntersectRayAxisAlignedBox(rayOrigin, rayDir,
    &mMeshBox, &tmin))
{
    // Find the nearest ray/triangle intersection.
    tmin = MathHelper::Infinity;
    for(UINT i = 0; i < mMeshIndices.size()/3; ++i)
    {
        // Indices for this triangle.
        UINT i0 = mMeshIndices[i*3+0];
        UINT i1 = mMeshIndices[i*3+1];
        UINT i2 = mMeshIndices[i*3+2];

        // Vertices for this triangle.
        XMVECTOR v0 = XMLoadFloat3(&mMeshVertices[i0].Pos);
        XMVECTOR v1 = XMLoadFloat3(&mMeshVertices[i1].Pos);
        XMVECTOR v2 = XMLoadFloat3(&mMeshVertices[i2].Pos);

        // We have to iterate over all the triangles in order to find
        // the nearest intersection.
        float t = 0.0f;
        if(XNA::IntersectRayTriangle(rayOrigin, rayDir, v0, v1, v2, &t))
        {
            if(t < tmin)
            {
                // This is the new nearest picked triangle.
                tmin = t;
                mPickedTriangle = i;
            }
        }
    }
}
```

In order to do picking, we keep a system memory copy of the mesh geometry (vertices and indices). This is because we cannot access a static vertex/index buffer for reading. It is common to store system memory copies of geometry for things like picking and collision detection. Sometimes a simplified version of the mesh is stored for these purposes to save memory and computation.

16.3.1 Ray/AABB Intersection

Observe that we first use the XNA collision library function `XNA::IntersectRayAxisAlignedBox` to see if the ray intersects the bounding box of the mesh. This is analogous to the frustum culling optimization. Performing a ray intersection test for every triangle in the scene adds up in computation time. Even for meshes not near the picking ray, we would still have to iterate over each triangle to conclude that the ray misses the mesh; this is wasteful and inefficient. A popular strategy is to approximate the mesh with a simple bounding volume, like a sphere or box. Then, instead of intersecting the ray with the mesh, we first intersect the ray with the bounding volume. If the ray misses the bounding volume, then the ray necessarily misses the triangle mesh and so there is no need to do further calculations. If the ray intersects the bounding volume, then we do the more precise ray/mesh test. Assuming that the ray will miss most bounding volumes in the scene, this saves us many ray/triangle intersection tests. The `XNA::IntersectRayAxisAlignedBox` function returns true if the ray intersects the box and false otherwise; it is prototyped as follows:

```
BOOL IntersectRayAxisAlignedBox(
    FXMVECTOR Origin,      // ray origin
    FXMVECTOR Direction,   // ray direction (must be unit length)
    const AxisAlignedBox* pVolume, // box
    FLOAT* pDist);  // ray intersection parameter
```

Given the ray $\mathbf{r}(t) = \mathbf{q} + t\mathbf{u}$, the last parameter outputs the ray parameter t_0 that yields the actual intersection point $\mathbf{p}$:

$$\mathbf{p} = \mathbf{r}(t_0) = \mathbf{q} + t_0\mathbf{u}$$

16.3.2 Ray/Sphere Intersection

There is also a ray/sphere intersection test given in the XNA collision library:

```
BOOL IntersectRaySphere(
    FXMVECTOR Origin,
    FXMVECTOR Direction,
    const Sphere* pVolume,
    FLOAT* pDist);
```

To give a flavor of these tests, we show how to derive the ray/sphere intersection test. The points $\mathbf{p}$ on the surface of a sphere with center $\mathbf{c}$ and radius r satisfy the equation:

$$\|\mathbf{p} - \mathbf{c}\| = r$$

Let $\mathbf{r}(t) = \mathbf{q} + t\mathbf{u}$ be a ray. We wish to solve for t_1 and t_2 such that $\mathbf{r}(t_1)$ and $\mathbf{r}(t_2)$ satisfy the sphere equation (i.e., the parameters t_1 and t_2 along the ray that yields the intersection points).

$$r = \| \mathbf{r}(t) - \mathbf{c} \|$$
$$r^2 = (\mathbf{r}(t) - \mathbf{c}) \times (\mathbf{r}(t) - \mathbf{c})$$
$$r^2 = (\mathbf{q} + t\mathbf{u} - \mathbf{c}) \times (\mathbf{q} + t\mathbf{u} - \mathbf{c})$$
$$r^2 = (\mathbf{q} - \mathbf{c} + t\mathbf{u}) \times (\mathbf{q} - \mathbf{c} + t\mathbf{u})$$

For notational convenience, let $\mathbf{m} = \mathbf{q} - \mathbf{c}$.

$$(\mathbf{m} + t\mathbf{u}) \cdot (\mathbf{m} + t\mathbf{u}) = r^2$$
$$\mathbf{m} \cdot \mathbf{m} + 2t\mathbf{m} \cdot \mathbf{u} + t^2 \mathbf{u} \cdot \mathbf{u} = r^2$$
$$t^2 \mathbf{u} \cdot \mathbf{u} + 2t\mathbf{m} \cdot \mathbf{u} + \mathbf{m} \cdot \mathbf{m} - r^2 = 0$$

This is just a quadratic equation with:

$$a = \mathbf{u} \cdot \mathbf{u}$$
$$b = 2(\mathbf{m} \cdot \mathbf{u})$$
$$c = \mathbf{m} \cdot \mathbf{m} - r^2$$

If the ray direction is unit length, then $a = \mathbf{u} \cdot \mathbf{u} = 1$. If the solution has imaginary components, the ray misses the sphere. If the two real solutions are the same, the ray intersects a point tangent to the sphere. If the two real solutions are distinct, the ray pierces two points of the sphere. A negative solution indicates an intersection point "behind" the ray. The smallest positive solution gives the nearest intersection parameter.

16.3.3 Ray/Triangle Intersection

For performing a ray/triangle intersection test, we use the XNA collision library function XNA:: IntersectRayTriangle:

```
BOOL IntersectRayTriangle(
    FXMVECTOR Origin,    // ray origin
    FXMVECTOR Direction, // ray direction (unit length)
    FXMVECTOR V0, // triangle vertex v0
    CXMVECTOR V1, // triangle vertex v1
    CXMVECTOR V2, // triangle vertex v2
    FLOAT* pDist); // ray intersection parameter
```

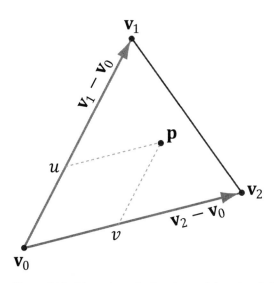

Figure 16.5. The point p in the plane of the triangle has coordinates (u, v) relative to the skewed coordinate system with origin v_0 and axes $v_1 - v_0$ and $v_2 - v_0$.

Let $\mathbf{r}(t) = \mathbf{q} + t\mathbf{u}$ be a ray and $\mathbf{T}(u, v) = \mathbf{v}_0 + u(\mathbf{v}_1 - \mathbf{v}_0) + v(\mathbf{v}_2 - \mathbf{v}_0)$ for $u \geq 0, v \geq 0, u + v \leq 1$ be a triangle (see Figure 16.5). We wish to simultaneously solve for t, u, v such that $\mathbf{r}(t) = \mathbf{T}(u, v)$ (i.e., the point the ray and triangle intersect):

$$\mathbf{r}(t) = \mathbf{T}(u, v)$$

$$\mathbf{q} + t\mathbf{u} = \mathbf{v}_0 + u(\mathbf{v}_1 - \mathbf{v}_0) + v(\mathbf{v}_2 - \mathbf{v}_0)$$

$$-t\mathbf{u} + u(\mathbf{v}_1 - \mathbf{v}_0) + v(\mathbf{v}_2 - \mathbf{v}_0) = \mathbf{q} - \mathbf{v}_0$$

For notational convenience, let $\mathbf{e}_1 = \mathbf{v}_1 - \mathbf{v}_0$, $\mathbf{e}_2 = \mathbf{v}_2 - \mathbf{v}_0$ and $\mathbf{m} = \mathbf{q} - \mathbf{v}_0$:

$$-t\mathbf{u} + u\mathbf{e}_1 + v\mathbf{e}_2 = \mathbf{m}$$

$$\begin{bmatrix} \uparrow & \uparrow & \uparrow \\ -\mathbf{u} & \mathbf{e}_1 & \mathbf{e}_2 \\ \downarrow & \downarrow & \downarrow \end{bmatrix} \begin{bmatrix} t \\ u \\ v \end{bmatrix} = \begin{bmatrix} \uparrow \\ \mathbf{m} \\ \downarrow \end{bmatrix}$$

Consider the matrix equation $\mathbf{Ax} = \mathbf{b}$, where $\mathbf{A}$ is invertible. Then Cramer's Rule tells us that $x_i = \det \mathbf{A}_i / \det \mathbf{A}$, where $\mathbf{A}_i$ is found by swapping the ith column vector in $\mathbf{A}$ with $\mathbf{b}$. Therefore,

$$t = \det \begin{bmatrix} \uparrow & \uparrow & \uparrow \\ \mathbf{m} & \mathbf{e}_1 & \mathbf{e}_2 \\ \downarrow & \downarrow & \downarrow \end{bmatrix} / \det \begin{bmatrix} \uparrow & \uparrow & \uparrow \\ -\mathbf{u} & \mathbf{e}_1 & \mathbf{e}_2 \\ \downarrow & \downarrow & \downarrow \end{bmatrix}$$

$$u = \det \begin{bmatrix} \uparrow & \uparrow & \uparrow \\ -\mathbf{u} & \mathbf{m} & \mathbf{e}_2 \\ \downarrow & \downarrow & \downarrow \end{bmatrix} / \det \begin{bmatrix} \uparrow & \uparrow & \uparrow \\ -\mathbf{u} & \mathbf{e}_1 & \mathbf{e}_2 \\ \downarrow & \downarrow & \downarrow \end{bmatrix}$$

$$v = \det \begin{bmatrix} \uparrow & \uparrow & \uparrow \\ -\mathbf{u} & \mathbf{e}_1 & \mathbf{m} \\ \downarrow & \downarrow & \downarrow \end{bmatrix} / \det \begin{bmatrix} \uparrow & \uparrow & \uparrow \\ -\mathbf{u} & \mathbf{e}_1 & \mathbf{e}_2 \\ \downarrow & \downarrow & \downarrow \end{bmatrix}$$

Using the fact that $\det \begin{bmatrix} \uparrow & \uparrow & \uparrow \\ \mathbf{a} & \mathbf{b} & \mathbf{c} \\ \downarrow & \downarrow & \downarrow \end{bmatrix} = \mathbf{a} \cdot (\mathbf{b} \times \mathbf{c})$ we can reformulate this as:

$$t = -\mathbf{m} \cdot (\mathbf{e}_1 \times \mathbf{e}_2) / \mathbf{u} \cdot (\mathbf{e}_1 \times \mathbf{e}_2)$$
$$u = \mathbf{u} \cdot (\mathbf{m} \times \mathbf{e}_2) / \mathbf{u} \cdot (\mathbf{e}_1 \times \mathbf{e}_2)$$
$$v = \mathbf{u} \cdot (\mathbf{e}_1 \times \mathbf{m}) / \mathbf{u} \cdot (\mathbf{e}_1 \times \mathbf{e}_2)$$

To optimize the computations a bit, we can use the fact that every time we swap columns in a matrix, the sign of the determinant changes:

$$t = \mathbf{e}_2 \cdot (\mathbf{m} \times \mathbf{e}_1) / \mathbf{e}_1 \cdot (\mathbf{u} \times \mathbf{e}_2)$$
$$u = \mathbf{m} \cdot (\mathbf{u} \times \mathbf{e}_2) / \mathbf{e}_1 \cdot (\mathbf{u} \times \mathbf{e}_2)$$
$$v = \mathbf{u} \cdot (\mathbf{m} \times \mathbf{e}_1) / \mathbf{e}_1 \cdot (\mathbf{u} \times \mathbf{e}_2)$$

And note the common cross products that can be reused in the calculations: $\mathbf{m} \times \mathbf{e}_1$ and $\mathbf{u} \times \mathbf{e}_2$.

16.4 DEMO APPLICATION

The demo for this chapter renders a car mesh and allows the user to pick a triangle by pressing the right mouse button. In our ray/triangle intersection loop (§16.3), we cache the index of the picked triangle in the variable `mPickedTriangle`. Once we know the index of the picked triangle, we can redraw this triangle again using a material that highlights the picked triangle (see Figure 16.6):

Figure 16.6. The picked triangle is highlighted green.

```
// Draw just the picked triangle again with a different material to
// highlight it.

if(mPickedTriangle != -1)
{
    // Change depth test from < to <= so that if we draw the same
    // triangle twice, it will still pass the depth test.  This
    // is because we redraw the picked triangle with a different
    // material to highlight it.  If we do not use <=, the triangle
    // will fail the depth test the 2nd time we try and draw it.

    md3dImmediateContext->OMSetDepthStencilState(
      RenderStates::LessEqualDSS, 0);

    Effects::BasicFX->SetMaterial(mPickedTriangleMat);
    activeMeshTech->GetPassByIndex(p)->Apply(0, md3dImmediateContext);

    // Just draw one triangle—3 indices.  Offset to the picked
    // triangle in the mesh index buffer.
    md3dImmediateContext->DrawIndexed(3, 3*mPickedTriangle, 0);

    // restore default
    md3dImmediateContext->OMSetDepthStencilState(0, 0);
}
```

Note: *You can press and hold the '1' key to view the mesh in wireframe mode.*

16.5 SUMMARY

1. Picking is the technique used to determine the 3D object that corresponds to the 2D projected object displayed on the screen that the user clicked on with the mouse.

2. The picking ray is found by shooting a ray, originating at the origin of the view space, through the point on the projection window that corresponds to the clicked screen point.

3. We can transform a ray $\mathbf{r}(t) = \mathbf{q} + t\mathbf{u}$ by transforming its origin $\mathbf{q}$ and direction $\mathbf{u}$ by a transformation matrix. Note that the origin is transformed as a point ($w = 1$) and the direction is treated as a vector ($w = 0$).

4. To test if a ray has intersected an object, we perform a ray/triangle intersection test for every triangle in the object. If the ray intersects one of the triangles, then it must have hit the mesh the triangle belongs to. Otherwise, the ray misses the mesh. Typically, we want the nearest triangle intersection, as it is possible for a ray to intersect several mesh triangles if the triangles overlap with respect to the ray.

5. A performance optimization for ray/mesh intersection tests is to first perform an intersection test between the ray and a bounding volume that approximates the mesh. If the ray misses the bounding volume, then the ray necessarily misses the triangle mesh and so there is no need to do further calculations. If the ray intersects the bounding volume, then we do the more precise ray/mesh test. Assuming that the ray will miss most bounding volumes in the scene, this saves us many ray/triangle intersection tests.

16.6 EXERCISES

1. Modify the "Picking" demo to use a bounding sphere for the mesh instead of an AABB.

2. Research the algorithm for doing a ray/AABB intersection test.

3. If you had thousands of objects in a scene, you would still have to do thousands of ray/bounding volume tests for picking. Research *octrees*, and explain how they can be used to reduce ray/bounding volume intersection tests. Incidentally, the same general strategy works for reducing frustum/bounding volume intersection tests for frustum culling.

Chapter 17 CUBE MAPPING

In this chapter, we study cube maps which are basically arrays of six textures interpreted in a special way. With cube mapping, we can easily texture a sky or model reflections.

Objectives:

1. To learn what cube maps are and how to sample them in HLSL code.
2. To discover how to create cube maps with the DirectX Texture Tool.
3. To find out how we can use cube maps to model reflections.
4. To understand how we can texture a sphere with cube maps to simulate a sky and distant mountains.

17.1 CUBE MAPPING

The idea of cube mapping is to store six textures and to visualize them as the faces of a cube—hence the name cube map—centered and axis aligned about some coordinate system. Because the cube texture is axis aligned, each face corresponds with a direction along the three major axes; therefore, it is natural to reference a particular face on a cube map based on the axis direction ($\pm X$, $\pm Y$, $\pm Z$,) that intersects the face. For the purposes of identifying a cube map face, Direct3D provides the D3D11_TEXTURECUBE_FACE enumerated type:

```
typedef enum D3D11_TEXTURECUBE_FACE {
    D3D11_TEXTURECUBE_FACE_POSITIVE_X   = 0,
    D3D11_TEXTURECUBE_FACE_NEGATIVE_X   = 1,
    D3D11_TEXTURECUBE_FACE_POSITIVE_Y   = 2,
    D3D11_TEXTURECUBE_FACE_NEGATIVE_Y   = 3,
    D3D11_TEXTURECUBE_FACE_POSITIVE_Z   = 4,
    D3D11_TEXTURECUBE_FACE_NEGATIVE_Z   = 5
} D3D11_TEXTURECUBE_FACE;
```

A cube map is stored in a texture array with six elements:

1. Index 0 refers to the +X face.
2. Index 1 refers to the –X face.
3. Index 2 refers to the +Y face.
4. Index 3 refers to the –Y face.
5. Index 4 refers to the +Z face.
6. Index 5 refers to the –Z face.

In contrast to 2D texturing, we can no longer identify a texel with 2D texture coordinates. To identify a texel in a cube map, we use 3D texture coordinates, which define a 3D *lookup* vector **v** originating at the origin. The texel of the cube map that **v** intersects (see Figure 17.1) is the texel corresponding to the 3D coordinates of **v**. The concepts of texture filtering discussed in Chapter 8 applies in the case **v** intersects a point between texel samples.

> **Note:** *The magnitude of the lookup vector is unimportant, only the direction matters. Two vectors with the same direction but different magnitudes will sample the same point in the cube map.*

In the HLSL, a cube texture is represented by the TextureCube type. The following code fragment illustrates how we sample a cube map:

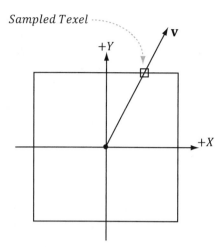

Figure 17.1. We illustrate in 2D for simplicity; in 3D the square becomes a cube. The square denotes the cube map centered and axis-aligned with some coordinate system. We shoot a vector v from the origin. The texel v intersects is the sampled texel. In this illustration, v intersects the cube face corresponding to the +*Y* axis.

```
TextureCube gCubeMap;

SamplerState gTriLinearSam
{
    Filter = MIN_MAG_MIP_LINEAR;
    AddressU = Wrap;
    AddressV = Wrap;
};

...

// in pixel shader
float3 v = float3(x,y,z); // some lookup vector
float4 color = gCubeMap.Sample(gTriLinearSam, v);
```

Note: *The lookup vector should be in the same space the cube map is relative to. For example, if the cube map is relative to the world space (i.e., the cube faces are axis aligned with the world space axes), then the lookup vector should have world space coordinates.*

17.2 ENVIRONMENT MAPS

The primary application of cube maps is *environment mapping*. The idea is to position a camera at the center of some object *0* in the scene with a 90° field of view angle (both vertically and horizontally). Then have the camera look down the positive x-axis, negative x-axis, positive y-axis, negative y-axis, positive z-axis, and negative z-axis, and to take a picture of the scene (excluding the object 0) from each of these six viewpoints. Because the field of view angle is 90°, these six images will have captured the entire surrounding environment (see Figure 17.2) from the perspective of the object 0. We then store these six images of the surrounding environment in a cube map, which leads to the name environment map. In other words, an *environment map* is a cube map where the cube faces store the surrounding images of an environment.

The previous description suggests that we need to create an environment map for each object that is to use environment mapping. However, often an environment map is used to only capture distant "background" information. Then many nearby objects can share the same environment map. In the demo for this chapter (Figure 17.3), all the spheres and skull share the environment map shown in Figure 17.2. Note that this environment map does not capture the local columns or floor of the scene; it only captures the distant mountains and sky (i.e., the scene background). Although the background environment map is, in some sense, incomplete, it works well in practice.

If the axis directions the camera looked down to build the environment map images were the world space axes, then the environment map is said to be generated relative to the world space. You could, of course, capture the environment from a

Figure 17.2. An example of an environment map after "unfolding" the cube map. Imagine refolding these six faces into a 3D box, and then imagine being at the center of the box. From every direction you look, you see the surrounding environment.

Figure 17.3. Screenshot of the "Cube Map" demo.

different orientation (say the local space of an object). However, the lookup vector coordinates must be in the space the cube map is relative to.

Note that the six images for the environment map are not necessarily taken in a Direct3D program, although they could be (we will see how to do this in §17.5). Because cube maps just store texture data, their contents are often pre-generated by an artist (just like the 2D textures we've been using). Consequently, we do not need to use real-time rendering to compute the images of a cube map. That is, we can create a scene in a 3D world editor, and then pre-render the six cube map face images in the editor. For outdoor environment maps, the program *Terragen* (http://www.planetside.co.uk/) is common to use (free for personal use), and can create photorealistic outdoor scenes. The environment maps we create for this book, such as the one shown in Figure 17.2, were made with *Terragen*.

Note: *If you choose to try out Terragen, you need to go to the **Camera Settings** dialog box and set the **zoom** factor to 1.0 to achieve a 90° field of view. Also, be sure to set your output image dimensions to be equal so that both the vertical and horizontal field of view angles are the same, namely 90°.*

Note: *There is a nice Terragen script on the Web (https://developer.valvesoftware.com/ wiki/Skybox_%282D%29_with_Terragen) that will use the current camera position, and render out the six surrounding images with a 90° field of view.*

Once you have created the six cube map images using some program, we need to create a cube map texture, which stores all six. The DDS texture image format we have been using readily supports cube maps, and we can use the DirectX Texture Tool to create a cube map from our six textures. Open the DirectX Texture Tool (ships with the DirectX SDK: *C:\DXSDKJune10\Utilities\bin\x86*) and first go to the **File** menu and select **New Texture.** From the dialog box that pops up (Figure 17.4), select **Cubemap Texture** as the texture type, enter the dimensions that match the dimensions of the six images, and choose a surface format (use a compressed format without alpha like DXT1 since high resolution cube maps can eat up a lot of memory because there are six textures being stored).

Now we have an empty cube map. Go to the **View** menu, select **Cube Map Face**, and pick the face along the axis you want to view in the window (Figure 17.5). (All of these faces are initially empty.) Select any face to start with, and then go to the **File** menu and select **Open Onto This Cubemap Face**, which will launch a

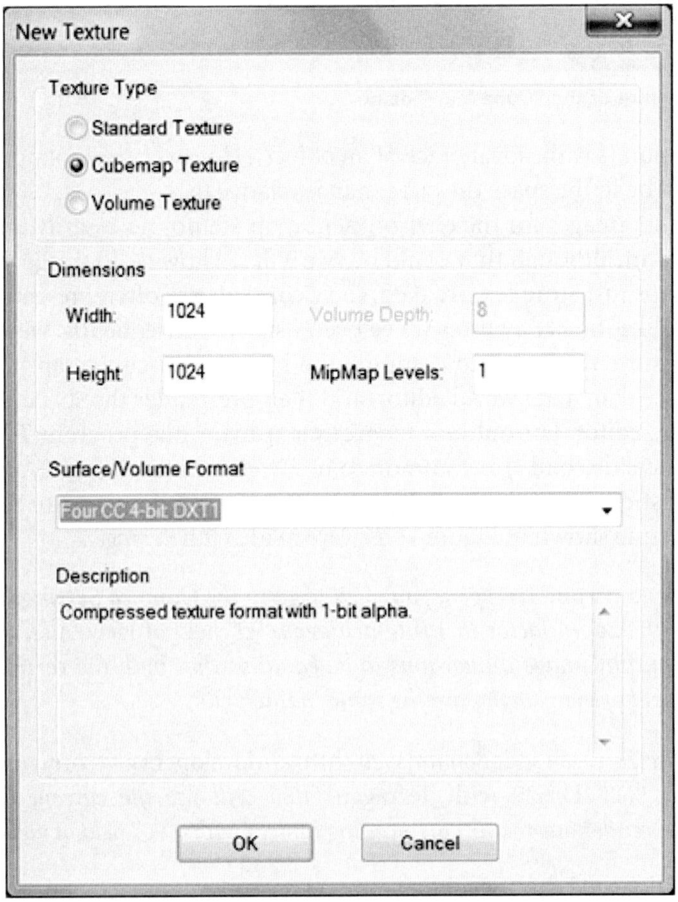

Figure 17.4. **Creating a new cube texture with the DirectX Texture Tool.**

Figure 17.5. Selecting a face of the cube map to view in the DirectX Texture Tool.

dialog box that asks you for the file you want to load onto the currently selected cube map face; choose the image corresponding to this cube map face. Repeat this process for the remaining five cube map faces so that each cube map face has the desired image inserted onto it. When you are done, save the DDS to file that now stores your cube map.

Note: *NVIDIA provides Photoshop plugins for saving .DDS and cubemaps in Photoshop; see* http://developer.nvidia.com/nvidia-texture-tools-adobe-photoshop.

17.2.1 Loading and Using Cube Maps in Direct3D

Conveniently, the `D3DX11CreateShaderResourceViewFromFile` function can load a DDS file that stores a cube map into an `ID3D11Texture2D` object and generate a shader resource view to it:

```
ID3D11ShaderResourceView* mCubeMapSRV;
HR(D3DX11CreateShaderResourceViewFromFile(device,
    cubemapFilename.c_str(), 0, 0, &mCubeMapSRV, 0));
```

An `ID3D11Texture2D` object stores the six textures of a cube map as a texture array.

After we have obtained an `ID3D11ShaderResourceView*` to the cube texture, we can set it to a `TextureCube` variable in an effect file with the `ID3DX11EffectShaderRe sourceVariable::SetResource` method:

```
// .fx variable
TextureCube gCubeMap;

// .cpp code
ID3DX11EffectShaderResourceVariable* CubeMap;


CubeMap        = mFX->GetVariableByName("gCubeMap")->AsShaderResource();

...

CubeMap->SetResource(cubemap);
```

17.3 TEXTURING A SKY

We can use an environment map to texture a sky. We create an ellipsoid that
surrounds the entire scene (we use an ellipsoid to create a flatter sky surface
which is more natural). To create the illusion of distant mountains far in the
horizon and a sky, we texture the ellipsoid using an environment map by the
method shown in Figure 17.6. In this way, the environment map is projected onto
the ellipsoid's surface.

We assume that the sky ellipsoid is infinitely far away (i.e., it is centered about the
world space but has infinite radius), and so no matter how the camera moves in the

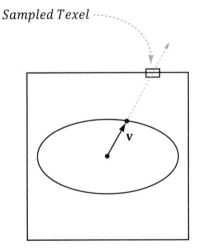

Figure 17.6. We illustrate in 2D for simplicity; in 3D the square becomes a cube and the
ellipse becomes an ellipsoid. We assume that the sky and environment map are centered
about the same origin. Then to texture a point on the surface of the ellipsoid, we use the
vector from the origin to the surface point as the lookup vector into the cube map. This
projects the cube map onto the ellipsoid.

world, we never appear to get closer or farther from the surface of the sky ellipsoid. To implement this infinitely faraway sky, we simply center the sky ellipsoid about the camera in world space so that it is always centered about the camera. Consequently, as the camera moves, we are getting no closer to the surface of the ellipsoid. If we did not do this, and we let the camera move closer to the sky surface, the whole illusion would break down, as the trick we use to simulate the sky would be obvious.

The effect file for the sky follows:

```
//===============================================================
// Sky.fx by Frank Luna (C) 2011 All Rights Reserved.
//
// Effect used to shade sky dome.
//===============================================================

cbuffer cbPerFrame
{
    float4x4 gWorldViewProj;
};

// Nonnumeric values cannot be added to a cbuffer.
TextureCube gCubeMap;

SamplerState samTriLinearSam
{
    Filter = MIN_MAG_MIP_LINEAR;
    AddressU = Wrap;
    AddressV = Wrap;
};

struct VertexIn
{
    float3 PosL : POSITION;
};

struct VertexOut
{
    float4 PosH : SV_POSITION;
    float3 PosL : POSITION;
};

VertexOut VS(VertexIn vin)
{
    VertexOut vout;

    // Set z = w so that z/w = 1 (i.e., skydome always on far plane).
    vout.PosH = mul(float4(vin.PosL, 1.0f), gWorldViewProj).xyww;

    // Use local vertex position as cubemap lookup vector.
    vout.PosL = vin.PosL;

    return vout;
}
```

```
float4 PS(VertexOut pin) : SV_Target
{
    return gCubeMap.Sample(samTriLinearSam, pin.PosL);
}

RasterizerState NoCull
{
    CullMode = None;
};

DepthStencilState LessEqualDSS
{
    // Make sure the depth function is LESS_EQUAL and not just LESS.
    // Otherwise, the normalized depth values at z = 1 (NDC) will
    // fail the depth test if the depth buffer was cleared to 1.
    DepthFunc = LESS_EQUAL;
};

technique11 SkyTech
{
    pass P0
    {
        SetVertexShader(CompileShader(vs_5_0, VS()));
        SetGeometryShader(NULL);
        SetPixelShader(CompileShader(ps_5_0, PS()));

        SetRasterizerState(NoCull);
        SetDepthStencilState(LessEqualDSS, 0);
    }
}
```

> Note: *In the past, applications would draw the sky first and use it as a replacement to clearing the render target and depth/stencil buffer. However, the "ATI Radeon HD 2000 Programming Guide" (http://developer.amd.com/media/ gpu_assets/ATI_Radeon_HD_2000_programming_guide.pdf) now advises against this for the following reasons. First, the depth/stencil buffer needs to be explicitly cleared for internal hardware depth optimizations to perform well. The situation is similar with render targets. Second, typically most of the sky is occluded by other geometry such as buildings and terrain. Therefore, if we draw the sky first, then we are wasting resources by drawing pixels that will only get overridden later by geometry closer to the camera. Therefore, it is now recommended to always clear, and to draw the sky last.*

17.4 MODELING REFLECTIONS

As described in the previous section, an environment map works well for the purposes of texturing a sky. However, the other main application of environment

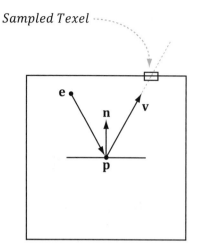

Sampled Texel

Figure 17.7. Here **e** is the eye point, and **n** is the surface normal at the point **p**. The texel that gets mapped to a point **p** on the surface is given by the reflection vector **v** (i.e., we use **v** as the lookup vector), which is the reflection of the vector from **e** to **p** about the surface. In this way, the eye sees the reflected environment.

maps is to model reflections for arbitrary objects (only the images in the environment map are reflected with this technique). Figure 17.7 illustrates how reflections are done with environment maps. The surface acts like a mirror: the eye looks at **p** and sees the environment reflected off **p**.

We compute the reflection vector per-pixel and then use it to sample the environment map:

```
litColor = texColor*(ambient + diffuse) + spec;

if(gReflectionEnabled)
{
    float3 incident = -toEye;
    float3 reflectionVector = reflect(incident, pin.NormalW);
    float4 reflectionColor  = gCubeMap.Sample(
samAnisotropic, reflectionVector);

    litColor += gMaterial.Reflect*reflectionColor;
}
```

In general, a pixel's color is not completely determined by the reflected color (only mirrors are 100% reflective). Therefore, we modify our lighting equation to include a reflection term $\mathbf{m}_R \otimes \mathbf{c}_R$. Here $\mathbf{c}_R$ is the color sampled from the environment map and $\mathbf{m}_R$ is an application controlled material value indicating how much of $\mathbf{c}_R$ the surface reflects into the eye. For example, if the surface only reflects red light then you could set $\mathbf{m}_R = (1, 0, 0)$ so that only red light from the environment map makes it into the eye. Recall that our `Material` structure already has a reflection property that we have not been using until this chapter:

```
struct Material
{
    float4 Ambient;
    float4 Diffuse;
    float4 Specular; // w = SpecPower
    float4 Reflect;
};
```

One issue with including the additional reflection term to the lighting equation is oversaturation. With the addition of the reflection term, we are now adding more color to the pixel which may brighten it up too much. Basically, if we are adding additional color from the reflection term, then we must take away color from one of the other terms to achieve a balance. This is usually done by scaling down the ambient and diffuse material factors so that less ambient and diffuse light are reflected off the surface. Another approach is to average the color sampled from the environment map with the usual lit pixel color **s**:

$$\mathbf{f} = t\mathbf{c}_R + (1 - t)\mathbf{s} \quad \text{for} \quad 0 \le t \le 1$$

In this way, as we add in the color sampled from the environment map with weight t, we equally take away color from the usual lit pixel color to keep a balance. So here the parameter t controls the reflectivity of the surface.

Figure 17.8 shows that reflections via environment mapping do not work well for flat surfaces. This is because the reflection vector does not tell the whole story,

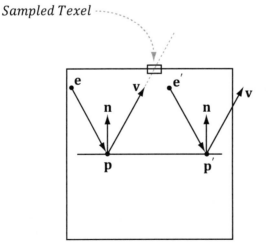

Figure 17.8. The reflection vector corresponding to two different points p and p' when the eye is at positions e and e', respectively.

as it does not incorporate position; we really need a reflection ray and to intersect the ray with the environment map. A ray has position and direction, whereas a vector just has direction. From the figure, we see that the two reflection rays, $\mathbf{r}(t) = \mathbf{p} + t\mathbf{v}$ and $\mathbf{r}'(t) = \mathbf{p}' + t\mathbf{v}$, intersect different texels of the cube map, and thus should be colored differently. However, because both rays have the same direction vector $\mathbf{v}$, and the direction vector $\mathbf{v}$ is solely used for the cube map lookup, the same texel gets mapped to $\mathbf{p}$ and $\mathbf{p}'$ when the eye is at $\mathbf{e}$ and $\mathbf{e}'$, respectively. For flat objects this defect of environment mapping is very noticeable. For curvy surfaces, this shortcoming of environment mapping goes largely unnoticed since the curvature of the surface causes the reflection vector to vary. See [Brennan02] for an approximate solution to this problem.

17.5 DYNAMIC CUBE MAPS

So far we have described static cube maps, where the images stored in the cube map are premade and fixed. This works for many situations and is relatively inexpensive. However, suppose that we want animated actors moving in our scene. With a pre-generated cube map, you cannot capture these animated objects, which means we cannot reflect animated objects. To overcome this limitation we can build the cube map at runtime. That is, every frame you position the camera in the scene that is to be the origin of the cube map, and then *render the scene six times into each cube map* face along each coordinate axis direction (see Figure 17.9). Since the cube

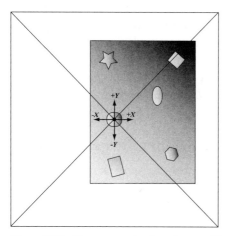

Figure 17.9. The camera is placed at position *0* in the scene, centered about the object we want to generate the dynamic cube map relative to. We render the scene six times along each coordinate axis direction with a field of view angle of 90° so that the image of the entire surrounding environment is captured.

Figure 17.10. Screenshot of the "Dynamic CubeMap" demo showing off dynamic reflections. The skull orbits the center sphere, and its reflection in the sphere animates accordingly. Moreover, because we are drawing the cube maps ourselves, we can model the reflections of the local objects as well, such as the columns, spheres, and floor.

map is rebuilt every frame, it will capture animated objects in the environment, and the reflection will be animated as well (see Figure 17.10).

Note: *Rendering a cube map dynamically is expensive. It requires rendering the scene to 6 render targets! Therefore, try to minimize the number of dynamic cube maps needed in a scene. For example, perhaps only use dynamic reflections for key objects in your scene that you want to show off or accentuate. Then use static cube maps for the less important objects where dynamic reflections would probably go unnoticed or not be missed. Normally, low resolution cube maps are used for dynamic cube maps, such as 256 × 256, to save fill rate.*

17.5.1 Building the Cube Map and Render Target Views

Creating a cube map texture is done by creating a texture array with six elements (one for each face) and specifying the D3D11_RESOURCE_MISC_TEXTURECUBE for the D3D11_TEXTURE2D_DESC::MiscFlags so that Direct3D knows to interpret the texture array as a cube map.

```
static const int CubeMapSize = 256;

//
// Cubemap is a special texture array with 6 elements.  We
```

```
// bind this as a render target to draw to the cube faces,
// and also as a shader resource, so we can use it in a pixel shader.
//

D3D11_TEXTURE2D_DESC texDesc;
texDesc.Width      = CubeMapSize;
texDesc.Height     = CubeMapSize;
texDesc.MipLevels = 0;
texDesc.ArraySize = 6;
texDesc.SampleDesc.Count = 1;
texDesc.SampleDesc.Quality = 0;
texDesc.Format = DXGI_FORMAT_R8G8B8A8_UNORM;
texDesc.Usage = D3D11_USAGE_DEFAULT;
texDesc.BindFlags = D3D11_BIND_RENDER_TARGET | D3D11_BIND_SHADER_RESOURCE;
texDesc.CPUAccessFlags = 0;
texDesc.MiscFlags = D3D11_RESOURCE_MISC_GENERATE_MIPS |
D3D11_RESOURCE_MISC_TEXTURECUBE;

ID3D11Texture2D* cubeTex = 0;
HR(md3dDevice->CreateTexture2D(&texDesc, 0, &cubeTex));
```

We also specify the `D3D11_RESOURCE_MISC_GENERATE_MIPS` flag. This flag allows us to call the `ID3D11DeviceContext::GenerateMips` method on the cube map, which has the hardware generate the lower mipmap levels of the texture. This is needed because we only render to the top mipmap level of the texture, and so the lower mipmap levels are undefined unless we generate them ourselves or use the `GenerateMips` method.

Next, we need to create a render target view to each element in the cube map texture array, so that we can render onto each cube map face. This is done as follows:

```
//
// Create a render target view to each cube map face
// (i.e., each element in the texture array).
//

ID3D11RenderTargetView* mDynamicCubeMapRTV[6];

D3D11_RENDER_TARGET_VIEW_DESC rtvDesc;
rtvDesc.Format = texDesc.Format;
rtvDesc.ViewDimension = D3D11_RTV_DIMENSION_TEXTURE2DARRAY;
rtvDesc.Texture2DArray.MipSlice = 0;

// Only create a view to one array element.
rtvDesc.Texture2DArray.ArraySize = 1;

for(int i = 0; i < 6; ++i)
{
    // Create a render target view to the ith element.
    rtvDesc.Texture2DArray.FirstArraySlice = i;
    HR(md3dDevice->CreateRenderTargetView(
      cubeTex, &rtvDesc, &mDynamicCubeMapRTV[i]));
}
```

Finally, we create a shader resource view to the cube map texture so that we can sample it in a pixel shader after it is built to render reflections.

```
//
// Create a shader resource view to the cube map.
//

ID3D11ShaderResourceView* mDynamicCubeMapSRV;

D3D11_SHADER_RESOURCE_VIEW_DESC srvDesc;
srvDesc.Format = texDesc.Format;
srvDesc.ViewDimension = D3D11_SRV_DIMENSION_TEXTURECUBE;
srvDesc.TextureCube.MostDetailedMip = 0;
srvDesc.TextureCube.MipLevels = -1;

HR(md3dDevice->CreateShaderResourceView(
    cubeTex, &srvDesc, &mDynamicCubeMapSRV));

// View saves reference.
ReleaseCOM(cubeTex);
```

17.5.2 Building the Depth Buffer and Viewport

Generally the cube map faces will have a different resolution than the main back buffer. Therefore, for rendering to the cube map faces, we need a depth buffer with dimensions that match the resolution of a cube map face. This is done with the following code (which should be familiar to you by now):

```
static const int CubeMapSize = 256;

ID3D11DepthStencilView* mDynamicCubeMapDSV;

D3D11_TEXTURE2D_DESC depthTexDesc;
depthTexDesc.Width = CubeMapSize;
depthTexDesc.Height = CubeMapSize;
depthTexDesc.MipLevels = 1;
depthTexDesc.ArraySize = 1;
depthTexDesc.SampleDesc.Count = 1;
depthTexDesc.SampleDesc.Quality = 0;
depthTexDesc.Format = DXGI_FORMAT_D32_FLOAT;
depthTexDesc.Usage = D3D11_USAGE_DEFAULT;
depthTexDesc.BindFlags = D3D11_BIND_DEPTH_STENCIL;
depthTexDesc.CPUAccessFlags = 0;
depthTexDesc.MiscFlags = 0;

ID3D11Texture2D* depthTex = 0;
HR(md3dDevice->CreateTexture2D(&depthTexDesc, 0, &depthTex));

// Create the depth stencil view for the entire buffer.
D3D11_DEPTH_STENCIL_VIEW_DESC dsvDesc;
dsvDesc.Format = depthTexDesc.Format;
dsvDesc.Flags  = 0;
```

```
dsvDesc.ViewDimension = D3D11_DSV_DIMENSION_TEXTURE2D;
dsvDesc.Texture2D.MipSlice = 0;
HR(md3dDevice->CreateDepthStencilView(depthTex,
    &dsvDesc, &mDynamicCubeMapDSV));

// View saves reference.
ReleaseCOM(depthTex);
```

Moreover, because the cube map faces will have a different resolution than the main back buffer, we need to define a new viewport that covers a cube map face:

```
D3D11_VIEWPORT mCubeMapViewport;
mCubeMapViewport.TopLeftX = 0.0f;
mCubeMapViewport.TopLeftY = 0.0f;
mCubeMapViewport.Width    = (float)CubeMapSize;
mCubeMapViewport.Height   = (float)CubeMapSize;
mCubeMapViewport.MinDepth = 0.0f;
mCubeMapViewport.MaxDepth = 1.0f;
```

17.5.3 Setting up the Cube Map Camera

Recall that to generate a cube map idea is to position a camera at the center of some object 0 in the scene with a 90° field of view angle (both vertically and horizontally). Then have the camera look down the positive x-axis, negative x-axis, positive y-axis, negative y-axis, positive z-axis, and negative z-axis, and to take a picture of the scene (excluding the object 0) from each of these six viewpoints. To facilitate this, we generate six cameras, one for each face, centered at the given position (x, y, z):

```
Camera mCubeMapCamera[6];

void DynamicCubeMapApp::BuildCubeFaceCamera(float x, float y, float z)
{
    // Generate the cube map about the given position.
    XMFLOAT3 center(x, y, z);
    XMFLOAT3 worldUp(0.0f, 1.0f, 0.0f);

    // Look along each coordinate axis.
    XMFLOAT3 targets[6] =
    {
      XMFLOAT3(x+1.0f, y, z),  // +X
      XMFLOAT3(x-1.0f, y, z),  // -X
      XMFLOAT3(x, y+1.0f, z),  // +Y
      XMFLOAT3(x, y-1.0f, z),  // -Y
      XMFLOAT3(x, y, z+1.0f),  // +Z
      XMFLOAT3(x, y, z-1.0f)   // -Z
    };

    // Use world up vector (0,1,0) for all directions except +Y/-Y.
    // In these cases, we are looking down +Y or -Y, so we need a
    // different "up" vector.
```

```
XMFLOAT3 ups[6] =
{
  XMFLOAT3(0.0f, 1.0f, 0.0f),   // +X
  XMFLOAT3(0.0f, 1.0f, 0.0f),   // -X
  XMFLOAT3(0.0f, 0.0f, -1.0f),  // +Y
  XMFLOAT3(0.0f, 0.0f, +1.0f),  // -Y
  XMFLOAT3(0.0f, 1.0f, 0.0f),   // +Z
  XMFLOAT3(0.0f, 1.0f, 0.0f)    // -Z
};

for(int i = 0; i < 6; ++i)
{
  mCubeMapCamera[i].LookAt(center, targets[i], ups[i]);
  mCubeMapCamera[i].SetLens(0.5f*XM_PI, 1.0f, 0.1f, 1000.0f);
  mCubeMapCamera[i].UpdateViewMatrix();
}
}
```

17.5.4 Drawing into the Cube Map

Finally, our `DrawScene` method first draws the scene to the cube map, except the center sphere which we are generating the cube map about, and then draws the scene as usual, with the dynamic cube map applied to the center sphere.

```
void DynamicCubeMapApp::DrawScene()
{
    ID3D11RenderTargetView* renderTargets[1];

    // Generate the cube map by rendering to each cube map face.
    md3dImmediateContext->RSSetViewports(1, &mCubeMapViewport);
    for(int i = 0; i < 6; ++i)
    {
      // Clear cube map face and depth buffer.
      md3dImmediateContext->ClearRenderTargetView(
        mDynamicCubeMapRTV[i],
        reinterpret_cast<const float*>(&Colors::Silver));
      md3dImmediateContext->ClearDepthStencilView(
        mDynamicCubeMapDSV,
        D3D11_CLEAR_DEPTH|D3D11_CLEAR_STENCIL, 1.0f, 0);

      // Bind cube map face as render target.
      renderTargets[0] = mDynamicCubeMapRTV[i];
      md3dImmediateContext->OMSetRenderTargets(
        1, renderTargets, mDynamicCubeMapDSV);

      // Draw the scene with the exception of the
      // center sphere, to this cube map face.
      DrawScene(mCubeMapCamera[i], false);
    }

    // Restore old viewport and render targets.
    md3dImmediateContext->RSSetViewports(1, &mScreenViewport);
    renderTargets[0] = mRenderTargetView;
```

```
md3dImmediateContext->OMSetRenderTargets(
  1, renderTargets, mDepthStencilView);

// Have hardware generate lower mipmap levels of cube map.
md3dImmediateContext->GenerateMips(mDynamicCubeMapSRV);

// Now draw the scene as normal, but with the center sphere.
md3dImmediateContext->ClearRenderTargetView(
  mRenderTargetView,
  reinterpret_cast<const float*>(&Colors::Silver));
md3dImmediateContext->ClearDepthStencilView(
  mDepthStencilView,
  D3D11_CLEAR_DEPTH|D3D11_CLEAR_STENCIL,
  1.0f, 0);

DrawScene(mCam, true);

HR(mSwapChain->Present(0, 0));
}
```

This code utilizes the overloaded `DrawScene` method to draw the actual objects; this overloaded method takes a `Camera` parameter, and a `bool` flag indicating whether to draw the center sphere or not.

```
void DrawScene(const Camera& camera, bool drawCenterSphere);
```

So we see in the previous code that we draw the scene six times, once to each cube map face with the corresponding camera for that face, while not drawing the center sphere to the cube map. Lastly, we draw the scene again this time with the center sphere drawn, and with our typical "player" camera. When the center sphere is drawn, it uses the cube map we just generated, so that animations reflect correctly.

17.6 DYNAMIC CUBE MAPS WITH THE GEOMETRY SHADER

In the previous section, we redrew the scene 6 times to generate the cube map—once for each cube map face. Draw calls are not free, and we should work to minimize them. There is a Direct3D 10 sample called "CubeMapGS," which the geometry shader uses to render a cube map by drawing the scene only once. (Direct3D 11 is a superset of 10, so the way this works also works in Direct3D 11.) In this section, we highlight the main ideas of how this sample works.

First, it creates a render target view to the *entire* texture array (not each individual face texture):

```
// Create the 6-face render target view
D3D10_RENDER_TARGET_VIEW_DESC DescRT;
DescRT.Format = dstex.Format;
```

```
DescRT.ViewDimension = D3D10_RTV_DIMENSION_TEXTURE2DARRAY;
DescRT.Texture2DArray.FirstArraySlice = 0;
DescRT.Texture2DArray.ArraySize = 6;
DescRT.Texture2DArray.MipSlice = 0;
V_RETURN(pd3dDevice->CreateRenderTargetView(
    g_pEnvMap, &DescRT, &g_pEnvMapRTV));
```

Moreover, this technique requires a cube map of depth buffers (one for each face). The depth stencil view to the *entire* texture array of depth buffers is created as follows:

```
// Create the depth stencil view for the entire cube
D3D10_DEPTH_STENCIL_VIEW_DESC DescDS;
DescDS.Format = DXGI_FORMAT_D32_FLOAT;
DescDS.ViewDimension = D3D10_DSV_DIMENSION_TEXTURE2DARRAY;
DescDS.Texture2DArray.FirstArraySlice = 0;
DescDS.Texture2DArray.ArraySize = 6;
DescDS.Texture2DArray.MipSlice = 0;
V_RETURN(pd3dDevice->CreateDepthStencilView(
    g_pEnvMapDepth, &DescDS, &g_pEnvMapDSV));
```

It then binds this render target and depth stencil view to the OM stage of the pipeline:

```
ID3D10RenderTargetView* aRTViews[ 1 ] = { g_pEnvMapRTV };
pd3dDevice->OMSetRenderTargets(sizeof(aRTViews)/sizeof(aRTViews[0]),
    aRTViews, g_pEnvMapDSV);
```

That is, we have bound a view to an array of render targets and a view to an array of depth stencil buffers to the OM stage, and we are going to render to each array slice simultaneously.

Now, the scene is rendered once and an array of six view matrices (one to look in the corresponding direction of each cube map face) is available in the constant buffers. The geometry shader replicates the input triangle six times, and assigns the triangle to one of the six render target array slices. Assigning a triangle to a render target array slice is done by setting the system value SV_RenderTargetArrayIndex. This system value is an integer index value that can only be set as an output from the geometry shader to specify the index of the render target array slice the primitive should be rendered onto. This system value can only be used if the render target view is actually a view to an array resource.

```
struct PS_CUBEMAP_IN
{
    float4 Pos : SV_POSITION;      // Projection coord
    float2 Tex : TEXCOORD0;        // Texture coord
    uint RTIndex : SV_RenderTargetArrayIndex;
};

[maxvertexcount(18)]
void GS_CubeMap(triangle GS_CUBEMAP_IN input[3],
inout TriangleStream<PS_CUBEMAP_IN> CubeMapStream)
```

```
{
    // For each triangle
    for(int f = 0; f < 6; ++f)
    {
        // Compute screen coordinates
        PS_CUBEMAP_IN output;

        // Assign the ith triangle to the ith render target.
        output.RTIndex = f;

        // For each vertex in the triangle
        for(int v = 0; v < 3; v++)
        {
            // Transform to the view space of the ith cube face.
            output.Pos = mul(input[v].Pos, g_mViewCM[f]);

            // Transform to homogeneous clip space.
            output.Pos = mul(output.Pos, mProj);

            output.Tex = input[v].Tex;
            CubeMapStream.Append(output);
        }
        CubeMapStream.RestartStrip();
    }
}
```

Thus we see that we have rendered the scene to each cube map face by rendering the scene only once instead of six times.

Note: *We have summarized the main idea of this sample, but refer to the "CubeMapGS" Direct3D 10 sample for the full source code to fill in any details.*

This strategy is interesting and demonstrates simultaneous render targets and the SV_RenderTargetArrayIndex system value; however, it is not a definite win. There are two issues that make this method unattractive:

1. It uses the geometry shader to output a large set of data. Recall from Chapter 11 that the geometry shader acts inefficiently when outputting a large set of data. Therefore, using a geometry shader for this purpose could hurt performance.

2. In a typical scene, a triangle will not overlap more than one cube map face (see again Figure 17.9). Therefore, the act of replicating a triangle and rendering it onto each cube face when it will be clipped by 5 out of 6 of the faces is wasteful. Admittedly, our demo in §5.4 also renders the entire scene to each cube map face for simplicity. However, in real applications (non-demo), we would use frustum culling (Chapter 15) and only render the objects visible to a particular cube map face. Frustum culling at the object level cannot be done by a geometry shader implementation.

On the other hand, a situation where this strategy does work well would be rendering a mesh that surrounds the scene. For example, suppose that you had a dynamic sky system where the clouds moved and the sky color changed based on the time of day. Because the sky is changing, we cannot use a prebaked cube map texture to reflect the sky, so we have to use a dynamic cube map. Because the sky mesh surrounds the entire scene, it *is visible by all six* cube map faces. Therefore, the second bullet point previously does not apply, and the geometry shader method could be a win by reducing draw calls from six to one, assuming usage of the geometry shader does not hurt performance too much.

17.7 SUMMARY

1. A cube map consists of six textures that we visualize as the faces of a cube. In Direct3D 11 a cube map can be represented by the `ID3D11Texture2D` interface as a texture array with the additional flag `D3D11_RESOURCE_MISC_TEXTURECUBE`. In the HLSL, a cube map is represented by the `TextureCube` type. To identify a texel in a cube map, we use 3D texture coordinates, which define a 3D *lookup* vector **v** originating at the center of the cube map. The texel of the cube map that **v** intersects is the texel corresponding to the 3D coordinates of **v**.

2. An environment map captures the surrounding environment about a point with six images. These images can then be stored in a cube map. With environment maps we can easily texture a sky or approximate reflections.

3. Cube maps can be made from six individual images using the DirectX Texture Tool. Cube maps can then be saved to file with the DDS image format. Because cube maps store six 2D textures, which can consume a lot of memory, a compressed DDS format should be used. The `D3DX11CreateShaderResourceViewFromFile` function can load a DDS file that stores a cube map and create a shader resource view to it.

4. Prebaked cube maps do not capture objects that move or objects in the scene that did not exist when the cube map was generated. To overcome this limitation we can build the cube map at runtime. That is, for every frame you position the camera in the scene that is to be the origin of the cube map, and then *render the scene six times into each cube map* face along each coordinate axis direction. Because the cube map is rebuilt every frame, it will capture animated objects and every object in the environment. Dynamic cube maps are expensive and their use should be minimized to key objects.

5. We can bind a render target view to a texture array to the OM stage. Moreover, we can render to each array slice in the texture array simultaneously. Assigning

a triangle to a render target array slice is done by setting the system value **sv_RenderTargetArrayIndex**. A render target view to a texture array, along with the **SV_RenderTargetArrayIndex** system value, allows generating a cube map dynamically by rendering the scene once instead of six times. However, this strategy might not always be a win over rendering the scene six times with frustum culling.

17.8 EXERCISES

1. Experiment with different **Material::Reflect** values in the "Cube Map" demo. Also try to make the cylinders and box reflective.

2. Find six image that capture an environment (either find cube map images online or use a program like *Terragen* to make them), and go through the process outlined in §17.2 using the Texture Tool to make your own cube map. Test your cube map out in the "Cube Map" demo.

3. A *dielectric* is a transparent material that refracts light; see Figure 17.11. When a ray strikes a dielectric, some light reflects and some light refracts based on

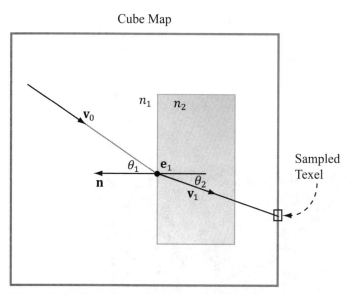

Figure 17.11. The incident vector v_0 travels through a medium with index of refraction n_1. The ray strikes a transparent material with index of refraction n_2, and refracts into the vector v_1. We use the refracted vector v_1 as a lookup into the cube map. This is almost like alpha blending transparency, except alpha blending transparency does not bend the incident vector.

Snell's Law of Refraction. The indices of refraction n_1 and n_2 determine how much the light bends:

(1) If $n_1 = n_2$, then $\theta_1 = \theta_2$ (no bending).

(2) If $n_2 > n_1$, then $\theta_2 < \theta_1$ (ray bends toward normal).

(3) If $n_1 > n_2$, then $\theta_2 > \theta_1$ (ray bends away from normal).

Thus, in Figure 17.11, $n_2 > n_1$ because the ray bends toward the normal when we enter the block. Physically, the light ray refracts again when leaving the block, but for real-time graphics, typically only the first refraction is modeled. The HLSL provides the intrinsic **refract** function to calculate the refraction vector:

```
float3 refract(float3 incident, float3 normal, float eta);
```

The incident vector is the incoming light ray vector ($\mathbf{v}_0$ in Figure 17.11), and the normal vector is the outward surface normal (**n** in Figure 17.11). The third parameter is the ratio of the indices of refraction n_1/n_2. The index of refraction of a vacuum is 1.0; some other index of refactions: water—1.33; glass—1.51. For this exercise, modify the "Cube Map" demo to do refraction instead of reflection (see Figure 17.12); you may need to adjust the **Material::Reflect** values. Try out **eta = 1.0**, **eta = 0.95**, **eta = 0.9**.

Figure 17.12. "Cube Demo" with refraction instead of reflection.

Chapter **18** # NORMAL MAPPING AND DISPLACEMENT MAPPING

In Chapter 8, we introduced texture mapping, which enabled us to map fine details from an image onto our triangles. However, our normal vectors are still defined at the coarser vertex level and interpolated over the triangle. For part of this chapter, we study a popular method for specifying surface normals at a higher resolution. Specifying surface normals at a higher resolution increases the detail of the lighting, but the mesh geometry detail remains unchanged. Displacement mapping, combined with tessellation, allows us to increase the detail of our meshes.

Objectives:

1. To understand why we need normal mapping.
2. To discover how normal maps are stored.
3. To learn how normal maps can be created.
4. To learn the coordinate system normal vectors in normal maps are specified relative to and how it relates to the object space coordinate system of a 3D triangle.
5. To find out how to implement normal mapping in a vertex and pixel shader.
6. To discover how displacement maps and tessellation can be combined to improve mesh detail.

18.1 MOTIVATION

Consider Figure 18.1. The specular highlights on the cone shaped columns do not look right—they look unnaturally smooth compared to the bumpiness of the brick texture. This is because the underlying mesh geometry is smooth, and we have merely applied the image of bumpy bricks over the smooth cylindrical surface. However, the lighting calculations are performed based on the mesh geometry (in particular, the interpolated vertex normals), and not the texture image. Thus the lighting is not completely consistent with the texture.

Ideally, we would tessellate the mesh geometry so much that the actual bumps and crevices of the bricks could be modeled by the underlying geometry. Then the lighting and texture could be made consistent. Hardware tessellation could help in this area, but we still need a way to specify the normals for the vertices generated by the tessellator (using interpolated normals does not increase our normal resolution).

Another possible solution would be to bake the lighting details directly into the textures. However, this will not work if the lights are allowed to move, as the texel colors will remain fixed as the lights move.

Figure 18.1. **Smooth specular highlights.**

Figure 18.2. **Bumpy specular highlights.**

Thus our goal is to find a way to implement dynamic lighting such that the fine details that show up in the texture map also show up in the lighting. Since textures provide us with the fine details to begin with, it is natural to look for a texture mapping solution to this problem. Figure 18.2 shows the same scene shown in Figure 18.1 with normal mapping; we can see now that the dynamic lighting is much more consistent with the brick texture.

18.2 NORMAL MAPS

A *normal map* is a texture, but instead of storing RGB data at each texel, we store a compressed x-coordinate, y-coordinate, and z-coordinate in the red component, green component, and blue component, respectively. These coordinates define a normal vector; thus a normal map stores a normal vector at each pixel. Figure 18.3 shows an example of how to visualize a normal map.

For illustration, we will assume a 24-bit image format, which reserves a byte for each color component, and therefore, each color component can range from

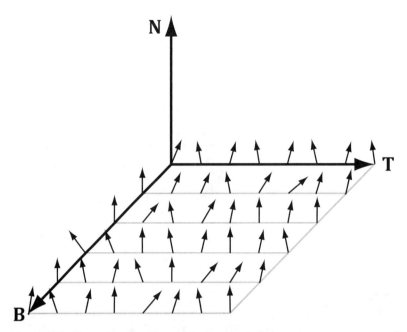

Figure 18.3. Normals stored in a normal map relative to a texture space coordinate system defined by the vectors T (*x*-axis), B (*y*-axis), and N (*z*-axis). The T vector runs right horizontally to the texture image; the B vector runs down vertically to the texture image; and N is orthogonal to the texture plane.

0–255. (A 32-bit format could be employed where the alpha component goes unused or stores some other scalar value such as a heightmap or specular map. Also, a floating-point format could be used in which no compression is necessary, but this requires more memory.)

Note: *As Figure 18.3 shows, the vectors are generally mostly aligned with the z-axis. That is, the z-coordinate has the largest magnitude. Consequently, normal maps usually appear mostly blue when viewed as a color image. This is because the z-coordinate is stored in the blue channel and because it has the largest magnitude, this color dominates.*

So how do we compress a unit vector into this format? First note that for a unit vector, each coordinate always lies in the range $[-1, 1]$. If we shift and scale this range to $[0, 1]$ and multiply by 255 and truncate the decimal, the result will be an integer in the range 0–255. That is, if x is a coordinate in the range $[-1, 1]$, then the integer part of $f(x)$ is an integer in the range 0–255, where f is defined by

$$f(x) = (0.5x + 0.5) \cdot 255$$

So to store a unit vector in a 24-bit image, we just apply f to each coordinate and write the coordinate to the corresponding color channel in the texture map.

The next question is how to reverse the compression process; that is, given a compressed texture coordinate in the range 0–255, how can we recover its true value in the interval $[-1, 1]$. The answer is to simply invert the function f, which after a little thought, can be seen to be:

$$f^{-1}(x) = \frac{2x}{255} - 1$$

That is, if x is an integer in the range 0–255, then $f^{-1}(x)$ is a floating-point number in the range $[-1, 1]$.

We will not have to do the compression process ourselves, as we will use a Photoshop plug-in to convert images to normal maps. However, when we sample a normal map in a pixel shader, we will have to do part of the inverse process to uncompress it. When we sample a normal map in a shader like this

```
float3 normalT = gNormalMap.Sample(gTriLinearSam, pin.Tex);
```

the color vector `normalT` will have normalized components (r, g, b) such that $0 \le r, g, b \le 1$.

Thus, the method has already done part of the uncompressing work for us (namely the divide by 255, which transforms an integer in the range 0–255 to the floating-point interval $[0, 1]$). We complete the transformation by shifting and scaling each component in $[0, 1]$ to $[-1, 1]$ with the function $g: [0,1] \rightarrow [-1,1]$ defined by:

$$g(x) = 2x - 1$$

In code, we apply this function to each color component like this:

```
// Uncompress each component from [0,1] to [-1,1].
normalT = 2.0f*normalT - 1.0f;
```

This works because the scalar 1.0 is augmented to the vector $(1, 1, 1)$ so that the expression makes sense and is done componentwise.

Note: *The Photoshop plug-in is available at* http://developer.nvidia.com/nvidia-texture-tools-adobe-photoshop. *There are other tools available for generating normal maps such as* http://www.crazybump.com/. *Also, there are tools that can generate normal maps from high resolution meshes (see* http://www.nvidia.com/object/melody_home.html).

Note: *If you want to use a compressed texture format to store normal maps, then use the BC7 (DXGI_FORMAT_BC7_UNORM) format for the best quality, as it significantly reduces the errors caused by compressing normal maps. For BC6 and BC7 formats, the DirectX SDK has a sample called "BC6HBC7EncoderDecoder11." This program can be used to convert your texture files to BC6 or BC7.*

18.3 TEXTURE/TANGENT SPACE

Consider a 3D texture mapped triangle. For the sake of discussion, suppose there is no distortion in the texture mapping; in other words, mapping the texture triangle onto the 3D triangle requires only a rigid body transformation (translation and rotation). Now, suppose that the texture is like a decal. So we pick the decal up, translate it, and rotate it onto the 3D triangle. So now Figure 18.4 shows how the texture space axes relate to the 3D triangle: they are tangent to the triangle and lie in the plane of the triangle. The texture coordinates of the triangle are, of course, relative to the texture space coordinate system. Incorporating the triangle face normal $\mathbf{N}$, we obtain a 3D *TBN-basis* in the plane of the triangle that we call

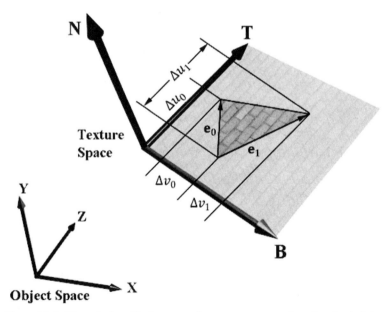

Figure 18.4. The relationship between the texture space of a triangle and the object space. The 3D tangent vector T aims in the *u*-axis direction of the texturing coordinate system, and the 3D tangent vector B aims in the *v*-axis direction of the texturing coordinate system.

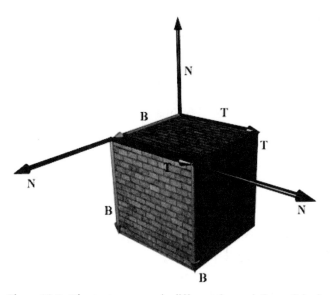

Figure 18.5. The texture space is different for each face of the box.

texture space or *tangent space*. Note that the tangent space generally varies from triangle-to-triangle (see Figure 18.5).

Now, as Figure 18.3 shows, the normal vectors in a normal map are defined relative to the texture space. But our lights are defined in world space. In order to do lighting, the normal vectors and lights need to be in the same space. So our first step is to relate the tangent space coordinate system with the object space coordinate system the triangle vertices are relative to. Once we are in object space, we can use the world matrix to get from object space to world space (the details of this are covered in the next section). Let $\mathbf{v}_0$, $\mathbf{v}_1$, and $\mathbf{v}_2$ define the three vertices of a 3D triangle with corresponding texture coordinates (u_0, v_0), (u_1, v_1), and (u_2, v_2) that define a triangle in the texture plane relative to the texture space axes (i.e., $\mathbf{T}$ and $\mathbf{B}$). Let $\mathbf{e}_0 = \mathbf{v}_1 - \mathbf{v}_0$ and $\mathbf{e}_1 = \mathbf{v}_2 - \mathbf{v}_0$ be two edge vectors of the 3D triangle with corresponding texture triangle edge vectors $(\Delta u_0, \Delta v_0) = (u_1 - u_0, v_1 - v_0)$ and $(\Delta u_1, \Delta v_1) = (u_2 - u_0, v_2 - v_0)$. From Figure 18.4, it is clear that

$$\mathbf{e}_0 = \Delta u_0 \, \mathbf{T} + \Delta v_0 \, \mathbf{B}$$
$$\mathbf{e}_1 = \Delta u_1 \, \mathbf{T} + \Delta v_1 \, \mathbf{B}$$

Representing the vectors with coordinates relative to object space, we get the matrix equation:

$$\begin{bmatrix} e_{0,x} & e_{0,y} & e_{0,z} \\ e_{1,x} & e_{1,y} & e_{1,z} \end{bmatrix} = \begin{bmatrix} \Delta u_0 & \Delta v_0 \\ \Delta u_1 & \Delta v_1 \end{bmatrix} \begin{bmatrix} T_x & T_y & T_z \\ B_x & B_y & B_z \end{bmatrix}$$

Note that we know the object space coordinates of the triangle vertices; hence we know the object space coordinates of the edge vectors, so the matrix

$$\begin{bmatrix} e_{0,x} & e_{0,y} & e_{0,z} \\ e_{1,x} & e_{1,y} & e_{1,z} \end{bmatrix}$$

is known. Likewise, we know the texture coordinates, so the matrix

$$\begin{bmatrix} \Delta u_0 & \Delta v_0 \\ \Delta u_1 & \Delta v_1 \end{bmatrix}$$

is known. Solving for the **T** and **B** object space coordinates we get:

$$\begin{bmatrix} T_x & T_y & T_z \\ B_x & B_y & B_z \end{bmatrix} = \begin{bmatrix} \Delta u_0 & \Delta v_0 \\ \Delta u_1 & \Delta v_1 \end{bmatrix}^{-1} \begin{bmatrix} e_{0,x} & e_{0,y} & e_{0,z} \\ e_{1,x} & e_{1,y} & e_{1,z} \end{bmatrix}$$

$$= \frac{1}{\Delta u_0 \Delta v_1 - \Delta v_0 \Delta u_1} \begin{bmatrix} \Delta v_1 & -\Delta v_0 \\ -\Delta u_1 & \Delta u_0 \end{bmatrix} \begin{bmatrix} e_{0,x} & e_{0,y} & e_{0,z} \\ e_{1,x} & e_{1,y} & e_{1,z} \end{bmatrix}$$

In the above, we used the fact that the inverse of a matrix $\mathbf{A} = \begin{bmatrix} a & b \\ c & d \end{bmatrix}$ is given by:

$$\mathbf{A}^{-1} = \frac{1}{ad - bc} \begin{bmatrix} d & -b \\ -c & a \end{bmatrix}$$

Note that the vectors **T** and **B** are generally not unit length in object space, and if there is texture distortion, they will not be orthonormal either.

The **T**, **B**, and **N** vectors are commonly referred to as the *tangent, binormal* (or *bitangent*), and *normal* vectors, respectively.

18.4 VERTEX TANGENT SPACE

In the previous section, we derived a tangent space per triangle. However, if we use this texture space for normal mapping, we will get a triangulated appearance since the tangent space is constant over the face of the triangle. Therefore, we specify tangent vectors per vertex, and we do the same averaging trick that we did with vertex normals to approximate a smooth surface:

1. The tangent vector **T** for an arbitrary vertex **v** in a mesh is found by averaging the tangent vectors of every triangle in the mesh that shares the vertex **v**.

2. The bitangent vector **B** for an arbitrary vertex **v** in a mesh is found by averaging the bitangent vectors of every triangle in the mesh that shares the vertex **v**.

Generally, after averaging, the TBN-bases will generally need to be orthonormalized, so that the vectors are mutually orthogonal and of unit length. This is usually done using the Gram-Schmidt procedure. Code is available on the Web for building a per-vertex tangent space for an arbitrary triangle mesh: http://www.terathon.com/code/tangent.html.

In our system, we will not store the bitangent vector **B** directly in memory. Instead, we will compute $\mathbf{B} = \mathbf{N} \times \mathbf{T}$ when we need **B**, where **N** is the usual averaged vertex normal. Hence, our vertex structure looks like this:

```
namespace Vertex
{
    struct NormalMap
    {
      XMFLOAT3 Pos;
      XMFLOAT3 Normal;
      XMFLOAT2 Tex;
      XMFLOAT3 TangentU;
    };
}
```

Recall that our procedurally generated meshes created by `GeometryGenerator` compute the tangent vector **T** corresponding to the u-axis of the texture space. The object space coordinates of the tangent vector **T** are easily specified at each vertex for box and grid meshes (see Figure 18.5). For cylinders and spheres, the tangent vector **T** at each vertex can be found by forming the vector-valued function of two variables $\mathbf{P}(u,v)$ of the cylinder/sphere and computing $\partial\mathbf{P}/\partial u$, where the parameter u is also used as the u-texture coordinate.

18.5 TRANSFORMING BETWEEN TANGENT SPACE AND OBJECT SPACE

At this point, we have an orthonormal TBN-basis at each vertex in a mesh. Moreover, we have the coordinates of the TBN vectors relative to the object space of the mesh. So now that we have the coordinates of the TBN-basis relative to the object space coordinate system, we can transform coordinates from tangent space to object space with the matrix:

$$\mathbf{M}_{object} = \begin{bmatrix} T_x & T_y & T_z \\ B_x & B_y & B_z \\ N_x & N_y & N_z \end{bmatrix}$$

Because this matrix is orthogonal, its inverse is its transpose. Thus, the change of coordinate matrix from object space to tangent space is:

$$\mathbf{M}_{tangent} = \mathbf{M}_{object}^{-1} = \mathbf{M}_{object}^{T} = \begin{bmatrix} T_x & B_x & N_x \\ T_y & B_y & N_y \\ T_z & B_z & N_z \end{bmatrix}$$

In our shader program, we will actually want to transform the normal vector from tangent space to world space for lighting. One way would be to transform the normal from tangent space to object space first, and then use the world matrix to transform from object space to world space:

$$\mathbf{n}_{world} = (\mathbf{n}_{tangent}\, \mathbf{M}_{object})\, \mathbf{M}_{world}$$

However, because matrix multiplication is associative, we can do it like this:

$$\mathbf{n}_{world} = \mathbf{n}_{tangent}\, (\mathbf{M}_{object}\, \mathbf{M}_{world})$$

And note that

$$\mathbf{M}_{object}\mathbf{M}_{world} = \begin{bmatrix} \leftarrow \mathbf{T} \rightarrow \\ \leftarrow \mathbf{B} \rightarrow \\ \leftarrow \mathbf{N} \rightarrow \end{bmatrix} \mathbf{M}_{world} = \begin{bmatrix} \leftarrow \mathbf{T}' \rightarrow \\ \leftarrow \mathbf{B}' \rightarrow \\ \leftarrow \mathbf{N}' \rightarrow \end{bmatrix} = \begin{bmatrix} T_x' & T_y' & T_z' \\ B_x' & B_y' & B_z' \\ N_x' & N_y' & N_z' \end{bmatrix}$$

where $\mathbf{T}' = \mathbf{T} \cdot \mathbf{M}_{world}$, $\mathbf{B}' = \mathbf{B} \cdot \mathbf{M}_{world}$, and $\mathbf{N}' = \mathbf{N} \cdot \mathbf{M}_{world}$. So to go from tangent space directly to world space, we just have to describe the tangent basis in world coordinates, which can be done by transforming the TBN-basis from object space coordinates to world space coordinates.

Note: We will only be interested in transforming vectors (not points). Thus, we only need a 3 × 3 matrix. Recall that the fourth row of an affine matrix is for translation, but we do not translate vectors.

18.6 NORMAL MAPPING SHADER CODE

We summarize the general process for normal mapping:

1. Create the desired normal maps from some art program or utility program and store them in an image file. Create 2D textures from these files when the program is initialized.

2. For each triangle, compute the tangent vector **T**. Obtain a per-vertex tangent vector for each vertex **v** in a mesh by averaging the tangent vectors of every triangle in the mesh that shares the vertex **v**. (In our demo, we use simple geometry and are able to specify the tangent vectors directly, but this averaging process would need to be done if using arbitrary triangle meshes made in a 3D modeling program.)

3. In the vertex shader, transform the vertex normal and tangent vector to world space and output the results to the pixel shader.

4. Using the interpolated tangent vector and normal vector, we build the TBN-basis at each pixel point on the surface of the triangle. We use this basis to transform the sampled normal vector from the normal map from tangent space to the world space. We then have a world space normal vector from the normal map to use for our usual lighting calculations.

To help us implement normal mapping, we have added the following function to *lighthelper.fx*:

```
//---------------------------------------------------------------------
// Transforms a normal map sample to world space.
//---------------------------------------------------------------------
float3 NormalSampleToWorldSpace(float3 normalMapSample,
                                float3 unitNormalW,
                                float3 tangentW)
{
    // Uncompress each component from [0,1] to [-1,1].
    float3 normalT = 2.0f*normalMapSample - 1.0f;

    // Build orthonormal basis.
    float3 N = unitNormalW;
    float3 T = normalize(tangentW - dot(tangentW, N)*N);
    float3 B = cross(N, T);

    float3x3 TBN = float3x3(T, B, N);

    // Transform from tangent space to world space.
    float3 bumpedNormalW = mul(normalT, TBN);

    return bumpedNormalW;
}
```

This function is used like this in the pixel shader:

```
float3 normalMapSample = gNormalMap.Sample(samLinear, pin.Tex).rgb;
float3 bumpedNormalW = NormalSampleToWorldSpace(
                        normalMapSample,
                        pin.NormalW,
                        pin.TangentW);
```

Two lines that might not be clear are these:

```
float3 N = unitNormalW;
float3 T = normalize(tangentW - dot(tangentW, N)*N);
```

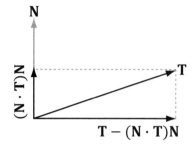

Figure 18.6. Since $\|N\| = 1$, $\text{proj}_N(T) = (T \cdot N)N$. The vector $T - \text{proj}_N(T)$ is the portion of T orthogonal to N.

After the interpolation, the tangent vector and normal vector may not be orthonormal. This code makes sure **T** is orthonormal to **N** by subtracting off any component of **T** along the direction **N** (see Figure 18.6). Note that there is the assumption that `unitNormalW` is normalized.

Once we have the normal from the normal map, which we call the "bumped normal," we use it for all the subsequent calculation involving the normal vector (e.g., lighting, cube mapping). The entire normal mapping effect is shown below for completeness, with the parts relevant to normal mapping in bold.

```
#include "LightHelper.fx"

cbuffer cbPerFrame
{
    DirectionalLight gDirLights[3];
    float3 gEyePosW;

    float  gFogStart;
    float  gFogRange;
    float4 gFogColor;
};

cbuffer cbPerObject
{
    float4x4 gWorld;
    float4x4 gWorldInvTranspose;
    float4x4 gWorldViewProj;
    float4x4 gTexTransform;
    Material gMaterial;
};

// Nonnumeric values cannot be added to a cbuffer.
Texture2D gDiffuseMap;
Texture2D gNormalMap;
TextureCube gCubeMap;

SamplerState samLinear
```

```
{
    Filter = MIN_MAG_MIP_LINEAR;
    AddressU = WRAP;
    AddressV = WRAP;
};

struct VertexIn
{
    float3 PosL     : POSITION;
    float3 NormalL  : NORMAL;
    float2 Tex      : TEXCOORD;
    float3 TangentL : TANGENT;
};

struct VertexOut
{
    float4 PosH     : SV_POSITION;
    float3 PosW     : POSITION;
    float3 NormalW  : NORMAL;
    float3 TangentW : TANGENT;
    float2 Tex      : TEXCOORD;
};

VertexOut VS(VertexIn vin)
{
    VertexOut vout;

    // Transform to world space space.
    vout.PosW     = mul(float4(vin.PosL, 1.0f), gWorld).xyz;
    vout.NormalW  = mul(vin.NormalL, (float3x3)gWorldInvTranspose);
    vout.TangentW = mul(vin.TangentL, (float3x3)gWorld);

    // Transform to homogeneous clip space.
    vout.PosH = mul(float4(vin.PosL, 1.0f), gWorldViewProj);

    // Output vertex attributes for interpolation across triangle.
    vout.Tex = mul(float4(vin.Tex, 0.0f, 1.0f), gTexTransform).xy;

    return vout;
}

float4 PS(VertexOut pin,
    uniform int gLightCount,
    uniform bool gUseTexure,
    uniform bool gAlphaClip,
    uniform bool gFogEnabled,
    uniform bool gReflectionEnabled) : SV_Target
{
    // Interpolating normal can unnormalize it, so normalize it.
    pin.NormalW = normalize(pin.NormalW);

    // The toEye vector is used in lighting.
    float3 toEye = gEyePosW - pin.PosW;

    // Cache the distance to the eye from this surface point.
```

```
float distToEye = length(toEye);

// Normalize.
toEye /= distToEye;

// Default to multiplicative identity.
float4 texColor = float4(1, 1, 1, 1);
if(gUseTexure)
{
  // Sample texture.
  texColor = gDiffuseMap.Sample(samLinear, pin.Tex);

  if(gAlphaClip)
  {
    // Discard pixel if texture alpha < 0.1.  Note
    // that we do this test as soon as possible so
    // that we can potentially exit the shader early,
    // thereby skipping the rest of the shader code.
    clip(texColor.a - 0.1f);
  }
}

//
// Normal mapping
//

float3 normalMapSample = gNormalMap.Sample(samLinear, pin.Tex).rgb;
float3 bumpedNormalW = NormalSampleToWorldSpace(
      normalMapSample, pin.NormalW, pin.TangentW);

//
// Lighting.
//

float4 litColor = texColor;
if(gLightCount > 0)
{
  // Start with a sum of zero.
  float4 ambient = float4(0.0f, 0.0f, 0.0f, 0.0f);
  float4 diffuse = float4(0.0f, 0.0f, 0.0f, 0.0f);
  float4 spec    = float4(0.0f, 0.0f, 0.0f, 0.0f);

  // Sum the light contribution from each light source.
  [unroll]
  for(int i = 0; i < gLightCount; ++i)
  {
    float4 A, D, S;
    ComputeDirectionalLight(gMaterial,
      gDirLights[i], bumpedNormalW, toEye,
      A, D, S);

    ambient += A;
    diffuse += D;
    spec    += S;
  }
```

```
        litColor = texColor*(ambient + diffuse) + spec;

    if(gReflectionEnabled)
    {
      float3 incident = -toEye;
      float3 reflectionVector = reflect(
        incident, bumpedNormalW);
      float4 reflectionColor  = gCubeMap.Sample(
        samLinear, reflectionVector);

      litColor += gMaterial.Reflect*reflectionColor;
    }
  }

  //
  // Fogging
  //

  if(gFogEnabled)
  {
    float fogLerp = saturate((distToEye - gFogStart) / gFogRange);

    // Blend the fog color and the lit color.
    litColor = lerp(litColor, gFogColor, fogLerp);
  }

  // Common to take alpha from diffuse material and texture.
  litColor.a = gMaterial.Diffuse.a * texColor.a;

  return litColor;
}
```

18.7 DISPLACEMENT MAPPING

Now that we have an understanding of normal mapping, we can improve the effect by combining it with tessellation and displacement mapping. The motivation for this is that normal mapping just improves the lighting detail, but it does not improve the detail of the actual geometry. So in a sense, normal mapping is just a lighting trick (see Figure 18.7).

The idea of displacement mapping is to utilize an additional map, called a *heightmap*, which describes the bumps and crevices of a surface. In other words, whereas a normal map has three color channels to yield a normal vector (x, y, z) for each pixel, the heightmap has a single color channel to yield a height value h at each pixel. Visually, a heightmap is just a grayscale image (gray because there is only one color channel), where each pixel is interpreted as a height value—it is basically a discrete representation of a 2D scalar field $h = f(x,z)$. When we tessellate the mesh, we sample the heightmap in the domain shader to offset the vertices in the normal vector direction to add geometric detail to the mesh (see Figure 18.8).

Figure 18.7. **The normal maps create the illusion of bumps and crevices, but if we look at the wireframe, we see that the geometry is smooth.**

While tessellating geometry adds triangles, it does not add detail on its own. That is, if you subdivide a triangle several times, you just get more triangles that lie on the original triangle plane. To add detail (e.g., bumps and crevices), then you need to offset the tessellated vertices in some way. A heightmap is one input source that can be used to displace the tessellated vertices. Typically, the following formula is used to displace a vertex position **p**, where we also utilize the outward surface normal vector **n** as the direction of displacement:

$$\mathbf{p}' = \mathbf{p} + s(h - 1)\mathbf{n}$$

The scalar $h \in [0,1]$ is the scalar value obtained from the heightmap. We subtract 1 from h to shift the interval $[0,1] \rightarrow [-1,0]$; because the surface normal is outward facing from the mesh, this means that *we displace "inward" instead of "outward."* This is common convention, as it is usually more convenient to "pop" geometry

Figure 18.8. **The tessellation stage creates additional triangles so that we can model small bumps and crevices in the geometry. The displacement map displaces the vertices to create true geometric bumps and crevices.**

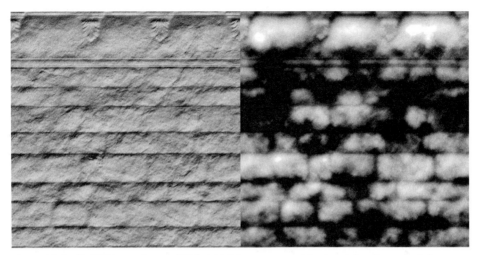

Figure 18.9. (Left) Normal map. (Right) Heightmap stored in the alpha channel of the normal map. A white value represents the highest height, and a black value represents the lowest height. Gray values represent intermediate heights.

in rather than "pop" geometry out. The scalar s is a scale factor to scale the overall height to some world space value. The height value h from the heightmap is in a normalized range where 0 means the lowest height (most inward displacement) and 1 means the highest height (no displacement). Say we want to at most offset by 5 world units. Then we take $s = 5$ so that $s(h - 1) \in [-5, 0]$. It is common to store the heightmap in the alpha channel of the normal map.

Generating heightmaps is an artistic task, and the texture artists can paint them or use tools to generate them (e.g., http://www.crazybump.com/).

18.8 DISPLACEMENT MAPPING SHADER CODE

The majority of the displacement mapping code occurs in the vertex shader, the hull shader, and the domain shader. The pixel shader is identical to the one we used for normal mapping.

18.8.1 Primitive Type

To integrate displacement mapping into our rendering, we need to support tessellation so that we can refine our geometry resolution to one that better matches the resolution of the displacement map. We can incorporate tessellation into our existing triangle meshes very easily by drawing our meshes with primitive type `D3D11_PRIMITIVE_TOPOLOGY_3_CONTROL_POINT_PATCHLIST` instead of

D3D11_PRIMITIVE_TOPOLOGY_TRIANGLELIST. This way, the three vertices of a triangle are interpreted as the 3 control points of a triangle patch, allowing us to tessellate each triangle.

18.8.2 Vertex Shader

When dealing with tessellation, we must decide how much to tessellate each triangle. We will employ a simple distance metric to determine the amount of tessellation. The closer the triangle is to the eye, the more tessellation it receives. The vertex shader helps with this distance calculation by computing a tessellation factor at each vertex that is then passed on to the hull shader.

We introduce the following variables in the constant buffer to control the distance calculation. The values you set to these variables are heavily scene dependent (how large your scene is and how much tessellation you want):

```
cbuffer cbPerFrame
{
    ...
    float gMaxTessDistance;
    float gMinTessDistance;
    float gMinTessFactor;
    float gMaxTessFactor;
};
```

1. **gMaxTessDistance**: The distance from the eye where maximum tessellation is achieved.

2. **gMinTessDistance**: The distance from the eye where minimum tessellation is achieved.

3. **gMinTessFactor**: The minimum amount of tessellation. For example, you may want each triangle to be tessellated at least 3 times no matter how far away it is.

4. **gMaxTessFactor**: The maximum amount of tessellation. For example, you may find that you do not need to tessellate more than 6 times, as the extra detail is not needed. The amount you need to tessellate will depend on how many triangles your input meshes have before tessellation. Also, remember the advice of Chapter 13, where it is inefficient to have triangles that cover less than 8 pixels.

Observe that **gMaxTessDistance** < **gMinTessDistance** as we increase the tessellation when the distance from the eye decreases.

Using these variables, we can create a linear function of distance to determine how much to tessellate based on distance (this function is analogous to the one used in §13.5).

```
struct VertexIn
{
    float3 PosL      : POSITION;
    float3 NormalL   : NORMAL;
    float2 Tex       : TEXCOORD;
    float3 TangentL  : TANGENT;
};

struct VertexOut
{
    float3 PosW        : POSITION;
    float3 NormalW     : NORMAL;
    float3 TangentW    : TANGENT;
    float2 Tex         : TEXCOORD;
    float  TessFactor  : TESS;
};

VertexOut VS(VertexIn vin)
{
    VertexOut vout;

    // Transform to world space space.
    vout.PosW     = mul(float4(vin.PosL, 1.0f), gWorld).xyz;
    vout.NormalW  = mul(vin.NormalL, (float3x3)gWorldInvTranspose);
    vout.TangentW = mul(vin.TangentL, (float3x3)gWorld);

    // Output vertex attributes for interpolation across triangle.
    vout.Tex = mul(float4(vin.Tex, 0.0f, 1.0f), gTexTransform).xy;

    float d = distance(vout.PosW, gEyePosW);

    // Normalized tessellation factor.
    // The tessellation is
    //   0 if d >= gMinTessDistance and
    //   1 if d <= gMaxTessDistance.
    float tess = saturate((gMinTessDistance - d) /
      (gMinTessDistance - gMaxTessDistance));

    // Rescale [0,1] --> [gMinTessFactor, gMaxTessFactor].
    vout.TessFactor = gMinTessFactor +
      tess*(gMaxTessFactor-gMinTessFactor);

    return vout;
}
```

18.8.3 Hull Shader

Recall that the constant hull shader is evaluated per patch, and is tasked with outputting the so-called tessellation factors of the mesh. The tessellation factors instruct the tessellation stage on how much to tessellate the patch. Most of the work for determining the tessellation factors was done by the vertex shader, but there is still a little work left for the constant hull shader. Specifically, the edge tessellation factors are computed by averaging the vertex tessellation factors. For the interior tessellation factor, we arbitrarily assign the first edge tessellation factor.

```
struct PatchTess
{
    float EdgeTess[3] : SV_TessFactor;
    float InsideTess  : SV_InsideTessFactor;
};

PatchTess PatchHS(InputPatch<VertexOut,3> patch,
    uint patchID : SV_PrimitiveID)
{
    PatchTess pt;

    // Average vertex tessellation factors along edges.
    // It is important to do the tessellation factor
    // calculation based on the edge properties so that edges shared by
    // more than one triangle will have the same tessellation factor.
    // Otherwise, gaps can appear.
    pt.EdgeTess[0] = 0.5f*(patch[1].TessFactor + patch[2].TessFactor);
    pt.EdgeTess[1] = 0.5f*(patch[2].TessFactor + patch[0].TessFactor);
    pt.EdgeTess[2] = 0.5f*(patch[0].TessFactor + patch[1].TessFactor);

    // Pick an edge tessellation factor for the interior tessellation.
    pt.InsideTess  = pt.EdgeTess[0];
    return pt;
}
```

It is important that edges shared by more than one triangle have the same tessellation factor, otherwise cracks in the mesh can appear (see Figure 18.10). One way to guarantee shared edges have the same tessellation factor is to compute the tessellation factor solely on properties of the edge like we did in the previous code. As an example of a way *not* to

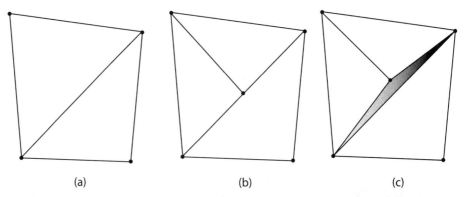

             (a)   (b)   (c)

Figure 18.10. (a) Two triangles that share an edge. (b) The top triangle gets tessellated so that an extra vertex along the edge is introduced. The bottom triangle does not get tessellated. (c) From displacement mapping, the newly created vertex gets moved. This creates a gap (denoted by the shaded region) between the two triangles that once shared an edge.

compute the tessellation factors, suppose that we compute the interior tessellation factor by looking at the distance between the eye and triangle centroid. Then we propagate the interior tessellation factor to the edge tessellation factors. If two adjacent triangles had different tessellation factors, then their edges would have different tessellation factors creating a T-junction that could lead to cracks after displacement mapping.

Recall that the control point hull shader inputs a number of control points and outputs a number of control points. The control point hull shader is invoked once per control point output. In our displacement mapping demo, the control point hull shader is simply a "pass through" shader:

```
struct HullOut
{
    float3 PosW       : POSITION;
    float3 NormalW    : NORMAL;
    float3 TangentW   : TANGENT;
    float2 Tex        : TEXCOORD;
};

[domain("tri")]
[partitioning("fractional_odd")]
[outputtopology("triangle_cw")]
[outputcontrolpoints(3)]
[patchconstantfunc("PatchHS")]
HullOut HS(InputPatch<VertexOut,3> p,
           uint i : SV_OutputControlPointID,
           uint patchId : SV_PrimitiveID)
{
    HullOut hout;

    // Pass through shader.
    hout.PosW     = p[i].PosW;
    hout.NormalW  = p[i].NormalW;
    hout.TangentW = p[i].TangentW;
    hout.Tex      = p[i].Tex;

    return hout;
}
```

18.8.4 Domain Shader

The domain shader is invoked for each vertex created by the tessellation stage; the hull shader is essentially the vertex shader for the tessellated patch. It is here that we do the displacement mapping by sampling the heightmap (which we store in the alpha channel of the normal map), and offsetting the vertices in the normal direction according to the formula discussed in §18.7.

```
struct DomainOut
{
    float4 PosH       : SV_POSITION;
    float3 PosW       : POSITION;
```

```
      float3 NormalW   : NORMAL;
      float3 TangentW  : TANGENT;
      float2 Tex       : TEXCOORD;
};

// The domain shader is called for every vertex created by the
//    tessellator.
// It is like the vertex shader after tessellation.
[domain("tri")]
DomainOut DS(PatchTess patchTess,
             float3 bary : SV_DomainLocation,
             const OutputPatch<HullOut,3> tri)
{
    DomainOut dout;

    // Interpolate patch attributes to generated vertices.
    dout.PosW     = bary.x*tri[0].PosW     +
                    bary.y*tri[1].PosW     +
                    bary.z*tri[2].PosW;
    dout.NormalW  = bary.x*tri[0].NormalW  +
                    bary.y*tri[1].NormalW  +
                    bary.z*tri[2].NormalW;
    dout.TangentW = bary.x*tri[0].TangentW +
                    bary.y*tri[1].TangentW +
                    bary.z*tri[2].TangentW;
    dout.Tex      = bary.x*tri[0].Tex      +
                    bary.y*tri[1].Tex      +
                    bary.z*tri[2].Tex;

    // Interpolating normal can unnormalize it, so normalize it.
    dout.NormalW = normalize(dout.NormalW);

    //
    // Displacement mapping.
    //

    // Choose the mipmap level based on distance to the eye;
    // specifically, choose the next miplevel every MipInterval units,
    // and clamp the miplevel in [0,6].
    const float MipInterval = 20.0f;
    float mipLevel = clamp(
      (distance(dout.PosW, gEyePosW) - MipInterval) /
        MipInterval, 0.0f, 6.0f);

    // Sample height map (stored in alpha channel).
    float h = gNormalMap.SampleLevel(samLinear, dout.Tex, mipLevel).a;

    // Offset vertex along normal.
    dout.PosW += (gHeightScale*(h-1.0))*dout.NormalW;

    // Project to homogeneous clip space.
    dout.PosH = mul(float4(dout.PosW, 1.0f), gViewProj);

    return dout;
}
```

One thing worth mentioning is that we need to do our own mipmap level selection in the domain shader. The usual pixel shader method `Texture2D::Sample` is not available in the domain shader, so we must use the `Texture2D::SampleLevel` method. This method requires us to specify the mipmap level.

Note: ➤ *The demo for this chapter has implementations for normal mapping and displacement mapping. The key controls are:*

1. Hold key '1' for wireframe mode.
2. Press '2' for basic rendering.
3. Press '3' for normal mapped rendering.
4. Press '4' for displacement mapped rendering.

18.9 SUMMARY

1. The strategy of normal mapping is to texture our polygons with normal maps. We then have per-pixel normals, which capture the fine details of a surface like bumps, scratches, and crevices. We then use these per-pixel normals from the normal map in our lighting calculations, instead of the interpolated vertex normal.

2. A normal map is a texture, but instead of storing RGB data at each texel, we store a compressed x-coordinate, y-coordinate, and z-coordinate in the red component, green component, and blue component, respectively. We use various tools to generate normal maps such as the ones located at http://developer.nvidia.com/nvidia-texture-tools-adobe-photoshop and http://www.crazybump.com/.

3. The coordinates of the normals in a normal map are relative to the texture space coordinate system. Consequently, to do lighting calculations, we need to transform the normal from the texture space to the world space so that the lights and normals are in the same coordinate system. The TBN-bases built at each vertex facilitates the transformation from texture space to world space.

4. The idea of displacement mapping is to utilize an additional map, called a *heightmap*, which describes the bumps and crevices of a surface. When we tessellate the mesh, we sample the heightmap in the domain shader to offset the vertices in the normal vector direction to add geometric detail to the mesh.

18.10 EXERCISES

1. Download the NVIDIA normal map plug-in (http://developer.nvidia.com/
    object/nv_texture_tools.html) and experiment with making different normal
    maps with it. Try your normal maps out in this chapter's demo application.

2. Download the trial version of *CrazyBump* (http://www.crazybump.com/).
    Load a color image, and experiment with making a normal and displacement
    map. Try your maps in this chapter's demo application.

3. Experiment with different values for the displacement mapping variables:

    ```
    cbuffer cbPerFrame
    {
        . . .
        float gHeightScale;
        float gMaxTessDistance;
        float gMinTessDistance;
        float gMinTessFactor;
        float gMaxTessFactor;
    };
    ```

4. If you apply a rotation texture transformation, then you need to rotate the
    tangent space coordinate system accordingly. Explain why. In particular,
    this means you need to rotate **T** about **N** in world space, which will require
    expensive trigonometric calculations (more precisely, a rotation transform
    about an arbitrary axis **N**). Another solution is to transform **T** from world
    space to tangent space, where you can use the texture transformation matrix
    directly to rotate **T**, and then transform back to world space.

5. Instead of doing lighting in world space, we can transform the eye and light vector
    from world space into tangent space and do all the lighting calculations in that space.
    Modify the normal mapping shader to do the lighting calculations in tangent space.

6. Displacement mapping can be used to implement ocean waves. The idea is to
    scroll two (or more) heightmaps over a flat vertex grid at different speeds and
    directions. For each vertex of the grid, we sample the heightmaps, and add the
    heights together; the summed height becomes the height (i.e., y-coordinate) of
    the vertex at this instance in time. By scrolling the heightmaps, waves continuously
    form and fade away giving the illusion of ocean waves (see Figure 18.11). For this
    exercise, implement the ocean wave effect just described using the two ocean wave
    heightmaps (and corresponding normal maps) available to download for this
    chapter (Figure 18.12). Here are a few hints to making the waves look good:

    (a) Tile the heightmaps differently so that one set can be used to model broad
        low frequency waves with high amplitude and the other can be used to
        model high frequency small choppy waves with low amplitude. So you

Figure 18.11. Ocean waves modeled with heightmaps, normal maps, and environment mapping.

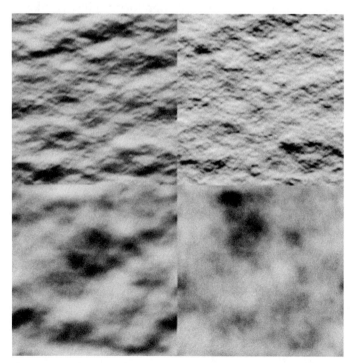

Figure 18.12. (Top Row) Ocean waves normal map and heightmap for high frequency choppy waves. (Bottom Row) Ocean waves normal map and heightmap for low frequency broad waves.

will need two sets of texture coordinates for the heightmaps maps and two texture transformations for the heightmaps.

(b) The normal map textures should be tiled more than the heightmap textures. The heightmaps give the shape of the waves, and the normal maps are used to light the waves per pixel. As with the heightmaps, the normal maps should translate over time and in different directions to give the illusion of new waves forming and fading. The two normals can then be combined using code similar to the following:

```
float3 normalMapSample0 = gNormalMap0.Sample(samLinear,
pin.WaveNormalTex0).rgb;
float3 bumpedNormalW0 = NormalSampleToWorldSpace(
        normalMapSample0, pin.NormalW, pin.TangentW);

float3 normalMapSample1 = gNormalMap1.Sample(samLinear,
pin.WaveNormalTex1).rgb;
float3 bumpedNormalW1 = NormalSampleToWorldSpace(
        normalMapSample1, pin.NormalW, pin.TangentW);

float3 bumpedNormalW = normalize(bumpedNormalW0 + bumpedNormalW1);
```

(c) Modify the waves' material to make it more ocean blue, and keep some reflection in from the environment map.

19 TERRAIN RENDERING

The idea of terrain rendering is to start off with a flat grid (top of Figure 19.1). Then we adjust the heights (i.e., the y-coordinates) of the vertices in such a way that the mesh models smooth transitions from mountain to valley, thereby simulating a terrain (middle of Figure 19.1). And, of course, we apply a nice texture to render sandy beaches, grassy hills, rocky cliffs, and snowy mountains (bottom of Figure 19.1).

Objectives:

1. To learn how to generate height info for a terrain that results in smooth transitions between mountains and valleys.

2. To find out how to texture the terrain.

3. To apply hardware tessellation to render the terrain with a continuous level of detail.

4. To discover a way to keep the camera or other objects planted on the terrain surface.

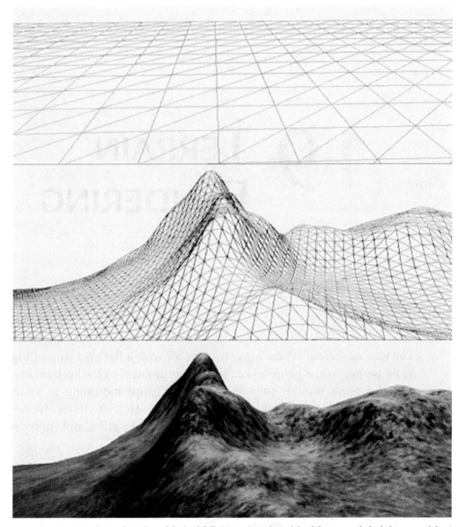

Figure 19.1. (Top) A triangle grid. (Middle) A triangle grid with smooth height transitions used to create hills and valleys. (Bottom) A lit and textured terrain.

19.1 HEIGHTMAPS

We use a *heightmap* to describe the hills and valleys of our terrain. A heightmap is a matrix, where each element specifies the height of a particular vertex in the terrain grid. That is, there exists an entry in the heightmap for each grid vertex, and the *ij*th heightmap entry provides the height for the *ij*th vertex. Typically, a heightmap is graphically represented as a grayscale map in an image editor, where

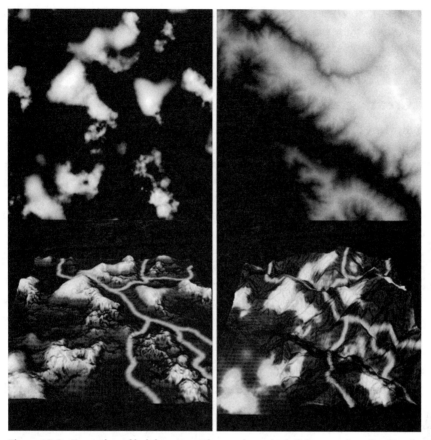

Figure 19.2. Examples of heightmaps. Observe how the heights, as described by the heightmaps, build different terrain surfaces.

black denotes the smallest height, white denotes the largest height, and shades of gray represent in-between heights. Figure 19.2 shows a couple examples of heightmaps and the corresponding terrains they construct.

When we store our heightmaps on disk, we usually allocate a byte of memory for each element in the heightmap, so the height can range from 0 to 255. The range 0 to 255 is enough to preserve the transition between heights of our terrain, but in our application we may need to scale out of the 0 to 255 range in order to match the scale of our 3D world. For example, if our unit of measure in the 3D world is feet, then 0 to 255 does not give us enough values to represent anything interesting. For this reason, when we load the data into our applications, we allocate a `float` for each height element. This allows us to then scale well outside the 0 to 255 range to match any scale necessary; moreover, it also enables us to filter the heightmap and generate height values in-between integer numbers.

Note: *In §6.11 we created a "terrain" using a mathematical function. That is an example of a procedurally generated terrain. However, it is difficult to come up with a function that precisely describes the terrain you want. Heightmaps give more flexibility because they can be edited by an artist in a paint program or heightmap editing tool.*

19.1.1 Creating a Heightmap

Heightmaps can be generated procedurally or in an image editor such as Adobe Photoshop. Using paint filters to generate different chaotic heightmap patterns can prove to be a good start; then the heightmap can be manually tweaked by taking advantage of your paint editor's tools. Applying the blur filter is useful to smooth out rough edges in the heightmap.

The program *Terragen* (http://www.planetside.co.uk/) can generate heightmaps procedurally, and it also provides tools for modifying the heightmap (or the heightmap can be exported, and then imported and modified in a separate paint program like Photoshop). The program *Bryce* (http://www.daz3d.com/i.x/software/bryce/-/) also has many procedural algorithms for generating heightmaps, as well as a built-in heightmap editor. Dark Tree (http://www.darksim.com/) is a powerful procedural texture authoring program, which, in particular, can be used for creating grayscale heightmaps.

Once you have finished drawing your heightmap, you need to save it as an 8-bit RAW file. RAW files simply contain the bytes of the image one after another. This makes it very easy to read the image into our programs. Your software may ask you to save the RAW file with a header; specify no header. Figure 19.3 shows the export dialog for *Terragen*.

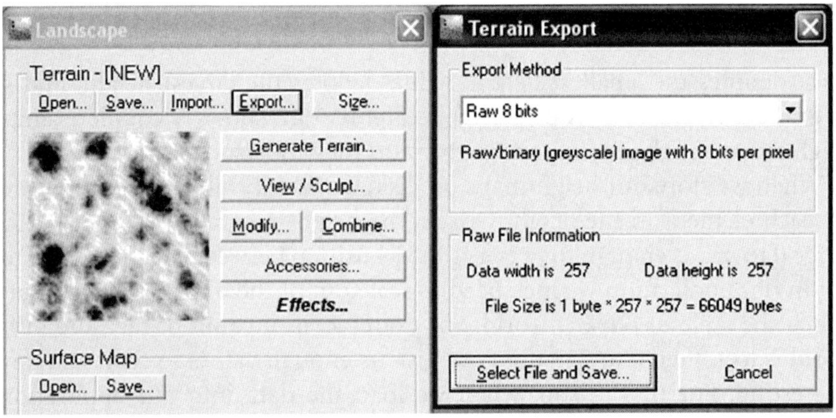

Figure 19.3. (Left) The landscape generator allows you to generate a random terrain procedurally and also to manually sculpt the terrain with brush tools. (Right) The export dialog for *Terragen*. Observe that the export method selected is the 8-bit RAW format.

> **Note:** You do not have to use the RAW format to store your heightmaps; you can use any format that suits your needs. The RAW format is just one example of a format that we can use. We decided to use the RAW format because many image editors can export to this format and it is very easy to load the data in a RAW file into our program demos. The demos in this book use 8-bit RAW files (i.e., each element in the heightmap is an 8-bit integer).

> **Note:** If 256 height steps is too coarse for your needs, you may consider storing 16-bit heightmaps, where each height entry is described by a 16-bit integer. Terragen can export 16-bit RAW heightmaps.

19.1.2 Loading a RAW File

Because a RAW file is nothing more than a contiguous block of bytes (where each byte is a heightmap entry), we can easily read in the block of memory with one `std::ifstream::read` call, as is done in this next method:

```
void Terrain::LoadHeightmap()
{
    // A height for each vertex
    std::vector<unsigned char> in(
      mInfo.HeightmapWidth * mInfo.HeightmapHeight);

    // Open the file.
    std::ifstream inFile;
    inFile.open(mInfo.HeightMapFilename.c_str(),
      std::ios_base::binary);

    if(inFile)
    {
      // Read the RAW bytes.
      inFile.read((char*)&in[0], (std::streamsize)in.size());

      // Done with file.
      inFile.close();
    }

    // Copy the array data into a float array and scale it.
    mHeightmap.resize(mInfo.HeightmapHeight * mInfo.HeightmapWidth, 0);
    for(UINT i = 0; i < mInfo.HeightmapHeight * mInfo.HeightmapWidth; ++i)
    {
      mHeightmap[i] = (in[i] / 255.0f)*mInfo.HeightScale;
    }
}
```

The `mInfo` variable, a member of the `Terrain` class, is an instance of the following structure which describes various properties of the terrain:

```
struct InitInfo
{
        // Filename of RAW heightmap data.
        std::wstring HeightMapFilename;

        // Texture filenames used for texturing the terrain.
        std::wstring LayerMapFilename0;
        std::wstring LayerMapFilename1;
        std::wstring LayerMapFilename2;
        std::wstring LayerMapFilename3;
        std::wstring LayerMapFilename4;
        std::wstring BlendMapFilename;

        // Scale to apply to heights after they have been
        // loaded from the heightmap.
        float HeightScale;

        // Dimensions of the heightmap.
        UINT HeightmapWidth;
        UINT HeightmapHeight;

        // The cell spacing along the x- and z-axes (see Figure (19.4)).
        float CellSpacing;
};
```

 *The reader may wish to review §5.11 for grid construction.*

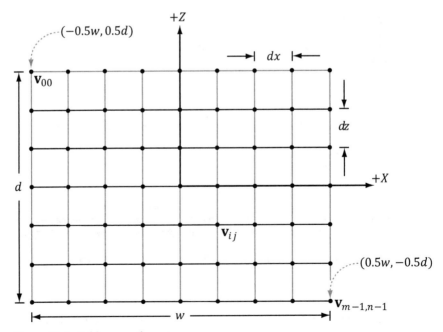

Figure 19.4. Grid properties.

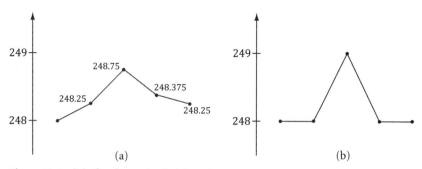

Figure 19.5. (a) Floating-point height values in the range [0, 255]. (b) Height values clamped to the nearest integer.

19.1.3 Smoothing

One of the problems of using an 8-bit heightmap is that it means we can only represent 256 discreet height steps. Consequently, we cannot model the height values shown in Figure 19.5a; instead, we end up with Figure 19.5b. This truncation creates a "rougher" terrain that was not intended. Of course, once we truncate we cannot recover the original height values, but by smoothing out Figure 19.5b, we can get something that is closer to 19.5a.

So what we do is load the heightmap into memory by reading the raw bytes. We then copy the byte array into a float array so that we have floating-point precision. Then we apply a filter to the floating-point heightmap, which smoothes the heightmap out, making the difference in heights between adjacent elements not so drastic. The filtering algorithm we use is quite basic. A new filtered heightmap pixel is computed by averaging itself along with its eight neighbor pixels (Figure 19.6):

$$\tilde{h}_{i,j} = \frac{h_{i-1,j-1} + h_{i-1,j} + h_{i-1,j+1} + h_{i,j-1} + h_{i,j} + h_{i,j+1} + h_{i+1,j-1} + h_{i+1,j} + h_{i+1,j+1}}{9}$$

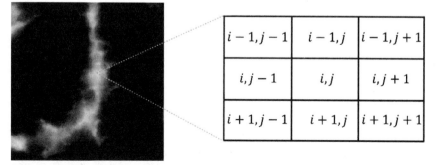

Figure 19.6. The heights of the *ij*th vertex are found by averaging the *ij*th heightmap entry together with its eight neighbor heights.

In the case that we are on the edge of the heightmap, where a pixel does not have eight neighboring pixels, then we just take the average with as many neighboring pixels as possible.

Here is the implementation of the function that averages the *ij*th pixel in the heightmap:

```
bool Terrain::InBounds(int i, int j)
{
    // True if ij are valid indices; false otherwise.
    return
      i >= 0 && i < (int)mInfo.HeightmapHeight &&
      j >= 0 && j < (int)mInfo.HeightmapWidth;
}

float Terrain::Average(int i, int j)
{
    // Function computes the average height of the ij element.
    // It averages itself with its eight neighbor pixels.  Note
    // that if a pixel is missing neighbor, we just don't include it
    // in the average--that is, edge pixels don't have a neighbor pixel.
    //
    // ----------
    // | 1| 2| 3|
    // ----------
    // |4 |ij| 6|
    // ----------
    // | 7| 8| 9|
    // ----------

    float avg = 0.0f;
    float num = 0.0f;

    // Use int to allow negatives.  If we use UINT, @ i=0, m=i-1=UINT_MAX
    // and no iterations of the outer for loop occur.
    for(int m = i-1; m <= i+1; ++m)
    {
      for(int n = j-1; n <= j+1; ++n)
      {
        if(InBounds(m,n))
        {
          avg += mHeightmap[m*mInfo.HeightmapWidth + n];
          num += 1.0f;
        }
      }
    }

    return avg / num;
}
```

The function inBounds returns true if the entry is on the heightmap and false otherwise. So if we try to sample an element adjacent to an entry on an edge that is not part of the heightmap, then inBounds returns false, and we do not include it in our average—it does not exist.

To smooth the entire heightmap, we just apply **average** to each heightmap entry:

```
void Terrain::Smooth()
{
    std::vector<float> dest(mHeightmap.size());

    for(UINT i = 0; i < mInfo.HeightmapHeight; ++i)
    {
      for(UINT j = 0; j < mInfo.HeightmapWidth; ++j)
      {
        dest[i*mInfo.HeightmapWidth+j] = Average(i,j);
      }
    }

    // Replace the old heightmap with the filtered one.
    mHeightmap = dest;
}
```

19.1.4 Heightmap Shader Resource View

As we will see in the next section, to support tessellation and displacement mapping, we will need to sample the heightmap in our shader programs. Hence, we must create a shader resource view to the heightmap. This should be a familiar exercise by now; the only trick to it is that to save memory, we use a 16-bit float instead of a 32-bit float. To convert a 32-bit float to a 16-bit float, we use the XNA math function XMConvertFloatToHalf.

```
void Terrain::BuildHeightmapSRV(ID3D11Device* device)
{
    D3D11_TEXTURE2D_DESC texDesc;
    texDesc.Width = mInfo.HeightmapWidth;
    texDesc.Height = mInfo.HeightmapHeight;
    texDesc.MipLevels = 1;
    texDesc.ArraySize = 1;
    texDesc.Format      = DXGI_FORMAT_R16_FLOAT;
    texDesc.SampleDesc.Count   = 1;
    texDesc.SampleDesc.Quality = 0;
    texDesc.Usage = D3D11_USAGE_DEFAULT;
    texDesc.BindFlags = D3D11_BIND_SHADER_RESOURCE;
    texDesc.CPUAccessFlags = 0;
    texDesc.MiscFlags = 0;

    // HALF is defined in xnamath.h, for storing 16-bit float.
    std::vector<HALF> hmap(mHeightmap.size());
    std::transform(mHeightmap.begin(), mHeightmap.end(),
           hmap.begin(), XMConvertFloatToHalf);

    D3D11_SUBRESOURCE_DATA data;
    data.pSysMem = &hmap[0];
    data.SysMemPitch = mInfo.HeightmapWidth*sizeof(HALF);
    data.SysMemSlicePitch = 0;
```

```
ID3D11Texture2D* hmapTex = 0;
HR(device->CreateTexture2D(&texDesc, &data, &hmapTex));

D3D11_SHADER_RESOURCE_VIEW_DESC srvDesc;
srvDesc.Format = texDesc.Format;
srvDesc.ViewDimension = D3D11_SRV_DIMENSION_TEXTURE2D;
srvDesc.Texture2D.MostDetailedMip = 0;
srvDesc.Texture2D.MipLevels = -1;
HR(device->CreateShaderResourceView(
        hmapTex, &srvDesc, &mHeightMapSRV));

// SRV saves reference.
ReleaseCOM(hmapTex);
}
```

19.2 TERRAIN TESSELLATION

Terrains cover large areas, and consequently, the number of triangles needed to build them is large. Generally, a *level of detail* (LOD) system is needed for terrains. That is, parts of the terrain further away from the camera do not need as many triangles because the detail goes unnoticed; see Figure 19.7.

Figure 19.7. The level of detail decreases with distance from the camera. Our strategy for terrain tessellation is as follows:

1. Lay down a grid of quad patches.
2. Tessellate the patches based on their distance from the camera.
3. Bind the heightmap as a shader resource. In the domain shader, perform displacement mapping from the heightmap to offset the generated vertices to their proper heights.

19.2.1 Grid Construction

Suppose our heightmap has dimensions $(2^m + 1) \times (2^n + 1)$. The most detailed terrain we can create from this heightmap would be a grid of $(2^m + 1) \times (2^n + 1)$ vertices; therefore, this represents our maximum tessellated terrain grid, which we shall refer to as T_0. The cell spacing between vertices of T_0 is given by the `InitInfo::CellSpacing` property (§9.1.2). That is, when we refer to cells, we are talking about cells of the most tessellated grid T_0.

We divide the terrain into a grid of patches such that each patch covers blocks of 65×65 vertices of T_0 (see Figure 19.8). We choose 65 because the maximum tessellation factor is 64, so we can dice up a patch into 64×64 cells, which intersect 65×65 vertices. So if a patch gets maximally tessellated, it has information from

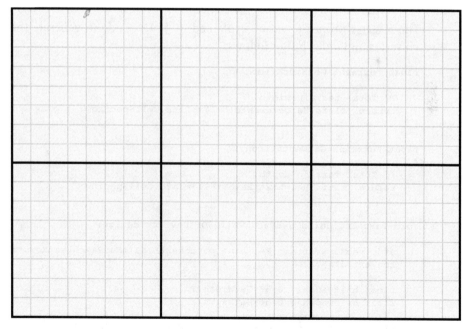

Figure 19.8. For illustration purposes, we use smaller numbers. The maximum tessellated terrain grid has 17 × 25 vertices and 16 × 24 cells. We divide the grid into a grid of patches such that each patch covers 8 × 8 cells or 9 × 9 vertices. This induces a 2 × 3 grid of patches.

the heightmap it needs for every generated vertex. If a patch has tessellation factor 1, then the patch is not subdivided and is merely rendered as two triangles. Therefore, the grid of patches can be thought of as the most coarsely tessellated version of the terrain.

The patch vertex grid dimensions are calculated by:

```
static const int CellsPerPatch = 64;

// Divide heightmap into patches such that each patch has CellsPerPatch.
mNumPatchVertRows = ((mInfo.HeightmapHeight-1) / CellsPerPatch) + 1;
mNumPatchVertCols = ((mInfo.HeightmapWidth-1) / CellsPerPatch) + 1;
```

And the total number of patch vertices and quad patch primitives are calculated by:

```
mNumPatchVertices  = mNumPatchVertRows*mNumPatchVertCols;
mNumPatchQuadFaces = (mNumPatchVertRows-1)*(mNumPatchVertCols-1);
```

Our terrain patch vertex structure looks like this:

```
struct Terrain
{
    XMFLOAT3 Pos;
    XMFLOAT2 Tex;
    XMFLOAT2 BoundsY;
};
```

The `BoundsY` property will be explained in §19.3. Code to generate the quad patch vertex and index buffer follows:

```
float Terrain::GetWidth()const
{
    // Total terrain width.
    return (mInfo.HeightmapWidth-1)*mInfo.CellSpacing;
}

float Terrain::GetDepth()const
{
    // Total terrain depth.
    return (mInfo.HeightmapHeight-1)*mInfo.CellSpacing;
}

void Terrain::BuildQuadPatchVB(ID3D11Device* device)
{
    std::vector<Vertex::Terrain> patchVertices(mNumPatchVertRows*mNumPa
tchVertCols);

    float halfWidth = 0.5f*GetWidth();
    float halfDepth = 0.5f*GetDepth();

    float patchWidth = GetWidth() / (mNumPatchVertCols-1);
    float patchDepth = GetDepth() / (mNumPatchVertRows-1);
    float du = 1.0f / (mNumPatchVertCols-1);
    float dv = 1.0f / (mNumPatchVertRows-1);
```

```
    for(UINT i = 0; i < mNumPatchVertRows; ++i)
    {
      float z = halfDepth - i*patchDepth;
      for(UINT j = 0; j < mNumPatchVertCols; ++j)
      {
        float x = -halfWidth + j*patchWidth;

        patchVertices[i*mNumPatchVertCols+j].Pos = XMFLOAT3(x, 0.0f, z);

        // Stretch texture over grid.
        patchVertices[i*mNumPatchVertCols+j].Tex.x = j*du;
        patchVertices[i*mNumPatchVertCols+j].Tex.y = i*dv;
      }
    }

    // Store axis-aligned bounding box y-bounds in upper-left patch corner.
    for(UINT i = 0; i < mNumPatchVertRows-1; ++i)
    {
      for(UINT j = 0; j < mNumPatchVertCols-1; ++j)
      {
        UINT patchID = i*(mNumPatchVertCols-1)+j;
        patchVertices[i*mNumPatchVertCols+j].BoundsY =
          mPatchBoundsY[patchID];
      }
    }

    D3D11_BUFFER_DESC vbd;
    vbd.Usage = D3D11_USAGE_IMMUTABLE;
    vbd.ByteWidth = sizeof(Vertex::Terrain) * patchVertices.size();
    vbd.BindFlags = D3D11_BIND_VERTEX_BUFFER;
    vbd.CPUAccessFlags = 0;
    vbd.MiscFlags = 0;
    vbd.StructureByteStride = 0;

    D3D11_SUBRESOURCE_DATA vinitData;
    vinitData.pSysMem = &patchVertices[0];
    HR(device->CreateBuffer(&vbd, &vinitData, &mQuadPatchVB));
}

void Terrain::BuildQuadPatchIB(ID3D11Device* device)
{
    std::vector<USHORT> indices(mNumPatchQuadFaces*4); // 4 indices per
    quad face

    // Iterate over each quad and compute indices.
    int k = 0;
    for(UINT i = 0; i < mNumPatchVertRows-1; ++i)
    {
      for(UINT j = 0; j < mNumPatchVertCols-1; ++j)
      {
        // Top row of 2x2 quad patch
        indices[k]   = i*mNumPatchVertCols+j;
        indices[k+1] = i*mNumPatchVertCols+j+1;

        // Bottom row of 2x2 quad patch
        indices[k+2] = (i+1)*mNumPatchVertCols+j;
        indices[k+3] = (i+1)*mNumPatchVertCols+j+1;
```

```
        k += 4; // next quad
    }
}

D3D11_BUFFER_DESC ibd;
ibd.Usage = D3D11_USAGE_IMMUTABLE;
ibd.ByteWidth = sizeof(USHORT) * indices.size();
ibd.BindFlags = D3D11_BIND_INDEX_BUFFER;
ibd.CPUAccessFlags = 0;
ibd.MiscFlags = 0;
ibd.StructureByteStride = 0;

D3D11_SUBRESOURCE_DATA iinitData;
iinitData.pSysMem = &indices[0];
HR(device->CreateBuffer(&ibd, &iinitData, &mQuadPatchIB));
}
```

19.2.2 Terrain Vertex Shader

Because we are using tessellation, the vertex shader operates per control point. Our vertex shader is almost a simple pass-through shader, except that we do displacement mapping for the patch control points by reading the heightmap value. This puts the y-coordinates of the control points at the proper height. The reason for doing this is that in the hull shader we are going to compute the distance between each patch and the eye; having the patch corners offset to the proper height makes this distance calculation more accurate than having the patch in the xz-plane.

```
Texture2D gHeightMap;

SamplerState samHeightmap
{
    Filter = MIN_MAG_LINEAR_MIP_POINT;

    AddressU = CLAMP;
    AddressV = CLAMP;
};

struct VertexIn
{
    float3 PosL     : POSITION;
    float2 Tex      : TEXCOORD0;
    float2 BoundsY  : TEXCOORD1;
};

struct VertexOut
{
    float3 PosW     : POSITION;
    float2 Tex      : TEXCOORD0;
    float2 BoundsY  : TEXCOORD1;
};
```

```
VertexOut VS(VertexIn vin)
{
    VertexOut vout;

    // Terrain specified directly in world space.
    vout.PosW = vin.PosL;

    // Displace the patch corners to world space.  This is to make
    // the eye to patch distance calculation more accurate.
    vout.PosW.y = gHeightMap.SampleLevel(samHeightmap, vin.Tex, 0).r;

    // Output vertex attributes to next stage.
    vout.Tex      = vin.Tex;
    vout.BoundsY  = vin.BoundsY;

    return vout;
}
```

19.2.3 Tessellation Factors

The hull shader constant function is responsible for calculating tessellation factors for each patch that indicate how much to subdivide each patch. In addition, we can use the hull shader constant function to do frustum culling on the GPU. We will explain GPU based patch frustum culling in §19.3.

We calculate the distance between the eye position and the midpoint of each patch edge to derive the edge tessellation factors. For the interior tessellation factors, we calculate the distance between the eye position and the midpoint of the patch. We use the following code to derive the tessellation factor from distance:

```
// When distance is minimum, the tessellation is maximum.
// When distance is maximum, the tessellation is minimum.
float gMinDist;
float gMaxDist;

// Exponents for power of 2 tessellation.  The tessellation
// range is [2^(gMinTess), 2^(gMaxTess)].  Since the maximum
// tessellation is 64, this means gMaxTess can be at most 6
// since 2^6 = 64, and gMinTess must be at least 0 since 2^0 = 1.
float gMinTess;
float gMaxTess;

float CalcTessFactor(float3 p)
{
    float d = distance(p, gEyePosW);

    float s = saturate((d - gMinDist) / (gMaxDist - gMinDist));

    return pow(2, (lerp(gMaxTess, gMinTess, s)));
}
```

Note that this formula is different than the one used in Chapter 18 when doing displacement mapping. We use power of 2 because this means at each finer level of detail, the number of subdivisions doubles. For example, say we are at a level of detail of $2^3 = 8$. The next refinement doubles the number of subdivisions to $2^4 = 16$, and the coarser level of detail is half the number of subdivisions $2^2 = 4$. Using the power of 2 function spreads out the levels of detail better with distance.

Now in the constant hull shader function, we apply this function to the patch midpoint, and the patch edge midpoints to compute the tessellation factors:

```
struct PatchTess
{
    float EdgeTess[4]    : SV_TessFactor;
    float InsideTess[2] : SV_InsideTessFactor;
};

PatchTess ConstantHS(InputPatch<VertexOut, 4> patch,
                     uint patchID : SV_PrimitiveID)
{
    PatchTess pt;

    //
    // Frustum cull
    //

    [... Omit frustum culling code]

    //
    // Do normal tessellation based on distance.
    //
    else
    {
      // It is important to do the tess factor calculation
      // based on the edge properties so that edges shared
      // by more than one patch will have the same
      // tessellation factor.  Otherwise, gaps can appear.

      // Compute midpoint on edges, and patch center
      float3 e0 = 0.5f*(patch[0].PosW + patch[2].PosW);
      float3 e1 = 0.5f*(patch[0].PosW + patch[1].PosW);
      float3 e2 = 0.5f*(patch[1].PosW + patch[3].PosW);
      float3 e3 = 0.5f*(patch[2].PosW + patch[3].PosW);
      float3  c = 0.25f*(patch[0].PosW + patch[1].PosW +
            patch[2].PosW + patch[3].PosW);

      pt.EdgeTess[0] = CalcTessFactor(e0);
      pt.EdgeTess[1] = CalcTessFactor(e1);
      pt.EdgeTess[2] = CalcTessFactor(e2);
      pt.EdgeTess[3] = CalcTessFactor(e3);

      pt.InsideTess[0] = CalcTessFactor(c);
      pt.InsideTess[1] = pt.InsideTess[0];

      return pt;
    }
}
```

19.2.4 Displacement Mapping

Recall that the domain shader is like the vertex shader for tessellation. The domain shader is evaluated for each generated vertex. Our task in the domain shader is to use the parametric (u, v) coordinates of the tessellated vertex positions to interpolate the control point data to derive the actual vertex positions and texture coordinates. In addition, we sample the heightmap to perform displacement mapping.

```
struct DomainOut
{
    float4 PosH     : SV_POSITION;
    float3 PosW     : POSITION;
    float2 Tex      : TEXCOORD0;
    float2 TiledTex : TEXCOORD1;
};

// How much to tile the texture layers.
float2 gTexScale = 50.0f;

[domain("quad")]
DomainOut DS(PatchTess patchTess,
            float2 uv : SV_DomainLocation,
            const OutputPatch<HullOut, 4> quad)
{
    DomainOut dout;

    // Bilinear interpolation.
    dout.PosW = lerp(
      lerp(quad[0].PosW, quad[1].PosW, uv.x),
      lerp(quad[2].PosW, quad[3].PosW, uv.x),
      uv.y);

    dout.Tex = lerp(
      lerp(quad[0].Tex, quad[1].Tex, uv.x),
      lerp(quad[2].Tex, quad[3].Tex, uv.x),
      uv.y);

    // Tile layer textures over terrain.
    dout.TiledTex = dout.Tex*gTexScale;

    // Displacement mapping
    dout.PosW.y = gHeightMap.SampleLevel(samHeightmap, dout.Tex, 0).r;

    // NOTE: We tried computing the normal in the domain shader
    // using finite difference, but the vertices move continuously
    // with fractional_even which creates noticable light shimmering
    // artifacts as the normal changes.  Therefore, we moved the
    // calculation to the pixel shader.

    // Project to homogeneous clip space.
    dout.PosH   = mul(float4(dout.PosW, 1.0f), gViewProj);

    return dout;
}
```

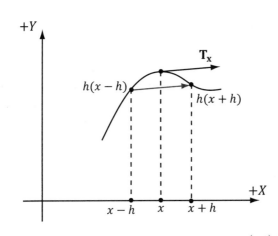

Figure 19.9. Central differences. The difference $\frac{h(x+h)-h(x-h)}{2h}$ gives the slope of the tangent vector in the x-direction. We use this difference as an estimate for the tangent vector at point x.

19.2.5 Tangent and Normal Vector Estimation

We estimate the tangent vectors (one in the $+x$ direction and one in the $-z$ direction) on the fly in the pixel shader from the heightmap using central differences (see Figure 19.9):

$$\mathbf{T}_x(x,z)=\left(1,\frac{\partial h}{\partial x},0\right)\approx\left(1,\frac{h(x+h,z)-h(x-h,z)}{2h},0\right)$$

$$\mathbf{T}_{-z}(x,z)=\left(0,-\frac{\partial h}{\partial z},-1\right)\approx\left(0,\frac{h(x,z-h)-h(x,z+h)}{2h},-1\right)$$

We take the negative z-direction because that direction corresponds to the texture space v-axis; so these vectors also help form the tangent space for normal mapping. Once we have estimates of the tangent vectors in the positive x- and negative z-directions, we compute the normal via the cross product:

```
// Spacing between height values in normalized uv-space [0,1].
float gTexelCellSpaceU;
float gTexelCellSpaceV;

// Spacing between cells in world space.
float gWorldCellSpace;

//
// Estimate normal and tangent using central differences.
//
float2 leftTex   = pin.Tex + float2(-gTexelCellSpaceU, 0.0f);
float2 rightTex  = pin.Tex + float2(gTexelCellSpaceU, 0.0f);
```

```
float2 bottomTex = pin.Tex + float2(0.0f, gTexelCellSpaceV);
float2 topTex    = pin.Tex + float2(0.0f, -gTexelCellSpaceV);

float leftY   = gHeightMap.SampleLevel(samHeightmap, leftTex, 0).r;
float rightY  = gHeightMap.SampleLevel(samHeightmap, rightTex, 0).r;
float bottomY = gHeightMap.SampleLevel(samHeightmap, bottomTex, 0).r;
float topY    = gHeightMap.SampleLevel(samHeightmap, topTex, 0).r;

float3 tangent = normalize(
float3(2.0f*gWorldCellSpace, rightY - leftY, 0.0f));
float3 bitan   = normalize(
float3(0.0f, bottomY - topY, -2.0f*gWorldCellSpace));
float3 normalW = cross(tangent, bitan);
```

We tried computing the normals in the domain shader using central difference, but the vertices move continuously with `fractional_even` tessellation, which creates noticeable light shimmering artifacts as the normal changes. Therefore, we moved the calculation to the pixel shader. Instead of computing the normals in the shader, you could also generate a normal map from the heightmap offline; this trades some GPU computation time with memory. If you decide to use a texture map, you can save memory by only storing $\frac{\partial h/\partial x}{\|T_x\|}$ and $-\frac{\partial h/\partial z}{\|T_{-z}\|}$. Then you can reconstruct $\frac{T_x}{\|T_x\|}$ and $\frac{T_{-z}}{\|T_{-z}\|}$ and the normal vector in the shader. This requires two bytes per element, and also gives you the tangent vectors in addition to the normal vector.

19.3 FRUSTUM CULLING PATCHES

Terrains generally cover a vast area and many of our patches will not be seen by the camera. This suggests that frustum culling will be a good optimization. If a patch has tessellation factors of all zero, then the GPU discards the patch from further processing; this means effort is not wasted tessellating a patch only for those triangles to later on be culled in the clipping stage.

In order to do frustum culling, we need two ingredients: we need the view frustum planes, and we need a bounding volume about each patch. Exercise 2 of Chapter 15 explained how to extract the view frustum planes. Code that implements the solution to this exercise is as follows (implemented in *d3dUtil.h/d3dUtil.cpp*):

```
void ExtractFrustumPlanes(XMFLOAT4 planes[6], CXMMATRIX M)
{
    //
    // Left
    //
    planes[0].x = M(0,3) + M(0,0);
    planes[0].y = M(1,3) + M(1,0);
    planes[0].z = M(2,3) + M(2,0);
    planes[0].w = M(3,3) + M(3,0);

    //
```

```
// Right
//
planes[1].x = M(0,3) - M(0,0);
planes[1].y = M(1,3) - M(1,0);
planes[1].z = M(2,3) - M(2,0);
planes[1].w = M(3,3) - M(3,0);

//
// Bottom
//
planes[2].x = M(0,3) + M(0,1);
planes[2].y = M(1,3) + M(1,1);
planes[2].z = M(2,3) + M(2,1);
planes[2].w = M(3,3) + M(3,1);

//
// Top
//
planes[3].x = M(0,3) - M(0,1);
planes[3].y = M(1,3) - M(1,1);
planes[3].z = M(2,3) - M(2,1);
planes[3].w = M(3,3) - M(3,1);

//
// Near
//
planes[4].x = M(0,2);
planes[4].y = M(1,2);
planes[4].z = M(2,2);
planes[4].w = M(3,2);

//
// Far
//
planes[5].x = M(0,3) - M(0,2);
planes[5].y = M(1,3) - M(1,2);
planes[5].z = M(2,3) - M(2,2);
planes[5].w = M(3,3) - M(3,2);

// Normalize the plane equations.
for(int i = 0; i < 6; ++i)
{
  XMVECTOR v = XMPlaneNormalize(XMLoadFloat4(&planes[i]));
  XMStoreFloat4(&planes[i], v);
}
}
```

Next, we need a bounding volume about each patch. Because each patch is rectangular, we choose an axis-aligned bounding box as our bounding volume. The patch control points inherently encode the x- and z-coordinate bounds because we construct the patches as rectangles in the xz-plane. What about the y-coordinate bounds? To obtain the y-coordinate bounds, we must do a preprocessing step. Each patch covers 65×65 elements of the heightmap. So for each patch, we scan the heightmap entries covered by the patch, and compute the minimum and maximum y-coordinates. We then store these values in the top-left control point of the patch, so that we have access to the y-bounds of the patch in the constant hull shader. The following code shows us computing the y-bounds for each patch:

```
// x-stores minY, y-stores maxY.
std::vector<XMFLOAT2> mPatchBoundsY;

void Terrain::CalcAllPatchBoundsY()
{
    mPatchBoundsY.resize(mNumPatchQuadFaces);

    // For each patch
    for(UINT i = 0; i < mNumPatchVertRows-1; ++i)
    {
      for(UINT j = 0; j < mNumPatchVertCols-1; ++j)
      {
        CalcPatchBoundsY(i, j);
      }
    }
}

void Terrain::CalcPatchBoundsY(UINT i, UINT j)
{
    // Scan the heightmap values this patch covers and
    // compute the min/max height.

    UINT x0 = j*CellsPerPatch;
    UINT x1 = (j+1)*CellsPerPatch;

    UINT y0 = i*CellsPerPatch;
    UINT y1 = (i+1)*CellsPerPatch;

    float minY = +MathHelper::Infinity;
    float maxY = -MathHelper::Infinity;
    for(UINT y = y0; y <= y1; ++y)
    {
      for(UINT x = x0; x <= x1; ++x)
      {
        UINT k = y*mInfo.HeightmapWidth + x;
        minY = MathHelper::Min(minY, mHeightmap[k]);
        maxY = MathHelper::Max(maxY, mHeightmap[k]);
      }
    }

    UINT patchID = i*(mNumPatchVertCols-1)+j;
    mPatchBoundsY[patchID] = XMFLOAT2(minY, maxY);
}

void Terrain::BuildQuadPatchVB(ID3D11Device* device)
{
    [...]

    // Store axis-aligned bounding box y-bounds in upper-left patch corner.
```

```
for(UINT i = 0; i < mNumPatchVertRows-1; ++i)
{
  for(UINT j = 0; j < mNumPatchVertCols-1; ++j)
  {
    UINT patchID = i*(mNumPatchVertCols-1)+j;
    patchVertices[i*mNumPatchVertCols+j].BoundsY =
      mPatchBoundsY[patchID];
  }
}

[...]
}
```

Now in the constant hull shader, we can construct our axis-aligned bound box, and perform box/frustum intersection test to see if the box lies outside the frustum. We use a different box/plane intersection test than we explained in Chapter 15. It is actually a special case of the OBB/plane test described in Exercise 4 of Chapter 15. Because the box is axis-aligned, the formula for the radius r simplifies:

$$a_0\mathbf{r}_0 = (a_0, 0, 0)$$
$$a_1\mathbf{r}_1 = (0, a_1, 0)$$
$$a_2\mathbf{r}_2 = (0, 0, a_2)$$
$$r = |a_0\mathbf{r}_0 \cdot \mathbf{n}| + |a_1\mathbf{r}_1 \cdot \mathbf{n}| + |a_2\mathbf{r}_2 \cdot \mathbf{n}|$$
$$= a_0|n_x| + a_1|n_y| + a_2|n_z|$$

We like this test over the one in §15.2.3.3 because it does not contain conditional statements.

```
float4 gWorldFrustumPlanes[6];

// Returns true if the box is completely behind (in negative
// half space) of plane.
bool AabbBehindPlaneTest(float3 center, float3 extents, float4 plane)
{
    float3 n = abs(plane.xyz); // (|n.x|, |n.y|, |n.z|)

    // This is always positive.
    float r = dot(extents, n);

    // signed distance from center point to plane.
    float s = dot(float4(center, 1.0f), plane);

    // If the center point of the box is a distance of e or more behind the
    // plane (in which case s is negative since it is behind the plane),
    // then the box is completely in the negative half space of the
    plane.
    return (s + e) < 0.0f;
}
```

```
// Returns true if the box is completely outside the frustum.
bool AabbOutsideFrustumTest(float3 center, float3 extents, float4
    frustumPlanes[6])
{
    for(int i = 0; i < 6; ++i)
    {
      // If the box is completely behind any of the frustum planes
      // then it is outside the frustum.
      if(AabbBehindPlaneTest(center, extents, frustumPlanes[i]))
      {
        return true;
      }
    }

    return false;
}

PatchTess ConstantHS(InputPatch<VertexOut, 4> patch, uint patchID :
    SV_PrimitiveID)
{
    PatchTess pt;

    //
    // Frustum cull
    //

    // We store the patch BoundsY in the first control point.
    float minY = patch[0].BoundsY.x;
    float maxY = patch[0].BoundsY.y;

    // Build axis-aligned bounding box.  patch[2] is lower-left corner
    // and patch[1] is upper-right corner.
    float3 vMin = float3(patch[2].PosW.x, minY, patch[2].PosW.z);
    float3 vMax = float3(patch[1].PosW.x, maxY, patch[1].PosW.z);

    // Center/extents representation.
    float3 boxCenter  = 0.5f*(vMin + vMax);
    float3 boxExtents = 0.5f*(vMax - vMin);
    if(AabbOutsideFrustumTest(boxCenter, boxExtents,
    gWorldFrustumPlanes))
    {
      pt.EdgeTess[0] = 0.0f;
      pt.EdgeTess[1] = 0.0f;
      pt.EdgeTess[2] = 0.0f;
      pt.EdgeTess[3] = 0.0f;

      pt.InsideTess[0] = 0.0f;
      pt.InsideTess[1] = 0.0f;

      return pt;
    }
    //
    // Do normal tessellation based on distance.
    //
    else
    {
      [...]
    }
```

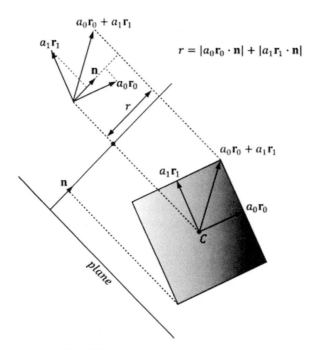

$$r = |a_0 \mathbf{r}_0 \cdot \mathbf{n}| + |a_1 \mathbf{r}_1 \cdot \mathbf{n}|$$

Figure 19.10. OBB/plane intersection test. We can use the same test for an AABB because an AABB is a special case of an OBB. Moreover, the formula for r simplifies in the case of an AABB.

19.4 TEXTURING

Recall §8.10 where we tiled a grass texture over hills. We tiled the texture to increase the resolution (i.e., to increase the number of texel samples that covered a triangle on the land mass). We want to do the same thing here; however, we do not want to be limited to a single grass texture. We would like to create terrains depicting sand, grass, dirt, rock, and snow, all at the same time. You might suggest creating one large texture that contains the sand, grass, dirt, etc., and stretch it over the terrain. But this would lead us back to the resolution problem—the terrain geometry is so large, we would require an impractically large texture to have enough color samples to get a decent resolution. Instead, we take a multitexturing approach that works like transparency alpha blending.

The idea is to have a separate texture for each terrain layer (e.g., one for grass, dirt, rock, etc.). These textures will be tiled over the terrain for high resolution. For the sake of example, suppose we have 3 terrain layers (grass, dirt, and rock); then these layers are then combined as shown in Figure 19.11.

The previous process should be reminiscent of transparency alpha blending. The blend map, which stores the source alpha of the layer we are writing, indicates

Terrain RGB	Layer Maps	Blend Maps

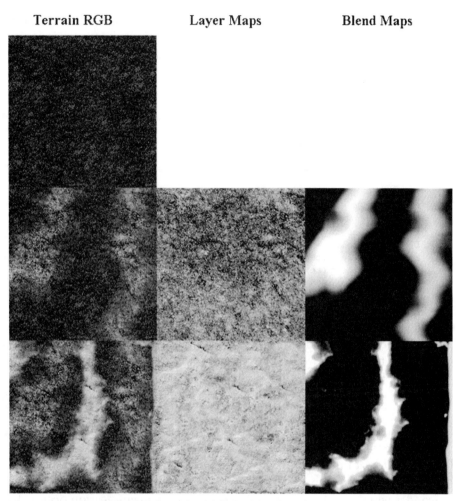

Figure 19.11. (Top) First lay down the 0th layer (grass) as the current terrain color. (Middle) Now blend the current terrain color with the 1st layer (dirt) via the transparency alpha blending equation; the blend map supplies the source alpha component. (Bottom) Finally, blend the current terrain color with the 2nd layer (rock) via the transparency alpha blending equation; the blend map supplies the source alpha component.

the opacity of the source layer, thereby allowing us to control how much of the source layer overwrites the existing terrain color. This enables us to color some parts of the terrain with grass, some parts with dirt, and others with snow, or various blends of all three.

Figure 19.11 illustrates the process with 3 color maps. In our code, we use 5. In order to combine the 5 color maps, we require 4 grayscale *blend maps.* We can pack these 4 grayscale blend maps into a single RGBA texture (the red channel stores the first blend map, the green channel the second blend map, the blue channel the third blend map, and the alpha channel the fourth blend map). Thus, a total of six textures are needed to implement this. The following terrain pixel shader code shows how our texture blending is implemented:

```
// Sample layers in texture array.
float4 c0 = gLayerMapArray.Sample(samLinear, float3(pin.TiledTex, 0.0f));
float4 c1 = gLayerMapArray.Sample(samLinear, float3(pin.TiledTex, 1.0f));
float4 c2 = gLayerMapArray.Sample(samLinear, float3(pin.TiledTex, 2.0f));
float4 c3 = gLayerMapArray.Sample(samLinear, float3(pin.TiledTex, 3.0f));
float4 c4 = gLayerMapArray.Sample(samLinear, float3(pin.TiledTex, 4.0f));

// Sample the blend map.
float4 t  = gBlendMap.Sample(samLinear, pin.Tex);

// Blend the layers on top of each other.
float4 texColor = c0;
texColor = lerp(texColor, c1, t.r);
texColor = lerp(texColor, c2, t.g);
texColor = lerp(texColor, c3, t.b);
texColor = lerp(texColor, c4, t.a);
```

The blend maps generally depend on the heightmap of the terrain. Therefore, we do not embed the blend maps into the alpha channels of the color maps. If we did, then the color maps would only work for a particular heightmap. By keeping the color maps and blend maps separate, we can reuse the color maps for many different terrains. On the other hand, different blend maps will be constructed for each terrain.

Unlike the layer textures, the blend maps are not tiled, as we stretch them over the entire terrain surface. This is necessary because we use the blend map to mark regions of the terrain where we want a particular texture to show through, so the blend map must be global and cover the whole terrain. You might wonder whether this is acceptable or if excessive magnification occurs. Indeed, magnification will occur and the blend maps will be distorted by the texture filtering when it is stretched over the entire terrain, but the blend maps are not where we get our details from (we get them from the tiled textures). The blend maps merely mark the general regions of the terrain where (and how much) a particular texture contributes. So if the blend maps get distorted and blurred, it will not significantly affect the end result—perhaps a bit of dirt will blend in with a bit of grass, for example, and this actually provides a smoother transition between layers.

Note: *You can add normal mapping support by tiling normal maps over the terrain as well. Materials like rocks could benefit from the higher detail normal maps provide. As we saw in §19.3, we do calculate the tangent frame per pixel.*

19.5 TERRAIN HEIGHT

A common task is to get the height of the terrain surface given the x- and z-coordinates. This is useful for placing objects on the surface of the terrain, or for placing the camera slighting above the terrain surface to simulate the player walking on the terrain.

The heightmap gives us the height of a terrain vertex at the grid points. However, we need the heights of the terrain between vertices. Therefore, we have to do interpolation to form a continuous surface $y = h(x, z)$ representing the terrain given the discrete heightmap sampling. Because the terrain is approximated by a triangle mesh, it makes sense to use linear interpolation so that our height function agrees with the underlying terrain mesh geometry.

To begin to solve this, our first goal is to figure out which cell the x- and z-coordinates lie in. (Note: We assume the coordinates x and z are relative to the local space of the terrain.) The following code does this; it tells us the row and column of the cell where the x- and z-coordinates are located.

```
// Transform from terrain local space to "cell" space.
float c = (x + 0.5f*width()) /  mInfo.CellSpacing;
float d = (z - 0.5f*depth()) / -mInfo.CellSpacing;

// Get the row and column we are in.
int row = (int)floorf(d);
int col = (int)floorf(c);
```

Figure 19.12*ab* explains what this code does. Essentially, we are transforming to a new coordinate system where the origin is at the upper-left most terrain vertex, the positive z-axis goes down, and each unit is scaled to that until it corresponds to one cell space. Now in this coordinate system, it is clear by Figure 19.12*b* that the row and column of the cell is just given by `floor(z)` and `floor(x)`, respectively. In the figure example, the point is in row four and column one (using zero based indices). (Recall that `floor(t)` evaluates to the greatest integer less than or equal to t.) Observe also that `row` and `col` give the indices of the upper-left vertex of the cell.

Now that we know the cell we are in, we grab the heights of the four cell vertices from the heightmap:

```
// Grab the heights of the cell we are in.
    // A*--*B
    //  | /|
    //  |/ |
    // C*--*D
    float A = mHeightmap[row*mInfo.HeightmapWidth + col];
    float B = mHeightmap[row*mInfo.HeightmapWidth + col + 1];
    float C = mHeightmap[(row+1)*mInfo.HeightmapWidth + col];
    float D = mHeightmap[(row+1)*mInfo.HeightmapWidth + col + 1];
```

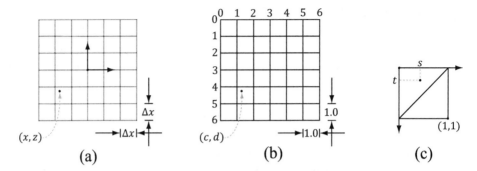

Figure 19.12. (a) The point in the *xz*-plane relative to the terrain coordinate system has coordinates (x, z). (b) We pick a new coordinate system where the origin is the upper-left most grid vertex, the positive *z*-axis goes down, and each unit is scaled so that it corresponds to one cell space. The point has coordinates (c, d) relative to this coordinate system. This transformation involves a translation and scaling. Once in this new coordinate system, finding the row and column of the cell we are in is trivial. (c) We introduce a third coordinate system, which has its origin at the upper-left vertex of the cell the point is in. The point has coordinates (s, t) relative to this coordinate system. Transforming the coordinates into this system involves only a simple translation to offset the coordinates. Observe that if $s + t \leq 1$ we are in the "upper" triangle, otherwise we are in the "lower" triangle.

At this point we know the cell we are in and we know the heights of the four vertices of that cell. Now we need to find the height (*y*-coordinate) of the terrain surface at the particular *x*- and *z*-coordinates. This is a little tricky because the cell can be slanted in a couple of directions; see Figure 19.13.

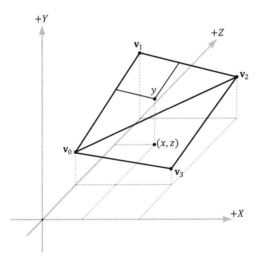

Figure 19.13. The height (*y*-coordinate) of the terrain surface at the particular *x*- and *z*-coordinates.

In order to find the height, we need to know which triangle of the cell we are in (recall our cells are rendered as two triangles). To find the triangle we are in, we are going to change our coordinates so that the coordinates (c, d) are described relative to the cell coordinate system (see Figure 19.12c). This simple change of coordinates involves only translations and is done as follows:

```
float s = c - (float)col;
float t = d - (float)row;
```

Then, if $s + t \leq 1$ we are in the "upper" triangle $\triangle ABC$, else we are in the "lower" triangle $\triangle DCB$.

Now we explain how to find the height if we are in the "upper" triangle. The process is similar for the "lower" triangle, and, of course, the code for both follows shortly. To find the height if we are in the "upper" triangle, we first construct two vectors $\mathbf{u} = (\Delta x, B - A, 0)$ and $\mathbf{v} = (0, C - A, -\Delta z)$ on the sides of the triangle originating from the terminal point $\mathbf{Q}$ as Figure 19.14a shows. Then we linearly interpolate along $\mathbf{u}$ by s, and we linearly interpolate along $\mathbf{v}$ by t. Figure 19.14b illustrates these interpolations. The y-coordinate of the point $\mathbf{Q} + s\mathbf{u} + t\mathbf{v}$ gives the height based on the given x- and z-coordinates (recall the geometric interpretation of vector addition to see this).

Note that because we are only concerned about the interpolated height value we can just interpolate the y-components and ignore the other components. Thus the height is obtained by the sum $A + su_y + tv_y$.

Thus the conclusion of the `Terrain::GetHeight` code is:

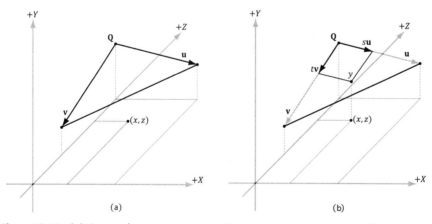

Figure 19.14. (a) Computing two vectors on the upper-triangle edges. (b) The height is the y-coordinate of the vector.

```
// If upper triangle ABC.
if(s + t <= 1.0f)
{
    float uy = B - A;
    float vy = C - A;
    return A + s*uy + t*vy;
}
else // lower triangle DCB.
{
    float uy = C - D;
    float vy = B - D;
    return D + (1.0f-s)*uy + (1.0f-t)*vy;
}
```

We can now clamp the camera above the terrain to simulate that the player is walking on the terrain:

```
void TerrainApp::UpdateScene(float dt)
{
    //
    // Control the camera.
    //
    if(GetAsyncKeyState('W') & 0x8000)
        mCam.Walk(10.0f*dt);

    if(GetAsyncKeyState('S') & 0x8000)
        mCam.Walk(-10.0f*dt);

    if(GetAsyncKeyState('A') & 0x8000)
        mCam.Strafe(-10.0f*dt);

    if(GetAsyncKeyState('D') & 0x8000)
        mCam.Strafe(10.0f*dt);

    //
    // Walk/fly mode
    //
    if(GetAsyncKeyState('2') & 0x8000)
        mWalkCamMode = true;
    if(GetAsyncKeyState('3') & 0x8000)
        mWalkCamMode = false;

    //
    // Clamp camera to terrain surface in walk mode.
    //
    if(mWalkCamMode)
    {
        XMFLOAT3 camPos = mCam.GetPosition();
        float y = mTerrain.GetHeight(camPos.x, camPos.z);
        mCam.SetPosition(camPos.x, y + 2.0f, camPos.z);
    }

    mCam.UpdateViewMatrix();
}
```

19.6 SUMMARY

1. We can model terrains using triangle grids where the height of each vertex is specified in such a way that hills and valleys are simulated.

2. A heightmap is a matrix where each element specifies the height of a particular vertex in the terrain grid. There exists an entry in the heightmap for each grid vertex, and the ijth heightmap entry provides the height for the ijth vertex. A heightmap is commonly represented visually as a grayscale map, where black denotes the smallest height, white denotes the largest height, and shades of gray represent in-between heights.

3. Terrains cover large areas, and consequently, the number of triangles needed to build them is large. If we use a uniformly tessellated grid, the screen space triangle density of the terrain will increase with distance due to the nature of perspective projection. This is actually the opposite of what we want: we want the triangle density to be large near the camera where the details will be noticed, and the triangle density to be smaller far away from the camera where the details will go unnoticed. We can use hardware tessellation to implement continuous level of detail based on the distance from the camera. The overall strategy for terrain tessellation can be summarized as follows:

   (a) Lay down a grid of quad patches.

   (b) Tessellate the patches based on their distance from the camera.

   (c) Bind the heightmap as a shader resource. In the domain shader, perform displacement mapping from the heightmap to offset the generated vertices to their proper heights.

4. We can implement frustum culling on the GPU to cull quad patches outside the frustum. This is done in the constant hull shader function by setting all the tessellation factors to zero for patches outside the frustum.

5. We texture the terrain by blending layers over each other (e.g., grass, dirt, rock, snow). Blend maps are used to control the amount each layer contributes to the final terrain image.

6. The heightmap gives us the height of a terrain vertex at the grid points, but we also need the heights of the terrain between vertices. Therefore, we have to do interpolation to form a continuous surface $y = h(x, z)$ representing the terrain given the discrete heightmap sampling. Because the terrain is approximated by a triangle mesh, it makes sense to use linear interpolation so that our height function agrees with the underlying terrain mesh geometry. Having the height function of the terrain is useful for placing objects on the surface of the terrain, or for placing the camera slightly above the terrain surface to simulate the player walking on the terrain.

19.7 EXERCISES

1. In our demo, we move the camera in the "look" direction as we did in previous chapters, then we apply the `Terrain::GetHeight` function to fix the camera slightly above the terrain surface to simulate that the camera is walking on the terrain. However, Figure 19.15 shows that you should move the camera in the direction tangent to the terrain surface, not in the "look" direction. Modify the "Terrain" demo to properly move the camera over the terrain so that there is no unnatural speedup when the player ascends or descends a hill.

2. Generally, some parts of a terrain will be rough and hilly with lots of details, and other parts will be flat and smooth. It is common to bias tessellation so that patches that contain high-frequency regions are more tessellated so the extra details show up. Likewise, flat areas do not need as much tessellation; for example, a flat quad patch does not need to be subdivided at all. Research ways to calculate a roughness factor per patch. The SDK sample "DetailTessellation11" would be a good starting point, which calculates a density map that indicates areas of the displacement map that have high-frequency regions.

3. Try generating your own heightmaps in *Terragen* and using them in the Terrain demo. Try authoring your own blend map.

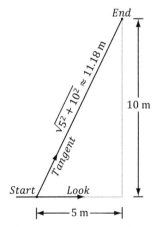

Figure 19.15. Suppose the camera is positioned at "Start" and moving in the "Look" direction. Also suppose that the camera has a speed of 5 m/s (meters per second). In one second, the camera will have traveled 5 m in the "Look" direction, but then the height will be adjusted to "End" so the camera stays on top of the terrain. In reality, then, the camera did not move 5 m in one second, it traveled a total distance of 11.18 m in one second, which is incorrect—the camera unnaturally sped up. To fix this, we always move the camera 5 m/s in a direction tangent to the surface.

4. We use continuous level of detail with the `fractional_even` tessellation mode. For debugging purposes, make the following changes to the `CalcTessFactor` function to make it easier to see the different LOD levels of the terrain.

```
float CalcTessFactor(float3 p)
{
    // max norm in xz plane (useful to see detail levels
    // from a bird's eye).
    float d = max(abs(p.x-gEyePosW.x), abs(p.z-gEyePosW.z));

    float s = saturate((d - gMinDist) / (gMaxDist - gMinDist));

    return pow(2, round(lerp(gMaxTess, gMinTess, s)));
}
```

We have made two changes. First, we use the max norm in the *xz*-plane to measure distance. This allows us to zoom out to a bird's eye view without affecting the distance (since *y*-coord is ignored). Second, we round the exponent to an integer so that the tessellation factor is always an integer power of 2. This gives us exactly seven discrete LOD levels: 2^0, $2^1, \ldots, 2^6$. For this exercise, make the above changes to the `CalcTessFactor` function, and zoom out to see something like Figure 19.7. It might help to disable drawing the sky, and to draw the terrain black in wireframe mode.

Chapter 20 PARTICLE SYSTEMS AND STREAM-OUT

In this chapter, we concern ourselves with the task of modeling a collection of particles (usually small) that all behave in a similar yet somewhat random manner; we call such a collection of particles a *particle system*. Particle systems can be used to simulate a wide range of phenomena such as fire, rain, smoke, explosions, sprinklers, magic spell effects, and projectiles.

Objectives:

1. To learn how to store and render particles efficiently using the geometry shader and stream out functionality.
2. To find out how we can make our particles move in a physically realistic way using basic physics concepts.
3. To design a flexible particle system framework that makes it easy to create new custom particle systems.

20.1 PARTICLE REPRESENTATION

A *particle* is a very small object that is usually modeled as a point mathematically. It follows then that a point primitive (D3D11_PRIMITIVE_TOPOLOGY_POINTLIST) would be a good candidate to display particles. However, point primitives are rasterized as a single pixel. This does not give us much flexibility, as we would like to have particles of various sizes and even map entire textures onto these particles. Therefore, we will take a strategy like we used for the tree billboards from Chapter 11: We will store the particles using points, but then expand them into quads that face the camera in the geometry shader. In contrast to the tree billboards, which were aligned with the world's *y*-axis, the particle billboards will fully face the camera (see Figure 20.1).

If we know the world coordinates of the world's up vector **j**, the billboard's center position **C**, and the eye position **E**, then we can describe the billboard's local frame in world coordinates, which gives us the billboard's world matrix:

$$\mathbf{w} = \frac{\mathbf{E} - \mathbf{C}}{\|\mathbf{E} - \mathbf{C}\|}$$

$$\mathbf{u} = \frac{\mathbf{j} \times \mathbf{w}}{\|\mathbf{j} \times \mathbf{w}\|}$$

$$\mathbf{v} = \mathbf{w} \times \mathbf{u}$$

$$\mathbf{W} = \begin{bmatrix} u_x & u_y & u_z & 0 \\ v_x & v_y & v_z & 0 \\ w_x & w_y & w_z & 0 \\ C_x & C_y & C_z & 1 \end{bmatrix}$$

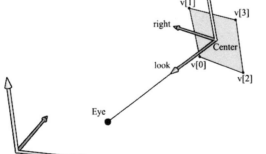

Figure 20.1. **The world and billboard frames. The billboard faces the eye position E.**

In addition to position and size, our particles will have other attributes. Our vertex structure for particles looks like this:

```
struct Particle
{
    XMFLOAT3 InitialPos;
    XMFLOAT3 InitialVel;
    XMFLOAT2 Size;
    float Age;
    unsigned int Type;
};
```

Note: *We need not expand a point into a quad, necessarily. For example, using line lists to render rain works pretty well. We can use a different geometry shader to expand points to lines. Basically, in our system, each particle system will have its own effect file. The effect file implements the details specific to the particular kind of particle system it is associated with.*

20.2 PARTICLE MOTION

We would like our particles to move in a physically realistic way. For simplicity, in this book, we restrict ourselves to a constant net acceleration; for example, acceleration due to gravity. (We can also make loose approximations by making acceleration due to other forces constant as well, such as wind.) In addition, we do not do any collision detection with our particles.

Let $\mathbf{p}(t)$ describe the position of a particle (at time t) moving along a curve. The instantaneous velocity of the particle at time t is:

$$\mathbf{v}(t) = \mathbf{p}'(t)$$

The instantaneous acceleration of the particle at time t is:

$$\mathbf{a}(t) = \mathbf{v}'(t) = \mathbf{p}''(t)$$

Recall the following from calculus:

1. An antiderivative of a function $\mathbf{f}(t)$ is any function $\mathbf{F}(t)$ such that the derivative of $\mathbf{F}(t)$ is $\mathbf{f}(t)$; that is, $\mathbf{F}'(t) = \mathbf{f}(t)$.

2. If $\mathbf{F}(t)$ is any antiderivative of $\mathbf{f}(t)$ and $\mathbf{c}$ is any constant, then $\mathbf{F}(t) + \mathbf{c}$ is also an antiderivative of $\mathbf{f}(t)$. Moreover, every antiderivative of $\mathbf{f}(t)$ has the form $\mathbf{F}(t) + \mathbf{c}$.

3. To denote an arbitrary antiderivative of $\mathbf{f}(t)$, we use the integral notation $\int \mathbf{f}(t)\, dt = \mathbf{F}(t) + \mathbf{c}$.

From the definitions of velocity and acceleration, it is evident that the velocity function is an antiderivative of the acceleration function, and the position function is an antiderivative of the velocity function. Thus we have:

$$\mathbf{p}(t) = \int \mathbf{v}(t)\, dt$$

$$\mathbf{v}(t) = \int \mathbf{a}(t)\, dt$$

Now, suppose that the acceleration is constant (i.e., it does not vary with time). Also suppose that we know the initial particle velocity $\mathbf{v}(0) = \mathbf{v}_0$ and the initial particle position $\mathbf{p}(0) = \mathbf{p}_0$ at time $t = 0$. Then the velocity function is found by integrating the constant acceleration:

$$\mathbf{v}(t) = \int \mathbf{a}(t)\, dt = t\mathbf{a} + \mathbf{c}$$

To find the constant $\mathbf{c}$, we use our initial velocity:

$$\mathbf{v}(0) = 0 \cdot \mathbf{a} + \mathbf{c} = \mathbf{c} = \mathbf{v}_0$$

So the velocity function is

$$\mathbf{v}(t) = t\mathbf{a} + \mathbf{v}_0$$

To find the position function, we integrate the just found velocity function:

$$\mathbf{p}(t) = \int \mathbf{v}(t)\, dt = \int (t\mathbf{a} + \mathbf{v}_0)\, dt = \frac{1}{2}t^2\mathbf{a} + t\mathbf{v}_0 + \mathbf{k}$$

To find the constant $\mathbf{k}$, we use our initial position:

$$\mathbf{p}(0) = \frac{1}{2} \cdot 0 \cdot \mathbf{a} + 0 \cdot \mathbf{v}_0 + \mathbf{k} = \mathbf{k} = \mathbf{p}_0$$

So the position function is

$$\mathbf{p}(t) = \frac{1}{2}t^2\mathbf{a} + t\mathbf{v}_0 + \mathbf{p}_0$$

In other words, the trajectory $\mathbf{p}(t)$ of a particle (i.e., its position at any time $t \geq 0$) is completely determined by its initial position, initial velocity, and the constant of acceleration. This is reasonable because if we know where we are starting, how fast and in which direction we are going initially, and we know how we are accelerating for all time, then we ought to be able to figure out the path we followed.

Let us look at an example. Suppose you have a mini-cannon sitting at the origin of a coordinate system and aimed at a 30° angle measured from the x-axis (see Figure 20.2). So in this coordinate system, $\mathbf{p}0 = (0, 0, 0)$ (i.e., the initial position

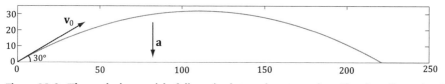

Figure 20.2. The path the particle follows in the *xy*-plane over time (the time dimension is not shown), given the initial position and velocity, and undergoing constant acceleration due to gravity.

of a cannon ball is at the origin), and the constant acceleration due to gravity is $\mathbf{a} = (0, -9.8, 0)$ m/s² (i.e., acceleration due to gravity is 9.8 meters per second squared). In addition, suppose that from previous tests, we have determined that at the instant the cannon fires, the cannon ball has an initial speed of 50 meters per second. Thus, the initial velocity is $\mathbf{v}_0 = 50(\cos 30°, \sin 30°, 0)$ m/s $\approx (43.3, 25.0, 0)$ m/s [remember velocity is speed and direction so we multiply the speed by the unit direction vector $(\cos 30°, \sin 30°, 0)$]. Thus the trajectory of the cannon ball is given by:

$$\mathbf{p}(t) = \frac{1}{2}t^2\mathbf{a} + t\mathbf{v}_0 + \mathbf{p}_0$$

$$= \frac{1}{2}t^2(0, -9.8, 0)\,\text{m}/\text{s}^2 + t(43.3, 25.0, 0)\,\text{m}/\text{s}$$

If we plot this in the *xy*-plane (*z*-coordinate is always zero), we get Figure 20.2, which is the trajectory we would expect with gravity.

Note: ▶ *You can also choose not to use the function derived previously. If you already know the trajectory function* $\mathbf{p}(t)$ *you want your particles to take, then you can just program it directly. For example, if you want your particles to follow an elliptical trajectory, then you can just use the parametric equations of an ellipse for* $\mathbf{p}(t)$.

20.3 RANDOMNESS

In a particle system, we want the particles to behave similarly, but not exactly the same; in other words, we want to add some randomness to the system. For example, if we are modeling raindrops, we do not want the raindrops to fall in exactly the same way; we want them to fall from different positions, at slightly different angles, and at slightly different speeds. To facilitate the randomness functionality required for particle systems, we use the **RandF** and **RandUnitVec3** functions implemented in *MathHelper.h/.cpp*:

```
// Returns random float in [0, 1).
static float RandF()
{
    return (float)(rand()) / (float)RAND_MAX;
}

// Returns random float in [a, b).
static float RandF(float a, float b)
{
    return a + RandF()*(b-a);
}

XMVECTOR MathHelper::RandUnitVec3()
{
    XMVECTOR One  = XMVectorSet(1.0f, 1.0f, 1.0f, 1.0f);
    XMVECTOR Zero = XMVectorZero();

    // Keep trying until we get a point on/in the hemisphere.
    while(true)
    {
      // Generate random point in the cube [-1,1]^3.
      XMVECTOR v = XMVectorSet(
        MathHelper::RandF(-1.0f, 1.0f),
        MathHelper::RandF(-1.0f, 1.0f),
        MathHelper::RandF(-1.0f, 1.0f), 0.0f);

      // Ignore points outside the unit sphere in order to
      // get an even distribution  over the unit sphere.  Otherwise
      // points will clump more on the sphere near the corners
      // of the cube.

      if(XMVector3Greater(XMVector3LengthSq(v), One))
        continue;

      return XMVector3Normalize(v);
    }
}
```

The previous functions work for C++ code, but we will also need random numbers in shader code. Generating random numbers in a shader is trickier because we do not have a shader random number generator. So what we do is create a 1D texture with four floating-point components (DXGI_FORMAT_R32G32B32A32_FLOAT). We fill the texture with random 4D vectors with coordinates in the interval $[-1,1]$. The texture will be sampled with the wrap address mode, so that we can use unbounded texture coordinates outside the interval $[0,1]$. The shader code will then sample this texture to get a random number. There are different ways to sample the random texture. If each particle has a different x-coordinate, we could use the x-coordinate as a texture coordinate to get a random number. However, this will not work very well if many of the particles have the same x-coordinate, as then they would all sample the same value in the texture, which would not be very random. Another approach is to use the current game time value as a texture coordinate. This way, particles generated at different times would get different random values. However, this means particles generated at the same time will have the same values. This can be a problem if the particle system needs to emit several particles at once. When generating many particles at the same time, we can add a different texture coordinate offset value to the game time so that we sample different points on the texture map, and hence get different random values. For example, if we were looping 20 times to create 20 particles, we could use the loop index (appropriately scaled) to offset the texture coordinate used to sample the random texture. This way, we would get 20 different random values.

The following code shows how to generate a random texture:

```
ID3D11ShaderResourceView* d3dHelper::CreateRandomTexture1DSRV(
    ID3D11Device* device)
{
    //
    // Create the random data.
    //
    XMFLOAT4 randomValues[1024];

    for(int i = 0; i < 1024; ++i)
    {
        randomValues[i].x = MathHelper::RandF(-1.0f, 1.0f);
        randomValues[i].y = MathHelper::RandF(-1.0f, 1.0f);
        randomValues[i].z = MathHelper::RandF(-1.0f, 1.0f);
        randomValues[i].w = MathHelper::RandF(-1.0f, 1.0f);
    }

    D3D11_SUBRESOURCE_DATA initData;
    initData.pSysMem = randomValues;
    initData.SysMemPitch = 1024*sizeof(XMFLOAT4);
    initData.SysMemSlicePitch = 0;

    //
    // Create the texture.
    //
    D3D11_TEXTURE1D_DESC texDesc;
    texDesc.Width = 1024;
    texDesc.MipLevels = 1;
    texDesc.Format = DXGI_FORMAT_R32G32B32A32_FLOAT;
    texDesc.Usage = D3D11_USAGE_IMMUTABLE;
    texDesc.BindFlags = D3D11_BIND_SHADER_RESOURCE;
    texDesc.CPUAccessFlags = 0;
    texDesc.MiscFlags = 0;
    texDesc.ArraySize = 1;

    ID3D11Texture1D* randomTex = 0;
    HR(device->CreateTexture1D(&texDesc, &initData, &randomTex));

    //
    // Create the resource view.
    //
    D3D11_SHADER_RESOURCE_VIEW_DESC viewDesc;
```

```
    viewDesc.Format = texDesc.Format;
    viewDesc.ViewDimension = D3D11_SRV_DIMENSION_TEXTURE1D;
    viewDesc.Texture1D.MipLevels = texDesc.MipLevels;
    viewDesc.Texture1D.MostDetailedMip = 0;

    ID3D11ShaderResourceView* randomTexSRV = 0;
    HR(device->CreateShaderResourceView(randomTex, &viewDesc,
    &randomTexSRV));

    ReleaseCOM(randomTex);

    return randomTexSRV;
}
```

Note that for a random texture, we only need one mipmap level. To sample a texture with only one mipmap, we use the `SampleLevel` intrinsic function. This function allows us to explicitly specify the mipmap level we want to sample. The first parameter to this function is the sampler; the second parameter is the texture coordinates (only one for a 1D texture); the third parameter is the mipmap level (which should be 0 in the case of a texture with only one mipmap level).

The following shader function is used to get a random vector on the unit sphere:

```
float3 RandUnitVec3(float offset)
{
    // Use game time plus offset to sample random texture.
    float u = (gGameTime + offset);

    // coordinates in [-1,1]
    float3 v = gRandomTex.SampleLevel(samLinear, u, 0).xyz;

    // project onto unit sphere
    return normalize(v);
}
```

20.4 BLENDING AND PARTICLE SYSTEMS

Particle systems are usually drawn with some form of blending. For effects like fire and magic spells, we want the color intensity to brighten at the location of the particles. For this effect, additive blending works well. That is, we just add the source and destination colors together. However, particles are also typically transparent; therefore, we must scale the source particle color by its opacity; that is, we use the blend parameters:

```
SrcBlend = SRC_ALPHA;
DestBlend = ONE;
BlendOp = ADD;
```

This gives the blending equation:

$$C = a_s C_{src} + C_{dst}$$

In other words, the amount of color the source particle contributes to the sum is determined by its opacity: the more opaque the particle is, the more color it contributes. An alternative approach is to premultiply the texture with its opacity (described by the alpha channel) so that the texture color is diluted based on its opacity. Then we use the diluted texture. In this case, we can use the blend parameters:

```
SrcBlend = ONE;
DestBlend = ONE;
BlendOp = ADD;
```

This is because we essentially precomputed *as* C_{src} and baked it directly into the texture data.

Additive blending also has the nice effect of brightening up areas proportional to the particle concentration there (due to additive accumulation of the colors); thus, areas where the concentration is high appear extra bright, which is usually what we want (see Figure 20.3).

For things like smoke, additive blending does not work because adding the colors of a bunch of overlapping smoke particles would eventually brighten up the smoke so that it is no longer dark. Blending with the subtraction operator (**D3D11_BLEND_OP_REV_SUBTRACT**) would work better for smoke, where the smoke particles would subtract color from the destination. In this way, higher concentrations of smoke particles would result in a blacker color, giving the illusion of thick smoke, whereas lower concentrations of smoke particles would result in a mild

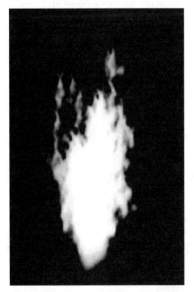

Figure 20.3. With additive blending, the intensity is greater near the source point where more particles are overlapping and being added together. As the particles spread out, the intensity weakens because there are fewer particles overlapping and being added together.

tint, giving the illusion of thin smoke. However, while this works well for black smoke, it does not work well for light gray smoke, or steam. Another possibility for smoke is to use transparency blending, where we just think of smoke particles as semi-transparent objects, and use transparency blending to render them. The main problem with transparency blending is sorting the particles in a system in back-to-front order with respect to the eye. This can be expensive and unpractical. Due to the random nature of particle systems, this rule can sometimes be broken without noticeable rendering errors. Note that if many particles systems are in a scene, the systems should still be sorted in back-to-front order; we just do not sort the particles of a system relative to each other. Note that when using blending, the discussions in §9.5.4 and §9.5.5 apply.

20.5 STREAM-OUT

We know that the GPU can write to textures. For example, the GPU handles writing to the depth/stencil buffer, and also the back buffer. A feature introduced in Direct3D 10 is the stream-out (SO) stage. The SO stage allows the GPU to actually write geometry (in the form of a vertex list) to a vertex buffer V bound to the SO stage of the pipeline. Specifically, the vertices output from the geometry shader are written (or streamed-out) to V. The geometry in V can then be drawn later. Figure 20.4 illustrates the idea (with the tessellation stages omitted). Stream-out will play an important role in our particle system framework.

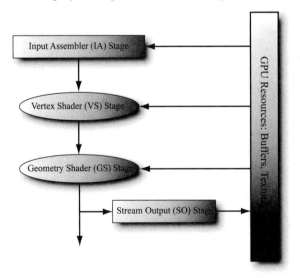

Figure 20.4. Primitives are pumped through the pipeline. The geometry shader outputs primitives which are streamed-out to vertex buffers in GPU memory.

20.5.1 Creating a Geometry Shader for Stream-Out

When using stream-out, the geometry shader must be created specially. The following code shows how this is done in an effect file:

```
GeometryShader gsStreamOut = ConstructGSWithSO(
    CompileShader(gs_5_0, GS()),
    "POSITION.xyz; VELOCITY.xyz; SIZE.xy; AGE.x; TYPE.x");

technique11 SOTech
{
    pass P0
    {
      SetVertexShader(CompileShader(vs_5_0, VS()));
      SetGeometryShader(gsStreamOut);
      SetPixelShader(CompileShader(ps_5_0, PS()));
    }
}
```

The first parameter of `ConstructGSWithSO` is just the compiled geometry shader. The second parameter is a string which describes the format of the vertices being streamed-out (i.e., the format of the vertices the geometry shader outputs). In the previous example, the vertex format is:

```
struct Vertex
{
    float3 InitialPosW : POSITION;
    float3 InitialVelW : VELOCITY;
    float2 SizeW       : SIZE;
    float Age          : AGE;
    uint Type          : TYPE;
};
```

20.5.2 Stream-Out Only

When using stream-out under normal conditions, the geometry shader output is streamed-out to the vertex buffer *and* still continues down to the next stage of the rendering pipeline (rasterization). If you want a rendering technique that only streams-out data, and does not render it, then the pixel shader and depth/stencil buffer must be disabled. (Disabling the pixel shader and depth/stencil buffer disables rasterization.) The following technique shows how this is done:

```
DepthStencilState DisableDepth
{
    DepthEnable = FALSE;
    DepthWriteMask = ZERO;
};

GeometryShader gsStreamOut = ConstructGSWithSO(
    CompileShader(gs_5_0, StreamOutGS()),
    "POSITION.xyz; VELOCITY.xyz; SIZE.xy; AGE.x; TYPE.x");
```

```
technique10 StreamOutTech
{
    pass P0
    {
        SetVertexShader(CompileShader(vs_5_0, StreamOutVS()));
        SetGeometryShader(gsStreamOut);

        // disable pixel shader for stream-out only
        SetPixelShader(NULL);

        // we must also disable the depth buffer for stream-out only
        SetDepthStencilState(DisableDepth, 0);
    }
}
```

Alternatively, you can bind a null render target and null depth/stencil buffer to the output-merger stage of the rendering pipeline.

In our particle system, we will use a stream-out only technique. This technique will be used solely to create and destroy particles (i.e., update the particle system). Every frame:

1. The current particle list will be drawn with stream-out only. This does not render any particles to the screen since the rasterization unit is disabled.

2. The geometry shader of this pass will create/destroy particles based on various conditions that vary from particle system to particle system.

3. The updated particle list will be streamed-out to a vertex buffer.

The application will then draw the updated particle list for that frame using a different rendering technique. The main reason for using two techniques is that the geometry shaders just do different things. For the stream-out only technique, the geometry shader inputs particles, updates them, and outputs particles. For the drawing technique, the geometry shader is tasked with expanding the point into a quad that faces the camera. So the geometry shaders do not even output the same type of primitives, thus we need two geometry shaders.

To summarize, we need two techniques for rendering our particle systems on the GPU:

1. A stream-out only technique used to update the particle system.

2. A rendering technique used to draw the particle system.

Note: *Particle physics could also be incrementally updated in the stream-out only pass. However, in our setup, we have an explicit position function $\mathbf{p}(t)$. So we do not need to incrementally update the position/velocity of the particle in the stream-out only pass. The ParticlesGS SDK sample does use the stream-out only pass for updating physics, however, because they use a different physics model.*

20.5.3 Creating a Vertex Buffer for Stream-Out

In order to bind a vertex buffer to the SO stage so that the GPU can write vertices to it, it must be created with the D3D11_BIND_STREAM_OUTPUT bind flag. Generally, a vertex buffer used as a stream-out target will also be used as an input into the pipeline later (i.e., it will be bound to the IA stage so that the contents can be drawn). Therefore, we must also specify the D3D11_BIND_VERTEX_BUFFER bind flag. The following code fragment shows an example of creating a vertex buffer for stream-out usage:

```
D3D11_BUFFER_DESC vbd;
vbd.Usage = D3D11_USAGE_DEFAULT;
vbd.ByteWidth = sizeof(Vertex) * MAX_VERTICES;
vbd.BindFlags = D3D11_BIND_VERTEX_BUFFER | D3D11_BIND_STREAM_OUTPUT;
    vbd.CPUAccessFlags = 0;
vbd.MiscFlags = 0;

HR(md3dDevice->CreateBuffer(&vbd, 0, &mStreamOutVB));
```

Note that the buffer memory is left uninitialized. This is because the GPU will be writing the vertex data to it. *Also note that the buffer has a finite size, so care should be taken not to stream-out so many vertices that the maximum is exceeded.*

20.5.4 Binding to the SO Stage

A vertex buffer created with the D3D11_BIND_STREAM_OUTPUT bind flag can be bound to the SO stage of the pipeline for writing with the following method:

```
void ID3D11DeviceContext::SOSetTargets(
    UINT NumBuffers,
    ID3D11Buffer *const *ppSOTargets,
    const UINT *pOffsets);
```

1. **NumBuffers**: The number of vertex buffers to bind to the SO stage as a target. The maximum is 4.

2. **ppSOTargets**: An array of vertex buffers to bind to the SO stage.

3. **pOffsets**: An array of offsets, one for each vertex buffer, indicating the start position the SO stage should begin writing vertices to.

Note: *There are four output slots for stream-out. If less than four buffers are bound to the SO stage, the other slots are set to null. For example, if you only bind to slot 0 (the first slot), then slots 1, 2, and 3 are set to null.*

20.5.5 Unbinding from the Stream-Out Stage

After we have streamed-out vertices to a vertex buffer, we may want to draw the primitives those vertices define. However, a vertex buffer cannot be bound to the SO stage and bound to the IA stage at the same time. To unbind a vertex buffer from the SO stage, we just need to bind a different buffer to the SO stage in its place (which can be null). The following code unbinds a vertex buffer from slot 0 by binding a null buffer:

```
ID3D11Buffer* bufferArray[1] = {0};
md3dDeviceContext->SOSetTargets(1, bufferArray, &offset);
```

20.5.6 Auto Draw

The geometry streamed out to a vertex buffer can be variable. So how many vertices do we draw? Fortunately, Direct3D keeps track of the count internally, and we can use the `ID3D11DeviceContext::DrawAuto` method to draw the geometry written to a vertex buffer with SO:

```
void ID3D11DeviceContext::DrawAuto();
```

Remarks:

1.   *Before calling* `DrawAuto`, *we must first bind the vertex buffer (which was used as a stream-out target) to input slot 0 of the IA stage. The* `DrawAuto` *method should only be used when a vertex buffer with the* `D3D11_BIND_STREAM_OUTPUT` *bind flag is bound to input slot 0 of the IA stage.*

2.   *We must still specify the vertex input layout of the vertices in the stream-out vertex buffer when drawing with* `DrawAuto`.

3.   `DrawAuto` *does not use indices, since the geometry shader only outputs entire primitives defined by vertex lists.*

20.5.7 Ping-Ponging Vertex Buffers

As already stated, a vertex buffer cannot be bound to the OS stage and bound to the IA stage at the same time. Therefore, a ping-pong scheme is used. When drawing with stream-out, we use two vertex buffers. One will serve as the input buffer, and the other will serve as the output buffer. On the next rendering frame, the roles of the two buffers are reversed. The buffer just streamed to becomes the new input buffer, and the old input buffer becomes the new stream-out target. The following table shows three iterations using vertex buffers V_0 and V_1.

	Input Vertex Buffer Bound to IA Stage	Output Vertex Buffer Bound to SO Stage
Frame i	V_0	V_1
Frame $i + 1$	V_1	V_0
Frame $i + 2$	V_0	V_1

20.6 GPU BASED PARTICLE SYSTEM

Particle systems generally emit and destroy particles over time. The seemingly natural way to do this would be to use a dynamic vertex buffer and keep track of spawning and killing particles on the CPU. Then the vertex buffer would be filled with the currently living particles and drawn. However, we now know from the previous section that a separate stream-out only pass can handle this spawn/kill update cycle completely on the GPU. The motivation for this is efficiency—there is some overhead whenever the CPU needs to upload data to the GPU; furthermore, it moves work from the CPU over to the GPU, which frees the CPU for other tasks like AI or physics. In this section, we explain the general details of our particle system framework.

20.6.1 Particle Effects

The specific details on how a particular particle system behaves are implemented in the effect file. That is, we will have a different (but similar) effect file for each particle system (e.g., rain, fire, smoke, etc.). The details of how particles are emitted, destroyed, and drawn are all scripted in the corresponding effect file because they vary from system to system. Examples:

1. We might destroy a rain particle when it hits the ground, whereas a fire particle would be destroyed after a few seconds.

2. A smoke particle may fade with time, whereas a rain particle would not. Likewise, the size of a smoke particle may expand with time, whereas a rain particle would not.

3. Line primitives generally work well for modeling rain, whereas a billboard quad would be used for fire/smoke particles. By using different effects for different particle systems, we can have the geometry shader expand points to lines for rain, and points to quads for fire/smoke.

4. The initial positions and velocities of rain and smoke particles would clearly be different.

To reiterate, these particle system specific details can be implemented in the effect files because in our system the shader code handles the creating, destroying, and updating of particles. This design is quite convenient because to add a new particle system, we just need to script a new effect file describing its behavior.

20.6.2 The Particle System Class

The class shown following handles the C++ related code for creating, updating, and drawing a particle system. This code is general and will apply to all the particle systems we create.

```
class ParticleSystem
{
public:

    ParticleSystem();
    ~ParticleSystem();

    // Time elapsed since the system was reset.
    float GetAge()const;

    void SetEyePos(const XMFLOAT3& eyePosW);
    void SetEmitPos(const XMFLOAT3& emitPosW);
    void SetEmitDir(const XMFLOAT3& emitDirW);

    void Init(ID3D11Device* device, ParticleEffect* fx,
      ID3D11ShaderResourceView* texArraySRV,
      ID3D11ShaderResourceView* randomTexSRV,
      UINT maxParticles);

    void Reset();
    void Update(float dt, float gameTime);
    void Draw(ID3D11DeviceContext* dc, const Camera& cam);

private:
    void BuildVB(ID3D11Device* device);

    ParticleSystem(const ParticleSystem& rhs);
    ParticleSystem& operator=(const ParticleSystem& rhs);

private:

    UINT mMaxParticles;
    bool mFirstRun;

    float mGameTime;
    float mTimeStep;
    float mAge;

    XMFLOAT3 mEyePosW;
    XMFLOAT3 mEmitPosW;
    XMFLOAT3 mEmitDirW;

    ParticleEffect* mFX;

    ID3D11Buffer* mInitVB;
    ID3D11Buffer* mDrawVB;
    ID3D11Buffer* mStreamOutVB;

    ID3D11ShaderResourceView* mTexArraySRV;
    ID3D11ShaderResourceView* mRandomTexSRV;
};
```

Except for the draw method, the implementations to the particle system class methods are quite routine by now (e.g., creating vertex buffers);

therefore, we do not show them in the book (see the corresponding chapter source code).

Note: ▶ *The particle system uses a texture array for texturing the particles. The idea is that we might not want all the particles to look exactly the same. For example, to implement a smoke particle system, we might want to use several smoke textures to add some variety; the primitive ID could be used in the pixel shader to alternate between the smoke textures in the texture array.*

20.6.3 Emitter Particles

Because the geometry shader is responsible for creating/destroying particles, we need to have special emitter particles. Emitter particles may or may not be drawn. For example, if you want your emitter particles to be invisible, then you just need the particle drawing geometry shader to not output them. Emitter particles behave differently than other particles in the system in that they can spawn other particles. For example, an emitter particle may keep track of how much time has passed, and when that time reaches a certain point, it emits a new particle. In this way, new particles are spawned over time. We use the `Type` member of the `Vertex::Particle` structure to indicate an emitter particle. Moreover, by restricting which particles are allowed to emit other particles, it gives us some control over how particles are emitted. For example, by having only one emitter particle, it is easy to control how many particles will get created per frame. The stream-only geometry shader should always output at least one emitter particle, for if the particle system loses all of its emitters, it effectively dies; however, for some particle systems this may be the desired result.

The particles system we demo in this book only uses one emitter particle for the life of the particle system. However, the particle system framework could be extended to use more if needed. Moreover, other particles can also emit particles. For example, the SDK's *ParticlesGS* demo has a launcher particle (an invisible particle that spawns shell particles), shell particles (unexploded fireworks that explode into new ember particles after some time), and some of these embers also explode into new secondary ember particles to create secondary explosions. In this sense, the emitter particle can emit other emitter particles. Exercise 1 asks you to explore this.

20.6.4 The Initialization Vertex Buffer

In our particle system, we have a special initialization vertex buffer. This vertex buffer contains only a single emitter particle. We draw this vertex buffer first to kick-off the particle system. This emitter particle will then start spawning other particles in subsequent frames. Note that the initialization vertex buffer is drawn only once (except when the system is reset). After the particle system has been initialized with a single emitter particle, we use the two stream-out vertex buffers in a ping-pong fashion.

The initialization vertex buffer is also useful if we need to restart the system from the beginning. We can use this code to restart the particle system:

```
void ParticleSystem::Reset()
{
    mFirstRun = true;
    mAge      = 0.0f;
}
```

Setting `mFirstRun` to true instructs the particle system to draw the initialization vertex buffer on the next draw call, thereby restarting the particle system with a single emitter particle.

20.6.5 The Update/Draw Method

Recall that we need two techniques for rendering our particle systems on the GPU:

1. A stream-out only technique used to update the particle system.
2. A rendering technique used to draw the particle system.

The following code does this, in addition to handling the ping-pong scheme of the two vertex buffers:

```
void ParticleSystem::Draw(ID3D11DeviceContext* dc, const Camera& cam)
{
    XMMATRIX VP = cam.ViewProj();

    //
    // Set constants.
    //
    mFX->SetViewProj(VP);
    mFX->SetGameTime(mGameTime);
    mFX->SetTimeStep(mTimeStep);
    mFX->SetEyePosW(mEyePosW);
    mFX->SetEmitPosW(mEmitPosW);
    mFX->SetEmitDirW(mEmitDirW);
    mFX->SetTexArray(mTexArraySRV);
    mFX->SetRandomTex(mRandomTexSRV);

    //
    // Set IA stage.
    //
    dc->IASetInputLayout(InputLayouts::Particle);
    dc->IASetPrimitiveTopology(D3D11_PRIMITIVE_TOPOLOGY_POINTLIST);
```

```
UINT stride = sizeof(Vertex::Particle);
UINT offset = 0;

// On the first pass, use the initialization VB.  Otherwise, use
// the VB that contains the current particle list.
if( mFirstRun )
  dc->IASetVertexBuffers(0, 1, &mInitVB, &stride, &offset);
else
  dc->IASetVertexBuffers(0, 1, &mDrawVB, &stride, &offset);

//
// Draw the current particle list using stream-out only to update them.
// The updated vertices are streamed-out to the target VB.
//
dc->SOSetTargets(1, &mStreamOutVB, &offset);

D3DX11_TECHNIQUE_DESC techDesc;
mFX->StreamOutTech->GetDesc(&techDesc);
for(UINT p = 0; p < techDesc.Passes; ++p)
{
  mFX->StreamOutTech->GetPassByIndex( p )->Apply(0, dc);

  if(mFirstRun)
  {
    dc->Draw(1, 0);
    mFirstRun = false;
  }
  else
  {
    dc->DrawAuto();
  }
}

// done streaming-out--unbind the vertex buffer
ID3D11Buffer* bufferArray[1] = {0};
dc->SOSetTargets(1, bufferArray, &offset);

// ping-pong the vertex buffers
std::swap(mDrawVB, mStreamOutVB);

//
// Draw the updated particle system we just streamed-out.
//
dc->IASetVertexBuffers(0, 1, &mDrawVB, &stride, &offset);

mFX->DrawTech->GetDesc(&techDesc);
for(UINT p = 0; p < techDesc.Passes; ++p)
{
  mFX->DrawTech->GetPassByIndex(p)->Apply(0, dc);

  dc->DrawAuto();
}
}
```

Figure 20.5. **Screenshot of particle system demo showing fire.**

20.7 FIRE

Following is the effect for rendering a fire particle system. It consists of two techniques:

1. A stream-out only technique used to update the particle system.
2. A rendering technique used to draw the particle system.

The logic programmed into these two techniques will generally vary from particle system to particle system, as the destroy/spawn/rendering rules will be different. The fire particles are emitted at the emit position, but are given random initial velocities to spread the flames out to create a fireball.

```
//***********************************************
// GLOBALS                                      *
//***********************************************

cbuffer cbPerFrame
{
    float3 gEyePosW;

    // for when the emit position/direction is varying
    float3 gEmitPosW;
    float3 gEmitDirW;
```

```
    float gGameTime;
    float gTimeStep;
    float4x4 gViewProj;
    };

cbuffer cbFixed
{
    // Net constant acceleration used to accerlate the particles.
    float3 gAccelW = {0.0f, 7.8f, 0.0f};

    // Texture coordinates used to stretch texture over quad
    // when we expand point particle into a quad.
    float2 gQuadTexC[4] =
    {
      float2(0.0f, 1.0f),
      float2(1.0f, 1.0f),
      float2(0.0f, 0.0f),
      float2(1.0f, 0.0f)
    };
};

// Array of textures for texturing the particles.
Texture2DArray gTexArray;

// Random texture used to generate random numbers in shaders.
Texture1D gRandomTex;

SamplerState samLinear
{
    Filter = MIN_MAG_MIP_LINEAR;
    AddressU = WRAP;
    AddressV = WRAP;
};

DepthStencilState DisableDepth
{
    DepthEnable = FALSE;
    DepthWriteMask = ZERO;
};

DepthStencilState NoDepthWrites
{
    DepthEnable = TRUE;
    DepthWriteMask = ZERO;
};

BlendState AdditiveBlending
{
    AlphaToCoverageEnable = FALSE;
    BlendEnable[0] = TRUE;
    SrcBlend = SRC_ALPHA;
    DestBlend = ONE;
    BlendOp = ADD;
    SrcBlendAlpha = ZERO;
    DestBlendAlpha = ZERO;
```

```
    BlendOpAlpha = ADD;
    RenderTargetWriteMask[0] = 0x0F;
};

//***********************************************
// HELPER FUNCTIONS                             *
//***********************************************
float3 RandUnitVec3(float offset)
{
    // Use game time plus offset to sample random texture.
    float u = (gGameTime + offset);

    // coordinates in [-1,1]
    float3 v = gRandomTex.SampleLevel(samLinear, u, 0).xyz;

    // project onto unit sphere
    return normalize(v);
}

//***********************************************
// STREAM-OUT TECH                              *
//***********************************************

#define PT_EMITTER 0
#define PT_FLARE 1

struct Particle
{
    float3 InitialPosW : POSITION;
    float3 InitialVelW : VELOCITY;
    float2 SizeW       : SIZE;
    float Age          : AGE;
    uint Type          : TYPE;
};

Particle StreamOutVS(Particle vin)
{
    return vin;
}

// The stream-out GS is just responsible for emitting
// new particles and destroying old particles.  The logic
// programed here will generally vary from particle system
// to particle system, as the destroy/spawn rules will be
// different.
[maxvertexcount(2)]
void StreamOutGS(point Particle gin[1],
                 inout PointStream<Particle> ptStream)
{
    gin[0].Age += gTimeStep;

    if(gin[0].Type == PT_EMITTER)
    {
      // time to emit a new particle?
      if(gin[0].Age > 0.005f)
```

```
        {
            float3 vRandom = RandUnitVec3(0.0f);
            vRandom.x *= 0.5f;
            vRandom.z *= 0.5f;

            Particle p;
            p.InitialPosW = gEmitPosW.xyz;
            p.InitialVelW = 4.0f*vRandom;
            p.SizeW       = float2(3.0f, 3.0f);
            p.Age         = 0.0f;
            p.Type        = PT_FLARE;

            ptStream.Append(p);

            // reset the time to emit
            gin[0].Age = 0.0f;
        }

        // always keep emitters
        ptStream.Append(gin[0]);
    }
    else
    {
        // Specify conditions to keep particle; this may vary
        // from system to system.
        if(gin[0].Age <= 1.0f)
            ptStream.Append(gin[0]);
    }
}

GeometryShader gsStreamOut = ConstructGSWithSO(
    CompileShader(gs_5_0, StreamOutGS()),
    "POSITION.xyz; VELOCITY.xyz; SIZE.xy; AGE.x; TYPE.x");

technique11 StreamOutTech
{
    pass P0
    {
        SetVertexShader(CompileShader(vs_5_0, StreamOutVS()));
        SetGeometryShader(gsStreamOut);

        // disable pixel shader for stream-out only
        SetPixelShader(NULL);

        // we must also disable the depth buffer for stream-out only
        SetDepthStencilState(DisableDepth, 0);
    }
}

//***********************************************
// DRAW TECH                                    *
//***********************************************

struct VertexOut
{
```

```
    float3 PosW  : POSITION;
    float2 SizeW : SIZE;
    float4 Color : COLOR;
    uint   Type  : TYPE;
};

VertexOut DrawVS(Particle vin)
{
    VertexOut vout;

    float t = vin.Age;

    // constant acceleration equation
    vout.PosW = 0.5f*t*t*gAccelW + t*vin.InitialVelW + vin.InitialPosW;

    // fade color with time
    float opacity = 1.0f - smoothstep(0.0f, 1.0f, t/1.0f);
    vout.Color = float4(1.0f, 1.0f, 1.0f, opacity);

    vout.SizeW = vin.SizeW;
    vout.Type  = vin.Type;

    return vout;
}

struct GeoOut
{
    float4 PosH  : SV_Position;
    float4 Color : COLOR;
    float2 Tex   : TEXCOORD;
};

// The draw GS just expands points into camera facing quads.
[maxvertexcount(4)]
void DrawGS(point VertexOut gin[1],
    inout TriangleStream<GeoOut> triStream)
{
    // do not draw emitter particles.
    if(gin[0].Type != PT_EMITTER)
    {
      //
      // Compute world matrix so that billboard faces the camera.
      //
      float3 look  = normalize(gEyePosW.xyz - gin[0].PosW);
      float3 right = normalize(cross(float3(0,1,0), look));
      float3 up    = cross(look, right);

      //
      // Compute triangle strip vertices (quad) in world space.
      //
      float halfWidth  = 0.5f*gin[0].SizeW.x;
      float halfHeight = 0.5f*gin[0].SizeW.y;

      float4 v[4];
```

```
     v[0] = float4(gin[0].PosW + halfWidth*right - halfHeight*up, 1.0f);
     v[1] = float4(gin[0].PosW + halfWidth*right + halfHeight*up, 1.0f);
     v[2] = float4(gin[0].PosW - halfWidth*right - halfHeight*up, 1.0f);
     v[3] = float4(gin[0].PosW - halfWidth*right + halfHeight*up, 1.0f);

     //
     // Transform quad vertices to world space and output
     // them as a triangle strip.
     //
     GeoOut gout;
     [unroll]
     for(int i = 0; i < 4; ++i)
     {
       gout.PosH  = mul(v[i], gViewProj);
       gout.Tex   = gQuadTexC[i];
       gout.Color = gin[0].Color;
       triStream.Append(gout);
     }
   }
}

float4 DrawPS(GeoOut pin) : SV_TARGET
{
     return gTexArray.Sample(samLinear, float3(pin.Tex, 0))*pin.Color;
}

technique11 DrawTech
{
    pass P0
    {
      SetVertexShader(CompileShader(vs_5_0, DrawVS()));
      SetGeometryShader(CompileShader(gs_5_0, DrawGS()));
      SetPixelShader(CompileShader(ps_5_0, DrawPS()));

      SetBlendState(AdditiveBlending, float4(0.0f, 0.0f, 0.0f, 0.0f), 0xffffffff);
      SetDepthStencilState(NoDepthWrites, 0);
    }
}
```

20.8 RAIN

We also implement a rain particle system. The behavior of the rain particle system is specified by the rain effect (*rain.fx*). It follows a similar pattern to *fire.fx*, but the destroy/spawn/rendering rules are different. For example, our rain drops accelerate downward at a slight angle, whereas the fire particles accelerated upward. Moreover, the rain particles are expanded into lines instead of quads (see Figure 20.6). The rain particles are emitted at random positions above the camera; the rain always "follows" the camera so that we do not have to emit rain particles all over the world. That is, just emitting rain particles near the camera

Figure 20.6. Screenshot of particle system demo showing rain.

is enough to give the illusion it is raining. Note that the rain system does not use any blending.

```
//************************************************
// GLOBALS                                       *
//************************************************

cbuffer cbPerFrame
{
    float3 gEyePosW;

    // for when the emit position/direction is varying
    float3 gEmitPosW;
    float3 gEmitDirW;

    float gGameTime;
    float gTimeStep;
    float4x4 gViewProj;
};

cbuffer cbFixed
{
    // Net constant acceleration used to accerlate the particles.
    float3 gAccelW = {-1.0f, -9.8f, 0.0f};
};

// Array of textures for texturing the particles.
Texture2DArray gTexArray;

// Random texture used to generate random numbers in shaders.
Texture1D gRandomTex;
```

```
SamplerState samLinear
{
    Filter = MIN_MAG_MIP_LINEAR;
    AddressU = WRAP;
    AddressV = WRAP;
};

DepthStencilState DisableDepth
{
    DepthEnable = FALSE;
    DepthWriteMask = ZERO;
};

DepthStencilState NoDepthWrites
{
    DepthEnable = TRUE;
    DepthWriteMask = ZERO;
};

//************************************************
// HELPER FUNCTIONS                              *
//************************************************
float3 RandUnitVec3(float offset)
{
    // Use game time plus offset to sample random texture.
    float u = (gGameTime + offset);

    // coordinates in [-1,1]
    float3 v = gRandomTex.SampleLevel(samLinear, u, 0).xyz;

    // project onto unit sphere
    return normalize(v);
}

float3 RandVec3(float offset)
{
    // Use game time plus offset to sample random texture.
    float u = (gGameTime + offset);

    // coordinates in [-1,1]
    float3 v = gRandomTex.SampleLevel(samLinear, u, 0).xyz;

    return v;
}

//************************************************
// STREAM-OUT TECH                               *
//************************************************

#define PT_EMITTER 0
#define PT_FLARE 1

struct Particle
{
    float3 InitialPosW : POSITION;
```

```
        float3 InitialVelW : VELOCITY;
        float2 SizeW       : SIZE;
        float Age          : AGE;
        uint Type          : TYPE;
};

Particle StreamOutVS(Particle vin)
{
    return vin;
}


// The stream-out GS is just responsible for emitting
// new particles and destroying old particles.  The logic
// programed here will generally vary from particle system
// to particle system, as the destroy/spawn rules will be
// different.
[maxvertexcount(6)]
void StreamOutGS(point Particle gin[1],
    inout PointStream<Particle> ptStream)
{
    gin[0].Age += gTimeStep;

    if(gin[0].Type == PT_EMITTER)
    {
      // time to emit a new particle?
      if(gin[0].Age > 0.002f)
      {
        for(int i = 0; i < 5; ++i)
        {
          // Spread rain drops out above the camera.
          float3 vRandom = 35.0f*RandVec3((float)i/5.0f);
          vRandom.y = 20.0f;

          Particle p;
          p.InitialPosW = gEmitPosW.xyz + vRandom;
          p.InitialVelW = float3(0.0f, 0.0f, 0.0f);
          p.SizeW       = float2(1.0f, 1.0f);
          p.Age         = 0.0f;
          p.Type        = PT_FLARE;

          ptStream.Append(p);
        }

        // reset the time to emit
        gin[0].Age = 0.0f;
      }

      // always keep emitters
      ptStream.Append(gin[0]);
    }
    else
    {
      // Specify conditions to keep particle; this may vary
      // from system to system.
      if( gin[0].Age <= 3.0f )
```

```
                    ptStream.Append(gin[0]);
        }
}

GeometryShader gsStreamOut = ConstructGSWithSO(
    CompileShader(gs_5_0, StreamOutGS()),
    "POSITION.xyz; VELOCITY.xyz; SIZE.xy; AGE.x; TYPE.x");

technique11 StreamOutTech
{
    pass P0
    {
      SetVertexShader(CompileShader(vs_5_0, StreamOutVS()));
      SetGeometryShader(gsStreamOut);

      // disable pixel shader for stream-out only
      SetPixelShader(NULL);

      // we must also disable the depth buffer for stream-out only
      SetDepthStencilState(DisableDepth, 0);
    }
}

//***********************************************
// DRAW TECH                                    *
//***********************************************

struct VertexOut
{
    float3 PosW  : POSITION;
    uint    Type  : TYPE;
};

VertexOut DrawVS(Particle vin)
{
    VertexOut vout;

    float t = vin.Age;

    // constant acceleration equation
    vout.PosW = 0.5f*t*t*gAccelW + t*vin.InitialVelW + vin.InitialPosW;

    vout.Type  = vin.Type;

    return vout;
}

struct GeoOut
{
    float4 PosH  : SV_Position;
    float2 Tex   : TEXCOORD;
};

// The draw GS just expands points into lines.
[maxvertexcount(2)]
```

```
void DrawGS(point VertexOut gin[1],
    inout LineStream<GeoOut> lineStream)
{
    // do not draw emitter particles.
    if(gin[0].Type != PT_EMITTER)
    {
        // Slant line in acceleration direction.
        float3 p0 = gin[0].PosW;
        float3 p1 = gin[0].PosW + 0.07f*gAccelW;

        GeoOut v0;
        v0.PosH = mul(float4(p0, 1.0f), gViewProj);
        v0.Tex = float2(0.0f, 0.0f);
        lineStream.Append(v0);

        GeoOut v1;
        v1.PosH = mul(float4(p1, 1.0f), gViewProj);
        v1.Tex  = float2(1.0f, 1.0f);
        lineStream.Append(v1);
    }
}

float4 DrawPS(GeoOut pin) : SV_TARGET
{
    return gTexArray.Sample(samLinear, float3(pin.Tex, 0));
}

technique11 DrawTech
{
    pass P0
    {
        SetVertexShader(CompileShader(vs_5_0, DrawVS()));
        SetGeometryShader(CompileShader(gs_5_0, DrawGS()));
        SetPixelShader(CompileShader(ps_5_0, DrawPS()));

        SetDepthStencilState(NoDepthWrites, 0);
    }
}
```

20.9 SUMMARY

1. A particle system is a collection of particles (usually small) that all behave in a similar, yet somewhat random, manner. Particle systems can be utilized to simulate a wide range of phenomena such as fire, rain, smoke, explosions, sprinklers, and magic spell effects.

2. We model our particles by points, but then expand them into quads that face the camera in the geometry shader prior to rendering. This means that we get the efficiency of working with a point: smaller memory footprint and we only have to apply physics to one point vertex instead of four quad vertices,

but furthermore, by later expanding the point into a quad we also get the ability to have different sized particles and to map textures on to them. Note that it is not necessary to expand a point into a quad. For example, lines can be used to model raindrops fairly well; we can use a different geometry to expand points to lines.

3. The trajectory of a particle undergoing constant acceleration is given by $\mathbf{p}(t) = \frac{1}{2}t^2\mathbf{a} + t\mathbf{v}_0 + \mathbf{p}_0$, where $\mathbf{a}$ is the constant acceleration vector, $\mathbf{v}_0$ is the initial velocity of the particle (i.e., the velocity at time $t = 0$), and $\mathbf{p}_0$ is the initial position of the particle (i.e., the position at time $t = 0$). With this equation, we can get the position of the particle at any time $t \geq 0$ by evaluating the function at t.

4. Use additive blending when you want the intensity of a particle system to be proportional with the particle density. Use transparency blending for transparent particles. Not sorting a transparent particle system in back to front order may or may not be a problem (i.e., the problems may or may not be noticeable). Commonly for particle systems, depth writes are disabled so that particles do not obscure each other. The depth test, however, is still enabled so that non-particle objects do obscure particles.

5. The stream-out (SO) stage allows the GPU to write geometry (in the form of a vertex list) to a vertex buffer V bound to the SO stage of the pipeline. Specifically, the vertices output from the geometry shader are written (or streamed-out) to V. The geometry in V can then be drawn later. We use this stream-out feature to implement a particle system that runs completely on the GPU. To do this, we use two techniques:

(a) A stream-out only technique used to update the particle system. In this rendering pass, the geometry shader spawns/destroys/updates particles based on various conditions that vary from particle system to particle system. The living particles are then streamed-out to a vertex buffer.

(b) A rendering technique used to draw the particle system. In this rendering pass, we draw the living particles that were streamed-out.

20.10 EXERCISES

1. Implement an explosion particle system where the emitter emits n shell particles in random directions. After a brief time, each shell particle should then explode into m particles. Each shell need not explode at the exact same time—to add some variety you can give them different countdown times. Experiment with

different *n* and *m* until you get good results. Note that after the emitter spawns the shell particles, destroy it so that no more shells are emitted.

2. Implement a fountain particle system. The particles should originate from a source point and emit randomly through a cone into the air. Eventually gravity should make them fall back to the ground. Note: Give the particles a high enough initial velocity magnitude to initially overcome gravity.

Chapter **21** # SHADOW MAPPING

Shadows indicate to the observer where light originates and help convey the relative locations of objects in a scene. This chapter provides an introduction to the basic shadow mapping algorithm, which is a popular method for modeling dynamic shadows in games and 3D applications. For an introductory book, we focus only on the basic shadow mapping algorithm; more sophisticated shadowing techniques, such as cascading shadow maps [Engel06] which give better quality results, are built by extending the basic shadow mapping algorithm.

Objectives:

1. To discover the basic shadow mapping algorithm.
2. To learn how projective texturing works.
3. To find out about orthographic projections.
4. To understand shadow map aliasing problems and common strategies for fixing them.

21.1 RENDERING SCENE DEPTH

The shadow mapping algorithm relies on rendering the scene depth from the viewpoint of the light source—this is essentially a variation of render-to-texture, which was first described in §12.7.2. By "rendering scene depth" we mean building the depth buffer from the viewpoint of the light source. Thus, after we have rendered the scene from the viewpoint of the light source, we will know the pixel fragments nearest to the light source—such fragments cannot be in shadow. In this section we review a utility class called ShadowMap that helps us store the scene depth from the perspective of the light source. It simply encapsulates a depth/stencil buffer, necessary views, and viewport. A depth/stencil buffer used for shadow mapping is called a *shadow map*.

```
class ShadowMap
{
public:
    ShadowMap(ID3D11Device* device, UINT width, UINT height);
    ~ShadowMap();

    ID3D11ShaderResourceView* DepthMapSRV();

    void BindDsvAndSetNullRenderTarget(ID3D11DeviceContext* dc);
private:
    ShadowMap(const ShadowMap& rhs);
    ShadowMap& operator=(const ShadowMap& rhs);

private:
    UINT mWidth;
    UINT mHeight;

    ID3D11ShaderResourceView* mDepthMapSRV;
    ID3D11DepthStencilView* mDepthMapDSV;

    D3D11_VIEWPORT mViewport;
};
```

The constructor creates the texture of the specified dimensions, views, and viewport. The resolution of the shadow map affects the quality of our shadows, but at the same time, a high resolution shadow map is more expensive to render into and requires more memory.

```
ShadowMap::ShadowMap(ID3D11Device* device, UINT width, UINT height)
: mWidth(width), mHeight(height), mDepthMapSRV(0), mDepthMapDSV(0)
{
    // Viewport that matches the shadow map dimensions.
    mViewport.TopLeftX = 0.0f;
    mViewport.TopLeftY = 0.0f;
    mViewport.Width    = static_cast<float>(width);
    mViewport.Height   = static_cast<float>(height);
    mViewport.MinDepth = 0.0f;
    mViewport.MaxDepth = 1.0f;
```

```
// Use typeless format because the DSV is going to interpret
// the bits as DXGI_FORMAT_D24_UNORM_S8_UINT, whereas the SRV is going
// to interpret the bits as DXGI_FORMAT_R24_UNORM_X8_TYPELESS.
D3D11_TEXTURE2D_DESC texDesc;
texDesc.Width      = mWidth;
texDesc.Height     = mHeight;
texDesc.MipLevels = 1;
texDesc.ArraySize = 1;
texDesc.Format     = DXGI_FORMAT_R24G8_TYPELESS;
texDesc.SampleDesc.Count    = 1;
texDesc.SampleDesc.Quality = 0;
texDesc.Usage            = D3D11_USAGE_DEFAULT;
texDesc.BindFlags        = D3D11_BIND_DEPTH_STENCIL |
                           D3D11_BIND_SHADER_RESOURCE;
texDesc.CPUAccessFlags = 0;
texDesc.MiscFlags      = 0;

ID3D11Texture2D* depthMap = 0;
HR(device->CreateTexture2D(&texDesc, 0, &depthMap));

D3D11_DEPTH_STENCIL_VIEW_DESC dsvDesc;
dsvDesc.Flags = 0;
dsvDesc.Format = DXGI_FORMAT_D24_UNORM_S8_UINT;
dsvDesc.ViewDimension = D3D11_DSV_DIMENSION_TEXTURE2D;
dsvDesc.Texture2D.MipSlice = 0;
HR(device->CreateDepthStencilView(depthMap, &dsvDesc,
&mDepthMapDSV));

D3D11_SHADER_RESOURCE_VIEW_DESC srvDesc;
srvDesc.Format = DXGI_FORMAT_R24_UNORM_X8_TYPELESS;
srvDesc.ViewDimension = D3D11_SRV_DIMENSION_TEXTURE2D;
srvDesc.Texture2D.MipLevels = texDesc.MipLevels;
srvDesc.Texture2D.MostDetailedMip = 0;
HR(device->CreateShaderResourceView(depthMap, &srvDesc,
&mDepthMapSRV));

// View saves a reference to the texture so we can release our
// reference.
ReleaseCOM(depthMap);
}
```

As we will see, the shadow mapping algorithm requires two render passes. In the first one, we render the scene depth from the viewpoint of the light into the shadow map; in the second pass, we render the scene as normal to the back buffer from our "player" camera, but use the shadow map as a shader input to implement the shadowing algorithm. We provide a method to access the shader resource view to the shadow map:

```
ID3D11ShaderResourceView* ShadowMap::DepthMapSRV()
{
    return mDepthMapSRV;
}
```

Finally, the following method prepares the OM stage for rendering to the shadow map. Observe that we set a null render target, which essentially disables color writes. This is because when we render the scene to the shadow map, all we care about is the depth values of the scene relative to the light source. Graphics cards are optimized for only drawing depth; a depth only render pass is significantly faster than drawing color and depth.

```
void ShadowMap::BindDsvAndSetNullRenderTarget(ID3D11DeviceContext* dc)
{
    dc->RSSetViewports(1, &mViewport);

    // Set null render target because we are only going to draw
    // to depth buffer.  Setting a null render target will disable
    // color writes.
    ID3D11RenderTargetView* renderTargets[1] = {0};
    dc->OMSetRenderTargets(1, renderTargets, mDepthMapDSV);

    dc->ClearDepthStencilView(mDepthMapDSV, D3D11_CLEAR_DEPTH, 1.0f, 0);
}
```

After we are done drawing to the shadow map, it is the responsibility of the calling application to restore the back buffer as the render target, the original depth/stencil buffer, and original viewport.

Note: *A better design for working with multiple render targets would be to implement a stack so that you can push and pop render targets. Popping would automatically restore the previous render targets, depth/stencil buffer, and viewport.*

21.2 ORTHOGRAPHIC PROJECTIONS

So far in this book we have been using a perspective projection. The key property of perspective projection is that objects are perceived as getting smaller as their distance from the eye increases. This agrees with how we perceive things in real life. Another type of projection is an orthographic projection. Such projections are primarily used in 3D science or engineering applications, where it is desirable to have parallel lines remain parallel after projection. However, orthographic projections will enable us to model shadows that parallel lights generate. With an orthographic projection, the viewing volume is a box axis-aligned with the view space with width w, height h, near plane n, and far plane f that looks down the positive z-axis of view space (see Figure 21.1). These numbers, defined relative to the view space coordinate system, define the box view volume.

With an orthographic projection, the lines of projection are parallel to the view space z-axis (Figure 21.2). And we see that the 2D projection of a vertex (x, y, z) is just (x, y).

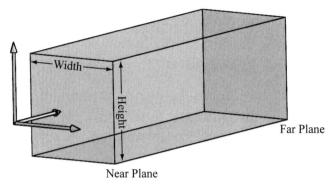

Figure 21.1. The orthographic viewing volume is a box that is axis aligned with the view coordinate system.

As with perspective projection, we want to maintain relative depth information, and we want normalized device coordinates. To transform the view volume from view space to NDC space, we need to rescale and shift to map the view space view volume $\left[-\frac{w}{2},\frac{w}{2}\right]\times\left[-\frac{h}{2},\frac{h}{2}\right]\times\left[n,f\right]$ to the NDC space view volume $\left[-1,1\right]\times\left[-1,1\right]\times\left[0,1\right]$. We can determine this mapping by working coordinate-by-coordinate. For the first two coordinates, it is easy to see that the intervals differ only by a scaling factor:

$$\frac{2}{w}\cdot\left[-\frac{w}{2},\frac{w}{2}\right]=\left[-1,1\right]$$

$$\frac{2}{h}\cdot\left[-\frac{h}{2},\frac{h}{2}\right]=\left[-1,1\right]$$

For the third coordinate, we need to map $[n,f]\rightarrow[0,1]$. We assume the mapping takes the form $g(z)=az+b$ (i.e., a scaling and translation). We have the conditions $g(n)=0$ and $g(f)=1$, which allow us to solve for a and b:

$$an+b=0$$
$$af+b=1$$

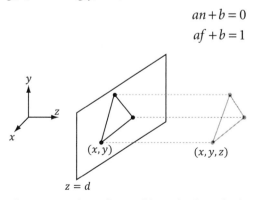

Figure 21.2. The orthographic projection of points onto the projection plane. The lines of projection are parallel to the view space z-axis with an orthographic projection.

The first equation implies $b = -an$. Plugging this into the second equation we get:

$$af - an = 1$$

$$a = \frac{1}{f-n}$$

And so:

$$-\frac{n}{f-n} = b$$

Thus,

$$g(z) = \frac{z}{f-n} - \frac{n}{f-n}$$

The reader may wish to graph $g(z)$ over the domain $[n, f]$ for various n and f such that $f > n$.

Finally, the orthographic transformation from view space coordinates (x, y, z) to NDC space coordinates (x', y', z') is:

$$x' = \frac{2}{w}x$$

$$y' = \frac{2}{h}y$$

$$z' = \frac{z}{f-n} - \frac{n}{f-n}$$

Or in terms of matrices:

$$[x', y', z', 1] = [x, y, z, 1]\begin{bmatrix} \frac{2}{w} & 0 & 0 & 0 \\ 0 & \frac{2}{h} & 0 & 0 \\ 0 & 0 & \frac{1}{f-n} & 0 \\ 0 & 0 & \frac{n}{n-f} & 1 \end{bmatrix}$$

The 4×4 matrix in the above equation is the *orthographic projection matrix*.

Recall that with the perspective projection transform, we had to split it into two parts: a linear part described by the projection matrix, and a nonlinear part described by the divide by w. In contrast, the orthographic projection transformation is completely linear—there is no divide by w. Multiplying by the orthographic projection matrix takes us directly into NDC coordinates.

21.3 PROJECTIVE TEXTURE COORDINATES

Projective texturing is so-called because it allows us to project a texture onto arbitrary geometry, much like a slide projector. Figure 21.3 shows an example of projective texturing.

Projective texturing can be useful on its own for modeling slide projector lights, but as we will see in §21.4, it is also used as an intermediate step for shadow mapping.

The key to projective texturing is to generate texture coordinates for each pixel in such a way that the applied texture looks like it has been projected onto the geometry. We will call such generated texture coordinates *projective texture coordinates*.

From Figure 21.4, we see that the texture coordinates (u, v) identify the texel that should be projected onto the 3D point **p**. But the coordinates (u, v) precisely identify the projection of **p** on the projection window, relative to a texture space coordinate system on the projection window. So the strategy of generating projective texture coordinates is as follows:

1. Project the point **p** onto the light's projection window and transform the coordinates to NDC space.

2. Transform the projected coordinates from NDC space to texture space, thereby effectively turning them into texture coordinates.

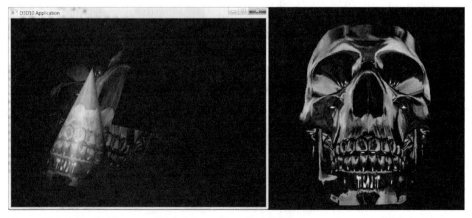

Figure 21.3. The skull texture (right) is projected onto the scene geometry (left).

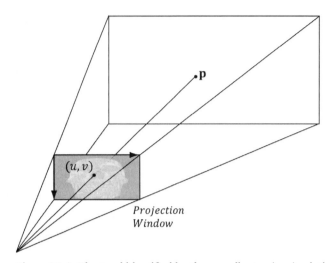

Figure 21.4. The texel identified by the coordinates (*u*, *v*) relative to the texture space on the projection window is projected onto the point p by following the line of sight from the light origin to the point p.

Step 1 can be implemented by thinking of the light projector as a camera. We define a view matrix $\mathbf{V}$ and projection matrix $\mathbf{P}$ for the light projector. Together, these matrices essentially define the position, orientation, and frustum of the light projector in the world. The matrix $\mathbf{V}$ transforms coordinates from world space to the coordinate system of the light projector. Once the coordinates are relative to the light coordinate system, the projection matrix, along with the homogeneous divide, are used to project the vertices onto the projection plane of the light. Recall from §5.6.3.5 that after the homogeneous divide, the coordinates are in NDC space.

Step 2 is accomplished by transforming from NDC space to texture space via the following change of coordinate transformation:

$$u = 0.5x + 0.5$$
$$v = -0.5y + 0.5$$

Here, $u, v \in [0,1]$ provided $x, y \in [-1,1]$. We scale the y-coordinate by a negative to invert the axis because the positive y-axis in NDC coordinates goes in the direction opposite to the positive v-axis in texture coordinates. The texture space transformations can be written in terms of matrices (recall Exercise 21 from Chapter 3):

$$\begin{bmatrix} x & y & 0 & 1 \end{bmatrix} \begin{bmatrix} 0.5 & 0 & 0 & 0 \\ 0 & -0.5 & 0 & 0 \\ 0 & 0 & 1 & 0 \\ 0.5 & 0.5 & 0 & 1 \end{bmatrix} = \begin{bmatrix} u & v & 0 & 1 \end{bmatrix}$$

Let us call the previous matrix **T** for "texture matrix" that transforms from NDC space to texture space. We can form the composite transform **VPT** that takes us from world space directly to texture space. After we multiply by this transform, we still need to do the perspective divide to complete the transformation; see Chapter 5, Exercise 8 for why we can do the perspective divide after doing the texture transform.

21.3.1 Code Implementation

The code for generating projective texture coordinates is shown as follows:

```
struct VertexOut
{
    float4 PosH      : SV_POSITION;
    float3 PosW      : POSITION;
    float3 TangentW  : TANGENT;
    float3 NormalW   : NORMAL;
    float2 Tex       : TEXCOORD0;
    float4 ProjTex   : TEXCOORD1;
};

VertexOut VS(VertexIn vin)
{
    VertexOut vout;

    [...]

    // Transform to light's projective space.
    vout.ProjTex = mul(float4(vIn.posL, 1.0f),
      gLightWorldViewProjTexture);

    [...]

    return vout;
}

float4 PS(VertexOut pin) : SV_Target
{
    // Complete projection by doing division by w.
    pin.ProjTex.xyz /= pin.ProjTex.w;

    // Depth in NDC space.
    float depth = pin.ProjTex.z;

    // Sample the texture using the projective tex-coords.
    float4 c = gTextureMap.Sample(sampler, pin.ProjTex.xy);

    [...]
}
```

21.3.2 Points Outside the Frustum

In the rendering pipeline, geometry outside the frustum is clipped. However, when we generate projective texture coordinates by projecting the geometry from the point of view of the light projector, no clipping is done—we simply project vertices. Consequently, geometry outside the projector's frustum receives projective texture coordinates outside the [0, 1] range. Projective texture coordinates outside the [0, 1] range function just like normal texture coordinates outside the [0, 1] range based on the enabled address mode (see (§8.8)) used when sampling the texture.

Generally, we do not want to texture any geometry outside the projector's frustum because it does not make sense (such geometry receives no light from the projector). Using the border color address mode with a zero color is a common solution. Another strategy is to associate a spotlight (see §7.10) with the projector so that anything outside the spotlight's field of view cone is not lit (i.e., the surface receives no projected light). The advantage of using a spotlight is that the light intensity from the projector is strongest at the center of the spotlight cone, and can smoothly fade out as the angle ϕ between $-\mathbf{L}$ and $\mathbf{d}$ increases (where $\mathbf{L}$ is the light vector to the surface point and $\mathbf{d}$ is the direction of the spotlight).

21.3.3 Orthographic Projections

So far we have illustrated projective texturing using perspective projections (frustum shaped volumes). However, instead of using a perspective projection for the projection process, we could have used an orthographic projection. In this case, the texture is projected in the direction of the z-axis of the light through a box.

Everything we have talked about with projective texture coordinates also applies when using an orthographic projection, except for a couple things. First, with an orthographic projection, the spotlight strategy used to handle points outside the projector's volume does not work. This is because a spotlight cone approximates the volume of a frustum to some degree, but it does not approximate a box. However, we can still use texture address modes to handle points outside the projector's volume. This is because an orthographic projection still generates NDC coordinates and a point (x, y, z) in NDC space is inside the volume if and only if:

$$-1 \leq x \leq 1$$
$$-1 \leq y \leq 1$$
$$0 \leq z \leq 1$$

Second, with an orthographic projection, we do not need to do the divide by w; that is, we do not need the line:

```
// Complete projection by doing division by w.
pin.ProjTex.xyz /= pin.ProjTex.w;
```

This is because after an orthographic projection, the coordinates are already in NDC space. This is faster, because it avoids the per-pixel division required for perspective projection. On the other hand, leaving in the division does not hurt because it divides by 1 (an orthographic projection does not change the w-coordinate, so w will be 1). If we leave the division by w in the shader code, then the shader code works for both perspective and orthographic projections uniformly. Though, the tradeoff for this uniformity is that you do a superfluous division with an orthographic projection.

21.4 SHADOW MAPPING

21.4.1 Algorithm Description

The idea of the shadow mapping algorithm is to render-to-texture the scene depth from the viewpoint of the light into a depth buffer called a *shadow map*. After this is done, the shadow map will contain the depth values of all the visible pixels from the perspective of the light. (Pixels occluded by other pixels will not be in the shadow map because they will fail the depth test and either be overwritten or never written.)

To render the scene from the viewpoint of the light, we need to define a light view matrix that transforms coordinates from world space to the space of the light and a light projection matrix, which describes the volume that light emits through in the world. This can be either a frustum volume (perspective projection) or box volume (orthographic projection). A frustum light volume can be used to model spotlights by embedding the spotlight cone inside the frustum. A box light volume can be used to model parallel lights. However, the parallel light is now bounded and only passes through the box volume; therefore, it may only strike a subset of the scene (see Figure 21.5). For a light source that strikes the entire scene (such as the sun), we can make the light volume large enough to contain the entire scene.

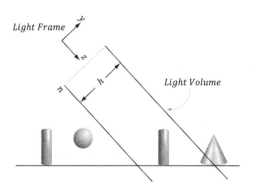

Figure 21.5. Parallel light rays travel through the light volume, so only a subset of the scene inside the volume receives light. If the light source needs to strike the entire scene, we can set the light volume size to contain the entire scene.

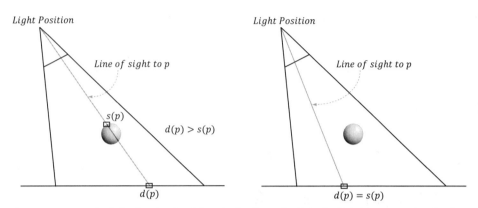

Figure 21.6. On the left, the depth of the pixel p from the light is $d(p)$. However, the depth of the pixel nearest to the light along the same line of sight has depth $s(p)$, and $d(p) > s(p)$. We conclude, therefore, that there is an object in front of p from the perspective of the light and so p is in shadow. On the right, the depth of the pixel p from the light is $d(p)$ and it also happens to be the pixel nearest to the light along the line of sight, that is, $s(p) = d(p)$, so we conclude p is not in shadow.

Once we have built the shadow map, we render the scene as normal from the perspective of the "player" camera. For each pixel p rendered, we also compute its depth from the light source, which we denote by $d(p)$. In addition, using projective texturing, we sample the shadow map along the line of sight from the light source to the pixel p to get the depth value $s(p)$ stored in the shadow map; this value is the depth of the pixel closest to the light along the line of sight from the position of the light to p. Then, from Figure 21.6, we see that a pixel p is in shadow if and only if $d(p) > s(p)$. Hence a pixel is not in shadow if and only if $d(p) \leq s(p)$.

Note: *The depth values compared are in NDC coordinates. This is because the shadow map, which is a depth buffer, stores the depth values in NDC coordinates. How this is done exactly will be clear when we look at the code.*

21.4.2 Biasing and Aliasing

The shadow map stores the depth of the nearest visible pixels with respect to its associated light source. However, the shadow map only has some finite resolution. So each shadow map texel corresponds to an area of the scene. Thus, the shadow map is just a discrete sampling of the scene depth from the light perspective. This causes aliasing issues known as *shadow acne* (see Figure 21.7).

Figure 21.7. Notice the aliasing on the floor plane with the "stair-stepping" alternation between light and shadow. This aliasing error is often called shadow acne.

Figure 21.8 shows a simple diagram to explain why shadow acne occurs. A simple solution is to apply a constant bias to offset the shadow map depth. Figure 21.9 shows how this corrects the problem.

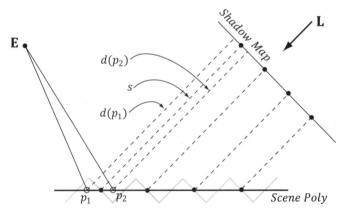

Figure 21.8. The shadow map samples the depth of the scene. Observe that due to finite resolution of the shadow map, each shadow map texel corresponds to an area of the scene. The eye E sees two points on the scene p_1 and p_2 that correspond to different screen pixels. However, from the viewpoint of the light, both points are covered by the same shadow map texel (that is, $s(p_1) = s(p_2) = s$). When we do the shadow map test, we have $d(p_1) > s$ and $d(p_2) \leq s$. Thus, p_1 will be colored as if it were in shadow, and p_2 will be colored as if it were not in shadow. This causes the shadow acne.

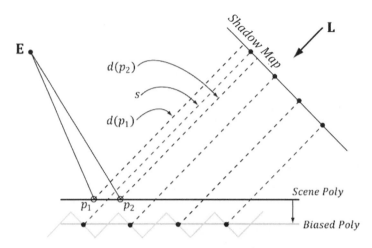

Figure 21.9. By biasing the depth values in the shadow map, no false shadowing occurs. We have that $d(p_1) \le s$ and $d(p_2) \le s$. Finding the right depth bias is usually done by experimentation.

Too much biasing results in an artifact called *peter-panning*, where the shadow appears to become detached from the object (see Figure 21.10).

Unfortunately, a fixed bias does not work for all geometry. In particular, Figure 21.11 shows that triangles with large slopes (with respect to the light source) need a larger bias. It is tempting to choose a large enough depth bias to handle all slopes. However, as Figure 21.10 showed, this leads to peter-panning.

Figure 21.10. Peter-panning—the shadow becomes detached from the column due to a large depth bias.

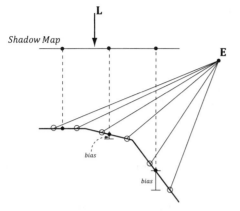

Figure 21.11. Polygons with large slopes, relative to the light source, require more bias than polygons with small slopes relative to the light source.

What we want is a way to measure the polygon slope with respect to the light source, and apply more bias for larger sloped polygons. Fortunately, graphics hardware has intrinsic support for this via the so-called *slope-scaled-bias* rasterization state properties:

```
typedef struct D3D11_RASTERIZER_DESC {
    [...]
    INT               DepthBias;
    FLOAT             DepthBiasClamp;
    FLOAT             SlopeScaledDepthBias;
    [...]
} D3D11_RASTERIZER_DESC;
```

1. `DepthBias`: A fixed bias to apply; see comments following for how this integer value is used for a UNORM depth buffer format.

2. `DepthBiasClamp`: A maximum depth bias allowed. This allows us to set a bound on the depth bias, for we can imagine that for very steep slopes, the bias slope-scaled-bias would be too much and cause peter-panning artifacts.

3. `SlopeScaledDepthBias`: A scale factor to control how much to bias based on the polygon slope; see comments following for the formula.

Note that we apply the slope-scaled-bias *when we are rendering the scene to the shadow map*. This is because we want to bias based on the polygon slope *with respect to the light source*. Consequently, we are biasing the shadow map values. In our demo we use the values:

```
RasterizerState Depth
{
    // [From MSDN]
    // If the depth buffer currently bound to the output-merger stage
```

```
        // has a UNORM format or no depth buffer is bound the bias value
        // is calculated like this:
        //
        // Bias = (float)DepthBias * r + SlopeScaledDepthBias *
        MaxDepthSlope;
        //
        // where r is the minimum representable value > 0 in the
        // depth-buffer format converted to float32.
        // [/End MSDN]
        //
        // For a 24-bit depth buffer, r = 1 / 2^24.
        //
        // Example: DepthBias = 100000 ==> Actual DepthBias = 100000/2^24 =
        .006

        // These values are highly scene dependent, and you will need
        // to experiment with these values for your scene to find the
        // best values.
        DepthBias = 100000;
        DepthBiasClamp = 0.0f;
        SlopeScaledDepthBias = 1.0f;
    };
```

> **Note:** *Depth bias happens during rasterization (after clipping), so does not affect geometry clipping.*

> **Note:** *For the complete details of depth bias, search the SDK documentation for "Depth Bias," and it will give all the rules for how it is applied, and how it works for floating-point depth buffers.*

21.4.3 PCF Filtering

The projective texture coordinates (u, v) used to sample the shadow map generally will not coincide with a texel in the shadow map. Usually, it will be between four texels. With color texturing, this is solved with bilinear interpolation (§8.4.1). However, [Kilgard01] points out that we should not average depth values, as it can lead to incorrect results about a pixel being flagged in shadow. (For the same reason, we also cannot generate mipmaps for the shadow map.) Instead of interpolating the depth values, we interpolate the results—this is called *percentage closer filtering (PCF)*. That is, we use point filtering (**MIN_MAG_MIP_POINT**) and sample the texture with coordinates (u, v), $(u + \Delta x, v)$, $(u, v + \Delta x)$, $(u + \Delta x, v + \Delta x)$, where $\Delta x = 1/\text{SHADOW\_MAP\_SIZE}$. Because we are using point sampling, these four points will hit the nearest four texels s_0, s_1, s_2, and s_3, respectively, surrounding (u, v), as shown in Figure 21.12. We then do the shadow map test for each of these sampled depths and bilinearly interpolate the shadow map results:

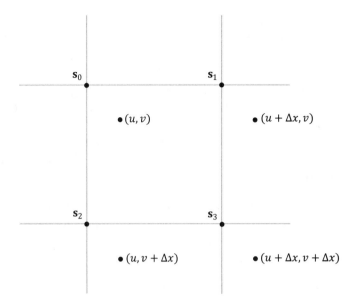

Figure 21.12. Taking four shadow map samples.

```
static const float SMAP_SIZE = 2048.0f;
static const float SMAP_DX = 1.0f / SMAP_SIZE;

...


// Sample shadow map to get nearest depth to light.
    float s0 = gShadowMap.Sample(gShadowSam,
      projTexC.xy).r;
    float s1 = gShadowMap.Sample(gShadowSam,
      projTexC.xy + float2(SMAP_DX, 0)).r;
    float s2 = gShadowMap.Sample(gShadowSam,
      projTexC.xy + float2(0, SMAP_DX)).r;
    float s3 = gShadowMap.Sample(gShadowSam,
      projTexC.xy + float2(SMAP_DX, SMAP_DX)).r;

    // Is the pixel depth <= shadow map value?
    float result0 = depth <= s0;
    float result1 = depth <= s1;
    float result2 = depth <= s2;
    float result3 = depth <= s3;

    // Transform to texel space.
    float2 texelPos = SMAP_SIZE*projTexC.xy;

    // Determine the interpolation amounts.
    float2 t = frac(texelPos);

    // Interpolate results.
    return lerp(lerp(result0, result1, t.x),
                lerp(result2, result3, t.x), t.y);
```

In this way, it is not an all-or-nothing situation; a pixel can be partially in shadow. For example, if two of the samples are in shadow and two are not in shadow, then the pixel is 50% in shadow. This creates a smoother transition from shadowed pixels to non-shadow pixels (see Figure 21.13).

The HLSL **frac** function returns the fractional part of a floating-point number (i.e., the mantissa). For example, if **SMAP_SIZE = 1024** and **projTex.xy = (0.23, 0.68)**, then **texelPos = (235.52, 696.32)** and **frac(texelPos) = (0.52, 0.32)**. These fractions tell us how much to interpolate between the samples. The HLSL **lerp(x, y, s)** function is the linear interpolation function and returns $x + s(y - x) = (1 - s)x + sy$.

> **Note:** *Even with our filtering, the shadows are still very hard and the aliasing artifacts can still be unsatisfactory close up. More aggressive methods can be used; see [Uralsky05], for example. We also note that using a higher-resolution shadow map helps, but can be cost prohibitive.*

The main disadvantage of PCF filtering as described previously is that it requires four texture samples. Sampling textures is one of the more expensive operations on a modern GPU because memory bandwidth and memory latency have not improved as much as the raw computational power of GPUs [Möller08]. Fortunately, Direct3D 11 graphics hardware has built in support for PCF via the **SampleCmpLevelZero** method:

Figure 21.13. In the top image, observe the "stairstepping" artifacts on the shadow boundary. On the bottom image, these aliasing artifacts are smoothed out a bit with filtering.

```
Texture2D gShadowMap;

SamplerComparisonState samShadow
{
    Filter   = COMPARISON_MIN_MAG_LINEAR_MIP_POINT;

    // Return 0 for points outside the light frustum
    // to put them in shadow.
    AddressU = BORDER;
    AddressV = BORDER;
    AddressW = BORDER;
    BorderColor = float4(0.0f, 0.0f, 0.0f, 0.0f);

    ComparisonFunc = LESS_EQUAL;
};

// Automatically does a 4-tap PCF.  The compare
percentLit = shadowMap.SampleCmpLevelZero(
samShadow, shadowPosH.xy, depth).r;
```

The Level Zero part of the method name means that it only looks at the top mipmap level, which is fine because that is what we want for shadow mapping (we do not generate a mipmap chain for the shadow map). This method does not use a typical sampler object, but instead uses a so-called *comparison sampler*. This is so that the hardware can do the shadow map comparison test, which needs to be done before filtering the results. For PCF, you need to use the filter COMPARISON_MIN_MAG_LINEAR_MIP_POINT and set the comparison function to LESS_EQUAL (LESS also works because we bias the depth). The first and second parameters are the comparison sampler and texture coordinates, respectively. The third parameter is the value to compare against the shadow map samples. So setting the compare value to depth and the comparison function to LESS_EQUAL we are doing the comparisons:

```
float result0 = depth <= s0;
float result1 = depth <= s1;
float result2 = depth <= s2;
float result3 = depth <= s3;
```

Then the hardware bilinearly interpolates the results to finish the PCF.

Note: *From the SDK documentation, only the following formats support comparison filters:* R32_FLOAT_X8X24_TYPELESS, R32_FLOAT, R24_UNORM_X8_TYPELESS, R16_UNORM.

So far in this section, we used a 4-tap PCF kernel. Larger kernels can be used to make the edges of shadows larger and even smoother, at the expense of extra SampleCmpLevelZero calls. In our demo, we call SampleCmpLevelZero in a 3 × 3 box filter pattern. Because each SampleCmpLevelZero call performs a 4-tap PCF, we are using 4 × 4 unique sample points from the shadow map (based on our pattern there is some overlap of sample points). Using large filtering kernels can cause the shadow acne problem to return; we explain why and describe a solution in §21.5.

An observation is that PCF really only needs to be performed at the shadow edges. Inside the shadow, there is no blending, and outside the shadow there is no blending. Based on this observation, methods have been devised to only do PCF at the shadow edges. [Isidoro06b] describes one way to do this. Such a technique requires a dynamic branch in the shader code: "If we are on a shadow edge, do expensive PCF, otherwise just take one shadow map sample."

Note that the extra expense of doing such a method makes it only worthwhile if your PCF kernel is large (say 5 × 5 or greater); however, this is just general advice and you will need to profile to verify the cost/benefit.

One final remark is that your PCF kernel need not be a box filter grid. Many articles have been written about randomly picking points to be in the PCF kernel.

21.4.4 Building the Shadow Map

The first step in shadow mapping is building the shadow map. To do this, we create a `ShadowMap` instance:

```
static const int SMapSize = 2048;
mSmap = new ShadowMap(md3dDevice, SMapSize, SMapSize);
```

We then define a light view matrix and projection matrix (representing the light frame and view volume). The light view matrix is derived from the primary light source, and the light view volume is computed to fit the bounding sphere of the entire scene.

```
// Estimate the scene bounding sphere manually since we know
// how the scene was constructed.  The grid is the "widest object"
// with a width of 20 and depth of 30.0f, and centered at the world
// space origin.  In general, you need to loop over every world space
// vertex position and compute the bounding sphere.

struct BoundingSphere
{
    BoundingSphere() : Center(0.0f, 0.0f, 0.0f), Radius(0.0f) {}
    XMFLOAT3 Center;
    float Radius;
};

BoundingSphere mSceneBounds;
mSceneBounds.Center = XMFLOAT3(0.0f, 0.0f, 0.0f);
mSceneBounds.Radius = sqrtf(10.0f*10.0f + 15.0f*15.0f);

void ShadowsApp::UpdateScene(float dt)
{
    [...]
```

```
    //
    // Animate the lights (and hence shadows).
    //

    mLightRotationAngle += 0.1f*dt;

    XMMATRIX R = XMMatrixRotationY(mLightRotationAngle);
    for(int i = 0; i < 3; ++i)
    {
      XMVECTOR lightDir = XMLoadFloat3(&mOriginalLightDir[i]);
      lightDir = XMVector3TransformNormal(lightDir, R);
      XMStoreFloat3(&mDirLights[i].Direction, lightDir);
    }

    BuildShadowTransform();
}

void ShadowsApp::BuildShadowTransform()
{
    // Only the first "main" light casts a shadow.
    XMVECTOR lightDir = XMLoadFloat3(&mDirLights[0].Direction);
    XMVECTOR lightPos = -2.0f*mSceneBounds.Radius*lightDir;
    XMVECTOR targetPos = XMLoadFloat3(&mSceneBounds.Center);
    XMVECTOR up = XMVectorSet(0.0f, 1.0f, 0.0f, 0.0f);

    XMMATRIX V = XMMatrixLookAtLH(lightPos, targetPos, up);

    // Transform bounding sphere to light space.
    XMFLOAT3 sphereCenterLS;
    XMStoreFloat3(&sphereCenterLS, XMVector3TransformCoord(targetPos,
    V));

    // Ortho frustum in light space encloses scene.
    float l = sphereCenterLS.x - mSceneBounds.Radius;
    float b = sphereCenterLS.y - mSceneBounds.Radius;
    float n = sphereCenterLS.z - mSceneBounds.Radius;
    float r = sphereCenterLS.x + mSceneBounds.Radius;
    float t = sphereCenterLS.y + mSceneBounds.Radius;
    float f = sphereCenterLS.z + mSceneBounds.Radius;
    XMMATRIX P = XMMatrixOrthographicOffCenterLH(l, r, b, t, n, f);

    // Transform NDC space [-1,+1]^2 to texture space [0,1]^2
    XMMATRIX T(
      0.5f, 0.0f, 0.0f, 0.0f,
      0.0f, -0.5f, 0.0f, 0.0f,
      0.0f, 0.0f, 1.0f, 0.0f,
      0.5f, 0.5f, 0.0f, 1.0f);

    XMMATRIX S = V*P*T;

    XMStoreFloat4x4(&mLightView, V);
    XMStoreFloat4x4(&mLightProj, P);
    XMStoreFloat4x4(&mShadowTransform, S);
}
```

Rendering the scene into the shadow map is done like so:

```
mSmap->BindDsvAndSetNullRenderTarget(md3dImmediateContext);

DrawSceneToShadowMap();

md3dImmediateContext->RSSetState(0);

//
// Restore the back and depth buffer to the OM stage.
//
ID3D11RenderTargetView* renderTargets[1] = {mRenderTargetView};
md3dImmediateContext->OMSetRenderTargets(1, renderTargets, mDepthStencilView);
md3dImmediateContext->RSSetViewports(1, &mScreenViewport);
```

The effect file we use for rendering the scene from the perspective of the light is quite simple because we are only building the shadow map, so we do not need to do any complicated pixel shader work.

```
cbuffer cbPerFrame
{
    float4x4 gLightWVP;
};

// Nonnumeric values cannot be added to a cbuffer.
Texture2D gDiffuseMap;

SamplerState samLinear
{
    Filter = MIN_MAG_MIP_LINEAR;
    AddressU = Wrap;
    AddressV = Wrap;
};

struct VertexIn
{
    float3 PosL     : POSITION;
    float3 NormalL  : NORMAL;
    float2 Tex      : TEXCOORD;
};

struct VertexOut
{
    float4 PosH : SV_POSITION;
    float2 Tex  : TEXCOORD;
};

VertexOut VS(VertexIn vin)
{
    VertexOut vout;

    vout.PosH = mul(float4(vin.PosL, 1.0f), gWorldViewProj);
    vout.Tex  = mul(float4(vin.Tex, 0.0f, 1.0f), gTexTransform).xy;

    return vout;
}
```

```
// This is only used for alpha cut out geometry, so that shadows
// show up correctly.  Geometry that does not need to sample a
// texture can use a NULL pixel shader for depth pass.
void PS(VertexOut pin)
{
    float4 diffuse = gDiffuseMap.Sample(samLinear, pin.Tex);

    // Don't write transparent pixels to the shadow map.
    clip(diffuse.a - 0.15f);
}
RasterizerState Depth
{
// [From MSDN]
// If the depth buffer currently bound to the output-merger stage has a UNORM
// format or no depth buffer is bound the bias value is calculated like this:
//
// Bias = (float)DepthBias * r + SlopeScaledDepthBias * MaxDepthSlope;
//
// where r is the minimum representable value > 0 in the depth-buffer format
// converted to float32.
// [/End MSDN]
//
// For a 24-bit depth buffer, r = 1 / 2^24.
//
// Example: DepthBias = 100000 ==> Actual DepthBias = 100000/2^24 = .006

    // You need to experiment with these values for your scene.
    DepthBias = 100000;
    DepthBiasClamp = 0.0f;
    SlopeScaledDepthBias = 1.0f;
};

technique11 BuildShadowMapTech
{
    pass P0
    {
      SetVertexShader(CompileShader(vs_5_0, VS()));
      SetGeometryShader(NULL);
      SetPixelShader(NULL);

    SetRasterizerState(Depth);
    }
}

technique11 BuildShadowMapAlphaClipTech
{
    pass P0
    {
      SetVertexShader(CompileShader(vs_5_0, VS()));
      SetGeometryShader(NULL);
      SetPixelShader(CompileShader(ps_5_0, PS()));
    }
}
```

Figure 21.14. **Leaf texture.**

Notice that the pixel shader does not return a value because we only need to output depth values. The pixel shader is solely used to clip pixel fragments with zero or low alpha values, which we assume indicate complete transparency. For example, consider the tree leaf texture in Figure 21.14; here, we only want to draw the pixels with white alpha values to the shadow map. To facilitate this, we provide two techniques: one that does the alpha clip operation, and one that does not. If the alpha clip does not need to be done, then we can bind a null pixel shader, which would be even faster than binding a pixel shader that only samples a texture and performs a clip operation.

> **Note:** *Although not shown for brevity, the shaders for rendering the depth for tessellated geometry are slightly more involved. When drawing tessellated geometry into the shadow map, we need to tessellate the geometry the same way we tessellate it when being drawn into the back buffer (i.e., based on the distance to the player's eye). This is for consistency; the geometry the eye sees should be the same that the light sees. That being said, if the tessellated geometry is not displaced too much, the displacement might not even be noticeable in the shadows; therefore, a possible optimization may be not to tessellate the geometry when rendering the shadow map. This optimization trades accuracy for speed.*

21.4.5 The Shadow Factor

The shadow factor is a new factor we add to the lighting equation. The shadow factor is a scalar in the range 0 to 1. A value of 0 indicates a point is in shadow, and a value of 1 indicates a point is not in shadow. With PCF (§21.4.3), a point can also be partially in shadow, in which case the shadow factor will be between 0 and 1. The `CalcShadowFactor` implementation is in *LightHelper.fx*.

```
static const float SMAP_SIZE = 2048.0f;
static const float SMAP_DX = 1.0f / SMAP_SIZE;
```

```
float CalcShadowFactor(SamplerComparisonState samShadow,
                       Texture2D shadowMap,
                       float4 shadowPosH)
{
    // Complete projection by doing division by w.
    shadowPosH.xyz /= shadowPosH.w;

    // Depth in NDC space.
    float depth = shadowPosH.z;

    // Texel size.
    const float dx = SMAP_DX;

    float percentLit = 0.0f;
    const float2 offsets[9] =
    {
      float2(-dx,  -dx), float2(0.0f,  -dx), float2(dx,  -dx),
      float2(-dx, 0.0f), float2(0.0f, 0.0f), float2(dx, 0.0f),
      float2(-dx,  +dx), float2(0.0f,  +dx), float2(dx,  +dx)
    };

    // 3x3 box filter pattern.  Each sample does a 4-tap PCF.
    [unroll]
    for(int i = 0; i < 9; ++i)
    {
      percentLit += shadowMap.SampleCmpLevelZero(samShadow,
        shadowPosH.xy + offsets[i], depth).r;
    }

    // Average the samples.
    return percentLit /= 9.0f;
}
```

In our model, the shadow factor will be multiplied against the diffuse and specular lighting terms:

```
// Only the first light casts a shadow.
float3 shadow = float3(1.0f, 1.0f, 1.0f);
shadow[0] = CalcShadowFactor(samShadow, gShadowMap, pin.ShadowPosH);

// Sum the light contribution from each light source.
[unroll]
for(int i = 0; i < gLightCount; ++i)
{
    float4 A, D, S;
    ComputeDirectionalLight(gMaterial, gDirLights[i],
bumpedNormalW, toEye, A, D, S);

    ambient += A;
    diffuse += shadow[i]*D;
    spec    += shadow[i]*S;
}
```

The shadow factor does not affect ambient light because that is indirect light, and it also does not affect reflective light coming from the environment map.

21.4.6 The Shadow Map Test

We now show the effect code used to draw the scene from the player camera viewpoint after the shadow map has been built. The key issue is computing $d(p)$ and $s(p)$ for each pixel p. The value $d(p)$ is found by transforming the point to the NDC space of the light; then the z-coordinate gives the normalized depth value of the point from the light source. The value is found by projecting the shadow map onto the scene through the light's view volume using projective texturing. Note that with this setup, both $d(p)$ and $s(p)$ are measured in the NDC space of the light, so they can be compared. The transformation matrix **gShadowTransform** transforms from local space to the shadow map texture space (§21.3).

The relevant code has been bolded.

```
#include "LightHelper.fx"

cbuffer cbPerFrame
{
    DirectionalLight gDirLights[3];
    float3 gEyePosW;

    float  gFogStart;
    float  gFogRange;
    float4 gFogColor;
};

cbuffer cbPerObject
{
    float4x4 gWorld;
    float4x4 gWorldInvTranspose;
    float4x4 gWorldViewProj;
    float4x4 gTexTransform;
    float4x4 gShadowTransform;
    Material gMaterial;
};

// Nonnumeric values cannot be added to a cbuffer.
Texture2D gShadowMap;
Texture2D gDiffuseMap;
Texture2D gNormalMap;

TextureCube gCubeMap;

SamplerState samLinear
{
    Filter = MIN_MAG_MIP_LINEAR;
    AddressU = WRAP;
    AddressV = WRAP;
};

SamplerComparisonState samShadow
{
```

```
    Filter   = COMPARISON_MIN_MAG_LINEAR_MIP_POINT;
    AddressU = BORDER;
    AddressV = BORDER;
    AddressW = BORDER;
    BorderColor = float4(0.0f, 0.0f, 0.0f, 0.0f);

    ComparisonFunc = LESS_EQUAL;
};

struct VertexIn
{
    float3 PosL      : POSITION;
    float3 NormalL   : NORMAL;
    float2 Tex       : TEXCOORD;
    float3 TangentL  : TANGENT;
};

struct VertexOut
{
    float4 PosH        : SV_POSITION;
    float3 PosW        : POSITION;
    float3 NormalW     : NORMAL;
    float3 TangentW    : TANGENT;
    float2 Tex         : TEXCOORD0;
    float4 ShadowPosH  : TEXCOORD1;
};

VertexOut VS(VertexIn vin)
{
    VertexOut vout;

    // Transform to world space space.
    vout.PosW     = mul(float4(vin.PosL, 1.0f), gWorld).xyz;
    vout.NormalW  = mul(vin.NormalL, (float3x3)gWorldInvTranspose);
    vout.TangentW = mul(vin.TangentL, (float3x3)gWorld);

    // Transform to homogeneous clip space.
    vout.PosH = mul(float4(vin.PosL, 1.0f), gWorldViewProj);

    // Output vertex attributes for interpolation across triangle.
    vout.Tex = mul(float4(vin.Tex, 0.0f, 1.0f), gTexTransform).xy;

    // Generate projective tex-coords to project shadow map onto scene.
    vout.ShadowPosH = mul(float4(vin.PosL, 1.0f), gShadowTransform);

    return vout;
}

float4 PS(VertexOut pin,
    uniform int gLightCount,
    uniform bool gUseTexure,
    uniform bool gAlphaClip,
    uniform bool gFogEnabled,
    uniform bool gReflectionEnabled) : SV_Target
{
```

```
// Interpolating normal can unnormalize it, so normalize it.
pin.NormalW = normalize(pin.NormalW);

// The toEye vector is used in lighting.
float3 toEye = gEyePosW - pin.PosW;

// Cache the distance to the eye from this surface point.
float distToEye = length(toEye);

// Normalize.
toEye /= distToEye;

// Default to multiplicative identity.
float4 texColor = float4(1, 1, 1, 1);
if(gUseTexure)
{
  // Sample texture.
  texColor = gDiffuseMap.Sample(samLinear, pin.Tex);

  f(gAlphaClip)
  {
    // Discard pixel if texture alpha < 0.1.  Note that we
    // do this test as soon as possible so that we can
    // potentially exit the shader early, thereby skipping
    // the rest of the shader code.
    clip(texColor.a - 0.1f);
  }
}

//
// Normal mapping
//

float3 normalMapSample = gNormalMap.Sample(samLinear, pin.Tex).rgb;
float3 bumpedNormalW = NormalSampleToWorldSpace(
        normalMapSample, pin.NormalW, pin.TangentW);

//
// Lighting.
//

float4 litColor = texColor;
if(gLightCount > 0)
{
  // Start with a sum of zero.
  float4 ambient = float4(0.0f, 0.0f, 0.0f, 0.0f);
  float4 diffuse = float4(0.0f, 0.0f, 0.0f, 0.0f);
  float4 spec    = float4(0.0f, 0.0f, 0.0f, 0.0f);

  // Only the first light casts a shadow.
  float3 shadow = float3(1.0f, 1.0f, 1.0f);
  shadow[0] = CalcShadowFactor(samShadow, gShadowMap, pin.ShadowPosH);

  // Sum the light contribution from each light source.
  [unroll]
```

```
    for(int i = 0; i < gLightCount; ++i)
    {
      float4 A, D, S;
      ComputeDirectionalLight(gMaterial, gDirLights[i],
            bumpedNormalW, toEye, A, D, S);

      ambient += A;
      diffuse += shadow[i]*D;
      spec    += shadow[i]*S;
    }

    litColor = texColor*(ambient + diffuse) + spec;

    if(gReflectionEnabled)
    {
      float3 incident = -toEye;
      float3 reflectionVector = reflect(incident, bumpedNormalW);
      float4 reflectionColor  = gCubeMap.Sample(
            samLinear, reflectionVector);

      litColor += gMaterial.Reflect*reflectionColor;
    }
  }

  //
  // Fogging
  //

  if(gFogEnabled)
  {
    float fogLerp = saturate((distToEye - gFogStart) / gFogRange);

    // Blend the fog color and the lit color.
    litColor = lerp(litColor, gFogColor, fogLerp);
  }

  // Common to take alpha from diffuse material and texture.
  litColor.a = gMaterial.Diffuse.a * texColor.a;

  return litColor;
}
```

21.4.7 Rendering the Shadow Map

For this demo, we also render the shadow map onto a quad that occupies the lower-right corner of the screen. This allows us to see what the shadow map looks like for each frame. Recall that the shadow map is just a depth buffer texture with the D3D11_BIND_SHADER_RESOURCE flag, so it can also be used to texture a surface. The shadow map is rendered as a grayscale image because it stores a one-dimensional value at each pixel (a depth value). Figure 21.15 shows a screenshot of the "Shadow Map" demo.

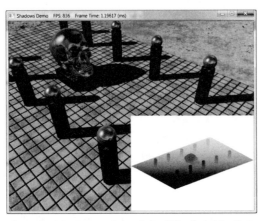

Figure 21.15. Screenshot of the "Shadow Map" demo.

21.5 LARGE PCF KERNELS

In this section, we discuss when a problem occurs when using a large PCF kernel. Our demos do not use a large PCF kernel, so this section is in some sense optional, but it introduces some interesting ideas.

Refer to Figure 21.16, where we are computing the shadow test for a pixel p visible by the eye. With no PCF, we compute the distance $d = d(p)$ of p from the light source and compare it to the corresponding shadow map value $s_0 = s(p)$. With PCF, we also compare neighboring shadow map values s_{-1} and s_1 against d. However, it is

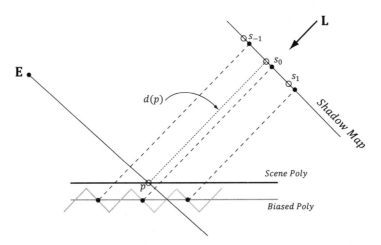

Figure 21.16. Comparing the depth $d(p)$ with s_0 is correct, because the texel s_0 covers the scene area p is contained in. However, it is not correct to compare $d(p)$ with s_{-1} and s_1, as those texels cover areas of the scene that are unrelated to p.

not valid to compare d with s_{-1} and s_1. The texels s_{-1} and s_1 describe the depths of different areas of the scene that may or may not be on the same polygon as p.

The scenario in Figure 21.16 actually results in an error in the PCF. Specifically, when we do the shadow map test we compute:

$$lit_0 = d \leq s_0 \, (true)$$
$$lit_{-1} = d \leq s_{-1} \, (true)$$
$$lit_1 = d \leq s_1 \, (false)$$

When the results are interpolated, we get that p is 1/3rd in shadow, which is incorrect as nothing is occluding p.

Observe from Figure 21.16 that more depth biasing would fix the error. However, in this example, we are only sampling the next door neighbor texels in the shadow map. If we widen the PCF kernel, then even more biasing is needed. Thus for small PCF kernels, simply doing the depth bias as explained in §21.4.2 is enough to counter this problem and it is nothing to worry about. But for large PCF kernels such as 5×5 or 9×9, which are used to make soft shadows, this can become a real problem.

21.5.1 The DDX and DDY Functions

Before we can look at an approximate solution to this problem, we first need to discuss the ddx and ddy HLSL functions. These functions estimate $\partial \mathbf{p}/\partial x$ and $\partial \mathbf{p}/\partial y$, respectively, where x is the screen space x-axis and y is the screen space y-axis. With these functions you can determine how per pixel quantities $\mathbf{p}$ vary from pixel to pixel. Examples of what the derivative functions could be used for:

1. Estimate how colors are changing pixel by pixel.
2. Estimate how depths are changing pixel by pixel.
3. Estimate how normals are changing pixel by pixel.

How the hardware estimates these partial derivatives is not complicated. The hardware processes pixels in 2×2 quads at a time in parallel. Then the partial derivative in the x-direction can be estimated by the forward difference equation $q_{x+1,y} - q_{x,y}$ (estimates how the quantity q changes from pixel (x, y) to pixel $(x+1, y)$), and similarly for the partial derivative in the y direction.

21.5.2 Solution to the Large PCF Kernel Problem

The solution we describe is from [Tuft10]. The strategy is to make the assumption that the neighboring pixels of p lie on the same plane as p. This assumption is not always true, but it is the best we have to work with.

Let $\mathbf{p} = (u, v, z)$ be the coordinates in light space. The coordinates (u, v) are used to index into the shadow map, and the value z is the distance from the light source used in the shadow map test. We can compute the vectors $\frac{\partial \mathbf{p}}{\partial x} = \left(\frac{\partial u}{\partial x}, \frac{\partial v}{\partial x}, \frac{\partial z}{\partial x}\right)$ and $\frac{\partial \mathbf{p}}{\partial y} = \left(\frac{\partial u}{\partial y}, \frac{\partial v}{\partial y}, \frac{\partial z}{\partial y}\right)$ with ddx and ddy, which lie in the tangent plane of the polygon. This tells us how we move in light space when we move in screen space. In particular, if we move $(\Delta x, \Delta y)$ units in screen space, we move $\Delta x \left(\frac{\partial u}{\partial x}, \frac{\partial v}{\partial x}, \frac{\partial z}{\partial x}\right) + \Delta y \left(\frac{\partial u}{\partial y}, \frac{\partial v}{\partial y}, \frac{\partial z}{\partial y}\right)$ units in light space in the directions of the tangent vectors. Ignoring the depth term for the moment, if we move $(\Delta x, \Delta y)$ units in screen space, we move $\Delta x \left(\frac{\partial u}{\partial x}, \frac{\partial v}{\partial x}\right) + \Delta y \left(\frac{\partial u}{\partial y}, \frac{\partial v}{\partial y}\right)$ units in light space *on the uv-plane*; this can be expressed by the matrix equation:

$$[\Delta x, \Delta y] \begin{bmatrix} \dfrac{\partial u}{\partial x} & \dfrac{\partial v}{\partial x} \\ \dfrac{\partial u}{\partial y} & \dfrac{\partial v}{\partial y} \end{bmatrix} = \Delta x \left(\frac{\partial u}{\partial x}, \frac{\partial v}{\partial x}\right) + \Delta y \left(\frac{\partial u}{\partial y}, \frac{\partial v}{\partial y}\right) = [\Delta u, \Delta v]$$

Therefore,

$$[\Delta x, \Delta y] = [\Delta u, \Delta v] \begin{bmatrix} \dfrac{\partial u}{\partial x} & \dfrac{\partial v}{\partial x} \\ \dfrac{\partial u}{\partial y} & \dfrac{\partial v}{\partial y} \end{bmatrix}^{-1}$$

$$= [\Delta u, \Delta v] \frac{1}{\dfrac{\partial u}{\partial x}\dfrac{\partial v}{\partial y} - \dfrac{\partial v}{\partial x}\dfrac{\partial u}{\partial y}} \begin{bmatrix} \dfrac{\partial v}{\partial y} & -\dfrac{\partial v}{\partial x} \\ -\dfrac{\partial u}{\partial y} & \dfrac{\partial u}{\partial x} \end{bmatrix} \qquad \text{(eq. 21.1)}$$

Recall from Chapter 2 that

$$\begin{bmatrix} A_{11} & A_{12} \\ A_{21} & A_{22} \end{bmatrix}^{-1} = \frac{1}{A_{11}A_{22} - A_{12}A_{21}} \begin{bmatrix} A_{22} & -A_{12} \\ -A_{21} & A_{11} \end{bmatrix}$$

This new equation tells us that if we move $(\Delta u, \Delta v)$ units in light space on the *uv-plane*, then we move $(\Delta x, \Delta y)$ units in screen space. So why is Equation 21.1 important to us? Well, when we build our PCF kernel, we offset our texture coordinates to sample neighboring values in the shadow map:

```
// Texel size.
   const float dx = SMAP_DX;

   float percentLit = 0.0f;
   const float2 offsets[9] =
```

```
{
    float2(-dx,   -dx), float2(0.0f,   -dx), float2(dx,   -dx),
    float2(-dx,  0.0f), float2(0.0f,  0.0f), float2(dx,  0.0f),
    float2(-dx,  +dx), float2(0.0f,  +dx), float2(dx,  +dx)
};

// 3x3 box filter pattern.  Each sample does a 4-tap PCF.
[unroll]
for(int i = 0; i < 9; ++i)
{
    percentLit += shadowMap.SampleCmpLevelZero(samShadow,
        shadowPosH.xy + offsets[i], depth).r;
}
```

In other words, we know how much we are displacing in light space in the *uv*-plane—we know $(\Delta u, \Delta v)$. Equation 21.1 tells us that when we move $(\Delta u, \Delta v)$ units in light space we are moving $(\Delta x, \Delta y)$ in screen space.

Now, let us return to the depth term we have been ignoring. If we move $(\Delta x, \Delta y)$ units in screen space, then the light space depth moves by $\Delta z = \Delta x \frac{\partial z}{\partial x} + \Delta y \frac{\partial z}{\partial y}$. Thus, when we offset our texture coordinates to do the PCF, we can modify the depth value used in the depth test accordingly: $z' = z + \Delta z$ (see Figure 21.17).

Let us summarize:

1. In our PCF implementation, we offset our texture coordinates to sample neighboring values in the shadow map. So for each sample, we know $(\Delta u, \Delta v)$.

2. We can use Equation 21.1 to find the screen space offset $(\Delta x, \Delta y)$ when we offset $(\Delta u, \Delta v)$ units in light space.

3. With $(\Delta x, \Delta y)$ solved for, apply $\Delta z = \Delta x \frac{\partial z}{\partial x} + \Delta y \frac{\partial z}{\partial y}$ to figure out the light space depth change.

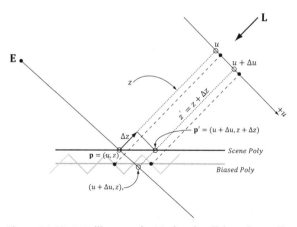

Figure 21.17. We illustrate in 2D for simplicity. If we offset from p = (*u*, *z*) by Δ*u* in the *u*-direction to get (*u* + Δ*u*, *z*), then we need to offset by Δ*z* in order to remain on the polygon to get p′ = (*u* + Δ*u*, *z*+Δ*z*).

The "CascadedShadowMaps11" demo in the DirectX 11 SDK implements this method in the `CalculateRightAndUpTexelDepthDeltas` and `CalculatePCFPercentLit` functions.

21.5.3 An Alternative Solution to the Large PCF Kernel Problem

This solution presented in [Isidoro06] is in the same spirit as the previous section, but takes a slightly different approach.

Let $\mathbf{p} = (u, v, z)$ be the coordinates in light space. The coordinates (u, v) are used to index into the shadow map, and the value z is the distance from the light source used in the shadow map test. We can compute $\frac{\partial \mathbf{p}}{\partial x} = \left(\frac{\partial u}{\partial x}, \frac{\partial v}{\partial x}, \frac{\partial z}{\partial x} \right)$ and $\frac{\partial \mathbf{p}}{\partial y} = \left(\frac{\partial u}{\partial y}, \frac{\partial v}{\partial y}, \frac{\partial z}{\partial y} \right)$ with `ddx` and `ddy`.

In particular, the fact that we can take these derivatives means $u = u(x, y), v = v(x, y)$, and $z = z(x, y)$ are all functions of x and y. However, we can also think of z as a function of u and v—that is, $z = z(u, v)$; as we move in light space in the u- and v-directions, the depth z changes along the polygon plane. By the chain rule, we have:

$$\frac{\partial z}{\partial x} = \frac{\partial z}{\partial u}\frac{\partial u}{\partial x} + \frac{\partial z}{\partial v}\frac{\partial v}{\partial x}$$

$$\frac{\partial z}{\partial y} = \frac{\partial z}{\partial u}\frac{\partial u}{\partial y} + \frac{\partial z}{\partial v}\frac{\partial v}{\partial y}$$

Or in matrix notation:

$$\begin{bmatrix} \dfrac{\partial z}{\partial x} & \dfrac{\partial z}{\partial y} \end{bmatrix} = \begin{bmatrix} \dfrac{\partial z}{\partial u} & \dfrac{\partial z}{\partial v} \end{bmatrix} \begin{bmatrix} \dfrac{\partial u}{\partial x} & \dfrac{\partial u}{\partial y} \\ \dfrac{\partial v}{\partial x} & \dfrac{\partial v}{\partial y} \end{bmatrix}$$

Taking the inverse yields:

$$\begin{bmatrix} \dfrac{\partial z}{\partial u} & \dfrac{\partial z}{\partial v} \end{bmatrix} = \begin{bmatrix} \dfrac{\partial z}{\partial x} & \dfrac{\partial z}{\partial y} \end{bmatrix} \begin{bmatrix} \dfrac{\partial u}{\partial x} & \dfrac{\partial u}{\partial y} \\ \dfrac{\partial v}{\partial x} & \dfrac{\partial v}{\partial y} \end{bmatrix}^{-1}$$

$$= \frac{\begin{bmatrix} \dfrac{\partial z}{\partial x} & \dfrac{\partial z}{\partial y} \end{bmatrix}}{\dfrac{\partial u}{\partial x}\dfrac{\partial v}{\partial y} - \dfrac{\partial u}{\partial y}\dfrac{\partial v}{\partial x}} \begin{bmatrix} \dfrac{\partial v}{\partial y} & -\dfrac{\partial u}{\partial y} \\ -\dfrac{\partial v}{\partial x} & \dfrac{\partial u}{\partial x} \end{bmatrix}$$

We now have solved for $\frac{\partial z}{\partial u}$ and $\frac{\partial z}{\partial v}$ directly (everything on the right-side of the equation is known). If we move $(\Delta u, \Delta v)$ units in light space on the *uv-plane*, then the light space depth moves by $\Delta z = \Delta u \frac{\partial z}{\partial u} + \Delta v \frac{\partial z}{\partial v}$.

So with this approach, we do not have to transform to screen space, but can stay in light space—the reason being that we figured out directly how depth changes when u and v change, whereas in the previous section, we only knew how depth changed when x and y changed in screen space.

21.6 SUMMARY

1. The back buffer need not always be the render target; we can render to a different texture. Rendering to texture provides an efficient way for the GPU to update the contents of a texture at runtime. After we have rendered to a texture, we can bind the texture as a shader input and map it onto geometry. Many special effects require render to texture functionality like shadow maps, water simulations, and general purpose GPU programming.

2. With an orthographic projection, the viewing volume is a box (see Figure 21.1) with width w, height h, near plane n, and far plane f, and the lines of projection are parallel to the view space z-axis. Such projections are primarily used in 3D science or engineering applications, where it is desirable to have parallel lines remain parallel after projection. However, we can use orthographic projections to model shadows that parallel lights generate.

3. Projective texturing is so-called because it allows us to project a texture onto arbitrary geometry, much like a slide projector. The key to projective texturing is to generate texture coordinates for each pixel in such a way that the applied texture looks like it has been projected onto the geometry. Such texture coordinates are called *projective texture coordinates*. We obtain the projective texture coordinates for a pixel by projecting it onto the projection plane of the projector, and then mapping it to the texture coordinate system.

4. Shadow mapping is a real-time shadowing technique, which shadows arbitrary geometry (it is not limited to planar shadows). The idea of shadow mapping is to render the depth of the scene from the light's viewpoint into a shadow map; thus, after which, the shadow map stores the depth of all pixels visible from the light's perspective. We then render the scene again from the camera's perspective, and we project the shadow map onto the scene using projective texturing. Let $s(p)$ be the depth value projected onto a pixel p from the shadow map and let $d(p)$ be the depth of the pixel from the light source. Then p is in shadow if $d(p) > s(p)$; that is, if the depth of the pixel is greater than the

projected pixel depth $s(p)$, then there must exist a pixel closer to the light which occludes p, thereby casting p in shadow.

5. Aliasing is the biggest challenge with shadow maps. The shadow map stores the depth of the nearest visible pixels with respect to its associated light source. However, the shadow map only has some finite resolution. So each shadow map texel corresponds to an area of the scene. Thus, the shadow map is just a discrete sampling of the scene depth from the light perspective. This causes aliasing issues known as *shadow acne*. Using the graphics hardware intrinsic support for *slope-scaled-bias* (in the rasterization render state) is a common strategy to fix shadow acne. The finite resolution of the shadow map also causes aliasing at the shadow edges. PCF is a popular solution to this. More advanced solutions utilized for the aliasing problem are *cascaded shadow maps* and *variance shadow maps*.

21.7 EXERCISES

1. Write a program that simulates a slide projector by projecting a texture onto the scene. Experiment with both perspective and orthographic projections.

2. Modify the solution to the previous exercise by using texture address modes so that points outside the projector's frustum do not receive light.

3. Modify the solution to Exercise 1 by using a spotlight so that points outside the spotlight cone do not receive any light from the projector.

4. Modify this chapter's demo application by using a perspective projection. Note that the slope-scaled-bias that worked for an orthographic projection might not work well for a perspective projection. When using a perspective projection, notice that the depth map is heavily biased to white (1.0). Does this make sense considering the graph in Figure 5.25?

5. Experiment with the following shadow map resolutions: 4096×4096, 1024×1024, 512×512, 256×256. Be sure to also update the effect constants that depend on the size:

   ```
   static const float SMAP_SIZE = 2048.0f;
   static const float SMAP_DX = 1.0f / SMAP_SIZE;
   ```

6. Derive the matrix that maps the box $[l,r] \times [b,t] \times [n,f] \rightarrow [-1,1] \times [-1,1] \times [0,1]$. This is an "off center" orthographic view volume (i.e., the box is not centered about the view space origin). In contrast, the orthographic projection matrix derived in §21.2 is an "on center" orthographic view volume.

7. In Chapter 16 we learned about picking with a perspective projection matrix. Derive picking formulas for an off-centered orthographic projection.

8. Modify the "Shadow Demo" to use a single point sampling shadow test (i.e., no PCF). You should observe hard shadows and jagged shadow edges.

9. Turn off the slope-scaled-bias to observe shadow acne.

10. Modify the slope-scaled-bias to have a very large bias to observe the peter-panning artifact.

11. Study the tessellation code in *BuildShadowMap.fx* for how to tessellate geometry being rendered into the shadow map.

12. An orthographic projection can be used to generate the shadow map for directional lights, and a perspective projection can be used to generate the shadow map for spotlights. Explain how cube maps and six 90° field of view perspective projections can be used to generate the shadow map for a point light.

 Recall how dynamic cube maps were generated in Chapter 17.) Explain how the shadow map test would be done with a cube map.

Chapter 22 AMBIENT OCCLUSION

Due to performance constraints, it is common for real-time lighting models not to take indirect light (i.e., light that has bounced off other objects in the scene) into consideration. However, much light we see in the real world is indirect. In Chapter 7 we introduced the ambient term to the lighting equation:

$$\mathbf{A} = \mathbf{l}_a \otimes \mathbf{m}_a$$

The color $\mathbf{l}_a$ specifies the total amount of indirect (ambient) light a surface receives from a light source. The ambient material color $\mathbf{m}_a$ specifies the amount of incoming ambient light that the surface reflects and absorbs. All ambient light does is uniformly brighten up the object a bit—there is no real physics calculation at all. The idea is that the indirect light has scattered and bounced around the scene so many times that it strikes the object equally in every direction. Figure 22.1 shows that if we draw a model using only the ambient term, it is rendered out as a constant color.

Figure 22.1 makes it clear that our ambient term could use some improvement. In this chapter, we discuss the popular technique of ambient occlusion to improve our ambient term.

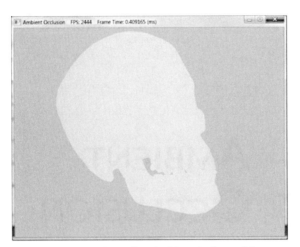

Figure 22.1. **A mesh rendered with only the ambient term appears as a solid color.**

Objectives:

1. To understand the basic idea behind ambient occlusion and how to implement ambient occlusion via ray casting.
2. To learn how to implement a real-time approximation of ambient occlusion in screen space called screen space ambient occlusion.

22.1 AMBIENT OCCLUSION VIA RAY CASTING

The idea of ambient occlusion is that the amount of indirect light a point **p** on a surface receives is proportional to how occluded it is to incoming light over the hemisphere about **p**—see Figure 22.2.

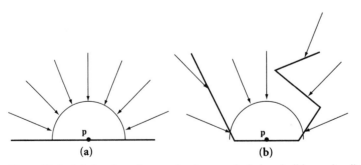

Figure 22.2. **(a) A point p is completely unoccluded and all incoming light over the hemisphere about p reaches p. (b) Geometry partially occludes p and blocks incoming light rays over the hemisphere about p.**

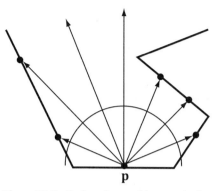

Figure 22.3. **Estimating ambient occlusion via ray casting.**

One way to estimate the occlusion of a point **p** is via ray casting. We randomly cast rays over the hemisphere about **p**, and check for intersections against the mesh (Figure 22.3). If we cast N rays, and h of them intersect the mesh, then the point has the occlusion value:

$$occlusion = \frac{h}{N} \in [0,1]$$

Only rays with an intersection point **q** whose distance from **p** is less than some threshold value d should contribute to the occlusion estimate; this is because an intersection point **q** far away from **p** is too far to occlude it.

The occlusion factor measures how occluded the point is (i.e., how much light it does not receive). For the purposes of calculations, we like to work with the inverse of this. That is, we want to know how much light the point does receive—this is called *accessibility* (or we call it ambient-access) and is derived from occlusion as:

$$accessiblity = 1 - occlusion \in [0, 1]$$

The "Ambient Occlusion" demo performs the ray cast per triangle, and then averages the occlusion results with the vertices that share the triangle. The ray origin is the triangle's centroid, and we generate a random ray direction over the hemisphere of the triangle.

```
void AmbientOcclusionApp::BuildVertexAmbientOcclusion(
    std::vector<Vertex::AmbientOcclusion>& vertices,
    const std::vector<UINT>& indices)
{
    UINT vcount = vertices.size();
    UINT tcount = indices.size()/3;

    std::vector<XMFLOAT3> positions(vcount);
    for(UINT i = 0; i < vcount; ++i)
        positions[i] = vertices[i].Pos;
```

```
Octree octree;
octree.Build(positions, indices);

// For each vertex, count how many triangles contain the vertex.
std::vector<int> vertexSharedCount(vcount);

// Cast rays for each triangle, and average triangle occlusion
0// with the vertices that share this triangle.
for(UINT i = 0; i < tcount; ++i)
{
  UINT i0 = indices[i*3+0];
  UINT i1 = indices[i*3+1];
  UINT i2 = indices[i*3+2];

  XMVECTOR v0 = XMLoadFloat3(&vertices[i0].Pos);
  XMVECTOR v1 = XMLoadFloat3(&vertices[i1].Pos);
  XMVECTOR v2 = XMLoadFloat3(&vertices[i2].Pos);

  XMVECTOR edge0 = v1 - v0;
  XMVECTOR edge1 = v2 - v0;

  XMVECTOR normal = XMVector3Normalize(
          XMVector3Cross(edge0, edge1));

  XMVECTOR centroid = (v0 + v1 + v2)/3.0f;

  // Offset to avoid self intersection.
  centroid += 0.001f*normal;

  const int NumSampleRays = 32;
  float numUnoccluded = 0;
  for(int j = 0; j < NumSampleRays; ++j)
  {
    XMVECTOR randomDir = MathHelper::RandHemisphereUnitVec3(normal);

    // Test if the random ray intersects the scene mesh.
    //
    // TODO: Technically we should not count intersections
    // that are far away as occluding the triangle, but
    // this is OK for demo.
    if(!octree.RayOctreeIntersect(centroid, randomDir))
    {
      numUnoccluded++;
    }
  }

  float ambientAccess = numUnoccluded / NumSampleRays;

  // Average with vertices that share this face.
  vertices[i0].AmbientAccess += ambientAccess;
  vertices[i1].AmbientAccess += ambientAccess;
  vertices[i2].AmbientAccess += ambientAccess;

  vertexSharedCount[i0]++;
  vertexSharedCount[i1]++;
  vertexSharedCount[i2]++;
}
```

```
// Finish average by dividing by the number of samples we added,
// and store in the vertex attribute.
for(UINT i = 0; i < vcount; ++i)
{
    vertices[i].AmbientAccess /= vertexSharedCount[i];
}
}
```

We are not going to go into detail of the "Ambient Occlusion" demo, as the ambient occlusion technique we really want is discussed in the next section. However, there are two points about the demo we will mention:

1. The demo uses an octree to speed up the ray/triangle intersection tests. For a mesh with thousands of triangles, it would be very slow to test each random ray with every mesh triangle. An octree sorts the triangles spatially, so we can quickly find only the triangles that have a good chance of intersecting the ray; this reduces the number of ray/triangle intersection tests substantially. An octree is a classic spatial data structure, and Exercise 1 asks you to research them further.

2. The demo uses the *xnacollision.h/cpp* utility library that was first mentioned in §15.2.1. These files are located at *Microsoft DirectX SDK (June 2010)\Samples\ C++\Misc\Collision*. They provide fast XNA math implementations to common geometric primitive intersection tests such as ray/triangle intersection, ray/ box intersection, box/box intersection, box/plane intersection, box/frustum, sphere/frustum, and much more.

Figure 22.4 shows a screenshot of a model rendered only with ambient occlusion generated by the previous algorithm (there are no light sources in the scene). The ambient occlusion is generated as a precomputation step during initialization

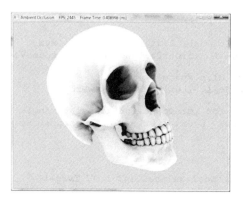

Figure 22.4. The mesh is rendered only with ambient occlusion—there are no scene lights. Notice how the crevices are darker; this is because when we cast rays out they are more likely to intersect geometry and contribute to occlusion. On the other hand, the skull cap is white (unoccluded) because when we cast rays out over the hemisphere for points on the skull cap, they will not intersect any geometry of the skull.

and stored as vertex attributes. As we can see, it is a huge improvement over Figure 22.1—the model actually looks 3D now.

Precomputing ambient occlusion works well for static models; there are even tools (http://www.xnormal.net) that generate *ambient occlusion maps*—textures that store ambient occlusion data. However, for animated models these static approaches break down. If you load and run the "Ambient Occlusion" demo, you will notice that it takes a few seconds to precompute the ambient occlusion for just one model. Hence, casting rays at runtime to implement dynamic ambient occlusion is not feasible. In the next section, we examine a popular technique for computing ambient occlusion in real-time using screen space information.

22.2 SCREEN SPACE AMBIENT OCCLUSION

The strategy of *screen space ambient occlusion* (SSAO) is, for every frame, render the scene view space normals and depths to a full screen render target, and then estimate the ambient occlusion at each pixel using only this render target as input.

22.2.1 Render Normals and Depth Pass

Render the scene to a screen-sized `DXGI_FORMAT_R16G16B16A16_FLOAT` normal/depth texture map, where RGB stores the view space normal and the alpha channel stores the view space depth (*z*-coordinate). The vertex/pixel shaders used for this pass are as follows:

```
VertexOut VS(VertexIn vin)
{
    VertexOut vout;

    // Transform to view space.
    vout.PosV   = mul(float4(vin.PosL, 1.0f), gWorldView).xyz;
    vout.NormalV = mul(vin.NormalL, (float3x3)gWorldInvTransposeView);

    // Transform to homogeneous clip space.
    vout.PosH = mul(float4(vin.PosL, 1.0f), gWorldViewProj);

    // Output vertex attributes for interpolation across triangle.
    vout.Tex = mul(float4(vin.Tex, 0.0f, 1.0f), gTexTransform).xy;

    return vout;
}

float4 PS(VertexOut pin, uniform bool gAlphaClip) : SV_Target
{
    // Interpolating normal can unnormalize it, so normalize it.
    pin.NormalV = normalize(pin.NormalV);

    if(gAlphaClip)
    {
        float4 texColor = gDiffuseMap.Sample(samLinear, pin.Tex);
```

```
        clip(texColor.a - 0.1f);
    }
    return float4(pin.NormalV, pin.PosV.z);
}
```

The vertex shader simply transforms the normal vector and position into view space. Then the view space normal and view space z-coordinate are written to the render target in the pixel shader. Observe that we are writing to floating-point render targets, so there is no problem writing out arbitrary floating-point data.

22.2.2 Ambient Occlusion Pass

After we have laid down the view space normals and depths to the render target, we disable the depth buffer (we do not need it for generating the ambient occlusion texture), and draw a full screen quad to invoke the SSAO pixel shader at each pixel. The pixel shader will then use the normal/depth buffer to generate an ambient accessibility value at each pixel. We call the generated texture map in this pass the *SSAO map*. Although we render the normal/depth map at full screen resolution (i.e., the resolution of our back buffer), we render to the SSAO map at half the width and height of the back buffer for performance reasons. Rendering at half the dimensions does not affect quality too much, as ambient occlusion is a low frequency effect. Refer to Figure 22.5 throughout the following subsections.

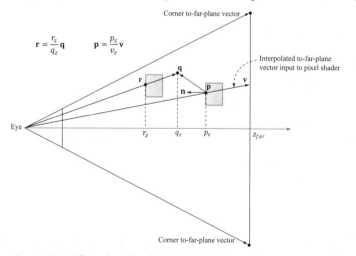

Figure 22.5. The points involved in SSAO. The point p corresponds to the current pixel we are processing, and it is reconstructed from the depth value stored in the normal/depth map and the interpolated to-far-plane vector v. The point q is a random point in the hemisphere of p. The point r corresponds to the nearest visible point along the ray from the eye to q. The point r contributes to the occlusion of p if $|p_z - r_z|$ is sufficiently small and the angle between r − p and n is less than 90°. In the demo, we take 14 random sample points and average the occlusion from each to estimate the ambient occlusion in screen space.

22.2.2.1 Reconstruct View Space Position

When we draw the full screen quad to invoke the SSAO pixel shader at each pixel of the SSAO map, we store at each of the four quad vertices an index to an array of far plane frustum corners. We fetch the frustum corner vector in the vertex shader and pass it on to the pixel shader. These to-far-plane vectors are interpolated and give us a vector **v** from the eye to the far plane for each pixel.

```
void Ssao::BuildFrustumFarCorners(float fovy, float farZ)
{
    float aspect = (float)mRenderTargetWidth / (float)mRenderTargetHeight;

    float halfHeight = farZ * tanf(0.5f*fovy);
    float halfWidth  = aspect * halfHeight;

    mFrustumFarCorner[0] = XMFLOAT4(-halfWidth, -halfHeight, farZ, 0.0f);
    mFrustumFarCorner[1] = XMFLOAT4(-halfWidth, +halfHeight, farZ, 0.0f);
    mFrustumFarCorner[2] = XMFLOAT4(+halfWidth, +halfHeight, farZ, 0.0f);
    mFrustumFarCorner[3] = XMFLOAT4(+halfWidth, -halfHeight, farZ, 0.0f);
}

cbuffer cbPerFrame
{
    float4    gFrustumCorners[4];

    . . .
};

VertexOut VS(VertexIn vin)
{
    VertexOut vout;

    // Already in NDC space.
    vout.PosH = float4(vin.PosL, 1.0f);

    // We store the index to the frustum corner in the normal x-coord slot.
    vout.ToFarPlane = gFrustumCorners[vin.ToFarPlaneIndex.x].xyz;

    // Pass onto pixel shader.
    vout.Tex = vin.Tex;

    return vout;
}
```

Now, for each pixel, we sample the normal/depth map so that we have the view space normal **n** and z-coordinate p_z of the nearest visible point to the eye. The goal is to reconstruct the view space position $\mathbf{p} = (p_x, p_y, p_z)$ from the sampled view space z-coordinate p_z and the interpolated to-far-plane vector **v**. This reconstruction is done as follows. Because the to-far-plane vector **v** passes through **p**, there exists a t such that $\mathbf{p} = t\mathbf{v}$. In particular, $p_z = tv_z$ so that $t = p_z/v_z$. Thus $\mathbf{p} = \frac{p_z}{v_z}\mathbf{v}$.

22.2.2.2 Generate Random Samples

This step is analogous to the random ray cast over the hemisphere. We randomly sample N points **q** about **p** that are also in front of **p** and within a specified occlusion radius. The occlusion radius is an artistic parameter to control how far away from **p** we want to take the random sample points. Choosing to only sample points in front of **p** is analogous to only casting rays over the hemisphere instead of the whole sphere when doing ray casted ambient occlusion.

The next question is how to generate the random samples. We can generate random vectors and store them in a texture map, and then sample this texture map at N different positions to get N random vectors. However, because they are random we have no guarantee that the vectors we sample will be uniformly distributed—they may all clump together in roughly the same direction. To overcome this, we do the following trick. In our implementation, we use $N = 14$ samples, and we generate 14 equally distributed vectors in the C++ code:

```cpp
void Ssao::BuildOffsetVectors()
{
    // Start with 14 uniformly distributed vectors.  We choose the
    // 8 corners of the cube and the 6 center points along each
    // cube face.  We always alternate the points on opposite sides
    // of the cubes.  This way we still get the vectors spread out
    // even if we choose to use less than 14 samples.

    // 8 cube corners
    mOffsets[0] = XMFLOAT4(+1.0f, +1.0f, +1.0f, 0.0f);
    mOffsets[1] = XMFLOAT4(-1.0f, -1.0f, -1.0f, 0.0f);

    mOffsets[2] = XMFLOAT4(-1.0f, +1.0f, +1.0f, 0.0f);
    mOffsets[3] = XMFLOAT4(+1.0f, -1.0f, -1.0f, 0.0f);

    mOffsets[4] = XMFLOAT4(+1.0f, +1.0f, -1.0f, 0.0f);
    mOffsets[5] = XMFLOAT4(-1.0f, -1.0f, +1.0f, 0.0f);

    mOffsets[6] = XMFLOAT4(-1.0f, +1.0f, -1.0f, 0.0f);
    mOffsets[7] = XMFLOAT4(+1.0f, -1.0f, +1.0f, 0.0f);

    // 6 centers of cube faces
    mOffsets[8] = XMFLOAT4(-1.0f, 0.0f, 0.0f, 0.0f);
    mOffsets[9] = XMFLOAT4(+1.0f, 0.0f, 0.0f, 0.0f);

    mOffsets[10] = XMFLOAT4(0.0f, -1.0f, 0.0f, 0.0f);
    mOffsets[11] = XMFLOAT4(0.0f, +1.0f, 0.0f, 0.0f);

    mOffsets[12] = XMFLOAT4(0.0f, 0.0f, -1.0f, 0.0f);
    mOffsets[13] = XMFLOAT4(0.0f, 0.0f, +1.0f, 0.0f);

    for(int i = 0; i < 14; ++i)
    {
```

```
    // Create random lengths in [0.25, 1.0].
    float s = MathHelper::RandF(0.25f, 1.0f);

    XMVECTOR v = s * XMVector4Normalize(XMLoadFloat4(&mOffsets[i]));

    XMStoreFloat4(&mOffsets[i], v);
    }
}
```

Note: *We use 4D homogeneous vectors just so we do not have to worry about any alignment issues when setting the array of offset vectors to the effect.*

Now, in the pixel shader we just sample the random vector texture map once, and use it to reflect our 14 equally distributed vectors. This results in 14 *equally distributed random vectors*.

22.2.2.3 Generate the Potential Occluding Points

We now have random sample points $\mathbf{q}$ surrounding $\mathbf{p}$. However, we know nothing about them—whether they occupy empty space or a solid object; therefore, we cannot use them to test if they occlude $\mathbf{p}$. To find potential occluding points, we need depth information from the normal/depth map. So what we do is generate projective texture coordinates for each $\mathbf{q}$ with respect to the camera, and use these to sample the normal/depth map to obtain the depth r_z of the nearest visible pixel along the ray from the eye to $\mathbf{q}$. With the z-coordinates r_z known, we can reconstruct the full 3D view space position $\mathbf{r}$ in an analogous way as we did in §22.2.2.1. Because the vector from the eye to $\mathbf{q}$ passes through $\mathbf{r}$ there exists a t such that $\mathbf{r} = t\mathbf{q}$. In particular, $r_z = tq_z$ so $t = r_z/q_z$. Therefore, $\mathbf{r} = \frac{r_z}{q_z}\mathbf{q}$. The points $\mathbf{r}$, one generated for each random sample point $\mathbf{q}$, are our potential occluding points.

22.2.2.4 Perform the Occlusion Test

Now that we have our potential occluding points $\mathbf{r}$, we can perform our occlusion test to estimate if they occlude $\mathbf{p}$. The test relies on two quantities:

1. The view space depth distance $|p_z - r_z|$. We linearly scale down the occlusion as the distance increases because points farther away have less of an occluding effect. If the distance is beyond some specified maximum distance, then no occlusion occurs. Also, if the distance is very small, then we assume $\mathbf{p}$ and $\mathbf{q}$ are on the same plane so $\mathbf{q}$ cannot occlude $\mathbf{p}$.

2. The angle between $\mathbf{n}$ and $\mathbf{r} - \mathbf{p}$ measured by $\max\left(\mathbf{n} \cdot \left(\frac{\mathbf{r}-\mathbf{p}}{\|\mathbf{r}-\mathbf{p}\|}\right), 0\right)$. This is to prevent self-intersection (see Figure 22.6).

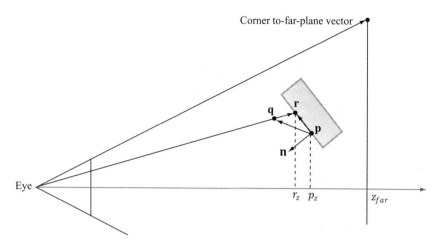

Figure 22.6. If r lies on the same plane as p, it can pass the first condition that the distance $|p_z - r_z|$ is small enough that r occludes p. However, the figure shows this is incorrect as r does not occlude p because they lie on the same plane. Scaling the occlusion by $\max\left(n \cdot \left(\frac{r-p}{\|r-p\|}\right), 0\right)$ prevents this situation.

22.2.2.5 Finishing the Calculation

After we have summed the occlusion from each sample, we compute the average occlusion by dividing by the sample count. Then we compute the ambient-access, and finally raise the ambient-access to a power to increase the contrast. You may also wish to increase the brightness of the ambient map by adding some number to increase the intensity. You can experiment with different contrast/brightness values.

```
occlusionSum /= gSampleCount;

float access = 1.0f - occlusionSum;

// Sharpen the contrast of the SSAO map to make the SSAO
// affect more dramatic.
return saturate(pow(access, 4.0f));
```

22.2.2.6 Implementation

The previous section outlined the key ingredients for generating the SSAO map. Following is the full effect code:

```
//=================================================================
// Ssao.fx by Frank Luna (C) 2011 All Rights Reserved.
//
// Computes SSAO map.
//=================================================================

cbuffer cbPerFrame
{
```

```
       float4x4 gViewToTexSpace; // Proj*Texture
       float4   gOffsetVectors[14];
       float4   gFrustumCorners[4];

       // Coordinates given in view space.
       float    gOcclusionRadius    = 0.5f;
       float    gOcclusionFadeStart  = 0.2f;
       float    gOcclusionFadeEnd    = 2.0f;
       float    gSurfaceEpsilon     = 0.05f;
   };

   // Nonnumeric values cannot be added to a cbuffer.
   Texture2D gNormalDepthMap;
   Texture2D gRandomVecMap;

   SamplerState samNormalDepth
   {
       Filter = MIN_MAG_LINEAR_MIP_POINT;

       // Set a very far depth value if sampling outside of
       // the NormalDepth map so we do not get false occlusions.
       AddressU = BORDER;
       AddressV = BORDER;
       BorderColor = float4(0.0f, 0.0f, 0.0f, 1e5f);
   };

   SamplerState samRandomVec
   {
       Filter = MIN_MAG_LINEAR_MIP_POINT;
       AddressU  = WRAP;
       AddressV  = WRAP;
   };

   struct VertexIn
   {
       float3 PosL             : POSITION;
       float3 ToFarPlaneIndex : NORMAL;
       float2 Tex              : TEXCOORD;
   };

   struct VertexOut
   {
       float4 PosH      : SV_POSITION;
       float3 ToFarPlane : TEXCOORD0;
       float2 Tex       : TEXCOORD1;
   };

   VertexOut VS(VertexIn vin)
   {
       VertexOut vout;

       // Already in NDC space.
       vout.PosH = float4(vin.PosL, 1.0f);

       // We store the index to the frustum corner in the normal x-coord slot.
       vout.ToFarPlane = gFrustumCorners[vin.ToFarPlaneIndex.x].xyz;
```

```
        // Pass onto pixel shader.
        vout.Tex = vin.Tex;

        return vout;
    }


    // Determines how much the sample point q occludes the point p as a function
    // of distZ.
    float OcclusionFunction(float distZ)
    {
    //
        // If depth(q) is "behind" depth(p), then q cannot occlude p.
        // Moreover, if depth(q) and depth(p) are sufficiently close,
        // then we also assume q cannot occlude p because q needs to
        // be in front of p by Epsilon to occlude p.
        //
        // We use the following function to determine the occlusion.
        //
        //
        //        1.0      -------------\
        //                 |           |  \
        //                 |           |   \
        //                 |           |    \
        //                 |           |     \
        //                 |           |      \
        //                 |           |       \
        //        ------|------|-----------|-------------|---------|--> zv
        //        0     Eps         z0           z1
        //

        float occlusion = 0.0f;
        if(distZ > gSurfaceEpsilon)
        {
            float fadeLength = gOcclusionFadeEnd - gOcclusionFadeStart;

            // Linearly decrease occlusion from 1 to 0 as distZ goes
            // from gOcclusionFadeStart to gOcclusionFadeEnd.
            occlusion = saturate((gOcclusionFadeEnd-distZ)/fadeLength);
        }

        return occlusion;
    }

    float4 PS(VertexOut pin, uniform int gSampleCount) : SV_Target
    {
        // p -- the point we are computing the ambient occlusion for.
        // n -- normal vector at p.
        // q -- a random offset from p.
        // r -- a potential occluder that might occlude p.

        // Get viewspace normal and z-coord of this pixel.  The tex-coords for
        // the fullscreen quad we drew are already in uv-space.
        float4 normalDepth = gNormalDepthMap.SampleLevel(
            samNormalDepth, pin.Tex, 0.0f);
```

```
float3 n = normalDepth.xyz;
float pz = normalDepth.w;

//
// Reconstruct full view space position (x,y,z).
// Find t such that p = t*pin.ToFarPlane.
// p.z = t*pin.ToFarPlane.z
// t = p.z / pin.ToFarPlane.z
//
float3 p = (pz/pin.ToFarPlane.z)*pin.ToFarPlane;

// Extract random vector and map from [0,1] --> [-1, +1].
float3 randVec = 2.0f*gRandomVecMap.SampleLevel(
  samRandomVec, 4.0f*pin.Tex, 0.0f).rgb - 1.0f;

float occlusionSum = 0.0f;

// Sample neighboring points about p in the hemisphere
// oriented by n.
[unroll]
for(int i = 0; i < gSampleCount; ++i)
{
  // Are offset vectors are fixed and uniformly
  // distributed (so that our offset vectors
  // do not clump in the same direction).  If we
  // reflect them about a random vector then we
  // get a random uniform distribution of offset vectors.
  float3 offset = reflect(gOffsetVectors[i].xyz, randVec);

  // Flip offset vector if it is behind the plane
  // defined by (p, n).
  float flip = sign(dot(offset, n));

  // Sample a point near p within the occlusion radius.
  float3 q = p + flip * gOcclusionRadius * offset;

  // Project q and generate projective tex-coords.
  float4 projQ = mul(float4(q, 1.0f), gViewToTexSpace);
  projQ /= projQ.w;

  // Find the nearest depth value along the ray from
  // the eye to q (this is not the depth of q, as q is
  // just an arbitrary point near p and might occupy
  // empty space).  To find the nearest depth we look
  // it up in the depthmap.

    float rz = gNormalDepthMap.SampleLevel(
      samNormalDepth, projQ.xy, 0.0f).a;

  // Reconstruct full view space position r = (rx,ry,rz).
  // We know r lies on the ray of q, so there exists a t
  // such that r = t*q.
  // r.z = t*q.z ==> t = r.z / q.z

  float3 r = (rz / q.z) * q;
```

```
//
// Test whether r occludes p.
//    * The product dot(n, normalize(r - p)) measures how
//        much in front of the plane(p,n) the occluder point
//        r is.   The more in front it is, the more occlusion
//        weight we give it.   This also prevents self shadowing
//        where a point r on an angled plane (p,n) could give a
//        false occlusion since they have different depth values
//        with respect to the eye.
//    * The weight of the occlusion is scaled based on how
//        far the occluder is from the point we are computing
//        the occlusion of.   If the occluder r is far away
//        from p, then it does not occlude it.
//

    float distZ = p.z - r.z;
    float dp = max(dot(n, normalize(r - p)), 0.0f);
    float occlusion = dp * OcclusionFunction(distZ);

    occlusionSum += occlusion;
}

occlusionSum /= gSampleCount;

float access = 1.0f - occlusionSum;

// Sharpen the contrast of the SSAO map to make the SSAO
// affect more dramatic.
return saturate(pow(access, 4.0f));

}

technique11 Ssao
{
    pass P0
    {
        SetVertexShader(CompileShader(vs_5_0, VS()));
        SetGeometryShader(NULL);
        SetPixelShader(CompileShader(ps_5_0, PS(14)));
    }
}
```

22.2.3 Blur Pass

Figure 22.7 shows what our ambient occlusion map currently looks like. The noise is due to the fact that we have only taken a few random samples. Taking enough samples to hide the noise is impractical for real-time. The common solution is to apply an edge preserving blur (i.e., bilateral blur) to the SSAO map to smooth it out. If we used a non-edge preserving blur, then we lose definition in the scene as sharp discontinuities become smoothed out. The edge preserving blur is similar to the blur we implemented in Chapter 12, except we add a conditional statement so that we do not blur across edges (edges are detected from the normal/depth map):

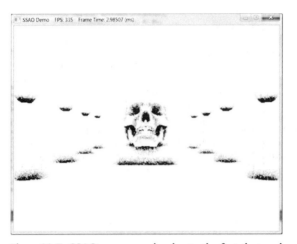

Figure 22.7. SSAO appears noisy due to the fact that we have only taken a few random samples.

```
//=====================================================================
// SsaoBlur.fx by Frank Luna (C) 2011 All Rights Reserved.
//
// Performs a bilateral edge preserving blur of the ambient map.  We use
// a pixel shader instead of compute shader to avoid the switch from
// compute mode to rendering mode.  The texture cache makes up for some
// of the loss of not having shared memory.  The ambient map uses
// 16-bit texture format, which is small, so we should be able to fit
// a lot of texels in the cache.
//=====================================================================

cbuffer cbPerFrame
{
    float gTexelWidth;
    float gTexelHeight;
};

cbuffer cbSettings
{
    float gWeights[11] =
    {
      0.05f, 0.05f, 0.1f, 0.1f, 0.1f, 0.2f, 0.1f,
      0.1f, 0.1f, 0.05f, 0.05f
    };
};

cbuffer cbFixed
{
    static const int gBlurRadius = 5;
};

// Nonnumeric values cannot be added to a cbuffer.
Texture2D gNormalDepthMap;
Texture2D gInputImage;
```

```
SamplerState samNormalDepth
{
    Filter = MIN_MAG_LINEAR_MIP_POINT;

    AddressU = CLAMP;
    AddressV = CLAMP;
};

SamplerState samInputImage
{
    Filter = MIN_MAG_LINEAR_MIP_POINT;

    AddressU  = CLAMP;
    AddressV  = CLAMP;
};

struct VertexIn
{
    float3 PosL    : POSITION;
    float3 NormalL : NORMAL;
    float2 Tex     : TEXCOORD;
};

struct VertexOut
{
    float4 PosH  : SV_POSITION;
    float2 Tex   : TEXCOORD;
};

VertexOut VS(VertexIn vin)
{
    VertexOut vout;

    // Already in NDC space.
    vout.PosH = float4(vin.PosL, 1.0f);

    // Pass onto pixel shader.
    vout.Tex = vin.Tex;

    return vout;
}

float4 PS(VertexOut pin, uniform bool gHorizontalBlur) : SV_Target
{
    float2 texOffset;
    if(gHorizontalBlur)
    {
      texOffset = float2(gTexelWidth, 0.0f);
    }
    else
    {
      texOffset = float2(0.0f, gTexelHeight);
    }

    // The center value always contributes to the sum.
    float4 color      = gWeights[5]*gInputImage.SampleLevel(
            samInputImage, pin.Tex, 0.0);
    float totalWeight = gWeights[5];
```

```
float4 centerNormalDepth = gNormalDepthMap.SampleLevel(
    samNormalDepth, pin.Tex, 0.0f);

for(float i = -gBlurRadius; i <=gBlurRadius; ++i)
{
  // We already added in the center weight.
  if(i == 0)
    continue;

  float2 tex = pin.Tex + i*texOffset;

  float4 neighborNormalDepth = gNormalDepthMap.SampleLevel(
      samNormalDepth, tex, 0.0f);

  //
  // If the center value and neighbor values differ too
  // much (either in normal or depth), then we assume we
  // are sampling across a discontinuity.  We discard
  // such samples from the blur.
  //

  if(dot(neighborNormalDepth.xyz, centerNormalDepth.xyz) >= 0.8f &&
     abs(neighborNormalDepth.a - centerNormalDepth.a) <= 0.2f)
  {
    float weight = gWeights[i+gBlurRadius];

    // Add neighbor pixel to blur.
    color += weight*gInputImage.SampleLevel(
      samInputImage, tex, 0.0);

    totalWeight += weight;
  }
}

// Compensate for discarded samples by making total weights sum to 1.
return color / totalWeight;
}

technique11 HorzBlur
{
    pass P0
    {
      SetVertexShader(CompileShader(vs_5_0, VS()));
      SetGeometryShader(NULL);
      SetPixelShader(CompileShader(ps_5_0, PS(true)));
    }
}

technique11 VertBlur
{
    pass P0
    {
      SetVertexShader(CompileShader(vs_5_0, VS()));
      SetGeometryShader(NULL);
      SetPixelShader(CompileShader(ps_5_0, PS(false)));
    }
}
```

Figure 22.8 shows the ambient map after an edge preserving blur.

Figure 22.8. An edge preserving blur smoothes out the noise. In our demo, we blur the image 4 times.

22.2.4 Using the Ambient Occlusion Map

Thus far we have constructed a nice ambient occlusion map. The final step is to apply it to the scene. One might think to use alpha blending and modulate the ambient map with the back buffer. However, if we do this, then the ambient map modifies not just the ambient term, but also the diffuse and specular term of the lighting equation, which is incorrect. Instead, when we render the scene to the back buffer, we bind the ambient map as a shader input. We then generate projective texture coordinates (with respect to the camera), sample the SSAO map, and apply it only to the ambient term of the lighting equation:

```
// In Vertex shader, generate projective tex-coords
// to project SSAO map onto scene.
vout.SsaoPosH = mul(float4(vin.PosL, 1.0f), gWorldViewProjTex);

// In pixel shader, finish texture projection and sample SSAO map.
pin.SsaoPosH /= pin.SsaoPosH.w;
float ambientAccess = gSsaoMap.Sample(samLinear, pin.SsaoPosH.xy,
    0.0f).r;

// Scale ambient term of lighting equation.
ambient += ambientAccess*A;
diffuse += shadow[i]*D;
spec    += shadow[i]*S;
```

Figure 22.9 shows the scene with the SSAO map applied. The SSAO can be subtle, and your scene has to reflect enough ambient light so that scaling it by

Figure 22.9. Screenshot of the demo. The effects are subtle as they only affect the ambient term, but you can see darkening at the base of the columns and box, under the spheres, and around the skull.

the ambient-access makes enough of a noticeable difference. If you want, you can consider multiplying the diffuse component by the ambient-access as well to make the effect more dramatic, although it is less accurate to do so.

The advantage of SSAO is most apparent when objects are in shadow. When objects are in shadow, the diffuse and specular terms are killed; thus only the ambient term shows up. Without SSAO, objects in shadow will appear flatly lit by a constant ambient term, but with SSAO they will keep their 3D definition.

When we render the scene to the normal/depth render target, we also build the depth buffer for the scene. Consequently, when we render the scene the second time with the SSAO map, we modify the depth comparison test to "EQUALS." This prevents any overdraw in the second rendering pass, as only the nearest visible pixels will pass this depth comparison test. Moreover, the second rendering pass does not need to write to the depth buffer because we already wrote the scene to the depth buffer in the normal/depth render target pass.

```
D3D11_DEPTH_STENCIL_DESC equalsDesc;
ZeroMemory(&equalsDesc, sizeof(D3D11_DEPTH_STENCIL_DESC));
equalsDesc.DepthEnable = true;
equalsDesc.DepthWriteMask = D3D11_DEPTH_WRITE_MASK_ZERO;
equalsDesc.DepthFunc = D3D11_COMPARISON_EQUAL;

HR(device->CreateDepthStencilState(&equalsDesc, &EqualsDSS));
...

//
// Render the view space normals and depths.  This render target has the
```

```
// same dimensions as the back buffer, so we can use the screen
//    viewport.
// This render pass is needed to compute the ambient occlusion.
// Notice that we use the main depth/stencil buffer in this pass.
//

md3dImmediateContext->ClearDepthStencilView(mDepthStencilView,
    D3D11_CLEAR_DEPTH|D3D11_CLEAR_STENCIL, 1.0f, 0);
md3dImmediateContext->RSSetViewports(1, &mScreenViewport);
mSsao->SetNormalDepthRenderTarget(mDepthStencilView);

DrawSceneToSsaoNormalDepthMap();

//
// Now compute the ambient occlusion.
//

mSsao->ComputeSsao(mCam);
mSsao->BlurAmbientMap(6);

//
// Restore the back and depth buffer and viewport to the OM stage.
//
ID3D11RenderTargetView* renderTargets[1] = {mRenderTargetView};
md3dImmediateContext->OMSetRenderTargets(1, renderTargets, mDepthStencilView);
md3dImmediateContext->RSSetViewports(1, &mScreenViewport);

md3dImmediateContext->ClearRenderTargetView(mRenderTargetView,
reinterpret_cast<const float*>(&Colors::Silver));

// We already laid down scene depth to the depth buffer in the
// Normal/Depth map pass, so we can set the depth comparison
// test to "EQUALS."  This prevents any overdraw in this rendering
// pass, as only the nearest visible pixels will pass this depth
// comparison test.
md3dImmediateContext->OMSetDepthStencilState(RenderStates::EqualsDSS, 0);

// ...draw scene to back buffer
```

Note: *In this demo, we computed the SSAO from the non-tessellated geometry. This simplification may work depending on the amount of displacement in the scene. If you want to use the tessellated geometry for computing the SSAO map, then you need to tessellate the geometry when it is rendered to the normal/depth render target.*

22.3 SUMMARY

1. The ambient term of the lighting equation models indirect light. In our lighting model, the ambient term is simply a constant value. Therefore, when an object is in shadow and only ambient light is applied to the surface, the model appears

very flat with no solid definition. The goal of ambient occlusion is to find a better estimate for the ambient term so that the object still looks 3D even with just the ambient term applied.

2. The idea of ambient occlusion is that the amount of indirect light a point **p** on a surface receives is proportional to how occluded it is to incoming light over the hemisphere about **p**. One way to estimate the occlusion of a point **p** is via ray casting. We randomly cast rays over the hemisphere about **p**, and check for intersections against the mesh. If the rays do not intersect any geometry, then the point is completely unoccluded; however, the more intersections there are, the more occluded **p** must be.

3. Ray casted ambient occlusion is too expensive to do in real-time for dynamic objects. Screen space ambient occlusion (SSAO) is a real-time approximation that is based on the view space normal/depth values. You can definitely find flaws and situations where it gives wrong results, but the results are very good in practice with the limited information it has to work with.

22.4 EXERCISES

1. Research on the Web, KD-Trees, quadtrees, and octrees.

2. Modify the "SSAO" demo to do a Gaussian blur instead of an edge preserving blur. Which one do you like better?

3. Can SSAO be implemented on the compute shader? If yes, sketch out an implementation.

4. Figure 22.10 shows what happens to the SSAO map if we do not include a check for self-intersection (§22.2.2.4). Modify the "SSAO" demo to remove the self-intersection check and reproduce the results in Figure 22.10.

Figure 22.10. **False occlusions everywhere.**

5. For the normal/depth pass, we used a DXGI_FORMAT_R16G16B16A16_FLOAT texture map, where RGB stores the view space normal and the alpha channel stores the view space depth (z-coordinate). This is 64-bits per pixel versus a 32-bit pixel format like DXGI_FORMAT_R8G8B8A8_UNORM. The 64-bit format takes double the bandwidth when writing to the texture and reading to the texture (and note that the blurring of the ambient map requires reading from the depth/normal map). Modify the "SSAO" demo to use the 32-bit pixel format DXGI_FORMAT_R8G8B8A8_UNORM, where RG stores the normal vector x- and y-coordinates (shifted and biased to $[0, 1]$ as with normal maps), and BA combined store a 16-bit depth value. The normal z-coordinate can be constructed in the shader by $n_z = -\sqrt{1 - x^2 + y^2}$ because the normal is unit length and we know front facing visible objects in view space will have normals with a negative z-coordinate. To store the view space depth over two 8-bit UNORM channels, z first needs to be normalized to $[0, 1]$ by dividing by some scaling factor, say the far plane depth z_{far}:

$$z' = \frac{z}{z_{far}} \in [0,1]$$

In binary, a 16-bit version of z' looks like $0.b_1 \ldots b_8 b_9 \ldots b_{16}$ and we need to spread this out over two 8-bit components. We can assign z' directly to the blue component, but it will only write the 8 most significant digits and truncate the others:

$$b = z' = 0.b_1 \ldots b_8$$

To save the remaining 8 bits, we do an 8-bit left shift (which can be done by multiplying by 256), and write the fractional part to the alpha channel:

$$a = \text{frac}(256 \cdot z') = \text{frac}(b_1 \ldots b_8 . b_9 \ldots b_{16}) = 0.b_9 \ldots b_{16}$$

In code:

```
z = depth / farZ;
normalDepth.ba = float2(z, frac(256*z));
```

Reforming the value is just the reverse process. We right-shift the alpha channel 8 bits to the right by dividing by 256:

$$a' = \frac{a}{256} = 0.00000000b_9 \ldots b_{16}$$

Then

$$z' = b + a' = 0 . b_1 \ldots b_8 + 0.00000000b_9 \ldots b_{16} = 0.b_1 \ldots b_8 b_9 \ldots b_{16}$$

In code:

```
float4 normalDepth = normalDepthTex.Sample(sampler, uv);
z = normalDepth.b + normalDepth.a/256.0f;
depth = z*farZ;
```

Note: *Instead of using a full screen normal/depth texture, another memory optimization is to use a normal/depth texture at a quarter of the screen resolution—just like we did with the SSAO map. However, for algorithms (such as the light prepass http://diaryofagraphicsprogrammer.blogspot.com/2008/03/light-pre-pass-renderer.html) that require a full screen normal/depth, we can write a short pixel shader to copy render the full screen normal/depth map to a quarter sized one, and use the smaller one for the SSAO.*

Chapter 23 MESHES

So far in this book we have worked with procedurally generated meshes (e.g., cylinders, grids, spheres), and some simple mesh data (e.g., the skull mesh) loaded from file. In this short chapter, we extend the *.m3d* format we have been using to support materials, and other information. In Chapter 25, we will extend this format again to support character animation.

The *.m3d* format is not a standard mesh format; it is a format we have developed for this book to make it relatively simple to load meshes into our demos. Studios generally have their own custom model formats that are specific to their application and rendering engine. Most 3D modeling programs provide tools for writing plugins so that you can export data from the modeling program into your own custom format. Another approach is to write a converter from a standard model format to your custom model format. For example, the "MeshFromOBJ10" SDK sample shows how to load *.obj* meshes to be rendered by Direct3D. As a second example, the XNA Game Studio content pipeline supports *.x* and *.fbx* file formats. The content pipeline loads the data into a game ready XNA `Model` class, which is ready to be rendered by the XNA framework. To avoid writing your own *.x* or *.fbx* converter, one could use XNA to load the file into the XNA `Model` class, extract the desired data, and then save it to your custom format. Readers may be interested in the *Open Asset Import Library* (http://assimp.sourceforge.net/index.html), which supports loading various standard model formats. Once the data is loaded, you can traverse the libraries' data structures, extract the data you want, and save it to your custom format. Regardless of whether you write a plugin or converter, it can be a significant effort and hard to make robust; therefore, using existing solutions like the XNA Game Studio content pipeline, or the *Open Asset Import Library* will save considerable time.

Objectives:

1. To learn how to load meshes and materials from the *.m3d* format.

2. To understand how a mesh can be broken up into different subsets.

23.1 *.M3D* FORMAT

The *.m3d* is text based for easy reading and editing by hand. In practice, using a binary format would be more memory efficient.

23.1.1 Header

The format begins with a header that specifies some global information that essentially tells our loader how much data it will need to read:

```
***************m3d-File-Header***************
#Materials 2
#Vertices 2258
#Triangles 1674
#Bones 0
#AnimationClips 0
```

1. `#Materials`: The number of distinct materials the mesh uses.

2. `#Vertices`: The number of vertices of the mesh.

3. `#Triangles`: The number of triangles in the mesh.

4. `#Bones`: The number of bones in the mesh—this will be used in Chapter 25; for now, none of our meshes will have bones, so these values will be 0.

5. `#AnimationClips`: The number of animation clips in the mesh—this will be used in Chapter 25; for now, none of our meshes will have animation data, so these values will be 0.

We load the header data as follows:

```
bool M3DLoader::LoadM3d(const std::string& filename,
        std::vector<Vertex::PosNormalTexTan>& vertices,
        std::vector<USHORT>& indices,
        std::vector<MeshGeometry::Subset>& subsets,
        std::vector<M3dMaterial>& mats)
{
```

```
std::ifstream fin(filename);

UINT numMaterials  = 0;
UINT numVertices   = 0;
UINT numTriangles  = 0;
UINT numBones      = 0;
UINT numAnimationClips = 0;

std::string ignore;

if(fin)
{
  fin >> ignore; // file header text
  fin >> ignore >> numMaterials;
  fin >> ignore >> numVertices;
  fin >> ignore >> numTriangles;
  fin >> ignore >> numBones;
  fin >> ignore >> numAnimationClips;
```

23.1.2 Materials

The next "chunk" in the .m3d format is a list of materials. In this particular example, the mesh has two materials:

```
***************Materials*********************
Ambient: 0.4 0.4 0.4
Diffuse: 0.9 0.9 0.9
Specular: 0.4 0.4 0.4
SpecPower: 16
Reflectivity: 0 0 0
AlphaClip: 1
Effect: Normal
DiffuseMap: tree01-leaves_diffuse.dds
NormalMap: tree01-leaves_normal.dds

Ambient: 0.4 0.4 0.4
Diffuse: 0.9 0.9 0.9
Specular: 0.4 0.4 0.4
SpecPower: 16
Reflectivity: 0 0 0
AlphaClip: 0
Effect: Normal
DiffuseMap: tree01-bark_diffuse.dds
NormalMap: tree01-bark_normal.dds
```

The file contains the material data we are familiar with (ambient, diffuse, specular, etc.), but also contains additional information such as the textures to apply, whether alpha clipping needs to be applied, and an effect name. We do not use the effect name in this book, but it could be used to specify a particular effect the geometry needs to be rendered with; for example, perhaps some geometry requires displacement mapping, another normal mapping, and another environment mapping.

We define a matching material structure to store the information we want, and load the material data as follows:

```cpp
struct M3dMaterial
{
    Material Mat;
    bool AlphaClip;
    std::string EffectTypeName;
    std::wstring DiffuseMapName;
    std::wstring NormalMapName;
};

void M3DLoader::ReadMaterials(std::ifstream& fin, UINT
                  numMaterials, std::vector<M3dMaterial>& mats)
{
    std::string ignore;
    mats.resize(numMaterials);

    std::string diffuseMapName;
    std::string normalMapName;

    fin >> ignore; // materials header text
    for(UINT i = 0; i < numMaterials; ++i)
    {
      fin >> ignore >> mats[i].Mat.Ambient.x  >>
          mats[i].Mat.Ambient.y  >> mats[i].Mat.Ambient.z;
      fin >> ignore >> mats[i].Mat.Diffuse.x  >>
           mats[i].Mat.Diffuse.y  >> mats[i].Mat.Diffuse.z;
      fin >> ignore >> mats[i].Mat.Specular.x >>
          mats[i].Mat.Specular.y >> mats[i].Mat.Specular.z;
      fin >> ignore >> mats[i].Mat.Specular.w;
      fin >> ignore >> mats[i].Mat.Reflect.x >>
          mats[i].Mat.Reflect.y >> mats[i].Mat.Reflect.z;
      fin >> ignore >> mats[i].AlphaClip;
      fin >> ignore >> mats[i].EffectTypeName;
      fin >> ignore >> diffuseMapName;
      fin >> ignore >> normalMapName;

      mats[i].DiffuseMapName.resize(diffuseMapName.size(), ' ');
      mats[i].NormalMapName.resize(normalMapName.size(), ' ');

      // convert to wstring
      std::copy(diffuseMapName.begin(),
          diffuseMapName.end(),
          mats[i].DiffuseMapName.begin());
      std::copy(normalMapName.begin(),
          normalMapName.end(),
          mats[i].NormalMapName.begin());
    }
}
```

23.1.3 Subsets

A mesh consists of one or more subsets. A *subset* is a group of triangles in a mesh that can all be rendered using the same material. By same *material* we mean the same effect, textures, and render states. Figure 23.1 illustrates how a mesh representing a car may be divided into several subsets.

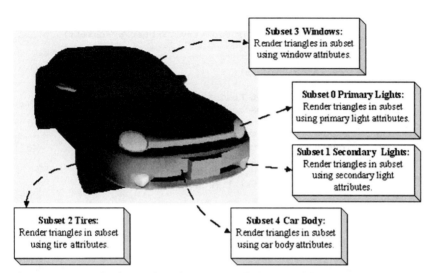

Figure 23.1. A car broken up by subset. Here only the materials per subset differ, but we could also imagine textures being added and differing as well. In addition, the render states may differ; for example, the glass windows may be rendered with alpha blending for transparency.

There is a subset corresponding to each material and the *i*th subset corresponds to the *i*th material. The *i*th subset defines a contiguous block of geometry that should be rendered with the *i*th material.

```
***************SubsetTable*******************
SubsetID: 0 VertexStart: 0 VertexCount: 1600 FaceStart: 0 FaceCount: 800
SubsetID: 1 VertexStart: 1600 VertexCount: 658 FaceStart: 800 FaceCount: 874
```

In the previous example, the first 800 triangles of the mesh (which reference vertices 0–1599) should be rendered with material 0, and the next 874 triangles of the mesh (which reference vertices 1600–2257) should be rendered with material 1.

```
struct Subset
{
    Subset() :
    Id(-1),
    VertexStart(0), VertexCount(0),
    FaceStart(0), FaceCount(0)
    {
    }

    UINT Id;
    UINT VertexStart;
    UINT VertexCount;
    UINT FaceStart;
    UINT FaceCount;
};
```

```
void M3DLoader::ReadSubsetTable(std::ifstream& fin, UINT numSubsets,
                std::vector<MeshGeometry::Subset>& subsets)
{
    std::string ignore;
    subsets.resize(numSubsets);

    fin >> ignore; // subset header text
    for(UINT i = 0; i < numSubsets; ++i)
    {
      fin >> ignore >> subsets[i].Id;
      fin >> ignore >> subsets[i].VertexStart;
      fin >> ignore >> subsets[i].VertexCount;
      fin >> ignore >> subsets[i].FaceStart;
      fin >> ignore >> subsets[i].FaceCount;
    }
}
```

23.1.4 Vertices and Triangle Indices

The last two chunks of data are just lists of vertices and indices (3 indices per triangle):

```
***************Vertices*********************
Position: 0.9207547 10.77502 -1.320696
Tangent: -0.2406725 0.05866166 -0.968832 1
Normal: 0.020704 0.9982551 0.05530001
Tex-Coords: 1 0

Position: -0.08739337 10.78203 -1.069832
Tangent: -0.2406725 0.05866166 -0.968832 1
Normal: 0.020704 0.9982551 0.05530001
Tex-Coords: 1 1
...

***************Triangles*********************
0 1 2
3 0 2
4 5 6
...
```

A limitation of our *.m3d* format is that we impose all vertices to have the same format (position, normal, tangent, texture coordinates). An application may have models that use different vertex formats. Adding such flexibility to the format complicates things, however, and the goal of our format is to keep it simple for demonstration purposes.

Code for loading the vertices and indices follows:

```
void M3DLoader::ReadVertices(std::ifstream& fin, UINT numVertices,
                std::vector<Vertex::PosNormalTexTan>& vertices)
{
    std::string ignore;
    vertices.resize(numVertices);

    fin >> ignore; // vertices header text
    for(UINT i = 0; i < numVertices; ++i)
```

```
{
  fin >> ignore >> vertices[i].Pos.x      >>
                   vertices[i].Pos.y      >>
                   vertices[i].Pos.z;
  fin >> ignore >> vertices[i].TangentU.x >>
                   vertices[i].TangentU.y >>
                   vertices[i].TangentU.z >>
                   vertices[i].TangentU.w;
  fin >> ignore >> vertices[i].Normal.x   >>
                   vertices[i].Normal.y   >>
                   vertices[i].Normal.z;
  fin >> ignore >> vertices[i].Tex.x >> vertices[i].Tex.y;
  }
}

void M3DLoader::ReadTriangles(std::ifstream& fin, UINT numTriangles,
    std::vector<USHORT>& indices)
{
  std::string ignore;
  indices.resize(numTriangles*3);

  fin >> ignore; // triangles header text
  for(UINT i = 0; i < numTriangles; ++i)
  {
    fin >> indices[i*3+0] >> indices[i*3+1] >> indices[i*3+2];
  }
}
```

23.2 MESH GEOMETRY

To organize mesh data, we define a low-level class called **MeshGeometry** that encapsulates the vertex and index buffers, as well as the subsets.

```
class MeshGeometry
{
public:
    struct Subset { ... };

public:
    MeshGeometry();
    ~MeshGeometry();

    template <typename VertexType>
    void SetVertices(ID3D11Device* device,
const VertexType* vertices, UINT count);

    void SetIndices(ID3D11Device* device,
const USHORT* indices, UINT count);

    void SetSubsetTable(std::vector<Subset>& subsetTable);

    void Draw(ID3D11DeviceContext* dc, UINT subsetId);
```

```
private:
    MeshGeometry(const MeshGeometry& rhs);
    MeshGeometry& operator=(const MeshGeometry& rhs);

private:
    ID3D11Buffer* mVB;
    ID3D11Buffer* mIB;

    DXGI_FORMAT mIndexBufferFormat; // Always 16-bit

    // Cache sizeof(VertexType) to pass to IASetVertexBuffers
    UINT mVertexStride;

    std::vector<Subset> mSubsetTable;
};
```

The implementations to the member functions are straightforward, so we will omit the code except for the **Draw** call. This function uses the subset table to draw only the triangles belonging to the specified subset:

```
void MeshGeometry::Draw(ID3D11DeviceContext* dc, UINT subsetId)
{
    UINT offset = 0;

    dc->IASetVertexBuffers(0, 1, &mVB, &mVertexStride, &offset);
    dc->IASetIndexBuffer(mIB, mIndexBufferFormat, 0);

    dc->DrawIndexed(
      mSubsetTable[subsetId].FaceCount*3,
      mSubsetTable[subsetId].FaceStart*3,
      0);
}
```

23.3 BASIC MODEL

At a higher-level, we define a **BasicModel** class; this contains a **MeshGeometry** instance specifying the geometry of the model as well as the materials needed to draw the mesh. Additionally, it keeps a system memory copy of the mesh. System memory copies are needed for when we need to read the mesh data such as for computing bounding volumes, picking, or collision detection.

```
class BasicModel
{
public:
    BasicModel(ID3D11Device* device,
      TextureMgr& texMgr,
      const std::string& modelFilename,
      const std::wstring& texturePath);
    ~BasicModel();

    UINT SubsetCount;
```

```
    std::vector<Material> Mat;
    std::vector<ID3D11ShaderResourceView*> DiffuseMapSRV;
    std::vector<ID3D11ShaderResourceView*> NormalMapSRV;

    // Keep CPU copies of the mesh data to read from.
    std::vector<Vertex::PosNormalTexTan> Vertices;
    std::vector<USHORT> Indices;
    std::vector<MeshGeometry::Subset> Subsets;

    MeshGeometry ModelMesh;
};

BasicModel::BasicModel(ID3D11Device* device,
                       TextureMgr& texMgr,
                       const std::string& modelFilename,
                       const std::wstring& texturePath)
{
    std::vector<M3dMaterial> mats;
    M3DLoader m3dLoader;
    m3dLoader.LoadM3d(modelFilename, Vertices, Indices, Subsets, mats);

    ModelMesh.SetVertices(device, &Vertices[0], Vertices.size());
    ModelMesh.SetIndices(device, &Indices[0], Indices.size());
    ModelMesh.SetSubsetTable(Subsets);

    SubsetCount = mats.size();

    for(UINT i = 0; i < SubsetCount; ++i)
    {
      Mat.push_back(mats[i].Mat);

      ID3D11ShaderResourceView* diffuseMapSRV = texMgr.CreateTexture(
        texturePath + mats[i].DiffuseMapName);
      DiffuseMapSRV.push_back(diffuseMapSRV);

      ID3D11ShaderResourceView* normalMapSRV = texMgr.CreateTexture(
        texturePath + mats[i].NormalMapName);
      NormalMapSRV.push_back(normalMapSRV);
    }
}
```

Now drawing a `BasicModel` amounts to looping over its subsets, setting the material for the *i*th subset, followed by submitting the *i*th subset geometry to the rendering pipeline:

```
for(UINT subset = 0; subset < mModelInstances[modelIndex].Model-
>SubsetCount; ++subset)
{
    Effects::NormalMapFX->SetMaterial(Model->Mat[subset]);
    Effects::NormalMapFX->SetDiffuseMap(Model->DiffuseMapSRV[subset]);
    Effects::NormalMapFX->SetNormalMap(Model->NormalMapSRV[subset]);

    tech->GetPassByIndex(p)->Apply(0, md3dImmediateContext);
    Model->ModelMesh.Draw(md3dImmediateContext, subset);
}
```

Because some meshes will share the same textures, these textures could be loaded more than once if care is not taken to prevent duplication. To prevent duplication, we introduce the `TextureMgr` class to create textures. This class prevents textures from being loaded and created twice using a `std::map` data structure. When the user tries to create a texture, the manager first checks to see if the texture already exists in the map. If it does, the manager just returns a pointer to the texture without loading it again. Otherwise, the manager loads the texture and returns a pointer to it. Note that the `TextureMgr` class also handles destroying the texture resources, so the main application code does not need to do this. The `TextureMgr` class is defined in *TextureMgr.h/.cpp* and lives in the *Common* directory.

We may wish to instance a `BasicModel` by drawing it multiple times but at different locations. We use the following simple structure to facilitate this:

```
struct BasicModelInstance
{
    BasicModel* Model;
    XMFLOAT4X4 World;
};
```

23.4 MESH VIEWER DEMO

Figure 23.2 shows a screenshot of our demo for this chapter. It loads and draws multiple meshes using the loading code and data structures we have discussed in this chapter.

Figure 23.2. Screenshot of "Mesh Viewer" demo.

23.5 SUMMARY

1. A mesh consists of one or more subsets. A subset is a group of triangles in a mesh that can all be rendered using the same effect, textures, and render states.

2. To organize mesh data, we define a low-level class called `MeshGeometry` that encapsulates the vertex and index buffers, as well as defining the subsets of the mesh.

3. The `BasicModel` class encapsulates a `MeshGeometry` instance as the materials needed to draw the mesh. Additionally, it keeps a system memory copy of the mesh. System memory copies are needed for when we need to read the mesh data such as for computing bounding volumes, picking, or collision detection.

23.6 EXERCISES

1. Manually create a *.m3d* file and fill it with cube data. Put the geometry of each face in its own subset so that there are six subsets. Texture each cube face with a different texture.

2. Study the "MeshFromOBJ10" Direct3D10 SDK demo to see how they load and render the *.obj* file format.

3. Download and set up the *Open Asset Import Library* (http://assimp. sourceforge.net/index.html). Find a free 3D model format on the Web that the library supports (or make your own model if you have access to a modeling program), and write a model viewer for it using Direct3D 11. In particular, the library supports the Blender 3D format (*.blend*), and Blender 3D (http:// www. blender. org/) is a free open source modeling program.

Chapter 24 QUATERNIONS

In Chapter 1, we introduced a new class of mathematical objects called vectors. In particular, we learned that a 3D vector consists of an ordered 3-tuple of real numbers, and we defined operators on vectors that are useful geometrically. Likewise, in Chapter 2 we introduced matrices, which are rectangular tables of real numbers with operations defined on them that are useful; for example, we saw how matrices can represent linear and affine transformations, and how matrix multiplication corresponds to transformation composition. In this chapter, we learn about another type of mathematical object called quaternions. We will see that a unit quaternion can be used to represent a 3D rotation, and has convenient interpolation properties. For readers looking for a comprehensive treatment of quaternions (and rotations), we like the book devoted to the topic by [Kuipers99].

Objectives:
1. To review the complex numbers and recall how complex number multiplication performs a rotation in the plane.
2. To obtain an understanding of quaternions and the operations defined on them.
3. To discover how the set of unit quaternions represent 3D rotations.
4. To find out how to convert between the various rotation representations.
5. To learn how to interpolate between unit quaternions, and understand that this is geometrically equivalent to interpolating between 3D orientations.
6. To become familiar with the XNA Math library's quaternion functions and classes.

24.1 REVIEW OF THE COMPLEX NUMBERS

The quaternions can be viewed as a generalization of the complex numbers; this motivates us to study complex numbers before quaternions. In particular, our main goal in this section is to show that multiplying a complex number **p** (thought of as a 2D vector or point) by a unit complex number results in a rotation of **p**. We will then show in §24.3 that a special quaternion product involving a unit quaternion results in a 3D rotation of a vector or point **p**.

24.1.1 Definitions

There are different ways to introduce complex numbers. We introduce them in such a way that they immediately cause us to think of complex numbers as 2D points or vectors.

An ordered pair of real numbers $\mathbf{z} = (a,b)$ is a complex number. The first component is called the *real* part and the second component is called the *imaginary* part. Moreover, equality, addition, subtraction, multiplication, and division are defined as follows:

1. $(a,b) = (c,d)$ if and only if $a = c$ and $b = d$
2. $(a,b) \pm (c,d) = (a \pm c, b \pm d)$
3. $(a,b)(c,d) = (ac - bd, ad + bc)$
4. $\frac{(a,b)}{(c,d)} = \left(\frac{ac+bd}{c^2+d^2}, \frac{bc-ad}{c^2+d^2} \right)$ if $(c,d) \neq (0,0)$

It is easy to verify that the usual arithmetic properties of real numbers also hold for complex arithmetic (e.g., commutativity, associativity, distributive laws); see Exercise 1.

If a complex number is of the form $(x,0)$ then it is customary to identify it by the real number x and write $x = (x,0)$; thus any real number can be thought of as a complex number with a zero imaginary component. Observe then that a real number times a complex number is given by $x(a,b) = (x,0)(a,b) = (xa,xb) = (a,b)(x,0) = (a,b)x$, which is reminiscent of scalar-vector multiplication.

We define the *imaginary unit* $i = (0,1)$. Using our definition of complex multiplication, observe that $i^2 = (0,1)(0,1) = (-1,0) = -1$, which implies $i = \sqrt{-1}$. This tells us that i solves the equation $x^2 = -1$.

The *complex conjugate* of a complex number $\mathbf{z} = (a,b)$ is denoted by $\bar{\mathbf{z}}$ and given by $\bar{\mathbf{z}} = (a,-b)$. A simple way to remember the complex division formula is to multiply the numerator and denominator by the conjugate of the denominator so that the denominator becomes a real number:

$$\frac{(a,b)}{(c,d)} = \frac{(a,b)}{(c,d)} \frac{(c,-d)}{(c,-d)} = \frac{(ac+bd, bc-ad)}{c^2+d^2} = \left(\frac{ac+bd}{c^2+d^2}, \frac{bc-ad}{c^2+d^2} \right)$$

Next, we show that a complex number (a,b) can be written in the form $a+ib$. We have $a=(a,0)$, $b=(b,0)$, and $i=(0,1)$, so

$$a+ib = (a,0)+(0,1)(b,0) = (a,0)+(0,b) = (a,b)$$

Using the form $a+ib$, we can recast the formulas for addition, subtraction, multiplication, and division as follows:

1. $(a+ib)\pm(c+id) = (a+c)+i(b+d)$
2. $(a+ib)(c+id) = (ac-bd)+i(ad+bc)$
3. $\frac{a+ib}{c+id} = \frac{ac+bd}{c^2+d^2} + i\frac{bc-ad}{c^2+d^2}$ if $(c,d) \neq (0,0)$

Furthermore, in this form, the complex conjugate of $\mathbf{z} = a+ib$ is given by $\bar{\mathbf{z}} = a-ib$.

24.1.2 Geometric Interpretation

The ordered pair form $a+ib = (a,b)$ of a complex number naturally suggests that we think of a complex number geometrically as a 2D point or vector in the complex plane. In fact, our definition of complex number addition matches our definition of vector addition; see Figure 24.1. We will give a geometric interpretation to complex number multiplication in the next section.

The *absolute value*, or *magnitude*, of the complex number $a + ib$ is defined as the length of the vector it represents (Figure 24.2), which we know is given by:

$$|a+ib| = \sqrt{a^2+b^2}$$

We say that a complex number is a *unit complex number* if it has a magnitude of one.

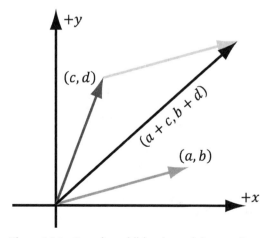

Figure 24.1. Complex addition is reminiscent of vector addition in the plane.

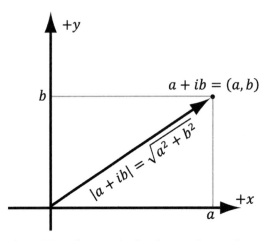

Figure 24.2. The magnitude of a complex number.

24.1.3 Polar Representation and Rotations

Because complex numbers can be viewed as just points or vectors in the 2D complex plane, we can just as well express their components using polar coordinates (see Figure 24.3):

$$r = |a + ib|$$
$$a + ib = r\cos\theta + ir\sin\theta = r(\cos\theta + i\sin\theta)$$

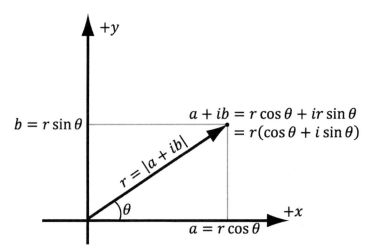

Figure 24.3. Polar representation of a complex number.

The right-hand-side of the equation is called the *polar representation* of the complex number $a+ib$.

Let us multiply two complex numbers in polar form. Let $\mathbf{z}_1 = r_1\left(\cos\theta_1 + i\sin\theta_1\right)$ and $\mathbf{z}_2 = r_2\left(\cos\theta_2 + i\sin\theta_2\right)$. Then

$$\mathbf{z}_1\mathbf{z}_2 = r_1 r_2\left(\cos\theta_1\cos\theta_2 - \sin\theta_1\sin\theta_2 + i\left(\cos\theta_1\sin\theta_2 + \sin\theta_1\cos\theta_2\right)\right)$$
$$= r_1 r_2\left(\cos\left(\theta_1 + \theta_2\right) + i\sin\left(\theta_1 + \theta_2\right)\right)$$

where we employed the trigonometric identities

$$\sin\left(\alpha+\beta\right) = \sin\alpha\cos\beta + \cos\alpha\sin\beta$$
$$\cos\left(\alpha+\beta\right) = \cos\alpha\cos\beta - \sin\alpha\sin\beta$$

Thus, geometrically, the product $\mathbf{z}_1\mathbf{z}_2$ is the complex number representing the vector with magnitude $r_1 r_2$ and which makes an angle $\theta_1 + \theta_2$ with the real axis. In particular, if $r_2 = 1$, then $\mathbf{z}_1\mathbf{z}_2 = r_1\left(\cos\left(\theta_1 + \theta_2\right) + i\sin\left(\theta_1 + \theta_2\right)\right)$, which, geometrically, rotates $\mathbf{z}_1$ by the angle θ_2; see Figure 24.4. *Therefore, multiplying a complex number $\mathbf{z}_1$ (thought of as a 2D vector or point) by a unit complex number $\mathbf{z}_2$ results in a rotation of $\mathbf{z}_1$.*

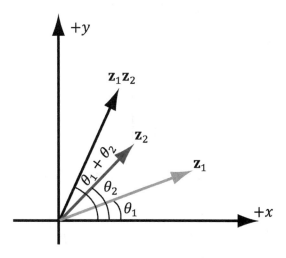

Figure 24.4. $\mathbf{z}_1 = r_1\left(\cos\theta_1 + i\sin\theta_1\right), \mathbf{z}_2 = \left(\cos\theta_2 + i\sin\theta_2\right)$. The product $z_1\, z_2$ rotates z_1 by the angle θ_2.

24.2 QUATERNION ALGEBRA

24.2.1 Definition and Basic Operations

An ordered 4-tuple of real numbers $\mathbf{q} = (x, y, z, w) = (q_1, q_2, q_3, q_4)$ is a quaternion. This is commonly abbreviated as $\mathbf{q} = (\mathbf{u}, w) = (x, y, z, w)$, and we call $\mathbf{u} = (x, y, z)$ the imaginary vector part and w the real part. Moreover, equality, addition, subtraction, multiplication, and division are defined as follows:

1. $(\mathbf{u}, a) = (\mathbf{v}, b)$ if and only if $\mathbf{u} = \mathbf{v}$ and $a = b$
2. $(\mathbf{u}, a) \pm (\mathbf{v}, b) = (\mathbf{u} \pm \mathbf{v}, a \pm b)$
3. $(\mathbf{u}, a)(\mathbf{v}, b) = (a\mathbf{v} + b\mathbf{u} + \mathbf{u} \times \mathbf{v}, ab - \mathbf{u} \cdot \mathbf{v})$

The definition of multiplication may seem "weird," but these operations are definitions, so we can *define* them however we want—and this definition turns out to be useful.

Let $\mathbf{p} = (\mathbf{u}, p_4) = (p_1, p_2, p_3, p_4)$ and $\mathbf{q} = (\mathbf{v}, q_4) = (q_1, q_2, q_3, q_4)$. Then $\mathbf{u} \times \mathbf{v} = (p_2 q_3 - p_3 q_2, p_3 q_1 - p_1 q_3, p_1 q_2 - p_2 q_1)$ and $\mathbf{u} \cdot \mathbf{v} = p_1 q_1 + p_2 q_2 + p_3 q_3$. Now, in component form, the quaternion product $\mathbf{r} = \mathbf{pq}$ takes on the form:

$$r_1 = p_4 q_1 + q_4 p_1 + p_2 q_3 - p_3 q_2 = q_1 p_4 - q_2 p_3 + q_3 p_2 + q_4 p_1$$

$$r_2 = p_4 q_2 + q_4 p_2 + p_3 q_1 - p_1 q_3 = q_1 p_3 + q_2 p_4 - q_3 p_1 + q_4 p_2$$

$$r_3 = p_4 q_3 + q_4 p_3 + p_1 q_2 - p_2 q_1 = -q_1 p_2 + q_2 p_1 + q_3 p_4 + q_4 p_3$$

$$r_4 = p_4 q_4 - p_1 q_1 - p_2 q_2 - p_3 q_3 = -q_1 p_1 - q_2 p_2 - q_3 p_3 + q_4 p_4$$

This can be written as a matrix product:

$$\mathbf{pq} = \begin{bmatrix} p_4 & -p_3 & p_2 & p_1 \\ p_3 & p_4 & -p_1 & p_2 \\ -p_2 & p_1 & p_4 & p_3 \\ -p_1 & -p_2 & -p_3 & p_4 \end{bmatrix} \begin{bmatrix} q_1 \\ q_2 \\ q_3 \\ q_4 \end{bmatrix}$$

Note: *If you prefer row vector-matrix multiplication, simply take the transpose:*

$$\left(\begin{bmatrix} p_4 & -p_3 & p_2 & p_1 \\ p_3 & p_4 & -p_1 & p_2 \\ -p_2 & p_1 & p_4 & p_3 \\ -p_1 & -p_2 & -p_3 & p_4 \end{bmatrix} \begin{bmatrix} q_1 \\ q_2 \\ q_3 \\ q_4 \end{bmatrix} \right)^T = \begin{bmatrix} q_1 \\ q_2 \\ q_3 \\ q_4 \end{bmatrix}^T \begin{bmatrix} p_4 & -p_3 & p_2 & p_1 \\ p_3 & p_4 & -p_1 & p_2 \\ -p_2 & p_1 & p_4 & p_3 \\ -p_1 & -p_2 & -p_3 & p_4 \end{bmatrix}^T$$

24.2.2 Special Products

Let $i = (1,0,0,0)$, $j = (0,1,0,0)$, $k = (0,0,1,0)$ be quaternions. Then we have the special products, some of which are reminiscent of the behavior of the cross product:

$$i^2 = j^2 = k^2 = ijk = -1$$
$$ij = k = -ji$$
$$jk = i = -kj$$
$$ki = j = -ik$$

These equations follow directly from our definition of quaternion multiplication. For example,

$$ij = \begin{bmatrix} 0 & 0 & 0 & 1 \\ 0 & 0 & -1 & 0 \\ 0 & 1 & 0 & 0 \\ -1 & 0 & 0 & 0 \end{bmatrix} \begin{bmatrix} 0 \\ 1 \\ 0 \\ 0 \end{bmatrix} = \begin{bmatrix} 0 \\ 0 \\ 1 \\ 0 \end{bmatrix} = k$$

24.2.3 Properties

Quaternion multiplication is *not* commutative; for instance, §24.2.2 showed that $ij = -ji$. Quaternion multiplication is associative, however; this can be seen from the fact that quaternion multiplication can be written using matrix multiplication and matrix multiplication is associative. The quaternion $e = (0,0,0,1)$ serves as a multiplicative identity:

$$pe = ep = \begin{bmatrix} p_4 & -p_3 & p_2 & p_1 \\ p_3 & p_4 & -p_1 & p_2 \\ -p_2 & p_1 & p_4 & p_3 \\ -p_1 & -p_2 & -p_3 & p_4 \end{bmatrix} \begin{bmatrix} 0 \\ 0 \\ 0 \\ 1 \end{bmatrix} = \begin{bmatrix} 1 & 0 & 0 & 0 \\ 0 & 1 & 0 & 0 \\ 0 & 0 & 1 & 0 \\ 0 & 0 & 0 & 1 \end{bmatrix} \begin{bmatrix} p_1 \\ p_2 \\ p_3 \\ p_4 \end{bmatrix} = \begin{bmatrix} p_1 \\ p_2 \\ p_3 \\ p_4 \end{bmatrix}$$

We also have that quaternion multiplication distributes over quaternion addition: $p(q+r) = pq + pr$ and $(q+r)p = qp + rp$. To see this, write the quaternion multiplication and addition in matrix form, and note that matrix multiplication distributes over matrix addition.

24.2.4 Conversions

We relate real numbers, vectors (or points), and quaternions in the following way: Let s be a real number and let $\mathbf{u} = (x, y, z)$ be a vector. Then

1. $s = (0, 0, 0, s)$

2. $\mathbf{u} = (x, y, z) = (\mathbf{u}, 0) = (x, y, z, 0)$

In other words, any real number can be thought of as a quaternion with a zero vector part, and any vector can be thought of as a quaternion with a zero real part. In particular, note that for the identity quaternion, $1 = (0, 0, 0, 1)$. A quaternion with a zero real part is called a *pure quaternion*.

Observe, using the definition of quaternion multiplication, that a real number times a quaternion is just "scalar multiplication" and it is commutative:

$$s(p_1, p_2, p_3, p_4) = (0, 0, 0, s)(p_1, p_2, p_3, p_4) = \begin{bmatrix} s & 0 & 0 & 0 \\ 0 & s & 0 & 0 \\ 0 & 0 & s & 0 \\ 0 & 0 & 0 & s \end{bmatrix} \begin{bmatrix} p_1 \\ p_2 \\ p_3 \\ p_4 \end{bmatrix} = \begin{bmatrix} sp_1 \\ sp_2 \\ sp_3 \\ sp_4 \end{bmatrix}$$

Similarly,

$$(p_1, p_2, p_3, p_4)s = (p_1, p_2, p_3, p_4)(0, 0, 0, s) = \begin{bmatrix} p_4 & -p_3 & p_2 & p_1 \\ p_3 & p_4 & -p_1 & p_2 \\ -p_2 & p_1 & p_4 & p_3 \\ -p_1 & -p_2 & -p_3 & p_4 \end{bmatrix} \begin{bmatrix} 0 \\ 0 \\ 0 \\ s \end{bmatrix} = \begin{bmatrix} sp_1 \\ sp_2 \\ sp_3 \\ sp_4 \end{bmatrix}$$

24.2.5 Conjugate and Norm

The conjugate of a quaternion $\mathbf{q} = (q_1, q_2, q_3, q_4) = (\mathbf{u}, q_4)$ is denoted by $\mathbf{q}^*$ and defined by

$$\mathbf{q}^* = -q_1 - q_2 - q_3 + q_4 = (-\mathbf{u}, q_4)$$

In other words, we just negate the imaginary vector part of the quaternion; compare this to the complex number conjugate. The conjugate has the following properties:

1. $(\mathbf{pq})^* = \mathbf{q}^* \mathbf{p}^*$

2. $(\mathbf{p} + \mathbf{q})^* = \mathbf{p}^* + \mathbf{q}^*$

3. $(\mathbf{q}^*)^* = \mathbf{q}$

4. $(s\mathbf{q})^* = s\mathbf{q}^*$ for $s \in \mathbb{R}$

5. $\mathbf{q} + \mathbf{q}^* = (\mathbf{u}, q_4) + (-\mathbf{u}, q_4) = (0, 2q_4) = 2q_4$

6. $\mathbf{qq}^* = \mathbf{q}^*\mathbf{q} = q_1^2 + q_2^2 + q_3^2 + q_4^2 = \| \mathbf{u} \|^2 + q_4^2$

In particular, note that $\mathbf{q} + \mathbf{q}^*$ and $\mathbf{qq}^* = \mathbf{q}^*\mathbf{q}$ evaluate to *real* numbers. The *norm* (or *magnitude*) of a quaternion is defined by:

$$\| \mathbf{q} \| = \sqrt{\mathbf{qq}^*} = \sqrt{q_1^2 + q_2^2 + q_3^2 + q_4^2} = \sqrt{\| \mathbf{u} \|^2 + q_4^2}$$

We say that a quaternion is a *unit quaternion* if it has a norm of one. The norm has the following properties:

1. $\| \mathbf{q}^* \| = \| \mathbf{q} \|$

2. $\| \mathbf{pq} \| = \| \mathbf{p} \| \| \mathbf{q} \|$

In particular, property 2 tells us that the product of two unit quaternions is a unit quaternion; also if $\| \mathbf{p} \| = 1$, then $\| \mathbf{pq} \| = \| \mathbf{q} \|$.

The conjugate and norm properties can be derived straightforwardly from the definitions. For example,

$$\left(\mathbf{q}^*\right)^* = \left(-\mathbf{u}, q_4\right)^* = \left(\mathbf{u}, q_4\right) = \mathbf{q}$$

$$\| \mathbf{q}^* \| = \| (-\mathbf{u}, q_4) \| = \sqrt{\| -\mathbf{u} \|^2 + q_4^2} = \sqrt{\| \mathbf{u} \|^2 + q_4^2} = \| \mathbf{q} \|$$

$$\| \mathbf{pq} \|^2 = (\mathbf{pq})(\mathbf{pq})^*$$

$$= \mathbf{pqq}^*\mathbf{p}^*$$

$$= \mathbf{p} \| \mathbf{q} \|^2 \mathbf{p}^*$$

$$= \mathbf{pp}^* \| \mathbf{q} \|^2$$

$$= \| \mathbf{p} \|^2 \| \mathbf{q} \|^2$$

The reader ought to try and derive the other properties (see Exercises).

24.2.6 Inverses

As with matrices, quaternion multiplication is not commutative, so we cannot define a division operator. (We like to reserve division only for when multiplication is commutative so that we have $\frac{a}{b} = ab^{-1} = b^{-1}a$.) However, every nonzero quaternion has an inverse. (The zero quaternion has zeros for all its components.) Let $\mathbf{q} = (q_1, q_2, q_3, q_4) = (\mathbf{u}, q_4)$ be a nonzero quaternion, then the inverse is denoted by $\mathbf{q}^{-1}$ and given by:

$$\mathbf{q}^{-1} = \frac{\mathbf{q}^*}{\| \mathbf{q} \|^2}$$

It is easy to check that this is indeed the inverse, for we have:

$$\mathbf{q}\mathbf{q}^{-1} = \frac{\mathbf{q}\mathbf{q}^*}{||\mathbf{q}||^2} = \frac{||\mathbf{q}||^2}{||\mathbf{q}||^2} = 1 = (0,0,0,1)$$

$$\mathbf{q}^{-1}\mathbf{q} = \frac{\mathbf{q}^*\mathbf{q}}{||\mathbf{q}||^2} = \frac{||\mathbf{q}||^2}{||\mathbf{q}||^2} = 1 = (0,0,0,1)$$

Observe that if $\mathbf{q}$ is a unit quaternion, then $||\mathbf{q}||^2 = 1$ and so $\mathbf{q}^{-1} = \mathbf{q}^*$.

The following properties hold for the quaternion inverse:

1. $\left(\mathbf{q}^{-1}\right)^{-1} = \mathbf{q}$
2. $\left(\mathbf{p}\mathbf{q}\right)^{-1} = \mathbf{q}^{-1}\mathbf{p}^{-1}$

24.2.7 Polar Representation

If $\mathbf{q} = (q_1, q_2, q_3, q_4) = (\mathbf{u}, q_4)$ is a unit quaternion, then

$$||\mathbf{q}||^2 = ||\mathbf{u}||^2 + q_4^2 = 1$$

This implies $q_4^2 \leq 1 \Leftrightarrow |q_4| \leq 1 \Leftrightarrow -1 \leq q_4 \leq 1$. Figure 24.5 shows there exists an angle $\theta \in [0, \pi]$ such that $q_4 = \cos\theta$. Employing the trigonometric identity $\sin^2\theta + \cos^2\theta = 1$, we have that

$$\sin^2\theta = 1 - \cos^2\theta = 1 - q_4^2 = ||\mathbf{u}||^2$$

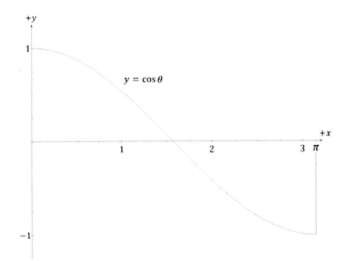

Figure 24.5. For a number $y \in [-1,1]$ there exists an angle θ such that $y = \cos\theta$.

This implies

$$\| \mathbf{u} \| = |\sin\theta| = \sin\theta \quad \text{for} \quad \theta \in [0,\pi]$$

Now label the unit vector in the same direction as $\mathbf{u}$ by $\mathbf{n}$:

$$\mathbf{n} = \frac{\mathbf{u}}{\| \mathbf{u} \|} = \frac{\mathbf{u}}{\sin\theta}$$

Hence, $\mathbf{u} = \sin\theta\mathbf{n}$ and we may therefore write the unit quaternion $\mathbf{q} = (\mathbf{u}, q_4)$ in the following *polar representation* where $\mathbf{n}$ is a unit vector:

$$\mathbf{q} = (\sin\theta\mathbf{n}, \cos\theta) \quad \text{for} \quad \theta \in [0,\pi]$$

For example, suppose we are given the quaternion $\mathbf{q} = \left(0, \frac{1}{2}, 0, \frac{\sqrt{3}}{2}\right)$. To convert to polar representation, we find $\theta = \arccos\frac{\sqrt{3}}{2} = \frac{\pi}{6}$, $\mathbf{n} = \frac{(0,\frac{1}{2},0)}{\sin\frac{\pi}{6}} = (0,1,0)$. So $\mathbf{q} = (\sin\frac{\pi}{6}(0,1,0), \cos\frac{\pi}{6})$.

Note: *The restriction of $\theta \in [0,\pi]$ is for when converting a quaternion $\mathbf{q} = (q_1, q_2, q_3, q_4)$ to polar representation. That is, we need the angle restriction in order to associate a unique angle with the quaternion $\mathbf{q} = (q_1, q_2, q_3, q_4)$. Nothing stops us, however, from constructing a quaternion $\mathbf{q} = (\sin\theta\mathbf{n}, \cos\theta)$ from any angle θ, but observe that $\mathbf{q} = (\sin(\theta + 2\pi n)\mathbf{n}, \cos(\theta + 2\pi n))$ for all integers n. So the quaternion does not have a unique polar representation without the angle restriction $\theta \in [0,\pi]$.*

Observe that substituting $-\theta$ for θ is equivalent to negating the vector part of the quaternion:

$$(\mathbf{n}\sin(-\theta), \cos(-\theta)) = (-\mathbf{n}\sin\theta, \cos\theta) = \mathbf{p}^*$$

In the next section we will see that $\mathbf{n}$ represents the axis of rotation, and so we can rotate in the other direction by negating the axis of rotation.

24.3 UNIT QUATERNIONS AND ROTATIONS

24.3.1 Rotation Operator

Let $\mathbf{q} = (\mathbf{u}, w)$ be a unit quaternion and let $\mathbf{v}$ be a 3D point or vector. Then we can think of $\mathbf{v}$ as the pure quaternion $\mathbf{p} = (\mathbf{v}, 0)$. Also recall that since $\mathbf{q}$ is a unit quaternion, we have that $\mathbf{q}^{-1} = \mathbf{q}^*$. Recall the formula for quaternion multiplication:

$$(\mathbf{m}, a)(\mathbf{n}, b) = (a\mathbf{n} + b\mathbf{m} + \mathbf{m} \times \mathbf{n}, ab - \mathbf{m} \cdot \mathbf{n})$$

Now consider the product:

$$qpq^{-1} = qpq^*$$
$$= (\mathbf{u}, w)(\mathbf{v}, 0)(-\mathbf{u}, w)$$
$$= (\mathbf{u}, w)(w\mathbf{v} - \mathbf{v} \times \mathbf{u}, \mathbf{v} \cdot \mathbf{u})$$

Simplifying this is a little lengthy, so we will do the real part and vector part separately. We make the symbolic substitutions:

$$a = w$$
$$b = \mathbf{v} \cdot \mathbf{u}$$
$$\mathbf{m} = \mathbf{u}$$
$$\mathbf{n} = w\mathbf{v} - \mathbf{v} \times \mathbf{u}$$

Real Part

$$ab - \mathbf{m} \cdot \mathbf{n}$$
$$= w(\mathbf{v} \cdot \mathbf{u}) - \mathbf{u} \cdot (w\mathbf{v} - \mathbf{v} \times \mathbf{u})$$
$$= w(\mathbf{v} \cdot \mathbf{u}) - \mathbf{u} \cdot w\mathbf{v} + \mathbf{u} \cdot (\mathbf{v} \times \mathbf{u})$$
$$= w(\mathbf{v} \cdot \mathbf{u}) - w(\mathbf{v} \cdot \mathbf{u}) + 0$$
$$= 0$$

Note that $\mathbf{u} \cdot (\mathbf{v} \times \mathbf{u}) = 0$ because $(\mathbf{v} \times \mathbf{u})$ is orthogonal to $\mathbf{u}$ by the definition of the cross product.

Vector Part

$$a\mathbf{n} + b\mathbf{m} + \mathbf{m} \times \mathbf{n}$$
$$= w(w\mathbf{v} - \mathbf{v} \times \mathbf{u}) + (\mathbf{v} \cdot \mathbf{u})\mathbf{u} + \mathbf{u} \times (w\mathbf{v} - \mathbf{v} \times \mathbf{u})$$
$$= w^2\mathbf{v} - w\mathbf{v} \times \mathbf{u} + (\mathbf{v} \cdot \mathbf{u})\mathbf{u} + \mathbf{u} \times w\mathbf{v} + \mathbf{u} \times (\mathbf{u} \times \mathbf{v})$$
$$= w^2\mathbf{v} + \mathbf{u} \times w\mathbf{v} + (\mathbf{v} \cdot \mathbf{u})\mathbf{u} + \mathbf{u} \times w\mathbf{v} + \mathbf{u} \times (\mathbf{u} \times \mathbf{v})$$
$$= w^2\mathbf{v} + 2(\mathbf{u} \times w\mathbf{v}) + (\mathbf{v} \cdot \mathbf{u})\mathbf{u} + \mathbf{u} \times (\mathbf{u} \times \mathbf{v})$$
$$= w^2\mathbf{v} + 2(\mathbf{u} \times w\mathbf{v}) + (\mathbf{v} \cdot \mathbf{u})\mathbf{u} + (\mathbf{u} \cdot \mathbf{v})\mathbf{u} - (\mathbf{u} \cdot \mathbf{u})\mathbf{v}$$
$$= (w^2 - \mathbf{u} \cdot \mathbf{u})\mathbf{v} + 2w(\mathbf{u} \times \mathbf{v}) + 2(\mathbf{u} \cdot \mathbf{v})\mathbf{u}$$
$$= (w^2 - \mathbf{u} \cdot \mathbf{u})\mathbf{v} + 2(\mathbf{u} \cdot \mathbf{v})\mathbf{u} + 2w(\mathbf{u} \times \mathbf{v})$$

where we applied the triple product identity $\mathbf{a} \times (\mathbf{b} \times \mathbf{c}) = (\mathbf{a} \cdot \mathbf{c})\mathbf{b} - (\mathbf{a} \cdot \mathbf{b})\mathbf{c}$ to $\mathbf{u} \times (\mathbf{u} \times \mathbf{v})$.
We have shown:

$$qpq^* = \left((w^2 - \mathbf{u} \cdot \mathbf{u})\mathbf{v} + 2(\mathbf{u} \cdot \mathbf{v})\mathbf{u} + 2w(\mathbf{u} \times \mathbf{v}), 0 \right) \qquad \text{(eq. 24.1)}$$

Observe that this results in a vector or point because the real component is zero (which is necessary if this operator is to rotate a vector or point—it must evaluate to a vector or point). Therefore, in the subsequent equations, we drop the real component.

Now, because **q** is a unit quaternion, it can be written as

$$\mathbf{q} = (\sin\theta\, \mathbf{n}, \cos\theta) \quad \text{for} \quad \|\mathbf{n}\| = 1 \quad \text{and} \quad \theta \in [0, \pi]$$

Substituting this into Equation 24.1 yields:

$$\mathbf{qpq}^{*} = \left(\cos^2\theta - \sin^2\theta\right)\mathbf{v} + 2\left(\sin\theta\, \mathbf{n}\cdot\mathbf{v}\right)\sin\theta\, \mathbf{n} + 2\cos\theta\left(\sin\theta\, \mathbf{n}\times\mathbf{v}\right)$$

$$= \left(\cos^2\theta - \sin^2\theta\right)\mathbf{v} + 2\sin^2\theta\left(\mathbf{n}\cdot\mathbf{v}\right)\mathbf{n} + 2\cos\theta\sin\theta\left(\mathbf{n}\times\mathbf{v}\right)$$

To simplify this further, we apply the trigonometric identities:

$$\cos^2\theta - \sin^2\theta = \cos(2\theta)$$
$$2\cos\theta\sin\theta = \sin(2\theta)$$
$$\cos(2\theta) = 1 - 2\sin^2\theta$$

$$\mathbf{qpq}^{*} = \left(\cos^2\theta - \sin^2\theta\right)\mathbf{v} + 2\sin^2\theta\left(\mathbf{n}\cdot\mathbf{v}\right)\mathbf{n} + 2\cos\theta\sin\theta\left(\mathbf{n}\times\mathbf{v}\right)$$

$$= \cos(2\theta)\mathbf{v} + \left(1 - \cos(2\theta)\right)\left(\mathbf{n}\cdot\mathbf{v}\right)\mathbf{n} + \sin(2\theta)\left(\mathbf{n}\times\mathbf{v}\right) \qquad \textbf{(eq. 24.2)}$$

Now, compare Equation 24.2 with the axis-angle rotation Equation 3.5 to see that this is just the rotation formula $\mathbf{R}_\mathbf{n}(\mathbf{v})$; that is, it rotates the vector (or point) **v** about the axis **n** by an angle 2θ:

$$\mathbf{R}_\mathbf{n}(\mathbf{v}) = \cos\theta\, \mathbf{v} + \left(1 - \cos\theta\right)\left(\mathbf{n}\cdot\mathbf{v}\right)\mathbf{n} + \sin\theta\left(\mathbf{n}\times\mathbf{v}\right)$$

Consequently, we define the quaternion rotation operator by:

$$R_\mathbf{q}(\mathbf{v}) = \mathbf{qvq}^{-1}$$
$$= \mathbf{qvq}^{*}$$
$$= \cos(2\theta)\mathbf{v} + \left(1 - \cos(2\theta)\right)\left(\mathbf{n}\cdot\mathbf{v}\right)\mathbf{n} + \sin(2\theta)\left(\mathbf{n}\times\mathbf{v}\right) \qquad \textbf{(eq. 24.3)}$$

We have shown that the quaternion rotation operator $R_\mathbf{q}(\mathbf{v}) = \mathbf{qvq}^{-1}$ rotates a vector (or point) **v** about the axis **n** by an angle 2θ.

So suppose you are given an axis **n** and angle θ to rotate about the axis **n**. You construct the corresponding rotation quaternion by:

$$\mathbf{q} = \left(\sin\!\left(\frac{\theta}{2}\right)\mathbf{n}, \cos\!\left(\frac{\theta}{2}\right)\right)$$

Then apply the formula $R_\mathbf{q}(\mathbf{v})$. The division by 2 is to compensate for the 2θ because we want to rotate by the angle θ, not 2θ.

24.3.2 Quaternion Rotation Operator to Matrix

Let $\mathbf{q} = (\mathbf{u}, w) = (q_1, q_2, q_3, q_4)$ be a unit quaternion. From Equation 24.1, we know

$$\mathbf{r} = R_{\mathbf{q}}(\mathbf{v}) = \mathbf{qpq}^* = (w^2 - \mathbf{u} \cdot \mathbf{u})\mathbf{v} + 2(\mathbf{u} \cdot \mathbf{v})\mathbf{u} + 2w(\mathbf{u} \times \mathbf{v})$$

Note that $q_1^2 + q_2^2 + q_3^2 + q_4^2 = 1$ implies that $q_4^2 - 1 = -q_1^2 - q_2^2 - q_3^2$, and so

$$(w^2 - \mathbf{u} \cdot \mathbf{u})\mathbf{v} = (q_4^2 - q_1^2 - q_2^2 - q_3^2)\mathbf{v}$$
$$= (2q_4^2 - 1)\mathbf{v}$$

The three terms in $R_{\mathbf{q}}(\mathbf{v})$ can be written in terms of matrices:

$$(w^2 - \mathbf{u} \cdot \mathbf{u})\mathbf{v} = \begin{bmatrix} v_x & v_y & v_z \end{bmatrix} \begin{bmatrix} 2q_4^2 - 1 & 0 & 0 \\ 0 & 2q_4^2 - 1 & 0 \\ 0 & 0 & 2q_4^2 - 1 \end{bmatrix}$$

$$2(\mathbf{u} \cdot \mathbf{v})\mathbf{u} = \begin{bmatrix} v_x & v_y & v_z \end{bmatrix} \begin{bmatrix} 2q_1^2 & 2q_1q_2 & 2q_1q_3 \\ 2q_1q_2 & 2q_2^2 & 2q_2q_3 \\ 2q_1q_3 & 2q_2q_3 & 2q_3^2 \end{bmatrix}$$

$$2w(\mathbf{u} \times \mathbf{v}) = \begin{bmatrix} v_x & v_y & v_z \end{bmatrix} \begin{bmatrix} 0 & 2q_4q_3 & -2q_4q_2 \\ -2q_4q_3 & 0 & 2q_4q_1 \\ 2q_4q_2 & -2q_4q_1 & 0 \end{bmatrix}$$

Summing the terms yields:

$$R_{\mathbf{q}}(\mathbf{v}) = \mathbf{v}Q = \begin{bmatrix} v_x & v_y & v_z \end{bmatrix} \begin{bmatrix} 2q_1^2 + 2q_4^2 - 1 & 2q_1q_2 + 2q_3q_4 & 2q_1q_3 - 2q_2q_4 \\ 2q_1q_2 - 2q_3q_4 & 2q_2^2 + 2q_4^2 - 1 & 2q_2q_3 + 2q_1q_4 \\ 2q_1q_3 + 2q_2q_4 & 2q_2q_3 - 2q_1q_4 & 2q_3^2 + 2q_4^2 - 1 \end{bmatrix}$$

The unit length property $q_1^2 + q_2^2 + q_3^2 + q_4^2 = 1$ of $\mathbf{q}$ implies:

$$2q_1^2 + 2q_4^2 = 2 - 2q_2^2 - 2q_3^2$$
$$2q_2^2 + 2q_4^2 = 2 - 2q_1^2 - 2q_3^2$$
$$2q_3^2 + 2q_4^2 = 2 - 2q_1^2 - 2q_2^2$$

We can, therefore, rewrite this matrix equation as:

$$R_q(\mathbf{v}) = \mathbf{vQ} = \begin{bmatrix} v_x & v_y & v_z \end{bmatrix} \begin{bmatrix} 1-2q_2^2-2q_3^2 & 2q_1q_2+2q_3q_4 & 2q_1q_3-2q_2q_4 \\ 2q_1q_2-2q_3q_4 & 1-2q_1^2-2q_3^2 & 2q_2q_3+2q_1q_4 \\ 2q_1q_3+2q_2q_4 & 2q_2q_3-2q_1q_4 & 1-2q_1^2-2q_2^2 \end{bmatrix} \quad \textbf{(eq. 24.4)}$$

Note: *Many graphics books use matrix-column vector ordering for transforming vectors. Hence you will see the transpose of the matrix* $\mathbf{Q}$ *in many graphics books for the perform* $R_q(\mathbf{v}) = \mathbf{Q}^T\mathbf{v}^T$.

24.3.3 Matrix to Quaternion Rotation Operator

Given the rotation matrix

$$\mathbf{R} = \begin{bmatrix} R_{11} & R_{12} & R_{13} \\ R_{21} & R_{22} & R_{23} \\ R_{31} & R_{32} & R_{33} \end{bmatrix}$$

we want to find the quaternion $q = (q_1, q_2, q_3, q_4)$ such that if we build the Equation 24.4 matrix $\mathbf{Q}$ from $\mathbf{q}$ we get $\mathbf{R}$. So our strategy is to set

$$\begin{bmatrix} R_{11} & R_{12} & R_{13} \\ R_{21} & R_{22} & R_{23} \\ R_{31} & R_{32} & R_{33} \end{bmatrix} = \begin{bmatrix} 1-2q_2^2-2q_3^2 & 2q_1q_2+2q_3q_4 & 2q_1q_3-2q_2q_4 \\ 2q_1q_2-2q_3q_4 & 1-2q_1^2-2q_3^2 & 2q_2q_3+2q_1q_4 \\ 2q_1q_3+2q_2q_4 & 2q_2q_3-2q_1q_4 & 1-2q_1^2-2q_2^2 \end{bmatrix}$$

and solve for q_1, q_2, q_3, q_4. Note that we are given $\mathbf{R}$, so all the elements on the left-hand-side of the equation are known.

We start by summing the diagonal elements (which is called the *trace* of a matrix):

$$\text{trace}(\mathbf{R}) = R_{11} + R_{22} + R_{33}$$
$$= 1-2q_2^2-2q_3^2+1-2q_1^2-2q_3^2+1-2q_1^2-2q_2^2$$
$$= 3-4q_1^2-4q_2^2-4q_3^2$$
$$= 3-4(q_1^2+q_2^2+q_3^2)$$
$$= 3-4(1-q_4^2)$$
$$= -1+4q_4^2$$
$$\therefore q_4 = \frac{\sqrt{\text{trace}(\mathbf{R})+1}}{2}$$

Now we combine diagonally opposite elements to solve for q_1, q_2, q_3 (because we eliminate terms):

$$R_{23} - R_{32} = 2q_2 q_3 + 2q_1 q_4 - 2q_2 q_3 + 2q_1 q_4$$
$$= 4q_1 q_4$$
$$\therefore q_1 = \frac{R_{23} - R_{32}}{4q_4}$$

$$R_{31} - R_{13} = 2q_1 q_3 + 2q_2 q_4 - 2q_1 q_3 + 2q_2 q_4$$
$$= 4q_2 q_4$$
$$\therefore q_2 = \frac{R_{31} - R_{13}}{4q_4}$$

$$R_{12} - R_{21} = 2q_1 q_2 + 2q_3 q_4 - 2q_1 q_2 + 2q_3 q_4$$
$$= 4q_3 q_4$$
$$\therefore q_3 = \frac{R_{12} - R_{21}}{4q_4}$$

If $q_4 = 0$ then these equations are undefined. In this case, we will find the largest diagonal element of $\mathbf{R}$ to divide by, and choose other combinations of matrix elements. Suppose R_{11} is the maximum diagonal:

$$R_{11} - R_{22} - R_{33} = 1 - 2q_2^2 - 2q_3^2 - 1 + 2q_1^2 + 2q_3^2 - 1 + 2q_1^2 + 2q_2^2$$
$$= -1 + 4q_1^2$$
$$\therefore q_1 = \frac{\sqrt{R_{11} - R_{22} - R_{33} + 1}}{2}$$

$$R_{12} + R_{21} = 2q_1 q_2 + 2q_3 q_4 + 2q_1 q_2 - 2q_3 q_4$$
$$= 4q_1 q_2$$
$$\therefore q_2 = \frac{R_{12} + R_{21}}{4q_1}$$

$$R_{13} + R_{31} = 2q_1 q_3 - 2q_2 q_4 + 2q_1 q_3 + 2q_2 q_4$$
$$= 4q_1 q_3$$
$$\therefore q_3 = \frac{R_{13} + R_{31}}{4q_1}$$

$$R_{23} - R_{32} = 2q_2q_3 + 2q_1q_4 - 2q_2q_3 + 2q_1q_4$$
$$= 4q_1q_4$$
$$\therefore q_4 = \frac{R_{23} - R_{32}}{4q_1}$$

A similar pattern is taken if R_{22} or R_{33} is the maximum diagonal.

24.3.4 Composition

Suppose $\mathbf{p}$ and $\mathbf{q}$ are unit quaternions with corresponding rotational operators given by $R_{\mathbf{p}}$ and $R_{\mathbf{q}}$, respectively. Letting $\mathbf{v}' = R_{\mathbf{p}}(\mathbf{v})$, the composition is given by:

$$R_{\mathbf{q}}\left(R_{\mathbf{p}}(\mathbf{v})\right) = R_{\mathbf{q}}(\mathbf{v}') = \mathbf{q}\mathbf{v}'\mathbf{q}^{-1} = \mathbf{q}\left(\mathbf{p}\mathbf{v}\mathbf{p}^{-1}\right)\mathbf{q}^{-1} = (\mathbf{qp})\mathbf{v}\left(\mathbf{p}^{-1}\mathbf{q}^{-1}\right) = (\mathbf{qp})\mathbf{v}(\mathbf{qp})^{-1}$$

Because $\mathbf{p}$ and $\mathbf{q}$ are both unit quaternions, the product $\mathbf{pq}$ is also a unit quaternion because $\|\mathbf{pq}\| = \|\mathbf{p}\|\|\mathbf{q}\| = 1$; thus, the quaternion product $\mathbf{pq}$ also represents a rotation; namely, the net rotation given by the composition $R_{\mathbf{q}}\left(R_{\mathbf{p}}(\mathbf{v})\right)$.

24.4 QUATERNION INTERPOLATION

Because quaternions are 4-tuples of real numbers, geometrically, we can visualize them as 4D vectors. In particular, unit quaternions are 4D unit vectors that lie on the 4D unit sphere. With the exception of the cross product (which is only defined for 3D vectors), our vector math generalizes to 4-space—and even n-space. Specifically, the dot product holds for quaternions. Let $\mathbf{p} = (\mathbf{u}, s)$ and $\mathbf{q} = (\mathbf{v}, t)$, then:

$$\mathbf{p} \cdot \mathbf{q} = \mathbf{u} \cdot \mathbf{v} + st = \|\mathbf{p}\|\|\mathbf{q}\|\cos\theta$$

where θ is the angle between the quaternions. If the quaternions $\mathbf{p}$ and $\mathbf{q}$ are unit length, then $\mathbf{p} \cdot \mathbf{q} = \cos\theta$. The dot product allows us to talk about the angle between two quaternions as a measure of how "close" they are to each other on the unit sphere.

For the purposes of animation, we want to interpolate from one orientation to another orientation. To interpolate quaternions, we want to interpolate on the arc of the unit sphere so that our interpolated quaternion is also a unit quaternion. To derive such a formula, consider Figure 24.6, where we want to interpolate between $\mathbf{a}$ to $\mathbf{b}$ by an angle $t\theta$. We want to find weights c_1 and c_2 such that

$\mathbf{p} = c_1\mathbf{a} + c_2\mathbf{b}$, where $\|\mathbf{p}\| = \|\mathbf{a}\| = \|\mathbf{b}\|$. We set up two equations for the two unknowns as follows:

$$\mathbf{a} \cdot \mathbf{p} = c_1 \mathbf{a} \cdot \mathbf{a} + c_2 \mathbf{a} \cdot \mathbf{b}$$
$$\cos(t\theta) = c_1 + c_2 \cos(\theta)$$

$$\mathbf{p} \cdot \mathbf{b} = c_1 \mathbf{a} \cdot \mathbf{b} + c_2 \mathbf{b} \cdot \mathbf{b}$$
$$\cos((1-t)\theta) = c_1 \cos(\theta) + c_2$$

This yields the matrix equation:

$$\begin{bmatrix} 1 & \cos(\theta) \\ \cos(\theta) & 1 \end{bmatrix} \begin{bmatrix} c_1 \\ c_2 \end{bmatrix} = \begin{bmatrix} \cos(t\theta) \\ \cos((1-t)\theta) \end{bmatrix}$$

Consider the matrix equation $\mathbf{A}\mathbf{x} = \mathbf{b}$, where $\mathbf{A}$ is invertible. Then Cramer's Rule tells us that $x_i = \det \mathbf{A}_i / \det \mathbf{A}$, where $\mathbf{A}_i$ is found by swapping the ith column vector in $\mathbf{A}$ with $\mathbf{b}$. Therefore:

$$c_1 = \frac{\det \begin{bmatrix} \cos(t\theta) & \cos(\theta) \\ \cos((1-t)\theta) & 1 \end{bmatrix}}{\det \begin{bmatrix} 1 & \cos(\theta) \\ \cos(\theta) & 1 \end{bmatrix}} = \frac{\cos(t\theta) - \cos(\theta)\cos((1-t)\theta)}{1 - \cos^2(\theta)}$$

$$c_2 = \frac{\det \begin{bmatrix} 1 & \cos(t\theta) \\ \cos(\theta) & \cos((1-t)\theta) \end{bmatrix}}{\det \begin{bmatrix} 1 & \cos(\theta) \\ \cos(\theta) & 1 \end{bmatrix}} = \frac{\cos((1-t)\theta) - \cos(\theta)\cos(t\theta)}{1 - \cos^2(\theta)}$$

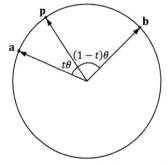

Figure 24.6. Interpolating along the 4D unit sphere from a to b by an angle $t\theta$. The angle between a and b is θ, the angle between a and p is $t\theta$, and the angle between p and b is $(1-t)\theta$.

From the trigonometric Pythagorean identity and addition formulas, we have:

$$1 - \cos^2(\theta) = \sin^2(\theta)$$

$$\cos((1-t)\theta) = \cos(\theta - t\theta) = \cos(\theta)\cos(t\theta) + \sin(\theta)\sin(t\theta)$$

$$\sin((1-t)\theta) = \sin(\theta - t\theta) = \sin(\theta)\cos(t\theta) - \cos(\theta)\sin(t\theta)$$

Therefore,

$$
\begin{aligned}
c_1 &= \frac{\cos(t\theta) - \cos(\theta)\big[\cos(\theta)\cos(t\theta) + \sin(\theta)\sin(t\theta)\big]}{\sin^2(\theta)} \\[2mm]
&= \frac{\cos(t\theta) - \cos(\theta)\cos(\theta)\cos(t\theta) - \cos(\theta)\sin(\theta)\sin(t\theta)}{\sin^2(\theta)} \\[2mm]
&= \frac{\cos(t\theta)\big(1 - \cos^2(\theta)\big) - \cos(\theta)\sin(\theta)\sin(t\theta)}{\sin^2(\theta)} \\[2mm]
&= \frac{\cos(t\theta)\sin^2(\theta) - \cos(\theta)\sin(\theta)\sin(t\theta)}{\sin^2(\theta)} \\[2mm]
&= \frac{\sin(\theta)\cos(t\theta) - \cos(\theta)\sin(t\theta)}{\sin(\theta)} \\[2mm]
&= \frac{\sin((1-t)\theta)}{\sin(\theta)}
\end{aligned}
$$

and

$$
\begin{aligned}
c_2 &= \frac{\cos(\theta)\cos(t\theta) + \sin(\theta)\sin(t\theta) - \cos(\theta)\cos(t\theta)}{\sin^2(\theta)} \\[2mm]
&= \frac{\sin(t\theta)}{\sin(\theta)}
\end{aligned}
$$

Thus we define the spherical interpolation formula:

$$\mathrm{slerp}(\mathbf{a}, \mathbf{b}, t) = \frac{\sin((1-t)\theta)\mathbf{a} + \sin(t\theta)\mathbf{b}}{\sin\theta} \quad \text{for} \quad t \in [0,1]$$

Thinking of unit quaternions as 4D unit vectors allows us to solve for the angle between the quaternions: $\theta = \arccos(\mathbf{a} \cdot \mathbf{b})$.

If θ, the angle between $\mathbf{a}$ and $\mathbf{b}$ is near zero, $\sin\theta$ is near zero, and the division can cause problems due to finite numerical precision. In this case, perform linear

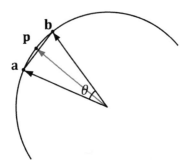

Figure 24.7. **For small angles θ between a and b, linear interpolation is a good approximation for spherical interpolation. However, when using linear interpolation, the interpolated quaternion no longer lies on the unit sphere, so you must normalize the result to project it back on to the unit sphere.**

interpolation between the quaternions and normalize the result, which is actually a good approximation for small θ (see Figure 24.7).

Observe from Figure 24.8 that linear interpolation followed by projecting the interpolated quaternion back on to the unit sphere results in a nonlinear rate of rotation. Thus if you use linear interpolation for large angles, the speed of rotation will speed up and slow down. This effect is often undesirable, and one reason why spherical interpolation is preferred (which rotates at a constant speed).

We now point out an interesting property of quaternions. Note that because $(s\mathbf{q})^* = s\mathbf{q}^*$ and scalar-quaternion multiplication is commutative, we have that:

$$R_{-\mathbf{q}}(\mathbf{v}) = -\mathbf{q}\mathbf{v}(-\mathbf{q})^*$$
$$= (-1)\mathbf{q}\mathbf{v}(-1)\mathbf{q}^*$$
$$= \mathbf{q}\mathbf{v}\mathbf{q}^*$$

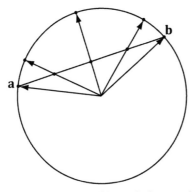

Figure 24.8. **Linear interpolation results in nonlinear interpolation over the unit sphere after normalization. This means the rotation speeds up and slows down as it interpolates, rather than moving at a constant speed.**

We therefore have $\mathbf{q}$ and $-\mathbf{q}$ representing the same rotation. To see this another way, if $\mathbf{q} = \left(\mathbf{n}\sin\frac{\theta}{2},\cos\frac{\theta}{2}\right)$, then

$$-\mathbf{q} = \left(-\mathbf{n}\sin\frac{\theta}{2},-\cos\frac{\theta}{2}\right)$$

$$= \left(-\mathbf{n}\sin\left(\pi-\frac{\theta}{2}\right),\cos\left(\pi-\frac{\theta}{2}\right)\right)$$

$$= \left(-\mathbf{n}\sin\left(\frac{2\pi-\theta}{2}\right),\cos\left(\frac{2\pi-\theta}{2}\right)\right)$$

That is, $R_{\mathbf{q}}$ rotates θ about the axis $\mathbf{n}$, and $R_{-\mathbf{q}}$ rotates $2\pi-\theta$ about the axis $-\mathbf{n}$. Geometrically, a unit quaternion $\mathbf{q}$ on the 4D unit sphere and its polar opposite $-\mathbf{q}$ represent the same orientation. Figure 24.9 shows that these two rotations take us to the same place. However, we see that one will take the shorter angle around and the other will take the longer angle around.

Because $\mathbf{b}$ and $-\mathbf{b}$ represent the same orientation, we have two choices for interpolation: slerp($\mathbf{a},\mathbf{b},t$) or slerp($\mathbf{a},-\mathbf{b},t$). One will interpolate between the orientations in the most direct way that minimizes spinning (analogous to Figure 24.9a), and one will take the long way around (analogous to Figure 24.9b). Referring to Figure 24.10, we want to choose $\mathbf{b}$ or $-\mathbf{b}$ based on which one interpolates over a shorter arc on the 4D unit sphere. Choosing the

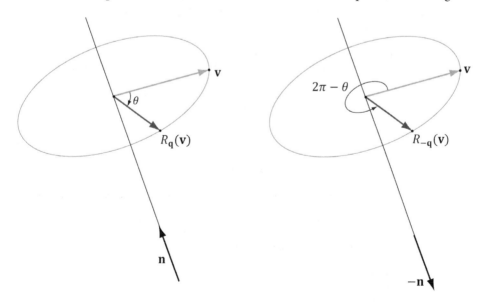

Figure 24.9. $R_{\mathbf{q}}$ rotates θ about the axis $\mathbf{n}$, and $R_{-\mathbf{q}}$ rotates $2\pi-\theta$ about the axis $-\mathbf{n}$.

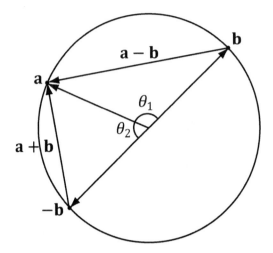

Figure 24.10. Interpolating from a to b results in interpolating over the larger arc θ_1 on the 4D unit sphere, whereas interpolating from a to −b results in interpolating over the shorter arc θ_2 on the 4D unit sphere. We want to choose the shortest arc on the 4D unit sphere.

shorter arc results in interpolating through the most direct path; choosing the longer arc results in extra spinning of the object [Eberly01], as it rotates the long way around.

From [Watt92], to find the quaternion that gives the shortest arc around the 4D unit sphere, we compare $\|\mathbf{a}-\mathbf{b}\|^2$ and $\|\mathbf{a}-(-\mathbf{b})\|^2 = \|\mathbf{a}+\mathbf{b}\|^2$. If $\|\mathbf{a}+\mathbf{b}\|^2 < \|\mathbf{a}-\mathbf{b}\|^2$ then we choose −b for interpolation instead of **b** because −**b** is closer to **a**, and thus will give the shorter arc.

```
// Linear interpolation (for small theta).
public static Quaternion LerpAndNormalize(Quaternion p, Quaternion q, float s)
{
    // Normalize to make sure it is a unit quaternion.
    return Normalize((1.0f - s)*p + s*q);
}

public static Quaternion Slerp(Quaternion p, Quaternion q, float s)
{
    // Recall that q and -q represent the same orientation, but
    interpolating
    // between the two is different: One will take the shortest arc and
    one
    // will take the long arc.  To find the shortest arc, compare the
    magnitude
    // of p-q with the magnitude p-(-q) = p+q.

    if(LengthSq(p-q) > LengthSq(p+q))
        q = -q;

    float cosPhi = DotP(p, q);
```

```
    // For very small angles, use linear interpolation.
    if(cosPhi > (1.0f - 0.001))
      return LerpAndNormalize(p, q, s);

    // Find the angle between the two quaternions.
    float phi = (float)Math.Acos(cosPhi);

    float sinPhi = (float)Math.Sin(phi);

    // Interpolate along the arc formed by the intersection of the 4D
    unit sphere and
    // the plane passing through p, q, and the origin of the unit
    sphere.
    return ((float)Math.Sin(phi*(1.0-s))/sinPhi)*p +
      ((float)Math.Sin(phi*s)/sinPhi)*q;
}
```

24.5 XNA MATH QUATERNION FUNCTIONS

The XNA math library supports quaternions. Because the "data" of a quaternion is 4 real numbers, XNA math uses the **XMVECTOR** type for storing quaternions. Then some of the common quaternion functions defined are:

// Returns the quaternion dot product $Q_1 \cdot Q_2$.
```
XMVECTOR XMQuaternionDot(XMVECTOR Q1, XMVECTOR Q2);
```

// Returns the identity quaternion $(0,0,0,1)$.
```
XMVECTOR XMQuaternionIdentity();
```

// Returns the conjugate of the quaternion Q.
```
XMVECTOR XMQuaternionConjugate(XMVECTOR Q);
```

// Returns the norm of the quaternion Q.
```
XMVECTOR XMQuaternionLength(XMVECTOR Q);
```

// Normalizes a quaternion by treating it as a 4D vector.
```
XMVECTOR XMQuaternionNormalize(XMVECTOR Q);
```
// Computes the quaternion product Q_1Q_2.
```
XMVECTOR XMQuaternionMultiply(XMVECTOR Q1, XMVECTOR Q2);
```

// Returns a quaternions from axis-angle rotation representation.
```
XMVECTOR XMQuaternionRotationAxis(XMVECTOR Axis, FLOAT Angle);
```

// Returns a quaternions from axis-angle rotation representation, where the axis
// vector is normalized—this is faster than **XMQuaternionRotationAxis**.
```
XMVECTOR XMQuaternionRotationNormal(XMVECTOR NormalAxis,FLOAT Angle);
```

// Returns a quaternion from a rotation matrix.

```
XMVECTOR XMQuaternionRotationMatrix(XMMATRIX M);
```

// Returns a rotation matrix from a unit quaternion.

```
XMMATRIX XMMatrixRotationQuaternion(XMVECTOR Quaternion);
```

// Extracts the axis and angle rotation representation from the quaternion **Q**.

```
VOID XMQuaternionToAxisAngle(XMVECTOR *pAxis, FLOAT *pAngle, XMVECTOR Q);
```

// Returns slerp($\mathbf{Q}1, \mathbf{Q}2, t$)

```
XMVECTOR XMQuaternionSlerp(XMVECTOR Q0, XMVECTOR Q1, FLOAT t);
```

24.6 ROTATION DEMO

For this chapter's demo, we animate a skull mesh around a simple scene. The position, orientation, and scale of the mesh are animated. We use quaternions to represent the orientation of the skull, and use slerp to interpolate between orientations. We use linear interpolation to interpolate between position and scale. This demo also serves as an animation "warm up" to the next chapter on character animation.

A common form of animation is called key frame animation. A *key frame* specifies the position, orientation, and scale of an object at an instance in time. In our demo (in *AnimationHelper.h/.cpp*), we define the following key frame structure:

```
struct Keyframe
{
    Keyframe();
    ~Keyframe();

    float TimePos;
    XMFLOAT3 Translation;
    XMFLOAT3 Scale;
    XMFLOAT4 RotationQuat;
};
```

An *animation* is a list of key frames sorted by time:

```
struct BoneAnimation
{
    float GetStartTime()const;
    float GetEndTime()const;

    void Interpolate(float t, XMFLOAT4X4& M)const;

    std::vector<Keyframe> Keyframes;

};
```

The reason for using the term "bone" will be made clear in the next section. For now you can just think of animating a single bone as animating a single object. The method GetStartTime just returns the time of the first key frame. For example, maybe the object does not start animating until after 10 seconds relative to some timeline. Similarly, the method GetEndTime returns the time of the last key frame. This is useful to know when the animation ends, and we can stop animating it.

We now have a list of key frames, which define the rough overall look of the animation. So how will the animation look at time between the key frames? This is where interpolation comes in. For times t between two key frames, say K_i and K_{i+1}, we interpolate between the two key frames K_i and K_{i+1}.

```
void BoneAnimation::Interpolate(float t, XMFLOAT4X4& M)const
{
    // t is before the animation started, so just return the first key
    frame.
    if(t <= Keyframes.front().TimePos)
    {
        XMVECTOR S = XMLoadFloat3(&Keyframes.front().Scale);
        XMVECTOR P = XMLoadFloat3(&Keyframes.front().Translation);
        XMVECTOR Q = XMLoadFloat4(&Keyframes.front().RotationQuat);

        XMVECTOR zero = XMVectorSet(0.0f, 0.0f, 0.0f, 1.0f);
        XMStoreFloat4x4(&M, XMMatrixAffineTransformation(S, zero, Q, P));
    }
    // t is after the animation ended, so just return the last key
    frame.
    else if(t >= Keyframes.back().TimePos)
    {
        XMVECTOR S = XMLoadFloat3(&Keyframes.back().Scale);
        XMVECTOR P = XMLoadFloat3(&Keyframes.back().Translation);
        XMVECTOR Q = XMLoadFloat4(&Keyframes.back().RotationQuat);

        XMVECTOR zero = XMVectorSet(0.0f, 0.0f, 0.0f, 1.0f);
        XMStoreFloat4x4(&M, XMMatrixAffineTransformation(S, zero, Q, P));
    }
    // t is between two key frames, so interpolate.
    else
    {
        for(UINT i = 0; i < Keyframes.size()-1; ++i)
        {
            if(t >= Keyframes[i].TimePos && t <= Keyframes[i+1].TimePos)
            {
                float lerpPercent = (t - Keyframes[i].TimePos) /
                    (Keyframes[i+1].TimePos - Keyframes[i].TimePos);

                XMVECTOR s0 = XMLoadFloat3(&Keyframes[i].Scale);
                XMVECTOR s1 = XMLoadFloat3(&Keyframes[i+1].Scale);

                XMVECTOR p0 = XMLoadFloat3(&Keyframes[i].Translation);
                XMVECTOR p1 = XMLoadFloat3(&Keyframes[i+1].Translation);

                XMVECTOR q0 = XMLoadFloat4(&Keyframes[i].RotationQuat);
                XMVECTOR q1 = XMLoadFloat4(&Keyframes[i+1].RotationQuat);
```

```
XMVECTOR S = XMVectorLerp(s0, s1, lerpPercent);
XMVECTOR P = XMVectorLerp(p0, p1, lerpPercent);
XMVECTOR Q = XMQuaternionSlerp(q0, q1, lerpPercent);

XMVECTOR zero = XMVectorSet(0.0f, 0.0f, 0.0f, 1.0f);
XMStoreFloat4x4(&M, XMMatrixAffineTransformation(S, zero, Q, P));

break;
            }
        }
    }
}
```

Figure 24.11 shows the in-between frames generated by interpolating from *Key 1* to *Key 2*.

Figure 24.11 appeared in the book by Frank D. Luna, *Introduction to 3D Game Programming with DirectX 9.0c: A Shader Approach*, 2006: Jones and Bartlett Learning, Burlington, MA. www.jblearning.com. Reprinted with permission.

After interpolation, we construct a transformation matrix because ultimately we use matrices for transformations in our shader programs. The **XMMatrixAffineTransformation** function is declared as follows:

```
XMMATRIX XMMatrixAffineTransformation(
    XMVECTOR Scaling,
    XMVECTOR RotationOrigin,
    XMVECTOR RotationQuaternion,
    XMVECTOR Translation);
```

Now that our simple animation system is in place, the next part of our demo is to define some key frames:

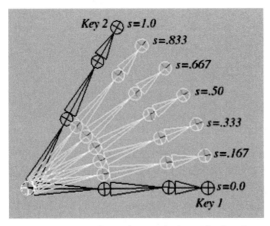

Figure 24.11. Key frame interpolation. The key frames define the "key" poses of the animation. The interpolated values represent the values between the key frames.

```
// Member data

float mAnimTimePos;
BoneAnimation mSkullAnimation;

//
// In constructor, define the animation keyframes
//

XMVECTOR q0 = XMQuaternionRotationAxis(XMVectorSet(0.0f, 1.0f, 0.0f, 0.0f),
    XMConvertToRadians(30.0f));
XMVECTOR q1 = XMQuaternionRotationAxis(XMVectorSet(1.0f, 1.0f, 2.0f, 0.0f),
    XMConvertToRadians(45.0f));
XMVECTOR q2 = XMQuaternionRotationAxis(XMVectorSet(0.0f, 1.0f, 0.0f, 0.0f),
    XMConvertToRadians(-30.0f));
XMVECTOR q3 = XMQuaternionRotationAxis(XMVectorSet(1.0f, 0.0f, 0.0f, 0.0f),
    XMConvertToRadians(70.0f));

mSkullAnimation.Keyframes.resize(5);
mSkullAnimation.Keyframes[0].TimePos = 0.0f;
mSkullAnimation.Keyframes[0].Translation = XMFLOAT3(-7.0f, 0.0f, 0.0f);
mSkullAnimation.Keyframes[0].Scale = XMFLOAT3(0.25f, 0.25f, 0.25f);
XMStoreFloat4(&mSkullAnimation.Keyframes[0].RotationQuat, q0);

mSkullAnimation.Keyframes[1].TimePos = 2.0f;
mSkullAnimation.Keyframes[1].Translation = XMFLOAT3(0.0f, 2.0f, 10.0f);
mSkullAnimation.Keyframes[1].Scale = XMFLOAT3(0.5f, 0.5f, 0.5f);
XMStoreFloat4(&mSkullAnimation.Keyframes[1].RotationQuat, q1);

mSkullAnimation.Keyframes[2].TimePos = 4.0f;
mSkullAnimation.Keyframes[2].Translation = XMFLOAT3(7.0f, 0.0f, 0.0f);
mSkullAnimation.Keyframes[2].Scale = XMFLOAT3(0.25f, 0.25f, 0.25f);
XMStoreFloat4(&mSkullAnimation.Keyframes[2].RotationQuat, q2);

mSkullAnimation.Keyframes[3].TimePos = 6.0f;
mSkullAnimation.Keyframes[3].Translation = XMFLOAT3(0.0f, 1.0f,
    -10.0f);
mSkullAnimation.Keyframes[3].Scale = XMFLOAT3(0.5f, 0.5f, 0.5f);
XMStoreFloat4(&mSkullAnimation.Keyframes[3].RotationQuat, q3);

mSkullAnimation.Keyframes[4].TimePos = 8.0f;
mSkullAnimation.Keyframes[4].Translation = XMFLOAT3(-7.0f, 0.0f, 0.0f);
mSkullAnimation.Keyframes[4].Scale = XMFLOAT3(0.25f, 0.25f, 0.25f);
XMStoreFloat4(&mSkullAnimation.Keyframes[4].RotationQuat, q0);
```

Our key frames position the skull at different locations in the scene, at different orientations, and at different scales. You can have fun experimenting with this demo by adding your own key frames or changing the key frame values. For example, you can set all the rotations and scaling to identity, to see what the animation looks like when only position is animated.

The last step to get the animation working is to perform the interpolation to get the new skull world matrix, which changes over time:

Figure 24.12. **Screenshot of the quaternion demo.**

```
void QuatApp::UpdateScene(float dt)
{
    ...

    // Increase the time position.
    mAnimTimePos += dt;
    if(mAnimTimePos >= mSkullAnimation.GetEndTime())
    {
        // Loop animation back to beginning.
        mAnimTimePos = 0.0f;
    }

    // Get the skull's world matrix at this time instant.
    mSkullAnimation.Interpolate(mAnimTimePos, mSkullWorld);
}
```

The skull's world matrix is now changing every frame in order to animate the skull.

24.7 SUMMARY

1.   An ordered 4-tuple of real numbers $\mathbf{q} = (x, y, z, w) = (q_1, q_2, q_3, q_4)$ is a quaternion. This is commonly abbreviated as $\mathbf{q} = (\mathbf{u}, w) = (x, y, z, w)$, and we call $\mathbf{u} = (x, y, z)$ the imaginary vector part and w the real part. Moreover, equality, addition, subtraction, multiplication, and division are defined as follows:

(a) $(\mathbf{u}, a) = (\mathbf{v}, b)$ if and only if $\mathbf{u} = \mathbf{v}$ and $a = b$

(b) $(\mathbf{u},a)\pm(\mathbf{v},b)=(\mathbf{u}\pm\mathbf{v},a\pm b)$

(c) $(\mathbf{u},a)(\mathbf{v},b)=(a\mathbf{v}+b\mathbf{u}+\mathbf{u}\times\mathbf{v},ab-\mathbf{u}\cdot\mathbf{v})$

2. Quaternion multiplication is *not* commutative, but it is associative. The quaternion $\mathbf{e}=(0,0,0,1)$ serves as a multiplicative identity. Quaternion multiplication distributes over quaternion addition: $\mathbf{p}(\mathbf{q}+\mathbf{r})=\mathbf{pq}+\mathbf{pr}$ and $(\mathbf{q}+\mathbf{r})\mathbf{p}=\mathbf{qp}+\mathbf{rp}$.

3. We can convert a real number s to quaternion space by writing $s=(0,0,0,s)$, and we can convert a vector $\mathbf{u}$ to quaternion space by writing $\mathbf{u}=(\mathbf{u},0)$. A quaternion with a zero real part is called a *pure quaternion*. It is then possible to multiply a scalar and a quaternion, and the result is $s(p_1,p_2,p_3,p_4)=(sp_1,sp_2,sp_3,sp_4)=(p_1,p_2,p_3,p_4)s$. The special case of scalar multiplication is commutative.

4. The conjugate of a quaternion $\mathbf{q}=(q_1,q_2,q_3,q_4)=(\mathbf{u},q_4)$ is denoted by $\mathbf{q}^*$ and defined by $\mathbf{q}^*=-q_1-q_2-q_3+q_4=(-\mathbf{u},q_4)$. The *norm* (or *magnitude*) of a quaternion is defined by: $\|\mathbf{q}\|=\sqrt{\mathbf{qq}^*}=\sqrt{q_1^2+q_2^2+q_3^2+q_4^2}=\sqrt{\|\mathbf{u}\|^2+q_4^2}$. We say that a quaternion is a *unit quaternion* if it has a norm of one.

5. Let $\mathbf{q}=(q_1,q_2,q_3,q_4)=(\mathbf{u},q_4)$ be a nonzero quaternion, then the inverse is denoted by $\mathbf{q}^{-1}$ and given by: $\mathbf{q}^{-1}=\frac{\mathbf{q}^*}{\|\mathbf{q}\|^2}$. If $\mathbf{q}$ is a unit quaternion, then $\mathbf{q}^{-1}=\mathbf{q}^*$.

6. A unit quaternion $\mathbf{q}=(\mathbf{u},q_4)$ can be written in the *polar representation* $\mathbf{q}=(\sin\theta\,\mathbf{n},\cos\theta)$, where $\mathbf{n}$ is a unit vector.

7. If $\mathbf{q}$ is a unit quaternion, then $\mathbf{q}=(\sin\theta\,\mathbf{n},\cos\theta)$ for $\|\mathbf{n}\|=1$ and $\theta\in[0,\pi]$. The quaternion rotation operator is defined by $R_\mathbf{q}(\mathbf{v})=\mathbf{qvq}^{-1}=\mathbf{qvq}^*$ and rotates the point/vector $\mathbf{v}$ around the axis $\mathbf{n}$ by an angle 2θ. $R_\mathbf{q}$ has a matrix representation, and any rotation matrix can be converted to a quaternion representing the rotation.

8. A common task in animation is to interpolate between two orientations. Representing each orientation by a unit quaternion, we can use spherical interpolation to interpolate the unit quaternions to find the interpolated orientation.

24.8 EXERCISES

1. Perform the indicated complex number operation.

(a) $(3+2i)+(-1+i)$

(b) $(3+2i)-(-1+i)$

(c) $(3+2i)(-1+i)$

(d) $4(-1+i)$

(e) $(3+2i)/(-1+i)$

(f) $(3+2i)^*$

(g) $|3+2i|$

2. Write the complex number $(-1,3)$ in polar notation.

3. Rotate the vector $(2,1)$ 30° using complex number multiplication.

4. Show using the definition of complex division that $\frac{a+ib}{a+ib} = 1$.

5. Let $\mathbf{z} = a + ib$. Show $|\mathbf{z}|^2 = \mathbf{z}\bar{\mathbf{z}}$.

6. Let $\mathbf{M}$ be a 2×2 matrix. Prove that $\det \mathbf{M} = 1$ and $\mathbf{M}^{-1} = \mathbf{M}^T$ if and only if
$\mathbf{M} = \begin{bmatrix} \cos\theta & \sin\theta \\ -\sin\theta & \cos\theta \end{bmatrix}$. That is, if and only if $\mathbf{M}$ is a rotation matrix. This gives
us a way of testing if a matrix is a rotation matrix.

7. Let $\mathbf{p} = (1,2,3,4)$ and $\mathbf{q} = (2,-1,1,-2)$ be quaternions. Perform the indicated
quaternion operations.

(a) $\mathbf{p} + \mathbf{q}$

(b) $\mathbf{p} - \mathbf{q}$

(c) $\mathbf{pq}$

(d) $\mathbf{p}^*$

(e) $\mathbf{q}^*$

(f) $\mathbf{p}^*\mathbf{p}$

(g) $\|\mathbf{p}\|$

(h) $\|\mathbf{q}\|$

(i) $\mathbf{p}^{-1}$

(j) $\mathbf{q}^{-1}$

8. Write the unit quaternion $\mathbf{q} = \left(\frac{1}{2}, \frac{1}{2}, 0, \frac{1}{\sqrt{2}}\right)$ in polar notation.

9. Write the unit quaternion $\mathbf{q} = \left(\frac{\sqrt{3}}{2}, 0, 0, -\frac{1}{2}\right)$ in polar notation.

10 . Find the unit quaternion that rotates 45° about the axis $(1,1,1)$.

11 . Find the unit quaternion that rotates 60° about the axis $(0,0,-1)$.

12 . Let $\mathbf{p} = \left(\frac{1}{2}, 0, 0, \frac{\sqrt{3}}{2}\right)$ and $\mathbf{q} = \left(\frac{\sqrt{3}}{2}, 0, 0, \frac{1}{2}\right)$. Compute $\text{slerp}\left(\mathbf{p}, \mathbf{q}, \frac{1}{2}\right)$ and verify it is
a unit quaternion.

13 . Show that a quaternion (x,y,z,w) can be written in the form $x\mathbf{i} + y\mathbf{j} + z\mathbf{k} + w$.

14 . Prove that $\mathbf{qq}^* = \mathbf{q}^*\mathbf{q} = q_1^2 + q_2^2 + q_3^2 + q_4^2 = \|\mathbf{u}\|^2 + q_4^2$.

15 . Let $\mathbf{p} = (\mathbf{u},0)$ and $\mathbf{q} = (\mathbf{v},0)$ be pure quaternions (i.e., real part 0). Show
$\mathbf{pq} = (\mathbf{p} \times \mathbf{q}, -\mathbf{p} \cdot \mathbf{q})$.

16 . Prove the following properties:

(a) $(pq)^* = q^* p^*$

(b) $(p+q)^* = p^* +q^*$

(c) $(sq)^* = sq^*$ for $s \in \mathbb{R}$

(d) $\|pq\| = \|p\|\|q\|$

17 . Prove $a \cdot \dfrac{\sin((1-t)\theta)a + \sin(t\theta)b}{\sin\theta} = \cos(t\theta)$ algebraically.

18 . Let a,b,c be 3D vectors. Prove the identities:

(a) $a \times (b \times c) = (a \cdot c)b - (a \cdot b)c$

(b) $(a \times b) \times c = -(c \cdot b)a + (c \cdot a)b$

Chapter 25 CHARACTER ANIMATION

Portions of this chapter appeared in the book by Frank D. Luna, *Introduction to 3D Game Programming with DirectX 9.0c: A Shader Approach*, 2006: Jones and Bartlett Learning, Burlington, MA. www.jblearning.com. Reprinted with permission.

In this chapter, we learn how to animate complex characters like a human or animal. Characters are complex because they have many moving parts that all move at the same time. Consider a human running—every bone is moving in some way. Creating such complicated animations is not practical by hand, and there are special modeling and animation tools for this task. Assuming we already have a character and its corresponding animation data created, in this chapter we will learn how to animate and render it using Direct3D.

Objectives:

1. To become familiar with the terminology of animated skinned meshes.
2. To learn the mathematics of mesh hierarchy transformations and how to traverse tree-based mesh hierarchies.
3. To understand the idea and mathematics of vertex blending.
4. To find out how to load animation data from the *.m3d* format.
5. To discover how to implement character animation in Direct3D.

25.1 FRAME HIERARCHIES

Many objects are composed of parts, with a parent-child relationship, where one or more child objects can move independently on their own (with possible physical motion constraints—e.g., human joints have a particular range of motion), but are also forced to move when their parent moves. For example, consider an arm divided into the parts: upper arm, forearm, and hand. The hand can rotate in isolation about its wrist joint; however, if the forearm rotates about its elbow joint, then the hand must rotate with it. Similarly, if the upper arm rotates about the shoulder joint, the forearm rotates with it, and if the forearm rotates, then the hand rotates with it (see Figure 25.1). Thus we see a definite object hierarchy: The hand is a child of the forearm; the forearm is a child of the upper arm, and if we extended our situation, the upper arm would be a child of the torso, and so on, until we have completed the skeleton (Figure 25.2 shows a more complex hierarchy example).

The aim of this section is to show how to place an object in the scene based on its position, and also the position of its *ancestors* (i.e., its parent, grandparent, great-grandparent, etc.).

25.1.1 Mathematical Formulation

Note: *The reader may wish to review Chapter 3 of this book, specifically the topic of change-of-coordinate transformations.*

To keep things simple and concrete, we work with the upper arm (the root), forearm, and hand hierarchy, which we label as Bone 0, Bone 1, and Bone 2, respectively (see Figure 25.3).

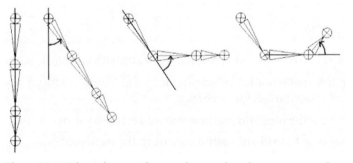

Figure 25.1. Hierarchy transforms; observe that the parent transformation of a bone influences itself and all of its children.

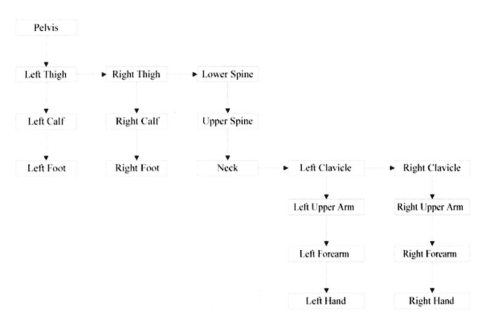

Figure 25.2. A more complex tree hierarchy to model a bipedal humanoid character. Down arrows represent "first child" relationships, and right arrows represent "sibling" relationships. For example, "Left Thigh," "Right Thigh," and "Lower Spine" are all children of the "Pelvis" bone.

Once the basic concept is understood, a straightforward generalization is used to handle more complex situations. So given an object in the hierarchy, how do we correctly transform it to world space? Obviously, we cannot just transform it directly into the world space because we must also take into consideration the transformations of its ancestors since they also influence its placement in the scene.

Each object in the hierarchy is modeled about its own local coordinate system with its pivot joint at the origin to facilitate rotation (see Figure 25.4).

Because all the coordinate systems exist in the same universe, we can relate them; in particular, for an arbitrary instant in time (we fix time and study a snapshot because, in general, these mesh hierarchies are animated and so these relationships change as a function of time), we describe each coordinate system relative to its parent coordinate system. (The parent coordinate system of the root

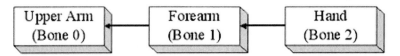

Figure 25.3. A simple hierarchy.

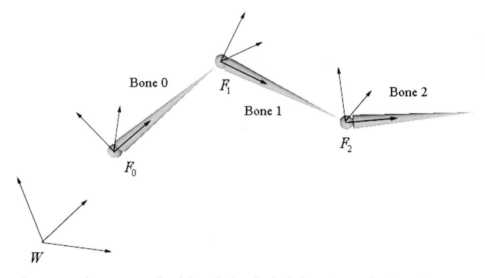

Figure 25.4. The geometry of each bone is described relative to its own local coordinate system. Furthermore, because all the coordinate systems exist in the same universe, we can relate them to one another.

frame F_0 is the world space coordinate system W; that is, the coordinate system F_0 is described relative to the world coordinate system.) Now that we have related the child and parent coordinate systems, we can transform from a child's space to its parent's space with a transformation matrix. (This is the same idea as the local-to-world transformation. However, instead of transforming from local space to world space, we transform from the local space to the space of the parent.) Let $\mathbf{A}_2$ be a matrix that transforms geometry from frame F_2 into F_1, let $\mathbf{A}_1$ be a matrix that transform geometry from frame F_1 into F_0, and let $\mathbf{A}_0$ be a matrix that transform geometry from frame F_0 into W. (We call $\mathbf{A}_i$ a *to-parent* matrix because it transforms geometry from a child's coordinate system into its parent's coordinate system.) Then, we can transform the ith object in the arm hierarchy into world space by the matrix $\mathbf{M}_i$ defined as follows:

$$\mathbf{M}_i = \mathbf{A}_i \mathbf{A}_{i-1} \cdots \mathbf{A}_1 \mathbf{A}_0 \qquad \text{(eq. 25.1)}$$

Specifically, in our example, $\mathbf{M}_2 = \mathbf{A}_2\,\mathbf{A}_1\,\mathbf{A}_0$, $\mathbf{M}_1 = \mathbf{A}_1\,\mathbf{A}_0$, and $\mathbf{M}_0 = \mathbf{A}_0$ transforms the hand into world space, the forearm into world space, and the upper arm into world space, respectively. Observe that an object inherits the transformations of its ancestors; this is what will make the hand move if the upper arm moves, for example.

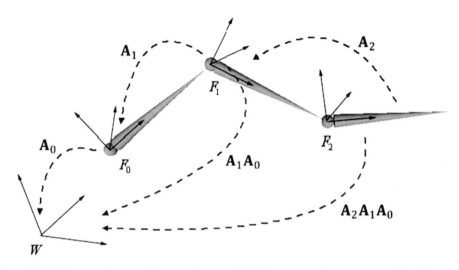

Figure 25.5. Because the coordinate systems exist in the same universe we can relate them, and therefore, transform from one to the other. In particular, we relate them by describing each bone's coordinate system relative to its parent's coordinate system. From that, we can construct a *to-parent* transformation matrix that transforms the geometry of a bone from its local coordinate system to its parent's coordinate system. Once in the parent's coordinate system, we can then transform by the parent's to-parent matrix to transform to the grandparent's coordinate system, and so on, until we have visited each ancestor's coordinate system and finally reached the world space.

Figure 25.5 illustrates what Equation 25.1 says graphically; essentially, to transform an object in the arm hierarchy, we just apply the to-parent transform of the object and all of its ancestors (in ascending order) to percolate up the coordinate system hierarchy until the object arrives in the world space.

The example we have been working with is a simple linear hierarchy. But the same idea generalizes to a tree hierarchy; that being, for any object in the hierarchy, its world space transformation is found by just applying the to-parent transform of the object and all of its ancestors (in ascending order) to percolate up the coordinate system hierarchy until the object arrives in the world space (we again stipulate that the parent coordinate system of the root is the world space). The only real difference is that we have a more complicated tree data structure to traverse instead of a linear list.

As an example, consider the left clavicle in Figure 25.2. It is a sibling of the neck bone, and therefore a child of the upper spine. The upper spine is a child of the lower spine, and the lower spine is a child of the pelvis. Therefore, the world transform of the left clavicle is formed by concatenating the left clavicle's to-parent transform, followed by the upper spine's to-parent transform, followed by the lower spine's to-parent transform, followed by the pelvis' to-parent transform.

25.2 SKINNED MESHES

25.2.1 Definitions

Figure 25.6 shows a character mesh. The highlighted chain of bones in the figure is called a *skeleton*. A skeleton provides a natural hierarchal structure for driving a character animation system. The skeleton is surrounded by an exterior *skin*, which we model as 3D geometry (vertices and polygons). Initially, the skin vertices are relative to the *bind space*, which is the local coordinate system that the entire skin is defined relative to (usually the root coordinate system). Each *bone* in the skeleton influences the shape and position of the subset of skin it influences (i.e., the vertices it influences), just like in real life. Thus, as we animate the skeleton, the attached skin is animated accordingly to reflect the current pose of the skeleton.

25.2.2 Reformulating a Bones To-Root Transform

One difference from §25.1 is that here we will transform from the root coordinate system to the world coordinate system in a separate step. So rather than finding the to-world matrix for each bone, we find the *to-root* (i.e., the transformation that transforms from the bone's local coordinate system to the root bone's coordinate system) matrix for each bone.

A second difference is that in §25.1, we traversed the ancestry of a node in a bottom-up fashion, where we started at a bone and moved up its ancestry. However, it is actually more efficient to take a top-down approach (see Equation 25.2),

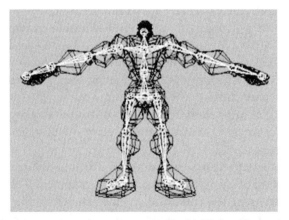

Figure 25.6. A character mesh. The highlighted bone chain represents the character's skeleton. The dark colored polygons represent the character's skin. The skin vertices are relative to the *bind space*, which is the coordinate system the mesh was modeled in.

where we start at the root and move down the tree. Labeling the n bones with an integer number $0,1,\ldots,n-1$, we have the following formula for expressing the ith bone's to-root transformation:

$$toRoot_i = toParent_i \cdot toRoot_p \qquad \text{(eq. 25.2)}$$

Here, p is the bone label of the parent of bone i. Does this make sense? Indeed, $toRoot_p$ gives us a direct map that sends geometry from the coordinate system of bone p to the coordinate system of the root. So to get to the root coordinate system, it follows that we just need to get geometry from the coordinate system of bone i to the coordinate system of its parent bone p, and $toParent_i$ does that job.

The only issue is that for this to work, when we go to process the ith bone, we must have already computed the to-root transformation of its parent. However, if we traverse the tree top-down, then a parent's to-root transformation will always be computed before its children's to-root transformation.

We can also see why this is more efficient. With the top-down approach, for any bone i, we already have the to-root transformation matrix of its parent; thus, we are only *one* step away from the to-root transformation for bone i. With a bottoms-up technique, we'd traverse the entire ancestry for each bone, and many matrix multiplications would be duplicated when bones share common ancestors.

25.2.3 The Offset Transform

There is a small subtlety that comes from the fact that the vertices influenced by a bone are not relative to the coordinate system of the bone (they are relative to the *bind space*, which is the coordinate system the mesh was modeled in). So before we apply Equation 15.2, we first need to transform the vertices from bind space to the space of the bone that influences the vertices. A so-called *offset transformation* does this; see Figure 25.7.

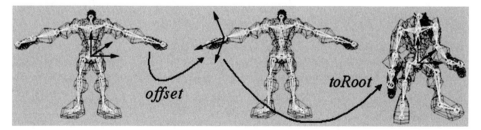

Figure 25.7. We first transform the vertices influenced by a bone from bind space to the space of the influencing bone via the offset transform. Then, once in the space of the bone, we apply the bone's to-root transformation to transform the vertices from the space of the bone to the space of the root bone. The final transformation is the combination of the offset transform, followed by the to-root transform.

Thus, by transforming the vertices by the offset matrix of some arbitrary bone *B*, we move the vertices from the bind space to the bone space of *B*. Then, once we have the vertices in the bone space of *B*, we can use *B*'s to-root transform to position it back in character space in its current animated pose.

We now introduce a new transform, call it the *final transform*, which combines a bone's offset transform with its to-root transform. Mathematically, the final transformation matrix of the *i*th bone $\mathbf{F}_i$ is given by:

$$\mathbf{F}_i = \textit{offset}_i \cdot \textit{toRoot}_i$$

(eq. 25.3)

25.2.4 Animating the Skeleton

In the demo of the last chapter, we showed how to animate a single object. We defined that a *key frame* specifies the position, orientation, and scale of an object at an instance in time, and that an *animation* is a list of key frames sorted by time, which roughly define the look of the overall animation. We then showed how to interpolate between key frames to calculate the placement of the object at times between key frames. We now extend our animation system to animating skeletons. These animation classes are defined in *SkinnedData.h/.cpp* in the "Skinned Mesh" demo of this chapter.

Animating a skeleton is not much harder than animating a single object. Whereas we can think of a single object as a single bone, a skeleton is just a collection of connected bones. We will assume that each bone can move independently. Therefore, to animate a skeleton, we just animate each bone locally. Then after each bone has done its local animation, we take into consideration the movement of its ancestors, and transform it to the root space.

We define an *animation clip* to be a list of animations (one for each bone in the skeleton) that work together to form a specific animation of the skeleton. For example, "walking," "running," "fighting," "ducking," and "jumping" are examples of animation clips.

```
///<summary>
/// Examples of AnimationClips are "Walk", "Run", "Attack", "Defend".
/// An AnimationClip requires a BoneAnimation for every bone to form
/// the animation clip.
///</summary>
struct AnimationClip
{
    // Smallest end time over all bones in this clip.
    float GetClipStartTime()const;

    // Largest end time over all bones in this clip.
    float GetClipEndTime()const;
```

```
        // Loops over each BoneAnimation in the clip and interpolates
        // the animation.
        void Interpolate(float t, std::vector<XMFLOAT4X4>& boneTransforms)const;

        // Animation for each bone.
        std::vector<BoneAnimation> BoneAnimations;
    };
```

A character will generally have several animation clips for all the animations the character needs to perform in the application. All the animation clips work on the same skeleton, however, so they use the same number of bones (although some bones may be stationary for a particular animation). We can use a map data structure to store all the animation clips and to refer to an animation clip by a readable name:

```
std::map<std::string, AnimationClip> mAnimations;
AnimationClip& clip = mAnimations["attack"];
```

Finally, as already mentioned, each bone needs an offset transform to transform the vertices from bind space to the space of the bone; and additionally, we need a way to represent the skeleton hierarchy (we use an array—see the next section for details). This gives us our final data structure for storing our skeleton animation data:

```
class SkinnedData
{
public:

    UINT BoneCount()const;

    float GetClipStartTime(const std::string& clipName)const;
    float GetClipEndTime(const std::string& clipName)const;

    void Set(
      std::vector<int>& boneHierarchy,
      std::vector<XMFLOAT4X4>& boneOffsets,
      std::map<std::string, AnimationClip>& animations);

    // In a real project, you'd want to cache the result if there
    // was a chance that you were calling this several times with
    // the same clipName at the same timePos.
    void GetFinalTransforms(const std::string& clipName, float timePos,
      std::vector<XMFLOAT4X4>& finalTransforms)const;

private:
    // Gives parentIndex of ith bone.  The ith bone corresponds to
    // the ith BoneAnimation in an animation clip.
    std::vector<int> mBoneHierarchy;

    // Offset transform of the ith bone.
    std::vector<XMFLOAT4X4> mBoneOffsets;

    std::map<std::string, AnimationClip> mAnimations;
};
```

25.2.5 Calculating the Final Transform

Our frame hierarchy for a character will generally be a tree, similar to the one in Figure 25.2. We model the hierarchy with an array of integers such that the *i*th array entry gives the parent index of the *i*th bone. Moreover, the *i*th entry corresponds to the *i*th BoneAnimation in the working animation clip and the *i*th entry corresponds to the *i*th offset transform. The root bone is always at element 0 and it has no parent. So for example, the animation and offset transform of the grandparent of bone *i* is obtained by:

```
int parentIndex  = mBoneHierarchy[i];
int grandParentIndex = mBoneHierarchy[parentIndex];

XMFLOAT4X4 offset = mBoneOffsets[grandParentIndex];

AnimationClip& clip = mAnimations["attack"];
BoneAnimation& anim = clip.BoneAnimations[grandParentIndex];
```

We can therefore compute the final transform for each bone like so:

```
void SkinnedData::GetFinalTransforms(const std::string& clipName,
float timePos,  std::vector<XMFLOAT4X4>& finalTransforms)const
{
    UINT numBones = mBoneOffsets.size();

    std::vector<XMFLOAT4X4> toParentTransforms(numBones);

    // Interpolate all the bones of this clip at the given time instance.
    auto clip = mAnimations.find(clipName);
    clip->second.Interpolate(timePos, toParentTransforms);

    //
    // Traverse the hierarchy and transform all the bones to the root space.
    //

    std::vector<XMFLOAT4X4> toRootTransforms(numBones);

    // The root bone has index 0.  The root bone has no parent, so
    // its toRootTransform is just its local bone transform.
    toRootTransforms[0] = toParentTransforms[0];

    // Now find the toRootTransform of the children.
    for(UINT i = 1; i < numBones; ++i)
    {
      XMMATRIX toParent = XMLoadFloat4x4(&toParentTransforms[i]);

      int parentIndex = mBoneHierarchy[i];
      XMMATRIX parentToRoot = XMLoadFloat4x4(&toRootTransforms[parentIndex]);

      XMMATRIX toRoot = XMMatrixMultiply(toParent, parentToRoot);

      XMStoreFloat4x4(&toRootTransforms[i], toRoot);
    }
```

```
// Premultiply by the bone offset transform to get the final transform.
for(UINT i = 0; i < numBones; ++i)
{
    XMMATRIX offset = XMLoadFloat4x4(&mBoneOffsets[i]);
    XMMATRIX toRoot = XMLoadFloat4x4(&toRootTransforms[i]);
    XMStoreFloat4x4(&finalTransforms[i], XMMatrixMultiply(offset, toRoot));
}
}
```

There is one requirement needed to make this work. When we traverse the bones in the loop, we look up the to-root transform of the bone's parent:

```
int parentIndex = mBoneHierarchy[i];
XMMATRIX parentToRoot = XMLoadFloat4x4(&toRootTransforms[parentIndex]);
```

This only works if we are guaranteed that the parent bone's to-root transform has already been processed earlier in the loop. We can, in fact, make this guarantee if we ensure that the bones are always ordered in the arrays such that a parent bone always comes before a child bone. Our sample 3D data has been generated such that this is the case. Here is some sample data of the first ten bones in the hierarchy array of some character model:

```
ParentIndexOfBone0: -1
ParentIndexOfBone1:  0
ParentIndexOfBone2:  0
ParentIndexOfBone3:  2
ParentIndexOfBone4:  3
ParentIndexOfBone5:  4
ParentIndexOfBone6:  5
ParentIndexOfBone7:  6
ParentIndexOfBone8:  5
ParentIndexOfBone9:  8
```

So take Bone9. Its parent is Bone8, the parent of Bone8 is Bone5, the parent of Bone5 is Bone4, the parent of Bone4 is Bone3, the parent of Bone3 is Bone2, and the parent of Bone2 is the root node Bone0. Notice that a child bone never comes before its parent bone in the ordered array.

25.3 VERTEX BLENDING

We have showed how to animate the skeleton. In this section we will focus on animating the skin of vertices that cover the skeleton. The algorithm for doing this is called *vertex blending*.

The strategy of vertex blending is as follows. We have an underlying bone hierarchy, but the skin itself is one continuous mesh (i.e., we do not break the mesh up into parts to correspond with each bone and animate them individually). Moreover, one or more bones can influence a vertex of the skin; the net result being determined by a weighted average of the influencing bones' final transforms (the

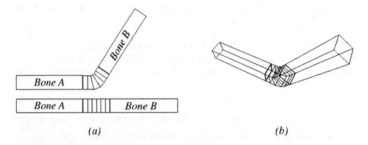

Figure 25.8. The skin is one continuous mesh that covers both bones. Observe that the vertices near the joint are influenced by both bone *A* and bone *B* to create a smooth transitional blend to simulate a flexible skin.

weights are specified by an artist when the model is being made and saved to file). With this setup, a smooth transitional blend can be achieved at joints (which are typically the troubled areas), thereby making the skin feel elastic; see Figure 25.8.

In practice, [Möller08] notes that we usually do not need more than four bone influences per vertex. Therefore, in our design we will consider a maximum of four influential bones per vertex. So to implement vertex blending, we model the character mesh's skin as one continuous mesh. Each vertex contains up to four indices that index into a *bone matrix palette*, which is the array of final transformation matrices (one entry for each bone in the skeleton). Additionally, each vertex also has up to four weights that describe the respective amount of influence each of the four influencing bones has on that vertex. Thus we have the following vertex structure for vertex blending (Figure 25.9):

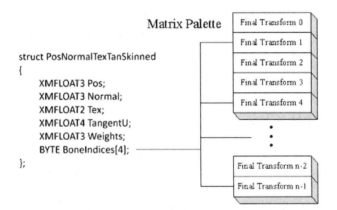

Figure 25.9. The matrix palette stores the final transformation for each bone. Observe how the four bone indices index into the matrix palette. The bone indices identify the bones of the skeleton that influence the vertex. Note that the vertex is not necessarily influenced by four bones; for instance, only two of the four indices might be used, thereby indicating that only two bones influence the vertex. We can set a bone weight to zero to effectively remove the bone from influencing the vertex.

A continuous mesh whose vertices have this format is ready for vertex blending, and we call it a *skinned mesh*.

The vertex-blended position $\mathbf{v}'$ of any vertex $\mathbf{v}$, relative to the root frame (remember we perform the world transformation as a last step once we have everything in the root coordinate system), can be calculated with the following weighted average formula:

$$\mathbf{v}' = w_0\mathbf{vF}_0 + w_1\mathbf{vF}_1 + w_2\mathbf{vF}_2 + w_3\mathbf{vF}_3$$

where $w_0 + w_1 + w_2 + w_3 = 1$; that is, the sum of the weights sums to one.

Observe that in this equation, we transform a given vertex $\mathbf{v}$ individually by all of the final bone transforms that influence it (i.e., matrices $\mathbf{F}_0$, $\mathbf{F}_1$, $\mathbf{F}_2$, $\mathbf{F}_3$). We then take a weighted average of these individually transformed points to compute the final vertex blended position $\mathbf{v}'$.

Transforming normals and tangents are done similarly:

$$\mathbf{n}' = \text{normalize}\left(w_0\mathbf{nF}_0 + w_1\mathbf{nF}_1 + w_2\mathbf{nF}_2 + w_3\mathbf{nF}_3\right)$$
$$\mathbf{t}' = \text{normalize}\left(w_0\mathbf{tF}_0 + w_1\mathbf{tF}_1 + w_2\mathbf{tF}_2 + w_3\mathbf{tF}_3\right)$$

Here we *assume* that the transformation matrices $\mathbf{F}_i$ do not contain any non-uniform scaling. Otherwise, we need to use the inverse-transpose $(\mathbf{F}_i^{-1})^T$ when transforming the normals (see §7.2.2).

The following vertex shader fragment shows the key code that does vertex blending with a maximum of two bone influences per vertex:

```
cbuffer cbSkinned
{
    // Max support of 96 bones per character.
    float4x4 gBoneTransforms[96];
};

struct SkinnedVertexIn
{
    float3 PosL        : POSITION;
    float3 NormalL     : NORMAL;
    float2 Tex         : TEXCOORD;
    float4 TangentL    : TANGENT;
    float3 Weights     : WEIGHTS;
    uint4 BoneIndices  : BONEINDICES;
};

VertexOut SkinnedVS(SkinnedVertexIn vin)
{
    VertexOut vout;

    // Init array or else we get strange warnings about SV_POSITION.
    float weights[4] = {0.0f, 0.0f, 0.0f, 0.0f};
    weights[0] = vin.Weights.x;
    weights[1] = vin.Weights.y;
```

```
weights[2] = vin.Weights.z;
weights[3] = 1.0f - weights[0] - weights[1] - weights[2];

// Do vertex blending.
float3 posL    = float3(0.0f, 0.0f, 0.0f);
float3 normalL = float3(0.0f, 0.0f, 0.0f);
float3 tangentL = float3(0.0f, 0.0f, 0.0f);
for(int i = 0; i < 4; ++i)
{
  // Assume no nonuniform scaling when transforming normals, so
  // that we do not have to use the inverse-transpose.

  posL    += weights[i]*mul(float4(vin.PosL, 1.0f),
                            gBoneTransforms[vin.BoneIndices[i]]).xyz;
  normalL += weights[i]*mul(vin.NormalL,
                            (float3x3)gBoneTransforms[vin.BoneIndices[i]]);
  tangentL += weights[i]*mul(vin.TangentL.xyz,
                            (float3x3)gBoneTransforms[vin.BoneIndices[i]]);
}

// Transform to world space space.
vout.PosW    = mul(float4(posL, 1.0f), gWorld).xyz;
vout.NormalW = mul(normalL, (float3x3)gWorldInvTranspose);
vout.TangentW = float4(mul(tangentL, (float3x3)gWorld), vin.TangentL.w);

// Transform to homogeneous clip space.
vout.PosH = mul(float4(posL, 1.0f), gWorldViewProj);

// Output vertex attributes for interpolation across triangle.
vout.Tex = mul(float4(vin.Tex, 0.0f, 1.0f), gTexTransform).xy;

// Generate projective tex-coords to project shadow map onto scene.
vout.ShadowPosH = mul(float4(posL, 1.0f), gShadowTransform);

// Generate projective tex-coords to project SSAO map onto scene.
vout.SsaoPosH = mul(float4(posL, 1.0f), gWorldViewProjTex);

return vout;
}
```

If the previous vertex shader does vertex blending with a maximum of four bone influences per vertex, then why do we only input three weights per vertex instead of four? Well, recall that the total weight must sum to one; thus, for four weights we have: $w_0 + w_1 + w_2 + w_3 = 1 \Longleftrightarrow w_3 = 1 - w_0 - w_1 - w_2$.

25.4 LOADING .M3D ANIMATION DATA

We now extend our .m3d file format to support skinned mesh data. Recall that the .m3d header has slots for the number of bones in the skeleton and the number of animation clips:

```
**************m3d-File-Header**************
#Materials 3
#Vertices 3121
#Triangles 4062
#Bones 44
#AnimationClips 15
```

The *.m3d* format is modified as follows for skinned mesh support:

1. Vertex blend weights and indices have been added to the vertex data chunk.

2. A new chunk for bone offset transformations (stored as a matrix).

3. A new chunk to store the hierarchy array.

4. A new chunk to store the animation clips.

25.4.1 Skinned Vertex Data

The first change is that our vertices now contain blend weights and bone indices, so we need a special method for reading skinned vertex data:

```
***************Vertices**********************
Position: -14.34667 90.44742 -12.08929
Tangent: -0.3069077 0.2750875 0.9111171 1
Normal: -0.3731041 -0.9154652 0.150721
Tex-Coords: 0.21795 0.105219
BlendWeights: 0.483457 0.483457 0.0194 0.013686
BlendIndices: 3 2 39 34

Position: -15.87868 94.60355 9.362272
Tangent: -0.3069076 0.2750875 0.9111172 1
Normal: -0.3731041 -0.9154652 0.150721
Tex-Coords: 0.278234 0.091931
BlendWeights: 0.4985979 0.4985979 0.002804151 0
BlendIndices: 39 2 3 0
...

void M3DLoader::ReadSkinnedVertices(std::ifstream& fin, UINT numVertices,
            std::vector<Vertex::PosNormalTexTanSkinned>& vertices)
{
    std::string ignore;
    vertices.resize(numVertices);

    fin >> ignore; // vertices header text
    int boneIndices[4];
    float weights[4];
    for(UINT i = 0; i < numVertices; ++i)
    {
      fin >> ignore >> vertices[i].Pos.x >>
                        vertices[i].Pos.y >>
                        vertices[i].Pos.z;
```

```
           fin >> ignore >> vertices[i].TangentU.x >>
                            vertices[i].TangentU.y >>
                            vertices[i].TangentU.z >>
                            vertices[i].TangentU.w;
           fin >> ignore >> vertices[i].Normal.x >>
                            vertices[i].Normal.y >>
                            vertices[i].Normal.z;
           fin >> ignore >> vertices[i].Tex.x >>
                            vertices[i].Tex.y;
           fin >> ignore >> weights[0] >> weights[1] >>
                            weights[2] >> weights[3];
           fin >> ignore >> boneIndices[0] >> boneIndices[1] >>
                            boneIndices[2] >> boneIndices[3];

       vertices[i].Weights.x = weights[0];
       vertices[i].Weights.y = weights[1];
       vertices[i].Weights.z = weights[2];

       vertices[i].BoneIndices[0] = (BYTE)boneIndices[0];
       vertices[i].BoneIndices[1] = (BYTE)boneIndices[1];
       vertices[i].BoneIndices[2] = (BYTE)boneIndices[2];
       vertices[i].BoneIndices[3] = (BYTE)boneIndices[3];
   }
}
```

25.4.2 Bone Offset Transforms

The bone offset transformation chunk just stores a list of matrices, one for each bone.

```
***************BoneOffsets*******************
BoneOffset0 -0.8669753 0.4982096 0.01187624 0
0.04897417 0.1088907 -0.9928461 0
-0.4959392 -0.8601914 -0.118805 0
-10.94755 -14.61919 90.63506 1

BoneOffset1 1 4.884964E-07 3.025227E-07 0
-3.145564E-07 2.163151E-07 -1 0
4.884964E-07 0.9999997 -9.59325E-08 0
3.284225 7.236738 1.556451 1
...

void M3DLoader::ReadBoneOffsets(std::ifstream& fin, UINT numBones,
                          std::vector<XMFLOAT4X4>& boneOffsets)
{
    std::string ignore;
    boneOffsets.resize(numBones);

    fin >> ignore; // BoneOffsets header text
    for(UINT i = 0; i < numBones; ++i)
    {
      fin >> ignore >>
        boneOffsets[i](0,0) >> boneOffsets[i](0,1) >>
        boneOffsets[i](0,2) >> boneOffsets[i](0,3) >>
        boneOffsets[i](1,0) >> boneOffsets[i](1,1) >>
```

```
          boneOffsets[i](1,2) >> boneOffsets[i](1,3) >>
          boneOffsets[i](2,0) >> boneOffsets[i](2,1) >>
          boneOffsets[i](2,2) >> boneOffsets[i](2,3) >>
          boneOffsets[i](3,0) >> boneOffsets[i](3,1) >>
          boneOffsets[i](3,2) >> boneOffsets[i](3,3);
   }
}
```

25.4.3 Hierarchy

The hierarchy chunk stores the hierarchy array—an array of integers such that the ith array entry gives the parent index of the ith bone.

```
***************BoneHierarchy*****************
ParentIndexOfBone0: -1
ParentIndexOfBone1: 0
ParentIndexOfBone2: 0
ParentIndexOfBone3: 2
ParentIndexOfBone4: 3
ParentIndexOfBone5: 4
ParentIndexOfBone6: 5
ParentIndexOfBone7: 6
ParentIndexOfBone8: 5
ParentIndexOfBone9: 8

void M3DLoader::ReadBoneHierarchy(std::ifstream& fin, UINT numBones,
                                  std::vector<int>& boneIndexToParentIndex)
{
    std::string ignore;
    boneIndexToParentIndex.resize(numBones);

    fin >> ignore; // BoneHierarchy header text
    for(UINT i = 0; i < numBones; ++i)
    {
      fin >> ignore >> boneIndexToParentIndex[i];
    }
}
```

25.4.4 Animation Data

The last chunk we need to read are the animation clips. Each animation has a readable name and a list of key frames for each bone in the skeleton. Each key frame stores the time position, the translation vector specifying the position of the bone, the scaling vector specifying the bone scale, and the quaternion specifying the orientation of the bone.

```
***************AnimationClips*****************
AnimationClip run_loop
{
    Bone0 #Keyframes: 18
    {
      Time: 0 Pos: 2.538344 101.6727 -0.52932
      Scale: 1 1 1
```

```
          Quat: 0.4042651 0.3919331 -0.5853591 0.5833637
          Time: 0.0666666
          Pos: 0.81979 109.6893 -1.575387
          Scale: 0.9999998 0.9999998 0.9999998
          Quat: 0.4460441 0.3467651 -0.5356012 0.6276384
          ...
        }

      Bone1 #Keyframes: 18
        {
          Time: 0
          Pos: 36.48329 1.210869 92.7378
          Scale: 1 1 1
          Quat: 0.126642 0.1367731 0.69105 0.6983587
          Time: 0.0666666
          Pos: 36.30672 -2.835898 93.15854
          Scale: 1 1 1
          Quat: 0.1284061 0.1335271 0.6239273 0.7592083
          ...
        }
      ...
  }

  AnimationClip walk_loop
  {
      Bone0 #Keyframes: 33
        {
          Time: 0
          Pos: 1.418595 98.13201 -0.051082
          Scale: 0.9999985 0.999999 0.9999991
          Quat: 0.3164562 0.6437552 -0.6428624 0.2686314
          Time: 0.0333333
          Pos: 0.956079 96.42985 -0.047988
          Scale: 0.9999999 0.9999999 0.9999999
          Quat: 0.3250651 0.6395872 -0.6386833 0.2781091
          ...
        }

      Bone1 #Keyframes: 33
        {
          Time: 0
          Pos: -5.831432 2.521564 93.75848
          Scale: 0.9999995 0.9999995 1
          Quat: -0.033817 -0.000631005 0.9097761 0.4137191
          Time: 0.0333333
          Pos: -5.688324 2.551427 93.71078
          Scale: 0.9999998 0.9999998 1
          Quat: -0.033202 -0.0006390021 0.903874 0.426508
          ...
        }
      ...
  }

  ...
```

```
void M3DLoader::ReadAnimationClips(std::ifstream& fin, UINT numBones,
    UINT numAnimationClips,
    std::map<std::string, AnimationClip>& animations)
{
    std::string ignore;
    fin >> ignore; // AnimationClips header text
    for(UINT clipIndex = 0; clipIndex < numAnimationClips; ++clipIndex)
    {
      std::string clipName;
      fin >> ignore >> clipName;
      fin >> ignore; // {

      AnimationClip clip;
      clip.BoneAnimations.resize(numBones);

      for(UINT boneIndex = 0; boneIndex < numBones; ++boneIndex)
      {
      ReadBoneKeyframes(fin, numBones, clip.BoneAnimations[boneIndex]);
      }
      fin >> ignore; // }

      animations[clipName] = clip;
    }
}

void M3DLoader::ReadBoneKeyframes(std::ifstream& fin,
    UINT numBones, BoneAnimation& boneAnimation)
{
    std::string ignore;
    UINT numKeyframes = 0;
    fin >> ignore >> ignore >> numKeyframes;
    fin >> ignore; // {

    boneAnimation.Keyframes.resize(numKeyframes);
    for(UINT i = 0; i < numKeyframes; ++i)
    {
      float t    = 0.0f;
      XMFLOAT3 p(0.0f, 0.0f, 0.0f);
      XMFLOAT3 s(1.0f, 1.0f, 1.0f);
      XMFLOAT4 q(0.0f, 0.0f, 0.0f, 1.0f);
      fin >> ignore >> t;
      fin >> ignore >> p.x >> p.y >> p.z;
      fin >> ignore >> s.x >> s.y >> s.z;
      fin >> ignore >> q.x >> q.y >> q.z >> q.w;

      boneAnimation.Keyframes[i].TimePos      = t;
      boneAnimation.Keyframes[i].Translation  = p;
      boneAnimation.Keyframes[i].Scale        = s;
      boneAnimation.Keyframes[i].RotationQuat = q;
    }

    fin >> ignore; // }
}
```

25.4.5 M3DLoader

We have added an overload of the LoadM3d function in *LoadM3D.h/.cpp* to load
SkinnedData:

```cpp
bool M3DLoader::LoadM3d(const std::string& filename,
        std::vector<Vertex::PosNormalTexTanSkinned>& vertices,
        std::vector<USHORT>& indices,
        std::vector<MeshGeometry::Subset>& subsets,
        std::vector<M3dMaterial>& mats,
        SkinnedData& skinInfo)
{
    std::ifstream fin(filename);

    UINT numMaterials = 0;
    UINT numVertices  = 0;
    UINT numTriangles = 0;
    UINT numBones     = 0;
    UINT numAnimationClips = 0;

    std::string ignore;

    if(fin)
    {
      fin >> ignore; // file header text
      fin >> ignore >> numMaterials;
      fin >> ignore >> numVertices;
      fin >> ignore >> numTriangles;
      fin >> ignore >> numBones;
      fin >> ignore >> numAnimationClips;

      std::vector<XMFLOAT4X4> boneOffsets;
      std::vector<int> boneIndexToParentIndex;
      std::map<std::string, AnimationClip> animations;

      ReadMaterials(fin, numMaterials, mats);
      ReadSubsetTable(fin, numMaterials, subsets);
      ReadSkinnedVertices(fin, numVertices, vertices);
      ReadTriangles(fin, numTriangles, indices);
      ReadBoneOffsets(fin, numBones, boneOffsets);
      ReadBoneHierarchy(fin, numBones, boneIndexToParentIndex);
      ReadAnimationClips(fin, numBones, numAnimationClips, animations);

      skinInfo.Set(boneIndexToParentIndex, boneOffsets, animations);

      return true;
    }
    return false;
}
```

25.5 CHARACTER ANIMATION DEMO

As a skinned mesh analog to BasicModel, which we defined in §23.3, we define SkinnedModel. This class is exactly like BasicModel except that it has a SkinnedData instance.

```
class SkinnedModel
{
public:
    SkinnedModel(ID3D11Device* device, TextureMgr& texMgr,
      const std::string& modelFilename,
      const std::wstring& texturePath);
    ~SkinnedModel();

    UINT SubsetCount;

    std::vector<Material> Mat;
    std::vector<ID3D11ShaderResourceView*> DiffuseMapSRV;
    std::vector<ID3D11ShaderResourceView*> NormalMapSRV;

    // Keep CPU copies of the mesh data to read from.
    std::vector<Vertex::PosNormalTexTanSkinned> Vertices;
    std::vector<USHORT> Indices;
    std::vector<MeshGeometry::Subset> Subsets;

    MeshGeometry ModelMesh;
    SkinnedData SkinnedData;
};
```

We may wish to instance a SkinnedModel by drawing it multiple times, with different animation clips and at different locations. We use the following simple structure to facilitate this:

```
struct SkinnedModelInstance
{
    SkinnedModel* Model;
    float TimePos;
    std::string ClipName;
    XMFLOAT4X4 World;
    std::vector<XMFLOAT4X4> FinalTransforms;

    void Update(float dt);
};
```

A SkinnedModel instance keeps track of its animation position, the name of the clip it is animating, and its final transforms. The Update method is called every frame and increments the time position, interpolates the animations for each bone based on the current animation clip, and generates the final transforms which are ultimately set to the effect for processing in the vertex shader. When we reach the end of the animation, we start the time position back at zero.

```
void SkinnedModelInstance::Update(float dt)
{
    TimePos += dt;
    Model->SkinnedData.GetFinalTransforms(
        ClipName, TimePos, FinalTransforms);

    // Loop animation
    if(TimePos > Model->SkinnedData.GetClipEndTime(ClipName))
        TimePos = 0.0f;
}
```

In our demo, we create a skinned model instance, call its `Update` method in the `SkinnedMeshApp::UpdateScene` method, and remember to set the final transforms array to the effect. Figure 25.10 shows a screenshot of our demo. The original animated model and textures were taken from the DirectX SDK and converted to the *.m3d* format for demoing purposes. This sample model only has one animation clip called *Take1*.

Figure 25.10. **Screenshot of the "Skinned Mesh" demo.**

25.6 SUMMARY

1. Many real world objects we wish to model graphically in a computer program consist of parts with a parent-children relationship, where a child object can move independently on its own, but is also forced to move when its parent moves. For example, a tank turret can rotate independently of the tank, but it is still fixed to the tank and moves with the tank. Another classic example is skeletons, in which bones are attached to other bones and must move when they move. Consider game characters on a train. The characters can move independently inside the train, but they also move as the train moves. This example illustrates how, in a game, the hierarchy can change dynamically and must be updated. That is, before a character enters a train, the train is not part of the character's hierarchy, but once the player does enter a train, the train does becomes part of the character's hierarchy (the character inherits the train transformation).

2. Each object in a mesh hierarchy is modeled about its own local coordinate system with its pivot joint at the origin to facilitate rotation. Because the coordinate systems exist in the same universe we can relate them, and therefore, transform from one to the other. In particular, we relate them by describing each object's coordinate system relative to its parent's coordinate system. From that, we can construct a *to-parent* transformation matrix that transforms the geometry of an object from its local coordinate system to its parent's coordinate system. Once in the parent's coordinate system, we can then transform by the parent's to-parent matrix to transform to the grandparent's coordinate system, and so on, until we have visited each ancestor's coordinate system and finally reach the world space. Stated in other words, to transform an object in a mesh hierarchy from its local space to world space, we apply the to-parent transform of the object and all of its ancestors (in ascending order) to percolate up the coordinate system hierarchy until the object arrives in the world space. In this way, the object inherits the transformations of its parents and moves when they move.

3. We can express the to-root transformation of the ith bone with the recurrence relation: $toRoot_i = toParent_i \cdot toRoot_p$, where p refers to the parent bone of the ith bone.

4. The bone-offset transformation transforms vertices from bind space to the space of the bone. There is an offset transformation for each bone in the skeleton.

5. In vertex blending, we have an underlying bone hierarchy, but the skin itself is one continuous mesh, and one or more bones can influence a vertex. The

magnitude in which a bone influences a vertex is determined by a bone weight. For four bones, the transformed vertex $\mathbf{v}'$, relative to the root of the skeleton, is given by the weighted averaging formula $\mathbf{v}' = w_0\mathbf{v}\mathbf{F}_0 + w_1\mathbf{v}\mathbf{F}_1 + w_2\mathbf{v}\mathbf{F}_2 + w_3\mathbf{v}\mathbf{F}_3$, where $w_0 + w_1 + w_2 + w_3 = 1$. By using a continuous mesh, and several weighted bone influences per vertex, a more natural elastic skin effect is achieved.

6. To implement vertex blending, we store an array of final transformation matrices for each bone (the array is called a *matrix palette*). (The ith bone's final transformation is defined as $\mathbf{F}_i = \textit{offset}_i \cdot \textit{toRoot}_i$—that is, the bone's offset transformation followed by its to-root transformation.) Then, for each vertex, we store a list of vertex weights and matrix palette indices. The matrix palette indices of a vertex identify the final transformations of the bones that influence the vertex.

25.7 EXERCISES

1. Model and render an animated linear hierarchy by hand. For example, you might model a simple robot arm built from sphere and cylinder meshes; the sphere could model a joint and the cylinder an arm.

2. Model and render an animated tree hierarchy by hand such as the one shown in Figure 25.11. You can again use spheres and cylinders.

3. If you have access to an animation package (*Blender* http:// www. blender.org/ is free), try learning how to model a simple animated character using bones and blend weights. Export your data to the .*x* file format which supports vertex blending, and try to convert the file data to the .*m3d* format for rendering in the "Skinned Mesh" demo. This is not a short project.

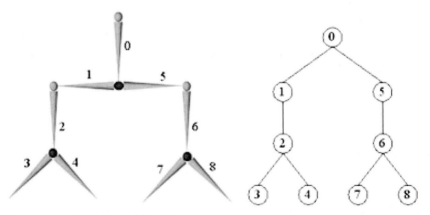

Figure 25.11. **Simple mesh hierarchy.**

INTRODUCTION TO WINDOWS PROGRAMMING

To use the Direct3D API (Application Programming Interface), it is necessary to create a Windows (Win32) application with a main window, upon which we will render our 3D scenes. This appendix serves as an introduction to writing Windows applications using the native Win32 API. Loosely, the Win32 API is a set of low-level functions and structures exposed to us in the C programming language that enables us to create Windows applications. For example, to define a window class, we fill out an instance of the Win32 API **WNDCLASS** structure; to create a window, we use the Win32 API **CreateWindow** function; to notify Windows to show a particular window, we use the Win32 API function **ShowWindow**.

Windows programming is a huge subject, and this appendix introduces only the amount necessary for us to use Direct3D. For readers interested in learning more about Windows programming with the Win32 API, the book *Programming Windows* by Charles Petzold, now in its fifth edition, is the standard text on the subject. Another invaluable resource when working with Microsoft technologies is the MSDN library, which is usually included with Microsoft's Visual Studio but can also be read online at www.msdn.microsoft.com. In general, if you come upon a Win32 function or structure that you would like to know more about, go to MSDN and search for that function or structure for its full documentation. If we mention a Win32 function or structure in this appendix and do not elaborate on it, it is an implicit suggestion that the reader look the function up in MSDN.

Objectives:

1. To learn and understand the event driven programming model used in Windows programming.

2. To learn the minimal code necessary to create a Windows application that is necessary to use Direct3D.

> **Note:** *To avoid confusion we will use a capital 'W' to refer to Windows the OS and we will use a lower case 'w' to refer to a particular window running in Windows.*

A.1 OVERVIEW

As the name suggests, one of the primary themes of Windows programming is programming windows. Many of the components of a Windows application are windows, such as the main application window, menus, toolbars, scroll bars, buttons, and other dialog controls. Therefore, a Windows application typically consists of several windows. These next subsections provide a concise overview of Windows programming concepts we should be familiar with before beginning a more complete discussion.

A.1.1 Resources

In Windows, several applications can run concurrently. Therefore, hardware resources such as CPU cycles, memory, and even the monitor screen must be shared amongst multiple applications. In order to prevent chaos from ensuing due to several applications accessing/modifying resources without any organization, Windows applications do not have direct access to hardware. One of the main jobs of Windows is to manage the presently instantiated applications and handle the distribution of resources amongst them. Thus, in order for our application to do something that might affect another running application, it must go through Windows. For example, to display a window you must call the Win32 API function `ShowWindow`; you cannot write to video memory directly.

A.1.2 Events, the Message Queue, Messages, and the Message Loop

A Windows application follows an *event-driven programming model*. Typically a Windows application sits and waits[1] for something to happen—an *event*. An event can be generated in a number of ways; some common examples are key presses,

---

[1] We note that an application can perform idle processing; that is, perform a certain task when no events are occurring.

mouse clicks, and when a window is created, resized, moved, closed, minimized, maximized, or becomes visible.

When an event occurs, Windows sends a *message* to the application the event occurred for, and adds the message to the application's *message queue*, which is simply a priority queue that stores messages for an application. The application constantly checks the message queue for messages in a *message loop* and, when it receives one, it dispatches the message to the *window procedure* of the particular window the message is for. (Remember, an application can contain several windows within it.) Every window has with it an associated function called a window procedure.[2] Window procedures are functions we implement which contain code that is to be executed in response to specific messages. For instance, we may want to destroy a window when the Escape key is pressed. In our window procedure we would write:

```
case WM_KEYDOWN:
    if(wParam == VK_ESCAPE)
      DestroyWindow(ghMainWnd);
    return 0;
```

The messages a window does not handle should be forwarded to the default window procedure, which then handles the message. The Win32 API supplies the default window procedure, which is called `DefWindowProc`.

To summarize, the user or an application does something to generate an event. The OS finds the application the event was targeted towards, and it sends that application a message in response. The message is then added to the application's message queue. The application is constantly checking its message queue for messages. When it receives a message, the application dispatches it to the window procedure of the window the message is targeted for. Finally, the window procedure executes instructions in response to the message.

Figure (A.1) summarizes the event driven programming model.

A.1.3 GUI

Most Windows programs present a GUI (Graphical User Interface) that users can work from. A typical Windows application has one main window, a menu, toolbar, and perhaps some other controls. Figure A.2 shows and identifies some common GUI elements. For Direct3D game programming, we do not need a fancy GUI. In fact, all we need is a main window, where the client area will be used to render our 3D worlds.

---

[2] Every window has a window procedure, but several windows can share the same window procedure; therefore, we do not necessarily have to write a unique window procedure for each window. Two different windows would have different window procedures if we wanted them to respond to messages differently.

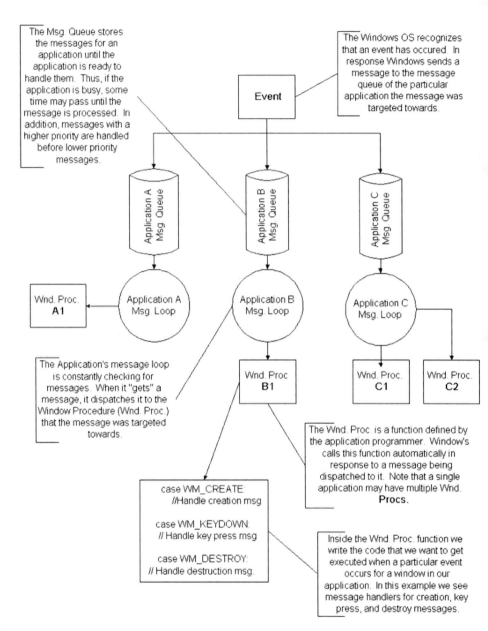

Figure A.1. The event driven programming model.

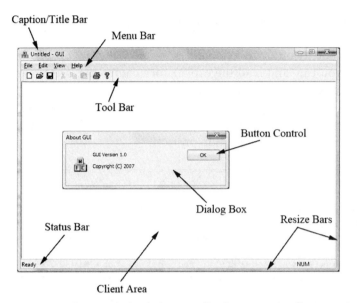

Caption/Title Bar

Menu Bar

Tool Bar

Button Control

Dialog Box

Resize Bars

Status Bar

Client Area

Figure A.2. The A typical Windows application GUI. The client area is the entire large white rectangular space of the application. Typically, this area is where the user views most of the program output. When we program our Direct3D applications, we render our 3D scenes into the client area of a window.

A.1.4 Unicode

Essentially, Unicode (http://unicode.org/) uses 16-bit values to represent a character. This allows us to represent a larger character set to support international characters, and other symbols. For Unicode in C++, we use the wide-characters type `wchar_t`. In 32- and 64-bit Windows, a `wchar_t` is 16-bits. When using wide characters, we must prefix a string literal with a capital L; for example:

```
const wchar_t* wcstrPtr = L"Hello, World!";
```

The L tells the compiler to treat the string literal as a string of wide-characters (i.e., as `wchar_t` instead of `char`). The other important issue is that we need to use the wide-character versions of the string functions. For example, to get the length of a string we need to use `wcslen` instead of `strlen`; to copy a string we need to use `wcscpy` instead of `strcpy`; to compare two strings we need to use `wcscmp` instead of `strcmp`. The wide-character versions of these functions work with `wchar_t` pointers instead of `char` pointers. The C++ standard library also provides a wide-character version of its string class: `std::wstring`. The Windows header file WinNT.h also defines:

```
typedef wchar_t WCHAR; // wc,   16-bit UNICODE character
```

A.2 BASIC WINDOWS APPLICATION

Following is the code to a fully functional, yet simple Windows program. Follow the code as best you can, and read the explanatory comments. The next section will explain the code a bit at a time. It is recommended that you create a project with your development tool, type the code in by hand, compile it, and execute it as an exercise. Note that for Visual C++, you must create a "Win32 application project," *not* a "Win32 console application project."

```cpp
//========================================================================
// Win32Basic.cpp by Frank Luna (C) 2008 All Rights Reserved.
//
// Illustrates the minimal amount of the Win32 code needed for
// Direct3D programming.
//========================================================================

// Include the windows header file; this has all the Win32 API
// structures, types,  and function declarations we need to program
// Windows.
#include <windows.h>

// The main window handle; this is used to identify a
// created window.
HWND ghMainWnd = 0;

// Wraps the code necessary to initialize a Windows
// application.  Function returns true if initialization
// was successful, otherwise it returns false.
bool InitWindowsApp(HINSTANCE instanceHandle, int show);

// Wraps the message loop code.
int  Run();

// The window procedure handles events our window receives.
LRESULT CALLBACK
WndProc(HWND hWnd, UINT msg, WPARAM wParam, LPARAM lParam);

// Windows equivalant to main()
int WINAPI
WinMain(HINSTANCE hInstance, HINSTANCE hPrevInstance,
        PSTR pCmdLine, int nShowCmd)
{
    // First call our wrapper function (InitWindowsApp) to create
    // and initialize the main application window, passing in the
    // hInstance and nShowCmd values as arguments.
    if(!InitWindowsApp(hInstance, nShowCmd))
            return 0;

    // Once our application has been created and initialized we
    // enter the message loop.  We stay in the message loop until
```

```
        // a WM_QUIT mesage is received, indicating the application
        // should be terminated.
        return Run();
}

bool InitWindowsApp(HINSTANCE instanceHandle, int show)
{
        // The first task to creating a window is to describe some of its
        // characteristics by filling out a WNDCLASS structure.
        WNDCLASS wc;

        wc.style         = CS_HREDRAW | CS_VREDRAW;
        wc.lpfnWndProc   = WndProc;
        wc.cbClsExtra    = 0;
        wc.cbWndExtra    = 0;
        wc.hInstance     = instanceHandle;
        wc.hIcon         = LoadIcon(0, IDI_APPLICATION);
        wc.hCursor       = LoadCursor(0, IDC_ARROW);
        wc.hbrBackground = (HBRUSH)GetStockObject(WHITE_BRUSH);
        wc.lpszMenuName  = 0;
        wc.lpszClassName = L"BasicWndClass";

        // Next, we register this WNDCLASS instance with Windows so
        // that we can create a window based on it.
        if(!RegisterClass(&wc))
        {
          MessageBox(0, L"RegisterClass FAILED", 0, 0);
          return false;
        }

        // With our WNDCLASS instance registered, we can create a
        // window with the CreateWindow function.  This function
        // returns a handle to the window it creates (an HWND).
        // If the creation failed, the handle will have the value
        // of zero.  A window handle is a way to refer to the window,
        // which is internally managed by Windows.  Many of the Win32 API
        // functions that operate on windows require an HWND so that
        // they know what window to act on.

        ghMainWnd = CreateWindow(
          L"BasicWndClass",    // Registered WNDCLASS instance to use.
          L"Win32Basic",       // window title
          WS_OVERLAPPEDWINDOW, // style flags
          CW_USEDEFAULT,       // x-coordinate
          CW_USEDEFAULT,       // y-coordinate
          CW_USEDEFAULT,       // width
          CW_USEDEFAULT,       // height
          0,                   // parent window
          0,                   // menu handle
          instanceHandle,      // app instance
          0);                  // extra creation parameters
```

```
    if(ghMainWnd == 0)
    {
      MessageBox(0, L"CreateWindow FAILED", 0, 0);
      return false;
    }

    // Even though we just created a window, it is not initially
    // shown.  Therefore, the final step is to show and update the
    // window we just created, which can be done with the following
    // two function calls.  Observe that we pass the handle to the
    // window we want to show and update so that these functions know
    // which window to show and update.
    ShowWindow(ghMainWnd, show);
    UpdateWindow(ghMainWnd);

    return true;
}

int Run()
{
    MSG msg = {0};

    // Loop until we get a WM_QUIT message.  The function
    // GetMessage will only return 0 (false) when a WM_QUIT message
    // is received, which effectively exits the loop.  The function
    // returns -1 if there is an error.  Also, note that GetMessage
    // puts the application thread to sleep until  there is a
    // message.
    BOOL bRet = 1;
    while((bRet = GetMessage(&msg, 0, 0, 0)) != 0)
    {
      if(bRet == -1)
      {
        MessageBox(0, L"GetMessage FAILED", L"Error", MB_OK);
        break;
      }
      else
      {
        TranslateMessage(&msg);
        DispatchMessage(&msg);
      }
    }

    return (int)msg.wParam;
}

LRESULT CALLBACK
WndProc(HWND hWnd, UINT msg, WPARAM wParam, LPARAM lParam)
{
    // Handle some specific messages.  Note that if we handle a
    // message, we should return 0.
    switch(msg)
```

```
{
   // In the case the left mouse button was pressed,
   // then display a message box.
case WM_LBUTTONDOWN:
  MessageBox(0, L"Hello, World", L"Hello", MB_OK);
  return 0;

   // In the case the escape key was pressed, then
   // destroy the main application window.
case WM_KEYDOWN:
  if(wParam == VK_ESCAPE)
    DestroyWindow(ghMainWnd);
  return 0;

   // In the case of a destroy message, then send a
   // quit message, which will terminate the message loop.
case WM_DESTROY:
  PostQuitMessage(0);
  return 0;
}

   // Forward any other messages we did not handle above to the
   // default window procedure.  Note that our window procedure
   // must return the return value of DefWindowProc.
   return DefWindowProc(hWnd, msg, wParam, lParam);
}
```

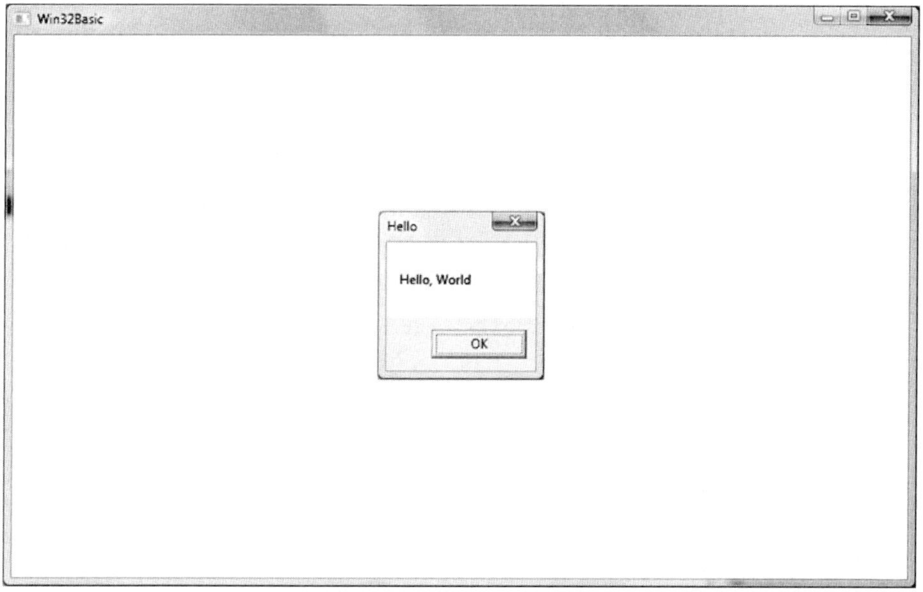

Figure A.3. A screenshot of the previous program. Note that the message box appears when you press the left mouse button in the window's client area. Also try exiting the program by pressing the Escape key.

A.3 EXPLAINING THE BASIC WINDOWS APPLICATION

We will examine the code from top to bottom, stepping into any function that gets called along the way. Refer back to the code listing in the "Basic Windows Application" section throughout the following subsections.

A.3.1 Includes, Global Variables, and Prototypes

The first thing we do is include the *windows.h* header file. By including the *windows.h* file we obtain the structures, types, and function declarations needed for using the basic elements of the Win32 API.

```
#include <windows.h>
```

The second statement is an instantiation of a global variable of type HWND. This stands for "handle to a window" or "window handle." In Windows programming, we often use handles to refer to objects maintained internally by Windows. In this sample, we will use an HWND to refer to our main application window maintained by Windows. We need to hold onto the handles of our windows because many calls to the API require that we pass in the handle of the window we want the API call to act on. For example, the call UpdateWindow takes one argument that is of type HWND that is used to specify the window to update. If we did not pass in a handle to it, the function would not know which window to update.

```
HWND ghMainWnd = 0;
```

The next three lines are function declarations. Briefly, InitWindowsApp creates and initializes our main application window; Run encapsulates the message loop for our application; and WndProc is our main window's window procedure. We will examine these functions in more detail when we come to the point where they are called.

```
bool InitWindowsApp(HINSTANCE instanceHandle, int show);
int  Run();
LRESULT CALLBACK
WndProc(HWND hWnd, UINT msg, WPARAM wParam, LPARAM lParam);
```

A.3.2 `WinMain`

WinMain is the Windows equivalent to the main function in normal C++ programming. WinMain is prototyped as follows:

```
int WINAPI
WinMain(HINSTANCE hInstance, HINSTANCE hPrevInstance,
        PSTR pCmdLine, int nShowCmd)
```

1. **hInstance**: Handle to the current application instance. It serves as a way of identifying and referring to this application. Remember there may be several Windows applications running concurrently, so it is useful to be able to refer to each one.

2. **hPrevInstance**: Not used in Win32 programming and is zero.

3. **pCmdLine**: The command line argument string used to run the program.

4. **nCmdShow**: Specifies how the application should be displayed. Some common commands that show the window in its current size and position, maximized, and minimized, respectively, are **SW_SHOW**, **SW_SHOWMAXIMIZED**, and **SW_SHOWMINIMIZED**. See the MSDN library for a complete list of show commands.

If **WinMain** succeeds, it should return the **wParam** member of the **WM_QUIT** message. If the function exits without entering the message loop, it should return zero. The **WINAPI** identifier is defined as:

```
#define WINAPI      __stdcall
```

This specifies the calling convention of the function, which means how the function arguments get placed on the stack.

A.3.3 WNDCLASS and Registration

Inside **WinMain** we call the function **InitWindowsApp**. As you can guess, this function does all the initialization of our program. Let us take a closer look at this function and its implementation. **InitWindowsApp** returns either **true** or **false**: **true** if the initialization was a success and **false** otherwise. In the **WinMain** definition, we pass as arguments a copy of our application instance and the show command variable into **InitWindowsApp**. Both are obtained from the **WinMain** parameter list.

```
if(!InitWindowsApp(hInstance, nShowCmd))
```

The first task at hand in initialization of a window is to describe some basic properties of the window by filling out a **WNDCLASS** (window class) structure. Its definition is:

```
typedef struct _WNDCLASS {
    UINT     style;
    WNDPROC  lpfnWndProc;
    int      cbClsExtra;
    int      cbWndExtra;
    HANDLE   hInstance;
    HICON    hIcon;
    HCURSOR  hCursor;
    HBRUSH   hbrBackground;
    LPCTSTR  lpszMenuName;
    LPCTSTR  lpszClassName;
} WNDCLASS;
```

1. **style:** Specifies the class style. In our example we use `CS_HREDRAW` combined with `CS_VREDRAW`. These two bit flags indicate that the window is to be repainted when either the horizontal or vertical window size is changed. For the complete list of the various styles with description, see the MSDN library.

```
wc.style = CS_HREDRAW | CS_VREDRAW;
```

2. **lpfnWndProc:** Pointer to the window procedure function to associate with this `WNDCLASS` instance. Windows that are created based on this `WNDCLASS` instance will use this window procedure. Thus, to create two windows with the same window procedure, you just create the two windows based on the same `WNDCLASS` instance. If you want to create two windows with different window procedures, you will need to fill out a different `WNDCLASS` instance for each of the two windows. The window procedure function is explained in section A.3.6.

```
wc.lpfnWndProc = WndProc;
```

3. **cbClsExtra** and **cbWndExtra:** These are extra memory slots you can use for your own purpose. Our program does not require any extra space and therefore sets both of these to zero.

```
wc.cbClsExtra = 0;
wc.cbWndExtra = 0;
```

4. **hInstance:** This field is a handle to the application instance. Recall the application instance handle is originally passed in through `WinMain`.

```
wc.hInstance = instanceHandle;
```

5. **hIcon:** Here you specify a handle to an icon to use for the windows created using this window class. You can use your own designed icon, but there are several built-in icons to choose from; see the MSDN library for details. The following uses the default application icon:

```
wc.hIcon = LoadIcon(0, IDI_APPLICATION);
```

6. **hCursor:** Similar to `hIcon`, here you specify a handle to a cursor to use when the cursor is over the window's client area. Again, there are several built-in cursors; see the MSDN library for details. The following code uses the standard "arrow" cursor.

```
wc.hCursor = LoadCursor(0, IDC_ARROW);
```

7. **hbrBackground:** This field is used to specify a handle to brush which specifies the background color for the client area of the window. In our sample code, we call the Win32 function `GetStockObject`, which returns a handle to a prebuilt white colored brush; see the MSDN library for other types of built in brushes.

```
wc.hbrBackground = (HBRUSH)GetStockObject(WHITE_BRUSH);
```

8. **lpszMenuName**: Specifies the window's menu. Because we have no menu in our application, we set this to zero.

    ```
    wc.lpszMenuName  = 0;
    ```

9. **lpszClassName**: Specifies the name of the window class structure we are creating. This can be anything you want. In our application, we named it "BasicWndClass". The name is simply used to identify the class structure so that we can reference it later by its name.

    ```
    wc.lpszClassName = L"BasicWndClass";
    ```

Once we have filled out a **WNDCLASS** instance, we need to register it with Windows so that we can create windows based on it. This is done with the **RegisterClass** function which takes a pointer to a **WNDCLASS** structure. This function returns zero upon failure.

```
if(!RegisterClass(&wc))
{
    MessageBox(0, L"RegisterClass FAILED", 0, 0);
    return false;
}
```

A.3.4 Creating and Displaying the Window

After we have registered a **WNDCLASS** variable with Windows, we can create a window based on that class description. We can refer to a registered **WNDCLASS** instance via the class name we gave it (**lpszClassName**). The function we use to create a window is the **CreateWindow** function, which is declared as follows:

```
HWND CreateWindow(
    LPCTSTR lpClassName,
    LPCTSTR lpWindowName,
    DWORD dwStyle,
    int x,
    int y,
    int nWidth,
    int nHeight,
    HWND hWndParent,
    HMENU hMenu,
    HANDLE hInstance,
    LPVOID lpParam
);
```

1. **lpClassName**: The name of the registered **WNDCLASS** structure that describes some of the properties of the window we want to create.

2. **lpWindowName**: The name we want to give our window; this is also the name that appears in the window's caption bar.

3. **dwStyle**: Defines the style of the window. **WS_OVERLAPPEDWINDOW** is a combination of several flags: **WS_OVERLAPPED, WS_CAPTION, WS_SYSMENU, WS_THICKFRAME, WS_MINIMIZEBOX,**

and **WS_MAXIMIZEBOX**. The names of these flags describe the characteristics of the window they produce. See the MSDN library for the complete list of styles.

4. **x**: The x position at the top left corner of the window relative to the screen. You can specify **CW_USEDEFAULT** for this parameter, and Windows will choose an appropriate default.

5. **y**: The y position at the top left corner of the window relative to the screen. You can specify **CW_USEDEFAULT** for this parameter, and Windows will choose an appropriate default.

6. **nWidth**: The width of the window in pixels. You can specify **CW_USEDEFAULT** for this parameter, and Windows will choose an appropriate default.

7. **nHeight**: The height of the window in pixels. You can specify **CW_USEDEFAULT** for this parameter, and Windows will choose an appropriate default.

8. **hWndParent**: Handle to a window that is to be the parent of this window. Our window has no relationship with any other windows, and therefore we set this value to zero.

9. **hMenu**: A handle to a menu. Our program does not use a menu, so we specify 0 for this field.

10. **hInstance**: Handle to the application the window will be associated with.

11. **lpParam**: A pointer to user-defined data that you want to be available to a **WM_CREATE** message handler. The **WM_CREATE** message is sent to a window when it is being created, but before **CreateWindow** returns. A window handles the **WM_CREATE** message if it wants to do something when it is created (e.g., initialization).

> Note: *When we specify the (x, y) coordinates of the window's position, they are relative to the upper-left corner of the screen. Also, the positive x-axis runs to the right as usual but the positive y-axis runs downward. Figure A.4 shows this coordinate system, which is called screen coordinates, or screen space.*

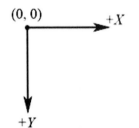

Figure A.4. Screen space. **CreateWindow** returns a handle to the window it creates (an **HWND**). If the creation failed, the handle will have the value of zero (null handle). Remember that the handle is a way to refer to the window, which is managed by Windows. Many of the API calls require a **HWND** so that it knows what window to act on.

```
ghMainWnd = CreateWindow(L"BasicWndClass", L"Win32Basic",
    WS_OVERLAPPEDWINDOW,
    CW_USEDEFAULT, CW_USEDEFAULT,
    CW_USEDEFAULT, CW_USEDEFAULT,
    0, 0, instanceHandle, 0);
if(ghMainWnd == 0)
{
    MessageBox(0, L"CreateWindow FAILED", 0, 0);
    return false;
}
```

The last two function calls in the InitWindowsApp function have to do with displaying the window. First we call ShowWindow and pass in the handle of our newly created window so that Windows knows which window to show. We also pass in an integer value that defines how the window is to be initially shown (e.g., minimized, maximized, etc.). This value should be nShowCmd, which is a parameter of WinMain. After showing the window, we should refresh it. UpdateWindow does this; it takes one argument that is a handle to the window we wish to update.

```
ShowWindow(ghMainWnd, show);
UpdateWindow(ghMainWnd);
```

If we made it this far in InitWindowsApp, then the initialization is complete; we return true to indicate everything went successfully.

A.3.5 The Message Loop

Having successfully completed initialization we can begin the heart of the program—the message loop. In our Basic Windows Application, we have wrapped the message loop in a function called Run.

```
int Run()
{
    MSG msg = {0};

    BOOL bRet = 1;
    while((bRet = GetMessage(&msg, 0, 0, 0)) != 0)
    {
      if(bRet == -1)
      {
        MessageBox(0, L"GetMessage FAILED", L"Error", MB_OK);
        break;
      }
      else
      {
        TranslateMessage(&msg);
        DispatchMessage(&msg);
      }
    }

    return (int)msg.wParam;
}
```

The first thing done in Run is an instantiation of a variable called msg of type MSG, which is the structure that represents a Windows message. Its definition is as follows:

```
typedef struct tagMSG {
    HWND    hwnd;
    UINT    message;
    WPARAM  wParam;
    LPARAM  lParam;
    DWORD   time;
    POINT   pt;
} MSG;
```

1. hwnd: The handle to the window whose window procedure is to receive the message.

2. message: A predefined constant value identifying the message (e.g., WM_QUIT).

3. wParam: Extra information about the message. This is dependent upon the specific message.

4. lParam: Extra information about the message. This is dependent upon the specific message.

5. time: The time the message was posted.

6. pt: The (x, y) coordinates of the mouse cursor, in screen coordinates, when the message was posted.

Next, we enter the message loop. The GetMessage function retrieves a message from the message queue, and fills out the msg argument with the details of the message. The second, third, and fourth parameters of GetMessage may be set to zero, for our purposes. If an error occurs in GetMessage, then GetMessage returns −1. If a WM_QUIT message is received, then GetMessage returns 0, thereby terminating the message loop. If GetMessage returns any other value, then two more functions get called: TranslateMessage and DispatchMessage. TranslateMessage has Windows perform some keyboard translations; specifically, virtual keys to character messages. DispatchMessage finally dispatches the message off to the appropriate window procedure.

If the application successfully exits via a WM_QUIT message, then the WinMain function should return the wParam of the WM_QUIT message (exit code).

A.3.6 The Window Procedure

We mentioned previously that the window procedure is where we write the code that we want to execute in response to a message our window receives. In the Basic Windows Application program, we name the window procedure WndProc and it is prototyped as:

```
LRESULT CALLBACK
WndProc(HWND hWnd, UINT msg, WPARAM wParam, LPARAM lParam);
```

This function returns a value of type **LRESULT** (defined as an integer), which indicates the success or failure of the function. The **CALLBACK** identifier specifies that the function is a callback function, which means that Windows will be calling this function outside of the code space of the program. As you can see from the Basic Windows Application source code, we never explicitly call the window procedure ourselves—Windows calls it for us when the window needs to process a message.

The window procedure has four parameters in its signature:

1. **hWnd:** The handle to the window receiving the message.

2. **msg:** A predefined value that identifies the particular message. For example, a quit message is defined as **WM_QUIT**. The prefix WM stands for "Window Message." There are over a hundred predefined window messages; see the MSDN library for details.

3. **wParam:** Extra information about the message which is dependent upon the specific message.

4. **lParam:** Extra information about the message which is dependent upon the specific message.

Our window procedure handles three messages: **WM_LBUTTONDOWN**, **WM_KEYDOWN**, and **WM_DESTROY** messages. A **WM_LBUTTONDOWN** message is sent when the user clicks the left mouse button on the window's client area. A **WM_KEYDOWN** message is sent to a window in focus when a key is pressed. A **WM_DESTROY** message is sent when a window is being destroyed.

Our code is quite simple; when we receive a **WM_LBUTTONDOWN** message we display a message box that prints out "Hello, World":

```
case WM_LBUTTONDOWN:
    MessageBox(0, L"Hello, World", L"Hello", MB_OK);
    return 0;
```

When our window gets a **WM_KEYDOWN** message, we test if the Escape key was pressed, and if it was, we destroy the main application window using the **DestroyWindow** function. The **wParam** passed into the window procedure specifies the virtual key code of the specific key that was pressed. Think of virtual key codes as an identifier for a particular key. The Windows header files have a list of virtual key code constants we can use to then test for a particular key; for example, to test if the escape key was pressed, we use the virtual key code constant **VK_ESCAPE**.

```
case WM_KEYDOWN:
    if(wParam == VK_ESCAPE)
      DestroyWindow(ghMainWnd);
    return 0;
```

Remember, the **wParam** and **lParam** parameters are used to specify extra information about a particular message. For the **WM_KEYDOWN** message, the **wParam** specifies the *virtual key code* of the specific key that was pressed. The MSDN library will specify the information the `wParam` and `lParam` parameters carry for each Windows message.

When our window gets destroyed, we post a `WM_QUIT` message with the `PostQuitMessage` function (which terminates the message loop):

```
case WM_DESTROY:
    PostQuitMessage(0);
    return 0;
```

At the end of our window procedure, we call another function named `DefWindowProc`. This function is the default window procedure. In our Basic Windows Application program, we only handle three messages; we use the default behavior specified in `DefWindowProc` for all the other messages we receive but do not necessarily need to handle ourselves. For example, the Basic Windows Application program can be minimized, maximized, resized, and closed. This functionality is provided to us through the default window procedure, as we did not handle the messages to perform this functionality.

A.3.7 The `MessageBox` Function

There is one last API function we have not yet covered, and that is the `MessageBox` function. This function is a very handy way to provide the user with information and to get some quick input. The declaration to the `MessageBox` function looks like this:

```
int MessageBox(
    HWND hWnd,         // Handle of owner window, may specify null.
    LPCTSTR lpText,    // Text to put in the message box.
    LPCTSTR lpCaption,// Text to put for the title of the message box.
    UINT uType         // Style of the message box.
);
```

The return value for the `MessageBox` function depends on the type of message box. See the MSDN library for a list of possible return values and styles; one possible style is a Yes/No message box; see Figure A.5.

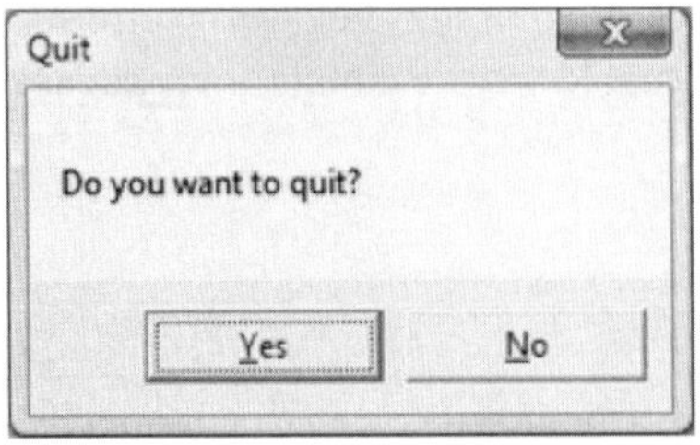

Figure A.5. Yes/No message box.

A.4 A BETTER MESSAGE LOOP

Games are very different applications than traditional Windows applications such as office type applications and Web browsers. Typically, games do not sit around waiting for a message, but are constantly being updated. This presents a problem, because if there are no messages in the message queue, the function `GetMessage` puts the thread to sleep and waits for a message. For a game, we do not want this behavior; if there are no Windows messages to be processed, then we want to run our own game code. The fix is to use the `PeekMessage` function instead of `GetMessage`. The `PeekFunction` message returns immediately if there are no messages. Our new message loop is as follows:

```
int Run()
{
    MSG msg = {0};

    while(msg.message != WM_QUIT)
    {
        // If there are Window messages then process them.
        if(PeekMessage(&msg, 0, 0, 0, PM_REMOVE))
        {
            TranslateMessage(&msg);
            DispatchMessage(&msg);
        }
        // Otherwise, do animation/game stuff.
        else
        {

        }
    }
    return (int)msg.wParam;
}
```

After we instantiate `msg`, we enter into an endless loop. We first call the API function `PeekMessage`, which checks the message queue for a message. See MSDN for the parameter descriptions. If there is a message it returns `true` and we handle the message. If there are no messages, `PeekMessage` returns `false` and we execute our own specific game code.

A.5 SUMMARY

1. To use Direct3D we must create a Windows application that has a main window onto which we can render our 3D scenes. Furthermore, for games we create a special message loop that checks for messages. If there are messages, it processes them; otherwise, it executes our game logic.

2. Several Windows applications can be run concurrently, and therefore Windows must manage resources between them and direct messages to the applications for which they were intended. Messages are sent to an application's message queue when an event (key press, mouse click, timer, etc.) has occurred for that application.

3. Every Windows application has a message queue in which messages an application receives are stored. The application's message loop constantly checks the queue for messages and dispatches them off to their intended window procedure. Note that a single application can have several windows within it.

4. The window procedure is a special callback function we implement that Windows calls when a window in our application receives a message. In the window procedure, we write the code we want to be executed when a window in our application receives a particular message. Messages we do not specifically handle are forwarded to a default window procedure for default handling.

A.6 EXERCISES

1. Modify the program in §A.2 to use a different icon, cursor, and background color.

   Look up the LoadIcon, LoadCursor, *and* GetStockObject *functions in MSDN.*

2. Modify the program in §A.2 by handling the WM_CLOSE message. This message is sent to a window or application indicating that the window or application should close. Use the message box function to ask the user if they really want to exit by displaying a Yes/No styled message box. If the user chooses "Yes," then destroy the window; otherwise do not destroy the window. You could also use this technique to ask the user if they want to save their work before closing.

3. Modify the program in §A.2 by handling the WM_CREATE message. This message is sent to a window when it is being created, but before CreateWindow returns. Output a message, via the message box function, indicating that the window has been created.

4. Look up the Sleep function in MSDN and summarize, in your own words, what the function does.

5. Look up the messages WM_SIZE and WM_ACTIVATE in MSDN and summarize, in your own words, when the messages are sent.

HIGH LEVEL SHADER LANGUAGE REFERENCE

VARIABLE TYPES

Scalar Types

1. `bool`: True or false value. Note that the HLSL provides the `true` and `false` keywords like in C++.
2. `int`: 32-bit signed integer.
3. `half`: 16-bit-floating point number.
4. `float`: 32-bit-floating point number.
5. `double`: 64-bit-floating point number.

Note: *Some platforms might not support* `int`, `half`, *and* `double`. *If this is the case these types will be emulated using* `float`.

Vector Types

1. `float2`: 2D vector, where the components are of type `float`.
2. `float3`: 3D vector, where the components are of type `float`.
3. `float4`: 4D vector, where the components are of type `float`.

Note: *You can create vectors where the components are of a type other than* `float`. *For example:* `int2, half3, bool4`.

We can initialize a vector using an array like syntax or constructor like syntax:

```
float3 v = {1.0f, 2.0f, 3.0f};
float2 w = float2(x, y);
float4 u = float4(w, 3.0f, 4.0f); // u = (w.x, w.y, 3.0f, 4.0f)
```

We can access a component of a vector using an array subscript syntax. For example, to set the *i*th component of a vector **vec** we would write:

```
vec[i] = 2.0f;
```

In addition, we can access the components of a vector **vec**, as we would access the members of a structure, using the defined component names **x, y, z, w, r, g, b**, and **a**.

```
vec.x = vec.r = 1.0f;
vec.y = vec.g = 2.0f;
vec.z = vec.b = 3.0f;
vec.w = vec.a = 4.0f;
```

The names **r, g, b**, and **a** refer to the exact same component as the names **x, y, z**, and **w**, respectively. When using vectors to represent colors, the RGBA notation is more desirable because it reinforces the fact that the vector is representing a color.

Swizzles

Consider the vector $\mathbf{u} = (u_x, u_y, u_z, u_w)$ and suppose we want to copy the components of **u** to a vector **v** such that $\mathbf{v} = (u_w, u_y, u_y, u_x)$. The most immediate solution would be to individually copy each component of **u** over to **v** as necessary. However, the HLSL provides a special syntax for doing these kinds of out of order copies called *swizzles*:

```
float4 u = {1.0f, 2.0f, 3.0f, 4.0f};
float4 v = {0.0f, 0.0f, 5.0f, 6.0f};

v = u.wyyx; // v = {4.0f, 2.0f, 2.0f, 1.0f}
```

Another example:

```
float4 u = {1.0f, 2.0f, 3.0f, 4.0f};
float4 v = {0.0f, 0.0f, 5.0f, 6.0f};

v = u.wzyx; // v = {4.0f, 3.0f, 2.0f, 1.0f}
```

When copying vectors, we do not have to copy every component over. For example, we can only copy the *x*- and *y*-components over as this code snippet illustrates:

```
float4 u = {1.0f, 2.0f, 3.0f, 4.0f};
float4 v = {0.0f, 0.0f, 5.0f, 6.0f};

v.xy = u; // v = {1.0f, 2.0f, 5.0f, 6.0f}
```

Matrix Types

We can define an $m \times n$ matrix, where m and n are between 1 and 4, using the following syntax:

```
floatmxn matmxn;
```

Examples:

1. **float2x2**: 2×2 matrix, where the entries are of type **float**.
2. **float3x3**: 3×3 matrix, where the entries are of type **float**.
3. **float4x4**: 4×4 matrix, where the entries are of type **float**.
4. **float3x4**: 3×4 matrix, where the entries are of type **float**.

Note: ▶ *You can create matrices where the components are of a type other than float. For example:* **int2x2**, **half3x3**, **bool4x4**.

We can access an entry in a matrix using a double array subscript syntax. For example, to set the *ij*th entry of a matrix **M** we would write:

```
M[i][j] = value;
```

In addition, we can refer to the entries of a matrix **M** as we would access the members of a structure. The following entry names are defined:

One-Based Indexing:

```
M._11 = M._12 = M._13 = M._14 = 0.0f;
M._21 = M._22 = M._23 = M._24 = 0.0f;
M._31 = M._32 = M._33 = M._34 = 0.0f;
M._41 = M._42 = M._43 = M._44 = 0.0f;
```

Zero-Based Indexing:

```
M._m00 = M._m01 = M._m02 = M._m03 = 0.0f;
M._m10 = M._m11 = M._m12 = M._m13 = 0.0f;
M._m20 = M._m21 = M._m22 = M._m23 = 0.0f;
M._m30 = M._m31 = M._m32 = M._m33 = 0.0f;
```

Sometimes we want to refer to a particular row vector in a matrix. We can do so using a single array subscript syntax. For example, to extract the *i*th row vector in a 3×3 matrix **M**, we would write:

```
float3 ithRow = M[i]; // get the ith row vector in M
```

In this next example, we insert three vectors into the first, second, and third row of a matrix:

```
float3 N = normalize(pIn.normalW);
float3 T = normalize(pIn.tangentW - dot(pIn.tangentW, N)*N);
float3 B = cross(N,T);
float3x3 TBN;
TBN[0] = T;   // sets row 1
TBN[1] = B;   // sets row 2
TBN[2] = N;   // sets row 3
```

We can also construct a matrix from vectors:

```
float3 N = normalize(pIn.normalW);
float3 T = normalize(pIn.tangentW - dot(pIn.tangentW, N)*N);
float3 B = cross(N,T);

float3x3 TBN = float3x3(T, B, N);
```

Note: *Instead of using* float4 *and* float4x4 *to represent 4D vectors and* 4×4 *matrices, you can equivalently use the* vector *and* matrix *type:*

```
vector u = {1.0f, 2.0f, 3.0f, 4.0f};
matrix M; // 4x4 matrix
```

Arrays

We can declare an array of a particular type using familiar C++ syntax, for example:

```
float  M[4][4];
half   p[4];
float3 v[12]; // 12 3D vectors
```

Structures

Structures are defined exactly as they are in C++. However, structures in the HLSL cannot have member functions. Here is an example of a structure in the HLSL:

```
struct SurfaceInfo
{
    float3 pos;
    float3 normal;
    float4 diffuse;
    float4 spec;
};

SurfaceInfo v;
litColor += v.diffuse;
dot(lightVec, v.normal);
float specPower   = max(v.spec.a, 1.0f);
```

The typedef Keyword

The HLSL typedef keyword functions exactly the same as it does in C++. For example, we can give the name point to the type vector<float, 3> using the following syntax:

```
typedef float3 point;
```

Then instead of writing:

```
float3 myPoint;
```

We can just write:

```
point myPoint;
```

Here is another example showing how to use the `typedef` keyword with the HLSL `const` keyword (which works as in C++):

```
typedef const float CFLOAT;
```

Variable Prefixes

The following keywords can prefix a variable declaration.

1. `static`: Essentially the opposite of `extern`; this means that the shader variable will not be exposed to the C++ application.

    ```
    static float3 v = {1.0f, 2.0f, 3.0f};
    ```

2. `uniform`: This means that the variable does not change per vertex/pixel—it is constant for all vertices/pixels until we change it at the C++ application level. Uniform variables are initialized from outside the shader program (e.g., by the C++ application).

3. `extern`: This means that the C++ application can see the variable (i.e., the variable can be accessed outside the shader file by the C++ application code). Global variables in a shader program are, by default, uniform and extern.

4. `const`: The `const` keyword in the HLSL has the same meaning it has in C++. That is, if a variable is prefixed with the `const` keyword then that variable is constant and cannot be changed.

    ```
    const float pi = 3.14f;
    ```

Casting

The HLSL supports a very flexible casting scheme. The casting syntax in the HLSL is the same as in the C programming language. For example, to cast a **float** to a **matrix** we write:

```
float f = 5.0f;
float4x4 m = (float4x4)f; // copy f into each entry of m.
```

What this scalar-matrix cast does is copy the scalar into each entry of the matrix. Consider the following example:

```
float3 n = float3(...);
float3 v = 2.0f*n - 1.0f;
```

The 2.0f*n is just scalar-vector multiplication, which is well defined. However, to make this a vector equation, the scalar 1.0f is augmented to the vector (1.0f, 1.0f, 1.0f). So the previous statement is like:

```
float3 v = 2.0f*n - float3(1.0f, 1.0f, 1.0f);
```

For the examples in this book, you will be able to deduce the meaning of the cast from the syntax. For a complete list of casting rules, search the SDK documentation index for "Casting and Conversion."

KEYWORDS AND OPERATORS

Keywords

For reference, here is a list of the keywords the HLSL defines:

```
asm, bool, compile, const, decl, do,
double, else, extern, false, float, for,
half, if, in, inline, inout, int,
matrix, out, pass, pixelshader, return, sampler,
shared, static, string, struct, technique, texture,
true, typedef, uniform, vector, vertexshader, void,
volatile, while
```

This next set of keywords displays identifiers that are reserved and unused, but may become keywords in the future:

```
auto, break, case, catch, char, class,
const_cast, continue, default, delete, dynamic_cast, enum,
explicit, friend, goto, long, mutable, namespace,
new, operator, private, protected, public, register,
reinterpret_cast, short, signed, sizeof, static_cast, switch,
template, this, throw, try, typename, union,
unsigned, using, virtual
```

Operators

HLSL supports many familiar C++ operators. With a few exceptions noted below, they are used exactly the same way as they are in C++. The following table lists the HLSL operators:

```
[]  .    >   <   <=  >=
!=  ==   !   &&  ||  ? :
+   +=   -   -=  *   *=
/   /=   %   %=  ++  --
=   ()   ,
```

Although the operators' behavior is very similar to C++, there are some differences. First of all, the modulus % operator works on both integer and floating-point types.

And in order to use the modulus operator, both the left-hand side value and right-hand side value must have the same sign (e.g., both sides must be positive or both sides must be negative).

Secondly, observe that many of the HLSL operations work on a per component basis. This is due to the fact that vectors and matrices are built into the language and these types consist of several components. By having the operations work on a component level, operations such as vector/matrix addition, vector/matrix subtraction, and vector/matrix equality tests can be done using the same operators we use for scalar types. See the following examples.

Note: *The operators behave as expected for scalars, that is, in the usual C++ way.*

```
float4 u = {1.0f, 0.0f, -3.0f, 1.0f};
float4 v = {-4.0f, 2.0f, 1.0f, 0.0f};

// adds corresponding components
float4 sum = u + v; // sum = (-3.0f, 2.0f, -2.0f, 1.0f)
```

Incrementing a vector increments each component:

```
// before increment: sum = (-3.0f, 2.0f, -2.0f, 1.0f)

sum++; // after increment: sum = (-2.0f, 3.0f, -1.0f, 2.0f)
```

Multiplying vectors componentwise:

```
float4 u = {1.0f, 0.0f, -3.0f, 1.0f};
float4 v = {-4.0f, 2.0f, 1.0f, 0.0f};

// multiply corresponding components
float4 product = u * v; // product = (-4.0f, 0.0f, -3.0f, 0.0f)
```

Warning: If you have two matrices:

```
float4x4 A;
float4x4 B;
```

the syntax A*B does componentwise multiplication, not matrix multiplication. You need to use the mul function for matrix multiplication.

Comparison operators are also done per component and return a vector or matrix where each component is of type bool. The resulting "bool" vector contains the results of each compared component. For example:

```
float4 u = { 1.0f, 0.0f, -3.0f, 1.0f};
float4 v = {-4.0f, 0.0f,  1.0f, 1.0f};

float4 b = (u == v); // b = (false, true, false, true)
```

Finally, we conclude by discussing variable promotions with binary operations:

1. For binary operations, if the left-hand side and right-hand side differ in dimension, then the side with the smaller dimension is promoted (cast) to have the same dimension as the side with the larger dimension. For example, if x is of type float and y is of type float3, in the expression (x + y), the variable x is promoted to float3 and the expression evaluates to a value of type float3. The promotion is done using the defined cast, in this case we are casting Scalar-to-Vector, therefore, after x is promoted to float3, x = (x, x, x) as the Scalar-to-Vector cast defines. Note that the promotion is not defined if the cast is not defined. For example, we can't promote float2 to float3 because there exists no such defined cast.

2. For binary operations, if the left-hand side and right-hand side differ in type, then the side with the lower type resolution is promoted (cast) to have the same type as the side with the higher type resolution. For example, if x is of type int and y is of type half, in the expression (x + y), the variable x is promoted to a half and the expression evaluates to a value of type half.

PROGRAM FLOW

The HLSL supports many familiar C++ statements for selection, repetition, and general program flow. The syntax of these statements is exactly like C++.

The *Return* statement:

```
return (expression);
```

The *If* and *If...Else* statements:

```
if(condition)
{
    statement(s);
}
```

```
if(condition)
{
    statement(s);
}
else
{
    statement(s);
}
```

The *for* statement:

```
for(initial; condition; increment)
{
    statement(s);
}
```

The while statement:

```
while(condition)
{
    statement(s);
}
```

The *do...while* statement:

```
do
{
    statement(s);
}while(condition);
```

FUNCTIONS

User-Defined Functions

Functions in the HLSL have the following properties:

1. Functions use a familiar C++ syntax.

2. Parameters are always passed by value.

3. Recursion is not supported.

4. Functions are always inlined.

Furthermore, the HLSL adds some extra keywords that can be used with functions. For example, consider the following function written in the HLSL:

```
bool foo(in const bool b, // input bool
         out int r1,       // output int
         inout float r2)   // input/output float
{
    if(b) // test input value
    {
      r1 = 5; // output a value through r1
    }
    else
    {
      r1 = 1; // output a value through r1
    }

    // since r2 is inout we can use it as an input
    // value and also output a value through it
    r2 = r2 * r2 * r2;

    return true;
}
```

The function is almost identical to a C++ function except for the in, out, and inout keywords.

1.   in: Specifies that the *argument* (particular variable we pass into a parameter) should be copied to the parameter before the function begins. It is not necessary to explicitly specify a parameter as in because a parameter is in by default. For example, the following are equivalent:

```
float square(in float x)
{
    return x * x;
}
```

And without explicitly specifying in:

```
float square(float x)
{
    return x * x;
}
```

2.   out: Specifies that the parameter should be copied to the argument when the function returns. This is useful for returning values through parameters. The out keyword is necessary because the HLSL doesn't allow us to pass by reference or to pass a pointer. We note that if a parameter is marked as out the argument is not copied to the parameter before the function begins. In other words, an out parameter can only be used to output data—it can't be used for input.

```
void square(in float x, out float y)
{
    y = x * x;
}
```

Here we input the number to be squared through x and return the square of x through the parameter y.

3.   inout: Shortcut that denotes a parameter as both in and out. Specify inout if you wish to use a parameter for both input and output.

```
void square(inout float x)
{
    x = x * x;
}
```

Here we input the number to be squared through x and also return the square of x through x.

Built-In Functions

The HLSL has a rich set of built-in functions that are useful for 3D graphics. The following describes an abridged list of them.

1.   abs(x) – Returns $|x|$.

2.   ceil(x) – Returns the smallest integer $\geq x$.

3.   cos(x) – Returns the cosine of x, where x is in radians.

4. `clamp(x, a, b)` – Clamps x to the range $[a, b]$ and returns the result.

5. `clip(x)` – This function can only be called in a pixel shader, and it discards the current pixel from further processing if x < 0.

6. `cross(u, v)` – Returns $\mathbf{u} \times \mathbf{v}$.

7. `ddx(p)` – Estimates screen space partial derivative $\partial \mathbf{p}/\partial x$. This allows you to determine how per pixel quantities $\mathbf{p}$ vary from pixel to pixel in the screen space x-direction.

8. `ddy(p)` – Estimates screen space partial derivative $\partial \mathbf{p}/\partial y$. This allows you to determine how per pixel quantities $\mathbf{p}$ vary from pixel to pixel in the screen space y-direction.

9. `degrees(x)` – Converts x from radians to degrees.

10 . `determinant(M)` – Returns the determinant of a matrix.

11 . `distance(u, v)` – Returns the distance $\|\mathbf{v}-\mathbf{u}\|$ between the points $\mathbf{u}$ and $\mathbf{v}$.

12 . `dot(u, v)` – Returns $\mathbf{u} \cdot \mathbf{v}$.

13 . `floor(x)` – Returns the greatest integer $\leq x$.

14 . `frac(x)` – This function returns the fractional part of a floating-point number (i.e., the mantissa). For example, if x = `(235.52, 696.32)` and `frac(x)` = `(0.52, 0.32)`.

15 . `length(v)` – Returns $\|\mathbf{v}\|$.

16 . `lerp(u, v, t)` – Linearly interpolates between $\mathbf{u}$ and $\mathbf{v}$ based on the parameter $t \in [0,1]$.

17 . `log(x)` – Returns $\ln(x)$.

18 . `log10(x)` – Returns $\log_{10}(x)$.

19 . `log2(x)` – Returns $\log_{2}(x)$.

20 . `max(x, y)` – Returns x if $x \geq y$, else returns y.

21 . `min(x, y)` – Returns x if $x \leq y$, else returns y.

22 . `mul(M, N)` – Returns the matrix product $\mathbf{MN}$. Note that the matrix product $\mathbf{MN}$ must be defined. If $\mathbf{M}$ is a vector, it is treated as a row vector so that the vector-matrix product is defined. Likewise, if $\mathbf{N}$ is a vector, it is treated as a column vector so that the matrix-vector product is defined.

23 . `normalize(v)` – Returns $\mathbf{v}/\|\mathbf{v}\|$.

24 . `pow(b, n)` – Returns $\mathbf{b}^{n}$.

25 . `radians(x)` – Converts x from degrees to radians.

26 . `saturate(x)` – Returns `clamp(x, 0.0, 1.0)`.

27 . `sin(x)` – Returns the sine of x, where x is in radians.

28 . `sincos(in x, out s, out c)` – Returns the sine and cosine of x, where x is in radians.

29 . `sqrt(x)` – Returns $\sqrt{x}$.

30 . `reflect(v, n)` – Computes the reflection vector given the incident vector **v** and the surface normal **n**.

31 . `refract(v, n, eta)` – Computes the refraction vector given the incident vector **v**, the surface normal **n**, and the ratio of the two indices of refraction of the two materials `eta`.

32 . `rsqrt(x)` – Returns $\frac{1}{\sqrt{x}}$.

33 . `tan(x)` – Returns the tangent of x, where x is in radians.

34 . `transpose(M)` – Returns the transpose $\mathbf{M}^T$.

35 . `Texture2D::Sample(S, texC)` – Returns a color from a 2D texture map based on the `SamplerState` object s, and 2D texture coordinates `texC`.

36 . `Texture2D::SampleLevel(S, texC, mipLevel)` – Returns a color from a 2D texture map based on the `SamplerState` object s, 2D texture coordinates `texC`, and mipmap level `mipLevel`. This function differs from `Texture2D::Sample` in that the third parameter manually specifies the mipmap level to use. For example, we would specify 0 to access the topmost mipmap LOD.

37 . `TextureCube::Sample(S, v)` – Returns a color from a cube map based on the `SamplerState` object s and 3D lookup vector **v**.

38 . `Texture2DArray::Sample(S, texC)` – Returns a color from a 2D texture array based on the `SamplerState` object s (recall a sampler state specifies texture filters and texture address modes) and 3D texture coordinates `texC`, where the first two coordinates are the usual 2D texture coordinates and the third coordinate specifies the array index.

Note: *Most of the functions are overloaded to work with all the built-in types that the function makes sense for. For instance, `abs` makes sense for all scalar types and so is overloaded for all of them. As another example, the cross product `cross` only makes sense for 3D vectors so it is only overloaded for 3D vectors of any type (e.g., 3D vectors of `int`s, `float`s, `double`s, etc.). On the other hand, linear interpolation, `lerp`, makes sense for scalars, 2D, 3D, and 4D vectors and therefore is overloaded for all types.*

Note: *If you pass in a non-scalar type into a "scalar" function, that is, a function that traditionally operates on scalars (e.g., `cos(x)`), the function will act per component. For example, if you write:*

```
float3 v = float3(0.0f, 0.0f, 0.0f);

v = cos(v);
```

then the function will act per component: $\mathbf{v} = (\cos(x), \cos(y), \cos(z))$.

Note: *For further reference, the complete list of the built-in HLSL functions can be found in the DirectX documentation. Search the index for "HLSL Intrinsic Functions."*

SOME ANALYTIC GEOMETRY

In this appendix, we use vectors and points as building blocks for more complicated geometry. These topics are used in the book, but not as frequently as vectors, matrices, and transformations; hence, we have put them in an appendix, rather than the main text.

C.1 RAYS, LINES, AND SEGMENTS

A line can be described by a point $\mathbf{p}_0$ on the line and a vector $\mathbf{u}$ that aims parallel to the line (see Figure C.1). The vector line equation is:

$$\mathbf{p}(t) = \mathbf{p}_0 + t\mathbf{u} \quad \text{for} \quad t \in \mathbb{R}$$

By plugging in different values for t (t can be any real number) we obtain different points on the line.

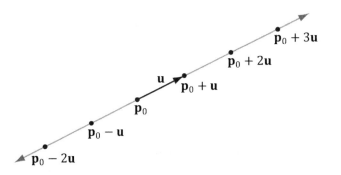

Figure C.1. A line described by a point $\mathbf{p}_0$ on the line and a vector $\mathbf{u}$ that aims parallel to the line. We can generate points on the line by plugging in any real number t.

If we restrict t to nonnegative numbers, then the graph of the vector line equation is a ray with origin $\mathbf{p}_0$ and direction $\mathbf{u}$ (see Figure C.2).

Now suppose we wish to define a line segment by the endpoints $\mathbf{p}_0$ and $\mathbf{p}_1$. We first construct the vector $\mathbf{u} = \mathbf{p}_1 - \mathbf{p}_0$ from $\mathbf{p}_0$ to $\mathbf{p}_1$; see Figure C.3. Then, for $t \in [0,1]$, the graph of the equation $\mathbf{p}(t) = \mathbf{p}_0 + t\mathbf{u} = \mathbf{p}_0 + t(\mathbf{p}_1 - \mathbf{p}_0)$ is the line segment defined by $\mathbf{p}_0$ and $\mathbf{p}_1$. Note that if you go outside the range $t \in [0,1]$, then you get a point on the line that coincides with the segment, but which is not on the segment.

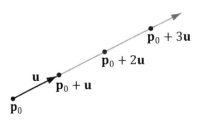

Figure C.2. A ray described by an origin $\mathbf{p}_0$ and direction $\mathbf{u}$. We can generate points on the ray by plugging in scalars for t that are greater than or equal to zero.

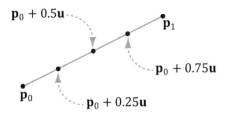

Figure C.3. We generate points on the line segment by plugging in different values for t in [0, 1]. For example, the midpoint of the line segment is given at $t = 0.5$. Also note that if $t = 0$, we get the endpoint p_0 and if $t = 1$, we get the endpoint p_1.

C.2 PARALLELOGRAMS

Let q be a point, and u and v be two vectors that are not scalar multiples of one another (i.e., $u \neq kv$ for any scalar k). Then the graph of the following function is a parallelogram (see Figure C.4):

$$p(s,t) = q + su + tv \quad \text{for} \quad s,t \in [0,1]$$

The reason for the "$u \neq kv$ for any scalar k" requirement can be seen as follows: If $u = kv$ then we could write:

$$p(s,t) = q + su + tv$$
$$= q + skv + tv$$
$$= q + (sk + t)v$$
$$= q + \bar{t}v$$

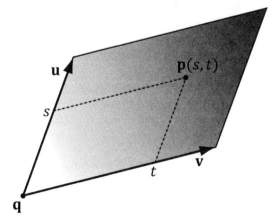

Figure C.4. Parallelogram. By plugging in different s, $t \in [0,1]$ we generate different points on the parallelogram.

which is just the equation of a line. In other words, we only have one degree of freedom. To get a 2D shape like a parallelogram, we need two degrees of freedom, so the vectors **u** and **v** must not be scalar multiples of each another.

C.3 TRIANGLES

The vector equation of a triangle is similar to that of the parallelogram equation, except that we restrict the domain of the parameters further:

$$\mathbf{p}(s,t) = \mathbf{p}_0 + s\mathbf{u} + t\mathbf{v} \quad \text{for} \quad s \geq 0, t \geq 0, s+t \leq 1$$

Observe from Figure C.5 that if any of the conditions on s and t do not hold, then $\mathbf{p}(s, t)$ will be a point "outside" the triangle, but on the plane of the triangle.

We can obtain the previous parametric equation of a triangle given three points defining a triangle. Consider a triangle defined by three vertices $\mathbf{p}_0, \mathbf{p}_1, \mathbf{p}_2$. Then for $s \geq 0, t \geq 0, s+t \leq 1$ a point on the triangle can be given by:

$$\mathbf{p}(s,t) = \mathbf{p}_0 + s(\mathbf{p}_1 - \mathbf{p}_0) + t(\mathbf{p}_2 - \mathbf{p}_0)$$

We can take this further and distribute the scalars:

$$\begin{aligned}
\mathbf{p}(s,t) &= \mathbf{p}_0 + s\mathbf{p}_1 - s\mathbf{p}_0 + t\mathbf{p}_2 - t\mathbf{p}_0 \\
&= (1-s-t)\mathbf{p}_0 + s\mathbf{p}_1 + t\mathbf{p}_2 \\
&= r\mathbf{p}_0 + s\mathbf{p}_1 + t\mathbf{p}_2
\end{aligned}$$

where we have let $r = (1-s-t)$. The coordinates (r, s, t) are called barycentric coordinates. Note that $r+s+t=1$ and the barycentric combination

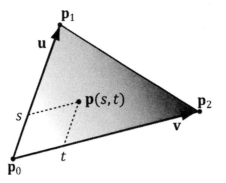

Figure C.5. **Triangle. By plugging in different s, t such that $s \geq 0$, $t \geq 0$, $s+t \leq 1$, we generate different points on the triangle.**

$p(r, s, t) = r\mathbf{p}_0 + s\mathbf{p}_1 + t\mathbf{p}_2$ expresses the point $\mathbf{p}$ as a weighted average of the vertices of the triangle. There are interesting properties of barycentric coordinates, but we do not need them for this book; the reader may wish to further research barycentric coordinates.

C.4 PLANES

A plane can be viewed as an infinitely thin, infinitely wide, and infinitely long sheet of paper. A plane can be specified with a vector $\mathbf{n}$ and a point $\mathbf{p}_0$ on the plane. The vector $\mathbf{n}$, not necessarily unit length, is called the plane's *normal vector* and is perpendicular to the plane; see Figure C.6. A plane divides space into a *positive half-space* and a *negative half-space*. The positive half-space is the space in front of the plane, where the *front* of the plane is the side the normal vector emanates from. The negative half-space is the space behind the plane.

By Figure C.6, we see that the graph of a plane is all the points $\mathbf{p}$ that satisfy the *plane equation*:

$$\mathbf{n} \cdot (\mathbf{p} - \mathbf{p}_0) = 0$$

When describing a particular plane, the normal $\mathbf{n}$ and a known point $\mathbf{p}_0$ on the plane are fixed, so it is typical to rewrite the plane equation as:

$$\mathbf{n} \cdot (\mathbf{p} - \mathbf{p}_0) = \mathbf{n} \cdot \mathbf{p} - \mathbf{n} \cdot \mathbf{p}_0 = \mathbf{n} \cdot \mathbf{p} + d = 0$$

where $d = -\mathbf{n} \cdot \mathbf{p}_0$. If $\mathbf{n} = (a, b, c)$ and $\mathbf{p} = (x, y, z)$, then the plane equation can be written as:

$$ax + by + cz + d = 0$$

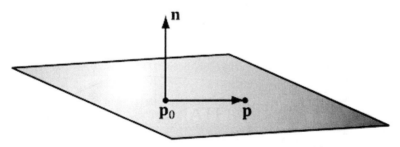

Figure C.6. A plane defined by a normal vector n and a point p_0 on the plane. If p_0 is a point on the plane, then the point p is also on the plane if and only if the vector p − p_0 is orthogonal to the plane's normal vector.

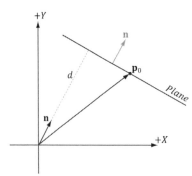

Figure C.7. **Shortest distance from a plane to the origin.**

If the plane's normal vector $\mathbf{n}$ is of unit length, then $d = -\mathbf{n} \cdot \mathbf{p}_0$ gives the shortest signed distance from the origin to the plane (see Figure C.7).

Note: *To make the pictures easier to draw, we sometimes draw our figures in 2D and use a line to represent a plane. A line, with a perpendicular normal, can be thought of as a 2D plane because the line divides the 2D space into a positive half-space and negative half-space.*

C.4.1 XNA Math Planes

When representing a plane in code, it suffices to store only the normal vector $\mathbf{n}$ and the constant d. It is useful to think of this as a 4D vector, which we denote as $(\mathbf{n}, d) = (a, b, c, d)$. Therefore, because the XMVECTOR type stores a 4-tuple of floating-point values, the XNA math library overloads the XMVECTOR type to also represent planes.

C.4.2 Point/Plane Spatial Relation

Given any point $\mathbf{p}$, observe from Figure C.6 and Figure C.8 that

1. If $\mathbf{n} \cdot (\mathbf{p} - \mathbf{p}_0) = \mathbf{n} \cdot \mathbf{p} + d > 0$ then $\mathbf{p}$ is in front of the plane.
2. If $\mathbf{n} \cdot (\mathbf{p} - \mathbf{p}_0) = \mathbf{n} \cdot \mathbf{p} + d < 0$ then $\mathbf{p}$ is behind the plane.

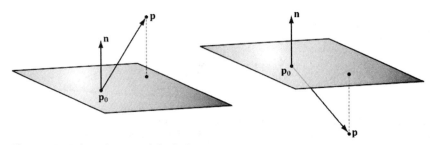

Figure C.8. **Point/plane spatial relation.**

3. If $\mathbf{n} \cdot (\mathbf{p} - \mathbf{p}_0) = \mathbf{n} \cdot \mathbf{p} + d = 0$ then $\mathbf{p}$ is on the plane.

These tests are useful for testing the spatial location of points relative to a plane. This next XNA math function evaluates $\mathbf{n} \cdot \mathbf{p} + d$ for a particular plane and point:

```
XMVECTOR XMPlaneDotCoord(// Returns n·p+d replicated in each coordinate
    XMVECTOR P,   // plane
    XMVECTOR V);  // point with w = 1

// Test the locality of a point relative to a plane.
XMVECTOR p = XMVectorSet(0.0f, 1.0f, 0.0f, 0.0f);

XMVECTOR v = XMVectorSet(3.0f, 5.0f, 2.0f);

float x = XMVectorGetX(XMPlaneDotCoord(p, v));

if(x approximately equals 0.0f) // v is coplanar to the plane.
if(x > 0)      // v is in positive half-space.
if(x < 0)      // v is in negative half-space.
```

Note: ➤ *We say approximately equals due to floating-point imprecision.*

A similar function is:

```
XMVECTOR XMPlaneDotNormal(XMVECTOR Plane, XMVECTOR Vec);
```

This returns the dot product of the plane normal vector and the given 3D vector.

C.4.3 Construction

Besides directly specifying the plane coefficients $(\mathbf{n}, d) = (a, b, c, d)$, we can calculate these coefficients in two other ways. Given the normal $\mathbf{n}$ and a known point on the plane $\mathbf{p}_0$ we can solve for the d component:

$$\mathbf{n} \cdot \mathbf{p}_0 + d = 0 \Rightarrow d = -\mathbf{n} \cdot \mathbf{p}_0$$

The XNA Math library provides the following function to construct a plane from a point and normal in this way:

```
XMVECTOR XMPlaneFromPointNormal(
    XMVECTOR Point,
    XMVECTOR Normal;)
```

The second way we can construct a plane is by specifying three distinct points on the plane. Given the points $\mathbf{P}_0, \mathbf{P}_1, \mathbf{P}_2$, we can form two vectors on the plane:

$$\mathbf{u} = \mathbf{p}_1 - \mathbf{p}_0$$

$$\mathbf{v} = \mathbf{p}_2 - \mathbf{p}_0$$

From that we can compute the normal of the plane by taking the cross product of the two vectors on the plane. (Remember the left-hand thumb rule.)

$$\mathbf{n} = \mathbf{u} \times \mathbf{v}$$

Then, we compute $d = -\mathbf{n} \cdot \mathbf{p}_0$.

The XNA Math library provides the following function to compute a plane given three points on the plane:

```
XMVECTOR XMPlaneFromPoints(
    XMVECTOR Point1,
    XMVECTOR Point2,
    XMVECTOR Point3;)
```

C.4.4 Normalizing a Plane

Sometimes we might have a plane and would like to normalize the normal vector. At first thought, it would seem that we could just normalize the normal vector as we would any other vector. But recall that the d component also depends on the normal vector: $d = -\mathbf{n} \cdot \mathbf{p}_0$. Therefore, if we normalize the normal vector, we must also recalculate d. This is done as follows:

$$d' = \frac{d}{\|\mathbf{n}\|} = -\frac{\mathbf{n}}{\|\mathbf{n}\|} \cdot \mathbf{p}_0$$

Thus, we have the following formula to normalize the normal vector of the plane $(\mathbf{n}, d)$:

$$\frac{1}{\|\mathbf{n}\|}(\mathbf{n}, d) = \left(\frac{\mathbf{n}}{\|\mathbf{n}\|}, \frac{d}{\|\mathbf{n}\|} \right)$$

We can use the following XNA Math function to normalize a plane's normal vector:

```
XMVECTOR XMPlaneNormalize(XMVECTOR P);
```

C.4.5 Transforming a Plane

[Lengyel02] shows that we can transform a plane $(\mathbf{n}, d)$ by treating it as a 4D vector and multiplying it by the inverse-transpose of the desired transformation matrix. Note that the plane's normal vector must be normalized first. We use the following XNA Math function to do this:

```
XMVECTOR XMPlaneTransform(XMVECTOR P, XMMATRIX M);
```

Sample code:

```
XMMATRIX T(...); // Initialize T to a desired transformation.
XMMATRIX invT = XMMatrixInverse(XMMatrixDeterminant(T), T);
XMMATRIX invTransposeT = XMMatrixTranspose(invT);

XMVECTOR p = (...); // Initialize Plane.
p = XMPlaneNormalize(p); // make sure normal is normalized.

XMVECTOR transformedPlane = XMPlaneTransform(p, &invTransposeT);
```

C.4.6 Nearest Point on a Plane to a Given Point

Suppose we have a point $\mathbf{p}$ in space and we would like to find the point $\mathbf{q}$ on the plane $(\mathbf{n},d)$ that is closest to $\mathbf{p}$. From Figure C.9, we see that

$$\mathbf{q} = \mathbf{p} - \text{proj}_\mathbf{n}(\mathbf{p} - \mathbf{p}_0)$$

Assuming $\|\mathbf{n}\|=1$ so that $\text{proj}_\mathbf{n}(\mathbf{p} - \mathbf{p}_0) = \left[(\mathbf{p} - \mathbf{p}_0)\cdot\mathbf{n}\right]\mathbf{n}$, we can rewrite this as:

$$\mathbf{q} = \mathbf{p} - \left[(\mathbf{p} - \mathbf{p}_0)\cdot\mathbf{n}\right]\mathbf{n}$$
$$= \mathbf{p} - (\mathbf{p}\cdot\mathbf{n} - \mathbf{p}_0\cdot\mathbf{n})\mathbf{n}$$
$$= \mathbf{p} - (\mathbf{p}\cdot\mathbf{n} + d)\mathbf{n}$$

C.4.7 Ray/Plane Intersection

Given a ray $\mathbf{p}(t) = \mathbf{p}_0 + t\mathbf{u}$ and the equation of a plane $\mathbf{n}\cdot\mathbf{p} + d = 0$, we would like to know if the ray intersects the plane and also the point of intersection. To do this, we plug the ray into the plane equation and solve for the parameter t that satisfies the plane equation, thereby giving us the parameter that yields the intersection point:

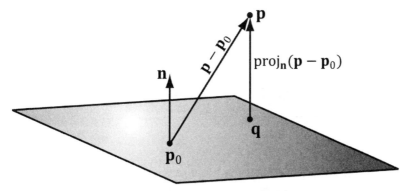

Figure C.9. The nearest point on a plane to a point p. The point $\mathbf{p}_0$ is a point on the plane.

$\mathbf{n} \cdot \mathbf{p}(t) + d = 0$	Plug ray into plane equation
$\mathbf{n} \cdot (\mathbf{p}_0 + t\mathbf{u}) + d = 0$	Substitute
$\mathbf{n} \cdot \mathbf{p}_0 + t\mathbf{n} \cdot \mathbf{u} + d = 0$	Distributive property
$t\mathbf{n} \cdot \mathbf{u} = -\mathbf{n} \cdot \mathbf{p}_0 - d$	Add $-\mathbf{n} \cdot \mathbf{p}_0 - d$ to both sides
$t = \dfrac{-\mathbf{n} \cdot \mathbf{p}_0 - d}{\mathbf{n} \cdot \mathbf{u}}$	Solve for t

If $\mathbf{n} \cdot \mathbf{u} = 0$ then the ray is parallel to the plane and there are either no solutions or infinite many solutions (infinite if the ray coincides with the plane). If t is not in the interval $[0,\infty)$, the ray does not intersect the plane, but the line coincident with the ray does. If t is in the interval $[0,\infty)$, then the ray does intersect the plane and the intersection point is found by evaluating the ray equation at $t_0 = \frac{-\mathbf{n} \cdot \mathbf{p}_0 - d}{\mathbf{n} \cdot \mathbf{u}}$.

The ray/plane intersection test can be modified to a segment/plane test. Given two points defining a line segment $\mathbf{p}$ and $\mathbf{q}$, then we form the ray $\mathbf{r}(t) = \mathbf{p} + t(\mathbf{q} - \mathbf{p})$. We use this ray for the intersection test. If $t \in [0,1]$, then the segment intersects the plane, otherwise it does not. The XNA Math library provides the following function:

```
XMVECTOR XMPlaneIntersectLine(
    XMVECTOR P,
    XMVECTOR LinePoint1,
    XMVECTOR LinePoint2);
```

C.4.8 Reflecting Vectors

Given a vector $\mathbf{I}$ we wish to reflect it about a plane with normal $\mathbf{n}$. Because vectors do not have positions, only the plane normal is involved when reflecting a vector. Figure C.10 shows the geometric situation, from which we conclude the reflection vector is given by:

$$\mathbf{r} = \mathbf{I} - 2(\mathbf{n} \cdot \mathbf{I})\mathbf{n}$$

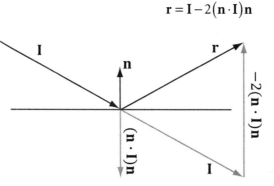

Figure C.10. **Geometry of vector reflection.**

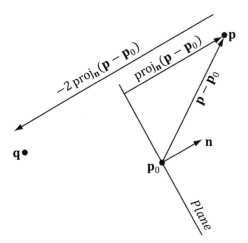

Figure C.11. **Geometry of point reflection.**

C.4.9 Reflecting Points

Points reflect differently from vectors because points have position. Figure C.11 shows that the reflected point **q** is given by:

$$\mathbf{q} = \mathbf{p} - 2\operatorname{proj}_{\mathbf{n}}(\mathbf{p} - \mathbf{p}_0)$$

C.4.10 Reflection Matrix

Let $(\mathbf{n}, d) = (n_x, n_y, n_z, d)$ be the coefficients of a plane, where $d = -\mathbf{n} \cdot \mathbf{p}_0$. Then, using homogeneous coordinates, we can reflect both points and vectors about this plane using a single 4×4 reflection matrix:

$$\mathbf{R} = \begin{bmatrix} 1 - 2n_x n_x & -2n_x n_y & -2n_x n_z & 0 \\ -2n_x n_y & 1 - 2n_y n_y & -2n_y n_z & 0 \\ -2n_x n_z & -2n_y n_z & 1 - 2n_z n_z & 0 \\ -2dn_x & -2dn_y & -2dn_z & 1 \end{bmatrix}$$

This matrix assumes the plane is normalized so that

$$\operatorname{proj}_{\mathbf{n}}(\mathbf{p} - \mathbf{p}_0) = \left[\mathbf{n} \cdot (\mathbf{p} - \mathbf{p}_0)\right]\mathbf{n}$$
$$= \left[\mathbf{n} \cdot \mathbf{p} - \mathbf{n} \cdot \mathbf{p}_0\right]\mathbf{n}$$
$$= \left[\mathbf{n} \cdot \mathbf{p} + d\right]\mathbf{n}$$

If we multiply a point by this matrix, we get the point reflection formula:

$$\begin{bmatrix} p_x, p_y, p_z, 1 \end{bmatrix} \begin{bmatrix} 1-2n_xn_x & -2n_xn_y & -2n_xn_z & 0 \\ -2n_xn_y & 1-2n_yn_y & -2n_yn_z & 0 \\ -2n_xn_z & -2n_yn_z & 1-2n_zn_z & 0 \\ -2dn_x & -2dn_y & -2dn_z & 1 \end{bmatrix}$$

$$= \begin{bmatrix} p_x - 2p_xn_xn_x - 2p_yn_xn_y - 2p_zn_xn_z - 2dn_x \\ -2p_xn_xn_y + p_y - 2p_yn_yn_y - 2p_zn_yn_z - 2dn_y \\ -2p_xn_xn_z - 2p_yn_yn_z + p_z - 2p_zn_zn_z - 2dn_z \\ 1 \end{bmatrix}^T$$

$$= \begin{bmatrix} p_x \\ p_y \\ p_z \\ 1 \end{bmatrix}^T + \begin{bmatrix} -2n_x\left(p_xn_x + p_yn_y + p_zn_z + d\right) \\ -2n_y\left(p_xn_x + p_yn_y + p_zn_z + d\right) \\ -2n_z\left(p_xn_x + p_yn_y + p_zn_z + d\right) \\ 0 \end{bmatrix}^T$$

$$= \begin{bmatrix} p_x \\ p_y \\ p_z \\ 1 \end{bmatrix}^T + \begin{bmatrix} -2n_x\left(\mathbf{n}\cdot\mathbf{p}+d\right) \\ -2n_y\left(\mathbf{n}\cdot\mathbf{p}+d\right) \\ -2n_z\left(\mathbf{n}\cdot\mathbf{p}+d\right) \\ 0 \end{bmatrix}^T$$

$$= \mathbf{p} - 2\left[\mathbf{n}\cdot\mathbf{p}+d\right]\mathbf{n}$$

$$= \mathbf{p} - 2\text{proj}_\mathbf{n}\left(\mathbf{p}-\mathbf{p}_0\right)$$

Note: *We take the transpose to turn row vectors into column vectors. This is just to make the presentation neater—otherwise, we would get very long row vectors.*

And similarly, if we multiply a vector by this matrix, we get the vector reflection formula:

$$\begin{bmatrix} v_x, v_y, v_z, 0 \end{bmatrix} \begin{bmatrix} 1-2n_xn_x & -2n_xn_y & -2n_xn_z & 0 \\ -2n_xn_y & 1-2n_yn_y & -2n_yn_z & 0 \\ -2n_xn_z & -2n_yn_z & 1-2n_zn_z & 0 \\ -2dn_x & -2dn_y & -2dn_z & 1 \end{bmatrix}$$

$$= \mathbf{v} - 2\left(\mathbf{n}\cdot\mathbf{v}\right)\mathbf{n}$$

The following XNA Math function can be used to construct the previous reflection matrix given a plane:

```
XMMATRIX XMMatrixReflect(XMVECTOR ReflectionPlane);
```

C.5 EXERCISES

1. Let $p(t) = (1,1) + t(2,1)$ be a ray relative to some coordinate system. Plot the points on the ray at $t = 0.0, 0.5, 1.0, 2.0,$ and 5.0.

2. Let p_0 and p_1 define the endpoints of a line segment. Show that the equation for a line segment can also be written as $p(t) = (1-t)p_0 + tp_1$ for $t \in [0,1]$.

3. For each part, find the vector line equation of the line passing through the two points.

    (a) $p_1 = (2,-1), p_2 = (4,1)$

    (b) $p_1 = (4,-2,1), p_2 = (2,3,2)$

4. Let $L(t) = p + tu$ define a line in 3-space. Let q be any point in 3-space. Prove that the distance from q to the line can be written as:

$$d = \frac{\|(q-p) \times u\|}{\|u\|}$$

5. Let $L(t) = (4,2,2) + t(1,1,1)$ be a line. Find the distance from the following points to the line:

    (a) $q = (0,0,0)$

    (b) $q = (4,2,0)$

    (c) $q = (0,2,2)$

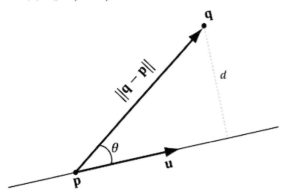

Figure C.12. Distance from q to the line.

6. Let $p_0 = (0,1,0)$, $p_1 = (-1,3,6)$, and $p_2 = (8,5,3)$ be three points. Find the plane these points define.

7. Let $\left(\frac{1}{\sqrt{3}}, \frac{1}{\sqrt{3}}, \frac{1}{\sqrt{3}}, -5\right)$ be a plane. Define the locality of the following points relative to the plane: $\left(3\sqrt{3}, 5\sqrt{3}, 0\right)$, $\left(2\sqrt{3}, \sqrt{3}, 2\sqrt{3}\right)$, and $\left(\sqrt{3}, -\sqrt{3}, 0\right)$.

8. Let $\left(-\frac{1}{\sqrt{2}}, \frac{1}{\sqrt{2}}, 0, \frac{5}{\sqrt{2}}\right)$ be a plane. Find the point on the plane nearest to the point $(0,1,0)$.

9. Let $\left(-\frac{1}{\sqrt{2}}, \frac{1}{\sqrt{2}}, 0, \frac{5}{\sqrt{2}}\right)$ be a plane. Find the reflection of the point $(0,1,0)$ about the plane.

10 . Let $\left(\frac{1}{\sqrt{3}}, \frac{1}{\sqrt{3}}, \frac{1}{\sqrt{3}}, -5\right)$ be a plane, and let $r(t) = (-1,1,-1) + t(1,0,0)$ be a ray. Find the point at which the ray intersects the plane. Then write a short program using the **XMPlaneIntersectLine** function to verify your answer.

SOLUTIONS TO
SELECTED EXERCISES

Solutions (including figures) to selected exercises in the text may be found on the companion DVD.

BIBLIOGRAPHY AND FURTHER READING

[Angel00] Angel, Edward, *Interactive Computer Graphics: A Top-Down Approach with OpenGL, Second Edition*, Addison-Wesley, Boston, MA, 2000.

[Bilodeau10] Bilodeau, Bill. "Efficient Compute Shader Programming," Game Developers Conference, AMD slide presentation, 2010. (*http://developer.amd.com/gpu_assets/Efficient%20Compute%20Shader%20Programming.pps*)

[Bilodeau10b] Bilodeau, Bill. "Direct3D 11 Tutorial: Tessellation," Game Developers Conference, AMD slide presentation, 2010. (*http://developer.amd.com/gpu_assets/Direct3D%2011%20Tessellation%20Tutorial.ppsx*)

[Blinn78] Blinn, James F., and Martin E. Newell. "Clipping Using Homogeneous Coordinates." In *Computer Graphics (SIGGRAPH '78 Proceedings)*, pages 245–251, New York, 1978.

[Blinn96] Blinn, Jim, *Jim Blinn's Corner: A Trip Down the Graphics Pipeline*, Morgan Kaufmann Publishers, Inc., San Francisco, CA, 1996.

[Boyd08] Boyd, Chas. "DirectX 11 Compute Shader," Siggraph slide presentation, 2008. (*http://s08.idav.ucdavis.edu/boyd-dx11-compute-shader.pdf*)

[Boyd10] Boyd, Chas. "DirectCompute Lecture Series 101: Introduction to DirectCompute," 2010. (*http://channel9.msdn.com/Blogs/gclassy/DirectCompute-Lecture-Series-101-Introduction-to-DirectCompute*)

[Brennan02] Brennan, Chris. "Accurate Reflections and Refractions by Adjusting for Object Distance," Direct3D ShaderX: Vertex and Pixel Shader Tips and Tricks, Wordware Publishing Inc., Plano, TX, 2002.

[Burg10] Burg, John van der, "Building an Advanced Particle System," Gamasutra, June 2000. (http://www.gamasutra.com/features/20000623/vanderburg_01.htm)

[De berg00] de Berg, M., M. van Kreveld, M. Overmars, and O. Schwarzkopf, Computational Geometry: Algorithms and Applications, Second Edition, Springer-Verlag Berlin Heidelberg, The Netherlands, 2000.

[Dietrich] Dietrich, Sim. "Texture Space Bump Maps," 2010. (http://developer.nvidia.com/object/texture_space_bump_mapping.html)

[Dunlop03] Dunlop, Robert. "FPS Versus Frame Time," 2003. (http://www.mvps.org/directx/articles/fps_versus_frame_time.htm)

[DXSDK10] Microsoft DirectX June 2010 SDK Documentation, Microsoft Corporation, 2010.

[Eberly01] Eberly, David H. 3D Game Engine Design, Morgan Kaufmann Publishers, Inc., San Francisco, CA, 2001.

[Engel02] Engel, Wolfgang (Editor), Direct3D ShaderX: Vertex and Pixel Shader Tips and Tricks, Wordware Publishing, Plano, TX, 2002.

[Engel04] Engel, Wolfgang (Editor), ShaderX2: Shader Programming Tips & Tricks with DirectX 9, Wordware Publishing, Plano, TX, 2004.

[Engel06] Engel, Wolfgang (Editor), ShaderX5: Shader Advanced Rendering Techniques, Charles River Media, Inc., Boston, MA, 2006.

[Engel08] Engel, Wolfgang (Editor), ShaderX6: Shader Advanced Rendering Techniques, Charles River Media, Inc., Boston, MA, 2008.

[Farin98] Farin, Gerald, and Dianne Hansford, The Geometry Toolbox: For Graphics and Modeling, AK Peters, Ltd., Natick, MA, 1998.

[Fernando03] Fernando, Randima, and Mark J. Kilgard, The CG Tutorial: The Definitive Guide to Programmable Real-Time Graphics, Addison-Wesley, Boston, MA, 2003.

[Fraleigh95] Fraleigh, John B., and Raymond A. Beauregard, Linear Algebra, Third Edition, Addison-Wesley, Boston, MA, 1995.

[Friedberg03] Friedberg, Stephen H., Arnold J. Insel, and Lawrence E. Spence, Linear Algebra, Fourth Edition, Pearson Education, Inc., Boston, MA, 2003.

[Fung10] Fung, James. "DirectCompute Lecture Series 210: GPU Optimizations and Performance," 2010. (http://channel9.msdn.com/Blogs/gclassy/DirectCompute-Lecture-Series-210-GPU-Optimizations-and-Performance)

[Halliday01] Halliday, David, Robert Resnick, and Jearl Walker, *Fundamentals of Physics, Sixth Edition*, John Wiley & Sons, Inc., Hoboken, NJ, 2001.

[Hausner98] Hausner, Melvin, *A Vector Space Approach to Geometry*, Dover Publications, Inc. (*http://www.doverpublications.com*), Englewood Cliffs, NJ, 1998.

[Hoffmann75] Hoffmann, Banesh, *About Vectors*, Dover Publications, Inc. (*http://www.doverpublications.com*), Englewood Cliffs, NJ, 1975.

[Isidoro06] Isidoro, John R. "Shadow Mapping: GPU-based Tips and Techniques," *Game Developers Conference*, ATI slide presentation, 2006. (*http://developer.amd.com/media/gpu_assets/Isidoro-ShadowMapping.pdf*)

[Isidoro06b] Isidoro, John R. "Edge Masking and Per-Texel Depth Extent Propagation for Computation Culling During Shadow Mapping," *ShaderX 5: Advanced Rendering Techniques*, Charles River Media, Boston, MA, 2007.

[Kilgard99] Kilgard, Mark J. "Creating Reflections and Shadows Using Stencil Buffers," *Game Developers Conference*, NVIDIA slide presentation, 1999. (*http://developer.nvidia.com/docs/IO/1407/ATT/stencil.ppt*)

[Kilgard01] Kilgard, Mark J. "Shadow Mapping with Today's OpenGL Hardware," *Computer Entertainment Software Association's CEDEC*, NVIDIA presentation, 2001. (*http://developer.nvidia.com/object/cedec_shadowmap.html*)

[Kryachko05] Kryachko, Yuri. "Using Vertex Texture Displacement for Realistic Water Rendering," *GPU Gems 2: Programming Techniques for High-Performance Graphics and General Purpose Computation*, Addison-Wesley, Boston, MA, 2005.

[Kuipers99] Kuipers, Jack B. *Quaternions and Rotation Sequences: A Primer with Applications to Orbits, Aerospace, and Virtual Reality*, Princeton University Press, Princeton, NJ, 1999.

[Lengyel02] Lengyel, Eric, *Mathematics for 3D Game Programming and Computer Graphics*. Charles River Media, Inc., Boston, MA, 2002.

[Möller08] Möller, Tomas, and Eric Haines, *Real-Time Rendering, Third Edition*, AK Peters, Ltd., Natick, MA, 2008.

[Mortenson99] Mortenson, M.E. *Mathematics for Computer Graphics Applications*, Industrial Press, Inc., New York, NY, 1999.

[NVIDIA05] *Antialiasing with Transparency*, NVIDIA Corporation, 2005. (*ftp://download.nvidia.com/developer/SDK/Individual_Samples/DEMOS/Direct3D9/src/AntiAliasingWithTransparency/docs/AntiAliasingWithTransparency.pdf*)

[NVIDIA08] *GPU Programming Guide GeForce 8 and 9 Series*, NVIDIA Corporation, 2008. (*http://developer.download.nvidia.com/GPU_Programming_Guide/GPU_Programming_Guide_G80.pdf*)

[NVIDIA09] *NVIDIA's Next Generation CUDA Compute Architecture: Fermi, NVIDIA Corporation, 2009.* (<u>http://www.nvidia.com/content/PDF/fermi_white_papers/NVIDIA_Fermi_Compute_Architecture_Whitepaper.pdf</u>)

[NVIDIA10] *DirectCompute Programming Guide, NVIDIA Corporation, 2007–2010.* (<u>http://developer.download.nvidia.com/compute/DevZone/docs/html/DirectCompute/doc/DirectCompute_Programming_Guide.pdf</u>)

[Oliveira10] *Oliveira, Gustavo. "Designing Fast Cross-Platform SIMD Vector Libraries," 2010.* (<u>http://www.gamasutra.com/view/feature/4248/designing_fast_crossplatform_simd_.php</u>)

[Parent02] *Parent, Rick, Computer Animation: Algorithms and Techniques, Morgan Kaufmann Publishers* (<u>http://www.mkp.com</u>), *Boston, MA, 2002.*

[Pelzer04] *Pelzer, Kurt. "Rendering Countless Blades of Waving Grass," GPU Gems: Programming Techniques, Tips, and Tricks for Real-Time Graphics, Addison-Wesley, Boston, MA, 2004.*

[Petzold99] *Petzold, Charles, Programming Windows, Fifth Edition, Microsoft Press, Redmond, WA, 1999.*

[Prosise99] *Prosise, Jeff, Programming Windows with MFC, Second Edition, Microsoft Press, Redmond, WA, 1999.*

[Santrock03] *Santrock, John W. Psychology 7, The McGraw-Hill Companies, Inc., Boston, MA, 2003.*

[Savchenko00] *Savchenko, Sergei. 3D Graphics Programming: Games and Beyond, Sams Publishing, 2000.*

[Schneider03] *Schneider, Philip J., and David H. Eberly, Geometric Tools for Computer Graphics, Morgan Kaufmann Publishers* (<u>http://www.mkp.com</u>), *Boston, MA, 2003.*

[Snook03] *Snook, Greg, Real-Time 3D Terrain Engines Using C++ and DirectX9, Charles River Media, Inc., Boston, MA, 2003.*

[Story10] *Story, Jon, and Cem Cebenoyan. "Tessellation Performance," Game Developers Conference, NVIDIA slide presentation, 2010.* (<u>http://developer.download.nvidia.com/presentations/2010/gdc/Tessellation_Performance.pdf</u>)

[Sutherland74] *Sutherland, I. E., and G. W. Hodgeman. Reentrant Polygon Clipping. Communications of the ACM, 17(1):32–42, 1974.*

[Tuft10] *Tuft, David. "Cascaded Shadow Maps," 2010.* (<u>http://msdn.microsoft.com/en-us/library/ee416307%28v=vs.85%29.aspx</u>)

[Uralsky05] *Uralsky, Yuri. "Efficient Soft-Edged Shadows Using Pixel Shader Branching," GPU Gems 2: Programming Techniques for High-Performance Graphics and General Purpose Computation, Addison-Wesley, Boston, MA, 2005.*

[Verth04] Verth, James M. van, and Lars M. Bishop, Essential Mathematics for Games & Interactive Applications: A Programmer's Guide. Morgan Kaufmann Publishers (http://www.mkp.com), Boston, MA, 2004.

[Vlachos01] Vlachos, Alex, Jörg Peters, Chas Boyd, and Jason L. Mitchell, "Curved PN Triangles," ACM Symposium on Interactive 3D Graphics 2001, pp. 159–166, 2001. (http://alex.vlachos.com/graphics/CurvedPNTriangles.pdf)

[Watt92] Watt, Alan, and Mark Watt, Advanced Animation and Rendering Techniques: Theory and Practice, Addison-Wesley, Boston, MA, 1992.

[Watt00] Watt, Alan, 3D Computer Graphics, Third Edition, Addison-Wesley, Boston, MA, 2000.

[Watt01] Watt, Alan, and Fabio Policarpo, 3D Games: Real-time Rendering and Software Technology, Addison-Wesley, Boston, MA, 2001.

[Weinreich98] Weinreich, Gabriel, Geometrical Vectors, The University of Chicago Press, Chicago, IL, 1998.

[Whatley05] Whatley, David. "Toward Photorealism in Virtual Botany," GPU Gems 2: Programming Techniques for High-Performance Graphics and General Purpose Computation, Addison-Wesley, Boston, MA, 2005.

[Wloka03] Wloka, Matthias. "Batch, Batch, Batch: What Does It Really Mean?" Presentation at Game Developers Conference, 2003. (http://developer.nvidia.com/docs/IO/8230/BatchBatchBatch.pdf)

[XNAMath10] DirectXMath Online Documentation, Microsoft Corporation. (http://msdn.microsoft.com/en-us/library/windows/desktop/hh437833%28v=VS.85%29.aspx)

INDEX